SCENOGRAPHY SZENOGRAFIE 2

STAGING THE SPACE
DER INSZENIERTE RAUM

PROJECTS AND PHILOSOPHY
1997 – 2018

ATELIER BRÜCKNER

CONTENTS

SCENOGRAPHY 2

Shirin Frangoul-Brückner

The list of publications is long–and pretty exciting: books in which projects by ATELIER BRÜCKNER are represented, themed essays, newspaper articles with the critical opinion of specialised journalists, and, last but not least, publications of our own. Why do we do that? Why don't we just work on our projects? Why do we speak and write about them?

Our book "Scenography 2" invites the reader to participate in ATELIER BRÜCKNER, in its projects and design theory. It offers the opportunity to have a look at what has been created in the past twenty years, to inspect and weigh up its significance–all in a very subjective manner, from a personal perspective. It wasn't always just the big projects that preoccupied and touched us. Sometimes it was the tasks involving the biggest challenges both in terms of content and organisationally that took us to surprising locations, bringing with them encounters and many years of friendship. And there were projects that were never realised, which we had put our hearts and souls into, only then to see them remain ideas, in our memories.

Our concepts want to be realised, and generally–whether temporarily or permanently–they become built reality, walk-in experiences. This path is strewn with surprises, challenges, and the aspiration to make the impossible possible. For us, holding other cultures in esteem is a fundamental prerequisite. Again and again, we need to be courageous, to consider things from another perspective, and to engage in changing constellations–always with an eye on the outcome, because ultimately that is what is perceived and results in a shared experience.

We are proud of the many opportunities and numerous projects which we have been fortunate enough to be able to tackle and realise together with our clients from around the world. And we are proud of our large, open team–an international and interdisciplinary team with well-versed personalities and in-depth know-how. We enjoy sensing the mutual trust and collective strength.

This book shows the milestones along our way and presents new projects and concepts. It is a reference work about our design methodology, which has been continuously honed and refined over the past two decades. My thanks at this point in particular to Uwe R. Brückner, who as originator of the design methodology has provided the basis for the way we work, and who–like Eberhard Schlag–teaches the theory of scenography as university professor.

Die Liste der Publikationen ist lang – und durchaus aufregend: Bücher, in denen Projekte von ATELIER BRÜCKNER vertreten sind, thematische Aufsätze, Zeitungsartikel mit kritischem Blick der Fachjournalisten und schließlich auch Veröffentlichungen, die wir selbst herausgegeben haben. Wieso machen wir das? Wieso realisieren wir nicht nur Projekte? Wieso reden und schreiben wir darüber?

Unser Buch „Scenography 2" lädt ein, am ATELIER BRÜCKNER teilzuhaben, an seinen Projekten und an seiner Gestaltungslehre. Es bietet die Möglichkeit, einen Blick zu werfen auf das, was in den vergangenen 20 Jahren entstand, zu sichten und zu gewichten – und das durchaus subjektiv und persönlich. Es waren nicht immer nur die großen Projekte, die uns beschäftigten und nahegingen. Manchmal waren es Aufgaben, die uns inhaltlich und organisatorisch herausforderten, die uns zu überraschenden Schauplätzen, Begegnungen und langjährigen Freundschaften führten. Und es waren Projekte, die nie realisiert wurden, die mit viel Herzblut erdacht und entwickelt wurden und dann nur als Ideen und in der Erinnerung präsent bleiben.

Unsere Konzepte streben nach Realisierung und werden meist – sei es temporär oder permanent – zur gebauten Realität, zu einem begehbaren Erlebnis. Auf diesem Weg gibt es durchaus Überraschungen, Herausforderungen und stets den Anspruch, das Unmögliche möglich zu machen. Die Wertschätzung anderer Kulturen ist uns grundlegende Voraussetzung. Immer wieder gilt es, mutig zu sein, unterschiedliche Perspektiven einzunehmen und sich auf sich verändernde Konstellationen einzulassen – stets mit Blick auf das Ergebnis, denn das ist es, was wahrgenommen wird und zum gemeinsamen Erleben führt.

Wir sind stolz auf die vielen Chancen und die zahlreichen Projekte, die wir gemeinsam mit unseren Auftraggebern aus aller Welt ergreifen und realisieren dürfen. Und wir sind stolz auf unser großes, aufgeschlossenes Team – ein internationales und interdisziplinäres Team mit versierten Persönlichkeiten und fundiertem Fachwissen. Es bereitet Freude, das gegenseitige Vertrauen und die gemeinsame Kraft zu spüren.

Das vorliegende Buch zeigt die Meilensteine unseres Wegs und es stellt neue Projekte und Konzepte vor. Und es ist ein Nachschlagewerk zu unserer Gestaltungslehre, die sich in den vergangenen zwei Jahrzehnten kontinuierlich weiterentwickelt hat. So gilt mein Dank an dieser Stelle insbesondere auch Uwe R. Brückner, der als Urheber der Gestaltungslehre die Basis unserer Arbeitsweise gelegt hat und der ebenso wie Eberhard Schlag als Professor die Theorie der Szenografie an der Hochschule lehrt.

PREFACE

Ruedi Baur, integral ruedi baur

ATELIER BRÜCKNER AND THE SOCIETY OF THE SPECTACLE

"For one to whom the real world becomes real images, mere images are transformed into real beings–tangible figments which are the efficient motor of trancelike behaviour." Guy Debord, "The Society of the Spectacle," 1967

Uwe R. Brückner was ten years old when the situationist artist and philosopher Guy Debord introduced the critical term of the spectacle in order to define the coming phase of capitalism. Thirty years later, in 1997, the designer with theatrical experience founded ATELIER BRÜCKNER together with his wife, Shirin Frangoul-Brückner–a workshop for the conception of exhibitions and museums. What followed was not only a series of fascinating stagings, but also in parallel to this the definition of a discipline that had to align itself internationally to the quality of the work. Barely twenty years later, this compendium is a rich corpus of staging design in this age of the society of the spectacle. In this time, the Atelier has been transformed into a performative company with multidisciplinary partners and international ambitions.

Looking back, one can define the work of ATELIER BRÜCKNER as an attempt to allow scenographers to work on a high level both in terms of form and content in an environment that is characterised by overstatement. It is a complex action to create a divergence within a system in which the image and visual narration have achieved an exaggerated power, rarely in the interest of the citizen. The power of the work lies not only in the execution, nor alone in the technical capabilities or good narration, but in the quality of the (not always respected) authors who allowed this part of the spectacle to stand out from the sober neutrality of the mass production of visual events.

The importance of such a disruptive factor is often underestimated both by the customer and also internally, by a team that seeks to satisfy the client. More important than this is the overarching desire to drag individual visitors out of the crowd–to explain to them the backstage construction and to thus give them the opportunity to think for themselves and to act, simply in order to regain power over reality.

The (inter-)action within the exhibition is one of the most discussed topics within the discipline, however, only in connection with the capacities of the digital technologies which allow us to immerse ourselves in an ever more coherent fictitious world. Of course, the interaction between man and object, signs, and spatial systems began long before the digital age.

ATELIER BRÜCKNER UND DIE GESELLSCHAFT DES SPEKTAKELS

„Wo die reale Welt in vereinfachte Bilder verwandelt wird, werden aus diesen einfachen Bildern reale Wesen und die effizienten Motive für hypnotisches Verhalten." Guy Debord, Die Gesellschaft des Spektakels, 1967.

Zehn Jahre alt war Uwe R. Brückner, als der situationistische Künstler und Philosoph Guy Debord den gesellschaftspolitisch kritischen Begriff des Spektakels einführte, um die kommende Phase des Kapitalismus zu definieren. 30 Jahre später, 1997, gründete der aus dem Theater kommende Gestalter gemeinsam mit seiner Frau Shirin Frangoul-Brückner das ATELIER BRÜCKNER – eine Werkstatt für die Konzeption von Ausstellungen und Museen. Es folgte nicht nur eine Serie von faszinierenden Inszenierungen, sondern parallel auch die Definition einer Disziplin, die sich an der Qualität des Werks international ausrichten musste. Kaum mehr als 20 Jahre später ist dieses Sammelwerk eines des reichsten Korpora der Gestaltung von Inszenierungen im Zeitalter der Gesellschaft des Spektakels. Das Atelier verwandelte sich in dieser Zeit in eine performative Gesellschaft mit multidisziplinären Partnern und internationalen Ambitionen.

Rückblickend kann man das Werk des ATELIER BRÜCKNER als einen Versuch definieren, in einem Umfeld, das von Zeichenüberflutung geprägt ist, Szenografen sowohl formal als auch inhaltlich auf hohem Niveau agieren zu lassen. Es ist eine komplexe Aktion, eine Divergenz, etwas Abweichendes, innerhalb eines Systems zu kreieren, in dem das Bild und die visuelle Narration eine übertriebene Macht – selten im Interesse des Bürgers – erreicht haben. Die Macht des Werks liegt nicht nur in der Ausführung, auch nicht allein in den technischen Fähigkeiten oder guter Narration, sondern in der Qualität, der (nicht immer respektierten) Autorenschaft, die ermöglichte, diesen Teil des Spektakels aus der nüchternen Neutralität der Massenproduktion visueller Events hervorzuheben.

Die Wichtigkeit eines solchen Störfaktors wird oft, sowohl vom Kunden als auch intern, von einem Team, das die Zufriedenheit der Auftraggeber sucht, unterschätzt. Wichtiger scheint aber der übergeordnete Wunsch, den individuellen Besucher aus der Masse zu reißen – ihm die Konstruktion der Hinterbühne bewusst zu machen und ihm dadurch die Möglichkeit zu geben, selbst zu denken und zu agieren, einfach um die Macht über die Realität wiederzugewinnen.

Das (Inter-)Agieren innerhalb der Ausstellung ist eines der am meisten diskutierten Themen innerhalb der Disziplin. Dies aber nur in Verbindung mit

The scenographer, like all other designers, has a central responsibility to the role, which he assigns to people in this exchange. Currently, the fascination of the designer mostly seems to lie in cultivating the machine that draws the visitor into the spectacle. He asks whether the goals of the designer match those of the spectacle society.

A good interactive installation within a staged narration can indeed help the visitor not only to leave the passive role of the spectator but also the spectacle of neo-liberal society. The situation can only be saved if democracy finally becomes truly democratic and the citizen is not merely viewed as a naïve spectator, but rather as a responsible player.

What does this mean for the future? Taking stock as in this compendium can under certain circumstances allow one to bid the past farewell in order to open up a new chapter of participation. The time is right; museums and exhibitions can take a new perspective in the coming society. It is then not about perfecting the spectacle within the spectacle but about using the capacity of such localities as a basis for new forms of consciousness of real democracy. Where history is processed, the future should also test better forms of democracy, solidarity, interrelations, and interdependencies.

As an internationally important representative of a discipline which defines itself as progressive, at the end of the day both Uwe R. Brückner as personality as well as ATELIER BRÜCKNER with its commitment bear a responsibility which goes far beyond the quality of the conception and realisation of individual assignments: a responsibility to the visitors of the staging they design, but also a responsibility to the discipline of scenographers.

“I didn’t want to judge, but to put the spectator in the position of a jury member or judge.” Jean-Luc Godard, “The Image Book,” 2012

den Kapazitäten der digitalen Technologien, die uns in eine immer stimmigere fiktive Welt eintauchen lassen. Die Interaktion zwischen Mensch und Objekt, Zeichen, Systemen oder Raum begann selbstverständlich lange vor der Digitalität. Der Szenograf, so wie alle anderen Designer auch, hat eine zentrale Verantwortung gegenüber der Rolle, die er dem Menschen in diesem Austausch zuschreibt. Die Faszination des Gestalters scheint momentan meist darin zu liegen, die Maschine zu kultivieren, die den Besucher weit in sein Spektakel zieht. Es fragt sich, ob die Ziele der Gestalter mit denen der Spektakelgesellschaft einhergehen.

In der Tat kann eine gute interaktive Installation innerhalb einer inszenierten Narration dem Besucher helfen, nicht nur aus der passiven Rolle des Zuschauers zu treten, sondern auch aus der des Spektakels der neoliberalen Gesellschaft. Die Situation kann nur gerettet werden, indem die Demokratie endlich demokratisch wird und den Bürger nicht nur als einen naiven Zuschauer betrachtet, sondern vielmehr als einen verantwortlichen Akteur.

Was heißt das für die Zukunft? Eine Bilanz wie die dieses Sammelwerks kann unter gewissen Umständen ermöglichen, die Vergangenheit zu verabschieden, um ein neues Kapitel der Partizipation zu eröffnen. Die Zeit passt. Museen und Ausstellungen können eine neue Perspektive in der kommenden Gesellschaft einnehmen. Es geht dann nicht mehr darum, das Spektakel innerhalb des Spektakels zu perfektionieren, sondern darum, die Kapazität solcher Örtlichkeiten als Basis für neue Formen von Bewusstsein realer Demokratie zu nutzen. Wo die Geschichte bearbeitet wird, sollte auch die Zukunft besserer Formen der Demokratie, der Solidarität, der Interrelationen, der Interdependenzen getestet werden.

Als international wichtige Vertreter einer Disziplin, die sich progressiv definiert, tragen schlussendlich sowohl Uwe R. Brückner als Persönlichkeit wie auch das ATELIER BRÜCKNER mit seinem Engagement eine Verantwortung, die weit über die Konzeptions- und Realisationsqualität der einzelnen Aufträge hinausgeht: eine Verantwortung gegenüber den Besuchern der gestalteten Inszenierungen, aber auch eine Verantwortung gegenüber der Disziplin der Szenografen.

„Ich wollte nicht urteilen, sondern den Zuschauer in die Position eines Geschworenen oder Richters versetzen." Jean-Luc Godard, Livre d'images, 2012.

EXPEDITION TITANIC

Temporary Exhibition, 3,500 sqm, Hamburg, Germany, 1997

Scenographically, “Expedition Titanic” is generally thought to be exemplary: it is object-oriented, it is emotional, and it is authentic–presented to a high museum-like standard. The exhibition is shaped by narrative spaces, combined with a sequence of specific themed rooms, associative, artistically designed interludes, and a connecting steel ship’s corridor which announces the sinking of the Titanic by subtly placed metronomes that tick faster and faster. The storyline is reminiscent of Akira Kurosawa’s anthology film “Rashomon” from 1950.

On a dramatized route that meanders along the corridor, the visitors themselves become passengers. They wander through the atmospherically dense rooms, each with its own light and sound choreography, and focused on original exhibits that were salvaged from 3,800 metres under the sea. They are accompanied by five protagonists and their conflicting memories of the events. Until the very end, it remains unclear whether the eyewitnesses survived the shipwreck.

The routing, starting with the boarding of the passengers, past reconstructed first- to third-class cabins to the salons, the “Lounges and Restaurants,” and the first interlude, the “Champagne Room”: an extremely bright room with an underlying bass tone that can be sensed rather than heard, reminiscent of the immense pressure underwater at a great depth. The dialectic juxtaposition of six bottles of Champagne and a workingman’s shoe is a metaphor for the classlessness of the sinking and a reference to the actual designation of the Titanic as an emigration ship.

The routing continues to the “Drama of the Sinking.” It is the most emotional room of the exhibition, devoted to the contradictory, deeply moving reports of survivors and optically shaped by Willy Stöwer’s famous painting of the sinking Titanic.

„Expedition Titanic“ gilt im szenografischen Sinne als exemplarisch: Die Ausstellung ist objektorientiert, emotional und authentisch – inszeniert auf hohem musealem Niveau. Geprägt von narrativen Raumbildern, kombiniert sie eine Abfolge spezifischer Themenräume, assoziativ-künstlerisch gestalteter Interludes und einen verbindenden stählernen Schiffskorridor, der den Untergang der Titanic durch subtil platzierte, immer schneller tickende Metronome ankündigt. Die Dramaturgie erinnert an Akira Kurosawas Episodenfilm „Rashomon“ von 1950.

Auf einer dramatisierten, über den Korridor mäandrierenden Route werden die Besucher selbst zu Passagieren. Sie wandeln durch die atmosphärisch dichten Räume mit jeweils spezifischer Licht- und Sound-Choreografie, fokussiert auf originale Exponate, die aus 3.800 Meter Meerestiefe geborgen wurden. Begleitet werden sie von fünf Protagonisten und deren widersprüchlichen Erinnerungen an die Ereignisse. Bis zuletzt bleibt unklar, ob die Zeitzeugen das Schiffsunglück überlebt haben.

Der Parcours führt, beginnend mit dem „Boarding“ der Passagiere, vorbei an rekonstruierten Kabinen der ersten bis dritten Klasse zu den Salons, dem „Öffentlichen Parkett“ und dem ersten Interlude, dem „Champagnerraum“ – ein gleißend heller Raum mit nicht hör-, aber spürbarem Basston, der an den immensen Wasserdruck in großer Tiefe erinnert. Die dialektische Gegenüberstellung von sechs Champagnerflaschen und einem Arbeiterschuh ist Metapher für die Klassenlosigkeit des Untergangs und Verweis auf die tatsächliche Bestimmung der Titanic als Auswandererschiff.

Weiter führt der Parcours zum sogenannten „Untergangsraum“. Er ist der emotionalste Raum der Ausstellung, gewidmet den einander widersprechenden, tief berührenden Berichten der Überlebenden und optisch geprägt von Willy Stöwers bekanntem Gemälde der sinkenden Titanic.

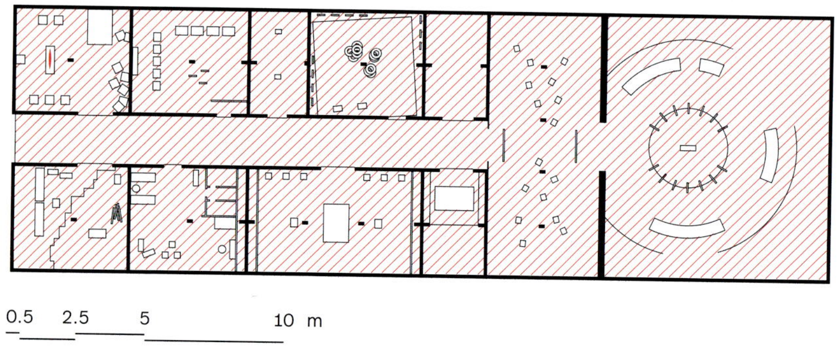

01 Floor Plan–Thematic Rooms in meandering order: “Welcome on Board,” “Coal and Steel,” “Life on Board,” “Lounges and Restaurants,” “Champagne Room,” “The Drama of the Sinking,” “Rescue,” “Streams of Fate,” “Room of Silence,” “Myth.” All rooms are linked by “The Corridor”–the lifeline of the Titanic.

02 “Welcome on Board”–an introduction by five protagonists, who serve as guides and interpreters by being quoted in the exhibition, no matter whether they survived or died.

The second interlude, the "Streams of Fate," contains an unrestored, broken clarinet; the hymn "Nearer, My God, to Thee" plays in the background, referring to the many ethnic groups who went down with the ship, supposedly united by music.

Subsequently, visitors are guided through the darkened room on the other side without sound and dimension, the "Room of Silence," with a large number of anonymous exhibits; and to the post-apocalyptic "Myth." The latter contains just one exhibit: the bell that Frederick Fleet very probably tolled when he saw the iceberg. It can only be reached by walking over white pebbles that crunch underfoot–a loud echo in contrast to the deathly silence that surrounds the wreck.

With 1.5 million visitors and huge media interest, "Expedition Titanic" is one of the most successful privately financed temporary exhibitions in the German-speaking world. It is shaped by an holistic design that addresses all the senses, a well-balanced density of exhibits, and narrative space which, together with the interludes, turns the expedition into a tour of suspense and a memorable experience.

Das zweite Interlude, der „Klarinettenraum," verweist mit einer unrestaurierten zerbrochenen Klarinette und dem Song „Nearer, My God, to Thee" auf die vielen Ethnien, die in der Musik geeint den Untergang erlebten.

Im Anschluss werden die Besucher durch den nachtdunklen, geräusch- und dimensionslosen Jenseitsraum, den „Raum der Stille", mit einer Vielzahl anonymer Exponate geführt und zum postapokalyptischen „Mythosraum" geleitet. Er präsentiert ein einziges Objekt: die Glocke, die höchstwahrscheinlich Frederick Fleet geläutet hat, als er den Eisberg sah. Sie ist nur über weißen, knirschenden Kies erreichbar – ein lautes Echo im Kontrast zur Totenstille rund um das Wrack zuvor.

Mit 1,5 Millionen Besuchern und einem riesigen Medieninteresse zählt Expedition Titanic zu den erfolgreichsten frei finanzierten temporären Ausstellungen im deutschsprachigen Raum. Sie zeichnet sich durch eine holistische, alle Sinne ansprechende Gestaltung, eine ausgewogene Exponatdichte und durch themenkonsistente Raumbilder aus. Diese bilden mit den Interludes einen spannungssteigernden Parcours und werden zum nachhaltigen Erlebnis.

03 "Room of Silence"–an acoustically insulated and absolutely dark space in reverence to anonymous personal objects provoking a lasting sense of empathy.

04 "Myth"–an after-wreckage public reflection. Flooded with overexposed light in extrem contrast to the space before, with jarring noisy gravel on the floor. Hidden audio players in the walls tell stories of other ship losses.

05 "Champagne Room"–a dialectic setting of six original Champagne bottles (obviously from 1st class) and a workingman's boot (3rd class) in an edgeless light box with imperceptible subwoofer tones hidden in the hollow walls. This means visitors feel the sensation of a room under pressure.

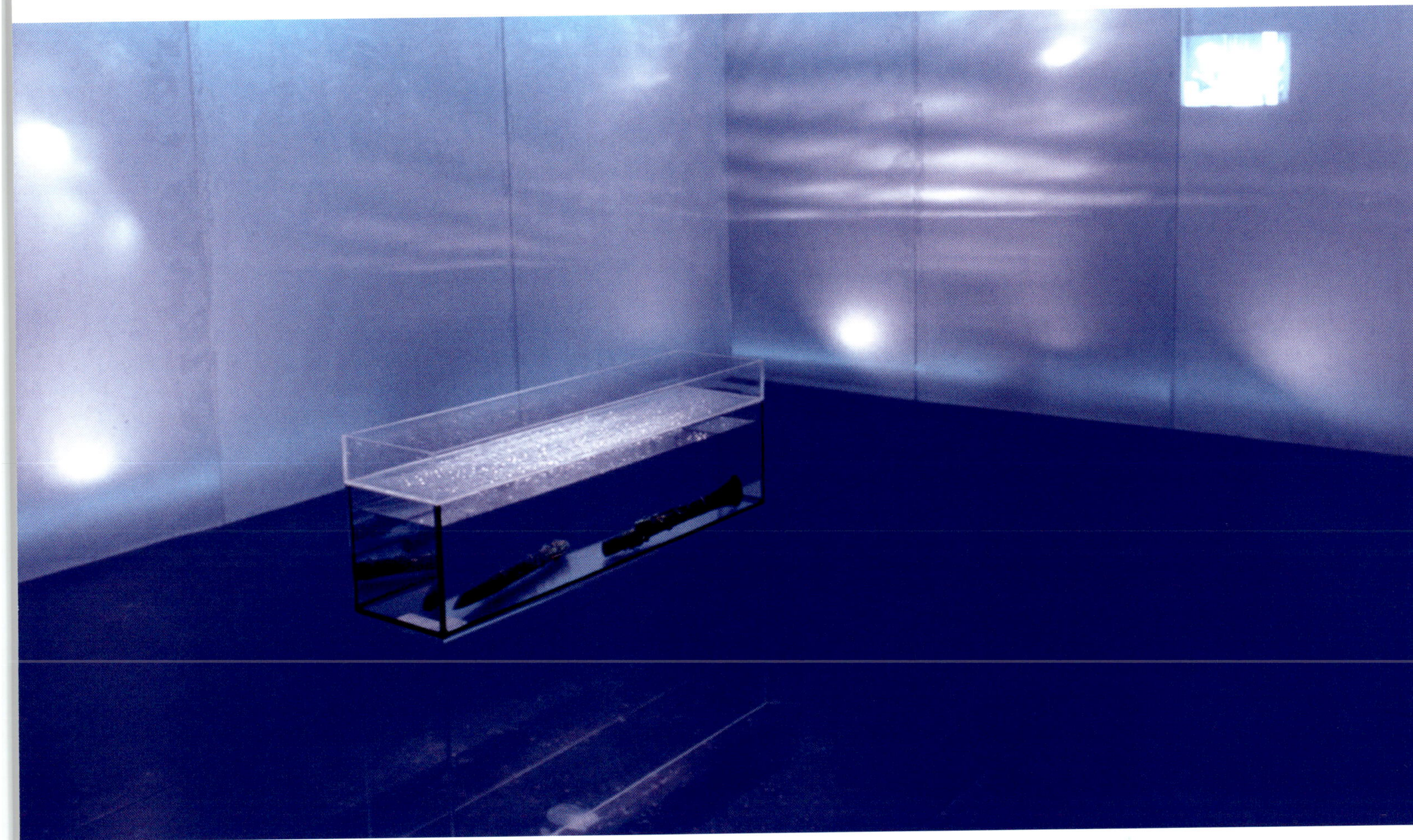

06 "Steams of Fate"–the untreated, broken instrument was a metaphor for the many languages travelling on the Titanic and the many ethnicities that were united in death. The room is filled with the haunting song "My Nearer to God by Thee."

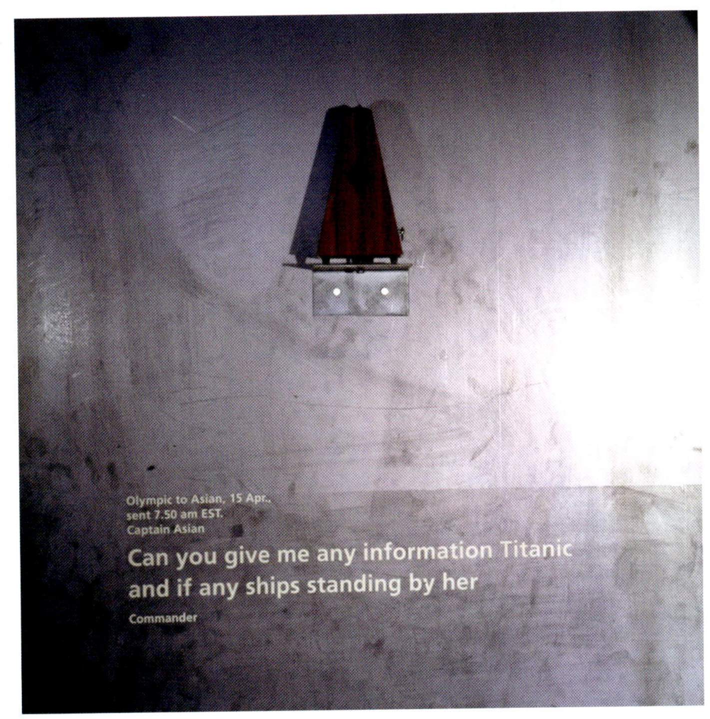

07 Metronomes along the corridor simulate the "pulse" of the Titanic. They are regular and in harmony at the beginning of the maiden voyage, becoming more frantic and the last one bound in silence. This spine of Titanic's lifeline was a sort of reminder to the inescapable fate of the ship.

CYCLEBOWL

Corporate Pavilion, 1,600 sqm, Expo Hanover, Germany, 2000

The Cyclebowl, the pavilion of Duales System Deutschland AG with a focus on cycles and the circular economy, was one of the most popular pavilions of the Expo Hanover. It offered an impressive, holistic experience with a real tornado as its main attraction, which visitors were prepared to wait hours to see.

The 25-metre-tall Cyclebowl is a scenographic experiment which stages the architecture and exhibition like a three-act opera. In the first act, visitors pass through a hedge labyrinth in which the first themes of the exhibition are introduced, shortening the time spent in queues by setting the mood for the experiences that await the curious visitors in the pavilion.

In the second act, visitors explore the exhibition inside the building via a spiral ramp. On three levels, it shows the past, present, and future of the circular economy, creating associations between this perspective and the three Expo themes—man, nature, and technology. Simulations, projections, and computer-animated exhibits, mirrored passages, and a laboratory full of experiments turn the tour around the exhibition into a themed experience. The focus is on the consumer habits of people and the way they handle natural resources as they become scarcer with the growing world population. An international breakfast table picks up this theme, showing not only the different meals with which people around the globe start their day, but also how much rubbish they produce.

In the third act, the lights are dimmed in the interior of the pavilion and the visitors experience a real tornado, a symbol for the indomitable force of nature and the dynamics of cycles. The story behind it is an abstract laboratory situation that gets out of control and goes up in a film of flames and smoke—a metaphor for the dangerous hubris of man wanting to solve problems it has caused by means of technical achievements alone.

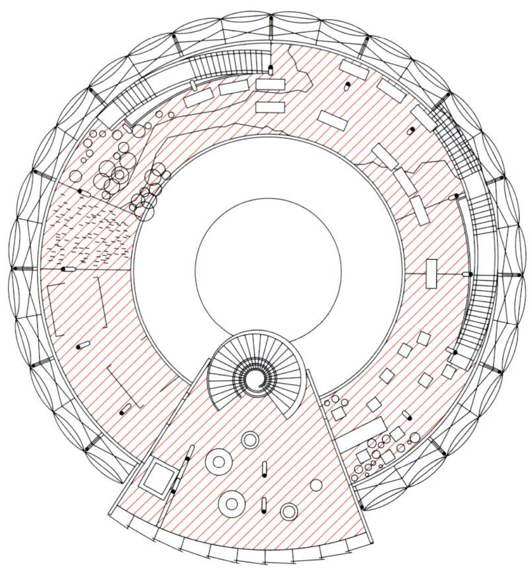

Der Cyclebowl genannte Pavillon der Duales System Deutschland AG zählte zu den meistbesuchten Pavillons der Expo Hannover. Er hatte das Thema „Kreisläufe und Kreislaufwirtschaft" und bot ein eindrückliches holistisches Erlebnis – mit einem realen Tornado als Hauptattraktion. Besucher nahmen stundenlange Wartezeiten in Kauf.

Die 25 Meter hohe Cyclebowl ist ein szenografisches Experiment, das Architektur und Ausstellung wie eine dreiaktige Oper inszeniert: Im ersten Akt gehen die Besucher durch ein Heckenlabyrinth, in dem bereits die Ausstellungsthemen angespielt werden. Sie nehmen das Warteschlangenmanagement als kurzweilige Einstimmung auf die Erlebnisse wahr, die im Pavillon auf sie warten.

Im zweiten Akt erkunden sie die Ausstellung im Inneren des Gebäudes über eine spiralförmige Rampe. Sie zeigt auf drei Ebenen Vergangenheit, Gegenwart und Zukunft der Kreislaufwirtschaft und verbindet diese Blickwinkel mit den drei Expo-Themen Mensch, Natur und Technik. Simulationen, Projektionen und computeranimierte Exponate, Spiegelgänge und ein Experimentierlabor machen den Rundgang zum Erlebnis. Der inhaltliche Fokus liegt dabei auf dem Konsumverhalten des Menschen und seinem Umgang mit den natürlichen Ressourcen in einer zunehmend enger werdenden Welt. So vermittelt ein internationaler Frühstückstisch nicht nur, mit welchen Mahlzeiten der Tag weltweit beginnt, sondern auch, wie viel Abfall dabei anfällt.

Im dritten Akt verdunkelt sich das Pavilloninnere und die Besucher erleben einen echten Tornado als Symbol für die unbezähmbare Kraft der Natur und die Dynamik von Kreisläufen. Der Tornado entwickelt sich im Zentrum des Pavillons narrativ aus einer abstrakten Laborsituation, die außer Kontrolle gerät und filmisch in Flammen und Rauch aufgeht – eine Metapher für die gefährliche Hybris der Menschen, selbst verschuldete Probleme allein durch technische Errungenschaften lösen zu wollen.

01 Floor plan.
02 "Cyclebowl" exterior with the pneumatic facade closed.

MILESTONES 2011 2012 2013 2014 2015 2016 2017 2018

03 Detail view of the pneumatic facade with spray-shields (closed: left, open: right). Triple layered ETFE-foil cushions with a silver print allow variable shading. The middle layer has a leaf print and the outer layer the negative of the print. By deflating one chamber and inflating the opposite these come together to create full shading coverage; the pillows can be inflated/deflated to vary this shading.

The cycle principle is reflected not only in the architecture and scenography, symbolised in the form of a bowl and a spiral ramp. It continues systematically in the fully recyclable building materials and natural air-conditioning and lighting technology. The Cyclebowl is, for instance, equipped with a pneumatic facade and roof system that allows the pavilion to be darkened automatically, transforming it from a building lit by daylight into a black box. In addition, it is naturally ventilated and has an energy-efficient air-conditioning system, the world's first system that visibly circulates water around the building by day, reducing the felt temperature; at night it is sprayed over the facade. Subsequently, the water that cools there naturally is collected belowground and fed back into the cooling cycle again during the day.

The synthesis of architecture, graphics, light, sound, film, and show, including the powerful message that responsibility is the key prerequisite alongside technical solutions for managing our waste problem, lets visitors experience the vision of an environmentally aware and sustainable society with all their senses.

Das Prinzip der Kreisläufe spiegelt sich nicht nur in Architektur und Szenografie, symbolisiert in der Form einer Bowl und der spiralförmigen Rampe. Es setzt sich auch konsequent in vollständig recycelbaren Baumaterialien und natürlicher Klima- und Lichttechnologie fort. So ist die Cyclebowl mit einem pneumatischen Fassaden- und Dachsystem ausgestattet, das eine stufenlose Verdunklung ermöglicht und sie innerhalb weniger Minuten von einem Tageslichtgebäude in eine Blackbox verwandelt. Zudem besitzt sie neben natürlicher Belüftung auch ein energieeffizientes Klimasystem – eine Weltneuheit. Wasser zirkuliert tagsüber sichtbar im gesamten Gebäude und senkt die empfundene Raumtemperatur, während es nachts auf die Fassade versprüht wird. Es kühlt dort auf natürliche Weise ab, wird unterirdisch gesammelt und tagsüber wieder in den Kühlkreislauf eingespeist.

Das Gesamtkunstwerk aus Architektur, Grafik, Licht, Ton, Film und Show – inklusive der starken Botschaft, dass neben technischen Lösungen Verantwortung das notwendige Fundament für die Überwindung unserer Abfallprobleme ist – lässt die Besucher mit allen Sinnen die Vision einer umweltbewussten und nachhaltigen Gesellschaft erfahren.

04 Nature 1–From natural to cultural landscape–a pathway through real plants.

05 "The International Breakfast Table" indicating the amount of packaging waste in various countries.

06 The spiralling and narrowing "Overpopulation" staircase is the last impressive gesture all visitors had to flow through. It was a metaphor for the depletion of resources while the world's population (visitors) is increasing uncontrollably.

07 The central void–with open facade (left)–closed facade, creating a black-box with tornado (right). Every full hour about 1,000 visitors could enjoy the transformation of the pavilion from a day-lit greenhouse into a black-box-cinema with a circular movie and a real 20 m high tornado.

INNOVARIUM

Feasibility Study for a Science Centre, 7,500 sqm, Oberhausen, Germany, 2000

The Innovarium, an international research and science museum project with a focus on renewable energies, which had been developed in 2000, was planned as the main attraction of the Science and Health Park by O.VISION. The park that extends over 54 hectares in Oberhausen combines research and exhibition in a highly innovative way. Scientific institutes and companies researching the use of sustainable energy run walk-in laboratories in the Innovarium. Their most recent findings and research results are incorporated directly into the exhibition where they are impressively staged for the public.

The exhibition tour is designed like an integrative hybrid of working laboratories and realistically dimensioned experimental arrangements for visitors to experience. The four elements –fire, water, air, and earth–offer visitors a metaphorical way to access the world of science. Just how important the sustainable energy industry is for the future is demonstrated spectacularly by a "Ventarium," an accessible solar updraught tower; an unfolding "Solarium," a solar power station that turns automatically to face the sun, an "Aquarium," a walk-in hydroelectric power station with sewage processing function; and a "Terrarium," with a biogas plant. The natural resources and their optimum use are at the same time content and exhibit. What is more, each of these four installations follows the concept of CO_2-neutral architecture. The building technology thus becomes an integral part of the exhibition and message.

Das Innovarium, ein internationales Forschungs- und Science-Museumsprojekt zum Thema erneuerbare Energien, das bereits im Jahr 2000 entwickelt wurde, war als Hauptattraktion des 54 Hektar großen Science- und Health-Parks von O.VISION in Oberhausen geplant. Es verbindet auf neuartige Art und Weise Forschung und Ausstellung. Wissenschaftsinstitute und Unternehmen, die über die Nutzung nachhaltiger Energie forschen, unterhalten im Innovarium begehbare Labore, in denen ihre neuesten Erkenntnisse und Forschungsergebnisse direkt in die Ausstellung eingespielt und dort publikumswirksam inszeniert werden.

Der Ausstellungsparcours ist wie ein integratives Hybrid aus aktiven Laboren und Versuchsanordnungen realistischer Dimension gestaltet. Die vier Elemente – Feuer, Wasser, Luft und Erde – bieten den Besuchern einen metaphorischen Zugang zur Wissenschaftswelt. Ihre spektakuläre Umsetzung als ein „Ventarium" (befahrbares Aufwindkraftwerk), ein entfaltbares „Solarium" (sich nach der Sonne ausrichtendes Solarkraftwerk), ein „Aquarium" (begehbares Wasserkraftwerk mit Klärfunktion) und ein „Terrarium" (mit Biogasanlage) steht für die notwendig nachhaltige Energiewirtschaft der Zukunft. Die natürlichen Ressourcen und deren optimale Nutzung sind Inhalt und Exponat zugleich. Jede dieser vier Installationen folgt dem Konzept einer CO_2-neutralen Architektur. So wird auch die Gebäudetechnik Gegenstand der Ausstellung und Vermittlung.

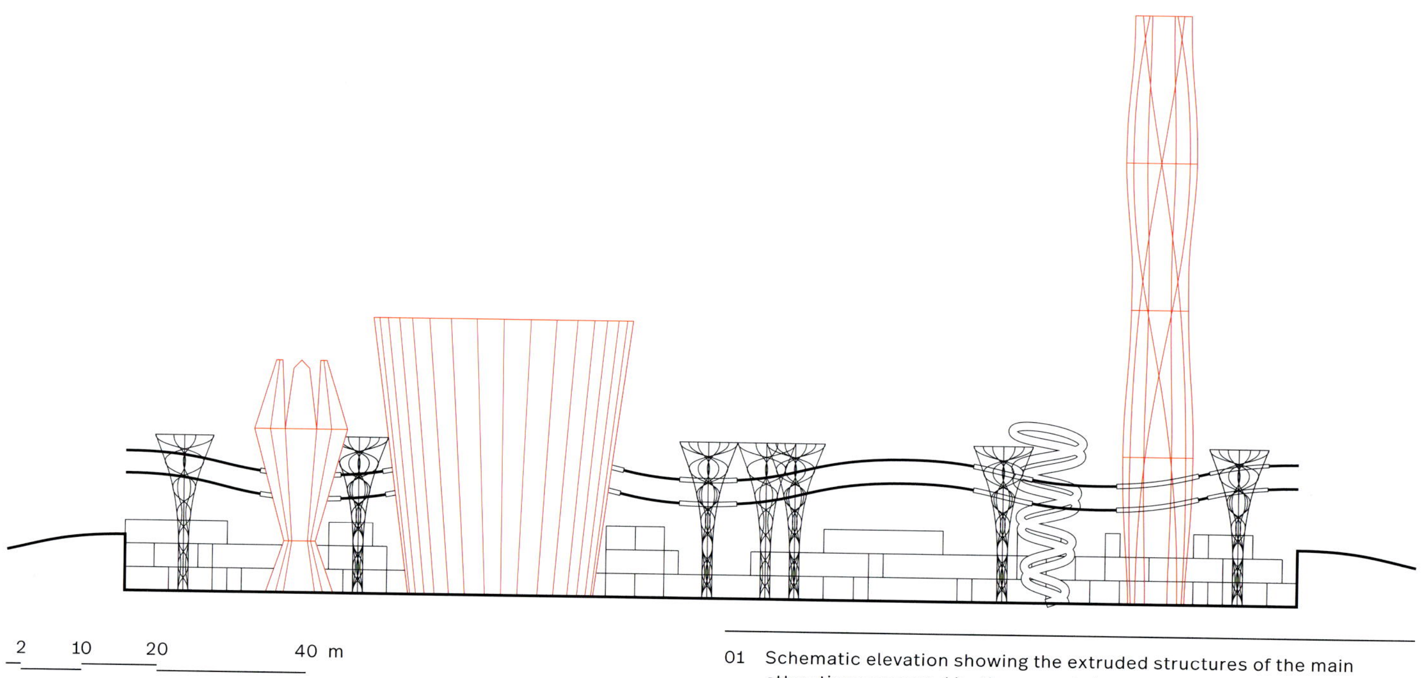

01 Schematic elevation showing the extruded structures of the main attractions powered by the sun, wind, water, and biomass energy.
02 Interactive public laboratories inviting visitors to explore the production of sustainable energies.

MILESTONES 2011 2012 2013 2014 2015 2016 2017 2018

03 Physical concept model at 1:200 scale, depicting the idea of extruding the building metaphorically from the ground.

Science, technology, and future topics are intended to get visitors to the Innovarium excited about the subject so that the message sticks in their minds. Research, presentation, and experience are closely combined here so that perspectives can be experienced beyond the normal field of vision: scientainment instead of conventional knowledge transfer–multimedial and interactive, fascinating and forward-looking.

Wissenschaft, Technik und Zukunftsthemen sollen die Besucher des Innovariums erinnerungswürdig begeistern. Forschen, Präsentieren und Erleben werden hier auf integrative Weise kombiniert, sodass jenseits traditioneller Sehgewohnheiten Visionen erlebbar werden. Scientainment statt konventioneller Wissensvermittlung – multimedial und interaktiv, faszinierend und zukunftsweisend.

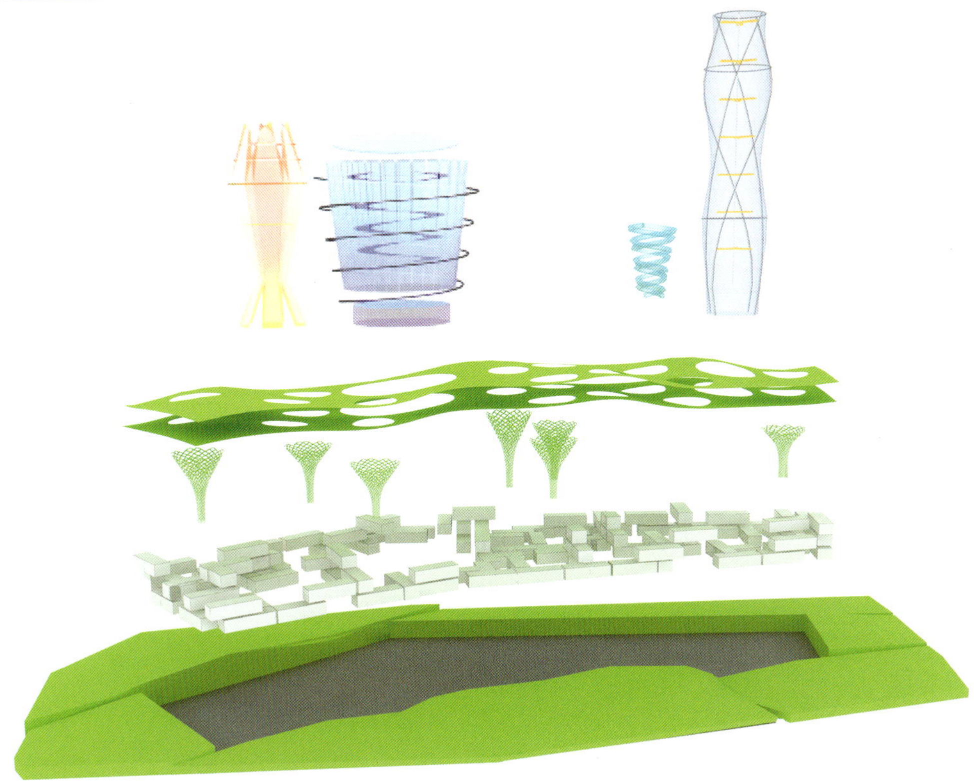

04 Exploded isometric view showing the solar tower, exhibition bowl, hydropower station, updraught tower, and tree-like supporting structure. The laboratories perforate the space with free-flowing public circulation around them.

PANASONIC—BLUE GARDENS

Trade Fair Stand, 3,500 sqm, IFA, Berlin, Germany, 2001

This trade fair stand—one of the most striking at the IFA 2001—does not at first glance show any products but instead a fascinating, endless projection along 300 metres of walls up to four metres in height. This spectacular gesture that unifies the booth into a single unit, pertinently symbolises the idea of a shared corporate identity. The underlying concept is based on a huge projected Möbius strip that not only serves as projection surface and control system, but also divides up the stand, separating the various project areas from one another.

A radical change of perspective: the focus is not on the product but on what the product can do—with the welcome effect that every visitor wants to know what devices were used to create such an impressive show.

The film projected using digital Panasonic high-performance projectors transforms the stand into an eye-catching, initially blue-shimmering, mystical underwater world. A woman in a red dress swims through the stand while the patterns on her dress are transformed in the rhythm of the music and in a choreography of colours into a surreal underwater world with mystical inhabitants—the "Blue Gardens."

The physical space fades into the background, replaced by the imagined space. With the speed and direction of the motifs, the film brings the architecture to life and provides navigation for the visitors—it becomes an accessible subject.

This early example of a huge moving-image installation aroused attention all over the world and demonstrates the performance and competence of the company by using its own devices to impressively create an imaginary world of images, sounds, and moods. A world of technology staged with emotion becomes a convincing and memorable experience.

Dieser Messestand – einer der auffälligsten auf der IFA 2001 – zeigt zunächst keine Produkte, sondern eine faszinierende Endlosprojektion auf 300 Meter langen und bis zu 4 Meter hohen Wänden – eine spektakuläre Geste, die den Messestand ganz im Sinne einer gemeinsamen Firmenidentität zu einer Einheit formt. Die Grundidee basiert auf einem überdimensionalen filmischen Möbius-Band, das nicht nur als Projektionsfläche und Leitsystem dient, sondern den Stand gliedert und die einzelnen Produktbereiche voneinander abgrenzt.

Ein radikaler Perspektivwechsel: Nicht das Produkt steht im Fokus, sondern das, was das Produkt leisten kann – mit dem willkommenen Effekt, dass jeder Besucher wissen will, mit welchen Geräten eine derartig beeindruckende Inszenierung umgesetzt werden kann.

Der mit digitalen Panasonic-Hochleistungsbeamern projizierte Film verwandelt den Stand in eine eindrucksvolle, zunächst blau schimmernde, mystische Unterwasserwelt. Eine Frau in einem roten Kleid durchschwimmt den Messestand, während sich die Muster ihres Kleides im Rhythmus der Musik und entsprechend der Choreografie der Farben zu surrealen Unterwassergärten mit mystischen Bewohnern transformieren – den „Blue Gardens".

Der physische Raum rückt völlig in den Hintergrund. An seine Stelle tritt der imaginierte Raum. Durch Geschwindigkeit und Bewegungsrichtung der Motive dynamisiert der Film die Architektur und übernimmt die Navigation der Besucher – er wird zum begehbaren Sujet.

Dieses frühe Beispiel einer raumgreifenden Bewegtbildinstallation erzeugte weltweite Aufmerksamkeit und beweist, nicht zuletzt durch die firmeneigenen Geräte, die eindrucksvoll eine imaginäre Welt aus Bildern, Klängen und Atmosphären schaffen, Leistungsfähigkeit und Kompetenz des Unternehmens. Eine emotional ansprechend inszenierte Technikwelt wird zum nachhaltig überzeugenden Erlebnis.

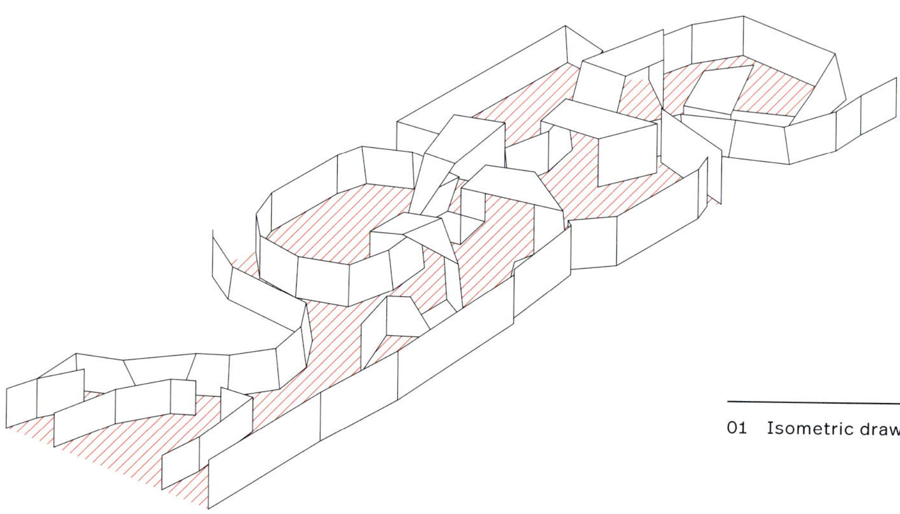

01 Isometric drawing of wall structure like a Möbius strip.

02 The 180-metre Möbius projection strip featuring the "Blue Gardens," a mysterious world of underwater environments and colourful patterns which convert the corridors into a dynamic film loop.

03 Narrative patterns from Panasonic's branding campaign alter the corridor and help to influence visitor movement.

EXPERIENCING FRONTIERS

Cantonal Pavilion, 900 sqm, Expo.02, Arteplage Biel/Bienne, Switzerland, 2002

When the eight border cantons chose the title for their pavilion at the Expo.02 in Switzerland–"Experiencing Frontiers"–they were not thinking so much of physical borders, but of limits from a social and cultural perspective. It was about a collective and individual experience of social and psychological limits. The idea was to make cultural and ethical limits, including bans, limits, and taboos such as marital violence, transsexuality, cloning, and euthanasia visible and tangible. How can this be done? How can borderline experiences be conveyed to Expo visitors who are seeking light entertainment and fun?

The pavilion, floating about three metres above the Arteplage in Biel, is conceived as a highly immersive, emotively staged experience that allows spatial access to the complexity of borderline situations. Passing through a labyrinth-like forest of poles, on the one hand a metaphor for barriers, on the other the load-bearing structure of the pavilion, the visitor reaches a cube whose silver-mirrored textile skin transports the film projection of the interior space to the outside as light choreography and inviting gesture.

Als die acht Schweizer Grenzkantone den Titel „Grenzen (er) leben" für ihren Pavillon auf der Expo.02 in der Schweiz wählten, hatten sie weniger physische Grenzen als soziokulturelle Grenzerfahrungen im Sinn. Es ging ihnen um kollektive und individuelle Erlebnisse sozialer und psychologischer Natur. Kulturelle und ethische Limits, darunter Verbote, Eingrenzungen und Tabus, wie Gewalt in der Ehe, Transsexualität, Klonen oder Sterbehilfe, sollten sichtbar und physisch erlebbar werden. Wie geht das? Wie lassen sich Grenzerfahrungen einem Expo-Publikum vermitteln, das kurzweilige, vergnügliche Unterhaltung sucht?

Der Pavillon, in etwa drei Metern Höhe über der Arteplage in Biel schwebend, ist als stark immersive, emotionalisierende Inszenierung erdacht, welche die Komplexität einer Grenzsituation real im Raum erfahrbar macht. Durch einen labyrinthischen Wald aus Stangen – einerseits Metapher für Schlagbäume, andererseits Tragstruktur des Pavillons – gelangt der Besucher in einen Kubus, dessen silbern verspiegelte Textilhülle die filmische Bespielung des Innenraums als Lichtchoreografie und einladende Geste nach draußen überträgt.

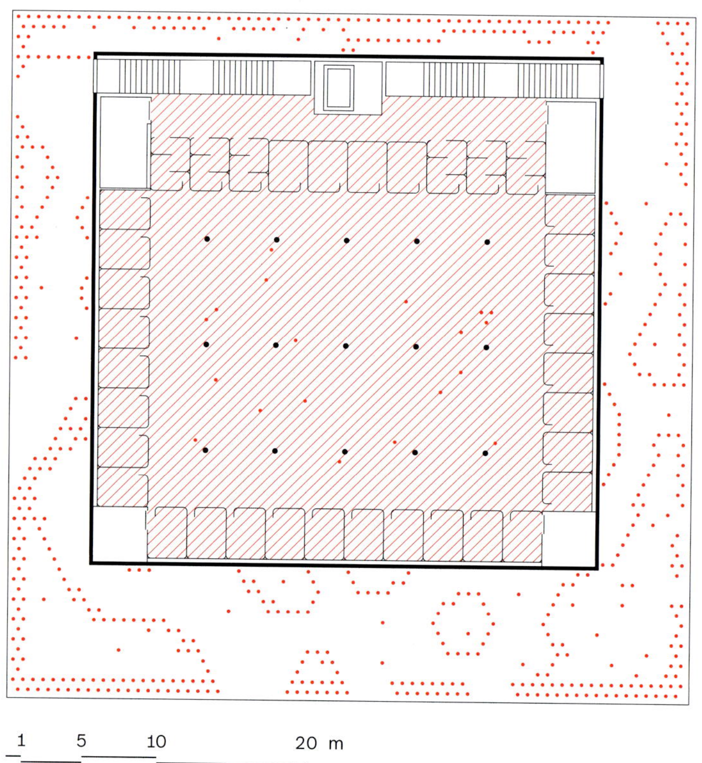

01 Plan view of the main exhibition level.
02 Pavilion "Experiencing Frontiers," hovering over the banks of Lake Biel.

MILESTONES 2011 2012 2013 2014 2015 2016 2017 2018

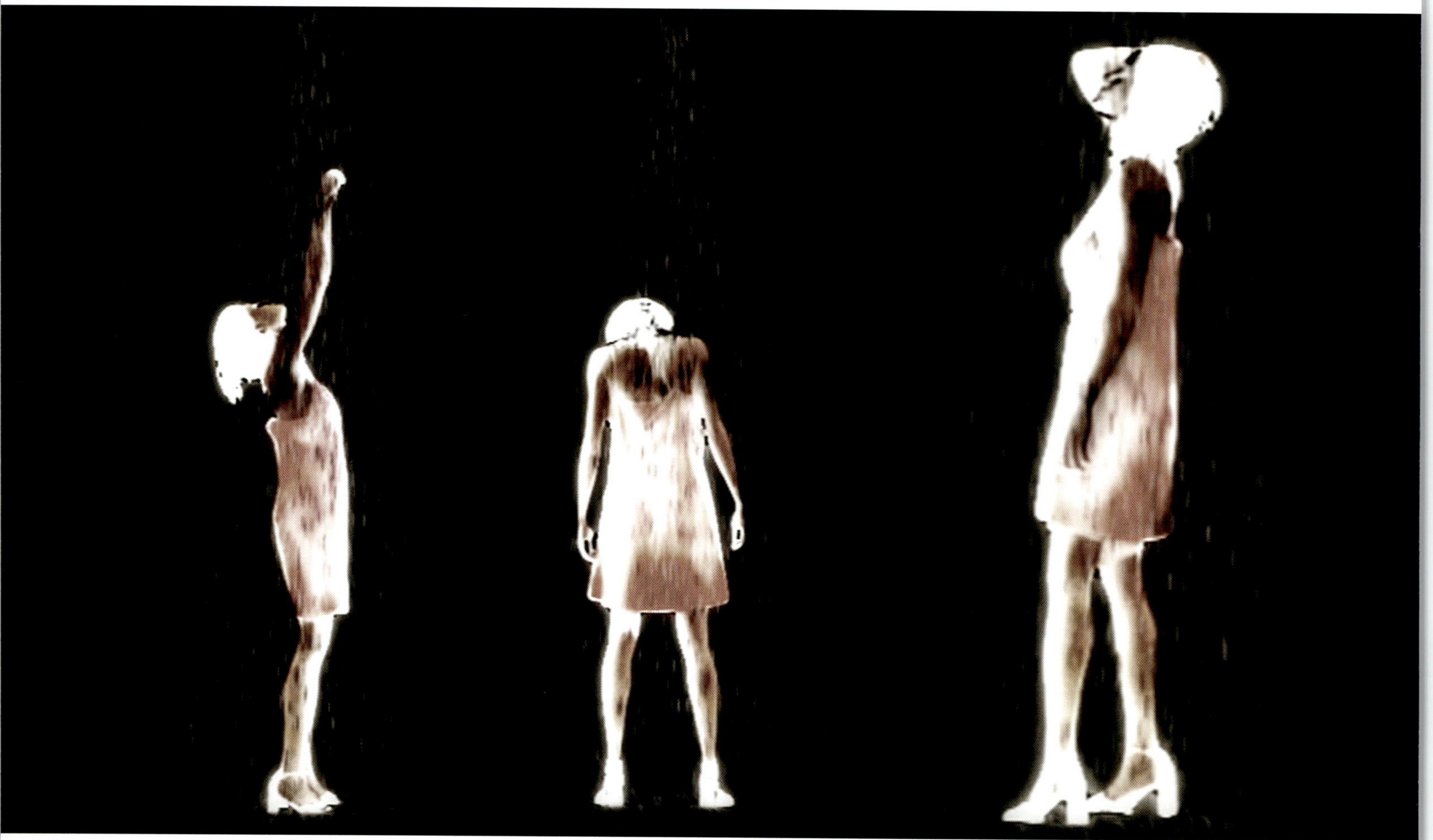

03 De-individualized character–one of seven different fringe-group protagonists: "Violence between spouses."

Initially visitors find themselves in individual cabins placed around the main space that is used as a film projection surface. From here, they see isolated figures as silhouettes, without any individual characteristics or personality. Through audio dramas they learn more about the seven protagonists. A sense of empathy evolves. For example, the listener, himself sitting in a wheelchair, hears the story of a paralysed bungee jumper, or in the adjacent cabin, the life story of a suicide victim is related to him.

In the central panorama room, the individual stories are contextualised into a collective happening. It becomes clear, for instance, that the bullet with which the person who tried to commit suicide hit another person. One after another, the figures become part of the interaction until finally, at the end of the 13-minute loop, they form a vociferously complaining fringe group–a social collective that holds up a mirror to the visitors, making it impossible for them to turn away.

The "Experiencing Frontiers" pavilion is a successful example of the integrative power of consistent scenography that is capable of translating complex, seemingly unattractive, hard-to-convey content into walk-in, self-explanatory subjects. The visitor is himself part of the spatial setting for the story. In the pavilion he himself crosses borders.

Die Besucher befinden sich zunächst in Einzelkabinen, die den filmisch bespielten Hauptraum umgeben. Von hier aus sehen sie isolierte Figuren als Silhouetten, ganz ohne jegliche Individualität. Über Hörspiele werden ihnen die sieben Protagonisten vertraut. Es entsteht Empathie. Beispielsweise erfährt der Zuhörer, selbst in einem Rollstuhl sitzend, von der Geschichte eines querschnittsgelähmten Bungeejumpers oder, in der Nachbarkabine, die Lebensgeschichte eines Selbstmörders.

Im zentralen Panoramaraum kontextualisieren sich dann die individuellen Geschichten zu einem kollektiven Ereignis. Unter anderem wird erzählt, dass die Kugel des Selbstmörders eine andere Person traf. Die Figuren treten nach und nach in Interaktion, bis sie sich zuletzt am Ende des 13-minütigen Loops zu einer lautstark anklagenden Randgruppe formieren – zu einem gesellschaftlichen Kollektiv, das den Besuchern den Spiegel vorhält und das Wegschauen unmöglich macht.

Der „Grenzen-(er)leben-Pavillon" ist ein erfolgreiches Beispiel für die integrative Kraft konsistenter Szenografie, die in der Lage ist, komplexe, vermeintlich unattraktive oder gar unvermittelbare Inhalte in begehbare, selbsterklärende Sujets zu übersetzen. Der Besucher ist selbst Teil der räumlich inszenierten Geschichte – er wird zum Grenzüberschreiter im Pavillon.

04 Central 360-degree panoramic projection on translucent membrane with 28 audio chambers behind.

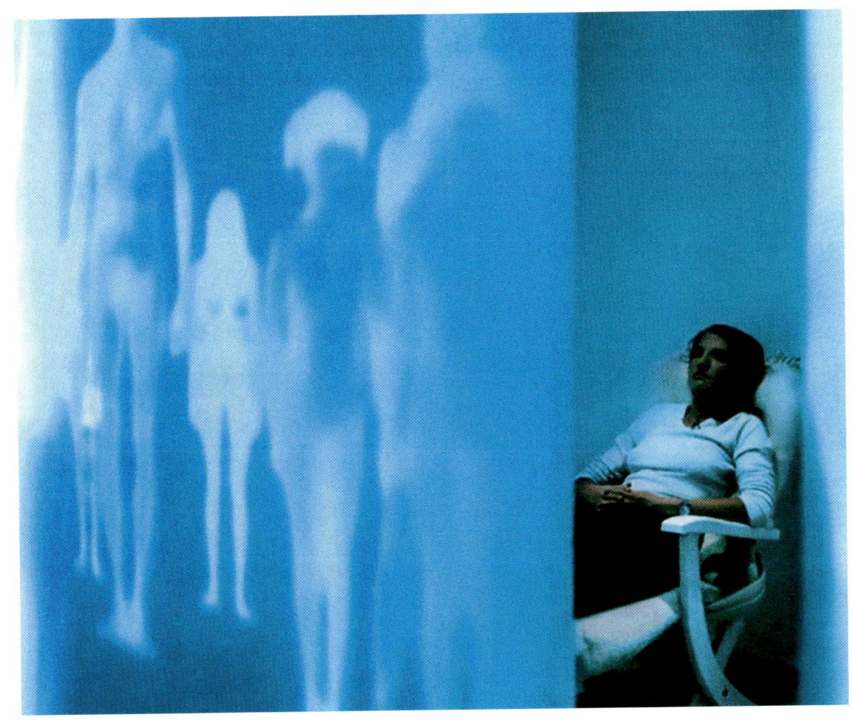

05 Audio chambers featuring seven real stories of borderline experiences performed by the protagonists in five languages each.

HOUSE OF HISTORY BADEN-WÜRTTEMBERG

Permanent Exhibition, 2,400 sqm, Stuttgart, Germany, 2002

The House of History by Wilford Schupp Architects in Stuttgart's museum district completes the ensemble of buildings, consisting of the State Gallery and Music College conceived by James Stirling, in a congenial way. The exhibition takes a critical look at 200 years of state history from the Napoleonic era through to the united Europe of today. It is divided into two routings, a chronological one and a thematic one.

The chronological routing welcomes visitors with an interactive, walk-on floor map that visualises the territorial power structures in Germany's southwest around the year 1790 and the reorganisation by Napoleon. Via a baroque staircase, which stages the rise of Baden and Württemberg, the visitor reaches the first floor. A varied visitor routing leads through the turbulent history of the state–from the Vormärz era before the revolution, the 1848 Revolution, via the world wars through to the present day.

Impressive narrative spaces generated era by era from the content support the story. For examample, wobbly floor tiles and flying leaflets convey the uncertain times around the 1848 Revolution. The projected quote "These times have been hit by a storm" can be tangibly experienced in the room.

A curated and scenographic device has been successfully applied in the much discussed and later highly praised "World War Block": the First and Second World Wars are presented here directly next to one another, separated merely by a 10-millimetre-thick glass pane on which at the same time–from the respective side–martial images of the war machine are projected without further commentary. Interestingly, the spatial sound works for both areas. The display cabinets around the walls are made of untreated steel; the hand- and fingerprints of the visitors build up into a warning patina.

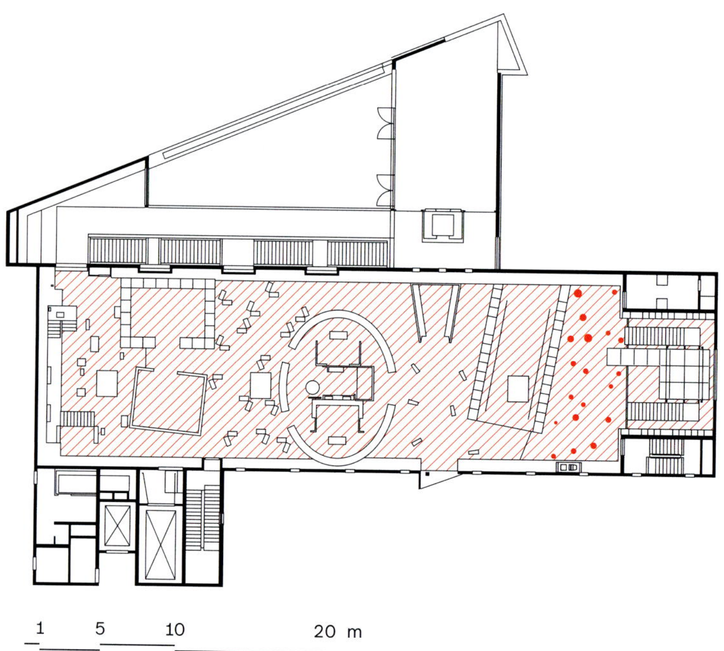

Das Haus der Geschichte von Wilford Schupp Architekten an der Stuttgarter Museumsmeile vervollständigt auf kongeniale Weise das von James Stirling erdachte bauliche Ensemble, bestehend aus Staatsgalerie und Musikhochschule. Die Ausstellung beleuchtet in kritischer Auseinandersetzung 200 Jahre Landesgeschichte, von der napoleonischen Zeit bis zum heutigen, geeinten Europa. Sie ist zweigeteilt in einen chronologischen und einen thematischen Parcours.

Der chronologische Parcours empfängt die Besucher mit einer interaktiven, begehbaren Bodenkarte, welche die territorialen Machtverhältnisse des deutschen Südwestens um das Jahr 1790 und die Neuordnung durch Napoleon veranschaulicht. Über ein barockes Treppenhaus, das den Aufstieg Badens und Württembergs inszeniert, erreicht der Besucher das erste Obergeschoss. Hier führt eine abwechslungsreich gestaltete Inzenierung durch die wechselvolle Geschichte des Landes – vom Vormärz und der Revolution 1848 über die Weltkriege bis in die Gegenwart.

Eindrucksvolle Raumbilder, die epochenweise aus den Inhalten generiert sind, unterstützen die Narration. So vermitteln gelockerte Bodenplatten und fliegende Flugblätter die unsichere, bewegte Zeit der Revolution 1848. Das projizierte Zitat „Ein Sturm ist in die Zeit gefahren" wird förmlich im Raum erlebbar.

Ein kuratorischer wie inszenatorischer Kunstgriff gelingt im viel diskutierten, später hochgelobten „Weltkriegsblock": Der Erste und Zweite Weltkrieg werden hier direkt nebeneinander präsentiert, lediglich getrennt von einer zehn Millimeter dicken Glasscheibe, auf die gleichzeitig – jeweils von der entsprechenden Seite – die martialischen Bilder der Kriegsmaschinerie kommentarlos projiziert werden. Interessanterweise passt der Raumton zu beiden Bereichen. Die raumumgrenzenden Vitrinenwände bestehen aus unbehandeltem Stahl, sodass sich die Hand- und Fingerabdrücke der Besucher wie eine mahnende Patina darauf legen.

01 Floor plan of the thematic exhibition–second floor.
02 Prologue–interactive floor surface powered by hundreds of capacitive sensors, responding to people standing on them. The coloured territories depict the dynasties which either survived or lost their estates after Napoleon politically restructured the German Southwest.

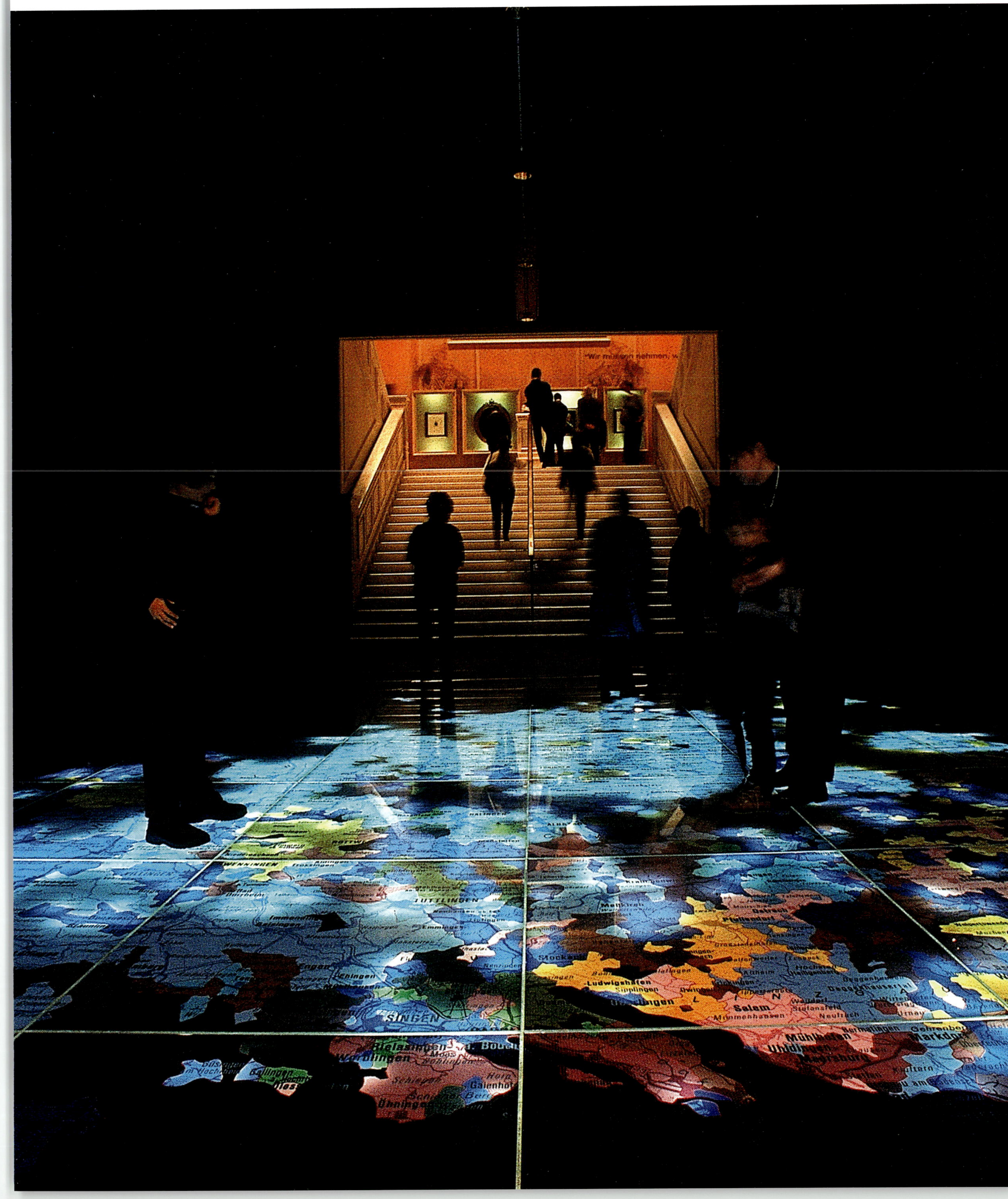
TUTTLINGEN
Emmingen
Ehingen
SINGEN
Ludwigshafen
Sipplingen
Salem
Mimmenhausen
Neufrach
Mühlhofen
Uhldingen
Meersburg
Wörblingen
Gailingen
Gaienhofen

03 First World War (left) and World War II (right) separated by a 10-millimetre glass panel with photographic imagery projected from either side. In the background the Weimar Republic integrated or squeezed in between the two World Wars. The untreated, partially corroded metal refers to the martial war and killing industry of the time.

HOUSE OF HISTORY BADEN-WÜRTTEMBERG

04 Economy. The metal shelf and the industrial objects tell many unique stories of how Baden-Württemberg became a venue of innovation and "Made in Germany" products, from Steiff teddy bears to the automotive industry.

Via the "Museum of the Present," a staged staircase with a view over Stuttgart that offers an interactive, always up-to-date platform for contemporary history and exhibits, the visitor arrives on the second floor of the museum. This is dedicated to eight themes typical for the region, including the Black Forest, Baden-Württemberg as business centre, religion, migration, and science. A specific narrative space was developed for each themed area. For instance, oversea trunks shape the migration section. Visitors can take a seat in them and listen to the fates of immigrants and emigrants.

Finally, the epilogue of the exhibition invites visitors on a journey through the topographical and cultural landscape of Baden-Württemberg. Seated in hanging bubble chairs, the 360-degree projection offers visitors a helicopter flight, woven into a collage with historical television recordings, such as John Cranko and his ballet.

The House of History does not try to tell every single detail of the 200 years of state history, but instead focuses on decisive political and social events. It offers a chronology of significant events with a staging suited to the exhibits placed in associative narrative spaces.

Über das „Museum der Gegenwart", ein inszeniertes Treppenhaus mit Ausblick auf Stuttgart, das eine interaktive, immer aktuelle Plattform für zeitgenössische Geschichte und Exponate bietet, gelangt der Besucher in die zweite Etage des Museums. Sie widmet sich acht landestypischen Themen, darunter dem Schwarzwald, Baden-Württemberg als Wirtschaftsstandort, den Religionen, Migration, und Wissenschaft. Für jeden Themenbereich wurde ein spezifisches Raumbild entwickelt. So prägen Reisekoffer den Bereich Migration. In ihnen kann der Besucher Platz nehmen und den Schicksalen von Ein- und Auswanderern lauschen.

Der Epilog der Ausstellung lädt schließlich zu einer Reise durch die topografisch wie kulturell geprägte Landschaft Baden-Württembergs ein. In hängenden Bubble-Chairs sitzend, erleben die Besucher einen Helikopterflug als 360-Grad-Projektion, collagiert mit historischen Fernsehaufzeichnungen, zum Beispiel von John Cranko und seinem Ballett.

Das Haus der Geschichte versucht nicht, 200 Jahre Landesgeschichte lückenlos zu erzählen, sondern es konzentriert sich auf prägende politische und gesellschaftliche Ereignisse.
Es bietet eine Bedeutungschronologie mit exponatadäquater Inszenierung in assoziativen Raumbildern.

05 The “Black Forest” on the first floor seems to fulfill the cliché of the authentic German forest, but boards sawed within the trees sophistically tell the real story, that the Black Forest always was an economically exploited wood.

LWL-MUSEUM OF ARCHAEOLOGY

Permanent Exhibition, 2,500 sqm, Herne, Germany, 2003

Who are we? Where do we come from? Where are we going? These unusual questions of the curators were the starting point for this museum. On top of that, they wanted to give an experiential dimension to the core tasks of a museum: collect, preserve, research, and communicate. The result was an integrative design approach that staged the permanent exhibition like a huge, accessible excavation site with archaeological survey grid, digging tents, ranging rods, and sites of archaeological finds. Three important design elements define the excavation landscape: a walkway presenting the time axis and all the educational information; themed cubes containing content not pertaining to a specific era, such as climate, origin, writing, and sexuality; and thirdly, the perforated museum wall that presents a cultural-comparative approach. The basic idea of the archaeological excavation field is supported by the architecture of the museum, which deliberately placed all the exhibition rooms belowground.

The visitor experiences the exhibition along a chronologically arranged route through 250,000 years of Westphalia's history: the caves of the Neanderthals, past the graves of the Bronze Age and Roman wells, or through a medieval town. Archaeology is memorably experienced at first hand: the cold of the ice age in a refrigerated cube with an original ice core from the Arctic, the warfare between Franconia and Saxony, or the smells and dirt of towns in the Middle Ages.

The excavation field puts the objects back into context. The way they are staged makes them self-explanatory. Some exhibits are presented in situ, where they were found–for example, 250,000-year-old stone tools in the scree of the ice age, bronze jewellery in the grave of a woman from the time around 550 BC, or a doll's head in the rubble left by the bombs of the Second World War. Other exhibits–for example, pieces of pottery–are shown in their former use. They all document history and they all tell stories.

Wer sind wir? Woher kommen wir? Wohin gehen wir? Diese ungewöhnlichen Fragestellungen der Kuratoren waren die Ausgangslage für dieses Museum. Darüber hinaus wollten sie die musealen Kernaufgaben „Sammeln, Bewahren, Forschen, Vermitteln" erlebbar machen. Daraus entstand der integrative Gestaltungsansatz, der die Dauerausstellung wie ein riesiges barrierefrei begehbares Ausgrabungsfeld inszeniert, mit archäologischem Vermessungsraster, Grabungszelten, Fluchtstangen und Fundorten. Drei wichtige Designelemente definieren die Grabungslandschaft: ein Steg, der die Zeitachse und alle didaktischen Informationen trägt. Themenkuben, die zeitübergreifende Inhalte wie Klima, Abstammung, Schrift und Sexualität beinhalten, und die perforierte Museumswand mit einem kulturvergleichenden Blick in die Welt. Unterstützt wird die Grundidee der Grabung durch die Museumsarchitektur, die alle Ausstellungsräume konsequent unter die Erde verlegt.

Der Besucher erlebt die Ausstellung als chronologische Route durch eine Viertelmillion Jahre westfälischer Geschichte: durch Höhlen der Neandertaler, vorbei an Gräbern der Bronzezeit und römischen Brunnen oder durch eine mittelalterliche Stadt. Archäologie wird unmittelbar und nachhaltig erlebbar: die Kälte der Eiszeit in einem gekühlten Kubus mit einem Original-Eisbohrkern aus der Arktis, die kriegerischen Auseinandersetzungen zwischen Franken und Sachsen oder die Gerüche und der Schmutz in den Städten des Mittelalters.

Das Grabungsfeld rekontextualisiert die Objekte. Durch die Inszenierung werden sie selbsterklärend. Einige Exponate sind in ihrem Fundzusammenhang, „in situ" präsentiert. Beispielsweise das 250.000 Jahre alte Steinwerkzeug im Geröll der Eiszeit, der Bronzeschmuck im Grab einer Frau aus der Zeit um 550 v. Chr. oder der Puppenkopf im Bombenschutt des Zweiten Weltkriegs. Andere Exponate, beispielsweise Keramiken, werden in ihrer einstigen Gebrauchssituation gezeigt. Sie alle dokumentieren Geschichte und erzählen Geschichten.

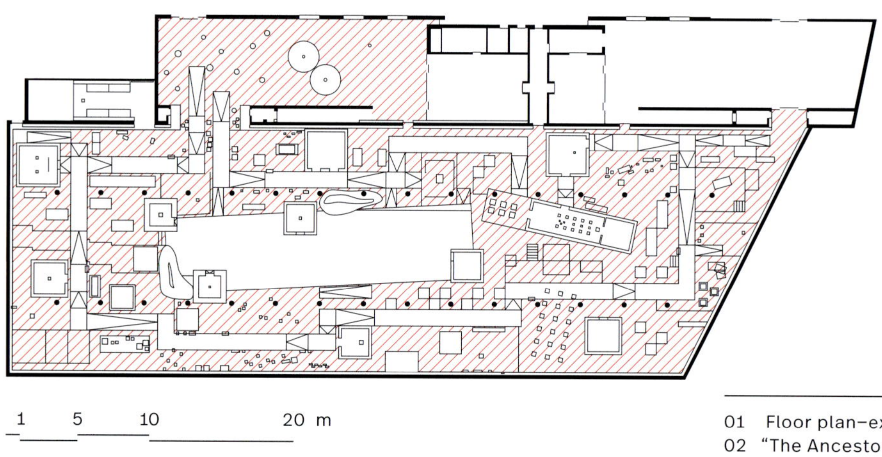

01 Floor plan–excavation field.
02 "The Ancestors"–skull fragments of Homo sapiens and Neanderthals alongside their digital reconstructions dominate the "Raumbild" (spatial image). These became the iconic image for the entire museum.

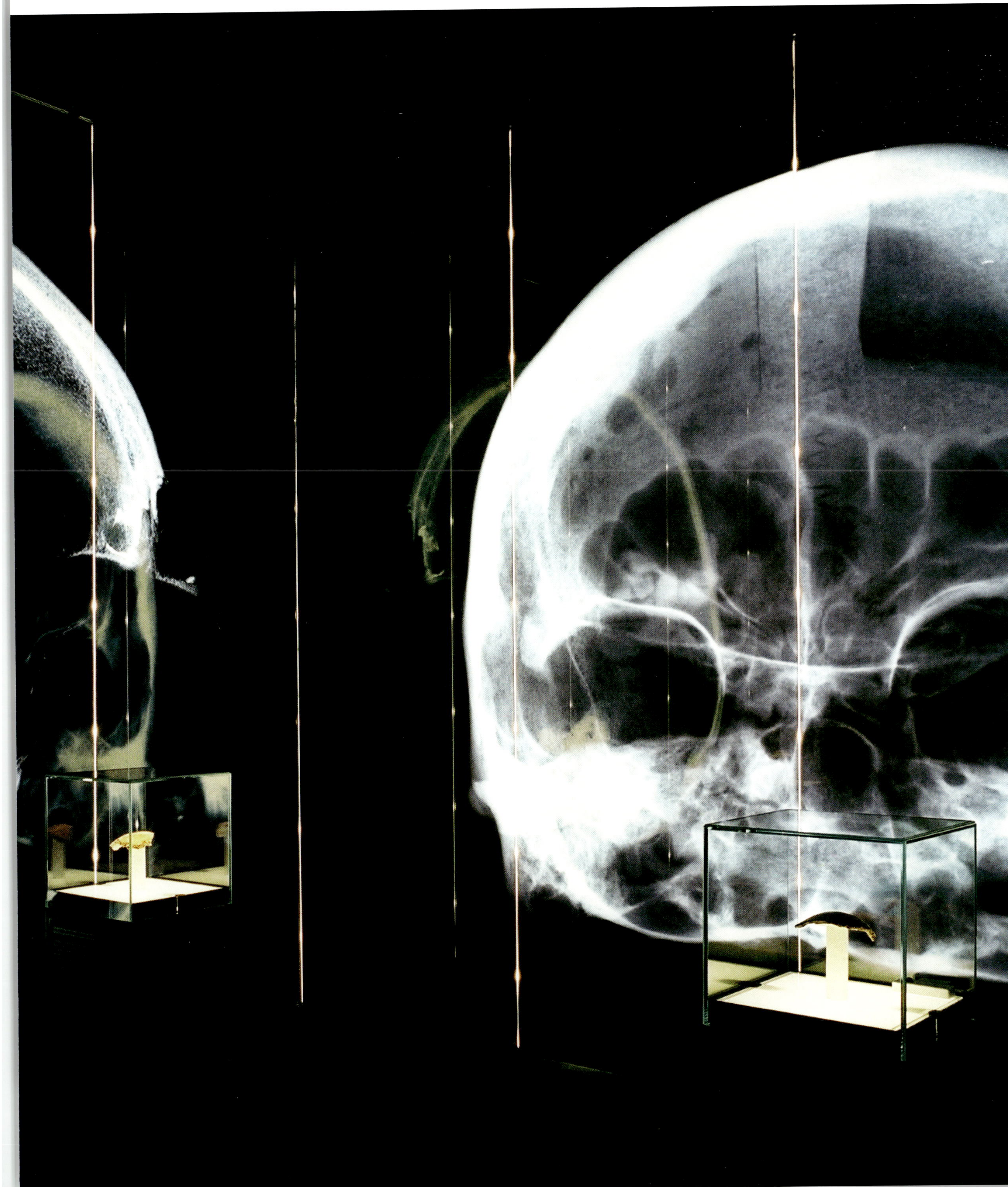

03 “The Romans in Westfalia”–glorious arrival and a disgraceful departure.

04 Themed cubes containing content not pertaining to a specific era, such as climate, origin, writing, and sexuality.

The archaeological excavation field as spatial image and the contextualisation of the artefacts not only offer the opportunity to provide educational information but above all allow visitors to experience archaeology, to create a dialogue between exhibits and visitors and to involve them in the history of their ancestors and the way they lived.

Das Grabungsfeld als Raumbild und die Kontextualisierung der Exponate bieten nicht nur die Möglichkeit didaktisch zu vermitteln, sondern Archäologie erlebbar zu machen: ein Dialog zwischen Exponat und Besuchern entsteht. Jene werden in die Geschichte ihrer Vorfahren und deren Lebensweisen involviert.

05 Excavation field with objects displayed "in situ" (as found).

06 Objects like these vases are displayed in a re-contextualised setting, showing how, where, and what they were used for.

SCIENCE LABORATORY

Permanent Exhibition, 140 sqm, LWL-Museum of Archaeology, Herne, Germany, 2005

Archaeology as thrilling as a criminal case—that is how visitors experience the research laboratory that forms a separate part of the permanent exhibition of the Museum of Archaeology in Herne. At the centre of the room is the crime scene—or rather the site of the archaeological find: a reconstructed section of a 5,000-year-old megalithic tomb. Above it, the archaeological finds hang in special bags as evidence.

After the find, as in criminology, follows the examination in the laboratory. Only there can the event be reconstructed from the results of the analysis of clues and the reassembly of smaller finds like the pieces of a puzzle.

Fourteen science containers reminiscent of laboratory tables offer visitors the opportunity to become detectives and researchers in hands-on experiments. For instance, they can date wood, analyse mammoth hairs under the microscope, reconstruct the appearance of people based on bones found in a grave, and find out more about their eating habits by examining seeds and leftovers. Step by step, they decipher the mystery.

As they explore, they experience how the clues of the past can be decrypted and at the same time learn how archaeologists go about their scientific work. In addition to historical and archaeological methods, nowadays this increasingly includes biological, chemical, medical, and physical analytics.

The science laboratory takes visitors on an exciting interactive journey of discovery through the world of archaeology. The aesthetically designed laboratory is a spatial expression of scientists' analytical approach and underlines the complexity of their work, while offering self-explanatory access to the subject.

Archäologie, spannend wie ein Kriminalfall – so erleben Besucher das Forscherlabor als eigenständigen Teil der Dauerausstellung des Archäologischen Museums in Herne. Mitten im Raum der Tatort bzw. Fundort: ein rekonstruierter Ausschnitt eines über 5.000 Jahre alten Großsteingrabs, über dem archäologische Grabungsfunde in speziellen Fundtüten wie Beweismittel hängen.

Nach dem Fund folgt wie in der Kriminalistik die Untersuchung im Labor. Erst durch die dortige Analyse der Spuren und Befunde sowie im Zusammensetzen vieler kleiner Fundstücke wie Puzzleteile lässt sich das Ereignis rekonstruieren.

Vierzehn Wissenschaftscontainer, die an Labortische erinnern, lassen Besucher über Hands-on-Experimente selbst zu Detektiven und Forschern werden. Sie können beispielsweise das Alter von Holz datieren, Mammuthaare unter dem Mikroskop analysieren, das Aussehen der Menschen anhand der Knochenfunde rekonstruieren und mehr über ihre Essgewohnheiten lernen, indem sie Samen und Speisereste untersuchen. So kommen sie dem Geheimnis nach und nach auf die Spur.

Explorativ erleben sie, wie die Spuren der Vergangenheit entschlüsselt werden, und lernen dabei zugleich die wissenschaftlichen Arbeitsweisen der Archäologen kennen. Neben historischen und archäologischen Methoden zählen dazu zunehmend biologische, chemische, medizinische und physikalische Analyseverfahren.

Das Forscherlabor bietet Besuchern eine spannende interaktive Entdeckungsreise in die Welt der Archäologie. Die räumliche Gestaltung als Laborsituation drückt das analytische Vorgehen der Wissenschaftler aus und steht für die Komplexität ihrer Arbeit. Das Raumbild eines ästhetisch gestalteten Labors bietet dazu den selbsterklärenden Zugang.

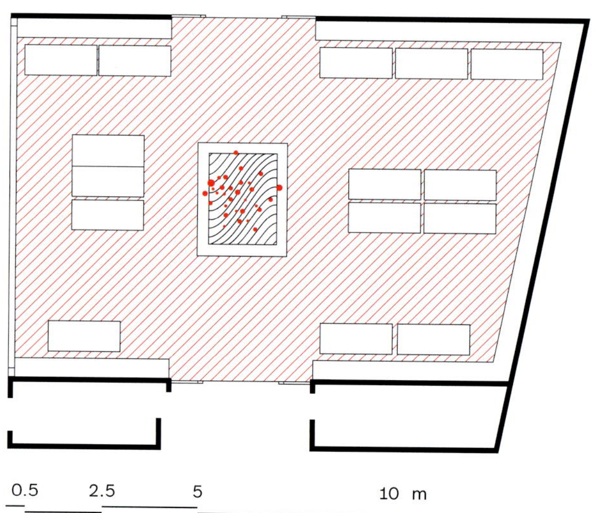

01 Floor plan.
02 Lab offering hands-on exploration for experiential learning on a high educational level.

SCIENCE LABORATORY

03 The Science Laboratory–14 containers styled as lab benches.

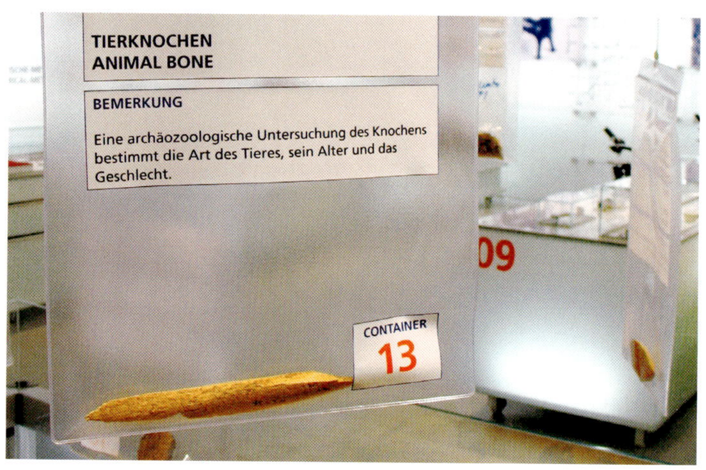

04|05 Young visitors can play the role of scientists by being encouraged to reconstruct species by following the methods of archaeologists.
06 Forensic reconstruction of a skull.

ANTHROPOLOGIE
ANTHROPOLOGY

DEUTSCHE BÖRSE– MAIN TRADING HALL

Corporate Scenography, 1,500 sqm, Frankfurt/Main, Germany, 2008

The main trading hall is the image of the Frankfurt Stock Exchange that the media present to the world. Its significance as visible brand space, but also as the workplace of many brokers and television teams as well as an attraction for 40,000 visitors per year were all aspects that the design concept took into account. In the course of the modernisation of the listed building, the multimedia and interactive visitors' gallery was added to extend the trading floor and foyer, and the electrics and IT technology were updated.

The clear, contemporary spatial impression and high-quality materials as an expression of a harmonious, representative corporate architecture, with careful use of the colours blue and white, give the Frankfurt Stock Exchange a worthy appearance.

Design elements that shape the space are the trading pits in the form of light-coloured circular structures that house ergonomic workplaces for 70 brokers and the historical display board, the hallmark of the Deutsche Börse.

The sophisticated dynamic lighting concept is an innovation. It allows the individual elements of the room to be illuminated individually, setting the scene for events like the IPO of a company: the light colour then changes from white to blue–from object illumination to creative staging light.

In order to accentuate the international importance of the Frankfurt Stock Exchange, a light installation was installed around the hall. The abstract map of the world is composed of LED lines and simulates day and night times worldwide in real time. Integrated news tickers provide important trading information from around the world–news and up-to-the-minute data from the leading indices on every continent: a visualisation of the global network of stock exchanges in the digital age.

The main trading hall has been given a coherent appearance that impressively represents the Deutsche Börse and underlines the key role it plays in the global financial market.

Der große Handelssaal prägt das Bild der Deutschen Börse in den Medien weltweit. Dieser großen Bedeutung als sichtbarer Markenraum, aber auch als Arbeitsplatz für zahlreiche Makler und Fernsehteams sowie als Anziehungspunkt für 40.000 Besucher pro Jahr trägt die gestalterische Konzeption Rechnung. Im Rahmen der Modernisierung im denkmalgeschützten Bestand wurden das Handelsparkett und das Foyer mit einer multimedialen, interaktiven Besuchergalerie erweitert sowie die komplette Elektro- und IT-Technik auf den neuesten Stand gebracht.

Der zeitgemäß klare Raumeindruck und hochwertige Materialien als Ausdruck einer stimmigen, aussagekräftigen Corporate Architecture mit gezielt eingesetzter Farbigkeit, vorwiegend in den Farben Weiß und Blau, verleihen der Börse Frankfurt ein adäquates Erscheinungsbild.

Raumbildprägende gestalterische Elemente sind die Handelsschranken in Form kreisrunder heller Körper mit ergonomischen Arbeitsplätzen für 70 Makler und die historische Anzeigetafel, das Markenzeichen der Deutschen Börse.

Eine Innovation ist das ausgeklügelte dynamische Lichtkonzept. Es erlaubt, die einzelnen Raumelemente individuell zu bespielen und Ereignisse wie den Börsengang eines Unternehmens szenografisch in Szene zu setzen: Die Lichtfarbe ändert sich dann von Weiß zu Blau – von der Objektbeleuchtung zum Inszenierungslicht.

Um die internationale Bedeutung der Börse zu akzentuieren, wurde eine umlaufende Lichtinstallation einer abstrahierten Weltkarte aus LED-Linien installiert. Sie simuliert Tages- und Nachtzeiten weltweit in Echtzeit. Integrierte Lauftexte liefern die wichtigen Informationen zum weltweiten Handelsgeschehen – News und aktuelle Leitindizes aus allen Kontinenten. So wird die globale Vernetzung des Börsenhandels im digitalen Zeitalter deutlich.

Der Große Handelssaal erhält ein stimmiges, aussagekräftiges Erscheinungsbild, das die Deutsche Börse eindrücklich repräsentiert und ihre Bedeutung im globalen Finanzmarkt unterstreicht.

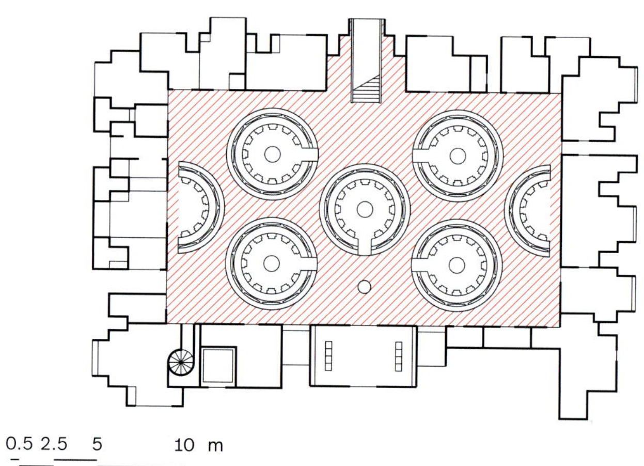

01 Floor plan.

02 The trading floor in event mode. Using the programmable light choreography allows different spatial atmospheres to be created.

DEUTSCHE BÖRSE
BÖRSE FRANKFURT

DEUTSCHE BÖRSE—MAIN TRADING HALL

03 The trading hall and visitors' balcony as seen from above. The interactive monitors depict the worldwide flow of trading activities, money, and information.

04|05 The visitors' balcony with LED spots, indicating values rising or falling in sync with real-time trading activities.

06 The trading floor in day mode. The abstract world map on the walls depicts worldwide trading activities in real time.

BMW MUSEUM

Architecture/Conversion and Permanent Exhibition, 5,000 sqm, Munich, Germany, 2008

The BMW Museum is located in the listed building that houses the corporate headquarters of the Munich-based automotive group. By extending the visitor routing of the museum to the west wing of the head office and lengthening the existing ramp system, the exhibition space was made five times larger and it was possible to completely realign the museum.

The overall conception that is based on the brand values "dynamic, challenging, cultivated" breaks new ground in the way it holistically combines architecture, exhibition design, and media staging–by way of an integrative Gesamtkunstwerk.

Visitors experience a routing without crossroads of around one kilometre in length. On what is called the "road in an enclosed space" they explore an urban, automotive, and dynamic city-shape with houses, squares, and bridges. In the two- to three-storey themed houses the history, innovations, and values of BMW are presented: design, company, motorcycle, technology, motor sport, series, and brand.

The centre and one of the highlights of the museum is the BMW central space, a 13-metre tall airspace surrounded by a huge mediatecture. The visitor encounters this central space on his tour several times from different directions and perspectives. Satin-finished glass walls, behind which lie 1.7 million LEDs, are used as a media surface for monochrome light choreographies that seemingly dematerialise the architecture.

Das BMW Museum befindet sich in der denkmalgeschützten Unternehmenszentrale des Münchner Automobilkonzerns. Durch die Ausweitung des Museumsparcours auf den Westflügel der Konzernzentrale und die Verlängerung des bestehenden Rampensystems konnte die Ausstellungsfläche um das Fünffache vergrößert und dem Museum eine völlig neue Ausrichtung gegeben werden.

Die Gesamtkonzeption, die auf den Markenwerten „dynamisch, herausfordernd, kultiviert" basiert, geht neue Wege bei der Verbindung von Architektur, Ausstellungsgestaltung und medialer Inszenierung – im Sinne eines integrativen Gesamtkunstwerks.

Die Besucher erleben einen kreuzungsfreien Parcours von rund einem Kilometer Länge. Auf der sogenannten „Straße im umbauten Raum" erkunden sie eine urbane, automobile und dynamische Stadtlandschaft mit Häusern, Plätzen und Brücken. In den zwei- bis dreigeschossigen Themenhäusern werden Geschichte, Innovationen und Werte von BMW vorgestellt: Gestaltung, Unternehmen, Motorrad, Technik, Motorsport, Baureihen und Marke.

Zentrum und einer der Höhepunkte des Museums ist der BMW Platz – ein 13 Meter hoher Luftraum, umgeben von einer raumgreifenden Mediatektur. Der Besucher erlebt diesen zentralen Raum auf seinem Rundgang mehrmals aus verschiedenen Richtungen und Perspektiven. Satinierte Glaswände, hinter denen 1,7 Millionen LEDs liegen, werden medial mit monochromen Lichtchoreografien bespielt. Die Architektur wird entmaterialisiert.

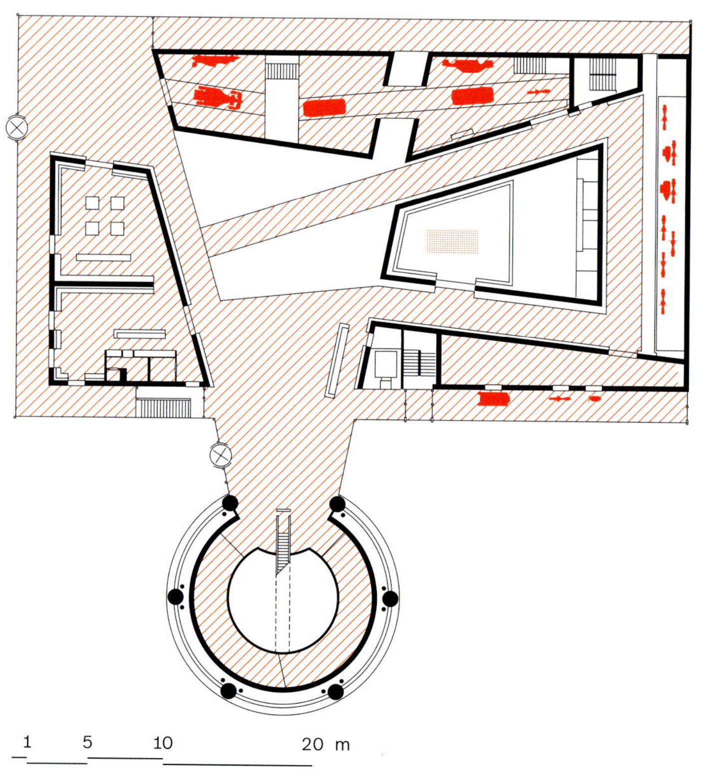

01 Floor plan–entrance floor.
02 Thematic cube with lightweight construction–featuring the first tubular frame structure for the racing car BMW 328 in the back.

03 Central space with circulation ramps flanked by the so-called “themed-houses” which contain one of the seven thematic exhibition areas. All facades are actually hiding a mega LED screen which can show a 360-degree spatial movie. The roadsters on the floor space are removable in order to host events right in the centre of the museum.

The cars, condemned to remain stationary, embark on an imaginary journey. This is a particularly good example of scenographic design as a symbiotic connection between media and architecture.

Another highlight of the exhibition is the kinetic sculpture in the “House of Design.” This mechatronic installation, with its more than 700 computer-controlled aluminium balls, forms a flowing transition between individual vehicle silhouettes and thus metaphorically gives the form finding part of the design process a spatial dimension.

Die zum Stehen verurteilten Automobile setzen sich in Bewegung und begeben sich auf eine imaginäre Reise. Szenografisches Gestalten als symbiotische Verbindung von Medien und Architektur wird hier besonders deutlich.

Ein weiterer Höhepunkt der Ausstellung ist die kinetische Skulptur im „Haus der Gestaltung“. Diese mechatronische Installation bildet mit über 700 computergesteuerten Aluminiumkugeln einen fließenden Übergang zwischen einzelnen Fahrzeugsilhouetten und übersetzt damit das Thema Formfindung im Designprozess metaphorisch in den Raum.

In the historical “museum bowl,” the routing ends in the epilogue, the “visual symphony”–a 360-degree panorama projection–picks up an idea of the architect Karl Schwanzer that back in the day had not been realisable. It offers an impressive spatial experience combined with sound.

Although media staging plays an important role, technology is largely hidden from sight in the BMW Museum. The focus is firmly on the exhibits and visitors’ interaction with them. The media design eliminates the limits of the space and creates a moving exhibition experience in both senses of the word–an automotive museum.

In der historischen „Museumsschüssel“ endet der Parcours im Epilog. Die „Visuelle Sinfonie“ – eine 360-Grad-Panorama-Projektion – greift eine ehedem technisch nicht realisierbare Idee des Architekten Karl Schwanzer auf. Zum Abschluss der Ausstellung bietet sie ein eindrucksvolles Raum-Klang-Erlebnis.

Obwohl mediale Inszenierungen eine große Rolle spielen, bleibt Technik im BMW Museum weitestgehend verborgen. Der Schwerpunkt liegt auf den Exponaten und der Interaktion der Besucher mit diesen. Die mediale Gestaltung hebt die Begrenzung durch den Raum auf und kreiert ein bewegtes und bewegendes Ausstellungserlebnis – ein auto-mobiles Museum.

04 Display showing the progress of the evolution of the legendary six-cylinder engines.

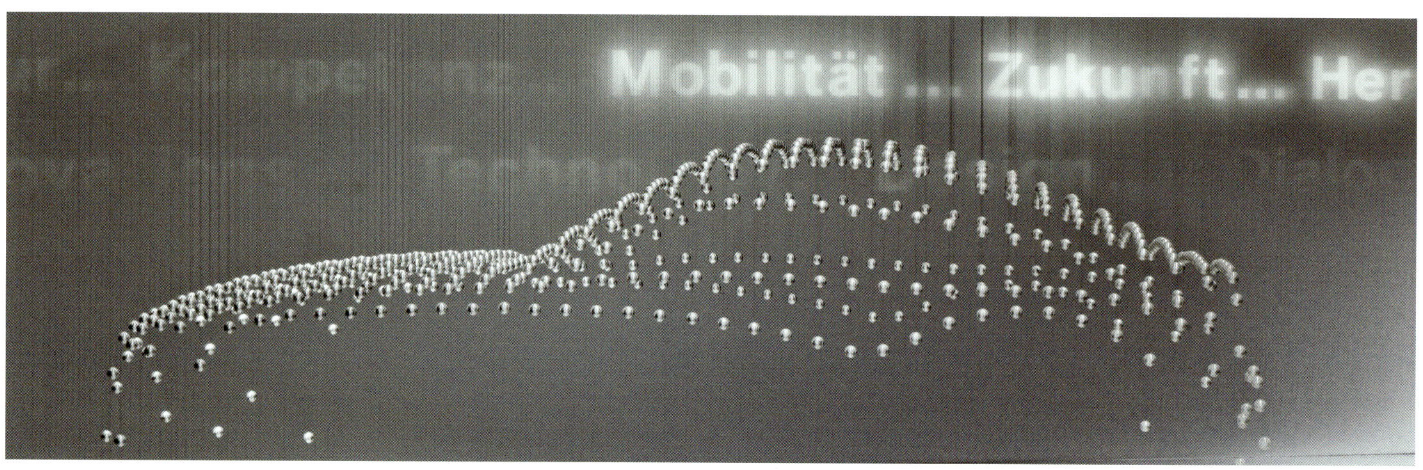

05 The kinetic sculpture (by ART+COM), which became the vivid icon of the entire museum, is able to artistically simulate any car shape ever created by BMW.

06 The classic cars, which were powering the postwar "Wirtschaftswunder" (post-war "economic boom")–Frontloader Isetta (left).

07 The revitalised exhibition bowl (designed by architect Karl Schwanzer) (left) with the posthumous realized visual symphony (right). A dynamic 360° panoramic projection featuring BMW's credo "Freude am Fahren" ("Sheer driving pleasure").

RAUTENSTRAUCH-JOEST-MUSEUM–CULTURES OF THE WORLD

Permanent Exhibition, 3,600 sqm, Cologne, Germany, 2010

Ethnological museums are normally organised by geographical region. The Rautenstrauch-Joest-Museum, by contrast, is based on the curated concept of cultural comparison, a contemporary new approach that focuses on content. Way of life, identity, faith, death–the exhibition picks up topics which move people the world over and provides insights into the cultures of the world in many different ways. Visitors to the exhibition embark on an insightful journey of discovery that is designed to arouse curiosity and encourage tolerance.

The themed visitor routing dedicated to "People in Their Worlds" is staged over three floors and shows some 2,000 exhibits, embedded in differentiated narrative spaces. The first exhibition area, "Comprehending the World," is devoted to the European view of other cultures and presents this as reflected in historical travel reports, in art, using museum methods of analysis, and also in prejudices. In the room "A Matter of Perception and Opinion: Art," visitors consider the objects on display initially as artistic artefacts, but on demand they can find out more about the original context, for example, the ritual designation. This information can be displayed on the rear walls of the showcases. It is up to the visitor to decide if and when he wants to activate it.

Why do the Maori have tattoos? What is the purpose of ancestor figures? What was practical about living in a tepee? These are the kinds of questions dealt within the second exhibition area, "Shaping the World." It conveys insights into the different forms and areas of life, including "Clothing and Adornment," "Death and the Afterlife," "Religion and Rituals." Each topic has been given its own narrative space. Concealed behind string curtains, "Death and the Afterlife," for instance, is completely white and bathed in searing light.

Ethnologische Museen sind üblicherweise nach geografischen Großräumen strukturiert. Das Rautenstrauch-Joest-Museum jedoch basiert auf dem kuratorischen Konzept des Kulturvergleichs, einem neuen, zeitgemäßen inhaltlichen Ansatz. Wohnen, Identität, Glaube, Tod – die Ausstellung greift Themen auf, die Menschen weltweit bewegen und Einblick in die Kulturen der Welt auf vielfältige Art und Weise geben. Die Besucher begeben sich auf eine erkenntnisreiche Entdeckungsreise, die Neugier wecken und Toleranz fördern soll.

Der inszenierte Themenparcours „Der Mensch in seinen Welten" erstreckt sich über drei Etagen und zeigt rund 2.000 Exponate, eingebettet in differenzierte Raumbilder. Das erste Hauptkapitel „Die Welt erfassen" widmet sich dem europäischen Blick auf andere Kulturen und stellt diesen gespiegelt in historischen Reiseberichten, der Perspektive auf Kunst, in museal-analytischen Methoden und auch in Vorurteilen vor. Im Raum „Ansichtssachen?!: Kunst" betrachten die Besucher die ausgestellten Objekte zunächst als künstlerische Artefakte, können dann aber auch „on-demand" mehr über den ursprünglichen Kontext, beispielsweise die rituelle Bestimmung, erfahren. Die Informationen werden auf der Vitrinenrückwand eingespielt. Der Besucher entscheidet selbst, ob und wann er diese Informationsebene aktivieren möchte.

Warum tragen die Maori Tätowierungen? Welchen Sinn haben Ahnenfiguren? Weshalb war das Wohnen im Tipi praktisch? Fragen wie diesen geht der zweite Ausstellungsbereich „Die Welt gestalten" nach. Er vermittelt Einblicke in unterschiedliche Formen und Bereiche der Lebensgestaltung, darunter „Kleidung und Schmuck", „Tod und Jenseits", „Religionen und Rituale". Jedes Thema konkretisiert sich in einem eigenständigen Raumbild. Der Bereich „Tod und Jenseits" ist beispielsweise ganz in Weiß gehalten und liegt in gleißendem Licht hinter Fadenvorhängen verborgen.

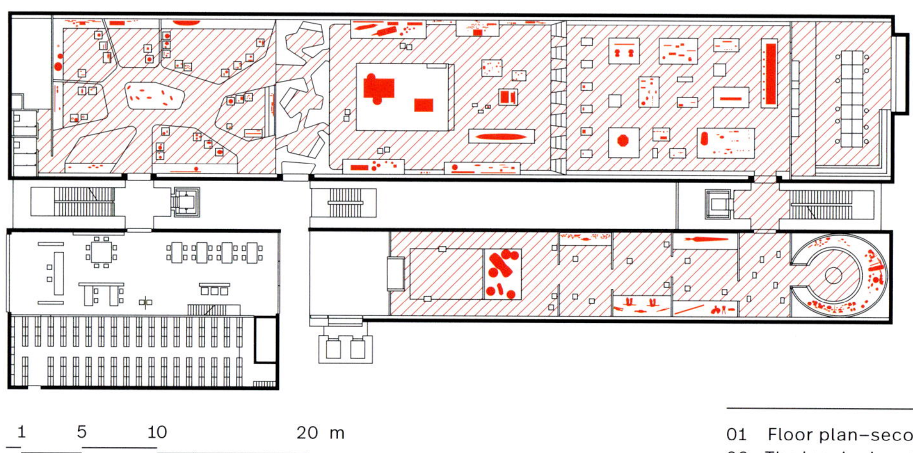

01 Floor plan–second floor.

02 The iconic rice storage at the exhibition entrance has interactive sliding monitors to give potential visitors a free preview of the exhibition. This is highly effective in enticing passers-by to visit.

03 Gamelan Orchestra–instruments displayed in front of film footage. This orchestra is periodically performed by passionate musicians.

Visitors experience the exhibition as a dynamic sequence of compact themed rooms. The museum surprises its visitors with an unconventional, content-oriented ethnological routing and with varied stagings that offer intuitive and interactive access to the cultures of the world. The visitors are directly addressed and called upon to explore differences and common features and thus to understand their own culture as one of many possible variants of equal value–a contribution to promoting understanding and tolerance.

Die Besucher erleben die Ausstellung als dynamische Abfolge kompakter Themenräume. Das Museum überrascht mit seinem unkonventionellen, inhaltskonsistenten ethnologischen Parcours und mit abwechslungsreichen Inszenierungen, die einen intuitiven und interaktiven Zugang zu den Kulturen der Welt bieten. Die Besucher werden direkt angesprochen und sind aufgefordert, Unterschiede und Gemeinsamkeiten zu erkunden und damit die eigene Kultur als eine mögliche Variante unter vielen gleichwertigen Möglichkeiten zu begreifen – ein Beitrag zur Förderung von Verständnis und Toleranz.

04 Rautenstrauch-Joest's private collection displayed in historic context with black and white backdrops but the objects and showcases in colour.

05 The sculpture gallery offers two approaches: an auratic, object-only display or an "Information on Demand" approach. By touching the object label the background information lights up, showing the objects' real purpose: sculptures created to worship the ancestors.

06 The "Museum within the Museum" where visitors can explore the four international criteria for museums: collecting, preserving, researching, and communicating. This became a much appreciated interactive zone in the museum.

07 Masks displayed in a panoramic showcase showing their origin and context related to the abstract map backdrop.

08 Collection of doors on open display as a metaphor of one of several transition areas in the collection.

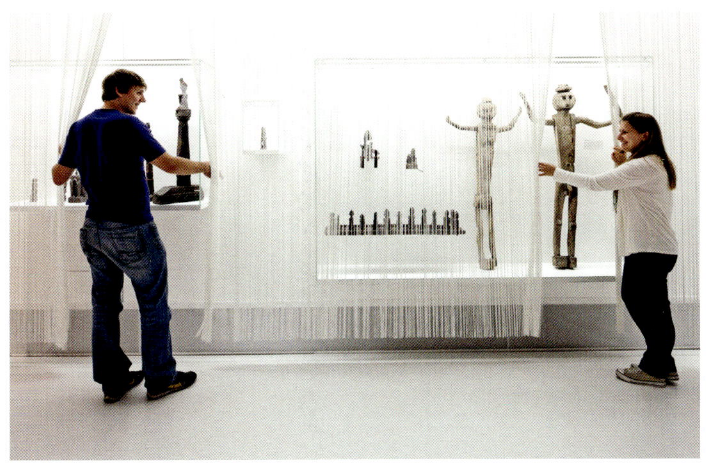

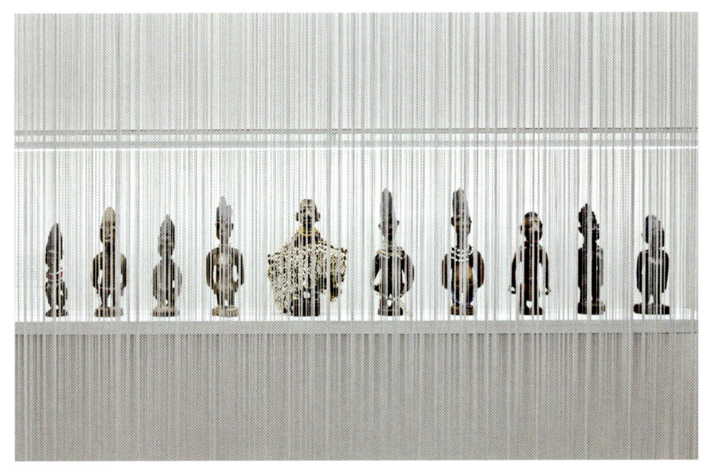

09 Objects of the afterlife behind a translucent curtain encourages the visitors to explore the vaguely visible objects.

STATE GRID PAVILION – MAGIC BOX

Corporate Pavilion, Main Show and Facade, Interior Magic Box: 15x15x13 m, Entire Facade: 4,700 sqm, Expo Shanghai, China, 2010

How can abstract topics such as energy generation and loss-free energy transmission be presented in an entertaining and yet easy-to-understand way? How can a memorable experience be achieved at a mass event like an Expo, where a visitor's attention span is just a few minutes long? The national Chinese energy supplier State Grid decided in favour of a presentation with an innovative approach that impressed millions with its technology and design: more than five million people visited the State Grid Pavilion, keen to immerse themselves in a spectacular spatial film.

The heart of the pavilion is the Magic Box, a cube-shaped cinema suspended in mid-air, 13 metres in height, which allows an immersive experience: films are projected onto all six sides using more than 17 million LEDs.

The visitor, standing on a glass bridge, finds himself in the middle of the film. Images flow around him and take him on a virtual journey from the resources used to produce energy in western China to its transport and use in the megacities of eastern China. Time and space dissolve.

The electricity network–a grid–is the guiding principle from which all the projections are generated. It is materialised in the prologue and epilogue of the film and enters into a symbiosis with the surrounding architecture. The whole building seems to be encompassed by pulsating grid lines–a metaphor for the all-encompassing electricity grid as prerequisite for the efficient transmission of energy without loss over huge distances.

Wie gelingt es, abstrakte Themen wie Energieerzeugung und verlustfreien Energietransport unterhaltsam und verständlich zu vermitteln? Wie kann auf einer Massenveranstaltung wie einer Expo und bei einer Aufmerksamkeitsspanne von nur wenigen Minuten ein memorables Erlebnis erzeugt werden? Der nationale chinesische Energieversorger State Grid hat sich für eine Inszenierung entschieden, deren technisch wie gestalterisch innovativer Ansatz ein Millionenpublikum begeisterte: Über fünf Millionen Menschen besuchten den State Grid Pavilion und tauchten hier in einen spektakulären Raumfilm ein.

Herzstück des Pavillons ist die Magic Box – ein frei im Pavillon schwebender Würfel, 13 Meter hoch, der ein immersives Erlebnis ermöglicht: Er ist auf allen sechs Seiten filmisch bespielt. Über 17 Millionen LEDs kommen zum Einsatz.

Der auf einer Glasbrücke stehende Besucher befindet sich mitten im Film. Filmische Bilder umfließen ihn und nehmen ihn mit auf eine virtuelle Reise, die von den Ressourcen der Energie in Chinas Osten über den Transport bis zur Nutzung der Energie in den Megastädten in Chinas Westen führt. Zeit und Raum lösen sich auf.

Das Elektrizitätsnetz – ein Grid – ist der Leitgedanke, aus dem heraus sich alle Bespielungen generieren. Es materialisiert sich im Prolog und Epilog des Films und geht hier eine Symbiose mit der umgebenden Architektur ein. Das gesamte Gebäude scheint gleichsam von stromdurchflossenen pulsierenden Netzlinien umspannt – Metapher für das allumfassende Stromnetz als Voraussetzung für den effizienten und verlustfreien Energietransport über große Distanzen hinweg.

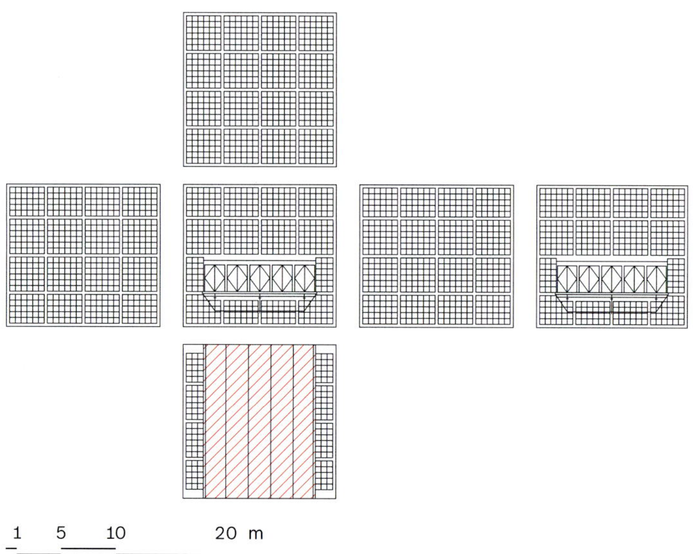

01 Floor plan and elevations of the "Magic Box" showing the glass bridge for the visitor experience.

02 "Magic Box"–the core-cube of the State Grid Pavilion containing the 720-degree cubic cinema.

国家电网馆
国家电网馆
STATE GRID PAVILION

03 Ultra-high-voltage energy transport from China's west to the megacities of the east.

At night, the projections seep from the interior to the outside facade, which becomes a membrane. During the day, the movable, semi-transparent tiles, whose movements are triggered by currents of air, stand for the natural energy resources wind and water.

With its walk-in film, the Magic Box offers a fascinating, holistic spatial experience that seems to transcend physical limits. The imagined replaces the physical space.

Nachts dringt die Bespielung aus dem Inneren nach außen und wird an der Fassade ablesbar – die Fassade wird zur Membran. Tagsüber stehen die beweglichen, semitransparenten Plättchen und deren durch Luftbewegungen ausgelöste Bewegungen symbolisch für die natürlichen Energieressourcen Wind und Wasser.

Die Magic Box bietet mit ihrem begehbaren Film ein faszinierendes holistisches Raumerlebnis, das physische Grenzen aufzuheben scheint. An die Stelle des physischen tritt der imaginierte Raum.

04 Mesmerizing experience provoked by a change of scale–creating a virtual journey through a meadow from an unexpected perspective.

05 The "energy stream" reaches a virtual collage of the east coast megacities ...

06 ... and supplies the inhabitants with energy and joy.

CERN – UNIVERSE OF PARTICLES

Permanent Exhibition, 450 sqm, CERN, Geneva, Switzerland, 2010

How can a non-scientist present science? How can the non-exhibitable be exhibited? How can a truly abstract and complex subject be made accessible? At CERN (Conseil Européen pour la Recherche Nucléaire), the world's largest research centre in the field of particle physics, the world's best physicists research the fundamentals of our existence.

Microcosm and macrocosm, CERN's diametric research fields, are united in the spatial narrative. All the exhibition elements are expressed in a spherical design idiom. Visitors are immersed in a world without measures; at the same time they are on the subatomic level and in the vast expanse of the solar system. At interactive display stations, they find out about the research facilities, CERN's worldwide network, the basics of its research, and even get to know some scientists. Spherical exhibition units display objects, and spherical touchscreens allow a virtual journey to the magnets weighing 80 tonnes far below at a depth of 100 metres. The exhibition's centre is a 24-square-metre display that visualises particle collisions in the Large Hadron Collider in real time. The visualisation stems from the computers of CERN's experts. The scientific experiment is the focus of attention. The fascination it exudes is conveyed intuitively.

The highlight of the free-flow exhibition is the main show, which offers a six-minute, multimedia spatial experience with sound every half hour: a virtual journey through time from the Big Bang via the history of the universe to the current scientific research at CERN.

Wie inszeniert man Wissenschaft, ohne ein Wissenschaftler zu sein? Wie das Unausstellbare ausstellen? Wie Zugang zu einem überaus abstrakten und schwer verständlichen Thema eröffnen? Im CERN – Conseil Européen pour la Recherche Nucléaire, dem weltweit größten Forschungszentrum auf dem Gebiet der Teilchenphysik, erforschen die weltbesten Physiker die Grundlagen unserer Existenz.

Mikro- und Makrokosmos, die beiden diametralen Forschungsbereiche des CERN, vereinen sich im Raumbild. Sämtliche Ausstellungselemente weisen eine sphärische Formensprache auf. Der Besucher taucht ein in eine Welt ohne Maßstäbe, er befindet sich zugleich auf subatomarer Ebene und in den unermesslichen Weiten des Sonnensystems. An interaktiven Displays lernt er die Forschungseinrichtungen, die weltweite Vernetzung des CERN, seine Forschungsgrundlagen und auch einzelne Wissenschaftler kennen. Kugelvitrinen zeigen Objekte und sphärische Touchscreens erlauben eine virtuelle Reise zum 80 Tonnen schweren Magneten in 100 Metern Tiefe. Zentrum der Ausstellung ist ein 24 Quadratmeter großes Display, das die Teilchenkollisionen des Large Hadron Colliders in Realzeit veranschaulicht. Die Visualisierung ist den Rechnern der CERN-Experten entsprungen. Das wissenschaftliche Experiment erhält die zentrale Aufmerksamkeit. Die Faszination, die von ihm ausgeht, vermittelt sich intuitiv.

Höhepunkt der Free-Flow-Ausstellung ist die Main Show, die jede halbe Stunde ein multimediales, dynamisches Raum-Klang-Erlebnis von sechs Minuten bietet: eine virtuelle Zeitreise vom Urknall über die Geschichte des Universums bis zur aktuellen wissenschaftlichen Forschung des CERN.

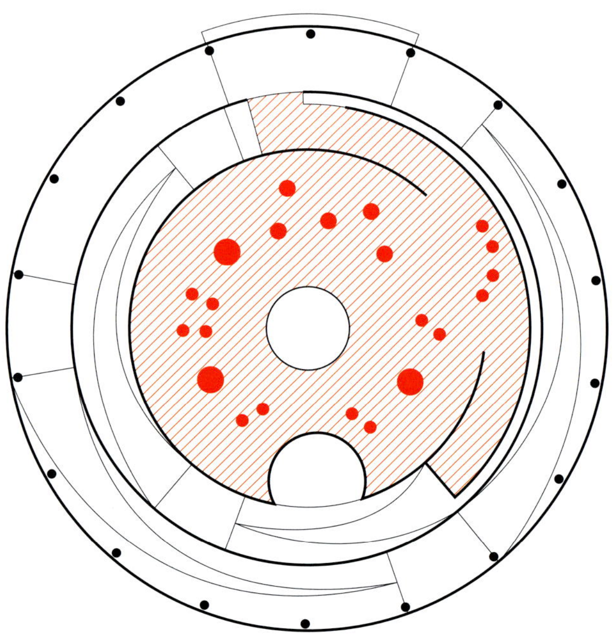

0.5 2.5 5 10 m

01 Floor plan–ground floor.
02 Via a virtual globe visitors can travel the global network of CERN.

03 Computer graphics, which depict particle collisions, make the invisible visible and complement the spatial gesture.

The choice of material and light, coupled with the three-dimensional sound landscape, ensure a memorable spatial experience. The technology is an integral part of the spherical forms. The way computer interfaces, projectors, and loudspeakers are embedded means that they are not perceived as technology.

The experience-oriented staging uses interactive multimedia stations to convey highly complex scientific topics to the uninitiated while the main show combines space, sound, and film to provide emotional access to the subject. The exhibition space itself becomes an exhibit.

Material- und Lichtwahl sowie die dreidimensional konzipierte Soundlandschaft führen zu einem nachhaltig memorierbaren Raumerlebnis. Die Technik ist integrierter Bestandteil der sphärischen Formen. Computer-Interfaces, Beamer und Lautsprecher sind eingebettet und werden nicht als Technik wahrgenommen.

Der erlebnisorientierten Inszenierung gelingt es mit multimedialen interaktiven Stationen, Laien hochwissenschaftliche komplexe Themen zu erschließen und ihnen mit dem Film-Raum-Klang-Erlebnis der Main Show einen emotionalen Zugang zu eröffnen. Der Raum wird selbst zum Exponat.

04|05 Interactive installations offer a large range of exploration of CERN's secrets.

TIM—STATE TEXTILE AND INDUSTRY MUSEUM

Permanent Exhibition, 2,500 sqm, Augsburg, Germany, 2010

The museum in the former spinning mill Augsburger Kammgarn-spinnerei AKS documents the history and technology of the once important Bavarian textile manufacturing industry. The centrepiece of the exhibition is the walk-in sample book archive. It sets the scene for the valuable fabric sample collection of the Neue Augsburger Kattunfabrik NAK from the years 1792 to 1995: Three larger-than-life Graces welcome visitors on a red carpet staged as a catwalk. Euphrosyne is wearing a dress made from original NAK fabric samples that reveals the feel of the different materials. Aglaia shows textile printing, while Thalia is about the design itself. The last two are designed as slowly rotating projection surfaces. Visitors choose designs from a digital sample book and project them in real time onto the revolving Thalia, thus creating new virtual dresses, again and again: the visitor as designer.

The walk-in sample book archive leads from both sides into the tour around the museum, which conveys the production process of textiles from the raw materials via their processing to the tailored end product. The tour begins in the shed halls and ends in the former head building of AKS. As a striking visual element and self-explanatory navigation system, a red thread in the form of floor graphics leads through the exhibition.

In the shed halls, visitors are immersed in an authentic factory situation. Restored machines in acoustically soundproofed glass boxes are witnesses of past working conditions. They are weaving again—now in the middle of the museum for the museum shop.

The head building that impresses with its rich collection of costumes, on the other hand, is staged as a darkened atelier: the processing of the materials through to the finished piece of clothing is presented here.

Das Museum in der ehemaligen Augsburger Kammgarn-spinnerei AKS dokumentiert Geschichte und Technik der einst bedeutenden bayerischen Textilherstellung. Herzstück der Ausstellung ist ein begehbares Musterbucharchiv. Es setzt die wertvolle Stoffmustersammlung der Neuen Augsburger Kattunfabrik NAK aus den Jahren 1792 bis 1995 in Szene: Drei überlebensgroße Grazien empfangen die Besucher auf einem als Laufsteg inszenierten roten Teppich. Euphrosyne trägt ein aus originalen Stoffmustern der NAK gefertigtes Kleid und verdeutlicht deren Haptik. Aglaia zeigt die Textilbedruckung, während es bei Thalia um den Entwurf an sich geht. Zwei der Figurinen sind als sich langsam drehende Projektionsflächen gestaltet. An einem digitalen Musterbuch wählen Besucher Dessins aus, projizieren diese in Echtzeit auf die rotierende Thalia und gestalten so immer neue virtuelle Kleider. Der Besucher wird selbst zum Entwerfer.

An das begehbare Musterbucharchiv schließt sich auf beiden Seiten der Rundgang durchs Museum an, der den Produktionsprozess der Textilien von den Rohstoffen über deren Verarbeitung bis zum geschneiderten Endprodukt vermittelt. Er beginnt in den Shed-Hallen und endet im ehemaligen Kopfbau der AKS. Als markantes visuelles Element und selbsterklärendes Leitsystem führt ein roter Faden in Form einer Bodengrafik durch die Ausstellung.

In den Shed-Hallen tauchen die Besucher in eine authentische Fabriksituation ein. Restaurierte Maschinen in einer gläsernen, akustisch abgeschirmten Box zeugen von ehemaligen Arbeitsbedingungen. Sie weben erneut – nun mitten im Museum für den Museumsshop.

Der Kopfbau, der mit seiner reichen Kostümsammlung beeindruckt, ist hingegen als abgedunkeltes Atelier inszeniert: Hier wird die Veredelung der Stoffe bis zum fertigen Kleidungsstück vorgestellt.

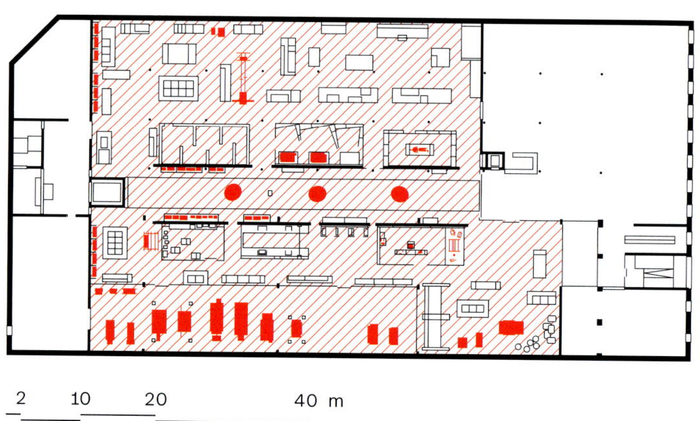

01 Floor plan—ground floor.
02 TIM's core installation: rotating oversize figurines.

03 Re-contextualisation of historical weaving machines on site.

04 Content-consistent installation featuring the fabric-printing-process.

05|06 Social history of entrepreneurs and workers, including the clashes between the classes in the nineteenth century.

07 Impressive collection of pattern-books and costumes.

In parallel to the production process, a second narrative strand conveys in individually staged cubes the turbulent social history of the Bavarian textile production from the early days of the weaving trade in the Middle Ages to its decline in the twentieth century and today's production of high-tech textiles.

The museum offers a holistic, multisensual exhibition experience in an authentic location. The concept of the hands-on museum turns visitors into protagonists, allowing them to actively get to grips with textile production.

Parallel zum Produktionsprozess vermittelt ein zweiter Erzählstrang in einzelnen, individuell inszenierten Kuben die bewegte Sozialgeschichte der bayerischen Textilherstellung von den Anfängen des Weberhandwerks im Mittelalter bis zum Niedergang im 20. Jahrhundert und zur heutigen Produktion von Hightech-Textilien.

Das Museum bietet ein ganzheitliches multisensuelles Ausstellungserlebnis am Originalschauplatz. Das Mitmach-Museum lässt die Besucher zu Akteuren werden und macht die Textilproduktion aktiv nachvollziehbar.

08 The interactive pattern-book allows visitors to select a pattern to be projected in real time onto the central figurine.

09 Young international designers travel to Augsburg to create new interpretations of historical patterns for the figurines.

GERMAN FILM MUSEUM

Permanent Exhibition, 800 sqm, Frankfurt/Main, Germany, 2011

The compact presentation makes conscious use of the film medium in all its facets. These references are to be found not only in the narrative plot of the museum, but also in the analogy to cinematic projection drawn by sensitive use of spotlights in the otherwise darkened rooms–a motif that creates the design frame on both floors of the permanent exhibition. The content has been developed into dense, memorable spatial images that give visitors intuitive and direct access to film and all the complex historical and technical themes that surround it.

On the first floor, the overall theme is “Filmic Vision” and is dedicated to technical discoveries and inventions, primarily from the nineteenth century. The individual theme-based stations–dealing with curiosity, movement, recording, projection, the moving image, and cinema–make use of film drums and rolls of film to convey their message. Visitors are able to use 14 functioning models of historical devices such as a zoetrope, a stroboscope, a magic lantern, and a walk-in camera obscura, and thus understand perceptual phenomena and how they are created technically.

On the second floor, which houses the “Filmic Narrative” section of the exhibition, visitors are able to take an active part in film-related technical processes. The focus is on the design of cinematic images and their emotional effect. At interactive media stations, they can mix film music, edit a film, create different light moods in a light box, or walk into an 8-metre-long green screen passage and stand at the top of a New York skyscraper. The four themes–namely, acting, sound, image, and editing–are arranged clockwise around a central film space, following the steps of the production process.

Die kompakte Inszenierung arbeitet bewusst mit den Mitteln des Films. Das zeigt sich nicht nur in der narrativen Dramaturgie, sondern auch in der Analogie zur Filmprojektion durch das sensitive und pointierte Licht sowie die dunkel gehaltenen Räume - ein Motiv, das über beide Etagen der Dauerausstellung den gestalterischen Rahmen bildet. Aus den Inhalten wurden dichte, einprägsame Raumbilder entwickelt, die den Besuchern den intuitiven und unmittelbaren Zugang zu den komplexen historischen und technischen Themen des Films erleichtern.

Der erste Stock hat das Thema „Filmisches Sehen“ und ist den technischen Entdeckungen und Erfindungen vor allem aus dem 19. Jahrhundert gewidmet. Die einzelnen Themenstationen - Schaulust, Bewegung, Aufnahme, Projektion, Laufbild und Kino - zitieren in ihrer Gestaltung Filmtrommel und Filmband. Allein 14 Funktionsmodelle historischer Apparaturen, wie eine Wundertrommel und ein Lebensrad, eine Laterna Magica und eine begehbare Camera Obscura, können Besucher selbst bedienen und erforschen dabei Wahrnehmungsphänomene sowie technische Zusammenhänge.

Im zweiten Obergeschoss mit der Ausstellungseinheit „Filmisches Erzählen“ nehmen die Besucher aktiv an heutigen filmtechnischen Prozessen teil. Der Fokus liegt dabei auf der Gestaltung von Filmbildern und ihrer emotionalen Wirkung. So können sie an interaktiven Medienstationen selbst Filmmusik mischen und einen Film schneiden, in einer Lichtbox verschiedene Lichtstimmungen erzeugen oder sich in einer acht Meter langen Greenscreen-Passage an den Abgrund eines New Yorker Wolkenkratzers stellen. Vier Themen - Schauspiel, Ton, Bild und Montage - reihen sich im Uhrzeigersinn analog zum Produktionsprozess um einen zentralen Filmraum.

01 Floor plan–first floor.
02 Thematically arranged cylindrical showcases connected by floor graphics.

BEWEGUNG MOVEMENT

03 Visitors can play with zoetropes to enjoy early motion pictures.

04 The collection includes fascinating original props like H.R. Giger's Alien.

05 Greenscreen passage: Visitors themselves are invited to play in a short film.

06 Central film space for temporary, thematically selected content.

The permanent exhibition offers a multisensory experience that combines seeing, experiencing, and trying things out, while promoting a dialogue between space and content, exhibition and observer.

Die Dauerausstellung bietet ein multisensuelles Erlebnis, das Sehen, Erfahren und Ausprobieren vereint und den Dialog zwischen Raum und Inhalt, Exponat und Betrachter fördert.

TEXTILWERK BOCHOLT

Architecture/Conversion, 8,500 sqm, Bocholt, Germany, 2011

The former spinning mill Spinnerei Herding, a four-storey building from 1907, was functionally overhauled and given a new usage. Where thread had been produced until 1973 is now the pulsating centre of a new urban district, a cultural centre with warehouse for shows and special exhibition areas, event spaces, and catering.

The design concept, guided by the maxim "reanimate and reinvent," was systematically developed from the old building structure. Careful architectural surgery interprets the industrial architecture and underlines the original functional interrelationships of the factory.

A bright red staircase that was installed in the reconstructed, 20-metre-tall former cable shaft is the central circulation element; where once transmission cables passed, visitors circulate between the floors.

The newly developed routing allows visitors to experience the former spinning mill as a huge machine and traces the route of the original energy axis. It leads from the generation of the energy in the boiler house via its transformation into movement in the machine house and the power transfer in the cable shaft to the generously dimensioned spinning halls and finally the former technical centre on the flat roof.

Die ehemalige Spinnerei Herding, ein viergeschossiges Gebäude aus dem Jahr 1907, wurde funktional ertüchtigt und einer neuen Verwendung zugeführt. Wo bis ins Jahr 1973 Garne produziert wurden, ist ein pulsierender Mittelpunkt eines neuen Stadtquartiers entstanden – ein Kulturzentrum mit Schaulager und Sonderausstellungsflächen, Veranstaltungsräumen und Gastronomie.

Das Gestaltungskonzept unter dem Leitgedanken „beleben und neu erlebbar machen" ist konsequent aus dem Altbestand heraus entwickelt. Gezielte architektonische Eingriffe interpretieren die Industriearchitektur und unterstreichen die ursprünglichen Funktionszusammenhänge der Fabrik.

Als zentrales Erschließungselement dient eine rot akzentuierte Treppe, die in den wiederhergestellten, 20 Meter hohen ehemaligen Seilgang eingebracht ist – anstelle von Transmissionsseilen zirkulieren nun die Besucher zwischen den Geschossen.

Der neu entwickelte Parcours macht die ehemalige Spinnerei als „große Maschine" erfahrbar und zeichnet den Weg der ursprünglichen Energieachse nach. Er führt von der Erzeugung der Energie im Kesselhaus über ihre Umwandlung in Bewegung im Maschinenhaus und die Kraftübertragung im Seilgang bis zu den großzügigen Spinnereisälen und schließlich der ehemaligen Technikzentrale auf dem Flachdach.

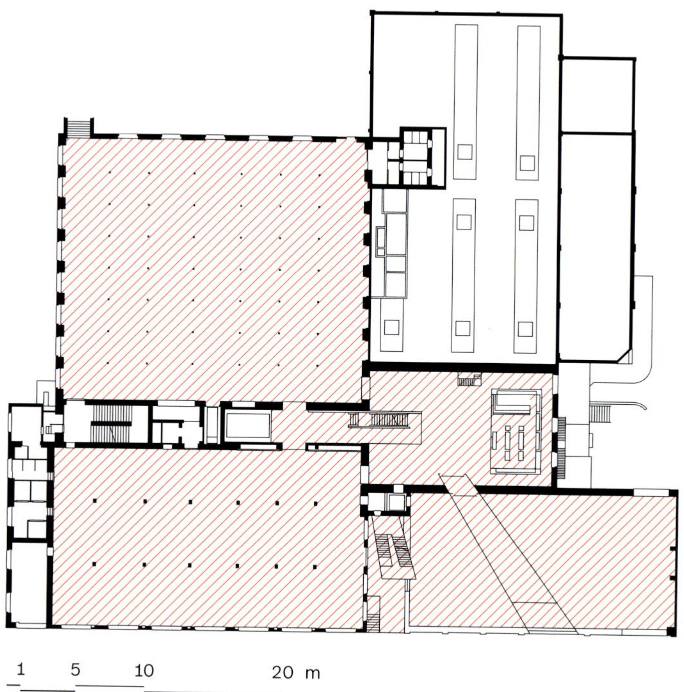

01 Floor plan.
02 New entrance to the former spinning mill.

LWL
TextilWerk Bocholt | Spinnerei
2. September bis
20. November 2011

03 The cable shaft was replaced by an expressive staircase representing the new power stream running through the building: the visitors.

04 Lecture hall equipped with coloured chairs based on colours found in the building.

This has been replaced by an airy, glazed cube whose contemporary architectural design idiom announces the former spinning mill and its new usage far beyond the city boundaries of Bocholt. The mounted facade of steel threads that reflect the light and weather moods is a metaphorical reference and attractive gesture. Inside, the installation of 88 historical ceiling lamps is reminiscent of the former factory.

An ihre Stelle tritt ein luftiger gläserner Kubus, der in seiner zeitgemäßen architektonischen Formensprache weit über Bocholt hinaus von der ehemaligen Spinnerei und deren neuer Nutzung kündet. Die vorgehängte Fassade aus stählernen Fäden, die Licht- und Wetterstimmungen reflektiert, ist metaphorischer Verweis und einladende Geste zugleich. Im Inneren erinnert eine Installation aus 88 historischen Deckenleuchten an die ehemalige Fabrik.

05 Rooftop restaurant overlooking the former production area, consequently dressed in metal threads reflecting both day- and artificial light.

06 Reception and shop as a box-in-a-box addition.

07 All additional rooms are placed like objects rather than interventions.

08 Restaurant and event venue, illuminated by lamps recovered from the historical building.

On all levels, the current usage and the history of the building enter into a dialogue. The old building structure, with the many traces of its former use, has been retained and a new time layer of equal value added. The new functional spaces for shop, counter, catering, warehouse, and WC areas have been incorporated as stand-alone elements, placed at a respectful distance from the old structure. Their pale grey outer surface forms a contrast to the heterogeneous surroundings with their patina, while each interior picks out one of the historical colours from the building. The movable furniture also uses this palette of colours: blue, red, green, white, and black.

The Textilwerk achieves a sensitive dialogue between the historical substance of the building that tells its stories as a documentation of a past era and the new fixtures and fittings that stand out clearly against the historical backdrop. They interpret the original usage of the industrial architecture—revitalised and revisited—with a sensitive dialogue between historical building structure and contemporary architectural accents.

Auf allen Etagen treten die aktuelle Nutzung und die Historie des Gebäudes in Dialog. Der Altbestand mit all seinen Gebrauchsspuren bleibt erhalten; gleichberechtigt hinzu kommt die neue Zeitschicht. Die neuen Funktionsräume für Shop, Counter, Catering, Lager und WC-Bereiche sind respektvoll vom Bestand abgerückt und als eigenständige Elemente eingestellt. Ihre hellgraue äußere Oberfläche bildet einen spannungsreichen Kontrast zur heterogenen, patinierten Umgebung, während das Innere jeweils eine der historischen Farben aus dem Gebäude aufgreift. Auch die bewegliche Möblierung bezieht sich auf diese Farbgebung: Blau, Rot, Grün, Weiß und Schwarz.

Dem Textilwerk gelingt ein feinsinniger Dialog zwischen historischer Bausubstanz, die als Zeitdokument ihre Geschichten erzählt, und den aktuellen Einbauten, die sich klar vom Bestand abheben. Sie interpretieren die ursprüngliche Nutzung der industriellen Architektur – neu belebt und neu erlebt.

HET SCHEEPVAARTMUSEUM

Permanent Exhibition, 1,230 sqm, Amsterdam, The Netherlands, 2011

Het Scheepvaartmuseum in Amsterdam is one of the world's largest maritime museums. Its outstanding collection demonstrates just how much Dutch culture has been influenced by the sea.

Since 1973 the museum has been housed in an arsenal of the Royal Netherlands Navy from the year 1656. Visitors access the exhibitions through the central, recently covered inner courtyard. Depending on what interests them, they can choose a tour through themed maritime worlds, through the historical development of seafaring, or through aptly named object galleries. The object galleries, which are located in the east wing, are mainly of interest for art lovers. On the first floor, three focal points of the collection are presented: model ships, globes, and items handcrafted from glass, silver, and porcelain; on the second floor there is a collection of navigation instruments and maritime paintings as well as ships' ornaments and photo albums.

A specific narrative space tailored to the content was developed for each of the seven object groups which recontextualises the group of exhibits based on their former use. The navigation instruments, for instance, are presented under a starlit sky, a reference to the way constellations were used to determine position and a ship's course. A sea panorama forms the backdrop for the collection of model ships, while a banquet hall offers the ideal ambiance for glass, silver, and porcelain. Individually designed media stations—for example, in the form of a projected place setting or a log book—make the historical objects accessible and understandable.

Das niederländische Schifffahrtsmuseum in Amsterdam zählt zu den größten maritimen Museen weltweit. Mit seiner herausragenden Sammlung demonstriert es, wie stark die niederländische Kultur durch das Meer geprägt wurde.

Seit 1973 ist das Museum in einem Arsenal der königlich-niederländischen Marine aus dem Jahr 1656 untergebracht. Die Besucher gelangen über den zentralen, neu überdachten Innenhof in die Gebäudeflügel. Je nach Interesse können sie einen Rundgang durch maritime Erlebniswelten, durch die historische Entwicklung der Seefahrt oder durch die sogenannten Objektgalerien wählen. Die Objektgalerien, die sich im Ostflügel befinden, wenden sich vor allem an kunstinteressierte Besucher. Im ersten Obergeschoss werden drei Sammlungsschwerpunkte präsentiert: Schiffsmodelle, Globen sowie kunsthandwerkliche Objekte aus Glas, Silber und Porzellan. Im zweiten Obergeschoss sind die Sammlung der Navigationsinstrumente, maritimer Gemälde sowie Schiffsornamente und Fotoalben ausgestellt.

Für jede dieser sieben Objektgruppen wurde ein individuelles, contentbasiertes Raumbild entwickelt, das die Exponatgruppen gemäß ihrer ehemaligen Verwendung atmosphärisch rekontextualisiert. So werden die Navigationsinstrumente unter einem Sternenhimmel präsentiert, der daran erinnert, dass in früheren Zeiten Sternbilder zur Positions- und Kursbestimmung der Schiffe genutzt wurden. Ein Meerespanorama bildet den Hintergrund für die Sammlung von Schiffsmodellen und ein Bankettraum bietet das ideale Ambiente für Glas, Silber und Porzellan. Individuell gestaltete Medienstationen, beispielsweise in Form eines projizierten Gedecks oder eines Logbuchs, erschließen die historischen Objekte, machen sie zugänglich und verständlich.

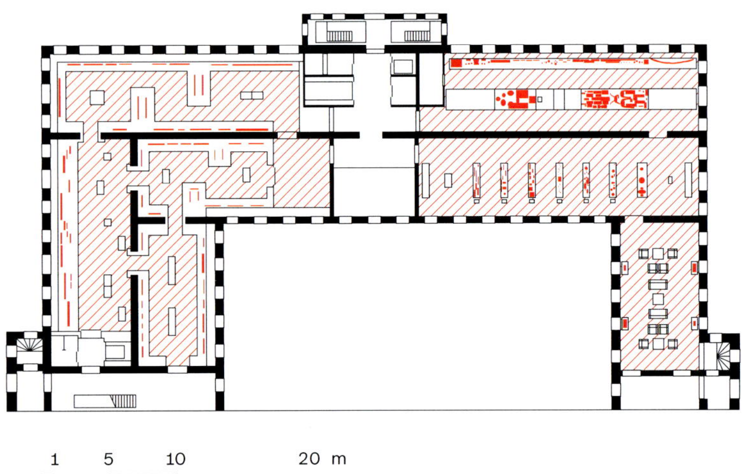

01 Floor plan—second floor.
02 Figureheads dynamically lit for better plasticity.

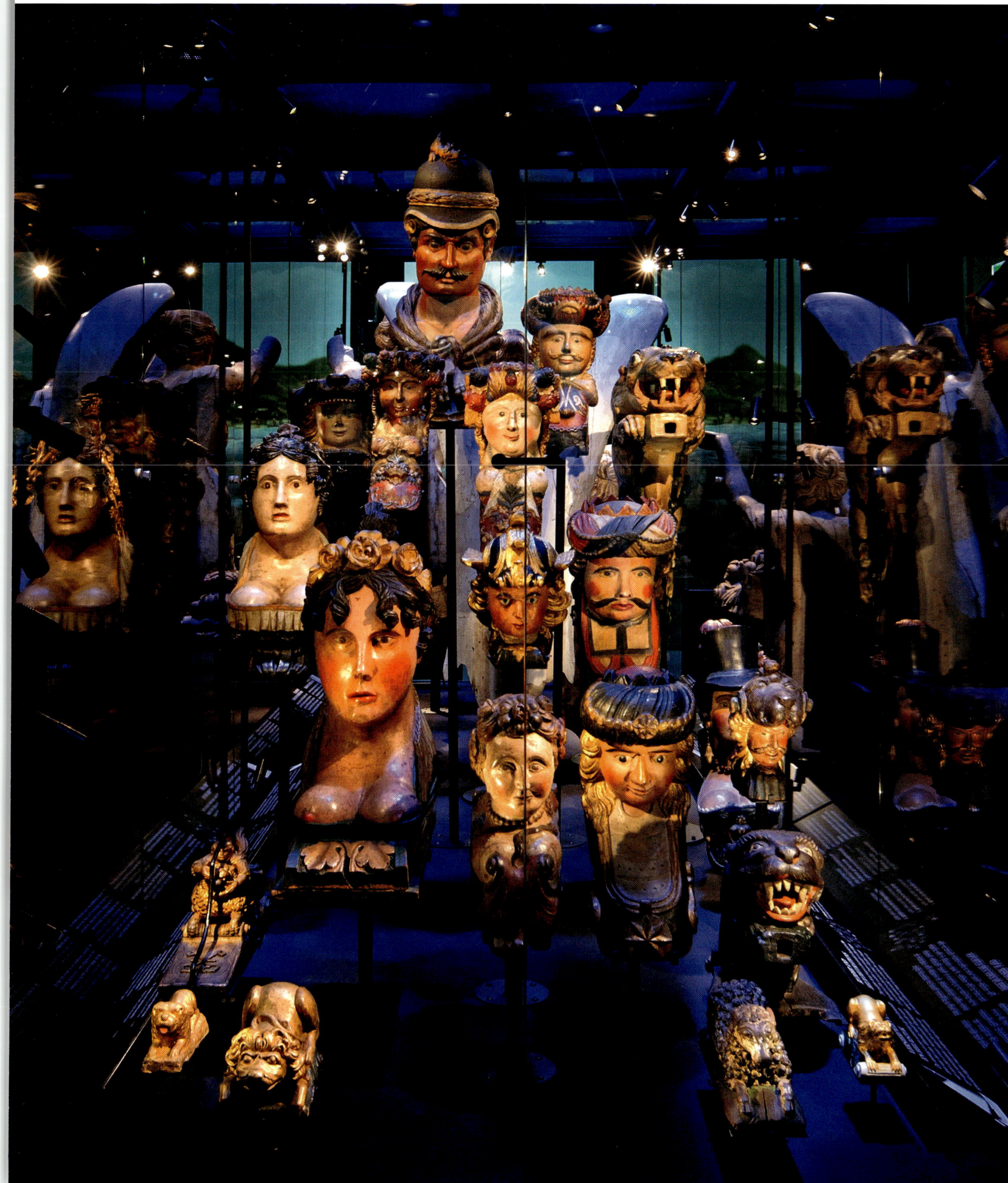

03 Navigational instruments under the artificial northern and southern star constellations.

The exhibition area with photo albums is like a private lounge in which visitors can immerse themselves in the everyday lives of ship's sailors and passengers. The personal stories with exotic destinations are conveyed via audio in the armchairs on which visitors sit as well as through images from the early years of photography and albums as chronicles.

Der Ausstellungsbereich der Fotoalben gleicht einer privaten Lounge, in der die Besucher in den Lebensalltag der Seeleute und Schiffsreisenden eintauchen. Vermittelt werden die privaten Geschichten, die zu exotischen Zielen führten, auditiv an Sesseln, auf denen die Besucher Platz nehmen, sowie durch Bilder aus den frühen Jahren der Fotografie und Alben als Chroniken.

When developing the narrative space, the exhibit is both starting point and at the same time also an integral part of the impressive scenography in which the aura of the objects can unfold. The permanent exhibition not only has a multimedia and multisensory set-up, but also invites visitors to participate and to join in themselves at interactive stations in order to experience maritime history.

Das Exponat ist bei der Entwicklung des Raumbilds Ausgangspunkt und zugleich auch integrativer Bestandteil der eindrucksvollen Szenografien, in denen sich die Aura der Objekte entfalten kann. Die Dauerausstellung ist nicht nur multimedial und multisensorisch angelegt, sondern lädt den Besucher dazu ein, zu partizipieren und an interaktiven Stationen selbst aktiv zu werden, um maritime Geschichte zu erleben.

04 Collection of model ships presented in front of a sea panorama.

05 Personal stories of sailors presented in a photo album collection.

06 The glas, silver and porcelain collection is presented in a banquet hall.

07 Presentation of precious globes in chronological order.

08 Climatized showcases provide all necessary conditions for the globes.

09 An interactive globe makes the precious globes explorable.

PARLAMENTARIUM

Visitor Centre of the European Parliament, 5,400 sqm, Brussels, Belgium, 2011

Transparent, informative, and experience-oriented: The Parlamentarium in Brussels uses impressive spatial narratives, media interactions, and personal contact to convey the way the European Parliament works and the history of the EU. All content is available in the 24 official EU languages. In addition, there are four sign languages and other options for persons with impaired hearing or eyesight. A storyline for children and young people rounds off the offerings.

A portable media guide is the personal companion through the exhibition. It allows visitors to choose from the huge volume of images, film, and text on offer and provides the content of the media stations in the requested language. More than 100 media installations show the history of and current events in European politics. The more than 500,000 visitors per year can immerse themselves in the world of the parliamentarians and obtain an understanding of political action.

The visitor centre was installed on three floors of an existing building located centrally in the EU district. The basic structure of the visitor routing is chronological from the eventful beginnings of the European idea to the current composition of the parliament and our wishes for the future of the EU. This is supplemented by rooms that introduce overarching themes.

The centrepiece is the "United in Diversity" room, representing the slogan of the European Union. Visitors explore a walk-on map without territorial borders and can activate films about a number of hot spots using a ground-of-stories scanner. The hot spots introduce EU institutions and show how the European Parliament has found solutions for cross-border challenges, for example the Seveso Directive that was enacted after a dioxin accident in Seveso in northern Italy in 1976. Above the map, the sky of opinions reflects the diversity of European opinions: 13,000 lights combine to create a unique voxel installation.

Transparent, informativ und erlebnisorientiert: Das Parlamentarium in Brüssel vermittelt Funktion und Arbeitsweise des Europäischen Parlaments sowie die Geschichte der EU über eindrucksvolle Raumbilder, mediale Interaktionen und persönliche Ansprache. Sämtliche Inhalte sind in den 24 EU-Amtssprachen aufbereitet. Hinzu kommen vier Gebärdensprachen und weitere Angebote für auditiv und visuell beeinträchtigte Menschen. Ein Erzählstrang für Kinder und Jugendliche ergänzt das Angebot.

Ein tragbarer Media-Guide ist der persönliche Begleiter durch die Ausstellung. Er ermöglicht den Besuchern, aus einem umfangreichen Bild-, Film- und Textangebot auszuwählen, und erschließt die Inhalte der Medienstationen in der jeweils gewünschten Sprache. Mehr als 100 Medieninstallationen zeigen Geschichte und aktuelles Geschehen der europäischen Politik. Die Besucher – über 500.000 jährlich – können in die Welt der Parlamentarier eintauchen und politisches Handeln nachvollziehen.

Für das Besucherzentrum wurden drei Etagen eines bereits bestehenden, zentral gelegenen Gebäudes im EU-Viertel erschlossen. Die Grundstruktur des Parcours ist chronologisch angelegt, von den bewegten Anfängen der europäischen Ideen bis hin zur aktuellen Zusammensetzung des Parlaments und unseren Wünschen für die Zukunft der EU. Hinzu kommen einzelne Themenräume, die übergeordnete Aspekte vorstellen.

Herzstück ist der Raum „United in Diversity". Er repräsentiert das Motto der Europäischen Union „In Vielfalt geeint". Die Besucher erkunden eine begehbare Landkarte ohne territoriale Grenzen und können mit einem Ground-of-Stories-Scanner Filme zu einzelnen Hotspots aufrufen. Diese stellen EU-Institutionen vor und zeigen, wie das Europäische Parlament Lösungen für länderübergreifende Herausforderungen gefunden hat, beispielsweise die Seveso-Richtlinien, die nach einem Dioxin-Unfall im norditalienischen Seveso 1976 verabschiedet wurden. Darüber spiegelt der „Sky of Opinions" europäische Meinungsvielfalt. 13.000 Lichter setzen sich zu einer einzigartigen Voxel-Installation zusammen.

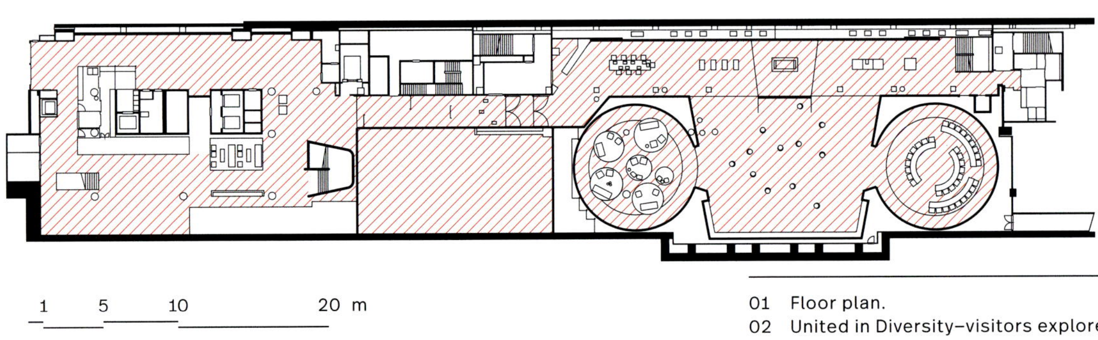

01 Floor plan.
02 United in Diversity–visitors explore a borderless map of Europe.

03 360-degree hemisphere enables visitors to participate in a debate and vote like a parliamentarian.

This area is flanked by two 360-degree panorama rooms. The first room leads into the political heart of Europe and illustrates in an impressively immersive way how the Parliament works. The visitor takes a seat in the plenum and, surrounded by a projection surface of 150 square metres, experiences at first hand how a law comes into being.

The second room reports about life in Europe. The panorama projection takes visitors on a cinematic journey through the culturally rich continent and its many different landscapes, while 54 Europeans tell about their lives and report how the work of the European Parliament impacts these—for example, as regards hygiene and export provisions.

The Parlamentarium offers its visitors a unique experience that addresses a number of senses to playfully combine knowledge sharing and entertainment. As a European co-production, it shows how the multilingual, -national, and -cultural spirit understands the diversity of various cultures, opinions, and histories. “Welcome to the Parlamentarium” means: Welcome to Europe.

Flankiert wird der Bereich von zwei 360-Grad-Panoramaräumen. Der erste Raum führt ins politische Herz Europas und veranschaulicht auf eindrucksvoll immersive Weise, wie das Parlament arbeitet. Der Besucher nimmt Platz im Plenum und erfährt umgeben von 150 Quadratmetern Filmfläche hautnah, wie ein Gesetz entsteht.

Der zweite Raum berichtet vom Leben in Europa. Die Panoramaprojektion nimmt die Besucher mit auf eine filmische Reise durch den kulturreichen Kontinent und seine vielfältigen Landschaften, während 54 Europäer aus ihrem Alltag erzählen und berichten, wie sich die Arbeit des Europäischen Parlaments darauf auswirkt, beispielsweise bezogen auf Hygiene- und Exportbestimmungen.

Das Parlamentarium eröffnet den Besuchern eine einzigartige Erfahrung, die Wissensvermittlung und Unterhaltung spielerisch und sinnlich vereint. Als europäische Koproduktion repräsentiert es die Besonderheit des multilingualen, -nationalen und -kulturellen europäischen Geistes, der die Vielfalt der unterschiedlichen Kulturen, Meinungen und Geschichten als Potenzial versteht. „Willkommen im Parlamentarium“ heißt: Willkommen in Europa.

04 Panorama projection and media stations: 54 Europeans talk about their lives.

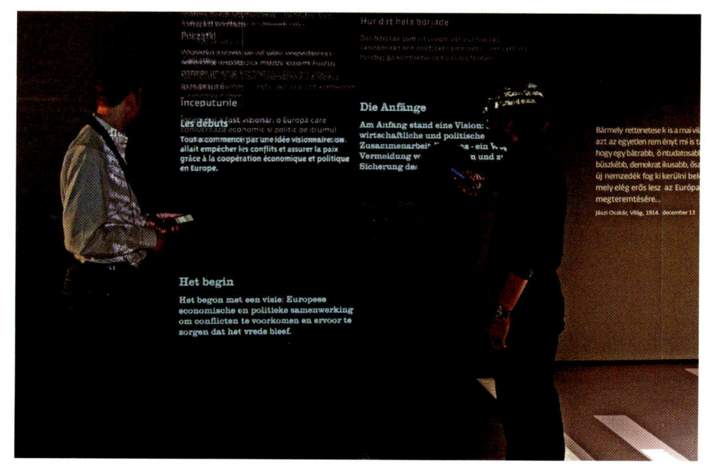

05 | 06 A personal digital device allows visitors to be addressed in their 24 national and 4 sign languages.

KUSCH+CO– PAST-PRESENT-FUTURE

Trade Fair Stand, 180 sqm, Milan, Italy, 2012

Like stars on the stage! That is how Kusch+Co presented their premium products at their debut appearance at the Milan Design Week. The spotlight is trained on 50 of the furniture manufacturer's seating objects. Design classics pay tribute to the 70-year history of the firm. Suspended in front of a mirrored wall, the red-coloured chairs form an ancestral gallery as a backdrop for more recent and current chairs of the present and future.

The visitor is not only an onlooker, but becomes part of the staging. By taking a seat, he finds himself on the stage. The perspective changes. The stage becomes the spectator stalls.

The seating objects also change their role: short films show them as the active protagonists in humorous scenes. The mirror of the ancestral gallery measures six by seven metres and reflects these stories into the installation.

The space becomes a lively setting for the spectacle of the history, present, and future of this heritage company.

Wie Stars auf der Bühne, so präsentiert Kusch+Co seine hochwertigen Produkte beim Premierenauftritt auf der Milan Design Week. Im Rampenlicht stehen 50 Sitzobjekte des Möbelherstellers, der auf eine über 70-jährige Firmengeschichte zurückblicken kann.

Designklassiker repräsentieren die Historie. Rot akzentuiert schweben sie vor einer Spiegelwand und bilden gleichsam eine Ahnengalerie, vor der neuere und aktuelle Sitzmöbel Gegenwart und Zukunft zeigen.

Der Besucher ist nicht nur Betrachter, sondern wird Teil der Inszenierung. Er nimmt Platz auf den Stühlen und steht damit selbst auf der Bühne. Die Perspektive ändert sich. Die Bühne wird zum Zuschauerparkett.

Auch die Sitzmöbel wechseln ihre Rolle: Projizierte Kurzfilme zeigen sie als aktive Hauptdarsteller humorvoller Szenen. Der sechs auf sieben Meter große Spiegel der Ahnengalerie reflektiert diese Geschichten in die Installation hinein.

Das Raumbild wird zum lebendigen Setting für das Schauspiel zu Geschichte, Gegenwart und Zukunft des traditionsreichen Unternehmens.

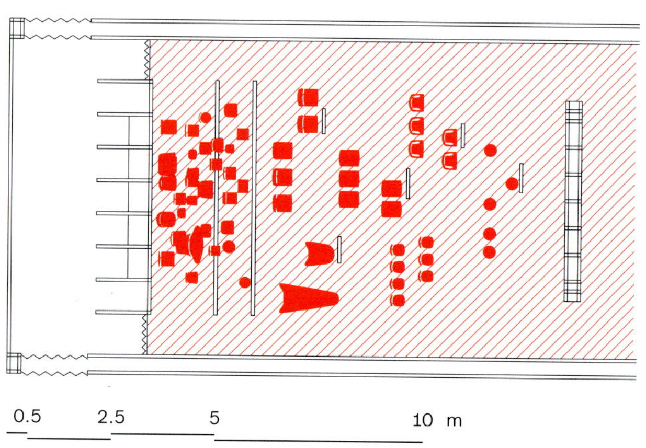

01 Floor plan.
02 All made from chairs: the stage, the backdrop, and the setting.

SERIES 8000
DESIGN BY PORSCHE DESIGN STUDIO

03 Chairs are the coulisse that populate the stage, act like protagonists, and serve as products to welcome and host the customers–the staged chairs offer a staged seating. Last but not least the chairs are the actors in an animated film featuring the company's tradition of high-quality products.

CARLSWORLD

Competition for a Permanent Brand Exhibition, 7,000 sqm, Copenhagen, Denmark, 2012

For more brand presence at home, the Carlsberg Group plans to sharpen its brand appearance at its traditional factory in Copenhagen and to create public appeal by redesigning the historical brewery and its famous elephant gate.

"The longest bar in the world" was developed as the central theme for this construction and marketing project, and is found as a flexible icon throughout the building. It connects various attractions to one another and changes to match the attractions and experiences: from the interactive digital timeline and a 3-D cinema labyrinth, via a football goal wall and a science lab through to a sky bar. A kinetic sculpture made of 1,400 Carlsberg bottles is one of the highlights. Illuminated from the inside, the sculpture acts as a three-dimensional dynamic screen.

Exploring and enjoying the Carlsberg brand along the longest bar in the world becomes a unique brand experience. The bar is a memorable symbol, an icon that sticks in the mind, which unites the entire building complex with a single identity, transforming the location with a humorous touch.

Mehr Markenpräsenz vor Ort: Der Carlsberg-Konzern plant, auf seinem angestammten Fabrikareal in Kopenhagen den eigenen Markenauftritt zu stärken und dazu das historische Brauhaus und das berühmte Elefanten-Tor publikumswirksam umzugestalten.

Als Leitidee für dieses Bau- und Marketingvorhaben wurde „die längste Bar der Welt" entwickelt, die sich als flexibles Icon durch das gesamte Gebäude zieht. Sie verbindet verschiedene Attraktionen miteinander und verändert sich entsprechend den Attraktionen und Erlebnissen: von der interaktiven digitalen Timeline und einem 3D-Kino-Labyrinth über eine Fußball-Torwand und ein Science-Lab bis hin zu einer Skybar. Eine kinetische Skulptur aus 1.400 Carlsberg-Flaschen ist als Highlight vorgesehen. Die Skulptur fungiert, von innen beleuchtet, als dreidimensionaler dynamischer Screen.

Das Erforschen und Genießen der Carlsberg-Marke entlang der längsten Bar der Welt wird zum einzigartigen Markenerlebnis. Die Bar ist ein erinnerungswürdiges Symbol – eine nachhaltig einprägsame Ikone, die den gesamten Gebäudekomplex identitätsstiftend verbindet und eine humorvolle Standorttransformation bewirkt.

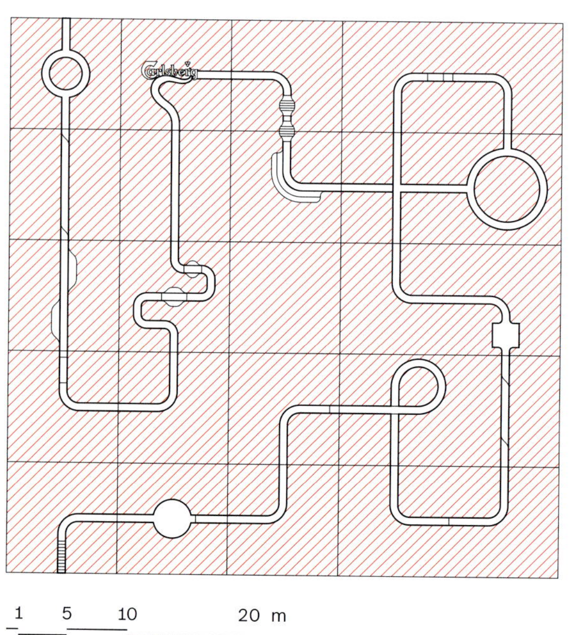

01 Floor plan.

02 Central kinetic installation of 1,400 LED-lit bottles has the potential to transport Carlsberg's brand philosophy in an iconic way.

03|04 Longest bar in the world, meandering through the historical brewery in a multifunctional, always surprising way.

LASCAUX IV—INTERNATIONAL CENTRE FOR CAVE ART

Concept for a Visitor Centre with a Permanent Exhibition, 8,400 sqm, Montignac-Lascaux, France, 2012

Lascaux, with its 20,000-year-old Stone Age cave paintings, is considered to be a cradle of mankind. For conservation reasons, the caves themselves can no longer be entered. A reproduction, an accurate copy of the original, supplements them.

The competition design conjures up a themed world that conveys the history and significance of Lascaux on many levels. The main theme and connecting element of the concept is light. Equipped with a flashlight, visitors can begin to explore the caves. Like the cave painters from back then, they hold a torch in their hands. Their movements are tracked so that suitable lighting and information can be cued at the right moment. Mysterious images and compositions appear on the scene.

In the second exhibition area, visitors themselves become researchers. They investigate the compositions and motifs of the drawings, compare cave paintings around the world, and take a look at scientific theories about the prehistoric age. The torch they have with them provides both images and content.

The interplay of light and shadow, of light and dark, stands for the cycle of time, or for the inside and outside of the caves, as well as for concealing, discovering, and deciphering. Such a holistic experience arouses a fascination for the roots of our culture and allows visitors to immerse themselves with all their senses into the synthesis of the arts that Lascaux represents.

Lascaux mit seinen 20.000 Jahre alten steinzeitlichen Wandmalereien gilt als eine Wiege der Menschheit. Die Höhle selbst kann aus konservatorischen Gründen nicht mehr betreten werden. Eine Reproduktion, ein originalgetreues Faksimile, wird sie ergänzen.

Der Wettbewerbsentwurf sieht eine Erlebniswelt vor, die Historie und Bedeutung Lascaux' vielschichtig vermittelt. Als Leitidee und verbindendes Element des Konzepts dient das Licht. Mit einer Taschenlampe ausgestattet können Besucher die Höhle erforschen. Es scheint, als hätten sie wie einst die Höhlenmaler eine Fackel in der Hand. Ihre Bewegungen werden getrackt, um passende szenische Beleuchtung und Informationen einzuspielen. Bildmotive und Kompositionen kommen lebendig und geheimnisvoll zum Vorschein.

Im zweiten Ausstellungsbereich werden die Besucher selbst zu Forschern. Sie untersuchen Kompositionen und Motive der Zeichnungen, vergleichen Höhlenmalereien weltweit und werfen einen Blick auf wissenschaftliche Theorien zur Prähistorie. Die Taschenlampe ist ihnen dabei abermals ein Bild- und Inhalte gebendes Medium.

Der Wechsel von Licht und Schatten, das Spiel von Dunkel und Hell, steht für den Zyklus der Zeit, für das Höhleninnere und -äußere und für das Verbergen, Entdecken und Entschlüsseln. Ein derartig ganzheitliches Erlebnis schafft Faszination für die Wurzeln unserer Kultur und ermöglicht dem Besucher, mit allen Sinnen in das Gesamtkunstwerk von Lascaux einzutauchen.

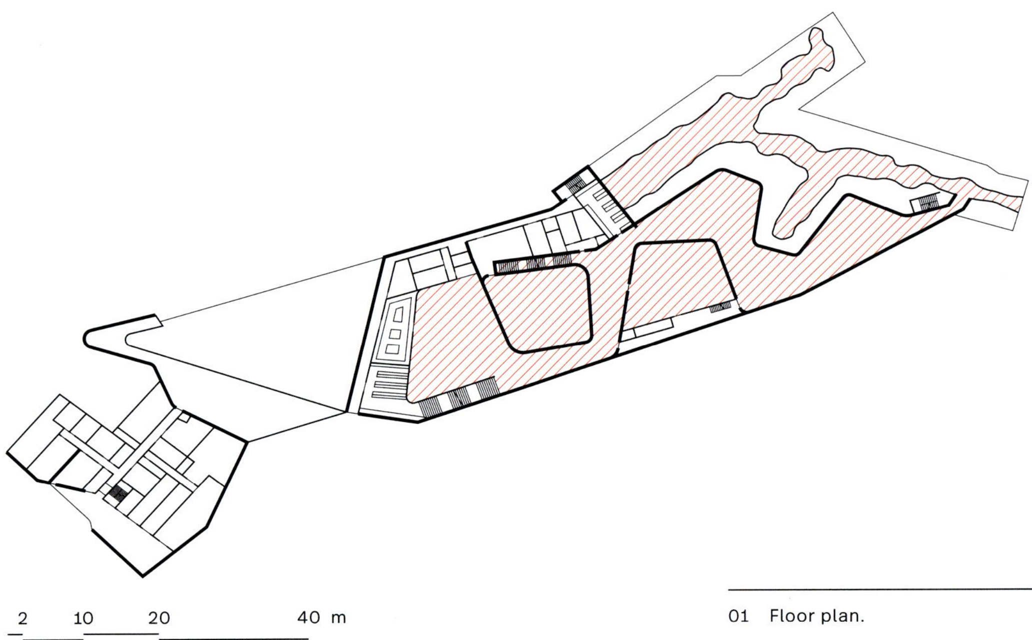

01 Floor plan.

02 Les fragments | Explore–compositions and motifs of drawings.

03 Tour de l'art pariétal | Compare–Cave painting worldwide.

04 Table des archéologues | Research–work of archaeologists.

GS CALTEX PAVILION

Corporate Pavilion, 1,960 sqm, Expo Yeosu, South Korea, 2012

"I am Your Energy": The GS Caltex pavilion translates the claim of the South Korean oil company into an impressive corporate scenography, expressing philosophical and social aspects related to the topic of energy.

First up, visitors–initially alone–explore an abstract, oversized paddy field: 18-metre-tall poles–400 so-called "blades"–bend like blades of grass in the wind. They visualise natural and human energy in equal parts. Individual blades can be activated. When touched, coloured light spreads over the whole field.

It is only at second glance that visitors discover the star-shaped pavilion hidden in the paddy field. Its mirrored outer skin multiplies the artificial blades and thus the image of the energy field into eternity. The entrance area opens beneath the raised corners of the star, a room without any feel for scale with a folded mirrored ceiling. Due to prismatic refractions, visitors are reflected many times, creating a sense of solidarity and social networking. The social community that is of great importance in Korean culture is perceived as collective energy.

The centrepiece of the exhibition is then to be found on the upper level, a 7-metre-tall round space with a 360-degree panorama projection. The animated film on the Expo slogan ("Living Ocean and Coast") uses simple black-and-white aesthetics. With reference to the grass blades of the energy field, it develops a poetical narration about a pearl diver and a whale. These are metaphors for the connection between land and sea, between man and nature–and ultimately a plea for a life in harmony with nature. Towards the end of the film, the shadows of the visitors become the projection surface for a rear projection, and it is at them that the message of sustainability is directed, thus closing the interactive cycle between visitors and staging.

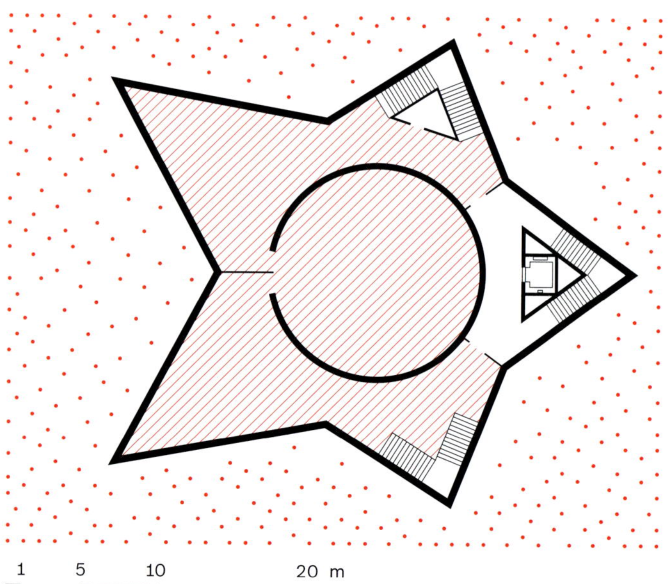

„I am Your Energy": Der GS Caltex Pavilion übersetzt den Claim des koreanisches Ölkonzerns in eine eindrucksvolle Corporate Scenography. Philosophische und soziale Aspekte, die mit dem Thema Energie in Zusammenhang stehen, kommen zum Ausdruck.

Der Besucher erkundet zunächst individuell ein abstraktes überdimensionales Reisfeld. 18 Meter hohe Stäbe - 400 sogenannte Blades - bewegen sich wie Grashalme im Wind. Sie visualisieren natürliche und menschliche Energie gleichermaßen. Einzelne Blades sind aktivierbar. Bei Berührung breitet sich farbiges Licht über das gesamte Feld aus.

Erst auf den zweiten Blick entdeckt der Besucher den im Reisfeld verborgenen sternförmigen Pavillonkörper. Seine verspiegelte Außenhaut multipliziert die künstlichen Halme und damit das Bild des Energiefelds ins Unendliche. Über die angehobenen Ecken des Sterns öffnet sich der Eingangsbereich - ein Raum ohne jegliche Maßstäblichkeit mit einer mehrfach gefalteten Spiegeldecke. Durch die prismatischen Brechungen spiegeln sich die Besucher vielfach. Ein Gefühl von Verbundenheit und sozialer Vernetzung entsteht. Die soziale Gemeinschaft, die in der koreanischen Kultur große Bedeutung hat, wird als kollektive Energie wahrgenommen.

Im Obergeschoss befindet sich das Herzstück der Ausstellung - ein sieben Meter hoher Rundraum mit einer 360-Grad-Panoramaprojektion. Der Animationsfilm zum Expo-Motto „Living Ocean and Coast" ist in reduzierter Schwarzweiß-Ästhetik gehalten. Er greift die Gräser des Energiefelds als Lichtlinien auf und entwickelt daraus eine poetische Narration rund um eine Perlentaucherin und einen Wal. Sie sind Metaphern für die Verbindung zwischen Land und Meer, zwischen Mensch und Natur - und letztlich ein Plädoyer für ein Leben im Einklang mit der Natur. Gegen Ende des Films wird der Schattenwurf der Besucher zur bespielten Fläche einer Rückprojektion. Damit richtet sich die Botschaft der Nachhaltigkeit direkt an jene. Der Interaktionskreislauf zwischen Besucher und Inszenierung schließt sich.

01 Floor plan.

02 The only pavilion on the Expo that did not look like a building but like an art installation.

03|04 The "energy field" was changing its colour and choreography according to the environmetal conditions or activity of the visitors.

05 LED-equipped blades sway in the wind, changing their mood in an aesthtic way and overcoming the line between reality and poetry.

06 10 percent of the blades were reactive—by touching them, visitors could change the light choreography.

07 Reflecting ceiling inviting visitors to explore the pavilion.

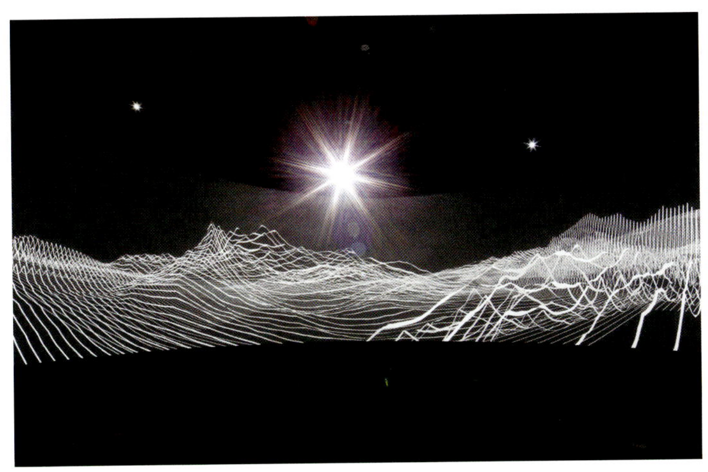

08 A 360-degree panoramic symphony composed of lightlines depicting the Korean coast and ocean life in a symphonic gesture.

DARWINEUM

Permanent Exhibition, 1,700 sqm, Rostock, Germany, 2012

A science centre in a zoo? The Darwineum in Rostock represents a new, entertaining way of conveying knowledge. It combines exhibition with a living zoological collection.

With Darwin's theory of evolution as the starting point, the permanent exhibition takes the visitor on a journey through the millions of years of Earth's history and its biodiversity: first through the "Evolution of Life" and then through the "Cultural Evolution" of man. The generously dimensioned tropical hall that houses Rostock Zoo's great apes is sandwiched between the two.

The "Evolution of Life" is presented in a round-shaped room with a family-tree game in the middle. At a circular media table, visitors learn about the relationships between the various living beings and find out, for example, to what extent man is in fact related to the ape. The surrounding cabinets offer access to different ages of the Earth, designed as reconstructive dioramas. Aquariums, paludariums, and terrariums house living animals that still have prehistoric characteristics or that embody stages of evolution, thus demonstrating biological evolution.

The content of the "Cultural Evolution" section rounds off the tour. Chronologically, it starts with the first tools and ends in a stem cell laboratory that takes a critical look at genetic engineering. After all, cultural evolution is what allows this intervention into biological evolution.

Ein Science Center in einem Zoo? Das Darwineum in Rostock repräsentiert einen neuen Typus unterhaltender Wissensvermittlung. Es verbindet Ausstellung und lebendige zoologische Sammlung.

Die Dauerausstellung schickt den Besucher, ausgehend von Darwins Evolutionstheorie, auf eine Reise durch die Jahrmillionen der Erd- und Artengeschichte, beginnend mit der „Evolution des Lebens" und dann durch die „Kulturelle Evolution" des Menschen. Dazwischen liegt die großzügige Tropenhalle, in der die Menschenaffen des Rostocker Zoos beheimatet sind.

Die „Evolution des Lebens" wird in einem Rundraum vorgestellt, in dessen Zentrum ein Stammbaumspiel steht. An einem runden Medientisch lernen die Besucher die Verwandtschaftsverhältnisse einzelner Lebewesen kennen und erfahren beispielsweise, inwieweit der Mensch tatsächlich mit dem Affen verwandt ist. Die umgebenden Kabinette bieten Zugang zu den einzelnen Erdzeitaltern, gestaltet als rekonstruierende Dioramen. In Aquarien, Paludarien und Terrarien leben Tiere, die noch urzeitliche Merkmale besitzen oder entsprechende Evolutionsstufen verkörpern und so die biologische Evolution veranschaulichen.

Der Bereich „Kulturelle Evolution" rundet den Parcours inhaltlich ab. Er setzt zeitlich mit den ersten Werkzeugen ein, welche die Menschen nutzten, und endet in einem Stammzellenlabor, das die Genforschung kritisch reflektiert. Schließlich ermöglicht es erst die kulturelle Entwicklung, in die biologische Evolution einzugreifen.

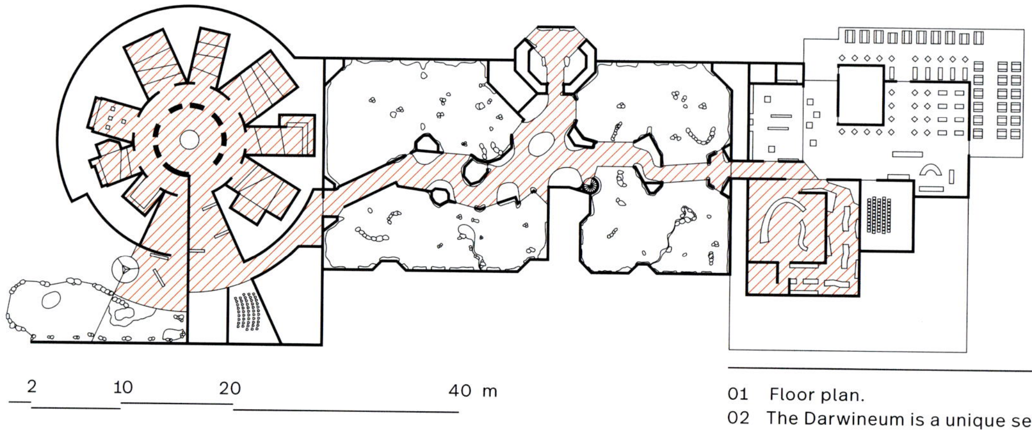

01 Floor plan.
02 The Darwineum is a unique setting of dioramas, scientific interpretation, live aquariums and vivariums.

Hör mal, wer da spricht!
Listen who's talking!

03 Museum, exploratorium, and zoo in one building provide exeptional experiences.

04 Exhibition area "Born from a Cell."

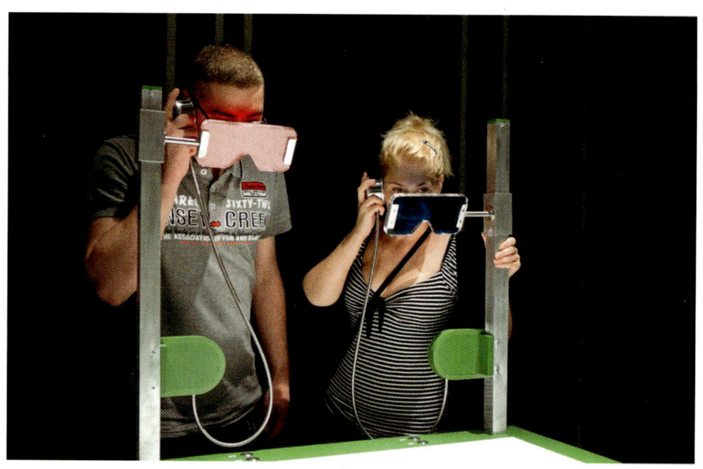

05 Playstation "Change of Perspective / Social Consciousness."

06 A central media table offers a contemporary and interactive journey through evolution.

07 “Blueprint of Life”–vivid family tree of species which have survived all extinctions.

GERMAN STEAM LOCOMOTIVE MUSEUM

Permanent Exhibition, Open Air Museum: 100,000 sqm, Engine Shed: 3,000 sqm, Neuenmarkt, Germany, 2013

Neuenmarkt, which was connected to the railway as early as 1848, was the starting point of the "Schiefe Ebene," the first European railway ramp with a steep gradient to be used by steam locomotives. As a result, prosperous railway works developed here, giving rise to new professions and a railway life that left its stamp on the place.

Visitors are plunged into this in three different ways: in a tour round the museum; through the turntable engine shed; and over the coal yard and the railway workers' village.

The centrepiece of the museum is the impressive turntable engine shed, whose original equipment and working atmosphere have been preserved. Visitors can sense the aura of the black giants. Along a timeline, they can dip into the history and be given the key facts about technical processes and developments using augmented reality to support the explanations. For instance, a one-to-one projection onto a steam locomotive visualises the functions and technical correlations concealed behind the steel outer skin.

As visitors continue their tour through the open-air space, they encounter a number of railwaymen. The signalman, for example, or the blacksmith and the worker on the water crane who tell visitors about their tasks. The life-sized silhouettes of these figures are points of attraction on the wide-ranging museum grounds while in the railway workers' village, information boards provide interesting facts about the various buildings and their inhabitants.

Neuenmarkt, das bereits im Jahr 1848 einen Bahnanschluss erhielt, war Ausgangspunkt der „Schiefen Ebenen", der ersten europäischen Steilrampe, die mit Dampflokomotiven befahren wurde. Hier entstand ein prosperierendes Bahnbetriebswerk, das neue Berufe hervorbrachte und zu einem den Ort prägenden Eisenbahnerleben führte.

In dieses taucht der Besucher über drei verschiedene Wege ein: beim Museumsrundgang durch den Ringlokschuppen und über den Kohlenhof sowie im Eisenbahnerdorf.

Herzstück des Museums ist der eindrucksvolle Ringlokschuppen, dessen ursprüngliche Ausstattung und Arbeitsatmosphäre erhalten blieben. Hier spürt der Besucher die Aura der schwarzen Giganten. Entlang einer Zeitlinie taucht er in die Historie ein und erfährt das Wichtigste zu den technischen Abläufen und Entwicklungen. Augmented Reality unterstützt die Erklärung. So verdeutlicht eine 1:1-Projektion auf eine Dampflok die Funktionen und technischen Zusammenhänge, die sich unter der stählernen Haut verbergen.

Einzelnen Eisenbahnern begegnet der Besucher auf seinem Rundgang über das Freigelände. Hier trifft er beispielsweise auf den Bahnwärter, den Schmied und den Arbeiter am Wasserkran, die ihm von ihren Aufgaben erzählen. Die lebensgroßen figurativen Silhouetten sind Anziehungspunkte auf dem weitläufigen Museumsareal, während im Eisenbahnerdorf Wissenswertes zu den einzelnen Gebäuden und zu deren Bewohnern auf Infotafeln angeboten wird.

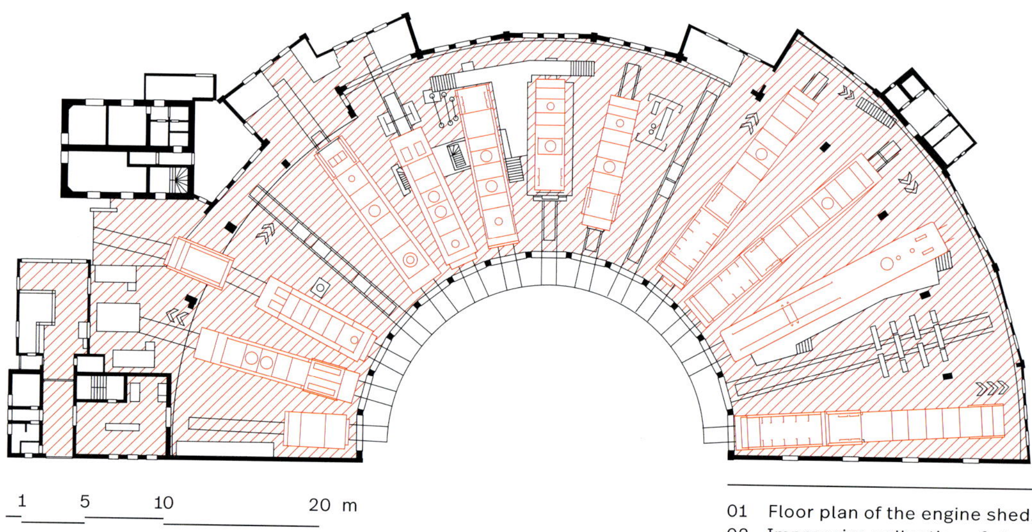

01 Floor plan of the engine shed.
02 Impressive collection of steam locomotives in front of the museum.

23 019

02 A precise projection mapping onto an original locomotive allows insights into its technical functions.

The stagings, interactive media installations, and life-sized figures convey the fascination associated with the black giants. The work on the railway and a place full of history and stories are brought to life.

Die Inszenierungen, interaktiven Medieninstallationen und lebensgroßen Figuren vermitteln die Faszination, die mit den schwarzen Giganten verbunden ist. Die Arbeit im Bahnbetriebswerk sowie ein Ort voller Geschichte und Geschichten werden lebendig.

03 “Pump changing workshop”–yellow lines indicate special areas of the railway depot in the engine shed.

04 Framing means emphasizing. In order to focus on technical details, yellow rectangles highlight functions to both amateurs and professionals.

05 Figures of workers in the vast outdoor area of the museum introduce the routines of the former railway depot.

LIVING THE FUTURE–THE DEMOGRAPHIC OPPORTUNITY

Touring Exhibition, 300 sqm, Berlin, Germany, 2013

We are living longer. There are fewer of us. We are becoming more diverse: scientific findings on these three core statements are the starting point for the exhibition that the Leibniz Association realised for the Year of Science 2013. In a very vivid and emotional way, it visualises the various aspects of demographic change–providing access to a topic that initially appears abstract and a long way off.

Nine walk-in themed cubes give the exhibition its appearance and provide navigation through it. The prologue consists of a demography pyramid that translates 100 years of change in population growth into a sculptural installation, giving it a tangible and understandable form. The following semi-transparent cubes have an outer and an inner narrative layer. Optically, the two layers overlap. Precisely designed graphics leak from the inside to the outside; for instance, a brightly coloured visualisation of the role of migration and the significance of work in demographic change. Large-scale portraits on the outer skin awaken interest in the people and the associated themes.

The cube "Ageing–An Achievement" places a scenographic accent. The dance performance "Kontakthof" by Pina Bausch is projected onto wrinkled strips of material, giving the subject, ageing, an experiential dimension through dance and materiality.

The information, experiences, and encounters in the exhibition invite visitors to consciously ponder the future and the opportunities that lie in demographic change.

Wir leben länger. Wir werden weniger. Wir werden vielfältiger: Wissenschaftliche Erkenntnisse zu diesen drei Kernaussagen sind der Ausgangspunkt der Ausstellung, welche die Leibniz-Gemeinschaft zum Wissenschaftsjahr 2013 realisierte. Sie verbildlicht auf sehr anschauliche und emotionale Weise verschiedene Aspekte des demografischen Wandels - ein Thema, das zunächst sehr abstrakt und weit entfernt erscheint.

Neun begehbare Themenkuben bilden Raumbild und Parcours. Der Prolog besteht aus einer Demografie-Pyramide, die 100 Jahre Wandel im Bevölkerungswachstum in eine skulpturale Rauminstallation übersetzt und damit physisch begreifbar macht. Die folgenden semitransparenten Kuben besitzen eine äußere und eine innere Erzählschicht. Beide überlagern sich optisch. Aus dem Inneren dringen präzise gestaltete Grafiken nach außen, die beispielsweise die Rolle der Migration und die Bedeutung der Arbeit beim demografischen Wandel farbenfroh visualisieren. Auf der Außenhaut sind es großformatige Porträts, die das Interesse an den Menschen und den damit verbundenen Themen wecken.

Einen szenografischen Akzent setzt der Kubus „Altern - eine Errungenschaft". Die Tanzperformance „Kontakthof" von Pina Bausch wird auf faltige Stoffbahnen projiziert und macht somit das Thema Altern tänzerisch und haptisch erlebbar.

Verschiedene Informationen, Erlebnisse und Begegnungen in der Ausstellung laden dazu ein, sich mit unserer Zukunft und den Chancen, die im demografischen Wandel liegen, intensiver auseinanderzusetzen.

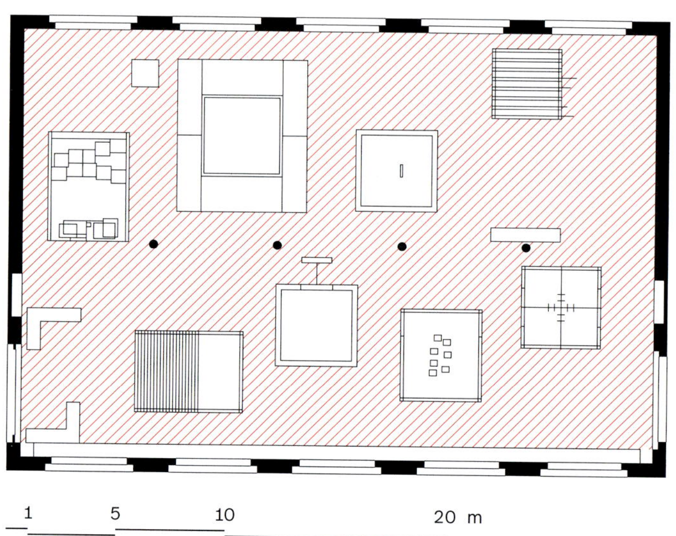

01 Floor plan.

02 Semi-transparent walk-in themed cubes provide two narrative layers.

03 Scientific research presented in a tangible exhibition.

04 Walk-in demography pyramid.

EXPERTISIUM

Permanent Exhibition, Showroom, 650 sqm, Aesculap Academy Bochum, Germany, 2013

In the Expertisium everything revolves around the human being. A 5-metre-tall human figure greets the specialist visitors and forms the focal point of the exhibition. The large-scale installation allows them to interactively experience the therapy areas for which the company offers medical-technical products. These are organised in a circle round the figure. At a terminal, visitors can pick the field that interests them and obtain detailed information, for example on the use of ultrasound in anaesthetics.

The Expertisium, which consists of a foyer and exhibition areas on several levels, is the heart of the Aesculap Academy on the Bochum Health Campus that offers training courses for medical carers and physicians.

A generously dimensioned and clearly structured spatial appearance, in which the corporate colour is used as an accent colour, shapes the showroom. Large graphics reminiscent of X-ray images provide insights into the human anatomy and form a scientific slide. This puts the medical-technical products, such as surgical instruments or prostheses, into the context of their applications.

The tour around the exhibition presents the company's innovations from clinical care via minimally invasive surgery and orthopaedic interventions through to neurosurgery, vascular surgery, and surgery of the spinal column.

Eleven stations along a 42-metre-long ramp look at milestones of the company's history, using objects illuminated from below to illustrate them. The growth rings of a tree trunk, for instance, stand for the growth of B. Braun Melsungen AG, to which Aesculap belongs as a separate segment with its head office in Tuttlingen. The ramp becomes a walkable timeline that connects the exhibition with the individual consultations on the second floor that take place in the "Competence Centre for Surgery."

Im Expertisium steht der Mensch im Zentrum. Dementsprechend begrüßt eine fünf Meter hohe menschliche Figur die Fachbesucher und bildet den Fokuspunkt der Ausstellung. Die Großinstallation macht die Therapiefelder, für die das Unternehmen medizintechnische Produkte anbietet, interaktiv erlebbar. Kreisförmig ordnen sie sich um die Figur. An einem Terminal kann der Besucher die Felder direkt ansteuern und Detailinformation erhalten, so beispielsweise zum Einsatz von Ultraschall in der Anästhesie.

Das Expertisium, das ein Foyer und Ausstellungsbereiche auf mehreren Ebenen umfasst, ist das Herz der Aesculap Akademie am Gesundheitscampus Bochum, deren Weiterbildungsangebot sich an medizinisches Pflegepersonal und Ärzte richtet.

Ein großzügiges und klar strukturiertes Raumbild, bei dem die Firmenfarbe als Akzentfarbe eingesetzt wird, prägt den Showroom. Großgrafiken, die an Röntgenbilder erinnern, geben Einblicke in die menschliche Anatomie und bilden eine wissenschaftliche Folie. Sie setzt die medizintechnischen Produkte, wie chirurgische Instrumente oder Prothesen, in Kontext zu deren Anwendungen.

Der Rundgang präsentiert die Innovationen des Unternehmens, von der klinischen Versorgung über die minimalinvasive Chirurgie und Orthopädie bis hin zur Neuro-, Gefäß- und Wirbelsäulenchirurgie.

Mit den Meilensteinen der Firmengeschichte befassen sich elf Stationen entlang einer 42 Meter langen Rampe. Entwicklung und Historie des Unternehmens werden anhand unterleuchteter Objekte anschaulich. So stehen beispielsweise die Jahresringe einer Baumscheibe für das Wachstum der B. Braun Melsungen AG, der Aesculap als eigenständige Sparte mit Hauptsitz in Tuttlingen angehört. Die Rampe wird zum begehbaren Zeitstrahl. Sie verbindet die Ausstellung mit der individuellen Beratung im zweiten Obergeschoss, dem Kompetenzzentrum Chirurgie.

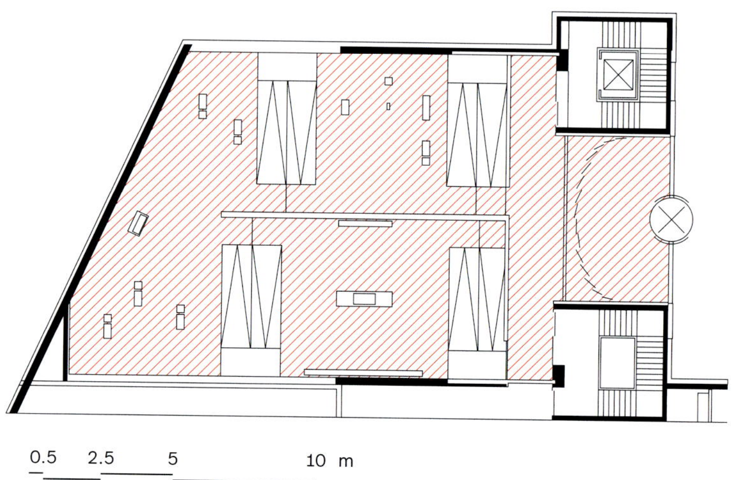

01 Floor plan of the entrance level.

02 The exhibition showcases and interactives were designed with precision equal to the high-end technical instruments on display.

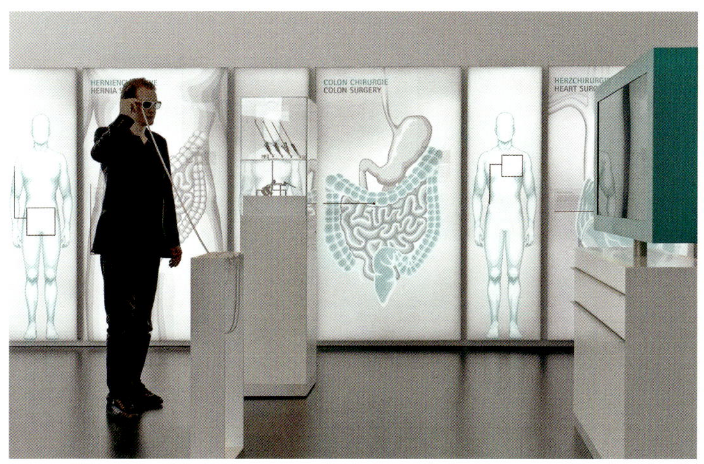

03 Scientific illustrations help to understand where and how instruments can be used.

04 “Competence Centre for Surgery”–more than 10,000 surgical instruments are stored and can be displayed on demand.

HAUS DER BERGE

Permanent Exhibition, Visitor Centre of the National Park, 900 sqm, Berchtesgaden, Germany, 2013

The Berchtesgaden National Park extends from the Königssee right up to the peak of the Watzmann. It is thus the only national park in Germany that contains four landscapes: water, forest, alpine pasture, and rock. It was precisely this stand-alone feature—the structure of the "vertical wilderness"—that inspired the exhibition concept to develop a narrative composition over an elevation gain of 2,300 metres.

The themed tour starts with a walk-on aerial photograph of the national park as prologue, after which the visitor climbs higher and higher through four successive exhibition areas—simultaneously a hike from the bottom of the lake to the top of the mountain. The sections offer information about flora and fauna specific to the different landscapes. Composed of white-varnished silhouettes, they provide a highly abstract landscape as backdrop for the very detailed exhibits, including numerous stuffed animals. Alternating sounds of nature and animals and changing light and colour moods convey the cold of winter and budding nature in spring, the interplay of light and shadow in summer, and the magnificent colours of autumn. Every three minutes the season changes, transforming the museum-like staging into a dynamic and cyclical spatial composition.

The highlight of the tour is a 16-metre-tall walk-in mountain sculpture that defines the striking form of the visitors' centre. Like a protective glass cabinet, a glass-sided cube is placed over the mountain. At first, visitors experience the cube as a closed structure. A panorama film shows the most spectacular photographs from the national park—a time-lapse of a year in the park. After 12 minutes, the projection wall opens up to reveal the Watzmann—an invitation to now go out and explore the area.

Visitors become a part of the holistic interplay of architecture, exhibition, and surrounding landscape.

Der Nationalpark Berchtesgaden erstreckt sich vom Königssee bis hinauf zum Gipfel des Watzmanns. Damit ist er der einzige Nationalpark Deutschlands, der vier Landschaftsräume umfasst: Wasser, Wald, Almwiesen und Fels. Genau diese Besonderheit – die Struktur der „vertikalen Wildnis" – greift die Ausstellungkonzeption auf und entwickelt eine narrative Dramaturgie über 2.300 Höhenmeter.

Der Erlebnisparcours beginnt mit einem begehbaren Luftbild des Nationalparks als Prolog und lässt den Besucher danach durch vier aufeinanderfolgende Ausstellungsbereiche stetig höher steigen – gleichsam in einer Wanderung vom Grund des Sees bis hinauf zur Bergspitze. Die Bereiche vermitteln die Besonderheiten von Flora und Fauna des jeweiligen Landschaftsraums. Sie sind mit weiß lasierten Silhouetten gestaltet, die den detailreichen Exponaten – darunter zahlreiche Tierpräparate – ein stark abstrahiertes Landschaftsambiente bieten. Wechselnde Naturgeräusche und Tierlaute sowie sich verändernde Licht- und Farbstimmungen vermitteln die Kälte des Winters und das Sprießen der Natur im Frühling, das Licht-Schatten-Spiel des Sommers und die Farbenpracht im Herbst. Alle drei Minuten ändert sich die Jahreszeit und überführt damit die museale Inszenierung in ein zyklisch-dynamisches Raumbild.

Höhepunkt des Parcours ist eine begehbare, 16 Meter hohe Bergskulptur, welche die markante Gebäudeform des Besucherzentrums bestimmt. Gleich einer schützenden Vitrine ist der seitlich verglaste Kubus über den Berg gestülpt. Der Besucher erlebt den Kubus zunächst geschlossen. Ein Panoramafilm zeigt spektakuläre Aufnahmen aus dem Nationalpark – einen Jahreszyklus im Zeitraffer. Nach zwölf Minuten öffnet sich die Projektionswand und gibt den Blick auf den Watzmann frei – eine Einladung, nun selbst die Natur zu erkunden.

Der Besucher wird Teil des ganzheitlichen Zusammenspiels aus Architektur, Ausstellung und umgebender Landschaft.

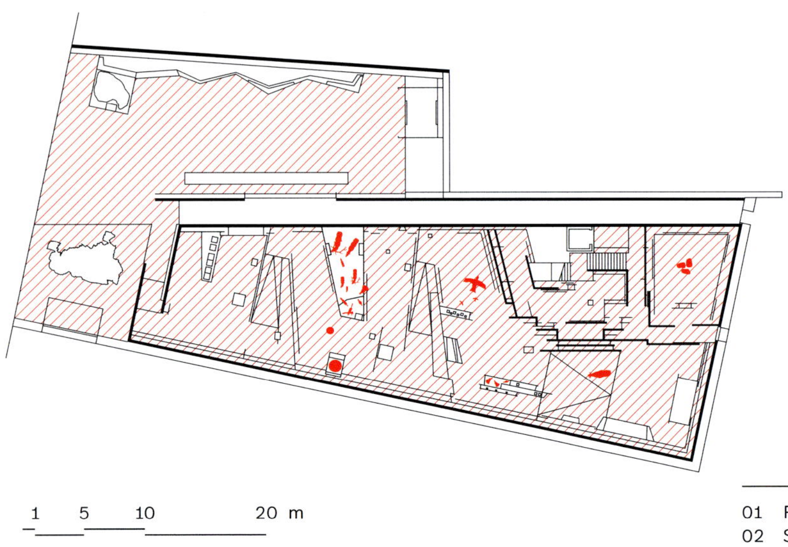

01 Floor plan.
02 Smart architecture can work as both a building and a showcase simultaneously. This offers glimpses in from the outside and allows amazing views from the inside outwards.

03 Abstracted nature cannot compete with the real thing, but it can still be impressive.
A dynamic time-lapse projection of the four seasons onto the trees of the National Park brings the outside in.

04 The spatial image enhances the aggregate condition of the seasons and creates a feeling of changing temperatures throughout the year.

05 At the peak of the route, visitors are amazed by a monumental projection screen that takes them on a year-long journey through the mountains, captured by seven simultaneously recording cameras.

06 At the end of the movie the screen opens to reveal a 10×15-metre window with an astonishing view to the real Watzmann.

CERN–VISIT POINTS

Permanent Exhibition, Visitor Centre, 800 sqm, Geneva, Switzerland, 2013

How did the universe evolve? What is it made of? Where do we come from? These are just some of the questions that visitors to the visitors' centre at CERN in Geneva can explore. Here they obtain instructive insights into the exciting world of particle physics.

After the great success of the permanent exhibition "Universe of Particles," the offering for visitors was extended to include several Visit Points dotted around the huge CERN campus. Each of them is docked onto one of the research centres, the order of which follows the underground ring-shaped Large Hadron Collider–the world's largest particle accelerator with a total length of 27 kilometres.

Making the real laboratories and their hidden levels of content accessible to visitors in professional guided tours is the core idea behind the Visit Points. One of the most fascinating stations is the CERN control room with its multiple projections onto switchable glass. First, visitors experience a vivid, virtual simulation of the experiments–fascinating and at the same time explained in an easy-to-understand way–and can then, as soon as the projection surface becomes transparent, take a direct look into the research facility that lies behind it. The Visit Points of the computer centre and the test centre for superconducting magnets SM18 function in much the same way.

Another highlight of the tour is the Synchro Cyclotron. The detector from 1957–the first of its kind–is reanimated by projecting a custom-fit animation onto the magnets, thus using augmented reality to make the inner processes visible and comprehensible.

In this way, CERN manages to make its complex scientific work accessible to a lay audience, allowing them to experience something that apparently defied exhibiting.

Wie ist das Universum entstanden? Woraus besteht es? Woher kommen wir? Fragen wie diesen können Besucher im Besucherzentrum des CERN in Genf nachgehen. Dort erhalten sie aufschlussreiche Einblicke in den wohl spannendsten Bereich der aktuellen Teilchenphysik.

Nach dem großen Erfolg der Dauerausstellung „Universe of Particles" wurde das Besucherangebot um mehrere Visit Points erweitert, die auf dem riesigen CERN-Areal liegen. Sie sind jeweils direkt bei den einzelnen Forschungszentren angedockt, deren Aufreihung dem unterirdisch verlegten ringförmigen Large Hadron Collider folgt – dem weltweit größten Teilchenbeschleuniger, der eine Gesamtlänge von 27 Kilometern hat.

Den Besuchern reale Labore und ihre verborgenen inhaltlichen Ebenen bei professionell geführten Touren zugänglich zu machen, ist die Kernidee der Visit Points. Eine faszinierende Station ist in dieser Hinsicht der CERN-Kontrollraum mit seinen Mehrfachprojektionen auf umschaltbarem Glas. Zuerst erleben die Besucher hier eine anschauliche virtuelle Simulation der Experimente – faszinierend und zugleich verständlich erklärt – und können dann, sobald die Projektionsfläche transparent wird, einen direkten Blick in die dahinterliegende Forschungseinrichtung werfen. Ähnlich funktioniert der Visit Point des Rechenzentrums und der Testanlage für supraleitende Magnete SM18.

Ein Highlight auf dem Rundgang ist ferner das Synchro Cyclotron. Der Teilchenbeschleuniger aus dem Jahre 1957 – der erste seiner Art – wird „reanimiert", indem eine passgenaue Animation auf den Magneten projiziert wird, welche die Vorgänge im Inneren via Augmented Reality sichtbar und nachvollziehbar macht.

Dem CERN gelingt es, einem Laienpublikum Zugang zu komplexer wissenschaftlicher Arbeit zu eröffnen und vermeintlich Nichtausstellbares erlebbar zu machen.

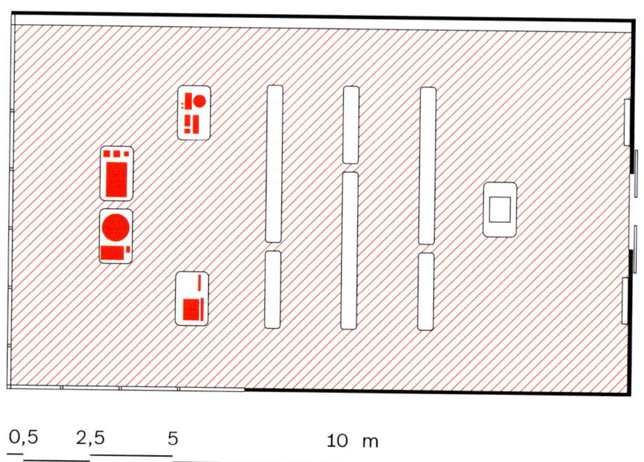

01 Floor plan of the control room.

02 The guided tours to viewing galleries within the functional labs offer a detailed insight into the tools used during the research process. Interactive wall screens illustrate the function and the impact of these tools.

03|04 At the end of the presentation the screen turns transparent to allow a surprising view over the labs and workshops.

GERMAN PAVILION

Competition for the German National Pavilion, Expo Milano 2015, Milan, Italy, 2013

For the German Pavilion "Germany's Garden–Laboratory of Ideas," the Expo slogan "Energy for Life" was interpreted as an overarching cycle of interconnected individual cycles. Three themes–"nature," "culture," and "technology"–dominate the routing round the pavilion. Like a "blue thread," the element of water guides visitors through the exhibition. The life-giving elixir is perceived by visitors in various different physical states.

The path first leads outside up to the pavilion from the coast, an area of water swathed in mist, meandering through an abstract landscape up to the alps and thus represents Germany's topography. Along the way, 16 state houses present the different federal states. The mountaintops are encircled by clouds that provide shade–symbolising the water cycle. Every now and then it rains, feeding a small stream and the high-tech irrigation system inside the pavilion.

The themed tour of the pavilion then takes the visitor into the central exhibition area–the "Laboratory of Ideas" that can be explored in greenhouses over several storeys. Eight laboratory gardens, set up as walk-in, interactive room narratives, visualise the whole vegetation cycle–from sowing, planting, and harvesting via marketing and cooking through to recycling. Water recycling is the focus of attention here.

Finally, the themed garden combines the individual concepts into a multisensual main show. Every half hour, the room is transformed physically, using different media, into a lush, surreal, and emotionally touching "greenhouse," a "Garden of Eden" of a special kind. Visitors experience a presentation of real and reactively animated worlds in which the seeds they catch develop into flowers in their hands.

In the German Pavilion the visitor is not only recipient and consumer, but also actor and idea generator. He takes his impressions home with him as a flow of inspiring ideas. Little bottles of mineral water from the various regions of Germany are a suitable giveaway.

Für den Deutschen Pavillon „Garten Deutschland - Labor der Ideen" wurde das Expo-Motto „Energy for Life" als ein Gesamtkreislauf zusammenhängender Einzelzyklen entworfen. Drei Themen - Natur, Kultur und Technologie - bestimmen den Rundgang. Als „Blauer Faden" leitet das Element Wasser durch die Ausstellung. Es ist das lebensspendende Elixier und wird von den Besuchern in verschiedenen Aggregatzuständen wahrgenommen.

Der Weg führt zunächst außen am Pavillon hinauf, von der Küste, einer von Nebel überzogenen Wasserfläche, mäandrierend durch eine abstrahierte Landschaft bis zu den Alpen - und repräsentiert damit Deutschlands Topografie. Am Wegesrand stellen 16 Länder-Häuser die einzelnen Bundesländer vor. Die Bergspitzen umkreisen schwebende, schattenspendende Wolken - Sinnbild für den Wasserkreislauf. Ab und zu regnen sie ab und speisen einen kleinen Bach sowie das Hightech-Bewässerungssystem im Inneren des Pavillons.

Der Erlebnisparcours führt sodann hinein in den zentralen Ausstellungsbereich - das Labor der Ideen, das sich in mehrgeschossigen Gewächshäusern unter der Landschaft explorieren lässt. Acht Laborgärten, angelegt als begehbare, interaktive Raumbilder, veranschaulichen den gesamten Vegetationskreislauf - vom Säen, Anbauen und Ernten über Vertreiben und Kochen bis zum Recycling. Eine Aufbereitungsanlage zur Rückgewinnung von Wasser steht hier im Mittelpunkt.

Der Erlebnisgarten fasst schließlich die einzelnen Themenbilder in einer multisensualen Main Show zusammen. Jeweils zur halben Stunde verwandelt sich der Raum physisch und medial in ein üppiges, surreales und emotional berührendes „Gewächshaus", in einen „Garten Eden" der besonderen Art. Der Besucher erlebt eine Inszenierung aus realer und reaktiv animierter Welt, in der er selbst Samen auffängt, die sich in seinen Händen zu Blumen entwickeln.

Im Deutschen Pavillon ist der Besucher nicht nur Rezipient und Konsument, sondern auch Akteur und Ideengeber. Er nimmt seine Eindrücke als fließend-inspirierende Ideen mit nach Hause. Mineralwasserfläschchen aus den verschiedenen Regionen Deutschlands sind das passende Give-away.

01 Floor plan.

02 The Prologue ramp represents a north-south section through the country, starting from the North Sea and landing on the Alps. The ramp on top of the greenhouses stands for both a statistical layout of Germany and the fragility of our future high-tech-controlled food production.

03 Visitors are encouraged to interact with the plants and laboratory installations.

04 The thematic spaces are organized according to the process of production and the method of consumption.

VIKING

Temporary Media Installation, Nationl Museum of Denmark,
1,000 sqm, Copenhagen, Denmark, 2013

The length of the wreck of the biggest Viking ship that has been recovered to date–the “Roskilde 6,” named after the site where it was found near Copenhagen–is 37 metres. The former warship, which could transport up to 100 people, is the centrepiece of the special exhibition “Viking.” Original parts integrated into a metal skeleton make it easy to visualise the original form and dimensions.

At certain intervals, a media installation sets the scene for the ship. A new technique called “liquid screen concept” developed especially for this purpose brings the “Roskilde 6” to live in a highly unusual way: Large-scale projections of animated films provide the theatrical backdrop for the exhibit. Short comic-strip sequences on an almost invisible projection gauze at the front and a 40-metre-wide background panorama bring the vessel to life and allow visitors to immerse themselves in seafaring stories and the culture of the Vikings. They experience how the “Roskilde 6” glides slowly through a fjord and how the vessel gets into a tempest. They are onlookers as the Vikings take a harbour town by storm and loot it, and how they afterwards return to their home port with the treasures.

The film does not make use of the photorealistic, computer-generated 3-D animation techniques commonly used today. The technique it uses instead is much like the traditional cartoon style, similar to the sophisticated animations that came out of Czech studios in the 1970s.

While the spatial set-up includes the visitors, who can move around freely between ship reconstruction and backdrop and immerse themselves in the narration, the animation style emphasises the artistic aspect. It is from this tension that the work draws its special charm.

Das Wrack des größten Wikingerschiffs, das bisher geborgen wurde, ist 37 Meter lang: die Roskilde 6, benannt nach ihrem Fundort nahe Kopenhagen. Das ehemalige Kriegsschiff, das bis zu 100 Personen tragen konnte, steht im Mittelpunkt der Sonderausstellung „Viking“. Die erhaltenen Originalteile sind in ein Metallskelett eingebunden, das die ursprüngliche Form und Dimension eindrucksvoll veranschaulicht.

Zeitlich getaktet setzt eine Medieninstallation das Schiff in Szene. Das dafür neu entwickelte „liquid screen concept“ macht die Roskilde 6 auf außergewöhnliche Weise erlebbar: Großformatige Filmprojektionen im Animationsstil geben den theatralen Hintergrund für das Exponat. Filmische Zeichentricksequenzen auf einer nahezu unsichtbaren Projektionsgaze im Vordergrund und einem 40 Meter breiten Hintergrundpanorama erwecken das Boot zum Leben und lassen die Besucher in die Geschichten der Seefahrt und in die Kultur der Wikinger eintauchen. Sie erleben, wie die Roskilde 6 langsam durch einen Fjord gleitet und auf hoher See in einen Sturm gerät. Und sie sind unmittelbar dabei, wenn die Wikinger eine Hafenstadt stürmen, sie plündern und schließlich mit den Schätzen wieder in ihrem Heimathafen anlegen.

Der Film greift nicht auf die heute gängigen fotorealistischen, computergenerierten 3-D-Animationstechniken zurück. Vielmehr bewegt er sich im Stil des traditionellen Zeichentrickfilms, ähnlich den anspruchsvollen Animationen aus tschechischen Ateliers der 1970er-Jahre.

Während das räumliche Set-up den Besucher inkludiert, der sich zwischen Schiffsrekonstruktion und Backdrop frei bewegen kann, und ihn immersiv in die Narration eintauchen lässt, betont der Animationsstil den künstlerischen Aspekt. Aus dieser Spannung zieht die Arbeit ihren besonderen Reiz.

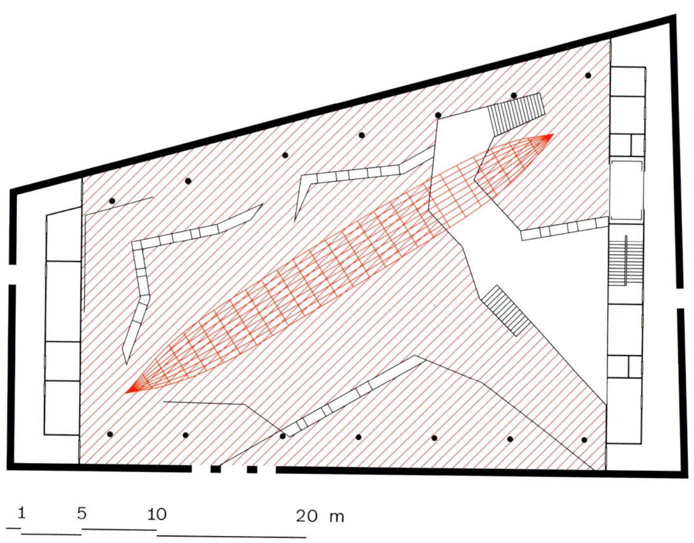

01 Floor plan.
02 The exhibition offers both a view on the original remnants of the ship as well as a re-contextualisation through a panoramic projection.

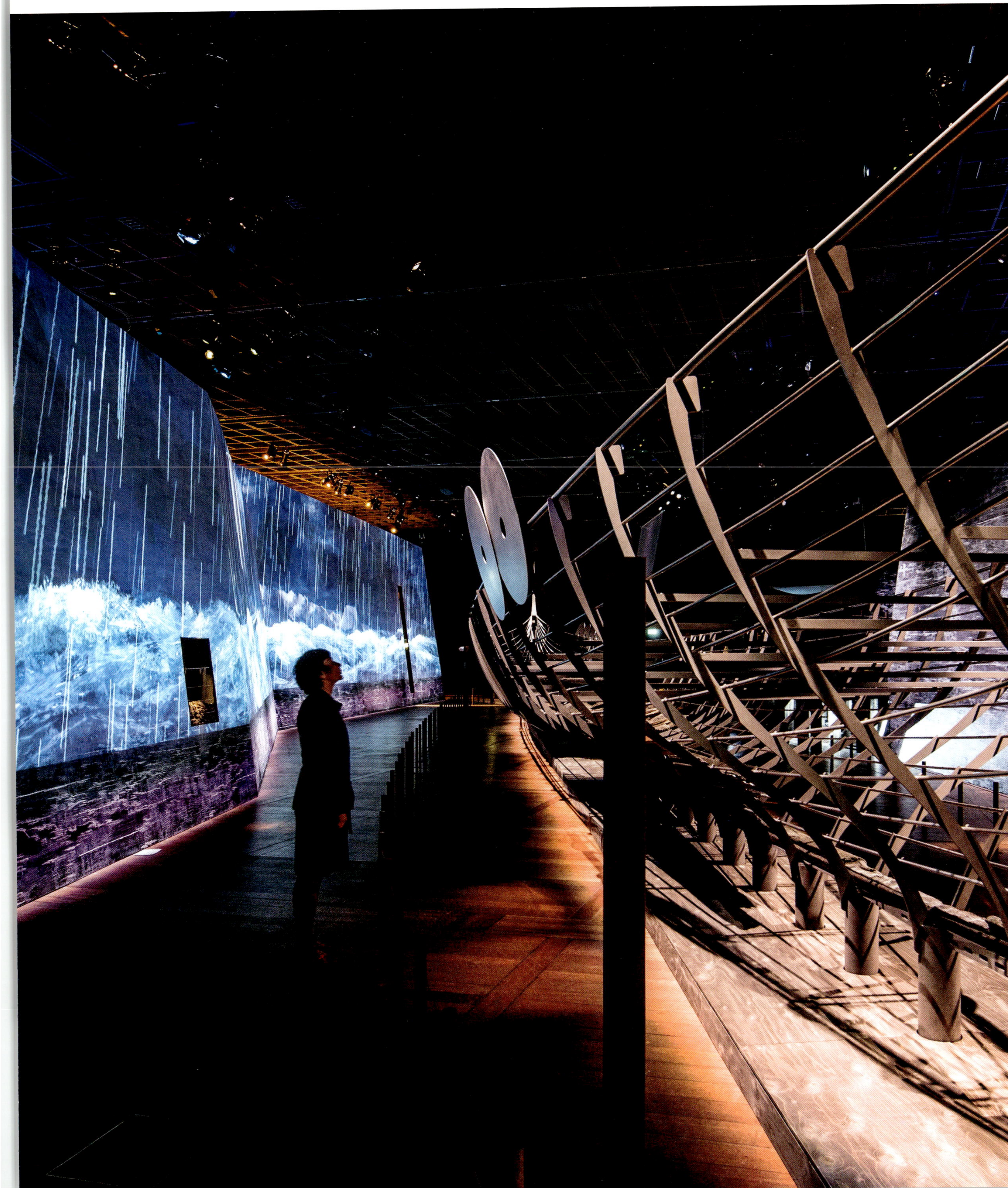

03 The impressive centrepiece supports the recovered original keel and plank fragments, supported by a scenographic illustration of how a foray could have happened. The animated hand sketches decipher the film as an interpolation of the historical background and an interpretation of how these ships were operated. The object-based exhibition spreads out behind the screens.

SCENOGRAPHY
THE ART OF HOLISTIC DESIGN
Uwe R. Brückner and Linda Greci

CONTENTS

Practice came before theory. Protagonists such as François Confino, Haus-Rucker-Co, Studio Azzurro, Mark Fischer, Peter Greenaway, Hans Dieter Schaal, Robert Wilson or Diller+Scofidio, to name but a few, served as models with their holistically choreographed and visually stunning staging that impressed with strong narration. This requires a consistent design approach and a striking signature conceived and developed from the content. Our credo is therefore "form follows content" and our concepts evolve with the help of our design method, the "Creativ(e) Structur(e)" [CS].

The [CS] is the basis, the spirit of the design philosophy of ATELIER BRÜCKNER (ATB). It aims to generate stagings as Gesamtkunstwerke, as holistic narrative spaces.

↗ p. 14

The "Expedition Titanic" exhibition from 1997, amidst the port warehouses of Hamburg's Speicherstadt, is considered to be the prototype for the early use of the [CS] and for all the ATB projects that followed. Content (story-telling) was transported in the form of quotations of protagonists who sailed on the Titanic (such as Frederik Fleet), with objects staged not as archaeological finds but conceived as subjects with narrative potential ("Room of Silence"), space as narrative space, staged as walk-in sets ("Public Floor–Lounges and Restaurants") and design tools such as light and sound carefully integrated and synchronised ("Champagne Room"). The recipient should feel like a passenger and experience the routing as a journey along the dramaturgy with its arc of suspense (ship's passageway with metronomes).

The [CS] as design method was to become a success story; refined in our definition of scenography, broken down into project phases, project structure, parameters, and instruments, referred to as the pillars. In the meantime, the [CS] has been supplemented by the parameters object, recipient, and dramaturgy/routing. On top of this, tools were added, design instruments for direct use. The expanded [CS] has become a navigation system that is used in the analysis and conception of projects as well as for their implementation.

The chapter "Scenography–The art of holistic design" gives an insight into the design philosophy practised at ATELIER BRÜCKNER, conveys our understanding of contemporary scenography, presents the Creativ(e) Structur(e), the design method used, and introduces the potential of design parameters and instruments, illustrated by exemplary projects from the formats museum, brand, and architecture.

Die Praxis kam vor der Theorie. Protagonisten wie François Confino, Haus-Rucker-Co, Studio Azzurro, Mark Fischer, Peter Greenaway, Hans Dieter Schaal, Robert Wilson, Diller+Scofidio und andere dienten als Vorbild mit Inszenierungen, die ganzheitlich choreografiert und bildgewaltig mit starker Narration beeindruckten. Dazu braucht es eine konsistente Gestaltungshaltung und eine markante Handschrift, die aus dem Inhalt heraus denkt und konzipiert. Entsprechend lautet unser Credo „form follows content" und unsere Gestaltungsmethode „Creativ(e) Structur(e)" [CS].

Die [CS] ist die Basis, der Spirit der Gestaltungsphilosophie des ATELIER BRÜCKNER (ATB). Sie hat den Anspruch, Inszenierungen als „Gesamtkunstwerke", als holistische Raumbilder, zu generieren.

Als Prototyp für die frühe Anwendung der [CS] und für alle folgenden ATB-Projekte gilt die Ausstellung „Expedition Titanic" in der Speicherstadt in Hamburg 1997. Inhalte (Storytelling) wurden in Form von Zitaten der auf der Titanic mitgefahrenen Protagonisten (wie Frederik Fleet) übermittelt, Objekte nicht als archäologische Fundstücke, sondern als Subjekte mit Erzählpotenzial („Raum der Stille") inszeniert, Raum als Raumbild, als begehbare Bühne („Öffentliches Parkett – Lounges and Restaurants") konzipiert und die Gestaltungsinstrumente, wie beispielsweise Licht und Sound, integrativ synchronisiert („Champagnerraum"). Der Rezipient sollte sich als Passagier und den Parcours als Reise entlang einer Dramaturgie mit Spannungskurve erleben (Schiffsgang mit Metronomen).

Die [CS] als Gestaltungsmethode wurde zur Erfolgsgeschichte; präzisiert in unserer Definition von Szenografie, strukturiert in Projektphasen, Projektstruktur, Parametern und Instrumenten, den sogenannten Pillars. Mittlerweile wurde die [CS] um die Parameter Objekt, Rezipient und Dramaturgie/Parcours und um die sogenannten Tools, Gestaltungsinstrumente zur direkten Anwendung, ergänzt. Die erweiterte [CS] wurde zu einem Navigationssystem, das bei der Analyse und Konzeption sowie der Umsetzung von Projekten anwendbar ist.

Das Kapitel „Scenography–The art of holistic design" soll Einblick in die im ATELIER BRÜCKNER praktizierte Gestaltungsphilosophie geben, unser Verständnis von zeitgemäßer Szenografie vermitteln, mit der angewandten [CS], der Gestaltungsmethodik, vertraut machen und die Potenziale der Gestaltungsparameter und -instrumente vorstellen. Dies geschieht anhand exemplarischer Projekte in den Formaten Museum, Marke und Architektur.

SCENOGRAPHY

DEFINITION, METHOD, TOOLS

Uwe R. Brückner and Linda Greci

"Scenography is the mother of all design disciplines. It is the sum of design thinking, acting, and receiving. It is philosophy, method, and signature–creating a spatial context between content, things and recipient."

Uwe R. Brückner

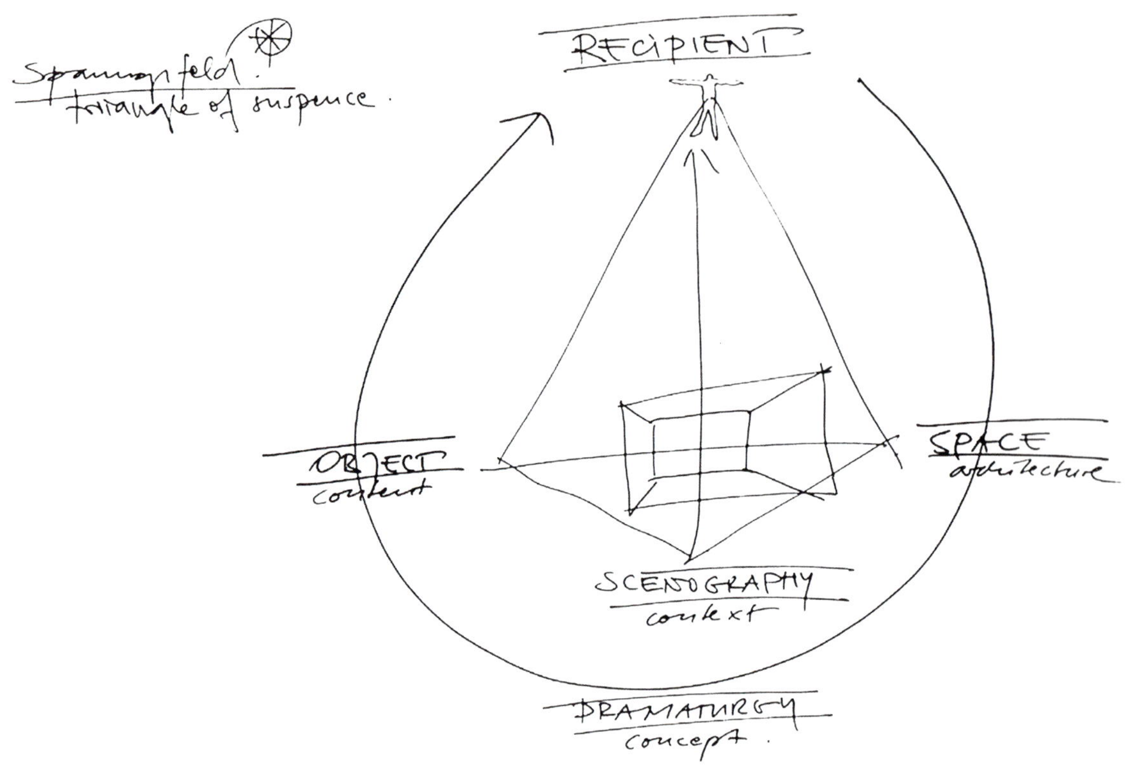

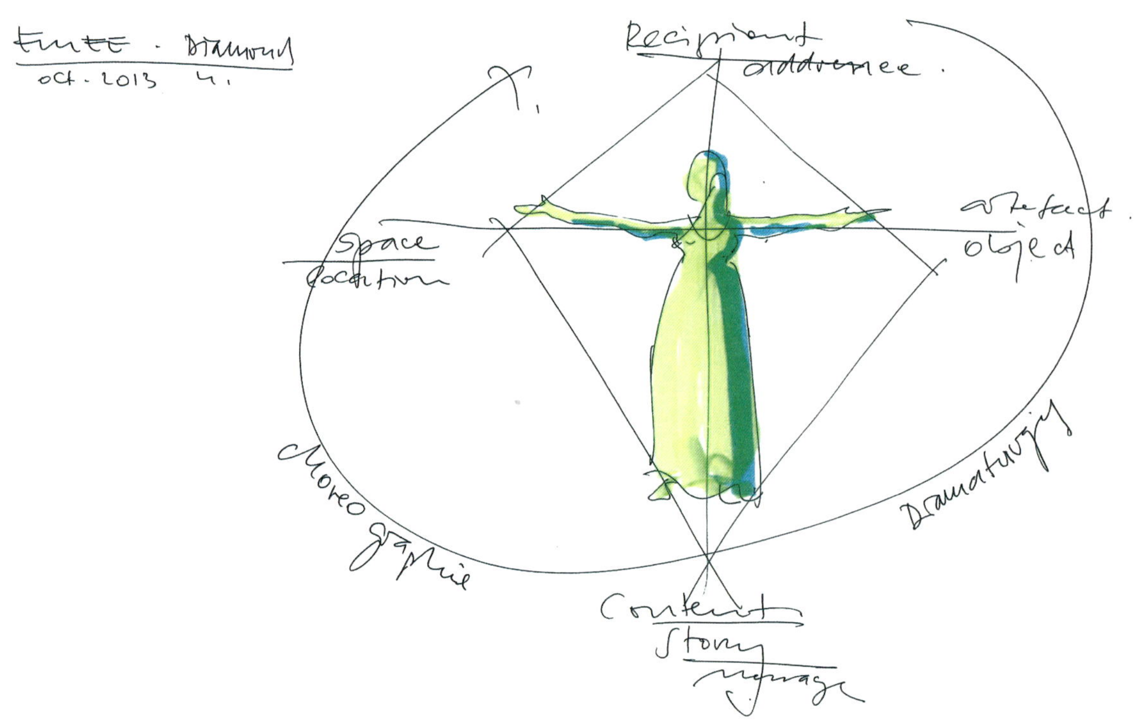

"Triangle of Suspense" (above)–Early version of design parameters, 2009.
"Diamond of Suspense" (below)–5 Parameters of scenography, 2013.

What is it about staged spaces that exerts such a fascination? Why do we see a need to give things a voice, what makes us give stories a stage and what is the added value of allowing visitors to experience this with several senses in walk-in narrative spaces? The journey ahead takes us to the core of scenography.

Scenography is a creative design philosophy that translates conceptional and material contents into three-dimensional, narrative themed spaces. It creates an overall composition which makes it possible to experience content with the senses, sets off objects, charges spaces with significance, choreographs them dramaturgically, and finally involves the visitors and encourages them to draw associations and think ahead. To achieve such a scene-setting force field, the scenographer uses a diverse range of staging tools, borrowed from various creative disciplines such as architecture and interior architecture, graphic, light, sound and media design, performing and pictorial arts, but also from genres like theatre, opera, and film. Increasingly, it can be observed how the traditional borders between these disciplines are being overstepped, dissolved, and reformed, and how new, sophisticated design options are emerging.

The term “scenography” stands for a multifaceted, holistic design approach, which is dedicated explicitly to space and the staging of this space. As integrative design philosophy, it addresses the interplay of various disciplines, but also the use and combination of various design instruments and parameters.[1] The instruments used by scenography include graphics, light, sound, digital media, projections, and film in order to combine the design parameters–content, object, space, recipient, and dramaturgy[2]–in a consistent composition to form a powerful and effective staging. Scenographic designing is also dynamic designing if visitors can move through a dramatized routing, often called upon to participate themselves (inter)actively in spatial subjects staged with analogue or digital elements, in a multilingual and

Was macht die Faszination von inszenierten Räumen aus? Warum sehen wir eine Notwendigkeit, den Dingen Sprache zu verleihen, was veranlasst uns, den Geschichten eine Bühne zu geben, und worin liegt der Mehrwert, dies für die Besucher multisensorisch, in begehbaren Raumbildern, erlebbar zu machen? Die anstehende Reise führt zum Kern der Szenografie.

Die Szenografie ist eine kreative Gestaltungsphilosophie, die konzeptionelle und materielle Inhalte in dreidimensionale, narrative Erlebnisräume übersetzt. Sie schafft eine Gesamtkomposition, die Inhalte sinnlich erfahrbar macht, Objekte inszeniert und Räume mit Bedeutung auflädt. Indem sie dramaturgisch choreografiert, involviert sie letztlich den Besucher und animiert zum assoziativen Weiterdenken. Um ein solches inszenatorisches Kräftefeld zu erreichen, nutzt die Szenografie ein vielfältiges Inszenierungsinstrumentarium, entlehnt aus verschiedenen Kreativdisziplinen wie Architektur und Innenarchitektur, Grafik-, Licht-, Sound- und Medien-Design, performativer und darstellender Kunst, aber auch aus Genres wie Theater, Oper und Film. Zunehmend lässt sich eine Überschreitung, Auflösung und Neuformierung der traditionellen Grenzen zwischen diesen Disziplinen beobachten und es entstehen anspruchsvolle neue Gestaltungsoptionen.

overall composition

Der Begriff „Szenografie“ steht für eine facettenreiche ganzheitliche Gestaltungshaltung, die sich explizit dem Raum und seiner Inszenierung widmet. Als integrative Gestaltungsphilosophie befasst sie sich mit dem Zusammenspiel verschiedener Disziplinen, aber auch mit der Verwendung und der Kombination unterschiedlicher Gestaltungsinstrumente und -parameter.[1] Die Szenografie setzt unter anderem Instrumente wie Grafik, Licht, Klang, digitale Medien, Projektion und Film ein, um die Gestaltungsparameter – Inhalt, Objekt, Raum, Rezipient und Dramaturgie[2] – in einer konsistenten Komposition zu einer wirkmächtigen Inszenierung zusammenzufügen. Szenografisches Gestalten heißt auch dynamisches Gestalten, wenn sich Besucher durch einen dramatisierten

design instruments and parameters

1 See Uwe R. Brückner and Linda Greci, eds., EMEE Toolkit 4: Synaesthetic Translation of Perspectives. Scenography: A Sketchbook (Vienna, 2016), pp. 25–79.

2 See also “The Five Parameters of Scenography: Content, Object, Space, Recipient and Dramaturgy.” Ibid.

"Translating content in an exciting way, allowing atmospheres to develop, evoking spatial images that arise from dramaturgic concepts, leading the visitor along a golden thread to the heart of a specific story: that is the dimension of scenography. Scenography is a holistic, integrative, multidisciplinary, and content-consistent design philosophy." Uwe R. Brückner

target-oriented way. The symbiotic interaction and the dynamic treatment of the space aim to transform physical exhibition and knowledge rooms into explorable spaces of significance and experience.

museum synaesthesia

Scenography has a long-term effect on visitor reception. In a good exhibition, understanding through observation and thus visual perception is not at the centre, but rather it offers an experience which addresses several senses at the same time. The term used for this is "museum synaesthesia" and means that the exhibition is perceived at the same time by seeing, moving, hearing, and sometimes even by touching and smelling.[3] This combination of sensory and motor aspects addresses several perception levels. Exhibitions are thus defined as "synaesthetic media."[4] The perception of an exhibition is thus a highly individual act. But every form of scenographic design is also individual and every project represents a new challenge for curators and designers alike. There are always various options, which have to be carefully sounded out, several ways of translating content into spatial subjects–depending on what is to be conveyed and presented. The scenographer as "author-designer"[5] is an interpreter of a concept for the content and transformer of stories in the real, three-dimensional exhibition space. He is responsible for translating complex content into walk-in narrative spaces and the staging of spaces with narrative qualities. If this all works, the result is a fascinating space that itself becomes a dramatic media, a transmitter of messages.

author-designer

3 See Jana Scholze, Medium Ausstellung. Lektüren musealer Gestaltung in Oxford, Leipzig, Amsterdam und Berlin (Bielefeld, 2004), p. 273.

4 Ibid.

5 See Atelier Brückner, ed., Scenography–Making spaces talk. Projects 2002–2010, 2nd ed. (Stuttgart, 2016), p. 18.

Parcours bewegen können, oft aufgefordert, sich selbst (inter)aktiv zu beteiligen, in analogen wie auch in digital inszenierten Raumsujets, multilingual und zielgruppenorientiert. Das symbiotische Zusammenwirken und der dynamische Umgang mit dem Raum zielen darauf ab, physische Ausstellungs- und Wissensräume in explorierbare Bedeutungs- und Erfahrungsräume zu verwandeln.

Szenografie nimmt nachhaltig Einfluss auf die Rezeption durch die Besucher. In einer guten Ausstellung steht nicht die Erkenntnis durch Anschauung und damit die visuelle Wahrnehmung im Zentrum, sondern ein Erlebnis, das mehrere Sinne zugleich anregt. Man spricht in diesem Zusammenhang von musealer Synästhesie und versteht darunter, dass die Ausstellungswahrnehmung gleichzeitig durch Sehen, Gehen, Hören und manchmal auch durch Fühlen und Riechen geprägt ist.[3] Diese Kombination sensorischer und motorischer Aspekte spricht mehrere Wahrnehmungsebenen an. Ausstellungen sind somit als „synästhetische Medien" definiert.[4] Die Wahrnehmung einer Ausstellung ist folglich ein höchst individueller Akt. Aber auch jegliche Form szenografischen Gestaltens erfolgt individuell und stellt immer wieder eine neue Herausforderung für die Kuratoren und Gestalter dar. Es gibt stets unterschiedliche Optionen, die sorgfältig auszuloten sind, mehrere Übersetzungsmöglichkeiten von Inhalten in räumliche Sujets – je nach Vermittlungs- und Darstellungsabsicht. Der Szenograf als „Autorengestalter"[5] ist Interpret eines

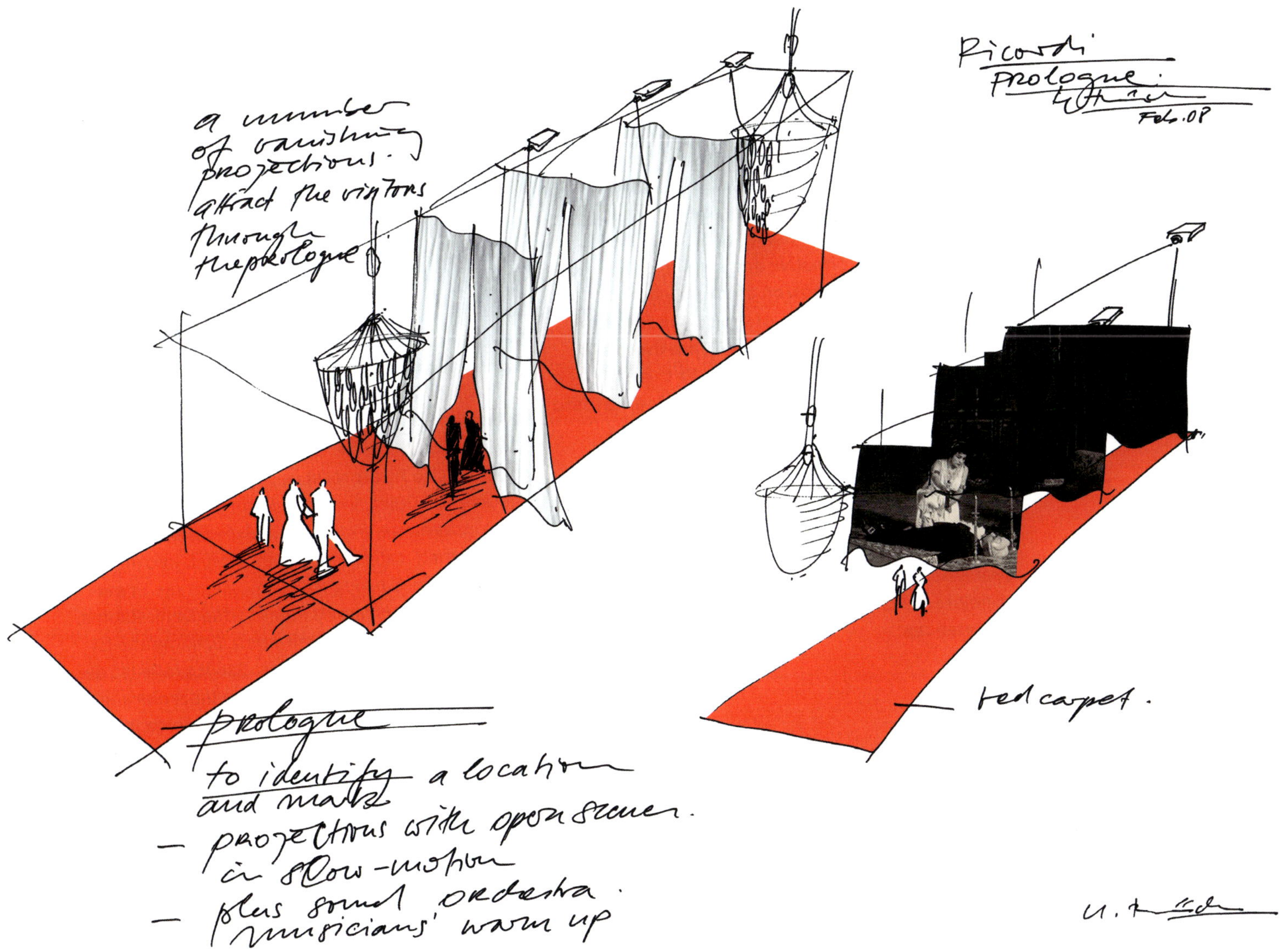

"That's Opera"–Prologue, 2008.

conception

reception

And yet there is often a discrepancy, a kind of orchestra pit, between the conception of the curator and designer on the one hand and the perception by the visitor on the other. Although the prerogative of interpretation lies with the curator and designer, the intention of the staging is not necessarily identical with the reception. The visitor perceives a staging individually, depending on his own cultural and social background, his experience (of life), and his accumulated knowledge. This gap gives the visitor space for new interpretations and perspectives and at the same time implies that a staging can work in multiple ways, from multiple perspectives. Scenography is an aesthetic interpretation, a subject charged with significance, a spatialised message–a staged reality. Scenography is real and virtual, rational and emotional, informative and sensuous. Scenography allows the expansion of the physical space, the contemplative space, of the scope for interpretation. Scenography is theory, method, and practice. Scenography is the key to the past, the staging in the present, and the virtual journey into the future.

aesthetic practice

Scenography is an aesthetic practice. It provides the logical and consistent answer to the design demands of our time and the constantly changing reception behaviour of our society. It is the adequate, necessary reaction to the desire for content-consistent staging and synaesthetic visitor experiences.

inhaltlichen Konzepts und Transformator von Geschichten in den realen, dreidimensionalen Ausstellungsraum. Er ist verantwortlich für die Übersetzung anspruchsvoller Inhalte in begehbare Raumbilder und das Inszenieren von Räumen mit narrativen Qualitäten. Gelingt all dies, entsteht das Faszinosum eines Raums, der selbst zum dramaturgischen Medium, zum Überbringer von Botschaften wird.

Doch es besteht oft eine Diskrepanz, eine Art Orchestergraben, zwischen der Konzeption des Kurators und Gestalters einerseits und der Wahrnehmung durch den Besucher andererseits. Obwohl dem Kurator und Gestalter eine Deutungshoheit zugesprochen wird, ist die Inszenierungsintention nicht zwingend identisch mit der Rezeption. Der Besucher nimmt eine Inszenierung individuell wahr, je nach eigenem kulturellem und sozialem Hintergrund, seiner (Lebens-)Erfahrung und seinem angesammelten Wissen. Dieser Zwischenraum lässt dem Besucher Raum für neue Interpretationen und Sichtweisen und impliziert gleichwohl multiple, multiperspektivische Wirkweisen von Inszenierungen. Szenografie ist eine ästhetische Interpretation, ein bedeutungsaufgeladenes Sujet, eine verräumlichte Botschaft – eine inszenierte Wirklichkeit. Szenografie ist real und virtuell, rational und emotional, informativ und sinnlich. Szenografie ermöglicht die Erweiterung des physischen Raums, des Denk-Raums, des Interpretations-Spielraums. Szenografie ist Theorie, Methode und Praxis. Szenografie ist der Schlüssel zur Vergangenheit, die Inszenierung in der Gegenwart und die virtuelle Reise in die Zukunft.

Szenografie ist eine ästhetische Praxis. Sie bildet die logische und konsequente Antwort auf die Gestaltungsanforderungen unserer Zeit und das sich ständig verändernde Rezeptionsverhalten unserer Gesellschaft. Sie ist die adäquate, notwendige Reaktion auf das Verlangen nach inhaltskonsistenten Inszenierungen und synästhetischen Besuchserlebnissen.

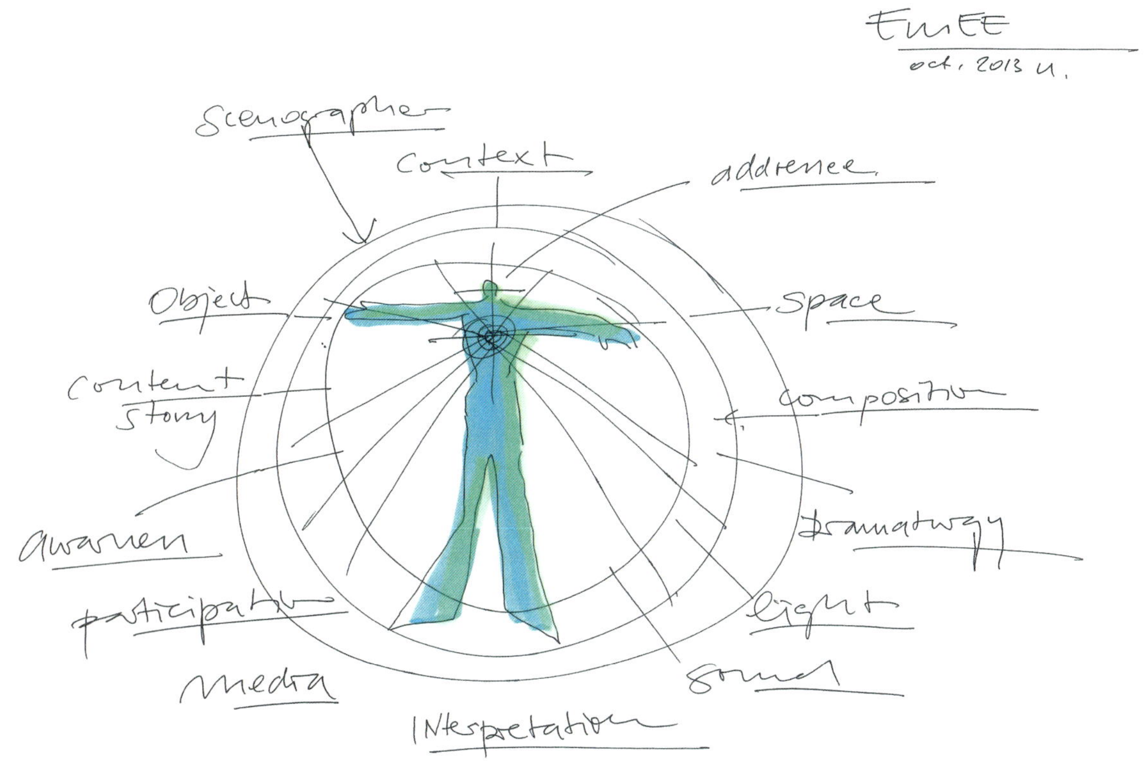

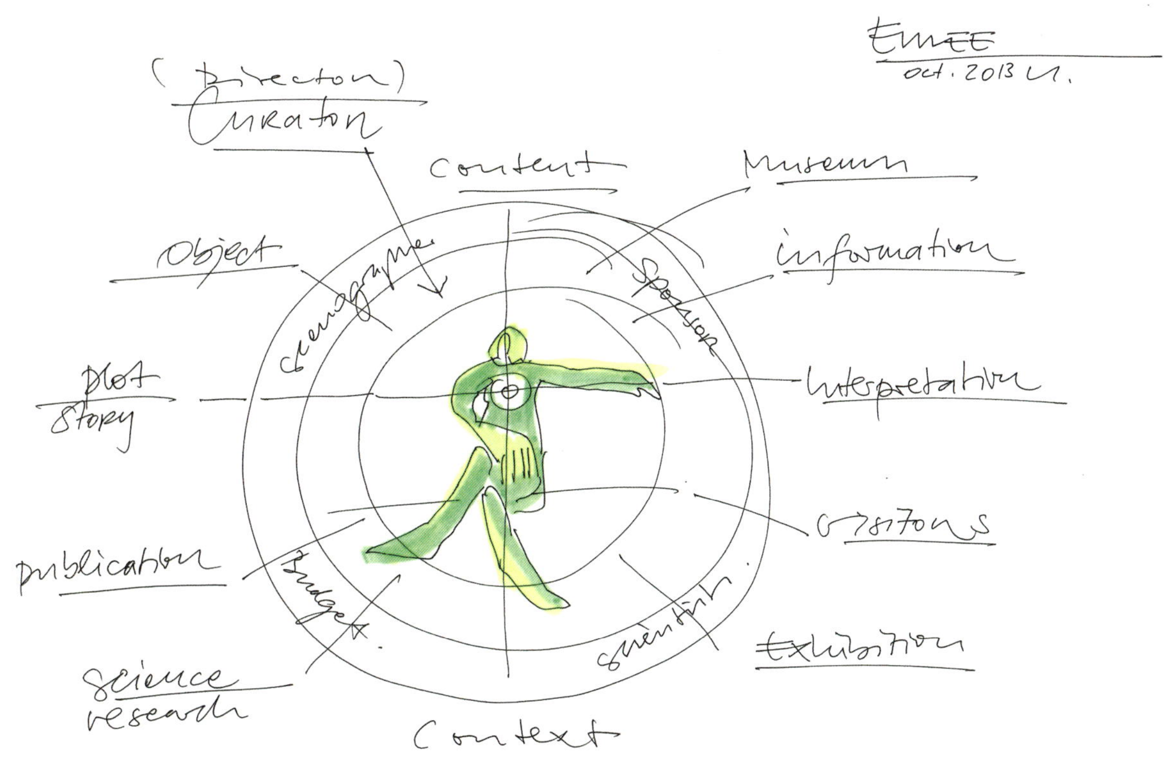

"Scenographer" (above), "Curator" (below)—Output and Input in Context, 2013.

“Scenography charges space with significance. With the patina of what has been experienced, with the fateful attestation of past or impending events–as on the Brechtian stage: give me a door, a window, and a chair, the protagonists will do the rest. On the stage, these are the actors; in the museum, the things.” Uwe R. Brückner

skené

Over the last few decades, scenography has successfully established itself as an independent, multidisciplinary design discipline–as documented by numerous national and international offices and ateliers as well as universities offering scenography courses. Its roots are to be found in the theatre of ancient Greece and the term “skené,” the classical Greek term for hut, tent, or arbour. The skené was originally a lean-to at the edge of the stage behind which actors could change their costumes and masks. It is a part of the stage that is not visible to the audience and forms off of the staging that stands for the need for illusion to ensure the credibility of a performance.[6]

theatre

Principles, methods, and instruments of the theatre, such as the interpretation of a play, the composition of a scene, the dramaturgy, the dramatic arc, and plot are to be found in many guises in exhibition design. The exhibits are the protagonists and storytellers–like the actors in the theatre. To set the scene for them and to offer them an appropriate stage, staging instruments are used as messengers and signifiers. Objects in walk-in exhibition space demand the same of actors and recipients as a stage performance. Everything that takes place in the actual or imaginary space of the staging is of significance and relevance. Without this agreement, the intention remains interchangeable, the effect arbitrary.

Im Laufe der letzten Jahrzehnte hat sich die Szenografie als eigenständige multidisziplinäre Gestaltungsdisziplin erfolgreich etabliert. Das belegen zahlreiche nationale und internationale Büros und Ateliers sowie Hochschulen mit Szenografie-Studiengängen. Ihre Wurzeln gehen auf das Theater des antiken Griechenlands und auf den Begriff der „skené“ zurück, den altgriechischen Begriff für Hütte, Zelt oder Laube. Die Skené war ursprünglich ein Verschlag am Bühnenrand, hinter dem die Schauspieler ihre Kleidung und Masken wechseln konnten. Sie ist eine für die Zuschauer unsichtbare Zone der Bühne und bildet das Off der Inszenierung, das für die Notwendigkeit der Illusion zugunsten der Glaubwürdigkeit einer Vorstellung steht.[6]

Prinzipien, Methoden und Instrumente des Theaters, wie etwa die Interpretation eines Stücks, die Komposition einer Szene, die Dramaturgie, der Spannungsbogen und Plot, spiegeln sich vielfältig in der Ausstellungsgestaltung wider. Die Exponate sind die Protagonisten und Geschichtenerzähler – wie die Schauspieler im Theater. Um diese in Szene zu setzen und ihnen eine angemessene Bühne zu bieten, werden gleichfalls Inszenierungsinstrumente als Botschaften- und Bedeutungsträger eingesetzt. Das Inszenieren von Objekten im begehbaren Ausstellungsraum stellt die gleichen Anforderungen an Akteure und Rezipienten wie das Geschehen auf der Bühne. Alles, was im tatsächlichen oder imaginierten Raum der Inszenierung stattfindet, hat Bedeutung und Relevanz. Ohne diese Verabredung bleibt die Absicht austauschbar, die Wirkung beliebig.

6 See Atelier Brückner 2016, p.18. For the genesis of the skené see also Stephan Trüby, “Die gesprengte Skene”, archithese (April 2010), pp. 36–41.

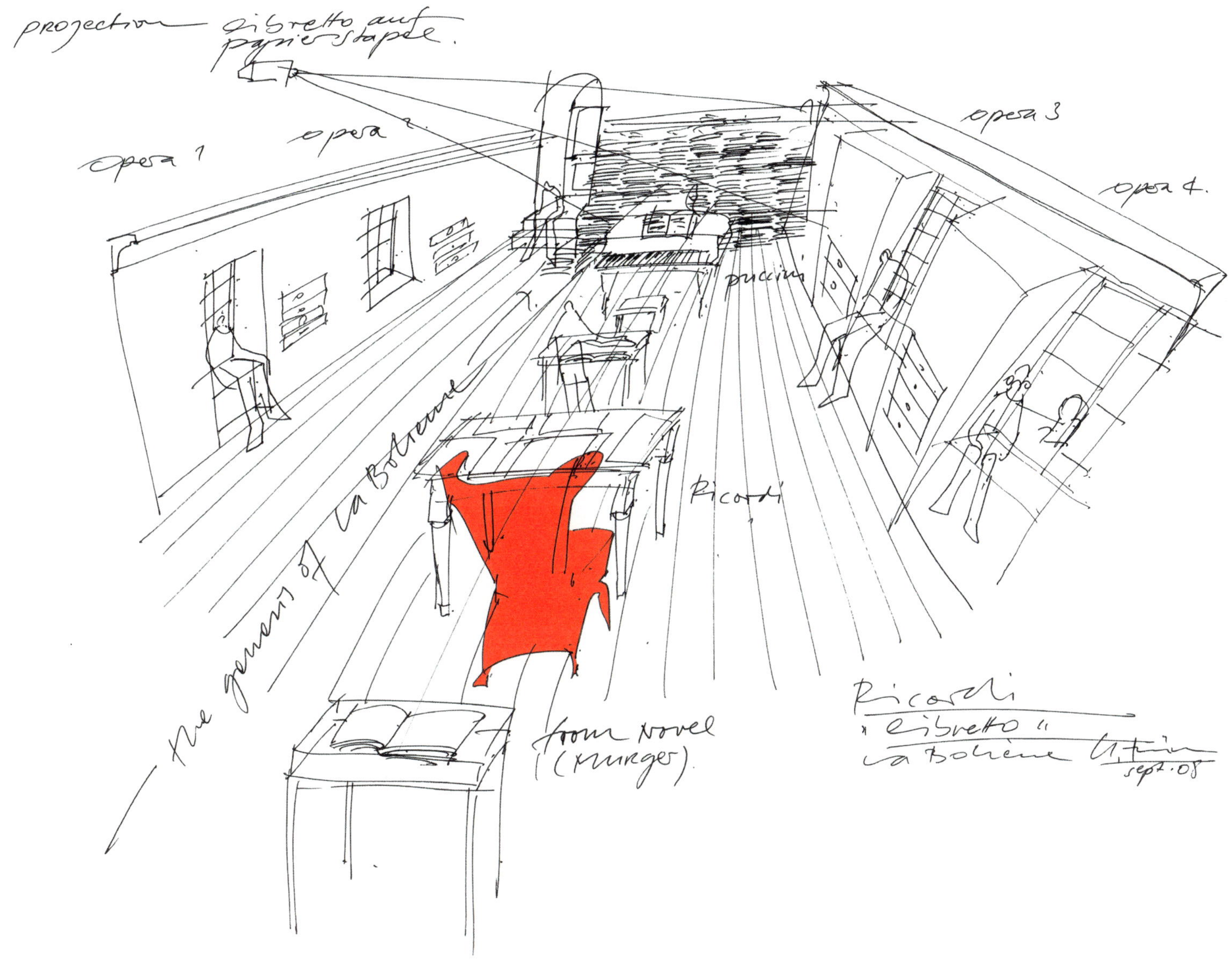

"That's Opera"–Libretto, 2008.

narrative format

reception alternatives

self-determined potential

Creativ(e) Structur(e)

Yet unlike in classical theatre, and also opera or film, the exhibition has produced its own narrative format. The classical theatre, which is our starting point, is characterised by staging formats, which offer a performance that is watched from the front and which usually separates stage and auditorium.[7] Visitors to an exhibition, on the other hand, can walk around the objects–they have various interaction possibilities and several reception alternatives.[8] An exhibition is thus a walk-in, democratic format in which the visitor with his freedom of movement represents self-determined potential and can only be conditioned to a certain extent–a circumstance which a designer can make good use of by building suspense via a sequence of staged interventions and dramaturgic structures. The pure visibility which classical theatre stage offers its audience becomes the individual immersion of the visitor while the visual perception becomes the multisensory exploration of the exhibition space.

Thanks to their shared roots, theatre and exhibition have a lot of things in common. The transfer and transformation of principles, design processes, methods, and instruments of the theatre into the practice of exhibition design are integral parts of the design philosophy of ATELIER BRÜCKNER and the Creativ(e) Structur(e) and are reflected in numerous projects.

Doch im Gegensatz zum klassischen Theater, aber auch zur Oper oder zum Film, hat die Ausstellung ein eigenes Erzählformat hervorgebracht. Das klassische Theater, von dem wir hier ausgehen, ist durch Inszenierungsformate geprägt, die ein frontal betrachtetes Schauspiel bieten und die meist den Bühnen- und Zuschauerraum voneinander trennen.[7] Im Unterschied dazu können die Besucher in einer Ausstellung um die Objekte herumgehen – sie haben verschiedene Interaktionsmöglichkeiten und mehrere Rezeptionsalternativen.[8] Eine Ausstellung ist demzufolge ein begehbares, demokratisches Format, in dem der Besucher in seiner freien Beweglichkeit ein selbstbestimmtes Potenzial besitzt und nur bedingt konditionierbar ist. Ein Umstand, den man sich als Gestalter durchaus zunutze machen kann, indem über eine Abfolge von inszenatorischen Interventionen und dramaturgischen Strukturen eine Spannung aufgebaut wird. Die reine Frontalansichtigkeit, die die klassische Theaterbühne den Zuschauern bietet, wird zum individuellen Eintauchen des Besuchers und die visuelle Wahrnehmung wird zur multisensorischen Erkundung des Ausstellungsraums.

Aufgrund ihrer gemeinsamen Wurzeln teilen das Theater und die Ausstellung viele Gemeinsamkeiten. Die Übertragung und die Transformation von Prinzipien, Gestaltungsprozessen, Methoden und Instrumenten des Theaters in die Praxis der Ausstellungsgestaltung sind integrativer Bestandteil der Gestaltungsphilosophie des ATELIER BRÜCKNER und der Creativ(e) Structur(e) und spiegeln sich in zahlreichen Projekten wider.

---

7 Note: Back in the 1980s, the artist group Studio Azzuro developed innovative concepts and staging forms that merged stage and audience, which involved the visitors, making them part of what is going on.

8 According to a 1970s thesis attributed to Gio Ponti, the visitor generates a sequence of scenes through their movement. This theory should be taken into account by the designer. That the visitor can stand still, that he turns and goes back sometimes. Accordingly the performance thus the narrative experience should work from various perspectives.

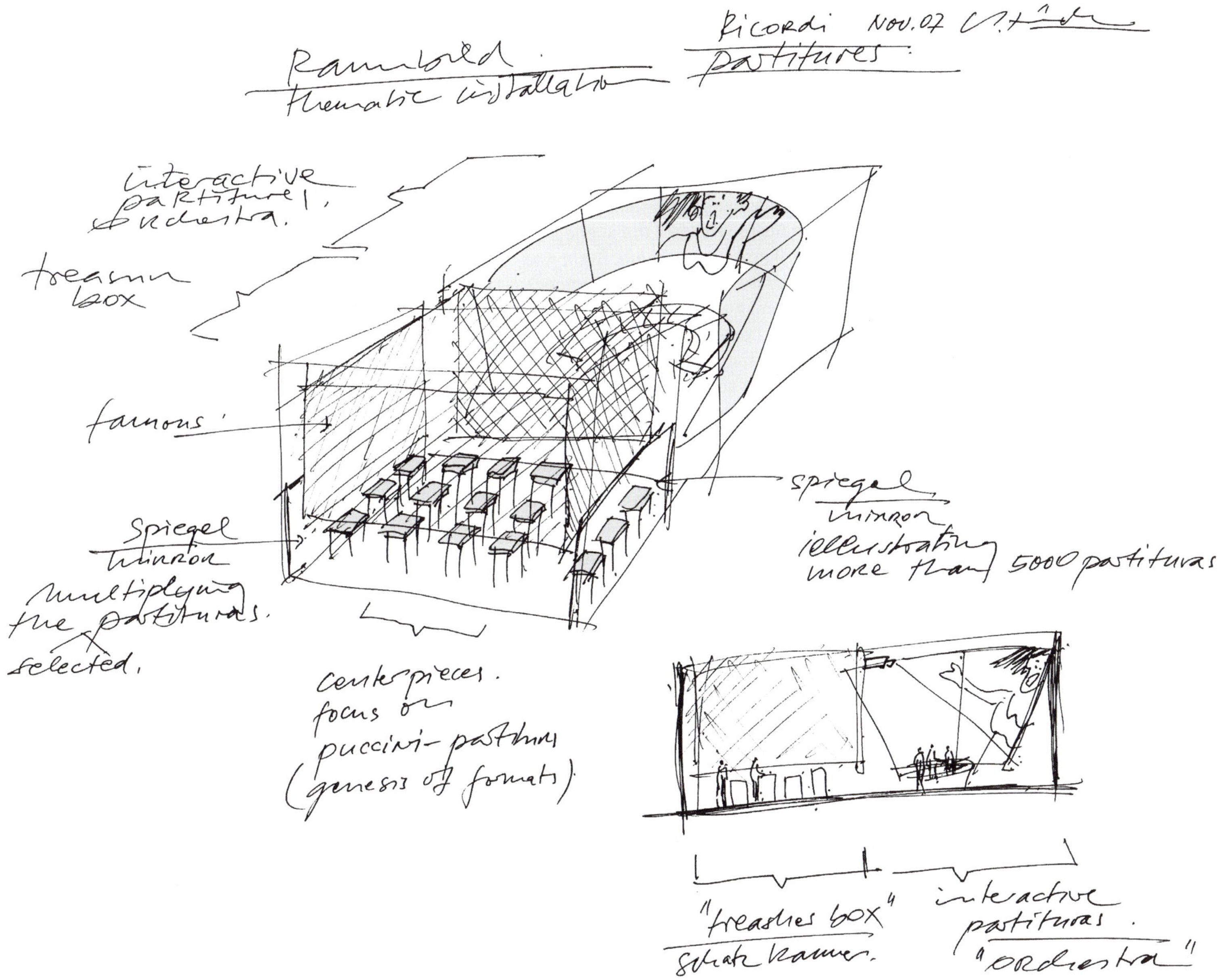

"That's Opera"–Partitura, Treasure Box, 2008. Sketch, 2007.

“Scenography creates form from content, endowing the latter with meaning and attitude. It generates narrative spaces from ideas, things, and stories and conveys their contents as messages.”[9]

Inszenierung (staging)

The German term “Inszenierung” (staging) stems etymologically from the French “mise en scène.” In the English language the equivalent would be to “set the scene.” The idea of “mise en scène” (staging) was introduced in the theatre in the first half of the nineteenth century and referred originally to decorating and equipping the stage for a scene of the performance. It was understood as the use of all means to interpret the scene, such as decoration, lighting, and sound. But it was also about the physicality, movement, and voices of the actors, verbal and non-verbal in space and time, stage, backdrop, costumes, make-up as well as the sequence of the scenes dictated by the dramaturgy.[10] Setting the scene in the context of theatre is, however, not only about visualising a work, staging it in order to strengthen its effect, but in the course of the twentieth century it started to be more about creating something new and expressing interpretations of their own.

(re-)presentation

In the middle of the twentieth century, the practice of staging migrated from the theatre and has since conquered other creative fields of (re-)presentation. This includes the museum as an institution that is no longer an archive of cultural legacy but a staged environment with sensory-aesthetic qualities, that conveys content, presents objects, and tells stories so that they leave a deep impression. According to Thomas Thiemeyer, the concept of staging was introduced to German museums in the course of the reform of the education system in the 1970s as they started to address potential visitors from all social classes and increasingly to tell stories on the basis of everyday

Der Begriff „Inszenierung“ leitet sich etymologisch vom französischen „mise en scène“ ab. Im deutschen Sprachgebrauch spricht man von „in Szene setzen“. Inszenierung wurde in der ersten Hälfte des 19. Jahrhunderts im Theater eingeführt und bezog sich ursprünglich auf die Ausstattung performativer Szenen. Inszenierung wurde als Gesamtheit der szenischen Interpretationsmittel verstanden, wie zum Beispiel Dekoration, Beleuchtung und Ton. Sie bezog sich aber auch auf Körperlichkeit, Bewegung und Stimme der Schauspieler, verbale und nonverbale Interaktion in Raum und Zeit, auf Bühne, Kulisse, Kostüm und Maske ebenso wie auf die dramaturgisch festgelegte Szenenabfolge.[10] Inszenierung im Theaterkontext bedeutet aber nicht nur, ein Werk zur Anschauung zu bringen, es szenisch aufzuführen, um seine Wirkung zu verstärken, sondern im Laufe des 20. Jahrhunderts geht es auch immer mehr darum, etwas Neues zu schaffen und eigene Interpretationen auszudrücken.

Mitte des 20. Jahrhunderts ist die Praxis der Inszenierung aus dem Theater migriert und hat weitere Kreativfelder der (Re-)Präsentation erobert. Das schließt auch das Museum als Institution ein, das nicht mehr länger ein Archiv kulturellen Erbes ist, sondern ein inszeniertes Environment mit sinnlich-ästhetischen Qualitäten, das Objekte präsentiert, Geschichte(n) erzählt und den Besuchern Inhalte so vermittelt, dass sie tiefe Eindrücke hinterlassen. Laut Thomas Thiemeyer wurde das Konzept der Inszenierung im Zuge der Bildungsreform in den 1970er-Jahren in deutschen Museen eingeführt, als diese damit anfingen, interessierte Besucher

9 See Atelier Brückner 2016, p. 59.
10 See Wolfgang Sting, “Inszenierung,” in Handbuch Kulturelle Bildung, ed. Bockhorst/Reinwand/Zacharias (Munich, 2012). Online at: http://www.kubi-online.de/artikel/inszenierung, accessed January 15, 2018.

"That's Opera"–Partitura, Walkthrough Orchestra Pit, 2008.

presentation forms

objects.[11] This made it necessary to find new forms of presentation. Staging replaced the conventional showcase exhibition and the educational reading museum, which explained the objects on long, often overloaded text banners. With the exhibition "Preußen: Versuch einer Bilanz" (The Prussia Exhibition) from 1981 at the Berlin Historical Museum, staging as a presentation form became popular in Germany. Following an alternative concept to the Staufer Exhibition from 1977, the exhibition about the history of Prussia reshaped the history of staging.[12]

social phenomenon

As a social phenomenon, staging left the boundaries of museums in the 1980s and has since become omnipresent. Staging concerns the artistic, public, and social areas and is expressed in many different formats, be it in new media, in advertising, in architecture, in shop window design, in performances, or on the catwalk. And it increasingly dominates more and more social areas such as politics, business, everyday life, sport, or pop culture. Staging is a trend which continues to this day.

The term "staging" also entered into the German-speaking museum discourse in the 1980s, but at that time with various, sometimes very different definitions. If one interprets the term broadly, every museum presentation can be described as staging because "the placing of an object for presentation already means 'staging'."[13] Interpreted more narrowly, it has come to mean spatial object presentations and arrangements as regards a certain meaning or message.[14] In contemporary exhibition design, the meaning of staging has been extended: The sensory experience by the visitor now plays a central role. Exhibits are no longer only displayed with the help of presentation furniture such as pedestals and showcases and explained with texts, but which

sensory experience

11 See Thomas Thiemeyer, "Inszenierung und Szenografie: Auf den Spuren eines Grundbegriffs des Museums und seinen Herausforderungen," Zeitschrift für Volkskunde 108, no. 2 (2012), pp. 199–214, here p. 199.

12 See Rosemarie Beier-de Haan, Erinnerte Geschichte – inszenierte Geschichte. Ausstellungen und Museen in der Zweiten Moderne (Frankfurt/Main, 2005), p. 187.

13 Scholze 2004, p. 149.

14 See Korff 2007, p. 144

aus allen sozialen Schichten anzusprechen und zunehmend Geschichten anhand von Alltagsobjekten zu erzählen.[11] Demzufolge wurden neue Präsentationsformen erforderlich. Die Inszenierung löste die konventionelle Vitrinenausstellung und das pädagogische Lesemuseum ab, das mit langen Texttapeten die Objekte erklärt und häufig überfrachtet. Mit der Ausstellung „Preußen – Versuch einer Bilanz" von 1981 im Berliner Historischen Museum wurde die Inszenierung als Präsentationsform in Deutschland populär. Die Ausstellung stellte einen Gegenentwurf zur Stuttgarter Staufer-Ausstellung von 1977 dar und prägte die Geschichte der Inszenierung.[12]

Als gesellschaftliches Phänomen hat das Inszenieren seit Mitte der 1980er-Jahre die Grenzen des Museums verlassen und ist allgegenwärtig geworden. Die Inszenierung betrifft den künstlerischen, den öffentlichen und den sozialen Bereich und findet in ganz unterschiedlichen Formaten Ausdruck – sei es in den neuen Medien, in der Werbung, der Architektur, im Schaufensterdesign, in der Performance oder auf dem Catwalk. Und sie dominiert mehr und mehr gesellschaftliche Bereiche, wie Politik, Wirtschaft, Alltag, Sport oder Populärkultur. Dieses (Sich-)In-Szene-Setzen entspricht einem Trend, der bis heute anhält.

Der Begriff „Inszenierung" etablierte sich im deutschsprachigen Museumsdiskurs ebenfalls in den 1980er-Jahren, jedoch mit verschiedener, teilweise stark differierender Definition. Fasst man den Begriff weit, kann jede museale Präsentation als Inszenierung bezeichnet werden, da „das Platzieren eines Objekts zur Präsentation immer schon dessen ‚In-Szene-Setzen' bedeutet."[13] Enger gefasst sind darunter Objektpräsentationen und -arrangements im Raum hinsichtlich einer bestimmten Bedeutung oder Botschaft zu verstehen.[14] In der zeitgenössischen Ausstellungsgestaltung hat das Verständnis von Inszenierung eine Bedeutungserweiterung erfahren: Das sinnliche Erleben durch den Besucher spielt heute eine zentrale Rolle. Exponate werden nicht nur mithilfe von Präsentationsmobiliar wie Podesten und Vitrinen ausgestellt und mit Texten erklärt, sondern mit

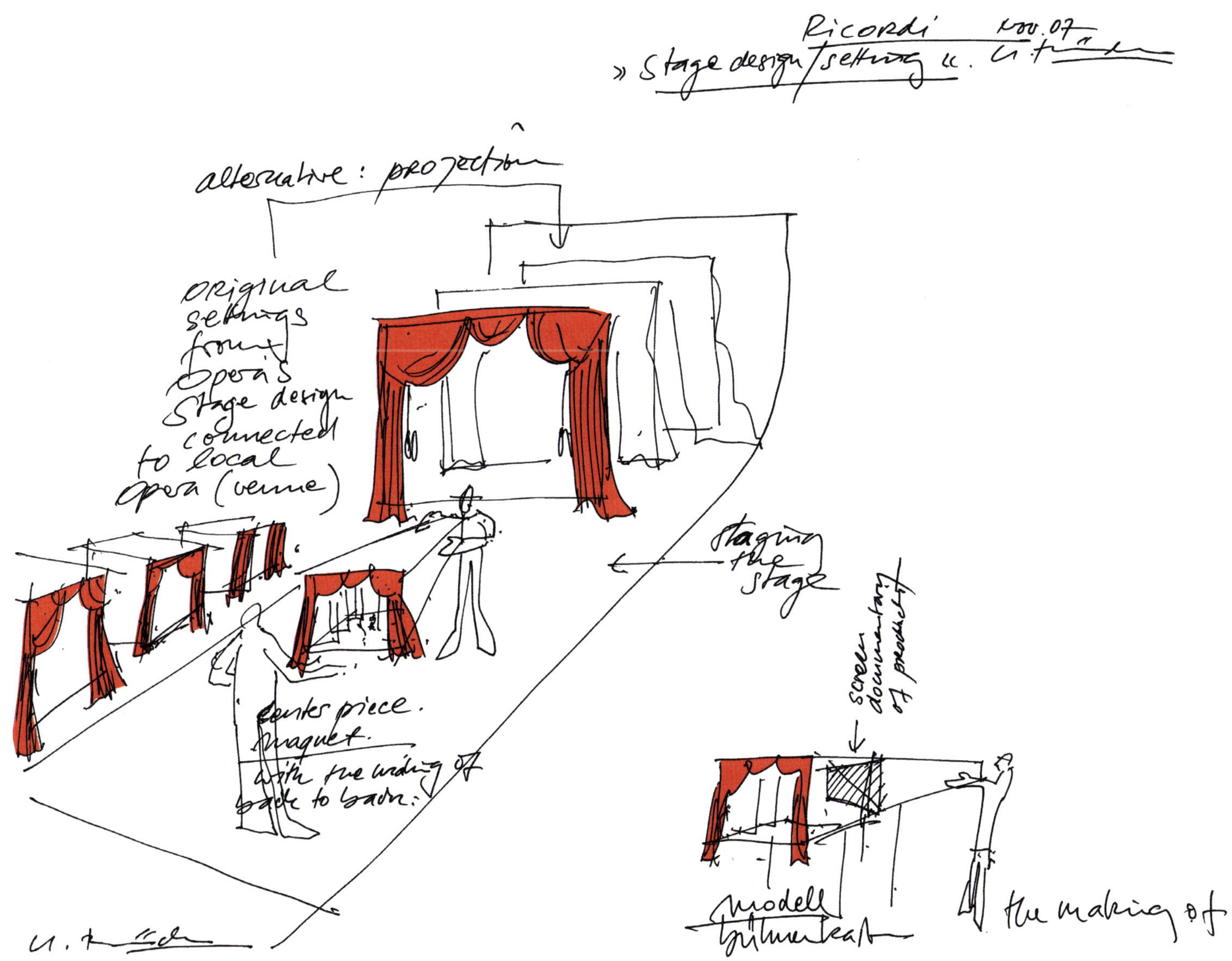

"That's Opera"–Scenografia, 2008. Sketch, 2007.

are narrated spatially with medial, audiovisual, and atmospheric means in order to allow the characteristics and meanings of an object to be experienced with several senses. With this type of staging, the visitor not only receives one-dimensional explanations, but considers the objects presented individually, interpreting them for himself and possibly also to critically question them and to think further.

scenography

In connection with experience with the senses, the term "scenography" came to the fore. It is often used synonymously with staging, even if there are subtle differences between the two terms. The term "scenography" originally also stems from the theatre context and it is a hybrid of the Greek words "skené" (scene) and "graphein" (to write). It took hold in the German-speaking world in the 1990s in the context of the Expo Hanover 2000; in particular with the definition of Martin Roth: Scenography is "[...] the craft to stage three-dimensional spaces, to set them up so that the effect of content is reinforced by design means, making it clearer and more striking and thus in its intended message."[15] According to Roth, scenography is the interpretation of the content using artistic means.[16] This definition is at the same time an expression of the fact that the classical understanding of staging is being replaced, bringing new staging strategies and techniques to the fore.

spatial experience

Incorporating the space and using various design instruments, scenography evokes content-driven, narrative themed rooms that are perceived on a sensually aesthetic level and focuses increasingly on the visitor or recipient. Scenography has since then been the term for scenic spatial design beyond the theatre and film and has long been recognised as a new creative discipline. The same applies for scenographers as multi- or trans-disciplinary designers for theatre performances, museums, and exhibitions, brand presentation, or architecture.

medialen, audiovisuellen und atmosphärischen Mitteln räumlich in Szene gesetzt, um Objekteigenschaften und -bedeutungen sinnlich erfahrbar zu machen. Diese Art der Inszenierung ermöglicht, dass der Besucher keine eindimensionalen Erklärungen bekommt, sondern sich mit dem Präsentierten individuell auseinandersetzen, es selbst interpretieren und es gegebenenfalls kritisch hinterfragen und weiterdenken kann.

Im Zusammenhang mit dem sinnlichen Erleben rückt der Begriff „Szenografie" in den Vordergrund. Er wird häufig als Synonym zu Inszenierung verwendet, auch wenn den Begriffen subtile Unterschiede innewohnen. Der Begriff Szenografie kommt ursprünglich auch aus dem Theaterkontext und ist ein Hybrid aus den griechischen Wörtern „skene" (Szene) und „graphein" (schreiben). Er etablierte sich im deutschen Sprachraum in den 1990er-Jahren im Kontext der Expo Hannover 2000, insbesondere mit der Definition von Martin Roth: Szenografie ist „[...] das Handwerk, dreidimensionale Räume so zu inszenieren, so einzurichten, dass Inhalte verstärkt durch gestalterische Mittel deutlicher und prägnanter in ihrer Wirkung und damit in der intendierten Aussage werden."[15] Laut Roth ist die Szenografie Interpretation der Inhalte mit künstlerischen Mitteln.[16] Diese Definition ist gleichwohl Ausdruck dessen, dass das klassische Inszenierungsverständnis abgelöst wurde und neue Inszenierungsstrategien und -techniken in den Vordergrund treten.

Unter Einbeziehung des Raums und der Verwendung verschiedener Gestaltungsinstrumente evoziert die Szenografie inhaltsgenerierte narrative Erlebnisräume, die auf einer sinnlich-ästhetischen Ebene wahrgenommen werden und zunehmend besucherorientiert sind. Szenografie ist seither der Begriff für die szenische Raumgestaltung jenseits des Theaters und des Films und ist längst als neue Kreativdisziplin anerkannt. Das Gleiche gilt für die Szenografen als multi- oder transdisziplinär qualifizierte Gestalter von Theaterinszenierungen, Museen und Ausstellungen, Markendarstellung oder Architektur.

15 Martin Roth, "Szenographie: Zur Entstehung von neuen Bildwelten im Themenpark der Expo 2000," in Museumskunde 1 (2001), pp. 25–32, here p. 25.

16 Ibid.

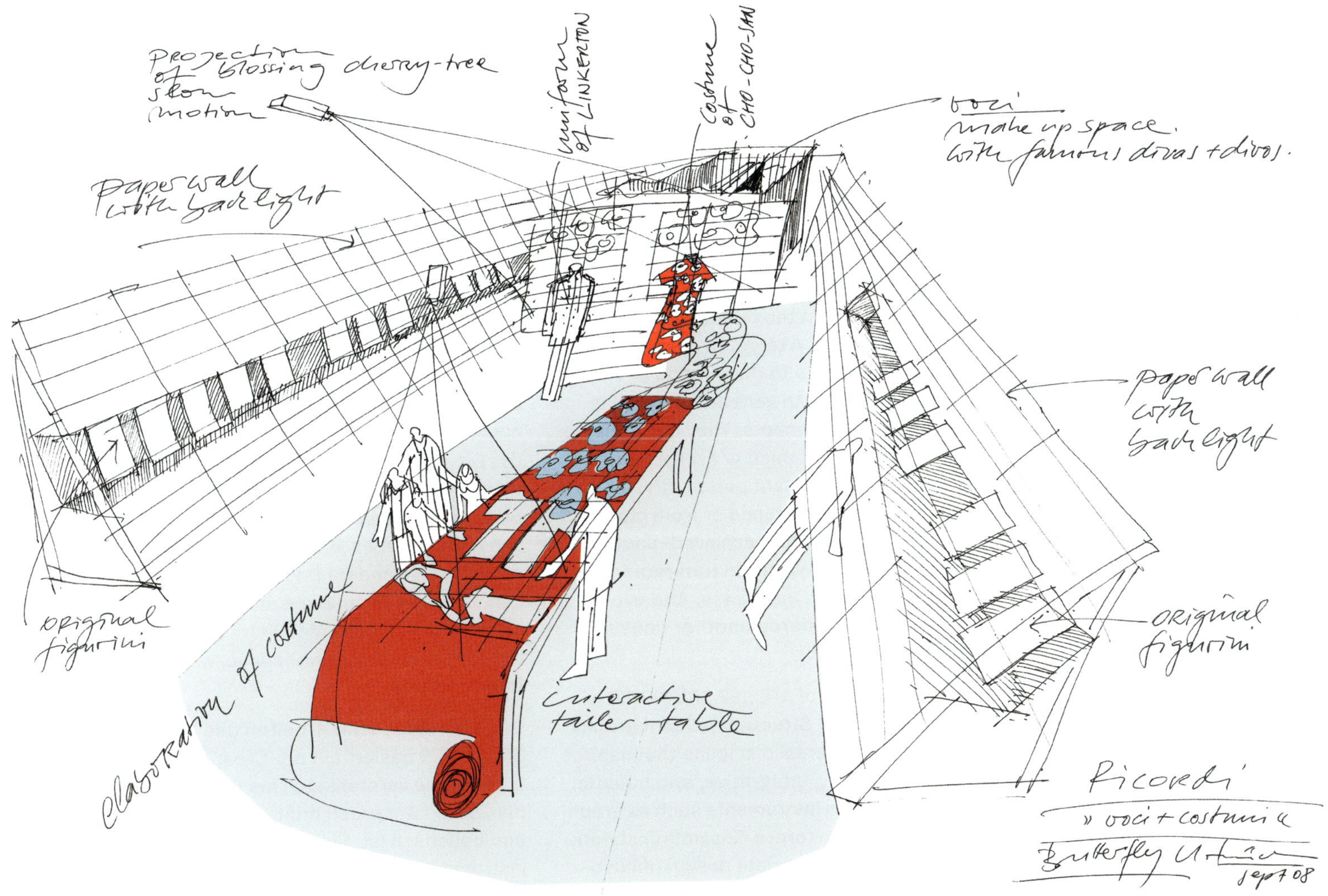

"That's Opera"–Voci e Costumi, 2008.

"When intuition and intellect pursue the same goals and the methodical use of dramaturgical principles determines the design process, when the choice of means is coherent and their application is consistent, a conception is on the right track to achieve a surprising, memorable scenography."[17]

scenographic design

Scenographic design is individual and for the designers poses a new challenge again and again. There is no such thing as an "automatic concept patent machine" that spews out the right and risk-free design solution when activated.[18] There are always different options and several translation possibilities of presenting content in spatial subjects–depending on the reason it is being conveyed or presented. A targeted change of perspective–from the inside to the outside or vice versa–allows designers to generate surprising and very memorable concepts. They can consider the thing as object, as artefact, or even as subject, from the aesthetic or content perspective, from above or below, from a distance or from close up. Every time, a new approach is achieved–another way of interpreting it–and this in turn requires a specific scenography in each case. And every time, the recipient is offered another unusual, powerful interpretation.

change of perspective

The scenographic work of ATELIER BRÜCKNER is based on the Creativ(e) Structur(e). Scenography considers itself a universal discipline that aspires to be multidisciplinary, integrative, and holistic. It orchestrates design instruments such as graphics, sound, or media to form a Gesamtkunstwerk. Scenography is the appropriate design philosophy in today's hybrid reality in which analogue and virtual experiences coexist.

↗ p. 180

↗ p. 152

content parameter

object parameter

Our scenographic work is defined by five basic parameters: content, object, space, recipient, and dramaturgy.[19] The content parameter represents the content as a resource, the overall narrative, the storytelling, the plot, and the message. The object parameter represents the

Szenografisches Gestalten erfolgt individuell und stellt immer wieder eine neue Herausforderung für die Gestalter dar. Es gibt keinen „Konzept-Patent-Automaten", der auf Anforderung die richtige und risikofreie Gestaltungslösung ausspuckt.[18] Es gibt immer unterschiedliche Optionen und mehrere Übersetzungsmöglichkeiten von Inhalten in räumliche Sujets – je nach Vermittlungs- und Darstellungsabsicht. Gezielte Perspektivwechsel – von innen nach außen oder vice verca – versetzen Gestalter in die Lage, überraschende und lang nachwirkende Konzepte zu generieren. Sie können das Ding als Objekt, als Artefakt oder gar als Subjekt betrachten, aus der ästhetischen oder inhaltlichen Sicht, von unten oder oben, aus der Ferne oder von Nahem. Jedes Mal wird eine neue Annäherung erreicht, eine andere Deutungsmöglichkeit gewonnen, die jeweils eine spezifische Szenografie erfordert. Und jedes Mal bietet sich dem Rezipienten eine andere ungewöhnliche, wirkmächtige Interpretation.

Das szenografische Arbeiten des ATELIER BRÜCKNER basiert auf der Creativ(e) Structur(e). Szenografie versteht sich als eine Universaldisziplin, deren Anspruch multidisziplinär, integrativ und holistisch ist. Sie orchestriert Gestaltungsinstrumente wie Grafik, Licht, Sound oder Medien zu einem Gesamtkunstwerk. Szenografie ist die adäquate Gestaltungsphilosophie in der heutigen hybriden Realität, in der sich analoge und virtuelle Erfahrungen mischen.

Unser szenografisches Arbeiten ist durch fünf grundlegende Parameter definiert: Inhalt, Objekt, Raum, Rezipient und Dramaturgie.[19] Der Inhaltsparameter repräsentiert die inhaltliche Ressource, die übergeordnete Erzählung, das Storytelling, den Plot und die Botschaft. Der Objektparameter repräsentiert die materielle Ressource, den Gegenstand der Betrachtung, den Bedeutungs-

17 See Atelier Brückner 2016, p. 111.
18 Uwe R. Brückner's answer to the question: "What makes good scenography?"
19 See also Brückner and Greci 2016, pp. 25–51.

material resource, the object that is being viewed, the bearer of meanings, and the storyteller of a project. The space parameter defines the physical borderlines of the venue and space; it defines proportion and dimension, materiality and surface, and it plays with the character of the space, its atmosphere, and its physical states.[20] The recipient as parameter focuses on the addressee, the visitor, and the recipient's perception in relation to the object, content, space, scenography, and dramaturgy. Dramaturgy as parameter represents the arrangement of the routing, a guiding thread through the exhibition and structures the visitor experience along a dramatic curve of suspense.[21] These parameters are the basic elements of scenographic design and are the starting point for any development of staging with a holistic concept. In the conception, the aim is to put them into a consistent context and to translate them into a spatial, narrative subject. Every single parameter has a specific quality and a powerful potential for the development of sophisticated scenographies.[22]

As a design approach, scenography is a very promising strategy to elaborate holistic concepts. But how do we get from an idea to a concept, from a concept to a conception? How do we navigate through a complex, creative design process? At the beginning there is always the meticulous analysis of the brief, the provided content and the anticipated key messages. From there we move on to a fundamental research of the content, always on the lookout for the obvious or hidden secrets. We look at every angle and explore various alternative approaches. Not to forget the investigation of the given spatial situation and architecture. Most concepts are elaborated during workshops with the curators, experts, artists, and colleagues from various design disciplines. From the outset we express our ideas in sketches. We believe in the power of storytelling, and we therefore write storyboards to create dynamic settings. We believe in spatial choreography,

20 See also Atelier Brückner 2016, p. 169.
21 Ibid., p. 117.
22 See Brückner and Greci 2016, p. 25.

träger und den Storyteller. Der Raumparameter definiert die physische Grenze von Ort und Raum, von Proportion und Dimension, von Materialität und Oberfläche und er spielt mit dem Charakter des Raums, seiner Atmosphäre und seinen Aggregatzuständen.[20] Der Rezipient als Parameter fokussiert sich auf den Adressaten, den Besucher und dessen Wahrnehmung in Beziehung zu Objekt, Inhalt, Raum, zur Szenografie und Dramaturgie. Die Dramaturgie als Parameter steht für die Anordnung des Parcours, für einen roten Faden durch die Ausstellung und die Strukturierung des Besuchererlebnisses entlang eines dramaturgischen Spannungsbogens.[21] Diese Parameter zählen zu den Grundelementen des szenografischen Gestaltens und sind Ausgangspunkt für jegliche Entwicklung von holistisch gedachten Inszenierungen. Es gilt, diese bei der Konzeption in einen konsistenten Kontext zu bringen und in ein räumliches, narratives Sujet zu übersetzen. Jeder einzelne Parameter hat eine spezifische Qualität und ein wirkmächtiges Potenzial für die Entwicklung anspruchsvoller Szenografien.[22]

Als Gestaltungshaltung ist die Szenografie eine vielversprechende Disziplin, um ganzheitliche Konzepte zu entwickeln. Aber wie gelangen wir von einer Idee zu einem Konzept, wie von einem Konzept zu einer Konzeption? Und wie navigieren wir durch komplexe kreative Gestaltungsprozesse? Wir beginnen immer mit der genauen Analyse des Briefings (Aufgabenstellung), den gegebenen Objekten und Inhalten oder intendierten Botschaften (Inhalt). Wir fahren fort mit einer grundlegenden Recherche zum Inhalt und den offensichtlichen Referenzen (Informationen) sowie verborgenen Geheimnissen. Wir wechseln häufig die Perspektive, um alternative Entwürfe zu untersuchen. Und wir analysieren die vorhandenen räumlichen Konditionen und die Architektur hinsichtlich ihrer verborgenen Potenziale. Die meisten Konzepte erarbeiten wir in Workshops mit den Kuratoren, Experten, Künstlern und Kollegen aus den verschiedenen Designdisziplinen. Von Anfang an entwickeln wir Ideen in Skizzenform. Wir glauben an die Kraft des Erzählens und entwickeln Storyboards für dynamische Inszenierungen. Wir vertrauen auf den choreografierten Raum, auf die Choreografie von Raumabfolgen und ver-

space parameter

recipient as parameter

dramaturgy as parameter

in the choreographed order of spaces, and in the dramaturgy of perception depicted in a partitura, the score. For the holistic presentation of complex concepts, the ATELIER BRÜCKNER develloped and uses the following productive templates: synopses, matrix, storyboard, and score.

synopses

The synopses or exposé is the first summary of a brief or task that we prepare.[23] Filmmakers use synopses, for instance, to prepare a film project. The narrative material of a novel or script is analysed by briefly summarising the plot. There is no prescribed length–a film synopses can range from a few sentences to a few pages of text. If the synopsis is only one sentence long, thus forming a pithy formulation that taps into the essence of the film, one refers to a log line.[24]

matrix

storyboard

score

The matrix or also content matrix is more of an analytical template in which the design parameters such as space, object, or content, and the design instruments are described and relationships established amongst them.[25] In the storyboard the matrix is supplemented by the narrative potential of the storytelling and a roughly sketched spatial image or a series of spatial images.[26] In the score, content matrix and storyboard are finally merged to form a synthesis,[27] a master document in which the whole project is presented in detail.[28] The score is the ideal instrument for the complex and holistic visualisation of the whole project. We read this horizontally, in the chronological order of the experiences (routing, spatial imagery), vertically in terms of content, form, and staging (parameters, instruments), and diagonally, the synchronisation of the events, the connecting of space, objects, narration, and perception by the recipient, along an arc of suspense and a certain dramaturgy.

23 Definition according to Longman: synopsis (Greek: sýnopsis): a condensed statement or outline (e.g., of a narrative or treatise); an abstract. See Longman Dictionary of the English Language, new edition published 1991, p. 1640.
24 See James Michael Thomas, Script Analysis for Actors, Directors, and Designers, 3rd ed. (Boston/Oxford, 2005).
25 See also Atelier Brückner 2016, p. 115.
26 Ibid., p. 120.
27 Definition according to Longman: synthesis (Greek: synthesis): a composition or combination of parts or elements so as to form a whole. See Longman Dictionary of the English Language, new edition published 1991, p. 1641.
28 See also Atelier Brückner 2016, p. 121.

wenden dafür eine Wahrnehmungsdramaturgie, beschrieben in einer Partitur. Das ATELIER BRÜCKNER entwickelte und verwendet für die ganzheitliche Darstellung komplexer Konzepte folgende operative Templates (Vorlagen): Synopse, Matrix, Storyboard und Partitur.

Die Synopse oder das Exposé ist die erste von uns erstellte Zusammenfassung eines Briefings, einer Aufgabenstellung.[23] Filmschaffende nutzen die Synopse beispielsweise zur Vorbereitung eines Filmprojekts. Das narrative Material eines Romans oder Skripts wird analysiert, indem der Plot knapp zusammengefasst wird. Die Länge ist hierbei nicht festgelegt – eine filmische Synopse kann wenige Sätze bis zu einigen Seiten Text umfassen. Ist die Synopse nur einen Satz lang und bildet somit eine prägnante Kürzestformel, nennt man sie Log Line.[24]

Die Matrix oder auch Inhaltsmatrix ist ein eher analytisches Template, in dem die Gestaltungsparameter, wie beispielsweise Raum, Objekt oder Inhalt, und die Gestaltungsinstrumente beschrieben und in Beziehung zueinander gesetzt werden.[25] Im Storyboard wird die Matrix um das narrative Potenzial des Storytelling und der meist skizzenhaften Beschreibung des Raumbildes oder einer Folge von Raumbildern erweitert.[26] In der Partitur (Score) fusionieren Inhaltsmatrix und Storyboard schließlich zu einer Synthese,[27] einem Masterdokument, in dem das gesamte Projekt erschöpfend dargestellt werden kann.[28] Die Partitur ist das ideale Instrumentarium für die komplexe und ganzheitliche Visualisierung des gesamten Projekts. Wir lesen diese im Horizontalen erlebnischronologisch (Parcours, Raumbilder), im Vertikalen inhaltlich, formal und inszenatorisch (Parameter, Instrumente), und in der Diagonalen die Synchronisierung der Ereignisse, die Verknüpfung von Raum, Objekten, Narration und der Wahrnehmung durch die Rezipienten entlang eines Spannungsbogens und einer bestimmten Dramaturgie.

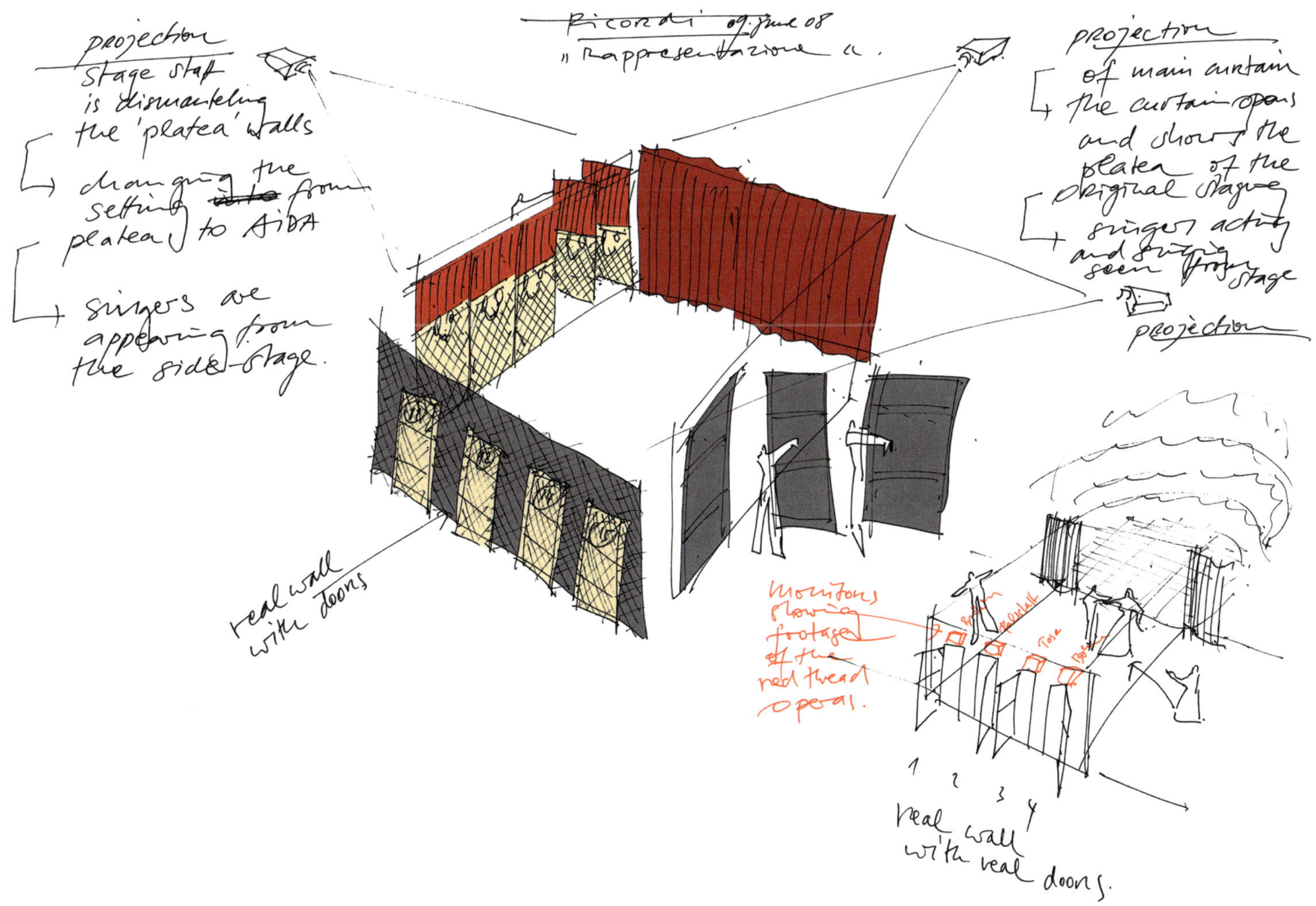

"That's Opera"–Rappresentazione, 2008.

"The Creativ(e) Structur(e) is the fundament of our design philosophy 'form follows content', it is method, navigational system, and curriculum at the same time. It helps to orchestrate all creative instruments in order to achieve a 'Gesamtkunstwerk', a holistic piece of art."

Uwe R. Brückner

Creativ(e) Structur(e) [CS]

CREATIV(E) STRUCTUR(E) [CS] The design methodology developed by Uwe R. Brückner back in the 1990s was compiled in the Creativ(e) Structur(e) [CS].[29] Originally the [CS] served as a training programme for staff. Since then the method has been used to implement the design philosophy of ATELIER BRÜCKNER in accordance with the credo of the Atelier "form follows content." The [CS] is navigation system, philosophy, methodology, and curriculum all rolled into one.

analytical tool

synopses

title, subtitle, content message

The [CS] is an effective analytical tool that helps the user to ask smart questions in order to get smart answers. Every project begins with the preparation of the synopses or exposé, in order to dissect the task thoroughly, to take a closer look at the content requirements and descriptions, to explore the motivation of the client, the intention of the project brief, and the way it is formulated and to examine the objective, the desired result, and the message to be conveyed. To do this–regardless of how complex, big, or demanding a task–requires only four answers to four core questions: as to the title, the subtitle, the content, and the message, each briefly formulated, in a nutshell so to speak.[30] This approach applies both for the analysis of the tasks at hand and also the development of new concepts.

CREATIV(E) STRUCTUR(E) [CS] Diese Gestaltungsmethodik hat Uwe R. Brückner seit den 1990er-Jahren in der Creativ(e) Structur(e) [CS] formuliert.[29] Sie diente ursprünglich als Ausbildungsprogramm für Mitarbeiter und wird seitdem als Methode zur Umsetzung der Gestaltungsphilosophie des ATELIER BRÜCKNER gemäß dem Credo des Ateliers „form follows content" angewendet. Die [CS] ist Navigationssystem, Philosophie, Methodik und Curriculum zugleich.

Die [CS] ist ein probates Analyseinstrument, weil sie hilft, kluge Fragen zu stellen, um intelligente Antworten zu bekommen. Jedes Projekt beginnt mit der Erstellung der Synopse oder des Exposés, um die Aufgabenstellung gründlich zu sezieren, inhaltliche Anforderungen und Beschreibungen zu beleuchten, die Motivation der Auftraggeber, die Intention der Aufgabenstellung eines Projekts und deren Formulierung zu ergründen sowie die Zielsetzung, das angestrebte Ergebnis und die zu überbringende Botschaft zu untersuchen. Dazu braucht es, egal wie komplex, groß oder anspruchsvoll eine Aufgabe sein mag, nur vier Antworten auf vier Kernfragen: die Frage nach dem Titel, dem Untertitel, dem Inhalt und der Botschaft mit jeweils knapper, auf den Punkt gebrachter Formulierung.[30] Das gilt sowohl für die Analyse gegebener Aufgabenstellungen als auch für die Entwicklung neuer Konzepte.

---

29 The [CS] – Creativ(e) Structur(e) was developed by Uwe R. Brückner over a period of twenty years and is a standard chapter in his lectures. In 2001, the curriculum of the Institute of Interior Architecture and Scenography at the Basel School of Design and Art (FHNW HGK) was developed on the basis of the [CS], and now forms the teaching basis for the design discipline scenography. More recently, the [CS] has been expanded to include the parameters recipient, object, and dramaturgy.
See Uwe R. Brückner and Linda Greci, eds., EMEE Toolkit 4: Synaesthetic Translation of Perspectives: Scenography–A Sketchbook (Vienna, 2016).

30 See also Atelier Brückner 2016, p. 114.

As navigation system, the [CS] allows users to find their way around complex projects, giving them orientation, allowing them to correctly assess the location, timing, and dimension of a task and, based on this, to independently develop scenic events from the conception via the design through to the implementation. The [CS] is an organisational system that helps to place engagement and the effect of creative processes in a promising relationship to one another and in a meaningful order. The [CS] is also a checklist with various, more or less chronological design steps which ask questions in the design phases about the input, but above all about the output. The [CS] contains a creative methodology which helps develop the conception by providing the user with useful suggestions. The [CS] describes project phases, that is, the genesis of creative design–design as translational approach in the development of concepts and their structured implementation in reality. The [CS] describes the main parameters like place, space, object, content, and recipient and the necessary field of tension in the interplay of these forces. The [CS] uses different dramatic compositions borrowed from literature, theatre, opera, or film. It also combines the potential of space and time and of perception and effect.[31]

The Creativ(e) Structur(e) is based on four pillars: project phases, project structure, scenographic parameters, and instruments. The project phases organise the whole design process from the briefing to the idea, from the concept to preliminary draft, from the planning to prototyping, from production to realisation–not to forget the opening. The project structure describes the main steps of the design process–from the detailed analysis of the task via the plot, the description of the intended experiences through to the conception, perfectly presented in a score. There are electronic templates for all the parameters, which serve as helpful checklists or operating instructions.[32]

Als Navigationssystem ermöglicht es die [CS], sich in komplexen Projekten zurechtzufinden, sich zu orientieren, Ort, Zeit und Dimension einer Aufgabe richtig einzuschätzen und szenische Ereignisse von der Konzeption über die Gestaltung bis hin zur Umsetzung selbstständig durchzuführen. Die [CS] ist ein Organisationssystem, das hilft, Engagement und Wirkung kreativer Prozesse in einem erfolgversprechenden Verhältnis und einer sinnstiftenden Reihenfolge zu organisieren. Die [CS] ist auch Checkliste mit verschiedenen, mehr oder minder chronologischen Gestaltungsschritten, die die Entwurfs- und Gestaltungsphasen nach dem Input, vor allem aber nach dem Output befragt. Die [CS] enthält eine Kreativmethodik, die mit entsprechenden Handlungsvorschlägen beim Konzeptionieren hilft. Die [CS] beschreibt Projektphasen, also die Genese kreativen Gestaltens, wobei Gestalten als übersetzerisches Vorgehen bei der Entwicklung von Konzepten und als strukturiertes Umsetzen in die Realität zu verstehen ist. Die [CS] beschreibt die wesentlichen Parameter, wie Ort, Raum, Objekt, Inhalt und Rezipient, und das erforderliche Spannungsfeld im Zusammenspiel dieser Kräfte. Die [CS] bedient sich unterschiedlicher Dramaturgien, entlehnt aus der Literatur, dem Theater, der Oper oder dem Film. Die [CS] verbindet die Potenziale von Raum und Zeit und von Wahrnehmung und Wirkung.[31]

Die Creativ(e) Structur(e) basiert auf insgesamt vier Säulen: Projektphasen, Projektstruktur, szenografische Parameter und Instrumente. Die Projektphasen organisieren den ganzen Gestaltungsprozess: vom Briefing zur Idee, vom Konzept zum Vorentwurf, von der Planung zum Prototyping, von der Produktion zur Realisierung – die Eröffnung nicht zu vergessen. Die Projektstruktur beschreibt die wesentlichen Schritte des Gestaltungsprozesses: von einer detaillierten Analyse der Aufgabenstellung über den Plot, die Beschreibung der intendierten Erlebnisse bis hin zur Konzeption, optimal dargestellt in einer Partitur. Für alle Parameter gibt es elektronische Templates, die als Checklisten oder als operative Anleitungen dienen.[32]

navigation system

organisational system

creative methodology

project phases, project structure
↗ p. 169 – 171

scenographic parameters
↗ p. 190 – 281

instruments
↗ p. 180 – 189

31 Ibid., p. 112.
32 Ibid., p. 118 – 119.

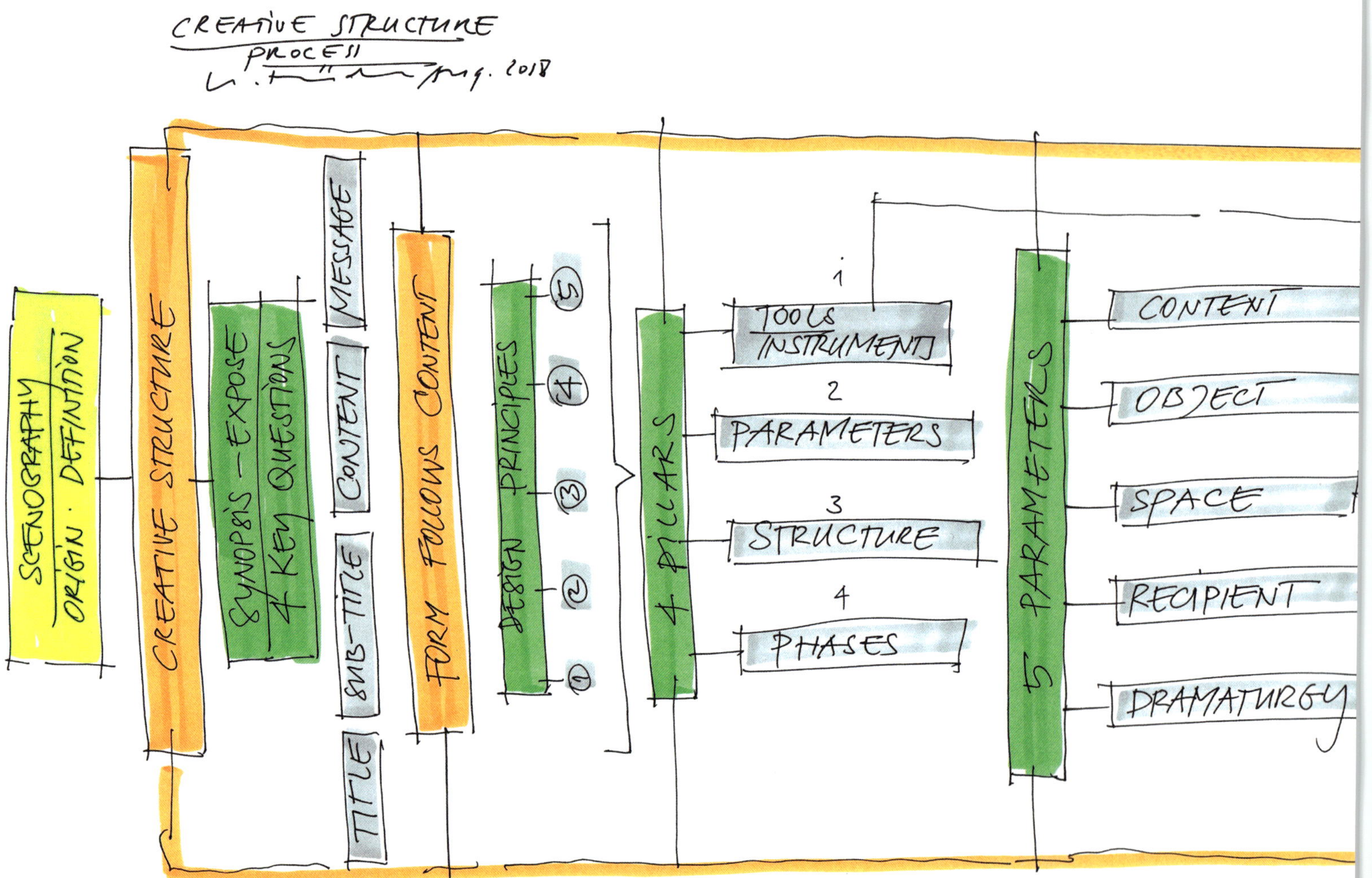
CREATIVE STRUCTURE
PROCESS
SCENOGRAPHY
ORIGIN · DEFINITION
CREATIVE STRUCTURE
SYNOPSIS – EXPOSE
4 KEY QUESTIONS
MESSAGE
CONTENT
SUB-TITLE
TITLE
FORM FOLLOWS CONTENT
DESIGN PRINCIPLES
1
2
3
4
5
4 PILLARS
1
TOOLS
INSTRUMENTS
2
PARAMETERS
3
STRUCTURE
4
PHASES
5 PARAMETERS
CONTENT
OBJECT
SPACE
RECIPIENT
DRAMATURGY

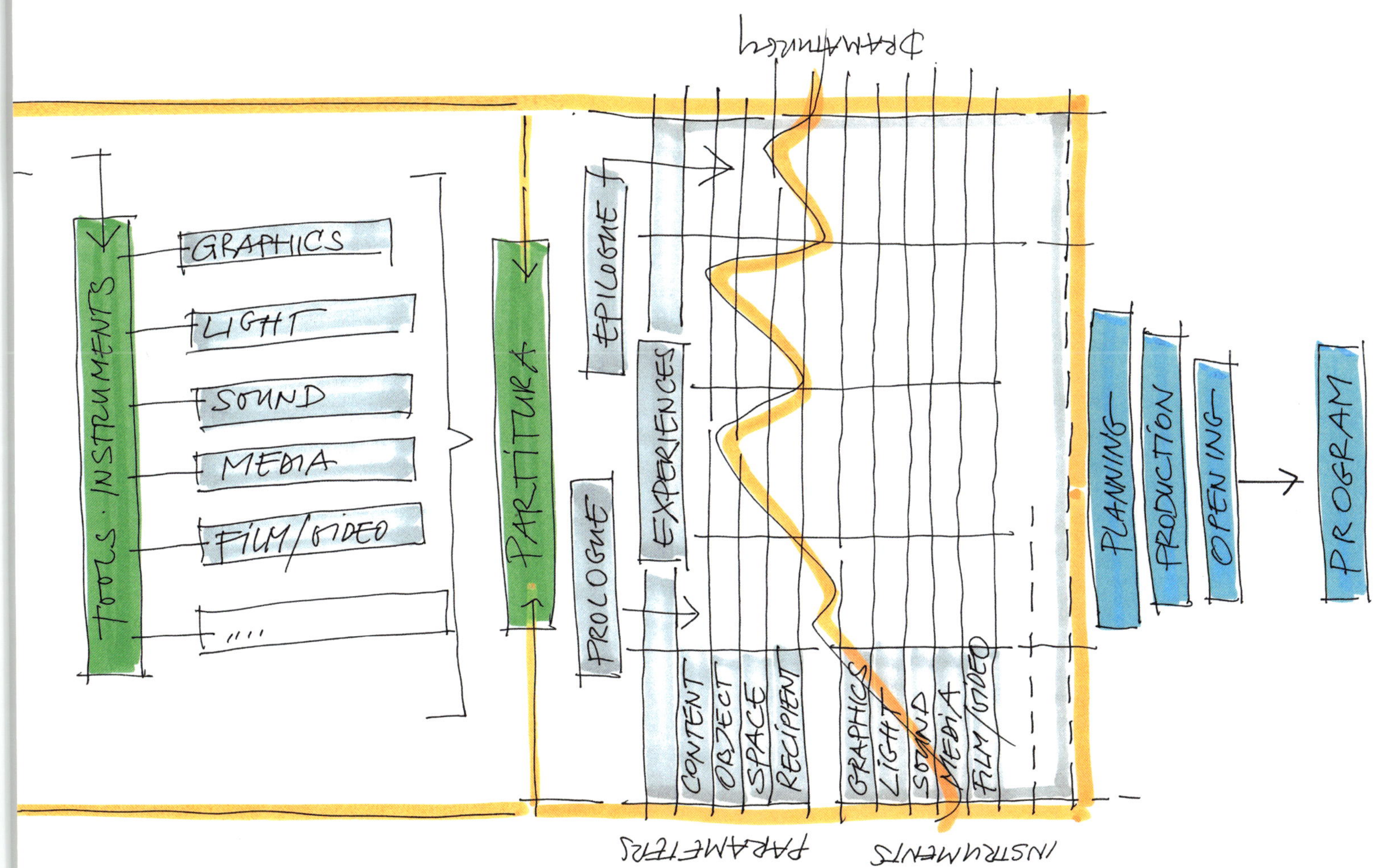

"Creativ(e) Structur(e)"– Map of Navigation, 2018.

DESIGN PRINCIPLES In its scenographic design work, ATELIER BRÜCKNER follows certain design principles alongside the Creativ(e) Structur(e), four of which are described here in more detail:

GESTALTUNGSGRUNDSÄTZE Beim szenografischen Gestalten folgt ATELIER BRÜCKNER neben der Creativ(e) Structur(e) bestimmten Gestaltungsgrundsätzen – vier seien hier hervorgehoben:

"You cannot not stage." Uwe R. Brückner

curatorial statement

A theatrical stage does not differ greatly from reality. Whenever birds of a feather flock together, they represent something, they show themselves off and consciously or unconsciously follow certain role patterns. The same applies to exhibitions. Adapted from the quote by Paul Watzlawick, "One cannot not communicate," we follow the credo "One cannot not stage." Exhibiting is always an act of staging and at the same time a commentary of the curators and designers or an expression of the times. Even if we only place a grain of rice in a showcase and illuminate it, that is already staging. Every choice of object is already a curatorial statement, and every spatial arrangement has an underlying intention to convey or present something with a certain effect. Scene setting is thus design authorship; the scenographer becomes an author designer ("Autorengestalter").[33]

Eine Theaterbühne unterscheidet sich nur bedingt von der Wirklichkeit. Wann immer Menschen sich unter ihresgleichen bewegen, stellen sie etwas dar, inszenieren sich selbst und folgen, bewusst oder unbewusst, bestimmten Rollenmustern. Vergleichbares trifft für Ausstellungen zu. In Anlehnung an das Zitat von Paul Watzlawick „Man kann nicht nicht kommunizieren", folgen wir dem Credo „Man kann nicht nicht inszenieren". Ausstellen ist immer ein Akt des Inszenierens und zugleich ein Kommentar der Kuratoren und Gestalter oder Ausdruck ihrer Zeit. Selbst wenn wir nur ein Reiskorn in eine Vitrine legen und Licht darauf ausrichten, ist das eine Inszenierung. Jede Auswahl von Objekten ist bereits ein kuratorisches Statement und jedes räumliche Arrangement hat Vermittlungs- oder Darstellungsabsicht mit intendierter Wirkung.
Das In-Szene-Setzen ist also gestalterisches Autorentum; und der Szenograf wird zum Autorengestalter.[33]

"Form follows content." Uwe R. Brückner

translation

Form follows content–this credo means the translation of content in the available space, giving it a spatial dimension. Good scenography always starts from the content. It is to be understood as the interpretation of content with design means, which introduces a transformation from something intangible, something non-material, into something physical or even to something with its own spatial self-conception. This design approach of the taking and giving of form to content has been a hallmark of the work of ATELIER BRÜCKNER for twenty years.

↗ p. 192

Die Form folgt dem Inhalt – dieses Credo bedeutet die Übersetzung von Inhalten in den Raum, in räumliche Gestaltung. Gute Szenografie geht stets vom Inhalt aus. Sie ist als Interpretation der Inhalte mit gestalterischen Mitteln zu verstehen, die eine Transformation einleitet, von etwas Immateriellem, nicht Greifbarem zu etwas Physischem oder gar zu einem Raum gewordenen Selbstverständnis. Diese Gestaltungshaltung des Formwerdens und Formgebens von Inhalten prägt die Arbeit des ATELIER BRÜCKNER bereits seit 20 Jahren.

---

33 Uwe R. Brückner describes scenographers as author designers ("Autorengestalter") with reference to the singer songwriter Bob Dylan who writes his texts himself, puts them to music and sings them or the author filmmakers from the 1970s like Wim Wenders.

"Form follows content" is the central guiding principle of the design philosophy of ATELIER BRÜCKNER and is applied to all formats–whether museum, brand, or architecture.

„Form follows content" ist der zentrale Leitsatz der Gestaltungsphilosophie von ATELIER BRÜCKNER und wird auf alle Formate – sei es im Bereich Museum, Marke oder Architektur – angewendet.

Uwe R. Brückner **"Start thinking from the End."**

anticipatory design

The designer should always start thinking from the result, an approach referred to as "anticipatory design," and from the outset consider how and with what statement the messages being transported are to reach the recipient. Ultimately, only the result counts, namely what the recipient perceives and remembers.

Der Gestalter sollte stets vom Ergebnis her denken, Gestaltung antizipatorisch anwenden und von vornherein überlegen, in welcher Weise und mit welcher Aussage die transportierten Botschaften den Rezipienten erreichen sollen. Am Ende zählt nur das Ergebnis, das was der Rezipient wahrnimmt und in Erinnerung behält.

Uwe R. Brückner **"Scenography–Or the Art of Holistic Design."**

Gesamtkunstwerk

Scenographic design is holistic design, which uses various design tools to combine the five parameters–content, object, space, recipient, and dramaturgy–to form a composition and to stage them, charged with meaning. A holistic approach always aims to become a "Gesamtkunstwerk" in the sense of Richard Wagner.[34] Like voices and instruments in the composition of a Wagnerian opera, the design instruments of scenography are combined into a whole and work together to form an holistic work of art. All elements of scenography are subordinated to a common purpose, namely the message designated to reach the visitor and the emotion that it should arouse in him. The ultimate goal is an overall composition of all design parameters and tools, expressed in an holistic staging.

These design principles are reflected in the projects of ATELIER BRÜCKNER. The first landmark project that shaped our scenography understanding and established our design philosophy is presented below.

Szenografisches Gestalten bedeutet holistisches Gestalten, das die fünf Parameter Inhalt, Objekt, Raum, Rezipient und Dramaturgie unter Verwendung von verschiedenen Gestaltungsinstrumenten in eine kompositorische Beziehung zueinander setzt und in einem bedeutungsvoll aufgeladenen Environment inszeniert. Es handelt sich um eine ganzheitliche Herangehensweise, die stets ein „Gesamtkunstwerk" im Sinne von Richard Wagner anstrebt.[34] Wie Stimmen und Instrumente bei der Komposition einer Wagner-Oper fügen sich die Gestaltungsinstrumente der Szenografie zu einem Ganzen und werden im Zusammenspiel zum Gesamtkunstwerk. Alle Elemente der Szenografie ordnen sich einem gemeinsamen Zweck unter, nämlich der Botschaft, die den Besucher erreicht, und der Emotion, die bei ihm ausgelöst werden soll. Das höchste Ziel ist eine Gesamtkomposition aller Gestaltungsparameter und -instrumente, die Ausdruck findet in einer holistischen Inszenierung.

Diese Gestaltungsprinzipien spiegeln sich in den Projekten von ATELIER BRÜCKNER. Im Nachfolgenden wird das erste, richtungsweisende Projekt, das unser Szenografieverständnis geprägt und unsere Gestaltungsphilosophie mitbegründet hat, vorgestellt.

34 In his essay "The Art-Work of the Future" Richard Wagner describes the concept of an integrative work of art consisting of various art forms. "The great United Art-Work, which must gather up each branch of art to use it as a mean, and in some sense to undo it for the common aim of all, for the unconditioned, absolute portrayal of perfected human nature–this great United Art-Work he cannot picture as depending on the arbitrary purpose of some human unit, but can only conceive it as the instinctive and associate product of the Manhood of the Future." Richard Wagner: Das Kunstwerk der Zukunft (Leipzig, 1850), p. 32, translation from Richard Wagner, The Art-Work of the Future and Other Works, trans. William Ashton Ellis (Lincoln, NE, 1994).

"We experience horizontally, archive vertically, and reflect and contextualise diagonally." Uwe R. Brückner

dramaturgical means

themed rooms
interludes

associative space

STAGING DIALOGUE BETWEEN EXHIBIT AND RECIPIENT The holistic aspiration of scenographic designing–the staging of the dialogue between object and space, between story and recipient along a dramaturgical arc of suspense–is perfectly illustrated by the exhibition "Expedition Titanic" realised in the warehouse district of Hamburg in 1997. It is an early example of an exhibition that was staged using dramaturgical means. Five protagonists guide the visitor in episodes through the routing that meanders along the imaginary ship's passageway, guided chronologically by the fate of the Titanic. The contradictory statements of the survivors formed the starting point for the concept.

The exhibits and the stories behind the objects are the centre of attention–the staging creates an emotional connection between objects and recipients. Alongside the themed rooms, spaces have been woven into the exhibition as interludes. These deal with the phenomenon Titanic on a meta level: in the "Champagne Room," for instance, six Champagne bottles from first class which were salvaged from the sea were juxtaposed dialectically with a worker's shoe from third class, presented on a par and without any explanation. The contrasting or positioning of objects in a dialectic relationship allows contrasting content to be conveyed in parallel, visually emphasising physical, tangible differences. Even the mere presence of the objects being compared can lead to a change of perspective and a reflection on what is on display.

The Champagne bottles and the worker's shoe were allotted a separate room–at the same time an associative space that offers direct access to the aura of the objects and subtly reminds the visitor that the Titanic set sail not only as a luxury liner, but also above all as an emigration ship. The bright light invalidates the dimension of the room and reflects where the objects were found, namely: the cold and dark depths of the West Atlantic. A subliminal ambient sound reminds the visitors ever so subtly of the unimaginable water

DIE INSZENIERUNG DES DIALOGS ZWISCHEN EXPONAT UND REZIPIENT Den holistischen Anspruch szenografischen Gestaltens – die Inszenierung des Dialogs zwischen Objekt und Raum, zwischen Story und Rezipient entlang eines dramaturgischen Spannungsbogens – verdeutlicht die 1997 in der Speicherstadt in Hamburg realisierte Ausstellung „Expedition Titanic" auf beispielhafte Weise. Sie zählt zu einer der frühen mit dramaturgischen Mitteln inszenierten Ausstellungen. Fünf Protagonisten führen episodisch durch den Parcours, der entlang eines imaginierten Schiffskorridors mäandriert und sich chronologisch am Schicksal der Titanic orientiert. Die widersprüchlichen Aussagen der Überlebenden waren Ausgangspunkt für das Konzept.

Die Exponate und die Geschichten hinter den Objekten stehen im Mittelpunkt – die Inszenierung stellt einen emotionalen Kontakt zwischen Objekten und Rezipienten her. Neben den Themenräumen sind Räume als Interludes, als Zwischenspiele, eingeflochten, die sich auf der Metaebene mit dem Phänomen Titanic beschäftigen: Im „Champagnerraum" wurden beispielsweise sechs aus dem Meer geborgene Champagnerflaschen der ersten Klasse dialektisch einem Arbeiterschuh der dritten Klasse gleichwertig und kommentarlos gegenübergestellt. Das Gegenüberstellen oder das Positionieren von Objekten in einem dialektischen Verhältnis vermag kontrastreiche Inhalte parallel zu vermitteln und physisch-materielle Unterschiede visuell zu verdeutlichen. Bereits die bloße Anwesenheit der im Vergleich zueinander stehenden Objekte kann einen Perspektivwechsel und eine innere Auseinandersetzung mit dem Gezeigten bewirken.

Den Champagnerflaschen und dem Arbeiterschuh wurde ein eigener Raum gewidmet – ein assoziativer Raum, der einen unmittelbaren, auratischen Zugang zu den Objekten bietet und subtil daran erinnert, dass die Titanic nicht nur als Luxusliner, sondern vorrangig als Auswandererschiff in See gestochen ist. Der Raum erfährt durch das gleißende Licht eine Entdimensionierung und reflek-

pressure almost four kilometres below sea level. The visitors cannot really hear the ambient sound, but—more importantly—they sense it. Thanks to its dialectic composition, its light mood and the subtle sound installation, the Champagne Room is a synaesthetic experience space.

This type of staging, which challenges visitors to form their own interpretation, was not common in the 1990s, known only from art exhibitions or stage sets. The aim of the exhibit-oriented exhibition was to unfold the aura of the (seemingly) everyday objects in an unexpected way and with a high emotional effect. It was about the permanent relationship in dialogue between the exhibit and its significance, but also between the exhibits and their observers. It was about amazing the visitors, converting provocation into positive awareness, and leaving a memorable impression.

tiert den Fundort der Objekte, nämlich: die kalte und lichtlose Tiefe des Westatlantiks. Ein unterschwelliger Raumton erinnert die Besucher ganz subtil an den unvorstellbaren Wasserdruck in annährend vier Kilometern Meerestiefe. Die Besucher konnten den Raumton zwar nicht wirklich hören, jedoch – umso wichtiger – spüren. Der „Champagnerraum" generiert durch seine dialektische Komposition, seine Lichtatmosphäre und die subtile Soundinstallation einen synästhetischen Erfahrungsraum.

experience space

interpretation

Diese Art der Inszenierung, welche die Besucher zur eigenen Interpretation herausfordert, war in den 1990er Jahren noch unüblich, in ihrer Konsequenz nur aus Kunstausstellungen oder von Bühnenbildern bekannt. Die eindeutig exponatorientierte Ausstellung hatte das Ziel, die Aura der (scheinbar) alltäglichen Gegenstände auf unerwartete Weise und mit hohem emotionalem Wirkungsgrad zur Entfaltung zu bringen. Es ging um eine nachhaltige und dialogische Beziehung zwischen dem Exponat und seiner Bedeutung, aber auch zwischen den Exponaten und ihren Betrachtern. Es ging darum, die Besucher zum Staunen zu bringen, Provokation in positive Betroffenheit zu wandeln und eine nachhaltige Erinnerungswürdigkeit zu erzeugen.

positive concern

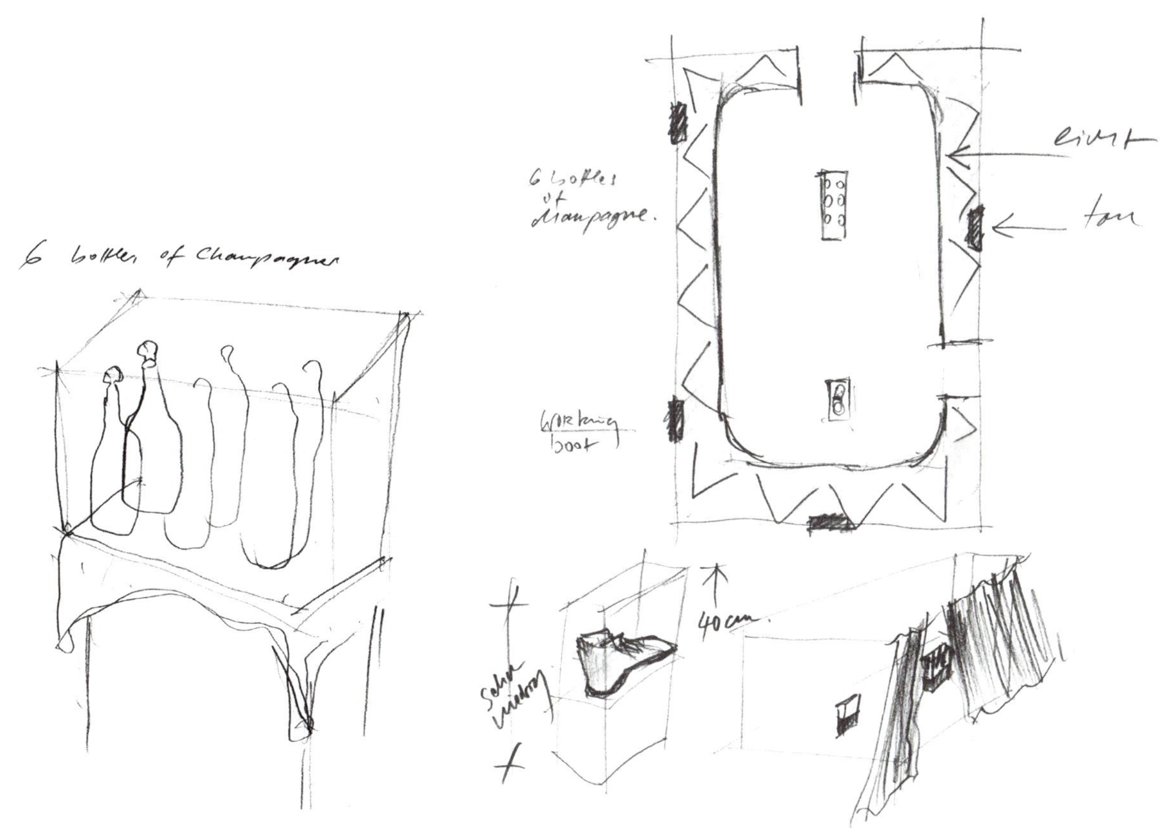

"Expedition Titanic"—Champagne Room—Dialectic setting of six bottles of Champagne and one worker's boot, 1997.

"Scenography is like a score: it orchestrates design tools like light, text, sound, or projection, and draws on dramaturgical structures from literature, film, theatre, or opera, combining all these elements into a choreography of space, narration, and experience." Uwe R. Brückner

Scenography as a holistic, multidisciplinary method of spatial design makes use of a multifaceted range of design tools.They can be applied in order to effectively combine the five basic parameters–content, object, space, recipient, and dramaturgy–and thus generate an integrative, scenographic setting.[35]

tools of scenography

The tools of scenography help to implement the key message and stage the objects and the conceptual ideas that have been derived from the content. Scenography instrumentalises media tools such as graphics, light, sound, digital media, projection, and film. These tools enable the designer to generate a synaesthetic experience that stimulates the senses. The tools can be used like instruments in an orchestra, as individual sounds are synchronised within a partitura to create a larger volume of sounds or music. The choice of instruments plays a decisive role in the realisation of a certain scenographic concept. They influence the way a staging is perceived as a design dominated by visual, acoustic, or multisensory aspects.

Als ganzheitliche und multidisziplinäre Methode für räumliches Gestalten bedient sich die Szenografie einer Vielzahl unterschiedlicher Gestaltungsinstrumente. Sie können in einer effektiven Kombination mit den fünf fundamentalen Parametern – Inhalt, Objekt, Raum, Rezipient und Dramaturgie – angewandt werden, um eine integrative Inszenierung mit szenografischen Qualitäten zu generieren. [35]

Die szenografischen Instrumente ermöglichen die Implementierung von Botschaften, die Inszenierung von Objekten und Konzepten, die aus den Inhalten abgeleitet oder entwickelt wurden. Szenografie instrumentalisiert Gestaltungsmedien wie Grafik, Licht, Ton/Klang/Musik, digitale Medien, Projektionen oder Film. Ihre Anwendung befähigt die Designer, synästhetische Erlebnisse zu erzeugen, die multisensorisch Sinne stimulieren. Sie können wie Instrumente eines Orchesters eingesetzt werden, als Solostimmen oder als synchronisiertes Ensemble, festgehalten in einer Partitur. Die Wahl der Instrumente spielt eine entscheidende Rolle, wenn es um die Umsetzung eines bestimmten szenografischen Konzepts geht. Sie beeinflussen die Wahrnehmung einer Inszenierung als eher visuell, akustisch oder multisensorisch.

35 See Atelier Brückner 2016, pp. 165 – 227; and Brückner and Greci 2016, pp. 54 – 79.

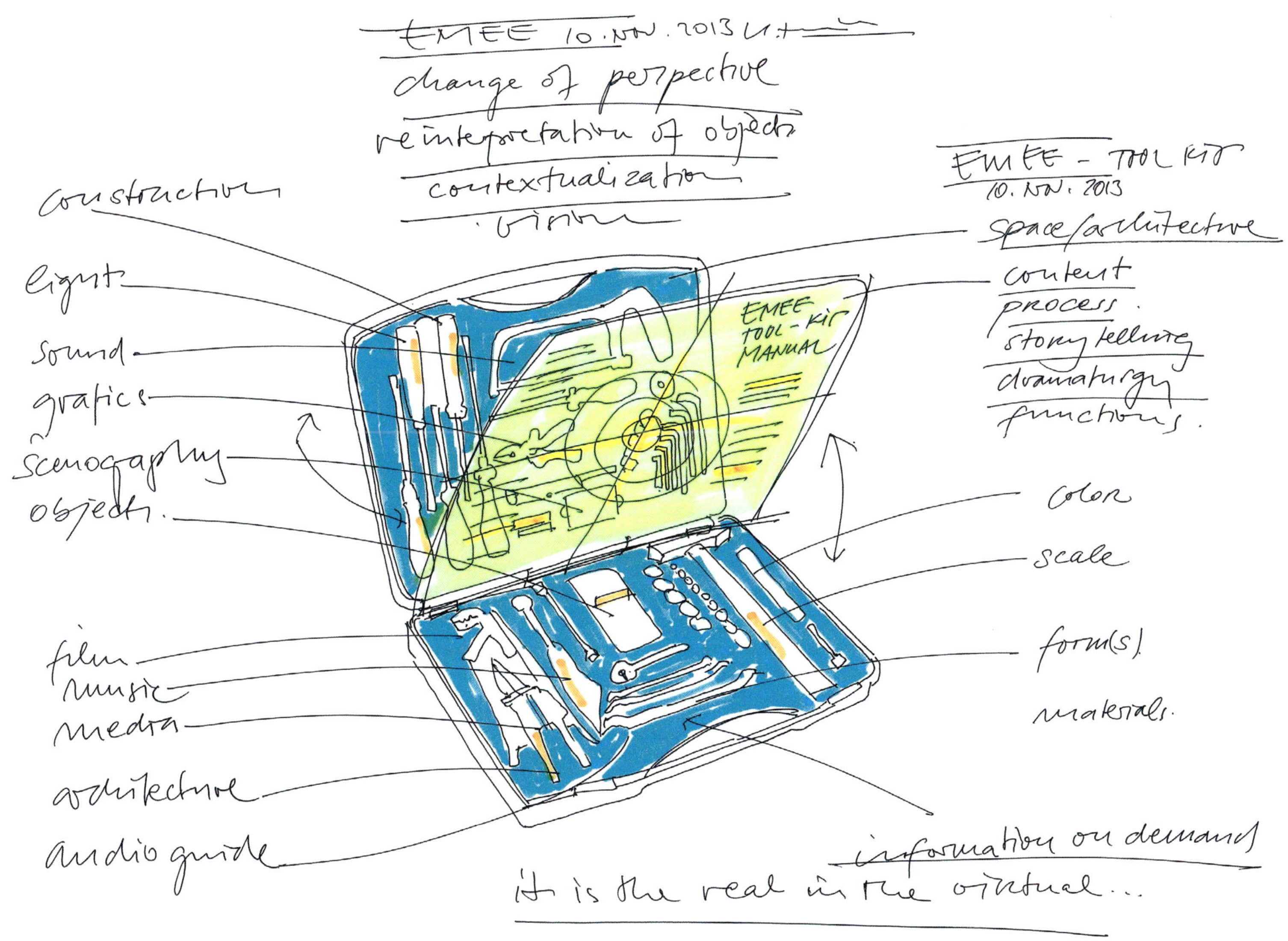

"EuroVision–Museum Exhibiting Europe (EMEE)"–Toolkit, 2013.

"Graphic design is an ubiquitous design medium: It is structure, layout, image, language or syntax– it's always there, even if you don't see it." Uwe R. Brückner

GRAPHIC DESIGN Graphic design is one of the most traditional design tools. Today, more than ever before, graphic design is constantly present in our everyday lives. Advertisements on the Internet, newspapers, and TV feed us constantly with designed messages delivered by means of pictures and typography. Ruedi Baur, a Swiss-French graphic designer, puts it in a nutshell when he says that everything is communication. As an interdisciplinary designer and pioneer in developing spatial graphic concepts, he emphasises the aspect of transience and permanence especially when it comes to the relationship between space and graphics. Baur mentions the flexibility of ever-changing messages in contrast to the finite nature of architecture.[36]

communication

In recent years, the discipline of exhibition graphics has developed at a very fast pace and has spread to all areas of design. Graphics are to be found everywhere, in the form of texts, images, illustrations, info graphics, and interactive media through to 3-D design. Graphic design can thus be described as a "space-forming medium" that is able to visualise and translate content, stories, and messages into narrative spaces.[37] The scenographic potential of graphic design is not restricted to the textual mediation of information.[38] But it is a tool that also helps to recontextualise objects and their stories. Graphic design can (co-)shape the character of a room and add value to it in the process. It can transform space into a narrative experience, into a walk-in story. Graphic design based on a consistently generated visualisation of content triggers an informative and emotional level of perception.

space-forming medium

36 Ruedi Baur, ed., Integral Ruedi Baur et Associés, Paris (Zurich, 2001).
37 See Atelier Brückner 2016, p. 217.
38 Ibid.

GRAFIK DESIGN Grafik ist eines der traditionellsten Gestaltungsinstrumente; heute ist sie omnipräsent. Werbung im Internet, Printmedien und TV-Spots füttern uns täglich mit Botschaften in Gestalt von Bilderfluten und Typografie. Ruedi Baur, der bekannte schweizerisch-französische Grafiker, bringt es auf den Punkt, wenn er sagt, dass (heute) alles Kommunikation sei. Als interdisziplinär arbeitender Pionier für Grafikkonzepte im Raum hebt er sowohl die Flüchtigkeit als auch die Dauerhaftigkeit der Zeichen hervor, speziell wenn es darum geht, eine Verbindung von Raum und Grafik herzustellen. Baur verweist auf die Flexibilität von sich ändernden Botschaften im Vergleich zur statischen Natur der Architektur.[36]

In den letzten Jahren hat sich die Ausstellungsgrafik rasant entwickelt und in fast alle Designfelder ausgebreitet. Grafik findet sich überall, in Texten, Bildgestaltung, Illustrationen, Informationsgrafiken, interaktiven Medien bis hinein ins 3-D-Design. Grafikdesign kann als „raumgestaltendes Medium" bezeichnet werden, das in der Lage ist, Inhalte zu visualisieren und Geschichten und Botschaften in narrative Räume zu übersetzen.[37] Das szenografische Potenzial von Grafikdesign ist dabei nicht reduziert auf die textliche Vermittlung von Inhalten, sondern hilft, Objekte und deren Geschichten zu rekontextualisieren.[38] So kann Grafik Charakter und Mehrwert eines Raums (mit)bestimmen. Sie kann Raum in ein Narrativum, in eine begehbare Story, transformieren. Inhaltskonsistente Grafik wirkt auf einer informativen und emotionalen Wahrnehmungsebene gleichermaßen.

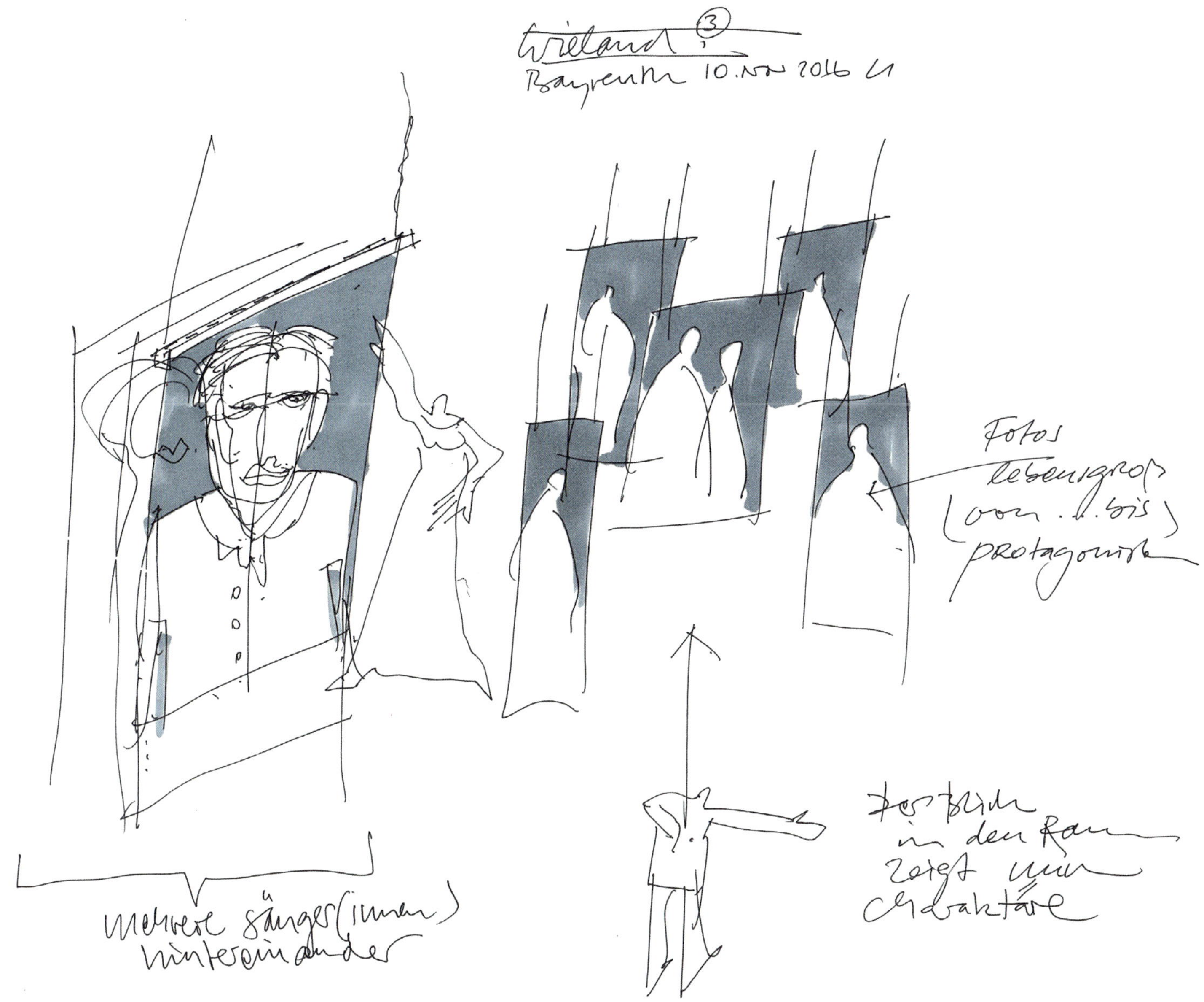

"Wieland Wagner"–Prelude, portraits of protagonists, 2016.

“Good scenography deeply depends on a light concept. Without light there is no reading, no taste, no lasting character. Three-dimensionality only comes with the light.” Uwe R. Brückner

aggregate states

LIGHT With the rapid development of connected technologies, light has become an influential design instrument for scenographers. Light is able to generate multifaceted aggregate states in a space that is valid for the object, the space itself, and the recipients. Light is bright or dimmed, warm or cold, diffuse or directed, documentary or mystical, static or dynamic. Light is a prerequisite for the ability to read and perceive things, subjects, spaces, or scenes. It tells stories and literally places objects in the right light.

Light is used as a tool of contemporary scenography and has physical, atmospheric, and narrative potential. First of all, we differentiate between daylight and artificial light–the former should be conditionable, the latter programmable. In the case of artificial or effect lighting we differentiate between static space light, precise exhibit light, dynamic scene-setting light, and a synchronised light choreography. Thanks to the development of LED technology and the programmability of individual light sources, designers have acquired a highly versatile and creative design tool.

space light

exhibit light

Space light creates the general atmosphere and ideally is adjusted to elements of the space such as ceilings, walls, and floor. It illuminates the space, and it can affect the spatial tonalities, colours, and temperatures as well as the character of the space or architecture. Exhibit light ensures the optimal plastic presentation of objects. It aims to reveal the object’s narrative potential, to emphasise its auratic character, and to integrate it into the dramaturgical structure. Exhibit light is, of course, used for museum objects in accordance with conservational requirements and needs to be used sensitively.[39]

scene-setting light

Scene-setting light plays a decisive role in how objects are perceived. For the objects it is not only necessary to be seen, but also to be understood or even admired. Smart scene-setting light can establish a relationship between object, space, and recipient and also convey messages

39 Idid, p. 181.

LICHT Mit der rapiden Entwicklung vernetzbarer Technologien ist das Licht zu einem einflussreichen Gestaltungsinstrument für Szenografen geworden. Licht ist in der Lage, diverse räumliche Aggregatzustände zu erzeugen – das gilt für das Objekt, den Raum selbst und die Rezipienten. Licht ist hell oder gedimmt, warm oder kalt, direkt oder diffus, dokumentarisch oder mystisch, statisch oder dynamisch. Licht ist Voraussetzung zum Lesen oder Erfahren von Dingen, Sujets, Räumen oder Szenen. Es beleuchtet Geschichten und setzt Objekte buchstäblich ins rechte Licht.

Zeitgenössische Szenografie benutzt die physischen, atmosphärischen und narrativen Potenziale des Instruments Licht. Wir unterscheiden zunächst zwischen Tageslicht und Kunstlicht – ersteres sollte konditionierbar sein, letzteres programmierbar. Beim Kunst- oder Effektlicht differenzieren wir zwischen statischem Raumlicht, präzisem Exponatlicht, dynamischem Inszenierungslicht und einer synchronisierten Lichtchoreografie. Mit der Entwicklung der LED-Technologie und der Möglichkeit, einzelne Lichtquellen individuell zu programmieren, haben die Gestalter ein vielseitiges Gestaltungsinstrument an die Hand bekommen.

Das Raumlicht bestimmt die elementare Atmosphäre und korrespondiert im besten Fall mit den Raumelementen wie Decke, Wand und Boden. Es illuminiert den Raum und bestimmt die Tonalität, die Farben, das Temperaturgefühl und somit den Charakter des Raums, der Architektur. Das Exponatlicht dient der optimalen, plastischen Präsentation von Objekten. Die narrativen Potenziale der Objekte sollen ans Licht gebracht, deren auratischer Charakter hervorgehoben und durch dynamische Beleuchtung die Objekte in eine dramaturgische Struktur eingebunden werden. Selbstverständlich muss das Exponatlicht den konservatorischen Anforderungen gerecht und entsprechend sensibel eingesetzt werden.[39]

Das Inszenierungslicht spielt eine entscheidende Rolle für die Wahrnehmung von Objekten – für

and narratives. Scene-setting light has an interpreting and commenting effect, thus helping to create contexts. Indeed it performs a dramaturgical function. Dynamic light is synchronised with other interactive media or follows a light choreography. Stage-setting light helps the visitor to experience the space, to structure the story, and to navigate the visitors. It has huge dramaturgical potential and synchronises the space light with the stage-setting light to form the entire lighting concept.[40] At the end of the day, it determines our and the things' perception.

diese geht es nicht nur darum, gesehen, sondern verstanden bzw. bewundert zu werden. Raffiniert eingesetzt kann Inszenierungslicht eine Beziehung zwischen Objekt, Raum und Betrachter erzeugen und Geschichten und Botschaften vermitteln.
Es kann interpretieren und kommentieren, es hilft zu kontextualisieren und hat eine dramaturgische Funktion. Dynamisches Licht ist mit anderen interaktiven Medien synchronisiert oder folgt einer Lichtchoreografie. Inszenierungslicht hilft, den Raum erfahrbar zu machen, die Erzählung zu strukturieren und die Besucher zu navigieren.
Es hat ein enormes dramaturgisches Potenzial und führt, synchronisiert mit dem Raumlicht, zu einem ganzheitlichen Lichtkonzept.[40] Letztlich steuert es unsere Wahrnehmung und die der Dinge.

light choreography

40 Ibid., p. 181.

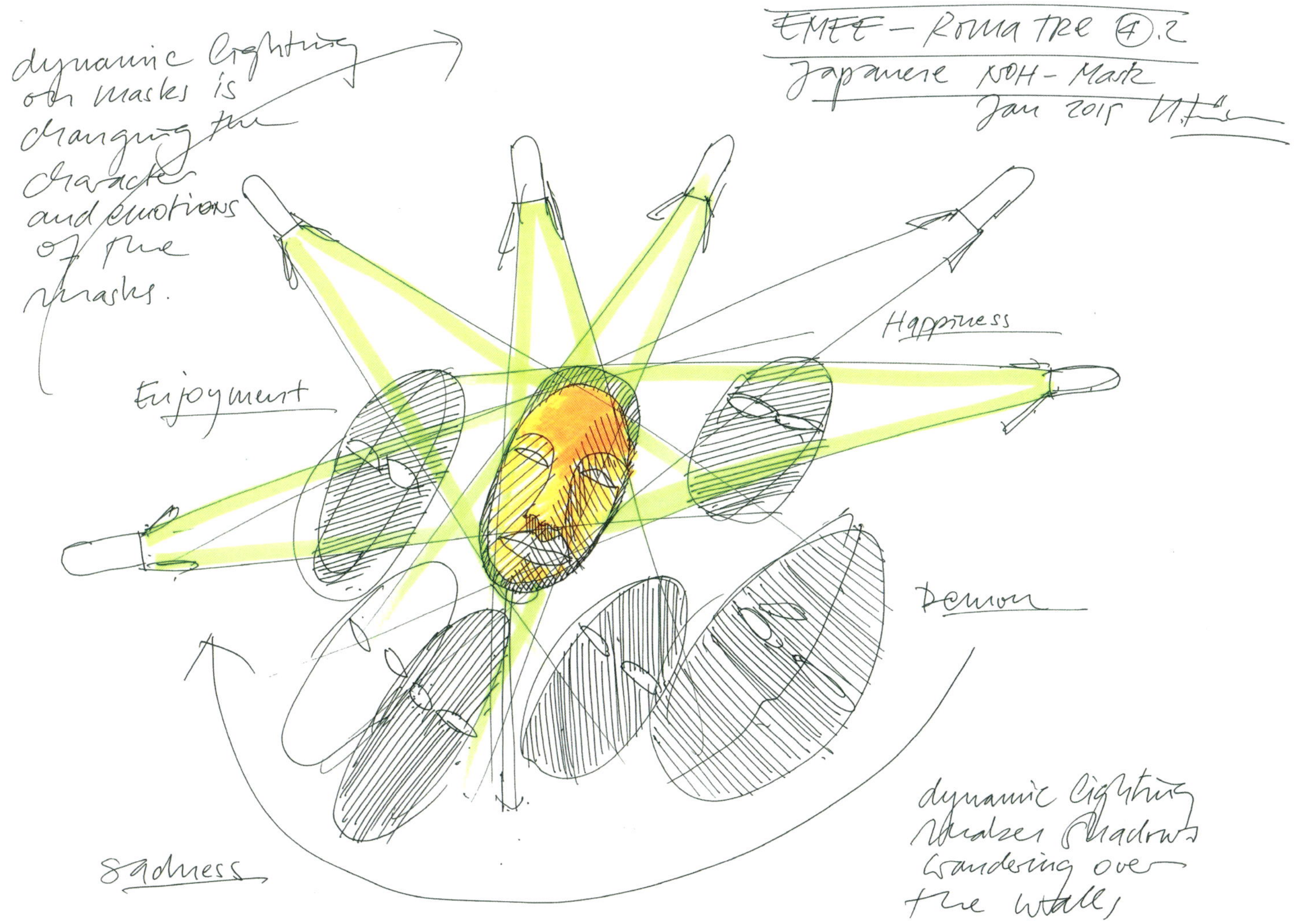

"EuroVision–Museums Exhibiting Europe (EMEE)"–Dynamic Lighting, 2015.

"More than any of our other senses, hearing, as an archaic level of reception, controls our awareness of our surroundings and, in the form of noise, sound, and music, appeals to the intuitive, noncognitive, and unconscious in us." [41]

SOUND Sound–tones, music, noises, or audio plays–was long underestimated as a tool of scenography–be it through its presence or absence–but is now increasingly attracting the attention of designers. New technologies are supporting the development of new narrative strategies and different kinds of sound concepts. Combined and synchronised with light or projections, sound has an enormous impact on synaesthetic reception. What is important is that the sound experiences are content-based and applied to guide what the visitors perceive. Sound can control their behaviour in the staging, condition their movements, or even generate an immersive sense of space. It can also support narration or create a certain atmosphere.

new technologies

Our ability of auditory perception–a complex interaction between the ear and the brain–is the tool that defines what we perceive beyond what we see. Sound installations are invisible, and yet their acoustic stimulation causes inner images to appear in the mind of the visitor. With each ring of the doorbell or the barking of a dog, they are directly connected to a picture based on what we have learned or experienced which appears immediately in our minds as the sound is heard. The things we hear evoke the things we see.[42]

sound installations

Sound can be divided into various categories: spatial sound, atmospheric sound, individual sound, soundtracks for several sources of sound, and audio plays. An open, spatial sound can give a space a certain rhythm, a more or less perceivable beat, which can enhance or even create the intended atmosphere. Atmospheric sound produces a kind of characteristic noise floor for themes or exhibits. It appeals to the emotional character

sound

41 See Atelier Brückner 2016, p. 209.
42 Ibid.

SOUND Ton – oder auch Klang, Musik, Geräusche und Hörspiele – als Gestaltungsinstrument der Szenografie war lange Zeit unterschätzt, sei es wegen seiner Präsenz oder Absenz, doch er wird zunehmend bedeutsam für die Gestalter. Neue Technologien ermöglichen die Entwicklung neuer Erzählstrategien und Soundkonzepte. Ton, kombiniert und synchronisiert mit Licht oder Projektionen, hat enormen Einfluss auf eine synästhetische Wahrnehmung. Dabei ist eine inhaltskongruente Verwendung entscheidend für die Wahrnehmung der Besucher. Ton kann ihr Verhalten in der Inszenierung steuern, Bewegungen konditionieren oder ein immersives Raumgefühl erzeugen. Ton kann die Narration unterstützen oder eine Atmosphäre erzeugen.

Unsere akustische Aufnahmefähigkeit – eine komplexe Interaktion zwischen Gehör und Gehirn – erzeugt Wahrnehmung jenseits des Sichtbaren. Soundinstallationen sind unsichtbar, doch ihre akustischen Reize provozieren Vorstellungen und erzeugen innere Bilder im Kopf des Besuchers. So verbinden wir jedes Türklingeln oder Hundebellen mit einem gelernten oder erfahrenen Bild, das synchron zum Hören erscheint. Dinge, die wir hören, evozieren, was wir sehen.[42]

Ton kann differenziert werden in Raumton, atmosphärischen Ton, individuell gerichteten Ton, Tonspuren für mehrere Tonquellen und Hörspiele. Ein offener Raumton kann einem Raum einen bestimmten Rhythmus geben, einen mehr oder minder wahrnehmbaren Beat, der die intendierte Atmosphäre verstärkt oder gar prägt. Atmosphärischer Ton erzeugt eine Art charakteristisches „Grundrauschen" für Themen oder Exponate. Er unterstützt das emotional, sinnlich erfahrbare Raumbild oder die empathische Stimmung der Besucher. Individuell gerichteter Ton konzentriert sich auf einen definierten Bereich, etwa durch Richtlautsprecher, oder er ist mit interaktiven

of the space and the empathetic mood of the visitors. Individual sound is focused on certain areas and is provided by loudspeakers, which have a directional focus or can be connected with interactive devices. Audio plays are narrative elements; voices or music mainly try to approach the listeners in a more intimate, dialogical way to convey stories and messages.

Sound can trigger emotions, can dynamically change the volume of the room, show absence or presence periodically to create a rhythm, and be combined skilfully to form a sound choreography or synchronised with lighting or other electronic media. Sound as scenographic tool can lead the visitor to another level of perception.

Stationen verknüpft. Soundtracks werden meist eingesetzt, um verschiedene Medien, wie Musik, Film, Animationen, mit einer Tonspur zu synchronisieren. Hörspiele sind narrative Instrumente, die über Stimmen und Geräusche einen intimeren, eher empathischen Zugang zu den Hörern ermöglichen, um Geschichten oder Botschaften zu vermitteln.

Ton kann Emotionen auslösen, Raumvolumen verändern, Rhythmus durch periodische An- oder Abwesenheit erzeugen und geschickt zu einer Soundchoreografie kombiniert werden oder Licht und andere elektronische Medien synchronisieren. Ton als Gestaltungsinstrument führt die Besucher auf eine höhere sinnliche Wahrnehmungsebene.

sound choreography

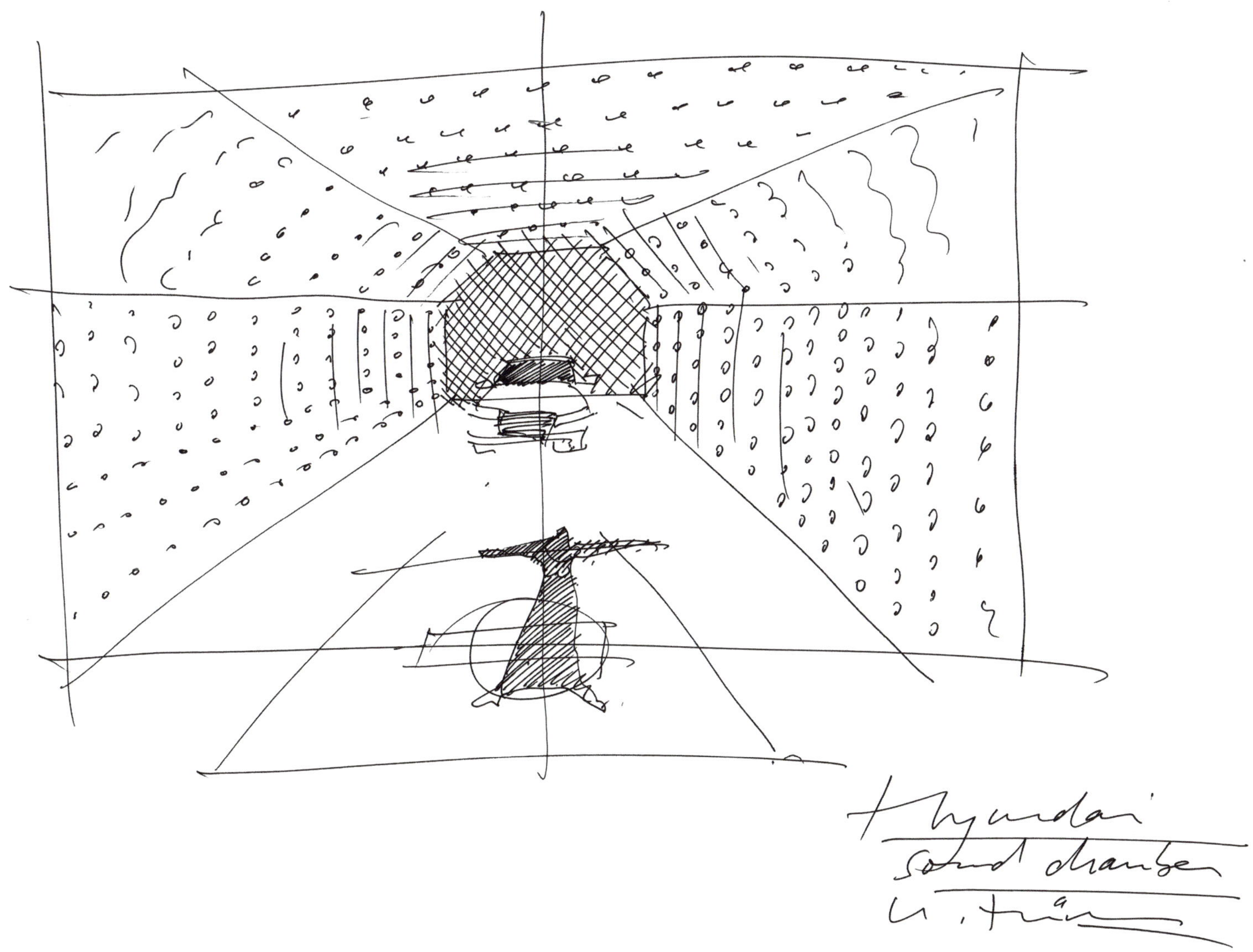

"Hyundai Motorstudio Goyang"–Sound Chamber, 2017.

"We never propose digital media for its own sake, but only use it if no other media is able to convey or express a certain content or message. At the end of the day it's a question of dosing." Uwe R. Brückner

communication technologies

DIGITAL MEDIA The increasing, at best carefully measured, use of contemporary digital media and electronic communication technologies makes it possible to convey complex or time-based content, for example, film or acoustic content. This technical achievement should be understood as a natural reaction to the constantly changing behaviour with regard to how messages are received and communicated within multicultural societies in a globalised world. Digital media have an instrumental character and achieve specific effects in the process of reception. The medium itself becomes the messenger. Digital media can be understood as a window to hidden worlds in that they make contents and objects accessible, decode complex interrelationships, and convey information and messages. They generate changing aggregate states[43] and enable leaps of time and scale.

individualised and participatory access

↗ p. 246

Furthermore, digital media enable individualised and participatory access to knowledge in real time. Visitors can individually explore several layers of information and decide where, when, and how much information they want to retrieve (information on demand).

media stations space-forming media

Digital media are able to transfer light, images, texts, films, sounds, and music, virtually or physically, playfully address various levels of perception, and allow an understanding of more sophisticated content. A general distinction can be made between "media stations" and "space-forming media"[44] or between spaces staged with media or media architectures. What they have in common is that they act as gateways for visitors to gain secret insights and explore content.

DIGITAL MEDIA Der zunehmende und bestenfalls wohldosierte Einsatz von zeitgemäßen digitalen Medien und elektronischen Kommunikationstechnologien macht es möglich, komplexe oder zeitbasierte, beispielsweise filmische oder akustische Inhalte zu vermitteln. Diese Errungenschaft sollte als natürliche Reaktion auf das sich ständig wandelnde Rezeptionsverhalten multikulturell geprägter Gesellschaften in einer globalisierten Welt verstanden werden. Digitale Medien haben instrumentalen Charakter und erzielen spezifische Wirkungen im Rezeptionsprozess. Das Medium wird selbst zum Botschafter, zum Botschaftenträger. Digitale Medien können als Fenster zu verborgenen Welten fungieren, indem sie Objekte inszenieren, Geschichten zugänglich machen, komplexe Zusammenhänge dekodieren, Informationen vermitteln und Botschaften erlebbar machen. Digitale Medien erlauben wechselnde Aggregatzustände[43] sowie Zeit- und Maßstabsprünge.

Darüber hinaus erlauben digitale Medien einen individuellen und partizipatorischen Zugang zu Wissen in Realzeit. Besucher können verschiedene Informationsebenen selbstbestimmt explorieren und dabei gewünschte Informationen abrufen (Information on Demand). Digitale Medien können Licht, Bilder, Texte, Filme, Klänge und Musik virtuell oder physisch übermitteln, verschiedene Wahrnehmungsebenen spielerisch ansprechen und vor allem komplexeres Verstehen ermöglichen. Grundsätzlich ist zwischen „Medienstationen" und „raumbildenden Medien"[44], medieninszenierten Räumen oder Mediatekturen zu unterscheiden. Gemeinsam ist ihnen, dass sie Einblicke in Verborgenes erlauben und Inhalte explorierbar machen.

43 In physics, the aggregate state describes the changing state of a material depending on pressure or temperature–solid, liquid or gas. Transferred to spaces, the Design Tools change a room to such an extent that they figuratively change their received aggregate state. The substance remains the same, but the feel of the space and the way it is perceived by the beholder change accordingly.

44 Ibid., p. 187.

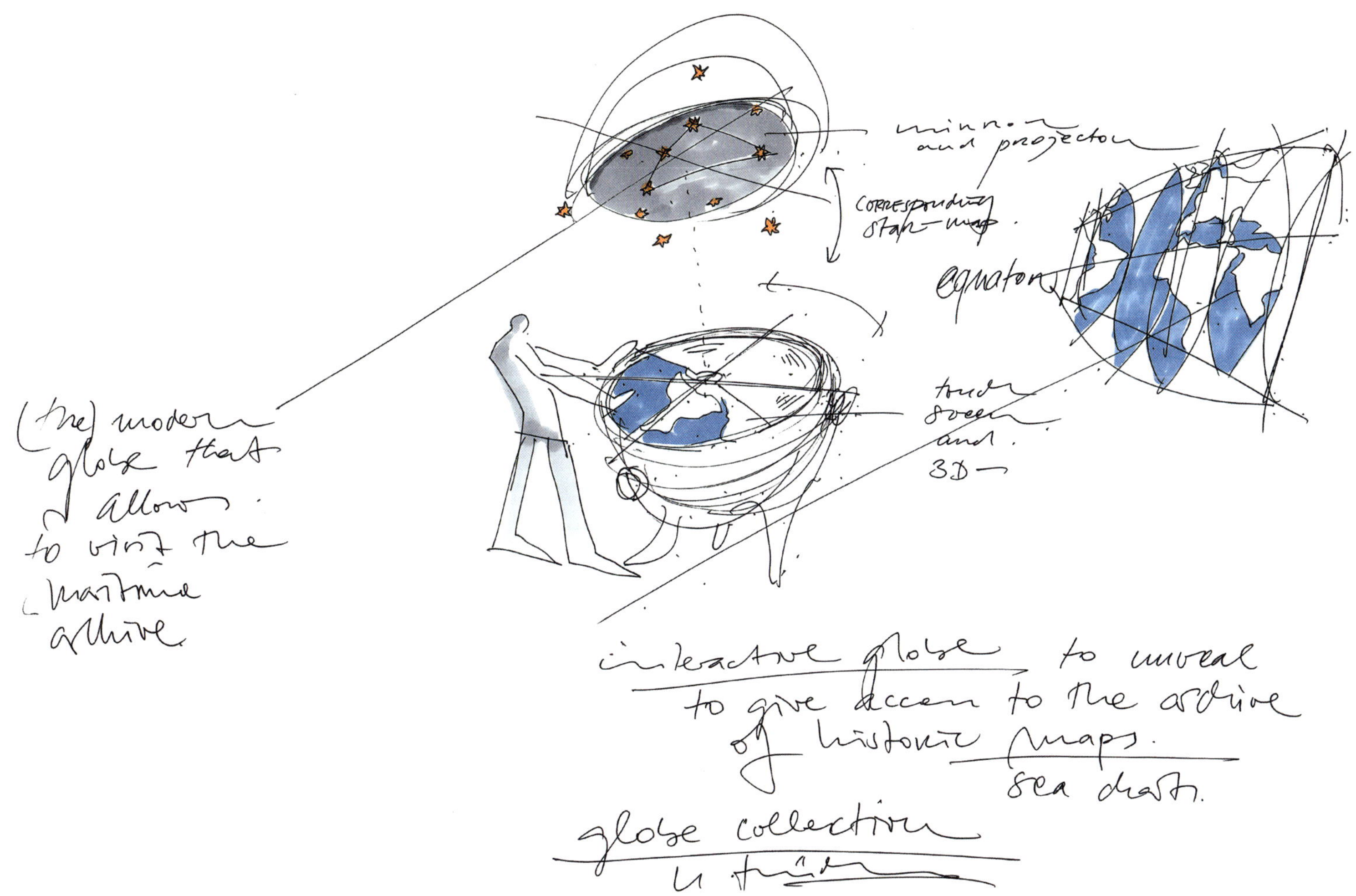

"Het Scheepvaartmuseum" – Interactive Globe, 2007.

CONTENT

FORM FOLLOWS CONTENT

Uwe R. Brückner and Linda Greci

“Form follows content is the design philosophy of ATELIER BRÜCKNER and the leading principle for all our projects.” Uwe R. Brückner

CONTENT

"FORM FOLLOWS CONTENT"

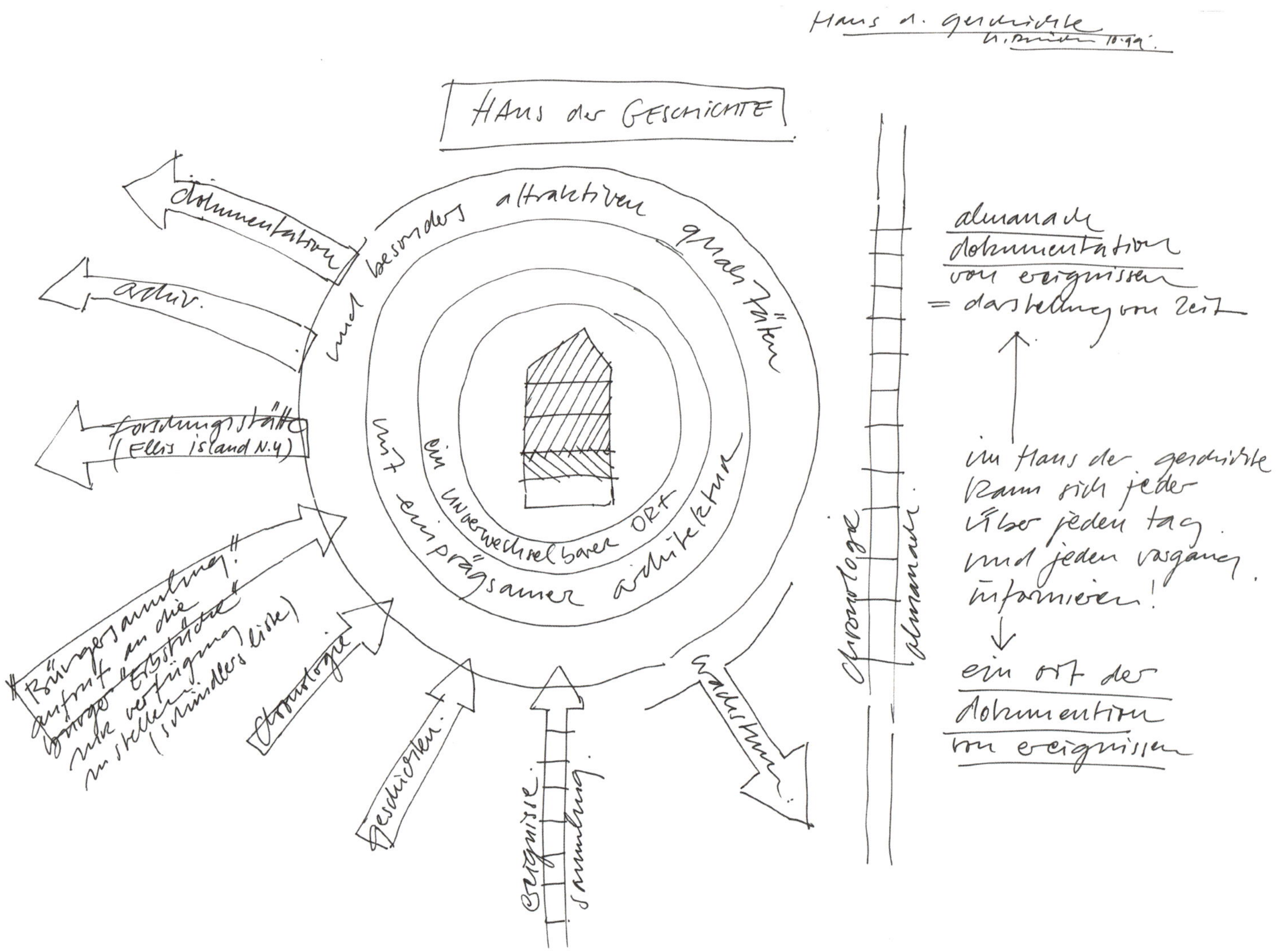

"House of History Baden-Württemberg"–The Self-perception, 1999.

“Form follows content” is the guiding principle of ATELIER BRÜCKNER, derived from Louis Sullivan’s maxim “form follows function.”[45] In his most famous essay, “The Tall Office Building Artistically Considered” (1896), Sullivan uses this dictum to describe his opinion that the outside shape of a building must follow the functions inside or, to put it another way, that form is derived from its function.[46] “Form follows content” should be understood as a transformation on a second level. It goes beyond the maxim that design is derived from its functionality in that it translates ideas, content, and messages into form, giving them not only form but also attitude and significance in the process.[47] It is an interpretation of content with design means and a translation of the non-physical into a walk-in, three-dimensional space. It is in this tradition of taking form and giving form to content that the work of ATELIER BRÜCKNER is rooted.

“Form follows content” is also the design approach of one of the most influential international contemporary schools of design, the Bauhaus. The close relationship of scenography to the Bauhaus movement is clear from its commitment to giving form to content and to a cross-disciplinary approach.[48] The Bauhaus aimed, amongst other things, to create a new, cross-disciplinary art of building, striving to reunite all types of artistic expression–sculpture, painting, arts and crafts. Scenography is also committed to a multidisciplinary approach.

Giving content form raises the question of what content is. Content means the narrative of an exhibition: source, storytelling, plot, and message. Content refers to objects, which are staged, but also to intangible, abstract information that is to be conveyed. Storytelling is a narrative and communication technique that transports knowledge and can involve the visitor actively, interactively, or reactively in a story. In this way, the content is experienced with all the senses and the story being told is the focus of attention. At ATELIER BRÜCKNER, “storytelling” has come to refer to the specific narrative means and techniques applied in the conception of the exhibition.[49]

45 See Atelier Brückner 2016, p. 60.
46 Louis Sullivan’s maxim “form follows function” was coined from a statement of his office partner Dankmar Adler, who had in turn taken his inspiration from Henri Labrouste.
47 See Atelier Brückner 2016, p. 60.
48 Ibid.
49 Ibid., p. 67.

form follows content

„Form follows content“ lautet der Leitsatz des ATELIER BRÜCKNER, der sich ableitet von Louis Sullivans Maxime „Form follows function“.[45] In einem seiner berühmtesten Aufsätze, „The Tall Office Building Artistically Considered“ (1896), beschreibt Sullivan damit, dass die äußeren Formen in einem Gebäude den inneren Funktionen folgen müssen oder dass sich die Form von seiner Funktion ableitet.[46] Entsprechend sollte „form follows content“ als eine Transformation zweiter Ordnung verstanden werden. Sie geht über die Maxime hinaus, dass sich Gestaltung aus ihrer Funktionalität ableitet, nämlich in dem Sinne, dass sie Ideen, Inhalte und Botschaften in Form übersetzt und ihnen dabei nicht nur Form, sondern auch Haltung und Bedeutung gibt.[47] Es handelt sich um eine Interpretation von Inhalten mit gestalterischen Mitteln und um eine Übersetzung von Nichtphysischem in einen begehbaren, dreidimensionalen Raum. Dieser Tradition von Formwerden und Formgeben von Inhalten ist die Arbeit des Ateliers verhaftet.

translation

Bauhaus

„Form follows content“ ist als Gestaltungshaltung auch von einer der einflussreichsten internationalen Gestaltungsschulen der Moderne geprägt, dem Bauhaus. In der Verpflichtung, Inhalten Form zu geben, und dem Postulat der Transdisziplinarität wird die Nähe der Szenografie zur Bauhaus-Bewegung deutlich.[48] Das Bauhaus strebte unter anderem nach einer neuen transdisziplinären Baukunst, nach der Wiedervereinigung aller werkkünstlerischen Disziplinen – Bildhauerei, Malerei, Kunstgewerbe und Handwerk. Diesem Streben nach Multidisziplinarität ist auch die Szenografie verpflichtet.

content

„Inhalten Form geben“ eröffnet schließlich auch die Frage danach, was Inhalt überhaupt ist. Inhalt bedeutet das Narrativ einer Ausstellung: Quelle, Storytelling, Plot und Botschaft. Inhalt bezieht sich auf die Objekte, die inszeniert werden, aber auch auf immaterielle, abstrakte Informationen, die vermittelt werden sollen. Storytelling ist eine Erzähl- und Kommunikationstechnik, die Wissen vermittelt und den Besucher aktiv, interaktiv oder reaktiv in eine Geschichte involvieren kann. So wird der Inhalt mit allen Sinnen erlebbar und die erzählte Geschichte erfährt Aufmerksamkeit und Konzentration. Storytelling hat sich im Atelier als Begriff etabliert, der sich auf die spezifischen narrativen Mittel und Techniken bei der Ausstellungskonzeption bezieht.[49]

storytelling

It is the refinement with which a story is narrated that arouses the necessary curiosity in the recipient, and it is the surprising staging which fulfills the thus provoked interest. Scenography supports and promotes the sensory approach to complex content and the emotional access to seemingly unwieldy topics. It builds a bridge to the object and provides the storyboard to its stories. The object becomes the subject, the protagonist, the combatants, or sportsmen on Greek vases start to run, to dance, to move rhythmically until the observer can almost hear the fast, heavy breathing of the athletes or the light-footed dance steps of the haetera.

storyboard

The staging sets the scene for the object and narrates the hidden, undiscovered stories; the imagination fills the gaps between the fragments; and the association provokes us to think up what is missing. The result is an image in the mind of the recipients; they are part of the staging and the story. And the designer has become the director. None of this works without a prelude, without dramaturgy with an arc of suspense, various acts, and a number of highlights; and none of this works without a congenial scenography.

design process

During the design process, the question that is raised again and again is how the content can be used as a creative resource and how the content can be expanded in the space or translated into a spatial experience. How can complex topics be approached?

title, subtitle, content and message

plot

The first thing is the examination of the sources, the objects, and possible stories. Then four questions have to be answered and described on no more than one page, regardless of how big or complex the project is: title, subtitle, content, and message. And we explore the questions: Which stories and messages are to be conveyed? How can a story be condensed into a plot? The plot should contain the most important events and actions which follows a narrative, often Aristotelian structure with prologue, main section, and epilogue. And a golden thread should be defined,

Es ist die Raffinesse des Erzählens, welche die notwendige Neugierde beim Rezipienten auslöst, und es ist die überraschende Inszenierung, die das provozierte Interesse stillt. Die Szenografie unterstützt und fördert die sinnliche Annäherung an komplexe Inhalte und den emotionalen Zugang zu vermeintlich sperrigen Themen. Sie baut eine Brücke zum Objekt und liefert das Storyboard zu seinen Geschichten. Das Objekt wird zum Subjekt, zum Protagonisten, die Kämpfer oder Sportler auf den griechischen Vasen beginnen zu laufen, zu tanzen, sich rhythmisch zu bewegen, bis der Betrachter vermeintlich den schnellen, heftigen Atem der Athleten hört oder die leichtfüßigen Tanzschritte der Hetären vernimmt.

Die Inszenierung setzt das Objekt in Szene und erzählt die verborgenen, unentdeckten Geschichten, die Imagination füllt die Lücke zwischen den Fragmenten und die Assoziation provoziert uns, das Fehlende weiterzudenken. Und schließlich entsteht das Bild im Kopf der Betrachter, sie seien Teil der Inszenierung und der Geschichte. Spätestens dann ist der Gestalter zum Regisseur geworden. All das geht nicht ohne Vorspiel, ohne Dramaturgie mit Spannungsbogen, diversen Akten und verschiedenen Höhepunkten, all das geht nicht ohne eine kongeniale Szenografie.

Während des Gestaltungsprozesses stellt sich somit immer wieder die Frage, wie Inhalt als Ressource der Kreativität genutzt wird und wie Inhalt in den Raum oder in ein räumliches Erlebnis übersetzt werden kann. Wie nähert man sich komplexen Themen an?

Zu Beginn werden immer die Quellen, die Objekte und die möglichen Geschichten untersucht. Dann sollten vier Fragen beantwortet und auf maximal einer Seite beschrieben werden, egal wie groß oder komplex das Projekt ist: Titel, Untertitel, Inhalt und Botschaft. Schließlich gehen wir den Fragen nach, welche Geschichten und Botschaften zu vermitteln sind und wie man die Geschichte zu einem Plot kondensieren kann. Der Plot sollte die wichtigsten Ereignisse und Handlungen

content matrix

which runs through the story and thus through the exhibition. A content matrix as methodological instrument can be used to develop a structure for the storyline and the plot. The matrix serves as reference system for the whole concept and comprises all the design parameters and instruments. The scenographer can thus "form" the parameter content in the context of a holistic conception.

At the end of the day, the main hallmark of a good exhibition is content, and it is the content that materially influences its form and design and conveys its significance and message.

beinhalten, die einer narrativen, oftmals aristotelischen Struktur mit Prolog, Hauptteil und Epilog folgt. Und es sollte ein roter Faden definiert werden, der durch die Geschichte und somit durch die Ausstellung führt. Mithilfe einer Inhaltsmatrix als methodologischem Instrument kann eine Struktur für die Storyline und den Plot entwickelt werden. Die Matrix dient als Bezugssystem für das Gesamtkonzept und umfasst alle Gestaltungsparameter und -instrumente. Der Szenograf vermag so den Parameter „Inhalt" im Kontext einer holistischen Konzeption zu „formen".

Inhalt ist schließlich das, was eine gute Ausstellung vornehmlich prägt, was ihre Form und Gestalt wesentlich bestimmt und was ihre Bedeutung und Aussage spiegelt.

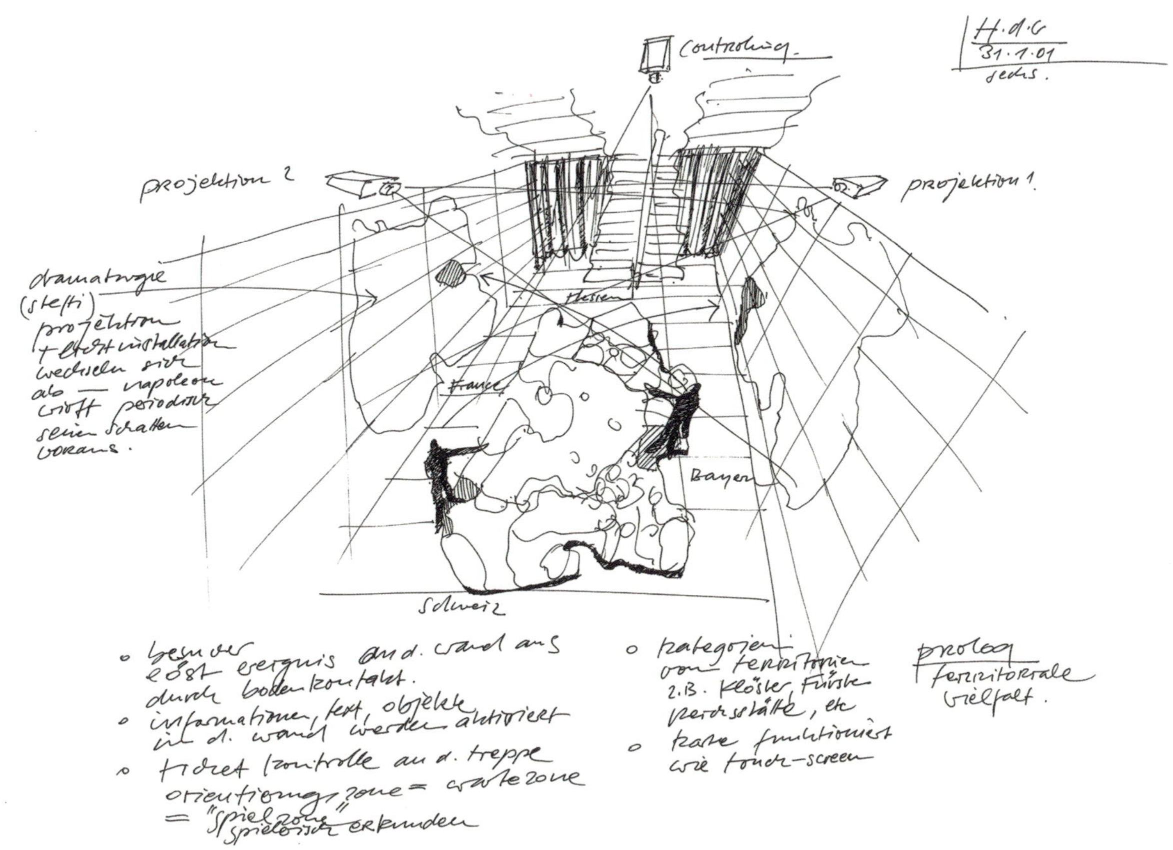

"House of History Baden-Württemberg"–Interactive Map, 2001.

MUSEUMS AS PERFORMATIVE SPACES "We are all actors" was the famous diagnosis of human interaction made in 1959 by Canadian sociologist Erving Goffman. According to him, social interaction determines a fundamentally theatrical moment which, depending on the situation, makes people act in a certain way at various stages of their lives. What Goffman discovered for microsociology was later claimed by the post-structuralist and the post-modernist movements and taken a step further, coming to the conclusion that all culture had a performative or a stage-setting dimension. This means that culture does not just depict reality but at the same time creates it. This paradigmatic new approach shifted the perspective from content to form or–to be more precise–to the content-shaping power of the cultural form. The classical preference of the internal was replaced by a new acknowledgement of the external. The essence shifted from the depths to the surface. From now on, attention no longer had to be drawn to the illusion of reality, but to the reality of the illusion.

It is thanks to this intellectual climate that museum scenography was established as a separate discipline and ATELIER BRÜCKNER advanced to a successful designer of museums and exhibitions. While older museum theory considered the content or the exhibits as decisive, Uwe R. Brückner correctly argues "You cannot not stage!" Indeed, it appears naïve to interpret, say, the "White Cube" of art galleries as a neutral space. The magic word in this context is "staging" that allowed the entry–beyond the enjoyment of art of the educated middle class–into a world of sensual perception, of emotional evocation, of the downright physical experience of culture. Such cultural experience is based on an anthropology, which understands people not just as cognitive but also as sensual beings whose sensory regime allows them to explore the world through a plethora of possibilities in order to obtain insights and experiences. In the context of staging, the expert in comparative studies Hans Ulrich Gumbrecht therefore talks about the "production of the presence" which places itself at the affective service of aesthetic experience.

It is this playful "production of the presence" which has been the hallmark of the work of ATELIER BRÜCKNER from the outset. Meanwhile more than 200 both narrative and multimedia exhibitions and themed worlds that the Stuttgart-based office has staged worldwide bear testimony to this. For ATELIER BRÜCKNER, the composition of (syn)aesthetic themed spaces makes interdisciplinary cooperation compulsory, involving directors, light designers, graphic designers, media designers, and many other artists.

MUSEEN ALS PERFORMATIVE RÄUME „Wir alle spielen Theater", so lautete 1959 die berühmte Diagnose der menschlichen Interaktion durch den kanadischen Soziologen Erving Goffman. Demnach bestimmt das soziale Miteinander ein grundsätzlich theatrales Moment, das den Menschen je nach Situation auf verschiedenen Bühnen des Lebens agieren lässt. Was Goffman für die Mikrosoziologie festgestellt hat, nahmen später der Poststrukturalismus und die Postmoderne – die zu dem Schluss gelangten, dass sämtliche Kultur eine performative bzw. eine inszenatorische eigene Dimension habe – für sich noch viel weitreichender in Anspruch. Kultur bildet demzufolge nicht nur die Wirklichkeit ab, sondern kreiert sie gleichermaßen. Dieser paradigmatisch neue Ansatz verschob die Perspektive vom Inhalt zur Form oder – präziser formuliert – zur inhaltlich formativen Kraft der kulturellen Form. Dadurch wich die klassische Bevorzugung des Inneren einer neuen Anerkennung des Äußeren. Die Essenz verlagerte sich von der Tiefe an die Oberfläche. Von nun an galt es, die Aufmerksamkeit nicht mehr auf die Illusion der Wirklichkeit, sondern auf die Wirklichkeit der Illusion zu richten.

Es ist dieses geistige Klima, dem die museale Szenografie ihre Etablierung als eigenständige Disziplin und das ATELIER BRÜCKNER seinen Aufstieg als erfolgreicher Gestalter von Museen und Ausstellungen verdankt. Hielt die ältere Museologie einzig die Inhalte oder die Exponate für ausschlaggebend, entgegnete ihnen Uwe R. Brückner zu Recht: „Man kann nicht nicht inszenieren!" In der Tat erscheint es geradezu naiv, etwa den „White Cube" von Kunstgalerien als einen neutralen Raum aufzufassen. Demgegenüber ist „Inszenierung" das Zauberwort, das – jenseits bildungsbürgerlichen Kunstgenusses – den Eintritt in eine Welt der sinnlichen Erkenntnis, der emotionalen Evokation, der geradezu körperlichen Erfahrung von Kultur eröffnet. Solche Kulturerfahrung geht von einer Anthropologie aus, die den Menschen nicht nur als ein kognitives, sondern als ein sinnliches Wesen begreift, dessen sensorisches Regime ihm die Welt in einer Fülle von Erkenntnis- und Erlebnismöglichkeiten erschließt. Im Kontext von Inszenierungen spricht der Komparatist Hans Ulrich Gumbrecht deshalb von der „Produktion von Präsenz", die sich in den affektiven Dienst des ästhetischen Erlebens stellt.

Es ist diese geradezu spielerische „Produktion von Präsenz", die die Arbeit des ATELIER BRÜCKNER von Anfang an auszeichnet. Davon zeugen inzwischen über 200 ebenso narrative wie multimediale Ausstellungen und Erlebniswelten, die das Stuttgarter Büro weltweit in Szene gesetzt hat. Die Komposition von (syn)ästhetischen Erlebnisräumen macht für das ATELIER BRÜCKNER die interdisziplinäre Kooperation zur Pflicht, die Regisseure, Lichtdesigner,

It is not surprising that Uwe R. Brückner himself started his scenographic career in the theatre, gripped by the idea of a "Gesamtkunstwerk."

At the end of the day, the stagings of ATELIER BRÜCKNER create performative spaces, which activate visitors. They allow a spatial practice, which aims to annex the spaces, spaces that will never be finished but will continue to evolve.

Those who grasp such museum spaces as public spaces will inevitably accord a political dimension to the spatial experiences this allows. For such spatial configurations require civil actors who use stagings in the museum to create a public sphere through performative means. Very much in the spirit of Jean-Christophe Ammann, this can produce places of poetic resistance, which place themselves in the service of a humane and just society. In any case, the museum scenographies of ATELIER BRÜCKNER create spaces and architectures which allow presentation on the one hand and perception on the other as a dialogue between equals.

Komponisten, Grafiker, Mediengestalter und viele weitere Künstler einbezieht. Kein Wunder, dass Uwe R. Brückner selbst seine szenografische Karriere beim Theater begann – von der Vorstellung eines „Gesamtkunstwerks“ in den Bann geschlagen.

Die Inszenierungen des ATELIER BRÜCKNER erzeugen letztlich performative Räume, welche die Besucher aktivieren. Sie erlauben eine Raumpraxis, die auf eine Aneignung der Räume zielt – Räume, die nie fertig, sondern immer im Entstehen sind.

Wer solchermaßen museale Räume als öffentliche Räume begreift, wird den dadurch ermöglichten Raumerfahrungen unweigerlich eine politische Dimension zuerkennen. Denn solche Raumkonfigurationen setzen zivilbürgerliche Akteure voraus, die Inszenierungen im Museum dazu nutzen, Öffentlichkeit performativ herzustellen. So können – ganz im Sinne von Jean-Christophe Ammann – Orte des poetischen Widerstands entstehen, die sich in den Dienst einer humanen und gerechten Gesellschaft stellen. Jedenfalls bieten die musealen Szenografien des ATELIER BRÜCKNER Räume und Architekturen, die das Darstellen einerseits und das Wahrnehmen andererseits als einen Dialog auf Augenhöhe ermöglichen.

Giving a three-dimensional aspect to intangible content such as historical, political, or social events of our time to protagonists and their biographies so that this content can be experienced by visitors requires a narrative and integrative design approach. Conventional exhibiting is replaced by contemporary staging. The translation of content into (walk-in) narrative spaces and the spatialised expression of messages shape the space. Form follows content.[50]

↗ p. 36

HOUSE OF HISTORY BADEN-WÜRTTEMBERG The narrative space in the House of History in Stuttgart (2002), the so-called "world wars' block," in which the two world wars and the Weimar Republic between the two wars have been combined, expresses both a bold curatorial concept as well as its unusual scenographic interpretation. The two world wars are separated physically by a pane of glass with projections of shockingly similar film footage and photographic material. The dynamics and the technical stage of development of the war machinery differ, but the horror and the madness stay the same.

Inhalte nichtdinglicher Art, wie historische, politische oder gesellschaftliche Ereignisse, die an das Zeitgeschehen, an Protagonisten und ihre Biografien gebunden sind, dreidimensional erlebbar zu machen, verlangt einen narrativen und integrativen Gestaltungsansatz. Das klassische Ausstellen wird von der zeitgemäßen Inszenierung abgelöst. Die Übersetzung von Inhalt in den (begehbaren) Erzählraum und der verräumlichte Ausdruck von Botschaften bestimmen den Raum. Inhalt generiert Raum – „Form follows content."[50]

HAUS DER GESCHICHTE BADEN-WÜRTTEMBERG Das Raumbild des sogenannten Weltkriegsblocks im Haus der Geschichte in Stuttgart (2002), in dem die zwei Weltkriege und die „Zwischenkriegszeit" der Weimarer Republik zusammengefasst wurden, ist sowohl ein mutiges kuratorisches Konzept als auch dessen ungewöhnliche szenografische Interpretation. Die beiden Weltkriege sind physisch getrennt durch eine Glasscheibe mit Projektionen von erschreckend ähnlichem Film- und Bildmaterial. Dynamik und technischer Entwicklungsstand der Kriegsmaschinerien unterscheiden sich, das Grauen und der Wahnsinn bleiben gleich.

50 See Atelier Brückner 2016, p. 60.

"House of History Baden-Württemberg"–First World War (left) and World War II (right) are simply divided by a ten-millimetre diffuse glass panel, projected with warlike images from both sides, bluntly demonstrating the machinery of war and its weapons of mass destruction without further commentary, 2002.

The untreated steel walls to each side stand for the industrialised war machinery. They provoke visible traces in the form of fingerprints of the visitors as a reminder of our responsibility for what happens in the world.

While the showcases on the side of the First World War are flush-mounted as a sign of loyalty to the German emperor and jingoism, on the side of the Second World War they jut out more aggressively, like stacked ammunition boxes.

One wall is dedicated to the Jewish citizens–on the one side there are flush-mounted showcases that show that German Jews fought for their country in the First World War as a matter of course, while the showcases of the German Jews on the side of the Second World War are broken out of the wall, strewn over the floor, together with objects which belong to the Holocaust–such as a beam from Kusterdingen on which Hungarian women left messages on their death march.

The narrative space thus subtly expresses the abstract content in a physical way but leaves enough scope for visitors to draw associations.

Die unbehandelten Stahlwände zu beiden Seiten stehen für die industrialisierte Kriegsmaschinerie. Sie provozieren bleibende Spuren in Form von Fingerabdrücken der Besucher als Erinnerung an unsere Verantwortung für das Zeitgeschehen.

Während die seriell eingeschnittenen Vitrinen auf der Seite des Ersten Weltkriegs noch bündig in die Wand eingelassen sind, als Zeichen der Loyalität zum Kaiser und des Hurra-Patriotismus, treten sie auf der Seite des Zweiten Weltkriegs aggressiver hervor, wie gestapelte Munitionskisten.

Eine Wand ist den jüdischen Mitbürgern gewidmet: Auf der einen Seite sind die Vitrinen wandgleich integriert und zeigen, dass deutsche Juden ganz selbstverständlich vaterlandstreu im Ersten Weltkrieg kämpften. Auf der Seite des Zweiten Weltkriegs sind die Vitrinen der deutschen Juden hingegen aus der Wand gebrochen, liegen auf dem Boden, bestückt mit Objekten aus dem Holocaust – wie die „Kusterdinger Balken", auf denen ungarische Frauen auf dem Todesmarsch ihre Botschaften hinterließen.

So drückt das Raumbild in subtiler Weise den abstrakten Inhalt physisch aus, lässt dem Besucher aber immer assoziativen Spielraum.

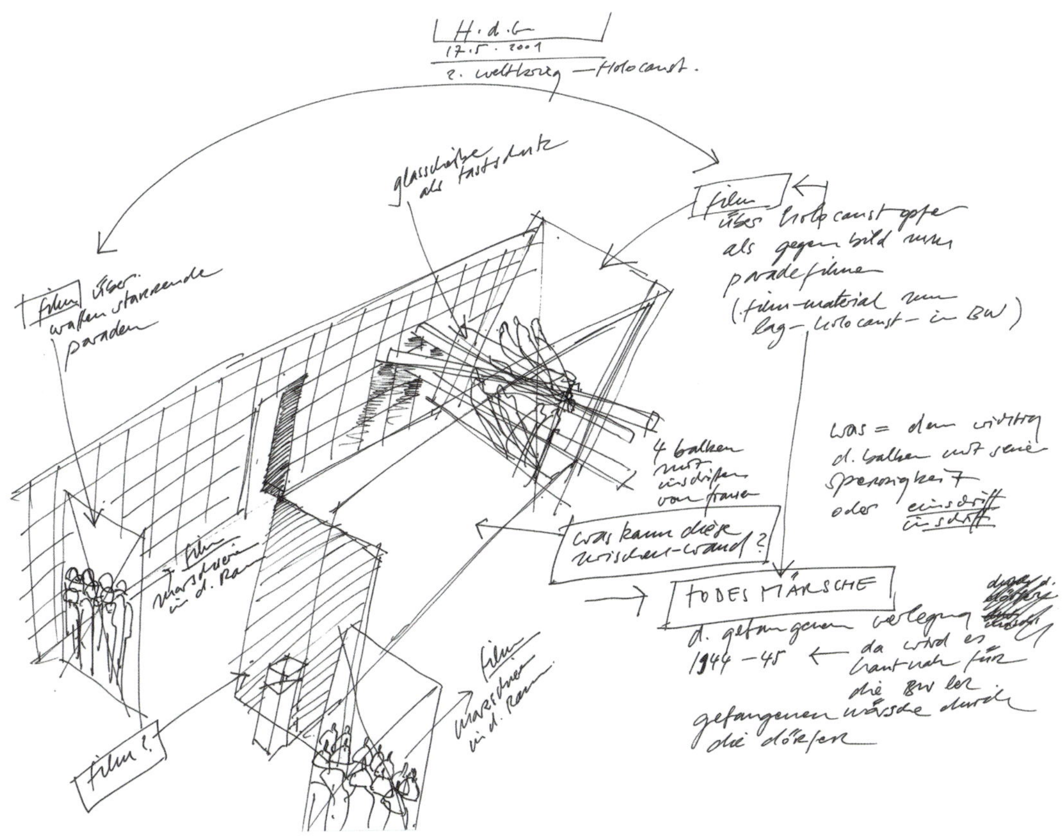

"House of History Baden-Württemberg"–World War II, 2001.

Information centres are not as a rule perceived on the museum level and are often developed with little curatorial and design ambition. They nevertheless usually have a similarly demanding task to master and are responsible for forming and enhancing the image of an institution. By means of consistent and clever scenography it is possible to set the scene for even a large body of information–often abstract, sometimes dry content–in a way which appeals to the audience, gives the centre an identity, and allows participation.

↗ p. 98

PARLAMENTARIUM–VISITOR CENTRE OF THE EUROPEAN PARLIAMENT What does this mean for the scenography in the Parlamentarium in Brussels (2011)? The central task was to reflect the many languages of Europe and to develop an exhibition in the 24 native languages of all Europeans. The actual challenge was, however, to convey the complex parliamentary debates and processes with only a few three-dimensional objects and reams of documents, photos, and documentaries. The task is to translate the mountains of content into memorable narrative spaces that convey the multifaceted work of the European Parliament in such a way that even young people get excited about their Europe. Conceptionally that means: Don't instruct, but

Informationszentren werden in der Regel nicht auf Museumsniveau wahrgenommen und oft mit geringerer kuratorischer oder gestalterischer Ambition entwickelt. Trotzdem haben sie meist einen ähnlich anspruchsvollen Auftrag und sind verantwortlich für Imagebildung und -gewinn einer Einrichtung. Durch eine konsistente und clevere Szenografie kann sogar eine große Informationsfülle von abstrakten, manchmal trockenen Inhalten publikumswirksam, identitätsbildend und partizipativ in Szene gesetzt werden.

PARLAMENTARIUM – BESUCHERZENTRUM DES EUROPÄISCHEN PARLAMENTS Was bedeutet das für die Szenografie im Parlamentarium in Brüssel (2011)? Der zentrale Anspruch ist es, die europäische Vielsprachigkeit zu reflektieren und eine Ausstellung in den 24 Muttersprachen aller Europäer zu entwickeln. Die eigentliche Herausforderung besteht allerdings darin, mit nur wenigen dreidimensionalen Objekten, aber unendlich vielen Dokumenten, Fotos und Dokumentationen komplexe parlamentarische Debatten und Prozesse zugänglich zu machen. Es gilt, die Berge von Inhalten in nachhaltig beeindruckende Raumbilder zu übersetzen, um das vielfältige Wirken des Europäischen Parlaments zu vermitteln, sodass sich

"Parlamentarium"-360-degree hemisphere enables visitors to participate in a debate and vote like a parliamentarian, 2011.

instead let them experience things and instead of didactics, let interaction and exploration take effect.

The scenographic translation uses the spatial metaphor of two closed circular hemispheres. The one entitled “A Parliament for Europe,” reflects the work of the members of parliament in a 360-degree panorama projection with authentic footage from debates in a legislative process. In the other, “Daily Life,” European citizens fill the multinational landscape panorama and relate in moving interviews of their experiences with the European legislation. The two are connected by the borderless map of Europe, “United in Diversity,” on which the work of the European Parliament can be explored with mobile scanners.

In both hemispheres, the content becomes space, the space becomes the carrier of messages, and the visitors become an immersive part of the staging.

auch junge Menschen für ihr Europa begeistern. Konzeptionell heißt das: nicht belehren, sondern erleben und statt Didaktik, Interaktion und Exploration wirken zu lassen.

Die szenografische Übersetzung bedient sich der räumlichen Metapher zweier geschlossener zirkulärer Hemisphären. Die eine, „A Parliament for Europe“, spiegelt die inhaltliche Arbeit der Abgeordneten in einer 360°-Panorama-Projektion mit authentischem Bildmaterial von Debatten in einem legislativen Prozess wider. In der anderen, in „Daily Life“, füllen die europäischen Bürger das multinationale Landschaftspanorama und erzählen in bewegenden Interviews von ihren Erfahrungen mit der europäischen Gesetzgebung. Verbunden sind die beiden mit der grenzenlosen Europakarte „United in Diversity“, auf der das Wirken des Europäischen Parlaments mit mobilen Scannern erkundet werden kann.

In beiden Hemisphären wird der Inhalt zum Raum, der Raum zum Vermittler von Botschaften und der Besucher zum Teil der immersiven Inszenierung.

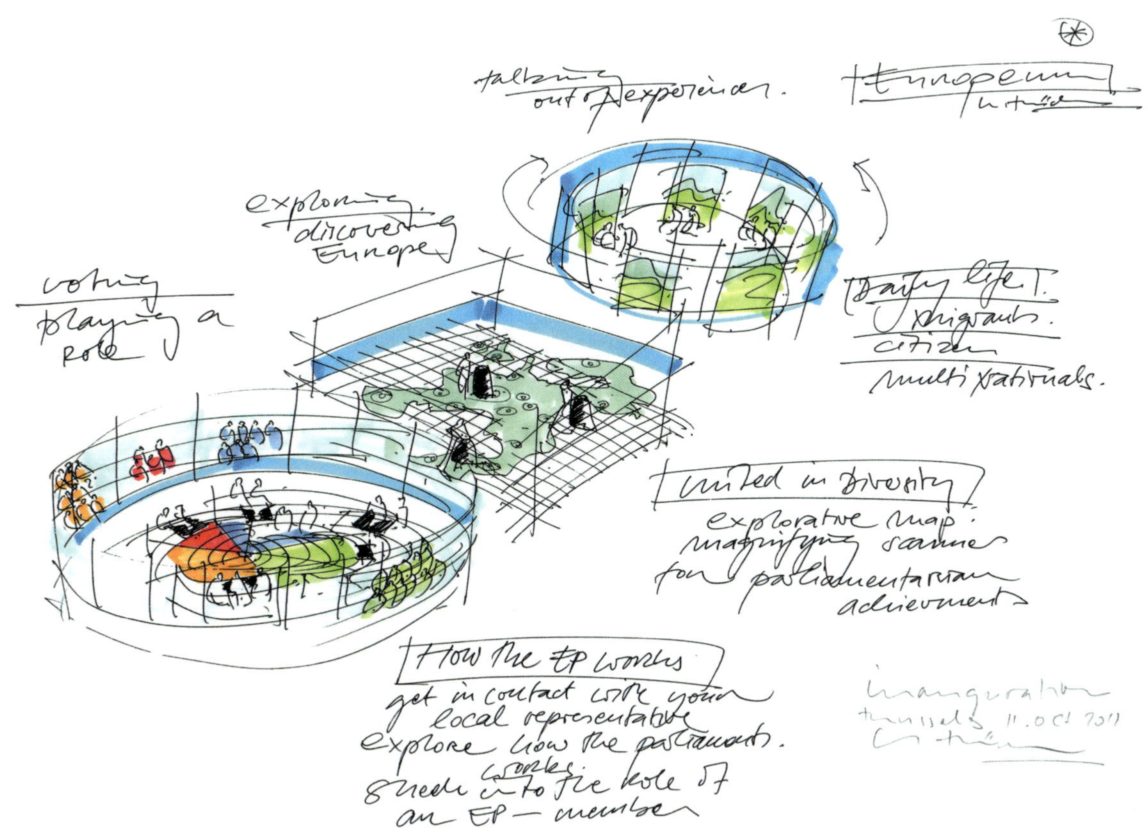

“Parlamentarium”–How the EP works | United in Diversity | Daily Life, 2007.

The on-going discussion about where architecture ends and scenography begins or whether architecture can develop scenographic–that is, spatial narrative–qualities or even transport content is usually reduced in the age of digitalisation to an applied facade projection. And yet, buildings can indeed transport content above and beyond the advertising billboards on the periphery of visually overloaded cities. Expo pavilions are welcome laboratories for designers, scenographic fields of experimentation, and walk-in public stages.

AFRICAN PAVILION, EXPO ZARAGOZA The African Pavilion at the Expo Saragossa 2008 was tasked with accommodating a group of African countries in one of the existing pavilions, so-called "beans," and at the same time to express this by means of the facade design.[51] The pavilion was a black box, ideal for staging on the inside, but hermetic as regards its legibility. How therefore could the content be brought from the inside to the outside without the conventional printed skins mounted on the facade?

Die anhaltende Diskussion darüber, wo Architektur endet und Szenografie beginnt oder ob Architektur szenografische, also räumlich-narrative Qualitäten entwickeln oder sogar Inhalte transportieren kann, wird im Zeitalter der Digitalisierung meist auf eine applizierte Fassadenbespielung reduziert. Dabei können die Gebäude sehr wohl selbst Inhalte vermitteln, jenseits werbetragender Billboards am Rande der visuell überfrachteten Städte. Expo-Pavillons sind Gestaltern willkommene Labore, szenografische Experimentierfelder und begehbare öffentliche Bühnen.

AFRIKANISCHER PAVILLON, EXPO ZARAGOZA Der Afrikanische Pavillon auf der Expo Saragossa 2008 präsentierte afrikanische Länder in einem der bestehenden Pavillons, den sogenannten Beans, und hatte die Aufgabe dies über die Fassadengestaltung auszudrücken.[51] Der Pavillon war eine Blackbox, ideal für das Inszenieren im Inneren, aber hermetisch, was seine Lesbarkeit nach außen anging. Wie also die Inhalte von innen nach außen bringen ohne die konventionellen bedruckten, vorgehängten Hüllen?

51 The countries that participated in the African pavilion were Sudan, Kenya, Tanzania, Ethiopia, Niger, Mali, Uganda, Cape Verde, Senegal, Equatorial Guinea, Cameroon, Mozambique, Namibia and South Africa.

"African Pavilion"–LED-based media facade 6 x 218 metres, resolution 10 x 10, 2008.

The solution was a visual membrane which lets content permeate from the inside to the outside, thus enticing passers-by to explore the interior. Thanks to the daylight-capable media facade, 6 metres high and 218 metres in length, which covered the whole building, the pavilion itself was turned into a mega screen. This consisted of an LED grid behind translucent flip tiles that moved in the wind, thus allowing two physical states: the printed tiles traced the movement of the wind in poetic patterns (wind clouds), while the LED grid provided an impressive panorama that evoked the impression of life-sized elephants, giraffes, and zebras emerging from the interior. All the cultural motifs, dances, or sounds were derived from the country stagings inside the pavilion.

The African pavilion not only became one of the liveliest icons of the Expo Saragossa, but also an exemplary study that showed not only that content and messages can be applied, but also that architecture itself can become narrator, a carrier of content.[52]

Die Lösung war eine visuelle Membran, welche die Inhalte permeabel von innen nach außen diffundieren lässt und so dazu einlädt, das Innere zu erkunden. Der Pavillon selbst wurde zum Mega-Bildschirm durch eine 6 Meter hohe und 218 Meter lange, tageslichtfähige Medienfassade, die das gesamte Gebäude einnahm. Diese bestand aus einem LED-Raster hinter windbewegten transluzenten Plättchen (flip-tiles) und erlaubte damit zwei Aggregatzustände: Die bedruckten Plättchen zeichneten die Windbewegung auf poetische Weise nach („Windwolken"). Das LED-Raster lieferte ein beeindruckendes Panorama, das den Eindruck vermittelte, es würden lebensgroße Elefanten, Giraffen oder Zebras aus dem Inneren heraustreten. Alle Kulturmotive, Tänze oder Klänge waren aus den Länderinszenierungen im Inneren des Pavillons abgeleitet.

Der Afrikanische Pavillon wurde nicht nur zu einer der lebendigsten Ikonen der Expo Saragossa, sondern auch zur exemplarischen Studie, die zeigte, dass Inhalte und Botschaften nicht nur appliziert werden können, sondern dass Architektur selbst zum Narrativum, zum Botschafter von Inhalten, werden kann.[52]

52 See Atelier Brückner 2016, p. 206.

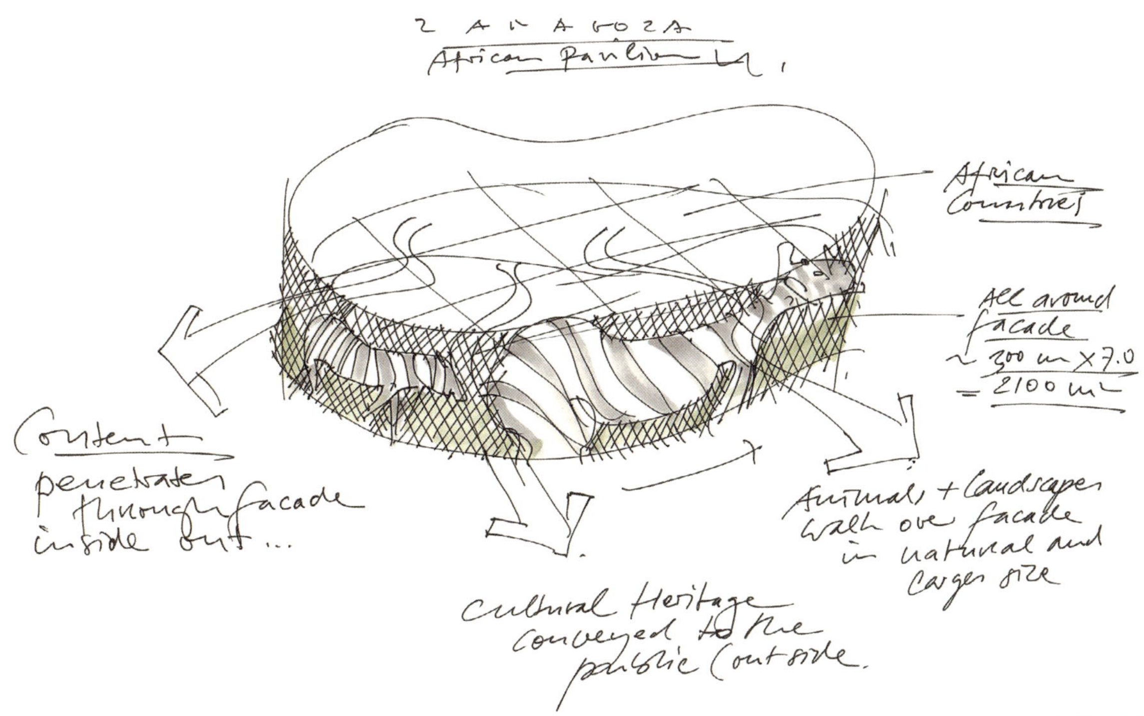

"African Pavilion"–Motives and patterns shown on screen refer to the African countries featured in the inside of the pavilion, 2007.

OBJECT

THE OBJECT IS THE SUBJECT

Uwe R. Brückner and Linda Greci

“From thing to object, from object to exhibit, from the real thing to its abstract significance. If you treat the object like a subject, you will get behind its hidden character. Good scenography (re)-contextualises and makes things talk.”

Uwe R. Brückner

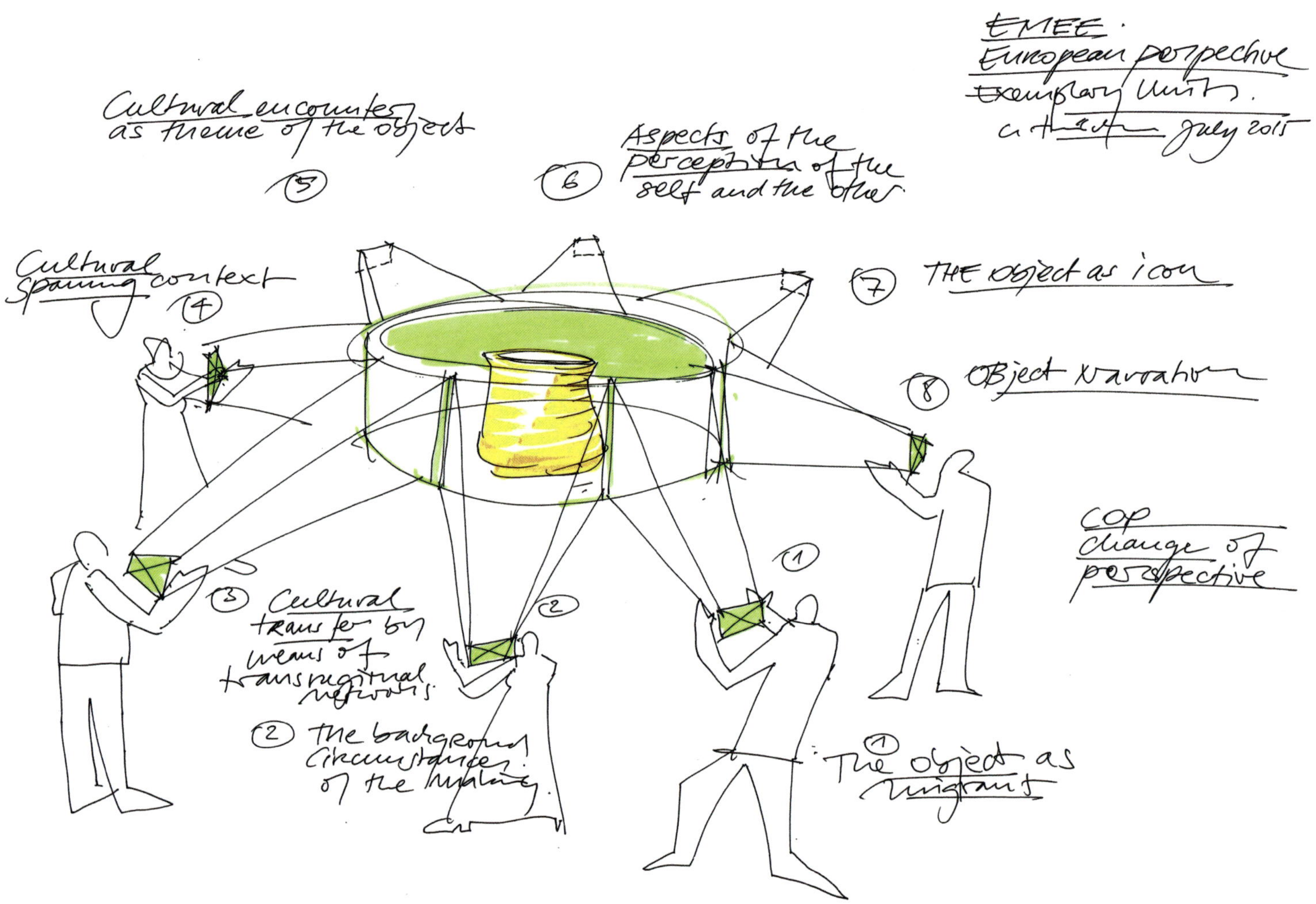

"EuroVision–Museums Exhibiting Europe (EMEE)"–Object as a Subject, 2015.

The object is thing, deposit, and exhibit; it is the third parameter of scenography.[53] The museum is a medium that, on the one hand, collects and preserves things in its repository as historical testimony and, on the other, exhibits and interprets them for the public in its exhibition space. Due to the relationship between depositing and exhibiting, the things of a museum are "agents of meaning formation that have been kept available."[54] They are witnesses, which mediate between the past and present, but they are also mediators between the visible and the invisible, between the materiality of the viewable and the immateriality of the memorable.[55] As "epistemic things," they are removed from their original, living context, robbed of their actual function and significance and then, in the context of the museum, recharged with significance.[56] This change in context and the transfer of significance allow a surprising change of perspective and promise new insights. Anyone involved in exhibiting is conscious of the fragmentary transfer of a thing and takes into account that things that are not self-explanatory need a recontextualisation in the museum.[57]

In the German-speaking museum discourse, (re-) contextualisation has been understood as a necessity because things only acquire meaning when placed in relationship to other things, content, texts, documents, and secondary material. They can only convey messages and information about the past if a context is created that generates a relational or conceptual connection.[58] Scenography (re-)contextualises objects not only in terms of content, but also spatially and synaesthetically. It stages objects in their original context, to bring long forgotten histories to life or to present them in unusual contexts in order to offer new interpretations. The (re-)contextualisation of objects can be effected through various presenta-

53 For this chapter see the research work: Linda Greci, Museale Markenpräsentation. Vergleichende Museumsanalyse. Magisterarbeit. (Tübingen, 2012), pp 15–19.
54 Gottfried Korff, "13 Anmerkungen zur aktuellen Situation des Museums als Einleitung zur 2. Auflage", in Gottfried Korff: Museumsdinge: deponieren – exponieren, ed. Martina Eberspächer, Gudrun Marlene König, and Bernhard Tschofen (Cologne, 2007), pp. ix–xxiv, here p. xvii.
55 See Krzystof Pomian, Der Ursprung des Museums: Vom Sammeln (Berlin, 1988), pp. 49–50.
56 Korff 2007, p. 143.
57 Ibid.
58 See Katharina Flügel, Einführung in die Museologie (Darmstadt, 2005), p. 27.

Das Objekt ist Ding, Deponat und Exponat; es ist der dritte Parameter der Szenografie.[53] Das Museum ist ein Medium, das einerseits Dinge als historische Zeugnisse in seinem Depot sammelt und bewahrt, andererseits diese in seinen Ausstellungsräumen der Öffentlichkeit zeigt und interpretiert. Aufgrund der wechselseitigen Beziehung zwischen Deponieren und Exponieren sind die Museumsdinge „verfügbar gehaltene Agenten einer Sinnbildung".[54] Sie sind Zeugen, die zwischen der Vergangenheit und der Gegenwart vermitteln, sie sind aber auch Mediatoren zwischen dem Sichtbaren und dem Unsichtbaren, zwischen der Materialität des Anschaubaren und der Immaterialität des Erinnerbaren.[55] Als „epistemische Dinge" werden sie aus ihrem lebendigen ursprünglichen Kontext herausgelöst, ihrer eigentlichen Funktion und Bedeutung beraubt und schließlich im Kontext des Museums erneut mit Bedeutung aufgeladen.[56] Diese Kontextänderung und der Bedeutungstransfer ermöglichen eine überraschende Perspektive und versprechen neue Erkenntnisse. Dabei ist man sich beim Ausstellen des fragmentarischen Charakters der Dingüberlieferung bewusst und berücksichtigt, dass die sich nicht selbst erklärenden Dinge eine „Re-Kontextualisierung" im Museum verlangen.[57]

Die (Re-)Kontextualisierung wird seit Jahren im deutschsprachigen Museumsdiskurs als Notwendigkeit verstanden, weil die Aussagekraft von Dingen erst durch das In-Beziehung-Setzen zu anderen Dingen, Inhalten, Texten, Dokumenten und Sekundärmaterial entsteht. Sie können Botschaften und Informationen über die Vergangenheit erst dann vermitteln, wenn ein Kontext hergestellt wird, der einen Beziehungs- und Bedeutungszusammenhang generiert.[58] Szenografie (re-)kontextualisiert Objekte konsequenterweise nicht nur inhaltlich, sondern auch räumlich und synästhetisch. Sie inszeniert Objekte in ihrem ursprünglichen Kontext, um vergessen geglaubte Geschichten lebendig zu machen, oder präsentiert sie in ungewohnten Zusammenhängen, um neue Interpretationen anzubieten. Die (Re-)Kontextualisierung von Objekten kann über verschiedene Präsentationsformate und Gestaltungsinstrumente erfolgen, zum Beispiel mithilfe von Grafik, Projektion, Film, digitalen Medien, Klang und Licht.

depositing and exhibiting

context

(re-)contextualisation

tion formats and design instruments, for example with the help of graphics, projection, film, digital media, sound, and light.

To do this, the object must first be examined, its history uncovered, and its significance revealed. The authentic object has, on the one hand, a source value, but, on the other, it also has a sensory, aesthetic value which triggers interest, fascination, and curiosity.[59] The source value of the authentic object effectively means being true to the facts. Based on this understanding, authenticity means the historical, testimonial character.[60]

authenticity

The terms "authenticity" or "authentic" can, however, also be understood as a category of the aesthetics of reception and used in the sense of credibility or being credible. In such cases, it is not decisive whether an object is in fact a material relict of a past event, but rather whether the object is perceived by the recipient as genuine.[61] Reference is made here to the term "aura" as used by Walter Benjamin: "The aura is not tied to the beautiful, but to being genuine and authentic. Authenticity is thus what actually gives an object meaning."[62]

atmosphere

Gernot Böhme, by contrast, introduced "atmosphere" as a synonym for aura and describes something indeterminate, diffuse[63]. It is unclear whether one should ascribe atmospheres to the objects or their surroundings or perhaps even to the subjects that experience them.[64] This still begs the question: Where and how does aura originate? Aura is "[...] not created in the object itself but is given it by another–social, in the past mainly transcendental–instance, or it evolves through the situational frame and due to the social role in which the auratic object is embedded."[65] This insight is of decisive importance because it examines the objects in the context of the museum. Gottfried Korff speaks in this context of "auratisation"[66] in the museum and thus directs attention to the means of staging which give the object an aura and thus allow aura experiences.[67]

auratisation

59 Uwe J. Reinhardt and Philipp Teufel, eds., Neue Ausstellungsgestaltung 02 (Ludwigsburg, 2010), p. 17.
60 See Korff 2007, p. 121.
61 Ibid.
62 Flügel 2005, pp. 29–30 (translation of the German original quotation taken from this source).
63 See Gernot Böhme, Atmosphäre. Essay zur neuen Ästhetik (Frankfurt, 1995), p. 27.
64 See Erika Fischer-Lichte, Ästhetik des Performativen (Frankfurt a. M., 2004), p. 201.
65 Peter M. Spangenberg, "Aura", in Ästhetische Grundbegriffe, vol. 4, Medien-Popular, ed. Karlheinz Barck (Stuttgart/Weimar, 2002), pp. 400–416, here p. 401 (translation of the German original quotation taken from this source).
66 Korff 2007, p. 131.
67 Ibid., pp. 126–139.

Dazu muss das Objekt jedoch vorab untersucht, seine Geschichte aufgedeckt und seine Bedeutung freigelegt werden. Das authentische Objekt hat einerseits einen Quellenwert, andererseits auch einen sinnlich-ästhetischen Reizwert, der Interesse, Faszination und Neugier auslöst.[59] Der Quellenwert des authentischen Objekts bedeutet soviel wie Tatsachentreue. Diesem Verständnis zufolge meint Authentizität den historischen Zeugnischarakter.[60] Die Begriffe „Authentizität" oder „authentisch" können aber auch als rezeptionsästhetische Kategorie gefasst und im Sinne von „Glaubwürdigkeit" oder „glaubwürdig" verwendet werden. Entscheidend ist dabei nicht, ob ein Objekt tatsächlich materielles Relikt eines vergangenen Ereignisses ist, sondern ob das Objekt vom Rezipienten als echt wahrgenommen wird.[61] An dieser Stelle sei auf den Begriff „Aura" von Walter Benjamin verwiesen: „Die Aura ist nicht an das Schöne gebunden, sondern an die Echtheit und Authentizität. Das Authentische macht demnach die eigentliche Bedeutung des Gegenstandes aus."[62]

Gernot Böhme dagegen hat für den Begriff „Aura" das Synonym „Atmosphäre" eingeführt und beschreibt damit etwas Unbestimmtes, Diffuses.[63] Es ist unklar, ob man Atmosphären den Objekten oder der räumlichen Umgebung zuschreiben soll oder vielleicht sogar den Subjekten, die sie erfahren.[64] So stellt sich immer noch die Frage: Wo und wie entsteht Aura? Aura ist: „[...] nicht im Objekt selbst angelegt, sondern sie wird ihm von einer anderen – gesellschaftlichen, früher vornehmlich transzendenten – Instanz verliehen, oder sie entsteht durch den situativen Rahmen und aufgrund der sozialen Rolle, in die das auratische Objekt eingebettet ist."[65] Diese Einsicht ist von maßgeblicher Bedeutung, weil sie den musealen Kontext der Objekte untersucht. Gottfried Korff spricht in diesem Zusammenhang von Auratisierung[66] im Museum und lenkt damit den Blick auf die Inszenierungsmittel, die dem Objekt eine Aura verleihen und somit Aura-Erlebnisse ermöglichen können.[67] Da die Aura-Erfahrung subjektive, rezeptionsästhetische Aspekte hat, ist sie vom Betrachter abhängig:

"EuroVision–Museums Exhibiting Europe (EMEE)"–Recontextualisation of Objects, 2014.

As the aura experience has subjective aspects relating to the aesthetics of reception, it is dependent on the observer: aura is thus more a perception mode, a museum experience rather than a performative act.[68] And in terms of aura, auratic is no more the object per se, but the reception situation as well.[69]

This performative redefinition of the idea of aura is part of the trend towards experience orientation currently being seen in contemporary exhibition design[70]; and in this context, attention has shifted to the concept of the performative space.

performative space

The performative space is not given, passive, and static like geometric space; rather it is permanently being recreated.[71] It plays an active role in the processes of determining meaning because it eliminates the divide between visitor and exhibit. This leaning towards performance concepts shows that the way the visitor aesthetically perceives and receives is at the forefront. This turn towards performative space suggests that attention is being shifted from the object to the subject. And as a result, the dialogue in the relationship and communication between object and recipient is in the foreground. By making the content of the things accessible, a reception space is created.

reception space

change of perspective

Apart from this shift in the focus of attention, another change of perspective in exhibition development and design can be observed against the current backdrop of global reality and an intermingling of cultures: a change of perspectives from a national to a transnational point of view.[72] The focus of the survey lies on transregional objects ranging from a national dimension to a European one. Understanding these objects simultaneously as parts of the local, regional, national, and European culture, embedded in different sociohistorical contexts, requires a multiperspective approach. Such an approach aims to expand the

68 Ibid., p. XVII.
69 Ibid.
70 Ibid., p. XVIII.
71 See Fischer-Lichte 2004, pp. 199–200.
72 EuroVision: Museums Exhibiting Europe (EMEE) is an European project for national and regional museums. It explores an innovative interdisciplinary approach for museums to reinterpret their objects in a broader context of European and transnational history. See more information on: www.museums-exhibiting-europe.de, accessed October 08, 2018.

Aura ist also mehr ein Wahrnehmungsmodus, ein Museumserlebnis als ein performativer Akt.[68] Und auratisch ist nicht mehr das Objekt per se, sondern die Rezeptionssituation.[69]

Diese performative Umdeutung des Begriffs „Aura“ liegt im gleichen Trend wie die Erlebnisorientierung[70] zeitgenössischer Ausstellungsgestaltung – in diesem Zusammenhang rückt das Konzept des performativen Raums ins Blickfeld der Betrachtung. Der performative Raum ist nicht wie der geometrische Raum gegeben, passiv und statisch, sondern er wird permanent neu hervorgebracht.[71] Er ist aktiv an den Bedeutungsprozessen beteiligt, weil er die Trennung zwischen Besucher und Exponat auflöst. Die Hinwendung zu Performancekonzepten macht deutlich, dass die rezeptionsästhetische Wahrnehmung des Besuchers im Vordergrund steht. Das heißt, dass mit dem Konzept des performativen Raums gegenwärtig eine Aufmerksamkeitsverschiebung vom Objekt zum Subjekt vollzogen wird. Und damit treten die dialogische Beziehung und Kommunikation zwischen Objekt und Rezipient in den Vordergrund. Ein Rezeptionsraum entsteht, in dem der Gehalt der Dinge verfügbar wird.

Abgesehen von dieser Aufmerksamkeitsverschiebung findet ein weiterer Perspektivenwechsel in der Ausstellungskonzeption und -gestaltung statt, der vor dem Hintergrund der gegenwärtigen globalen Realität und Kulturvermischung zu sehen ist: ein Perspektivenwechsel von einer nationalen zu einer transnationalen Perspektive.[72] Der Fokus der Untersuchung liegt dabei auf transregionalen Objekten, die zwischen einer nationalen und einer europäischen Dimension rangieren. Das gleichzeitige Verständnis dieser Objekte als Bestandteile der lokalen, regionalen, nationalen und europäischen Kultur, eingebettet in unterschiedliche soziohistorische Kontexte, erfordert einen multiperspektivischen Gestaltungsansatz. Ein solcher Ansatz zielt auf eine Erweiterung der Perspektive ab, ohne die lokale, regionale oder nationale Bedeu-

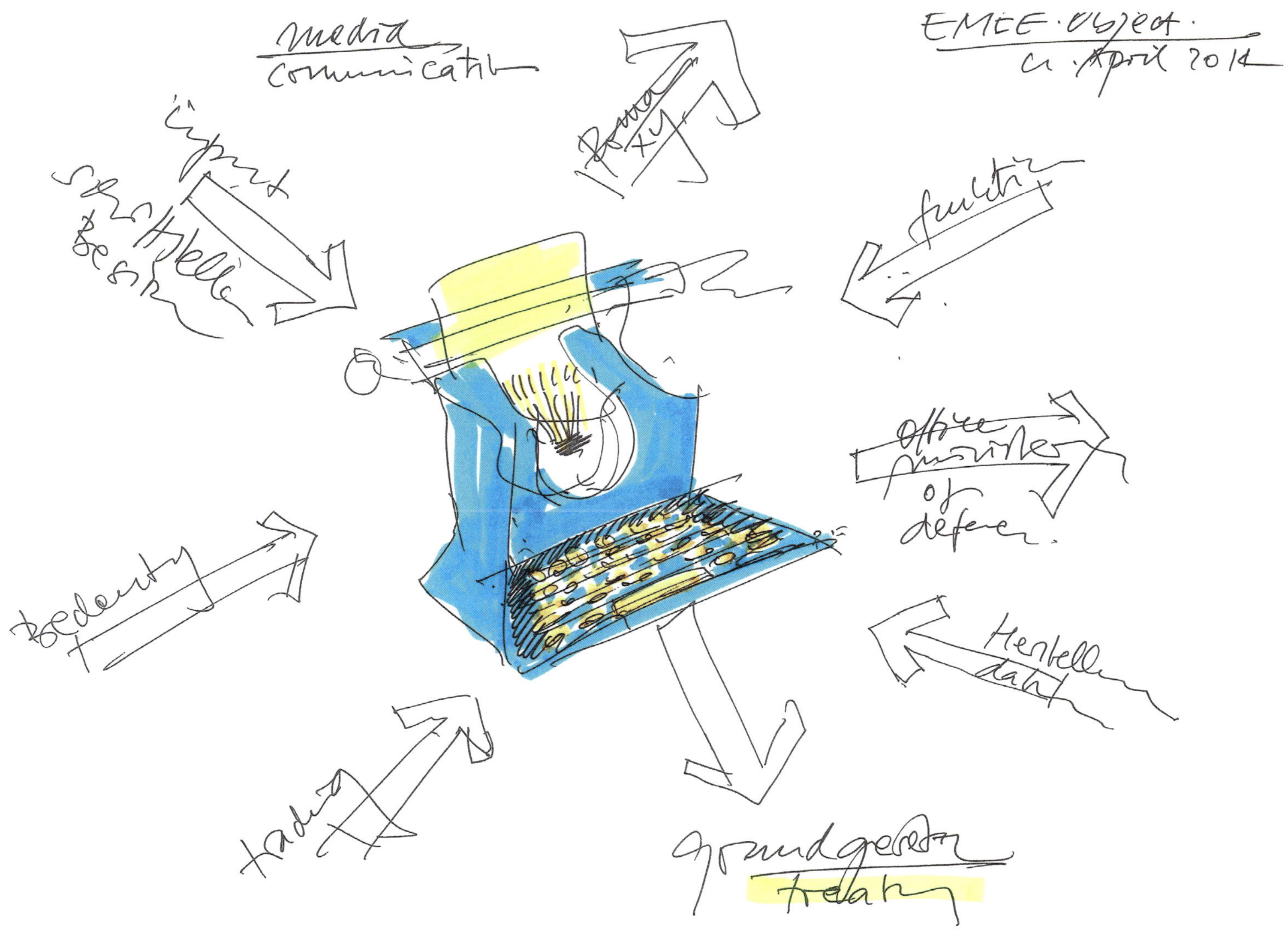

"EuroVision–Museums Exhibiting Europe (EMEE)"–Object's Potentials, 2014.

perspective without denying the local, regional, and national level of meaning. In this way, the commonly used one-dimensional presentation of museum objects can be overcome, replaced by multidimensional staging, possibly revealing a transnational perspective in the process.[73]

The genesis of an object, beginning with the research into the object by the curator and the identification of its purpose, is staged by the scenographer and completed by the perception of the object by the visitor. However, the visitor cannot recognise the potential of an object through its mere existence; to understand the origins, cultural and historical significance, relevance, symbolism, original function, and value of an object requires staging consistent with content. Scenography puts the object into context and conveys its various layers of meaning and stories within a staged environment–some self-explanatory or with the help of narrative structures. The aim is to make the object speak for itself, to convey information, ideas, and messages and to allow visitors to enjoy this in a synaesthetic spatial experience.

synaesthetic spatial experience

Good scenography closes the gap between object and recipient. The object becomes an exhibit, the carrier of meaning, eyewitness, the object of desire; and it appears as storyteller, as protagonist, subject with personality and destiny. Its aura becomes an ether, a captivating carrier of an emotional and sensual meta-level into which visitors can dive–its aura becomes a space for experience and imagination.

tungsebene zu leugnen. Eine gewöhnlich eindimensionale Präsentation von Museumsobjekten kann damit überwunden werden und eine multidimensionale Inszenierung, die eine neue, gegebenenfalls transnationale Perspektive enthüllt, tritt in den Vordergrund.[73]

Die Genese eines Objekts, die mit der Erforschung und Bedeutungsbestimmung durch den Kurator beginnt, wird durch die Inszenierung seitens des Szenografen vermittelt und mit der Wahrnehmung durch den Besucher vollendet. Der Besucher vermag das Potenzial eines Objekts allerdings nicht aufgrund seiner bloßen Anwesenheit zu erkennen, vielmehr bedarf es einer inhaltskonsistenten Inszenierung, die ihn für die Herkunft, kulturhistorische Bedeutung, Relevanz, Symbolik, ehemalige Funktion und den Wert des Objekts sensibilisiert. Szenografie kontextualisiert das Objekt und vermittelt dessen verschiedene Bedeutungsebenen und Geschichten innerhalb eines gestalteten Environments - möglichst selbsterklärend und mithilfe von narrativen Strukturen. Ziel ist es, das Objekt zum Sprechen zu bringen. Es gilt, Informationen, Ideen und Botschaften zu vermitteln und diese in einem synästhetischen Raumerlebnis nachhaltig erlebbar zu machen.

Gute Szenografie hebt die Distanz zwischen Objekt und Rezipient auf. Das Objekt wird zum Exponat, zum Bedeutungsträger, zum Zeitzeugen, zum Gegenstand der Begierde; und es tritt in Erscheinung als Geschichtenerzähler, als Protagonist, als Subjekt mit Charakter und Schicksal. Seine Aura wird zum Äther, zum fesselnden Träger einer emotionalen und sinnlichen Metaebene, in die der Besucher eintauchen kann - seine Aura wird zum Erfahrungs- und Imaginationsraum.

73 See also Brückner and Greci 2016.

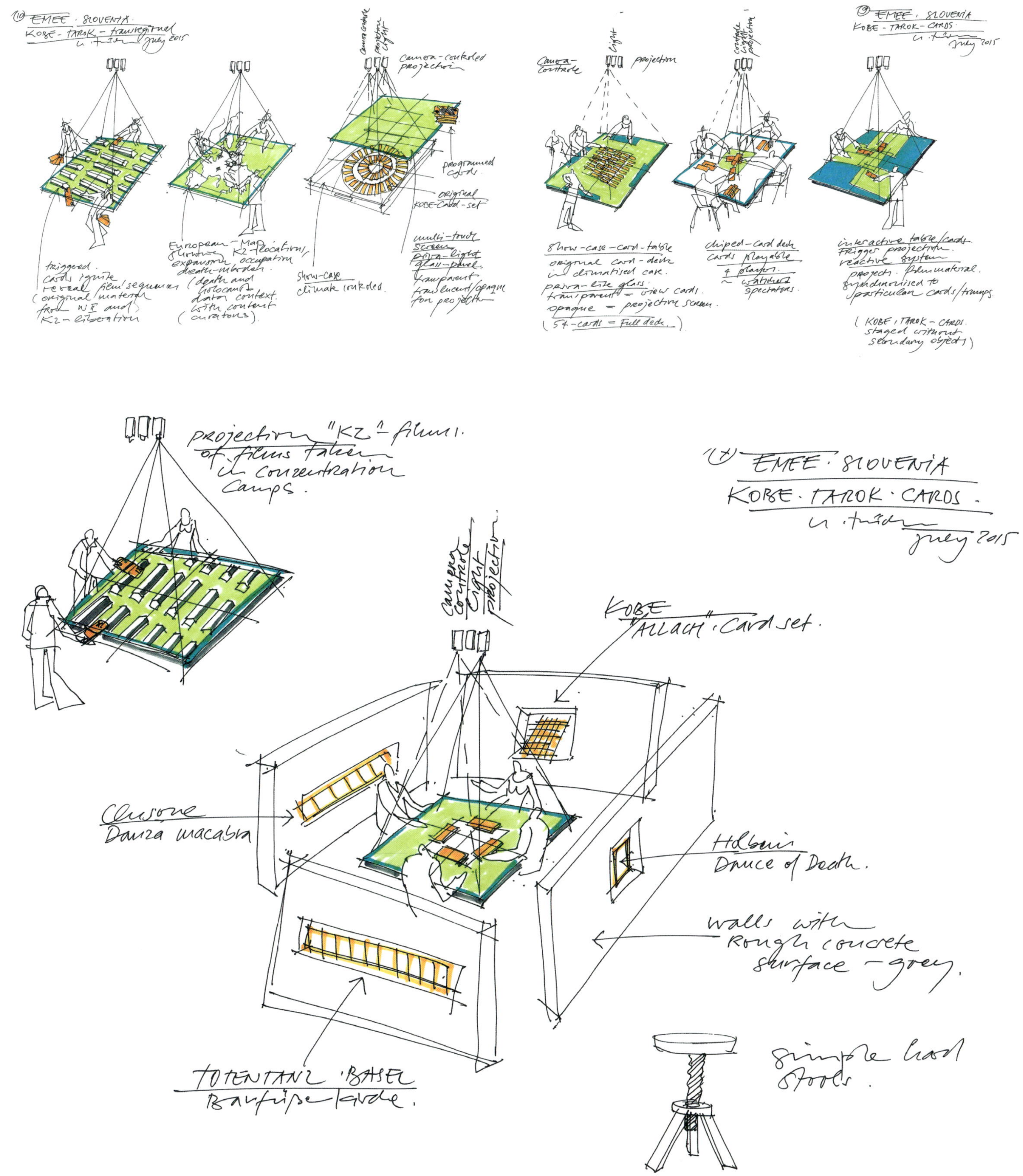

"EuroVision–Museums Exhibiting Europe (EMEE)"–Staging Kobe tarot cards, 2015.

Exploration is a participatory staging strategy, which enables sensitive objects, abstract content, and complex contexts to be experienced. It puts the visitor in the role of a researcher who can not only explore the object interactively, but also its whole potential. Often, the objects in question have to be stored in the museum's repository for conservation reasons or can only be presented in the exhibition in a protected showcase, behind glass or in dimmed light. Or things which for various reasons cannot be brought to the museum in their original condition.

↗ p. 92

HET SCHEEPVAARTMUSEUM This Museum is home to an impressive collection of maritime objects: model ships, figureheads, paintings of sea battles and ships, nautical charts, navigation instruments, and globes, that is, things which have long lost their relevance for today's seafaring. How therefore can an internationally unique collection of globes or other navigation instruments in a time of GPS[74] and Google Maps be made appealing to a younger generation of museum visitors? How can the globes be staged so that the generally unseen Southern Hemisphere becomes visible and how to make the globes turnable? An inter-

74 Global Positioning System.

Exploration ist eine partizipative Inszenierungsstrategie, die empfindliche Objekte, abstrakte Inhalte und komplexe Zusammenhänge erfahrbar macht. Sie versetzt den Besucher in die Rolle eines Forschers, der interaktiv nicht nur das Objekt, sondern dessen gesamtes Potenzial erkunden kann. Oftmals handelt es sich um Objekte, die aus konservatorischen Gründen im Museumsdepot lagern müssen oder in der Ausstellung lediglich in einer geschützten Vitrine, hinter Glas und bei gedimmtem Licht präsentiert werden können. Oder es sind Dinge, die aus verschiedenen Gründen in ihrem Originalzustand nicht ins Museum geholt werden können.

HET SCHEEPVAARTMUSEUM Dieses Museum beherbergt eine beeindruckende Sammlung maritimer Objekte: Schiffsmodelle, Galionsfiguren, Schlachten- und Schiffsgemälde, Seekarten, Navigationsinstrumente und Globen, alles Dinge, deren Relevanz für die Seefahrt heute längst obsolet geworden ist. Wie schafft man es also in Zeiten von GPS[74] und Google Maps eine junge Generation mit einer international einzigartigen Globensammlung oder anderen Navigationsinstrumenten zu begeistern? Wie kann man die

"Het Scheepvaartmuseum"–Globes, originals in chronological order (left) | Interactive globe (right), 2011.

active globe (track-ball), which can be rotated in all directions, makes it possible to navigate various globes via virtual projected scans and to go on a journey back in time, through the history of cartography.

Equally mysterious, the large painting depicting "The naval battle at Gibraltar on 25 April 1607" contains dozens of small stories just waiting to be deciphered with a digital facsimile. Here the visitor learns that compared to the small model painting to the left of the painting, lots of politically or privately motivated modifications were made during the painting process, changes with a high degree of anecdotal value.

Exploratory installations like these actively integrate visitors in the routing. They are not only fascinating but also highly sustainable because they are so memorable.

Globen inszenieren, um auch die meist nicht einsehbare Südhalbkugel sichtbar und die Globen drehbar zu machen? Ein interaktiver Globus (track-ball), der in alle Richtungen rotierbar ist, erlaubt es, über virtuelle projizierte Scans verschiedene Globen zu navigieren und auf eine Zeitreise durch die Geschichte der Kartografie zu gehen.

Mindestens so geheimnisvoll gibt sich das große Seeschlachten-Gemälde „The Naval Battle at Gibraltar on 25 April 1607", in dem sich Dutzende von kleinen Geschichten verbergen, die man mit einem digitalen Faksimile dechiffrieren kann. Dabei kann man erfahren, dass im Vergleich zu dem kleinen Mustergemälde links daneben beim Malen etliche politisch oder privat motivierte Modifikationen entstanden, Änderungen mit hohem anekdotischem Wert.

Explorative Installationen wie diese binden die Besucher aktiv in den Parcours ein. Sie sind nicht nur faszinierend, sondern auch in besonderem Maße nachhaltig, weil erinnerungswürdig.

"Het Scheepvaartmuseum"–Maritime masters sea battle painting "The Naval Battle at Gibraltar on 25 April 1607" of Cornelis Claesz van Wieringen; Original and interactive digital copy, 2011.

"The object is the star" is a popular formula used to direct the focus to the object and to preserve it in showcases, because stars are sensitive, need protection, and must not be touched. The museum attracts visitors with the argument that they can see the exhibits–as a rule, originals–close up, but then isolates them again in closed display cabinets. How can this anachronism be scenographically solved? How can the necessary conservatory distance be observed and nevertheless create a proximity to the exhibits that make them talk?

↗ p. 330

ARCHAEOLOGY SWITZERLAND A huge challenge in this respect was the permanent archaeological exhibition in the Swiss National Museum (2016), with more than 1,000 artefacts on just 500 square metres' exhibition space. This demands precision, well-dosed and accurate use of design instruments, an orchestration of graphics, light, and media–a chamber play at the most ambitious level, in which every instrument has to play a solo. This applies all the more so for the staging of the objects themselves. In the epochal showcases, they are arranged as individual pieces and collectively in aesthetic tableaux, consistently themed and chronological, to form powerful images. They create a visual draw and train the attention thus gained directly on themselves.

„Das Objekt ist der Star" ist eine beliebte Formel, um den Fokus auf das Objekt zu lenken und es in sicheren Vitrinen zu verwahren, denn Stars sind sensibel, brauchen Schutz und dürfen nicht berührt werden. Man holt die Besucher ins Museum mit dem Argument, den Exponaten – in der Regel Originalen – nah sein zu können, aber isoliert sie dann wieder in geschlossenen Vitrinen. Wie kann man diesen Anachronismus szenografisch auflösen? Wie kann man die notwendige konservatorische Distanz einhalten und trotzdem Nähe zu den Exponaten herstellen, diese zum Sprechen bringen?

ARCHÄOLOGIE SCHWEIZ Eine enorme Herausforderung in dieser Hinsicht war die Archäologische Dauerausstellung im Schweizer Nationalmuseum (2016) mit über 1.000 Objekten auf nur 500 Quadratmetern Ausstellungsfläche. Das verlangt Präzision, wohldosierten und treffsicheren Einsatz aller Gestaltungsinstrumente, eine Orchestrierung von Grafik, Licht und Medien – ein Kammerspiel auf anspruchsvollstem Niveau, in dem jedes Instrument ein Solo spielen können muss. Das gilt umso mehr für die Inszenierung der Objekte selbst. In den Epochenvitrinen sind sie als Einzelstücke und im Kollektiv themenkonsistent und chronologisch in ästhetischen Tableaus bildmächtig arrangiert.

"Archaeology Switzerland–National Museum"–Epochal showcase, Early Middle Ages (476 – 800) with movable scanner, 2016.

The subtle object presentation and the discreet object mounts underline the high design standards. Anyone who is interested in the stories and the content beyond the auratic charisma of the exhibits can dive into further information levels via sliding, digital scanner monitors. Then, at the latest, an auratic and media-based presentation in the museum is no longer a contradiction in terms. Visitors decide for themselves when, where, and how much information they want to retrieve, that is, as "information on demand."

At the end of the central epochal strip, visitors find themselves seated in a showcase—as an "exhibit," reflecting on Stefan Zweig's question: "Is it really me who is sitting here?"

Sie erzeugen einen visuellen Sog und lenken die so gewonnene Aufmerksamkeit unmittelbar auf sich selbst.

Die subtile Objektpräsentation und die dezenten Objekthalterungen unterstreichen den hohen gestalterischen Anspruch. Wer sich für die Geschichten und Inhalte jenseits der auratischen Ausstrahlung der Exponate interessiert, kann sich über die verschiebbaren digitalen Scannermonitore in weitere Informationsebenen vertiefen. Spätestens dann ist eine auratische und mediale Präsentation im Museum kein Widerspruch mehr. Die Besucher entscheiden selbst, wann, wo und wie viel Information sie abrufen wollen, auf Anforderung, also als „Information on Demand".

Am Ende des zentralen Epochenbands findet sich der Besucher selbst in einer Vitrine sitzend – als „Exponat" und über Stefan Zweigs Frage reflektierend: „Bin das eigentlich wirklich ich, der da sitzt?"

↗ p. 242

"Archaeology Switzerland–National Museum"–Concept "Chamber Museum." The central epochal strip is dedicated to the human species; it starts with the earliest humans found in Switzerland and ends with the visitor placing himself like an artefact listening to philosopher Stefan Zweig asking: "Is it really me who is sitting here?", 2016.

Exhibiting objects that are in fact products on a museum level means not only promoting their monetary value or symbolic status. Rather, it is about staging their design, their innovative added value, and their public or even social relevance. And, of course, to enable visitors to experience their narrative, often even iconic potential, and scenographically to translate the stories and legends they contain.

↗ p. 54

BMW MUSEUM, LIGHTWEIGHT CONSTRUCTION The first aluminium lightweight construction of a BMW 328 Millemiglia racing vehicle was more than a note in the margin for the curators of the BMW Museum (2008). The idea was to allow visitors to physically experience the separation of frame and shell, the huge saving of materials, and the additional rigidity of the tubular frame and bodywork, and to put this technological advancement into a visual context. An original BMW 328 is therefore exhibited in dialogue with a suspended 328 tubular frame as an exhibit on a par with the whole vehicle. What is more, it is hanging at a height as if it were being carried by a fitter. Four spring scales show that the tubular frame weighs just 28 kilograms. The object thus becomes a carrier of its message and an exhibit with contextualised meaning, while at the same time exuding maximum auratic presence.

Objekte, die eigentlich Produkte sind, auf Museumsniveau auszustellen, heißt, nicht nur ihren monetären Wert oder Symbolstatus zu bewerben, sondern ihr Design, ihren innovativen Mehrwert und ihre öffentliche oder gar gesellschaftliche Relevanz zu inszenieren. Natürlich geht es auch darum, ihre narrativen, häufig auch ihre ikonografischen Potenziale erlebbar zu machen und die ihnen eingeschriebenen Geschichten oder Legenden szenografisch zu übersetzen.

BMW MUSEUM, LEICHTBAU Nicht nur für die Kuratoren des BMW Museums (2008) war die erste Aluminium-Leichtbauweise eines BMW-328-Millemiglia-Rennfahrzeugs mehr als nur eine Randnotiz. Die Trennung von Rahmen und Hülle, die enorme Materialeinsparung und die zusätzliche Steifigkeit von Rohrrahmen und Karosserie sollten physisch erlebbar und visuell kontextualisiert werden. Ein originaler BMW 328 steht daher in dialogischer Aufstellung einem hängenden 328-Rohrrahmen gegenüber, als wollte man zum Ausdruck bringen, dass das Korsett so wichtig ist wie das Kleid – der Elektron-Rohrrahmen als gleichwertiges Exponat zum ganzen Fahrzeug. Noch dazu hängt er in einer Höhe, als würde er gerade von einem Monteur getragen. Vier Federwaagen weisen das Gewicht des Rohrrahmens mit nur 28 Kilogramm aus.

"BMW Museum"–BMW 328, lightweight cage. To demonstrate the perfection and lightness of the 328 aluminium frame the object is suspended from springscales, which show a total weight of just 28 kilograms, 2008.

BMW SCULPTURE The ephemeral process of design was to be given a physical dimension in the themed cube devoted to design. The brief: to transform a sheet of paper with a sketch into a three-dimensional vehicle. The solution lay in a radical change of perspective–not showing the individual steps of the design, but thinking back from the result, the finished model. The form of the chassis was deconstructed into vector points and translated into 714 aluminium balls that can move around completely freely thanks to the computer-controlled kinetics and be put together in different forms.[75]

The result is a dynamic, abstract object, a substitute for many objects that, as artistically translated sculpture, can subsume the many shape-finding steps and historical and current vehicle silhouettes in a single installation. The "BMW-Sculpture" has meanwhile itself become a museum object–the sculpture has developed into the iconographic symbol of the brand.

If one talks of architecture as an object that is to be staged as an exhibit, two categories of build-

75 A truly artistic translation by ART+COM, Berlin. For further information go to: www.artcom.de.

Das Objekt wird so zum Träger seiner Botschaft und zum Exponat mit kontextualisierter Bedeutung, bei gleichzeitig maximaler auratischer Präsenz.

BMW SKULPTUR Im Themenkubus „Design" sollte der ephemere Prozess des Gestaltens physisch erlebbar gemacht, ein Blatt Papier mit einer Skizze in ein dreidimensionales Fahrzeug verwandelt werden. Die Lösung lag in dem radikalen Perspektivwechsel, nicht die einzelnen Entwurfsschritte zu zeigen, sondern vom Ergebnis, vom fertigen Modell her zu denken. Die Form des Chassis wurde in Vektorpunkte zerlegt und in 714 Aluminiumkugeln übersetzt, die über eine computergesteuerte Kinetik völlig frei und zu unterschiedlichen Formen zusammengesetzt werden können.[75]

Dadurch entstand ein dynamisches, abstraktes Objekt, ein Substitut für viele Objekte, das als künstlerisch übersetzte Skulptur die Vielzahl von Formfindungsschritten sowie historische und aktuelle Fahrzeugsilhouetten in einer einzigen Installation subsumiert. Die „BMW-Skulptur" ist inzwischen selbst zum musealen Objekt geworden – die Skulptur hat sich zum ikonografischen Zeichen der Marke entwickelt.

Wenn man von Architektur als Objekt spricht, das als Ausstellungsstück inszeniert werden soll, kommen einem zwei Kategorien von Gebäuden

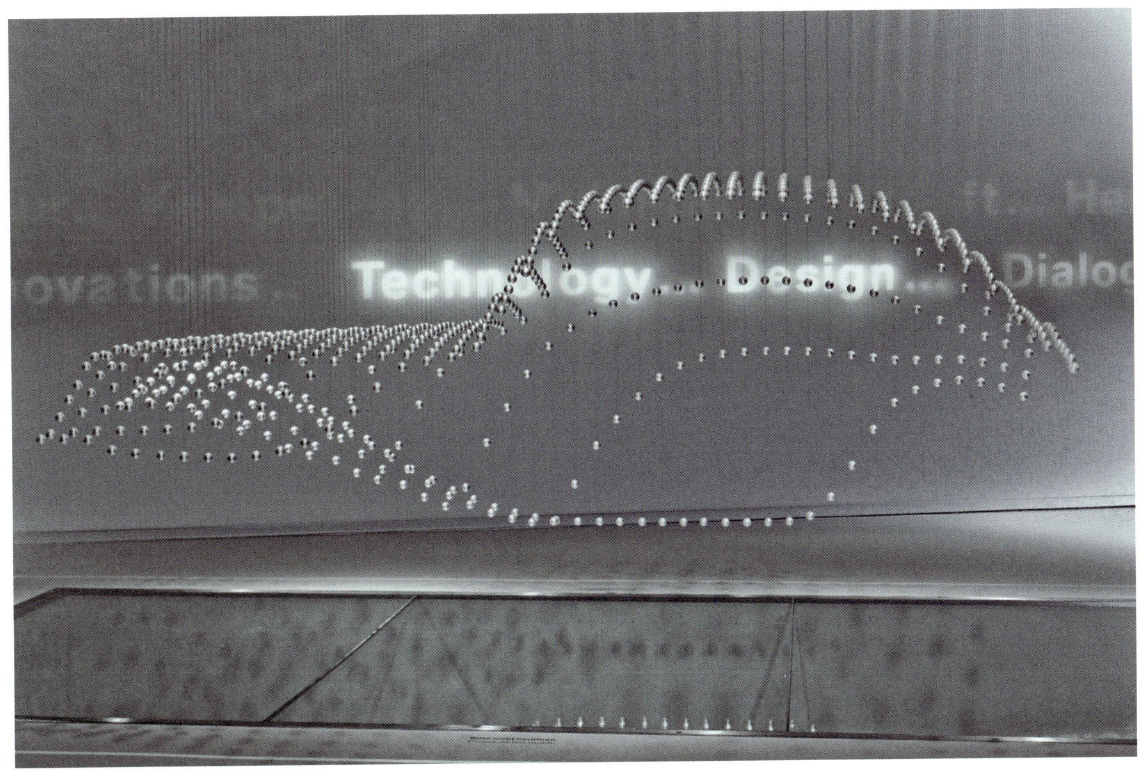

"BMW Museum"–In a computer-controlled installation, 714 aluminium balls configure ever-changing BMW vehicle models, 2008.

ing spring to mind. First, historical buildings which are given a new purpose and a new character through conversion, such as the smac–State Museum of Archaeology Chemnitz. Second, spectacular examples of architecture like the Guggenheim Bilbao; or third, Expo pavilions like the Cyclebowl, which themselves have the character of an exhibit and trigger associations or convey content through their appearance alone.

↗ p. 290

↗ p. 86

TEXTILWERK BOCHOLT The Textilwerk Bocholt (2011), a former spinning mill, was converted into a cultural centre with warehouse for shows, exhibition galleries, and catering. The original character was retained by making the various phases of use and time layers of and in the building legible. The Textilwerk opens to the street with a new ramp, which leads into a generous foyer, the gutted former energy centre. In the former shaft, which transported energy to the spinning halls, a red carpet leads visitors to the event rooms.

The building breathes the past and lives the present. An intelligent architectural intervention converted the ventilation unit on the roof into a restaurant with a roof terrace and a wonderful view. The Textilwerk has thus itself become an exhibit within the ensemble of buildings that make up the former industrial district.

in den Sinn. Zum einen historische Gebäude, die durch Konversion einen neuen Zweck und einen neuen Charakter erhalten, etwa das smac – Staatliches Museum für Archäologie Chemnitz. Zum anderen spektakuläre Architektur wie das Guggenheim Bilbao oder Expo-Pavillons wie die Cyclebowl, die selbst Exponatcharakter haben und Assoziationen auslösen oder Inhalte vermitteln sollen durch ihren bloßen Auftritt.

TEXTILWERK BOCHOLT Das Textilwerk Bocholt (2011), eine ehemalige Spinnerei, wurde in ein Kulturzentrum mit Schaulager, Ausstellungsgalerien und Gastronomie konvertiert. Durch die Ablesbarkeit der verschiedenen Nutzungsphasen und Zeitschichten am und im Gebäude blieb der ursprüngliche Charakter erhalten. Das Textilwerk öffnet sich zur Straße hin mit einer neuen Rampe, die in ein großzügiges Foyer, die entkernte frühere Energiezentrale, führt. Im ehemaligen Seilgang, der die Energie in die Säle der Spinnerei transportierte, leitet nun eine expressive rote Treppe die Besucher in die Veranstaltungsräume.

Im Gebäude atmet die Vergangenheit und lebt die Gegenwart. Eine intelligente Intervention verwandelte die Lüftungsanlage auf dem Dach in ein Restaurant mit Dachterrasse und herrlichem Blick. So wird das Textilwerk selbst zum Exponat im Ensemble des ehemaligen Industriequartiers.

"Textilwerk Bocholt"–In the new foyer, the impressive red stairs mark the central distribution zone–formerly housing the power distribution shaft, now directing visitors to the various galleries and venues, 2011.

WAGENHALLEN The Wagenhallen, former engine sheds of the German Railway from the 1890s, also have the character of an object.

Damaged in the war, rebuilt several times, converted and occupied by artists, the Wagenhallen have survived, due amongst other reasons to the unique flair of the shed roof halls with a footprint of more than 14,000 square metres. Users, architects, and the City of Stuttgart agreed that this unmistakable ambiance and the many time layers needed to be made legible in order to make the building talk. Restoration, upgrading, and architectural interventions take place in dialogue with the historical substance of the building. The new firewalls of fair-faced concrete are self-assuredly visible but reflect the language of the historical building.

As reference to the former usage, the old tracks should be reactivated and be used to move atelier containers out of the hall into the outer space. These flexible artist ateliers give the building room to breathe–dimension, structure, and historical function remain legible. The Wagenhallen will become an exemplary conversion object and the nucleus of a new city district.

WAGENHALLEN Auch die Stuttgarter Wagenhallen, eine ehemalige Lokomotivremise der Bundesbahn aus den 1890er-Jahren, haben Objektcharakter.

Im Krieg beschädigt, mehrmals umgebaut, umgenutzt und von Künstlern besetzt, haben die Wagenhallen überlebt, auch aufgrund des einzigartigen Flairs der Sheddach-Hallen mit über 14.000 Quadratmetern Grundfläche. Nutzer, Architekten und die Stadt Stuttgart waren sich einig, dieses unverwechselbare Ambiente zu erhalten und die vielen Zeitschichten ablesbar zu machen, um so das Gebäude zum Sprechen zu bringen. Sanierung, Ertüchtigung und architektonische Interventionen finden im Dialog mit der historischen Bausubstanz statt. Die neuen Brandwände aus Sichtbeton zeigen sich selbstbewusst, greifen aber die Sprache des historischen Gebäudes auf.

Als Referenz an die ehemalige Nutzung sollen die alten Schienen, auf denen Ateliercontainer aus der Halle in den Außenraum fahren können, reaktiviert werden. Diese flexiblen Künstlerateliers lassen dem Gebäude Raum zum Atmen – Dimension, Struktur und historische Funktion bleiben ablesbar. Die Wagenhallen werden zum exemplarischen Konversionsobjekt und zum Nukleus eines neuen Stadtviertels.

"Wagenhallen"–Fair-faced concrete with historical steel roof construction, in progress.

SPACE

THE SPACE IS THE MEDIUM

Uwe R. Brückner and Linda Greci

“All staged spaces are based on the same spatial parameters:
1. the physically substantive,
2. the atmospherically adjectival,
3. the narratively verbal and
4. the dramatised syntactical.
These four parameters share the purpose of making appropriate space available for the content to be conveyed, the objects to be exhibited and the intended messages.”

Uwe R. Brückner

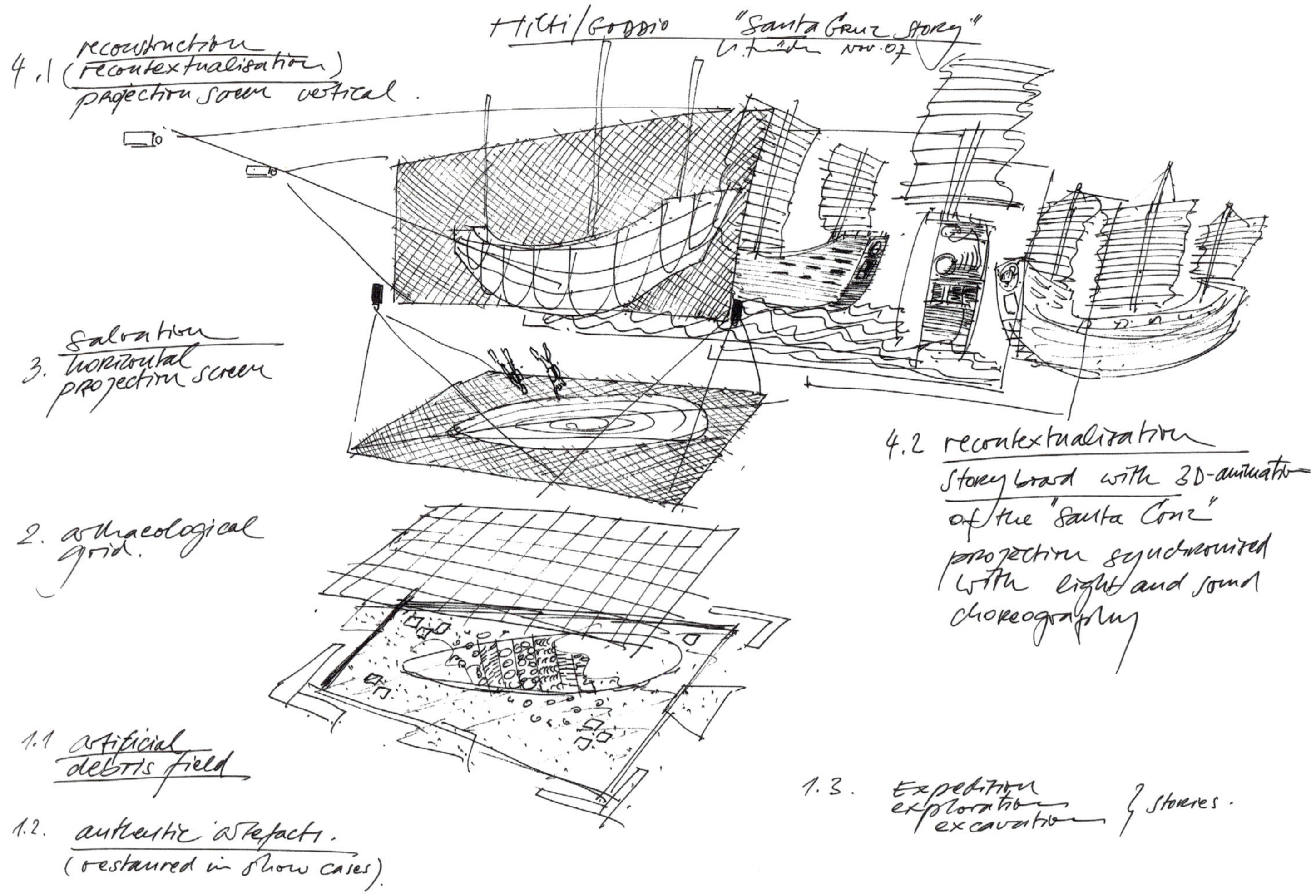

"Never work against the architecture—adopt the space and play it like an instrument." Uwe R. Brückner

"Goddio"–Storyboard of animated recontruction, 2007.

The space, with its potential for stage setting and narrative, is one of the foremost design parameters of scenography and serves as its central medium. Every space has its own language and its own message; it has a wide range of jargon, styles, and subjects. The space is environment, place, and stage; it can exclude, include, and frame and it can inform, convince, or deceive. Space is a place that endows meaning like a stage set in the theatre, on which interpretation and imagination enter a relationship. Staging a space also means the transformation of content and narration into atmosphere and emotion and the conversion of space in time. The staged space can have different dimensions and states of aggregation—including architectural, media-related, sculptural, and performative. It is a space for thought, a space for associations, a temporal space, a space for movement, an art space, an illusion space, an imagination space, an exploratory and narrative space.

Space is perceived intuitively, cognitively, and associatively; as a rule, the visitor experience is the sum of all these types of perception. Moreover, the way space is perceived is shaped by the individual experience of each person and by social, cultural, economic, and historical aspects. This way, the recipient can understand, experience, and feel subjectively.

The staged space as real space, capable of being shaped, can be a virtual or virtually extended space. Storytelling film spaces, projections, or images can, for example, dissolve or blur the physical borders of the space and create a new, additional spatial dimension in which visitors can immerse themselves. Virtually extended space creates a reality generated by media; it allows a metaphysical spatial experience and an extrasensory visitor experience.

Consistently staged spaces achieve a symbiotic interplay between content, object, space, recipient, and dramaturgy. For scenography, the focus is on the transformation of the physical space into a dramatized, atmospherically charged narrative space. For the scenographer, this entails using the opportunities to be found in the dialogue between (existing) architecture and design intervention. The built, physical space can always be the same and nevertheless always receive a different interpretation, staging, and message.

All staged spaces are the sum of the same four spatial parameters: 1. the physically substantive; 2. the atmospherically adjectival; 3. the narratively verbal; and 4. the dramatized syntactical

Der Raum mit seinem inszenatorischen und narrativen Potenzial ist einer der vorrangigen Gestaltungsparameter der Szenografie und fungiert als zentrales Medium. Jeder Raum besitzt seine eigene Sprache und seine eigene Aussage, er hat eine Vielfalt an Jargons, Stilen und Sujets. Der Raum ist Environment, Ort und Bühne, er kann aus-, ein- oder umgrenzen und er kann mitteilen, überzeugen oder täuschen. Der Raum ist ein Bedeutungsraum wie eine Theaterbühne, auf der inszeniert wird, auf der Interpretation und Imagination eine Beziehung eingehen. Das Inszenieren eines Raums meint auch die Transformation von Inhalten und Narration in Atmosphäre und Emotion und die Verwandlung von Raum in Abhängigkeit von Zeit. Der inszenierte Raum kann unterschiedlichste Dimensionen und Aggregatzustände einnehmen – unter anderem architektonische, mediale, skulpturale und performative. Er ist Denk-Raum, Assoziations-Raum, Emotions-Raum, Zeit-Raum, Bewegungs-Raum, Kunst-Raum, Illusions-Raum, Imaginations-Raum, Explorations-Raum und Narrations-Raum.

Raum wird intuitiv, kognitiv und assoziativ wahrgenommen. Das Besuchserlebnis entspricht in der Regel der Summe dieser Wahrnehmungsformen. Darüber hinaus ist die Raumwahrnehmung durch die individuelle Erfahrung eines jeden Menschen geprägt und durch soziale, kulturelle, ökonomische und historische Aspekte beeinflusst. So kann der Rezipient Räume ganz subjektiv begreifen, erfahren und empfinden.

Der inszenierte Raum als realer, formbarer Raum kann ein virtueller oder virtuell erweiterbarer Raum sein. Film-Räume, Projektions-Räume oder Bild-Räume können beispielsweise physische Raumgrenzen auflösen oder verschwimmen lassen und eine neue, zusätzliche Raumdimension schaffen, in die der Besucher eintauchen kann. Die virtuelle Raumerweiterung erzeugt eine medial konstruierte Wirklichkeit. Sie ermöglicht eine metaphysische Raumerfahrung und ein übersinnliches Besuchserlebnis.

Konsistent inszenierten Räumen gelingt eine symbiotische Wechselwirkung zwischen Inhalt, Objekt, Raum, Rezipient und Dramaturgie. Für die Szenografie steht die Transformation des physischen Raums in einen dramatisierten, atmosphärisch aufgeladenen Narrationsraum im Fokus. Für den Szenografen heißt das, die Chance zu nutzen, die im Dialog zwischen (bestehender) Architektur und gestalterischer Intervention steckt. Ein und derselbe gebaute, physische Raum kann

space

dimensions

states of aggregation

perception of space

virtual space

space.[76] The shared purpose of these four parameters is to provide an adequate space for content, objects, intended messages, and for the reception. Each of these four space parameters reveals a specific quality of the space, and the way they work together in a dramaturgical conception entices the visitor to engage with the staging.

physical space

1. THE PHYSICAL SPACE—OR THE PHYSICALLY SUBSTANTIVE PARAMETER The physical space is determined by its borders, the exclusion of the surroundings, the demarcation of the scope for action and thought. It acts as a boundary between the inside and the outside, between content and context. Its dimension, its spatial shell, materiality, and its capability of displaying content is the focus of attention and form a space for intervention. The volume capable of displaying content is defined by the physical presence of the surfaces framing the space—wall, floor, and ceiling. The space is characterised by its openings such as entrance and exit, but also by the windows, which transform the space into a daylight space, or, if closed off, a black box. It is a substantive parameter because the briefing mainly uses nouns to describe the features of the physical space such as wall, floor, ceiling, entrance, and exit. An architectonic space in an existing building is particularly effective if it is not just a functional shell or a built sculpture for content inserted subsequently but if it consistently develops content or is itself generated directly from the content, thus applying the credo "form follows content." "Well-staged space unifies or breaks down boundaries; it admits rather than excludes."[77]

76 Atelier Brückner 2016, p. 171.
77 Uwe R. Brückner

immer wieder eine andere Interpretation, Inszenierung und Botschaft erhalten.

Allen inszenierten Räumen liegen in der Summe dieselben vier Raumparameter zugrunde: 1. der physisch-substantivische, 2. der atmosphärisch-adjektivische, 3. der narrativ-verbische und 4. der dramatisiert-syntaktische. Diese vier Parameter haben die gemeinsame Bestimmung, einen adäquaten Raum für Inhalte, Objekte, intendierte Botschaften und für die Rezeption zu erschaffen.[76] Jeder dieser vier Raumparameter zeigt eine spezifische Qualität des Raums auf, und ihr Zusammenspiel in einer dramaturgischen Konzeption verführt die Besucher, sich auf die Inszenierung einzulassen.

1. DER PHYSISCHE RAUM – ODER DER PHYSISCH-SUBSTANTIVISCHE PARAMETER Die Bestimmung des physischen Raums erfolgt durch seine Umgrenzung, die Ausgrenzung des Umfelds, die Eingrenzung des Handlungs-, Denk- und Spielraums. Er fungiert als Grenze zwischen innen und außen, zwischen Inhalt und Kontext. Seine Dimension, seine Raumhülle, Materialität und seine Bespielbarkeit stehen im Fokus und bilden einen Interventionsraum. Durch die physische Präsenz der umgrenzenden Oberflächen – Wand, Boden und Decke – definiert sich das bespielbare Volumen. Der Raum wird durch seine Öffnungen wie Eingang und Ausgang, aber auch durch Fenster, die den Raum zu einem Tageslichtraum oder bei Abschottung zu einer Black Box verwandeln, charakterisiert. Er ist ein substantivischer Parameter, weil die Eigenheiten des physischen Raums im Briefing meist mit Substantiven wie Wand, Boden, Decke, Eingang oder Ausgang beschrieben werden. Ein architektonisch-baulicher Raum ist besonders wirkungsvoll, wenn er nicht nur eine funktionale Hülle ist oder eine gebaute Skulptur für einen nachträglich eingebrachten Inhalt darstellt, sondern wenn er Inhalte konsistent konzipiert oder direkt aus dem Inhalt generiert wird und somit das Credo „Form follows content" einlöst. „Gut inszenierter Raum umgrenzt oder entgrenzt, schließt nicht aus, sondern lässt zu."[77]

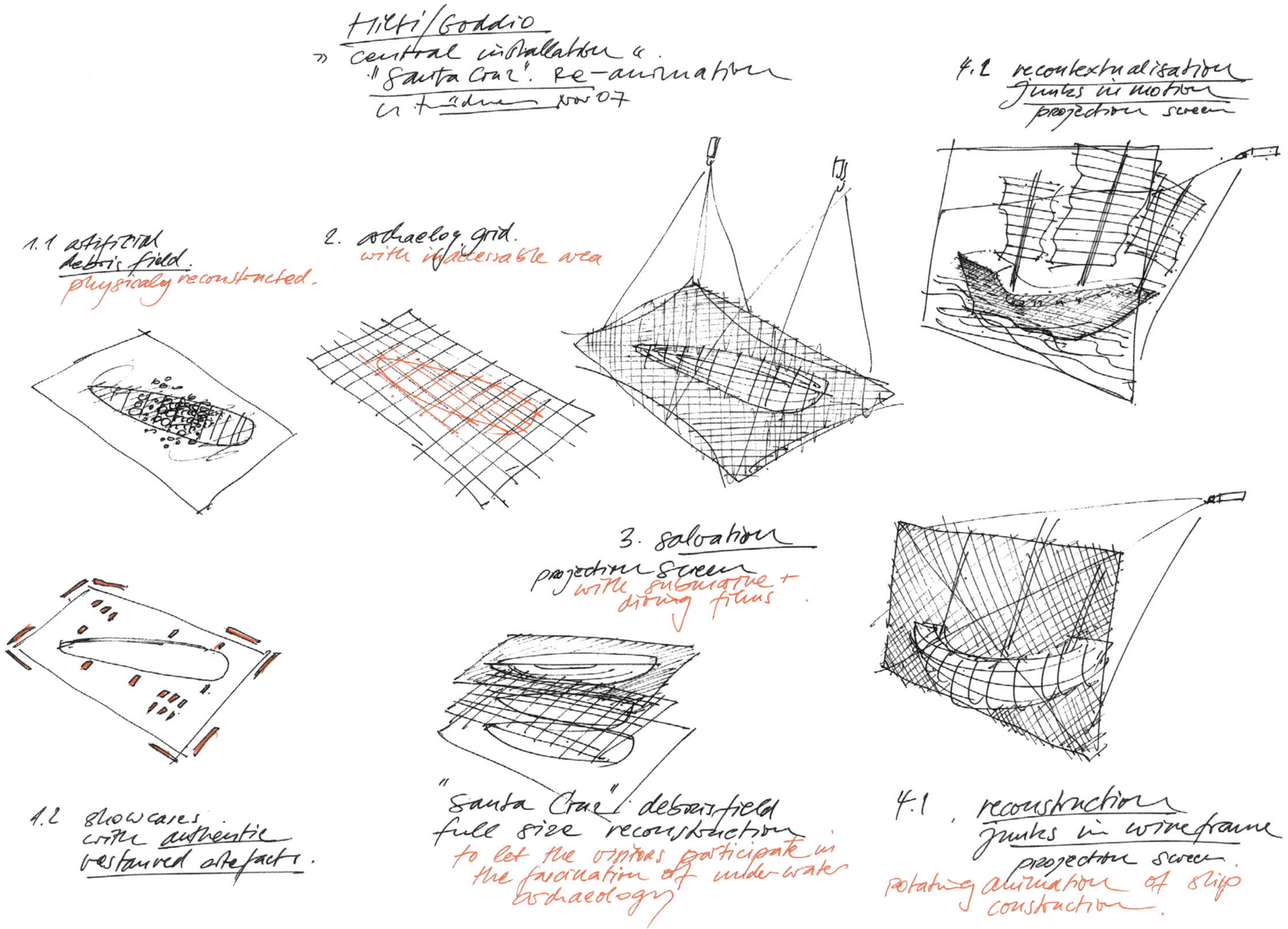

"Goddio"–Concept of projection mapping, 2007.

atmospheric space

2. THE ATMOSPHERIC SPACE—OR THE ATMOSPHERICALLY ADJECTIVAL The atmospheric space is a tuned, emotionalised space. Its aggregate states can be changed, its features can be declined, and it is perceived with the senses. It is about materiality and surface (structures), the temperatures in the room, light and its tonality, but also about colours, shapes, scents, acoustics, and sound. It is described with the help of adjectives like light, dark, noisy, quiet, poetic, distanced, or dynamic. Depending on the way these characteristics are used, the space is given a particular atmosphere and performative aura. The creation of a specific spatial atmosphere facilitates access to complex topics and supports the willingness of visitors to approach content via the intuitive experience and sensory perception. Ideally, a consistent field of tension is created between the spatial atmosphere, the object, the content, and the recipient. "The atmospheric space is synaesthetic, emotional, and intravenous–sensed, not read."[78]

narrative space

3. THE NARRATIVE SPACE—OR THE NARRATIVELY VERBAL PARAMETER The narrative space is shaped by its storytelling characteristics and poetic aspects. It is a space that tells or triggers stories. It uses verbal means–language, words, texts, signs, and symbols–to tell stories which refer to action and change. The narration generates spaces, and spaces become a narrative medium. And when the space itself becomes a narrative medium, when the staging using text, graphics, or sound makes the space into a carrier of information, then the result is a walk-in narrative and a dialogue between space and recipient. Free to move around in the exhibition room, the recipient can influence and change the story. The exhibition design has to use the narrative potential to create an experiential level. Like a verb, a narrative space can be conjugated and adjusted to match its subject. It is a verbal volume, a talking medium, a built message: a space with past, present, and future. "The narrative space always has a before, a now and after."[79]

78 Uwe R. Brückner
79 Uwe R. Brückner

2. DER ATMOSPHÄRISCHE RAUM – ODER DER ATMOSPHÄRISCH-ADJEKTIVISCHE PARAMETER Der atmosphärische Raum ist ein gestimmter, emotionalisierter Raum. Seine Aggregatzustände sind veränderbar, seine Eigenschaften deklinierbar und seine Wahrnehmung ist sinnlich. Es geht um Materialität und Oberflächen(-strukturen), um Temperaturen des Raums, um Licht und dessen Tonalitäten, aber auch um Farben, Formen, Gerüche, Akustik und Klang. Seine Beschreibung erfolgt über Adjektive wie hell, dunkel, laut, leise, poetisch, distanziert oder dynamisch. Je nach unterschiedlicher Ausgestaltung dieser Eigenschaften bekommt der Raum eine spezifische Atmosphäre und eine performative Aura. Durch das Herstellen spezifischer Raummilieus wird der Zugang zu komplexen Themen erleichtert und die Bereitschaft unterstützt, dass die Besucher sich den Inhalten über die intuitive Erfahrung und sinnliche Wahrnehmung nähern. Es entsteht im optimalen Fall ein konsistentes Spannungsfeld zwischen der Raumstimmung, dem Objekt, dem Inhalt und dem Rezipienten. „Der atmosphärische Raum ist synästhetisch, emotional und ‚intravenös' – gefühlt, nicht gelesen."[78]

3. DER NARRATIVE RAUM – ODER DER NARRATIV-VERBALE PARAMETER Der narrative Raum ist über seine erzählerischen Eigenschaften und poetischen Aspekte charakterisiert. Er ist ein Geschichten erzählender oder Geschichten auslösender Raum. Er bedient sich des Verbalen – Sprache, Worte, Texte, Zeichen und Symbole – und erzählt Geschichten, die auf Handlung und Veränderung verweisen. Die Erzählung generiert Räume, und Räume werden zu erzählerischen Medien. Und wenn der Raum selbst zum erzählenden Medium wird, wenn durch die Inszenierung mit Text, Grafik oder Ton der Raum zum Träger von Information avanciert, dann entstehen eine begehbare Story und ein Dialog zwischen Raum und Rezipient. Durch seine autarke Beweglichkeit im Ausstellungsraum kann der Rezipient die Geschichte beeinflussen und verändern. Das Erlebbarmachen muss die Ausstellungsgestaltung leisten, indem sie die erzählerischen Potenziale nutzt und einlöst. Der narrative Raum ist wie ein Verb konjugierbar und lässt sich seinem Sujet anpassen. Er ist ein „verbales Volumen", ein sprechendes Medium, eine gebaute Botschaft; ein Raum mit Vergangenheit, Gegenwart oder Zukunft. „Der narrative Raum hat immer ein Davor, ein Jetzt und ein Danach."[79]

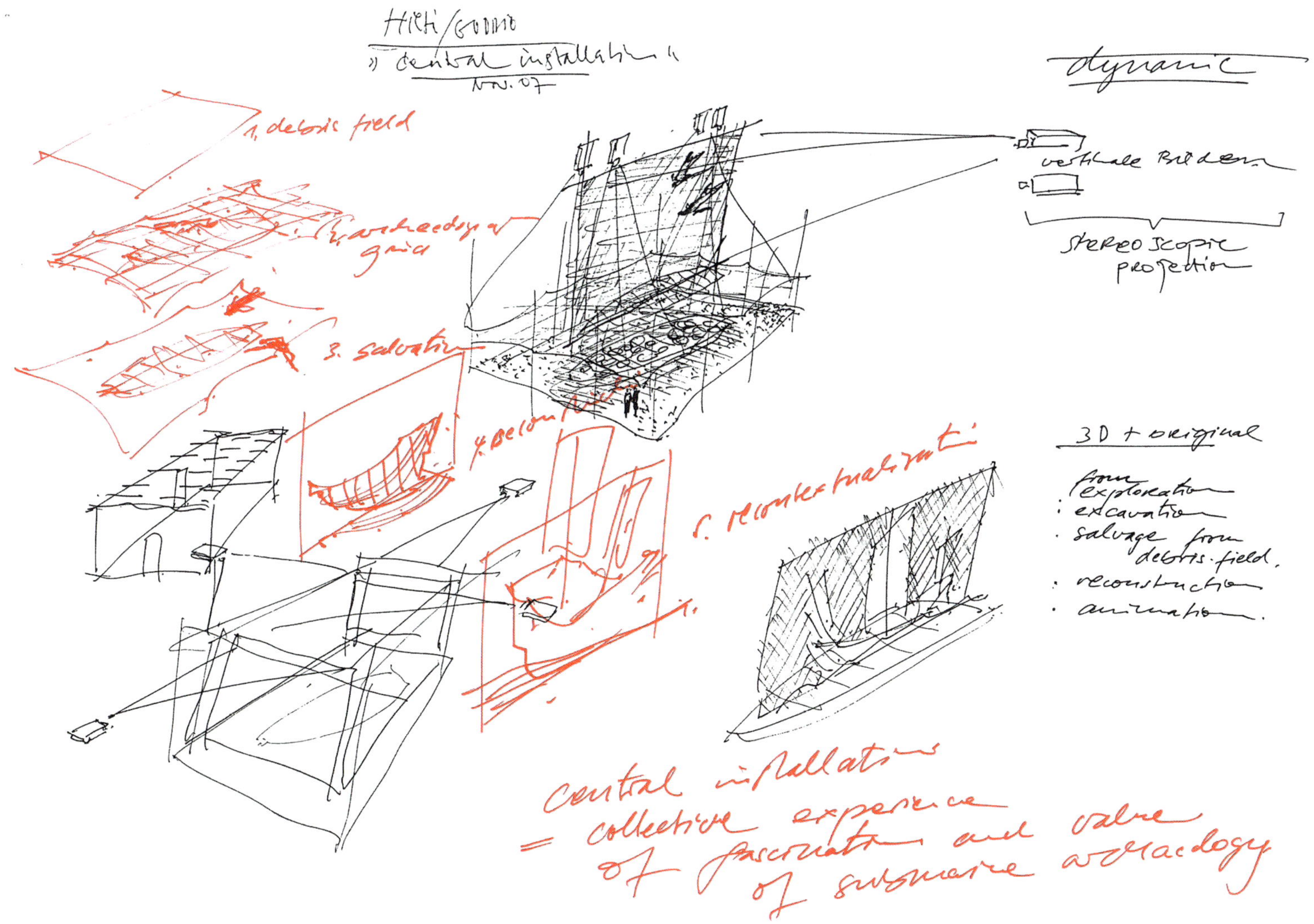

"Goddio"–Concept for screen setting, 2007.

dramatized space

4. THE DRAMATIZED SPACE—OR THE DRAMATIZED, SYNTACTICAL PARAMETER The dramatized space implies structure, suspense, rhythm, and dynamics. It is a choreographed space with an arc of suspense, the sequence of topics skilfully chosen for dramaturgical effect, the dramaturgical interpretation of things and their stories, their perception or effect on the recipient. And it is about the synchronised use of various scenographic instruments, usually described in a score. It is about the place and its ability to be transformed, and time as a design factor. The dramatized parameter can create movement in a space, thus bringing it to life as a medium. The dramatized space follows its own syntax of a narrative structure, a way of reading and classifying experiences, which builds suspense, provokes expectations, and converts these into a climax. "The dramatized space allows choreographed experience."[80]

narrative space

5. THE STAGED SPACE—OR THE SPATIAL IMAGE AS GESAMTKUNSTWERK We call the symbiosis and interplay of these four spatial parameters the spatial image. It orchestrates the many different staging instruments and creates an overall composition that allows a dialogue between space and content, between object and recipient.[81] The spatial image is a large gesture and forms a walk-in milieu—the subject for everything that is to be conveyed informatively, sensually, or emotionally. It allows the visitor to get to grips with an idea, to decipher content, to get to the bottom of things, or to find the soul of matter. Spatial images are not the illustration or decoration of content; they generate content and make it self-explanatory. They are able to (re-)contextualise objects and convey their stories and messages—directly or through association. They explore the narrative quintessence of an exhibition's theme, looking ahead and creating metaphors; they offer space for the stories to be narrated. Spatial images appeal above all to the deeper layers of consciousness and influence the non-cognitive perception with a sustainable effect. They astound, excite, captivate, and seduce. They allow the past to be rediscovered, shed a new light on known facts, and provoke involvement in the sense of a collective relevance and individual enthusiasm.[82]

80 Uwe R. Brückner
81 See Atelier Brückner 2016, p. 69.
82 See Brückner and Greci 2016, p. 43.

4. DER DRAMATISIERTE RAUM – ODER DER DRAMATISIERT-SYNTAKTISCHE PARAMETER Der dramatisierte Raum impliziert Struktur, Spannung, Rhythmus und Dynamik. Es handelt sich um den choreografierten Raum mit Spannungsbogen, die dramaturgisch geschickt gewählte Abfolge von Themen, die dramaturgische Fassung von Dingen und deren Geschichten, ihrer Wahrnehmung oder Wirkung auf die Adressaten. Und es geht um den synchronisierten Einsatz verschiedener szenografischer Instrumentarien, deren Beschreibung in der Regel in einer Partitur erfolgt. Es geht um den Ort und seine Verwandlungsfähigkeit und die Zeit als Gestaltungsfaktor. Der dramatisierte Parameter kann Raum in Bewegung versetzen und zum lebendigen Medium machen. Der dramatisierte Raum folgt einer eigenen Syntax einer Erzählstruktur, einer Lesart und Erlebensgliederung, die Spannung aufbaut, Erwartungen provoziert und diese in einer Erlebnisklimax einlöst. „Der dramatisierte Raum ermöglicht choreografiertes Erleben."[80]

5. DER INSZENIERTE RAUM – ODER DAS RAUMBILD ALS GESAMTKUNSTWERK Die Symbiose und das Zusammenspiel dieser vier Raumparameter nennen wir das Raumbild. Es orchestriert vielfältige Inszenierungs-Instrumente und schafft eine Gesamtkomposition, die einen Dialog zwischen Raum und Inhalt, zwischen Objekt und Rezipient ermöglicht.[81] Das Raumbild ist eine große Geste und bildet ein begehbares Milieu – das Sujet für all das, was informativ, sinnlich oder emotional transportiert werden soll. Es verleitet die Besucher dazu, sich einer Idee anzunähern, Inhalte zu dechiffrieren, den Dingen auf den Grund zu gehen oder die Seele einer Sache aufzuspüren. Raumbilder sind keine Illustration oder Dekoration von Inhalten, sondern in besonderem Maße inhaltsgeneriert und selbsterklärend. Sie ermöglichen die (Re-)Kontextualisierung von Objekten und die Vermittlung ihrer Geschichten und Botschaften – unmittelbar und assoziativ. Sie erschließen die erzählerische Quintessenz eines Ausstellungsthemas, sie sind Vorschau und Metapher, sie sind Spielräume der Erzählung. Raumbilder sprechen vor allem die tieferen Schichten des Bewusstseins an und beeinflussen die nicht kognitive Wahrnehmung mit nachhaltigem Effekt. Sie verblüffen, begeistern, entführen und verführen. Sie lassen Vergangenes wiederentdecken, belichten Bekanntes neu und provozieren Betroffenheit im Sinne einer kollektiven Relevanz und individuellen Begeisterung.[82]

Spatial images create images of remembrance that instantly become memories. Finding and inventing spatial images is the trademark of the Atelier. Like “form follows content,” “from content to spatial image” has become a guiding principle of scenographic work.

Scenography transforms space and all things spatial. It translates content into a spatial dimension and generates spatial images as poetic environments, making the visitors part of the staging in the process. The space parameter with all its facets is able to convey knowledge and generate authentic experiences for visitors. In addition, the space–beyond its physical function–becomes a stage, a place to stage messages, a carrier of messages. It is thus not just available, it itself becomes a medium that talks.

Raumbilder sind Erinnerungsbilder, die sich augenblicklich ins Gedächtnis einbrennen. Das Finden und Erfinden von Raumbildern ist Markenzeichen des ATELIER BRÜCKNER. „Vom Inhalt zum Raumbild“ ist wie „Form follows content“ zum Leitsatz des szenografischen Arbeitens geworden.

Szenografie transformiert Raum und alles Räumliche. Sie vollzieht eine raumgenerierende Übersetzung der Inhalte und erzeugt Raumbilder als poetische Environments, die die Besucher zum Teil der Inszenierung machen. Der Parameter Raum in all seinen Facetten ist dazu befähigt, Wissen zu vermitteln und authentische Erlebnisse für die Besucher zu generieren. Außerdem wird der Raum – jenseits seiner physischen Funktion – zur Bühne, zum Ort der Inszenierung von Botschaften, zum Botschaftenträger. Er stellt sich also nicht nur zur Verfügung, sondern wird selbst zum sprechenden Medium.

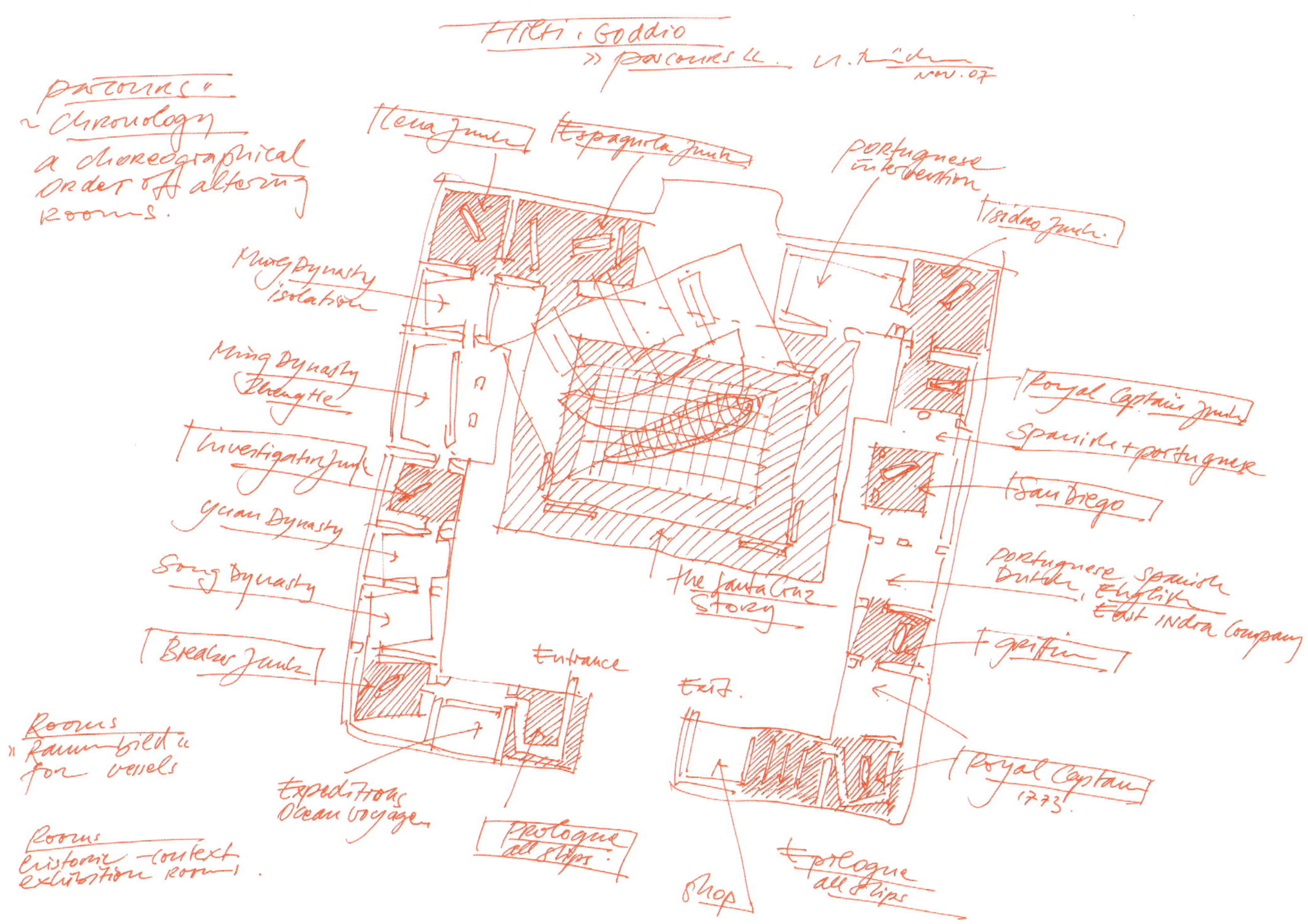

“Goddio”–scheme floor plan of thematic parcours and central installation, 2007.

Fritz Auer, Auer Weber Assoziierte

STORYTELLER ON THE ARCHITECTURAL STAGE ATELIER BRÜCKNER is an exceptional phenomenon, even from the perspective of a "pure play" architect. Why? Via predefined programs and existing situations—be they geographical, social, or even political constellations—the "pure play" architect is used to developing facilities and buildings with his professional tools which pick up these premises as closely as possible and realise them in the best possible way.

One could call this kind of architect a "service provider" without disqualifying this term as a reduction to what is "strictly necessary."

Even ATELIER BRÜCKNER cannot avoid this level in their projects. But the many projects that have been realised—and what is more, the projects that have not been realised—show that for the Atelier team, the pure "service" is not enough to inspire and convince the client. What is the surplus that drives them to go beyond this level of the strictly necessary?

ATELIER BRÜCKNER has the ability to sort the hard facts of a task, indeed to stage them, in such a way that they become "stories" which—and this is what makes the approach special—are initially developed and told in a series of sketches in such a way that they boost the imaginative power and emotional intensity of those for whom it is intended, taking them beyond the purely factual, beyond what is strictly necessary. This extraordinary and ambitious design approach is what has rightly made ATELIER BRÜCKNER successful internationally.

Uwe R. Brückner is far more than a "pure play" architect, because after his architecture studies he made his way to scenography and exhibition design, as befits a storyteller.

This is where, in my opinion, the special quality of his and the work of the Atelier lies—which in every project, each in its own way, gives us an idea of and lets us experience the versatility that emerges from this fusion of stupendous professionalism and the theatrical exaggeration of the field of work of a "pure" architect, managing again and again to surprise and astonish us.

DIE GESCHICHTENERZÄHLER AUF DER BÜHNE DER ARCHITEKTUR

Das ATELIER BRÜCKNER ist, auch aus Sicht eines „reinen“ Architekten, eine Ausnahmeerscheinung. Warum? Der „reine“ Architekt ist gewohnt, über vorgegebene Programme und vorgefundene Situationen – seien es geografische, soziale oder gar politische Konstellationen – mit seinen fachlichen Mitteln Anlagen und Baulichkeiten zu entwickeln, die möglichst genau diese Prämissen aufgreifen und sie im besten Sinne umsetzen.

Man könnte diese Art von Architekten auch „Dienstleister“ nennen, ohne diese Bezeichnung als Herabsetzung nur ins „Notwendige“ abzuqualifizieren.

Auch das ATELIER BRÜCKNER wird bei seinen Projekten nicht um diese Ebene herumkommen. Aber die vielfältigen realisierten, mehr noch die nicht realisierten Projekte zeigen, dass dem Team des Ateliers die reine „Dienstleistung“ nicht reicht, um seine Auftraggeber davon einzunehmen und zu überzeugen. Was ist also das Mehr, das „Surplus“, was es antreibt, um über diese Ebene des Notwendigen hinauszukommen?

ATELIER BRÜCKNER hat die Fähigkeit, die harten Fakten einer Aufgabenstellung so zu sortieren, ja auch in Szene zu setzen, dass daraus „Geschichten“ werden, die – und das ist das Besondere an der Herangehensweise – zunächst in skizzenhaften Bildern entwickelt und erzählt werden, sodass sie für diejenigen, für die sie gedacht sind, eben das Mehr an Vorstellungskraft und Erlebnishaftigkeit bewirken, welches über das rein Sachliche, das nur Notwendige hinausführt. Diese außergewöhnliche und ambitionierte Gestaltungshaltung hat das ATELIER BRÜCKNER zu Recht international erfolgreich gemacht.

Uwe R. Brückner ist also weit mehr als ein „reiner“ Architekt, weil er über das Architekturstudium hinaus – wie könnte es bei einem Geschichtenerzähler anders sein – zur Szenografie und zur Ausstellungsgestaltung gefunden hat.

Darin liegt aus meiner Sicht die besondere Qualität seiner und der Arbeit des Ateliers – die bei jedem Projekt auf jeweils eigene Art die Vielseitigkeit erahnen und erleben lässt, die aus dieser Verbindung von stupender Professionalität und schauspielerischer Überhöhung des Arbeitsfeldes des „reinen“ Architekten entsteht und uns immer wieder aufs Neue überrascht und in Erstaunen versetzt.

Architecture can, of course, have scenographic qualities–as demonstrated by museums, galleries, or public buildings–or can be designed taking scenographic aspects into account. Architecture can be used as a projection surface for light, film, or sound, can change physically, or take on various different appearances. The architectural space can be used for scenographic interventions, can transform into a meeting point, open theatre, or urban stage. It has character, it can show attitude, can invite or radiate, can give identity, can express itself, and itself become the carrier of a message, entering into a dialogue with the place and the people.

Selbstverständlich kann Architektur, wie Museen, Galerien oder öffentliche Gebäude beweisen, szenografische Qualitäten haben oder unter szenografischen Gesichtspunkten gestaltet werden. Architektur kann dynamisch bespielt werden, mit Licht, Film oder Sound, sich physisch wandeln oder verschiedene Erscheinungsformen annehmen. Der architektonische Raum kann szenografisch bespielt werden, kann sich zum Treffpunkt, offenen Theater, zur urbanen Bühne wandeln. Er hat Charakter, kann Haltung zeigen, kann einladen oder ausstrahlen, kann Identität stiften, kann sich äußern und selbst zum Träger einer Botschaft werden, einen Dialog mit dem Ort und den Menschen eingehen.

“Scenographic space is narrative space–it gives space relevance and personality, it becomes a messenger.” Uwe R. Brückner

“Troisdorf City Gate”–Rendering featuring Kindergarten (left) and City Gate (right), in progress.

TROISDORF CITY GATE As city gate, the new parish centre of the Catholic church parish of Saint Hippolytus creates a prominent urban planning highlight in the heterogeneous cityscape of Troisdorf. As a new entrance to the city, the three large approaches of the "city gate" open up to form the newly designed, star-shaped city plaza. They enter into a dialogue with the city and as an ensemble with the kindergarten and church make an inviting gesture. The plaza flows into the interim space and passes straight through the building. The interior space becomes a city space. The generous, tripartite ground floor can be used in many different ways and can be subdivided into several units. These include the parish hall, the foyer, and café for the local Troisdorf Tafel e.V., and as venues for any manner of cultural events.

A wide range of usages are combined in this place that adapts to the needs of the community. The Troisdorf City Gate is parish centre and district stage, an urban meeting place, a house for everyone, a place for community.

TROISDORF STADTTOR Das neue Pfarrzentrum der katholischen Kirchengemeinde St. Hippolytus setzt als Stadttor einen prominenten städtebaulichen Akzent im heterogenen Stadtraum von Troisdorf. Als neuer Stadteingang öffnen sich die drei großen Zugänge des „Stadttors" sternförmig zum neu gestalteten Stadtplatz. Sie treten in Dialog mit der Stadt und bilden als Ensemble mit Kindergarten und Kirche eine einladende Geste. Der Platz fließt in den Zwischenraum hinein und führt geradewegs durch das Gebäude hindurch. Der Innenraum wird zum Stadtraum. Das großzügige dreigliedrige Erdgeschoss ist vielfach bespielbar und kann in mehrere Raumeinheiten unterteilt werden. Sie dienen unter anderem als Pfarrsaal, als Foyer und Café für die ortsansässige Troisdorfer Tafel e.V. und als Orte für vielfältige kulturelle Veranstaltungen.

Die verschiedensten Nutzungen werden an diesem Ort, der sich den Bedürfnissen der Gemeinschaft anpasst, zusammengeführt. Das Troisdorfer Stadttor ist Pfarrzentrum und Stadtteilbühne zugleich, ein urbaner Treffpunkt, ein Haus für alle, ein Ort für die Gemeinschaft.

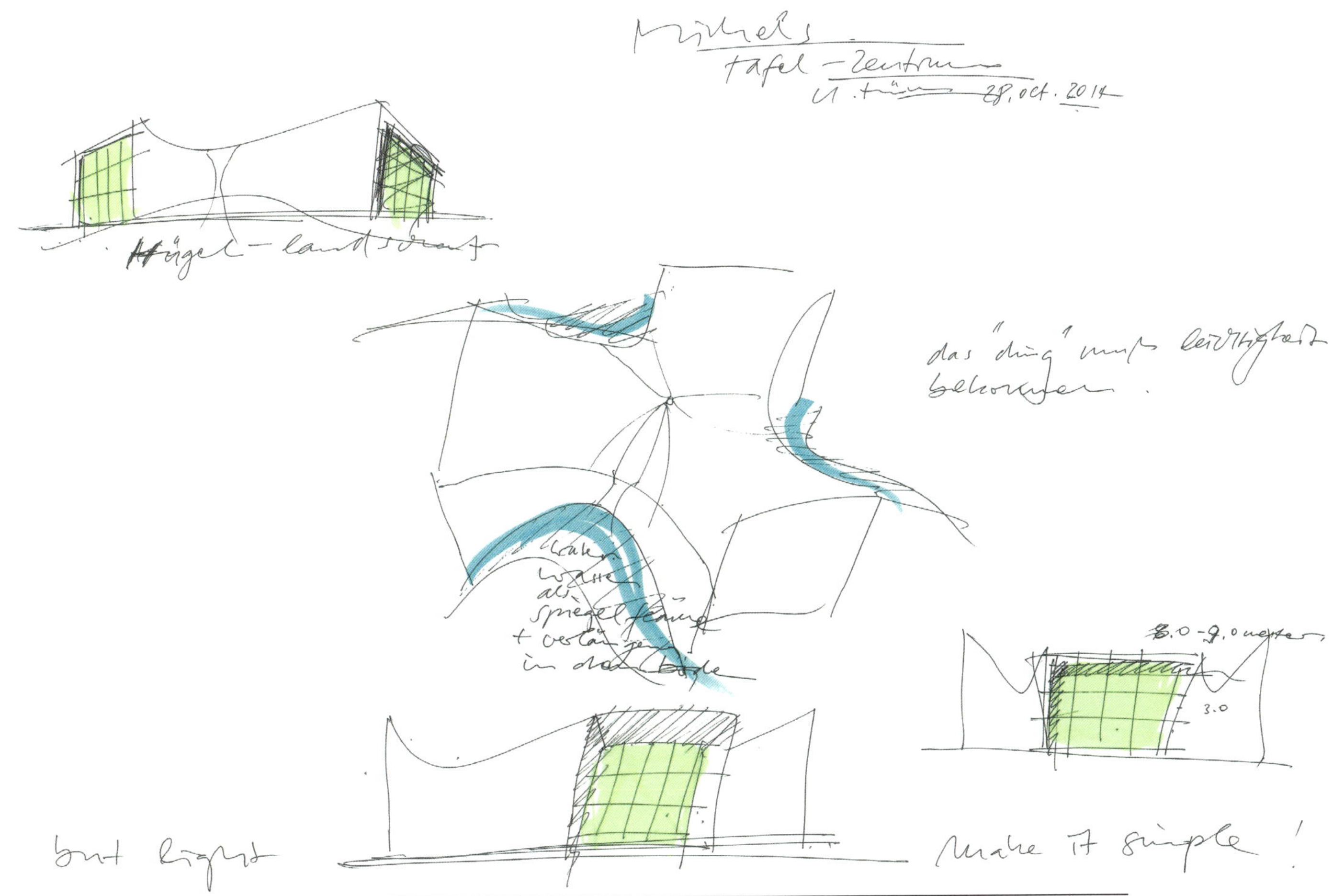

"Troisdorf City Gate," 2017.

When production plants are to be merged with visitor centres, a scenography with a strong identity is needed alongside an iconographic architecture (if possible) if the brand values are to be transported with emotion. The combination of product and production plant, the making-of and the showroom, lend the product authenticity and draw attention to the production location. Then a symbiosis has been achieved which has marketing potential, that motivates employees, that welcomes guests and wins them as brand fans. This requires an integrative concept of architectural and scenographic spaces, which can be staged autonomously, but enrich one another in context–with an unmistakable ambiance and a shared signature.

↗ p. 364

THE MACALLAN VISITOR EXPERIENCE The new Macallan distillery in Craigellachie, Scotland (2018), and the roughly 40 by 40-metre "Whisky Experience" are housed under a spectacular 240-metre-long roof. With respect for the strong architecture a symbiotic room-in-room constellation was selected. The "Mastery," the scenographic part of the tour, is a continuation of the impressively staged arrangement of the stills in the form of cylindrical pavilions.

Wenn Produktionsstätten mit Besucherzentren verschmelzen sollen, braucht es neben einer möglichst ikonografischen Architektur eine identitätsstarke Szenografie, um Markenwerte emotional zu vermitteln. Die Kombination von Produkt und Produktionsstätte, von Making-of und Showroom verleihen dem Produkt Authentizität und dem Produktionsort Aufmerksamkeit. Auf diese Weise glückt eine Symbiose, die Vermarktungspotenzial besitzt, die Mitarbeiter motiviert, die Kunden als Gäste willkommen heißt und zu Markenfans werden lässt. Dafür empfiehlt sich ein integratives Konzept von architektonischen und szenografischen Räumen, die autark inszeniert werden können, aber im Kontext bereichernd wirken – mit einem unverwechselbaren Ambiente und einer gemeinsamen Handschrift.

THE MACALLAN VISITOR EXPERIENCE Die neue Macallan-Destillerie in Craigellachie, Schottland (2018), und die etwa 40 auf 40 Meter große „Whisky Experience" sind unter einem 240 Meter langen, spektakulären Dach vereint. Mit Respekt vor der starken Architektur wurde eine symbiotische Raum-im-Raum-Konstellation gewählt. Die „Mastery", der szenografische Teil der Tour, setzt die eindrucksvoll inszenierte Anordnung der „Stills" (Destillieranlage) in Form zylindrischer Pavillons fort.

"The Macallan"–The Wood Story, 2018 (Left) | "The Macallan"–The Wisky Story, 2018 (Right).

The three pavilions stage the most important ingredients and production steps in "Experiences." In "The Wood Story," a dynamically opening and closing cylinder of wooden slats, the visitor finds out how barrels are made and burned out, a decisive step for the later taste and colour. In "The Whisky Story," a cylindrical pavilion of original oak wood, the "Blending" is projected in impressive film images directly onto the wooden wall. And in "The Peerless Spirit," an open, glazed cylinder, the "Whisky Spirit" floats as a metaphorical whisky drop in the room.

Each pavilion surprises with another narrative space derived from the production process of whisky, with its own choreography. In each of the Experiences, light, sound, and projections are used dynamically to change the aggregate status during the performance, synchronised with the dramaturgy of the narration. By placing the pavilions freely in the space, the architectural space is not obscured; the entry of daylight through the floor-to-ceiling glass facade is negigibly, and "Experiences" can be staged individually. The scenographic space becomes a carrier of a concept–itself a brand ambassador.

In den „Experiences", den drei Pavillons, werden die wichtigsten Ingredenzien und Herstellungsschritte in Szene gesetzt. In „The Wood Story", einem sich dynamisch öffnenden und schließenden Zylinder aus Holzlamellen, erfährt der Besucher, wie die Fässer hergestellt und ausgebrannt werden, was für den späteren Geschmack und die Farbe entscheidend ist. In „The Whisky Story", einem zylindrischen Pavillon aus originalem Eichenholz, wird das „Blending" mit beeindruckenden Filmbildern direkt auf die Holzwand projiziert. Und im „The Peerless Spirit", einem offenen gläsernen Zylinder, schwebt der „Whisky Spirit" als metaphorischer Whiskytropfen im Raum.

Jeder Pavillon überrascht mit einem anderen, aus dem Herstellungsprozess des Whiskys abgeleiteten Raumbild, mit einer eigenen Choreografie. Alle „Experiences" werden dynamisch bespielt, sodass sich ihre Aggregatzustände während der Performance mittels Licht, Sound und Projektionen ändern, synchron zur Dramaturgie des Erzählens. Durch die frei im Raum positionierten Pavillons bleibt der architektonische Raum unverstellt, wird der Tageslichteinfall durch die gebäudehohe Glasfassade kontrollierbar und sind die „Experiences" individuell inszenierbar. Der szenografische Raum wird zum Träger eines Konzepts – zum Markenbotschafter selbst.

"The Macallan"–The Wisky Story, 2018 (Left) | "The Macallan"–The Peerless Spirit, 2018 (Right).

What does a museum space have to be capable of? Inclusion instead of exclusion and limitation, a strong spatial gesture and the visualisation of content and messages as well as the staging of a subject as walk-in stage. What sticks in our minds? Perhaps a big gesture like the obligatory "crocodile in historical cabinets of curiosities." Perhaps a memorable narrative space, such as a walk-in archaeological dig, a kinetic sculpture, or explosive object like that in the Rautenstrauch-Joest-Musuem, flanked by a tableau of aesthetically arranged exhibits. This is how the narrative space becomes a memorable picture.

↗ p. 60
↗ p. 258

RAUTENSTRAUCH-JOEST-MUSEUM Architects love big windows in museums: the daylight, the connection to the outside, and free glimpses of the inside from outside–the scenographer then has to get this daylight, which makes sensitive objects fade, under control. Cologne's Rautenstrauch-Joest-Museum (2010) has such a huge, two-storey window on the routing of the permanent exhibition. None of the collections with sensitive objects could move in here due to the extreme light conditions, not the sculptures, not the costumes, neither the tents nor the masks. The only thing that was left was the museum education. The answer was a rice barn; an impressive gesture

Was muss Museumsraum können? Umgrenzung statt Ausgrenzung oder Eingrenzung, eine starke räumliche Geste und die Visualisierung von Inhalten oder Botschaften im Raum und die Inszenierung eines Sujets als begehbare Bühne. Was bleibt davon im Gedächtnis? Vielleicht eine große Geste wie das obligatorische „Krokodil in historischen Wunderkammern", vielleicht ein einprägsames Raumbild, wie eine begehbare Grabungslandschaft, eine kinetische Skulptur oder im Rautenstrauch-Joes-Musuem, ein Explosionsobjekt, flankiert von einem Tableau ästhetisch arrangierter Exponate. So wird das Raumbild zum einprägsamen Erinnerungsbild.

RAUTENSTRAUCH-JOEST-MUSEUM Architekten lieben große Fenster im Museum, das Tageslicht, den Außenbezug und den kostenlosen Blick von außen nach innen – die Szenografen müssen dieses Tageslicht dann in den Griff bekommen, das mit ausbleichenden Lux nach den sensiblen Objekten greift. Auch im Rautenstrauch-Joest-Museum in Köln (2010) gibt es ein derartig riesiges, zweigeschossiges Fenster im Parcours der Dauerausstellung. Keine der Sammlungen mit sensiblen Objekten konnte dort wegen der extremen Lichtverhältnisse einziehen, die Skulpturen nicht, nicht die Kostüme, noch die Zelte oder die Masken.

"Rautenstrauch-Joest-Museum"–"The Museum in the Museum". Interactive table featuring a fractalised rice barn divided in the four museological principles: 1. collecting, 2. preserving, 3. researching, 4. communicating, 2010.

and an object that could be explored as an example. It was deconstructed into its individual parts and suspended from the ceiling like an exploding sculpture. Below it is a four-part table with integrated display cases and sliding monitors, which work like scanners. Without didactic pointers, largely self-explanatory, the four basic principles of the museum–collecting, preserving, researching, and comunicating–can be explored in an entertaining but sophisticated way. The two-storey narrative space is dominated by the central rice barn and the exhibit walls, which are staged like a walk-in object archive. Like a butterfly collection sorted by species, the objects are pinned to the wall with aesthetic meticulousness. The arrangement dominates the narrative space, surrounds the central table with scientific exploration, and removes the borders of the museum room through the exotic nature of their origin and the optical extension to the outside through the museum window. The result is a place of exploration–a museum within the museum.

Also blieb nur die Museumsdidaktik. Als eindrucksstarke Geste und als exemplarisch explorierbares Objekt bot sich ein Reisspeicher an. Dieser wurde in seine Einzelteile dekonstruiert und wie eine explodierende Skulptur von der Decke gehängt. Darunter ein vierteiliger Tisch mit eingebauten Vitrinen und Schiebemonitoren, die wie Scanner funktionieren. Ohne didaktischen Fingerzeig, weitestgehend selbsterklärend, können dort die vier Grundprinzipien des Museums – Sammeln, Bewahren, Forschen und Vermitteln – auf kurzweilige, aber niveauvolle Weise exploriert werden. Das zweigeschossige Raumbild wird dominiert vom zentralen Reisspeicher und den Exponatwänden, die wie ein begehbares Objektarchiv inszeniert sind. Dort sind die Objekte in ästhetischer Akribie, wie in einer Schmetterlingssammlung nach Arten sortiert, an die Wand gepinnt. Das Arrangement dominiert das Raumbild, umgrenzt den zentralen Tisch mit der wissenschaftlichen Exploration und entgrenzt den musealen Raum durch die Exotik ihrer Provenienz und durch seine optische Expansion nach draußen durch das Museumsfenster. Es entsteht ein Ort der Exploration – ein Museum im Museum.

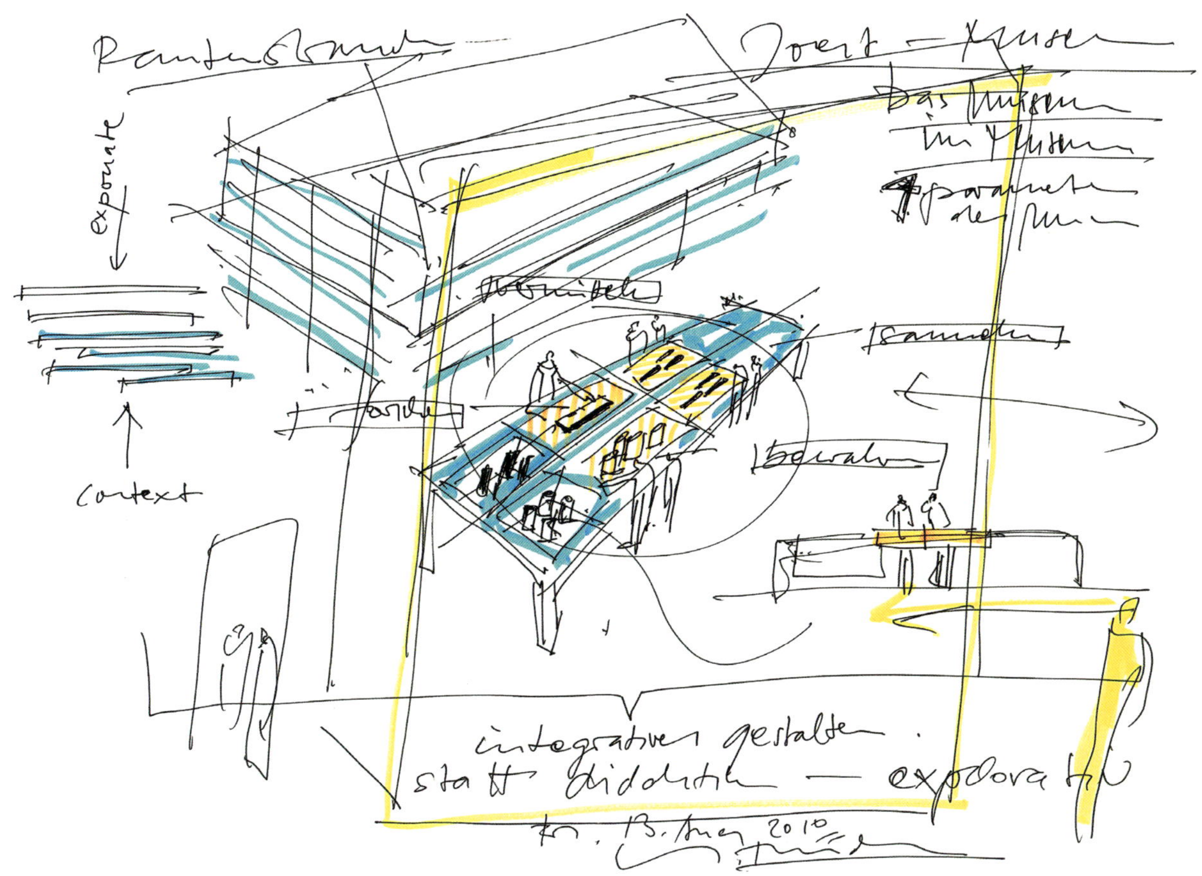

"Rautenstrauch-Joest-Museum"–Interactive table beneath an 'exploding' rice barn, 2010.

RECIPIENT

THE RECIPIENT IS THE ADDRESSEE

Uwe R. Brückner and Linda Greci

"The visitor is the anarchistic element in the exhibition: never foreseeable, hard to gauge; rather a social projection surface with uncertain receptive behaviour."

Uwe R. Brückner

RECIPIENT

THE RECIPIENT IS THE ADDRESSEE

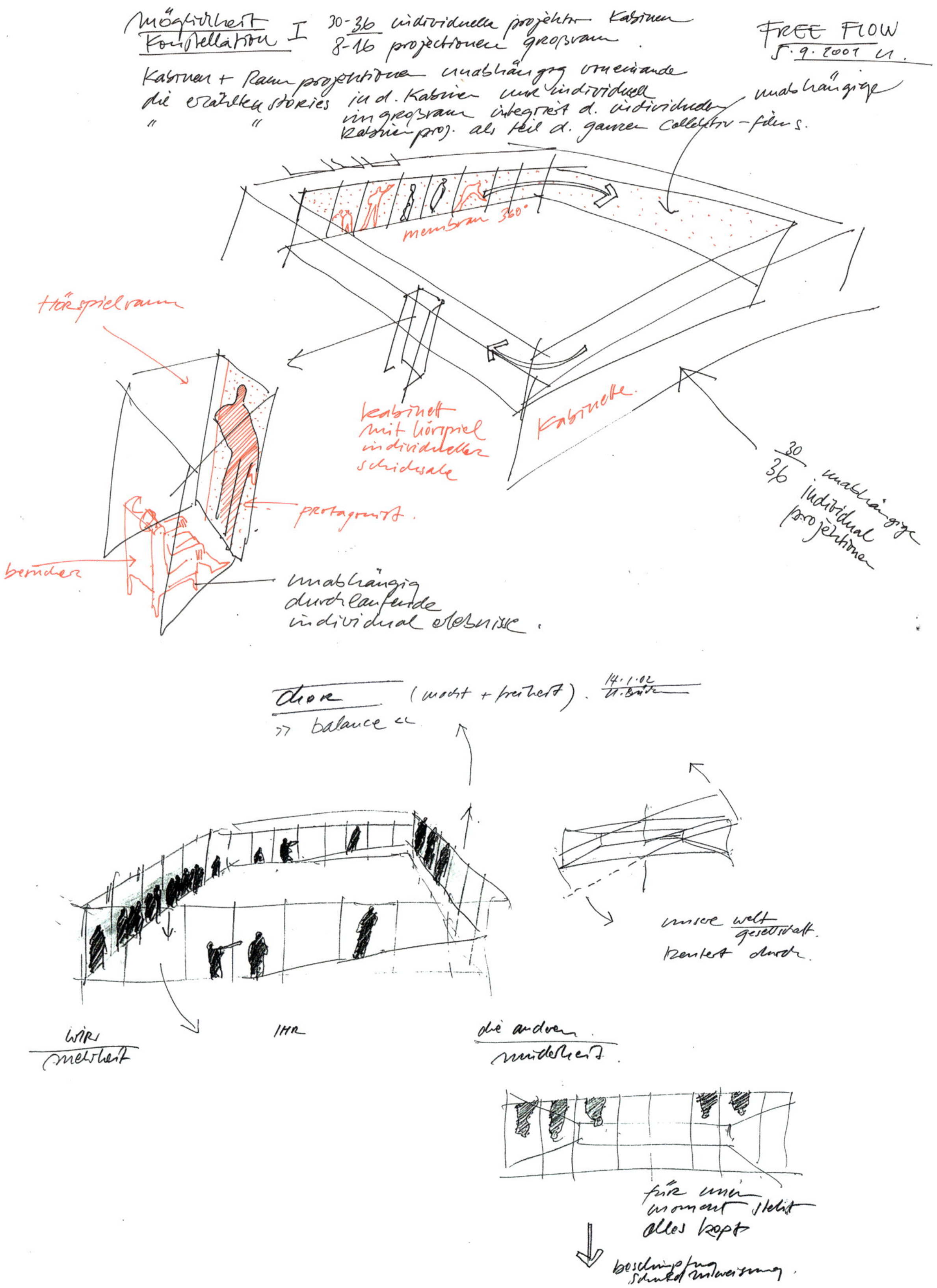

"Experiencing Frontiers"–Central panoramic projection–"The Chorus," 2002. Sketches, 2001.

The recipient and his perception play a central role in the contemporary understanding of scenography. Staged settings always have an "information-conveying and/or referencing function" and exert a major impact on the meaning-assigning processes that take place in exhibitions.[83] This not only concerns the (re-)contextualisation of objects and the presentation of complex contents and the design of narrative spaces, but also the involvement of the recipient in communication in the museum. In the 1970s the linear and unilateral model of communication–from the curator to the recipient via the object–was replaced by a new model and since then has been understood as a "dialogue-based relationship."[84] The visitor is no longer a passive recipient, but rather actively takes part in the process of assigning meaning.

A contemporary understanding from the perspective of exhibition design goes far beyond this: The recipient is understood as a design parameter of scenography. He is the starting point of all conceptional and design deliberations. Understood in this way, scenography places the focus on the recipient, even in the design process. He stands within the field of tension of the staged setting, in a reciprocal relationship with the three design parameters–space, object, and content–embedded in dramaturgical and spatially choreographed structures. The recipient is thus not only evaluated with hindsight as protagonist in the exhibition, as is often the case in visitor research, but anticipated as part of the staging.

The visitor reception is not necessarily identical to the intention of the curator or designer–there is always room for interpretation. The visitors, who have different national, cultural, social, and demographic backgrounds, perceive the objects and content differently and dive into immersive configurations of meaning in different, individual ways. Seeing, viewing, perceiving is always a subjective process. The recipient always has certain prerequisites, attitudes, which control or "colour" the result of the seeing process.[85] Communication in the museum deeply relies on the visual.

Der Rezipient und seine Wahrnehmung spielen im zeitgemäßen Verständnis von Szenografie eine zentrale Rolle. Inszenierungen haben immer eine „Vermittlungs- und/oder Verweisfunktion" und beteiligen sich an den Deutungsprozessen, die in Ausstellungen stattfinden.[83] Dabei geht es nicht nur um die (Re-)Kontextualisierung von Objekten, um die Vermittlung komplexer Inhalte und die Gestaltung narrativer Räume, sondern auch um die Einbindung des Rezipienten in die museale Kommunikation. Das lineare und einseitige Kommunikationsmodell – vom Kurator über das Objekt zum Rezipienten – wurde in den 1970er-Jahren von einem neuen Modell abgelöst und wird seither als „dialogisches Verhältnis" verstanden.[84] Der Besucher ist kein passiver Rezipient mehr, sondern nimmt aktiv an Bedeutungsprozessen teil.

communication in the museum

dialogue-based relationship

Ein zeitgemäßes Verständnis aus Perspektive der Ausstellungsgestaltung geht darüber noch hinaus: Der Rezipient wird als Gestaltungsparameter der Szenografie begriffen. Er ist Ausgangspunkt für alle konzeptionellen wie gestalterischen Überlegungen. Eine so verstandene Szenografie rückt den Rezipienten bereits im Entwurfsprozess in den Fokus. Er steht im Spannungsfeld der Inszenierung, im wechselwirksamen Verhältnis zu den drei Gestaltungsparametern Raum, Objekt und Inhalt, eingebettet in dramaturgische und raumchoreografische Strukturen. Der Rezipient wird also nicht nur im Nachhinein als Protagonist in der Ausstellung evaluiert, wie es in der Besucherforschung oft der Fall ist, sondern als Teil der Inszenierung antizipiert.

protagonist

visitor reception intention

Die Besucherrezeption ist nicht zwingend identisch mit der Vermittlungsintention des Kurators oder des Gestalters – immer besteht ein Spielraum für Interpretation. Die Besucher, die unterschiedliche nationale, kulturelle, soziale und demografische Hintergründe haben, nehmen Objekte und Inhalte verschieden wahr und tauchen individuell in immersive Bedeutungskonfigurationen ein. Sehen, Anschauen, Wahrnehmen sind immer subjektive Vorgänge. Jeder Betrachter bringt schon gewisse Voraussetzungen und Einstellungen mit, die das Ergebnis seines Sehens steuern oder „färben".[85] Die Kommunikation im Museum ist stark auf das Visuelle angewiesen.

83 Scholze 2004, p. 11.
84 Flügel 2005, p. 98.
85 See ibid., p. 99.

However, it is not just about the externally visible, but also always about the "inner involvement" of the person.[86] The task of the scenographer is to enable people to experience things and to evoke an associative scope.

autonomously

The visitor moves in a scenographically charged environment autonomously and passes through exhibitions independently; he can influence and change content and stories in terms of sequence and meaning. Contrary to a classical drama, where the action takes place "behind the so-called fourth wall or in the cinema on the big screen which the audience stares at [...]. In the exhibition room, the visitors are not excluded from the action, they walk through the space and thus through the action, are themselves moving on the stage. They define the distance to and thus the communication with the things themselves [...]."[87]

fourth wall

A visitor to an exhibition is also invited to interpret, participate, and accumulate knowledge. In staged exhibitions he can decide when, where and how much information he wants to receive. This individual, autonomous immersion in the content is referred to by Uwe R. Brückner as democratic approach. "Information on demand" is a form of content sharing wich allows visitors to be encountered as equals; it allows a personal access and a specific form of becoming aware, encouraging visitors to get to grips with seemingly dull things or complex content. The curators decide what and how much content is to be conveyed, and the designers decide how this content is to be offered to allow visitors to retrieve the information individually as they wish. "Information on demand" overcomes the additive approach to design, replacing it, in a scenographic sense, with an integrative, self-explanatory design attitude.

information on demand

Doch gleichwohl geht es nicht nur um das äußerlich Sichtbare, sondern immer auch um das „innere Beteiligtsein" des Menschen.[86] Das Erlebbarmachen und das Evozieren eines assoziativen Spielraums sind Aufgaben der Szenografie.

Der Besucher bewegt sich in einem szenografisch aufgeladenen Environment selbstbestimmt und durchläuft Ausstellungen autark. Er kann Inhalte und Geschichten in ihrer Abfolge und Aussage beeinflussen und verändern. Die Handlung findet nicht wie im klassischen Drama „hinter der sogenannten vierten Wand oder wie im Kino auf einer Leinwand statt, auf die die Zuschauer gebannt schauen [...]. Im Ausstellungsraum sind die Besucher nicht von der Handlung ausgeschlossen, sie durchschreiten den Raum und somit die Handlung, bewegen sich also selbst auf der Bühne. Sie definieren den Abstand, die Distanz und damit die Kommunikation zu den Dingen selbst [...]."[87]

Der Ausstellungsbesucher ist zudem eingeladen zur Interpretation, Partizipation und Wissensaneignung. In inszenierten Ausstellungen kann er entscheiden, wann, wo und wie viel Information er abrufen möchte. Das individuelle, selbstbestimmte Eintauchen in die Inhalte bezeichnet Uwe R. Brückner als demokratischen Zugang, als „Information on Demand". Es ist eine Form der Inhaltsvermittlung die Begegnung mit den Besuchern auf Augenhöhe erlaubt. Sie ermöglicht einen persönlichen Zugang und eine spezifische Form des Bewusstwerdens, die dazu anregt, sich auf vermeintlich uninteressante Dinge oder komplexe Inhalte einzulassen. Die Kuratoren bestimmen, welche und wie viele Inhalte es zu vermitteln gilt, und die Gestalter entscheiden, auf welche Art und Weise diese individuell abrufbar angeboten werden. „Information on Demand" vermag den additiven Gestaltungsansatz zu überwinden und eine im szenografischen Sinne integrative, selbsterklärende Gestaltungshaltung einzunehmen.

86 See Flügel 2005, p. 100.
87 Werner Hanak-Lettner, Die Ausstellung als Drama: Wie das Museum aus dem Theater entstand (Bielefeld, 2011), p. 20.

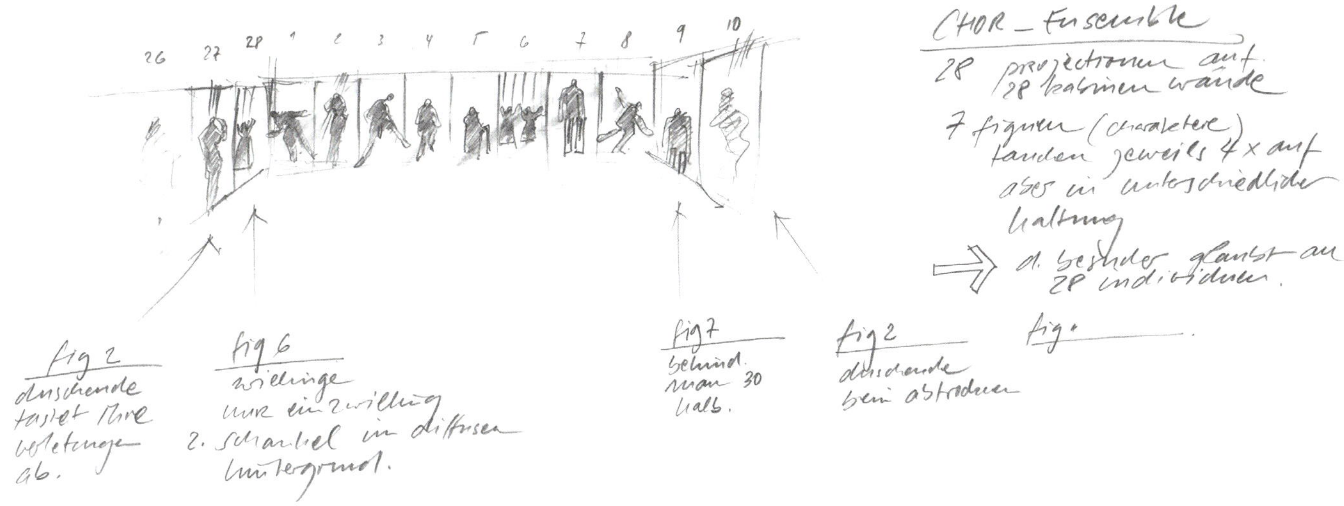

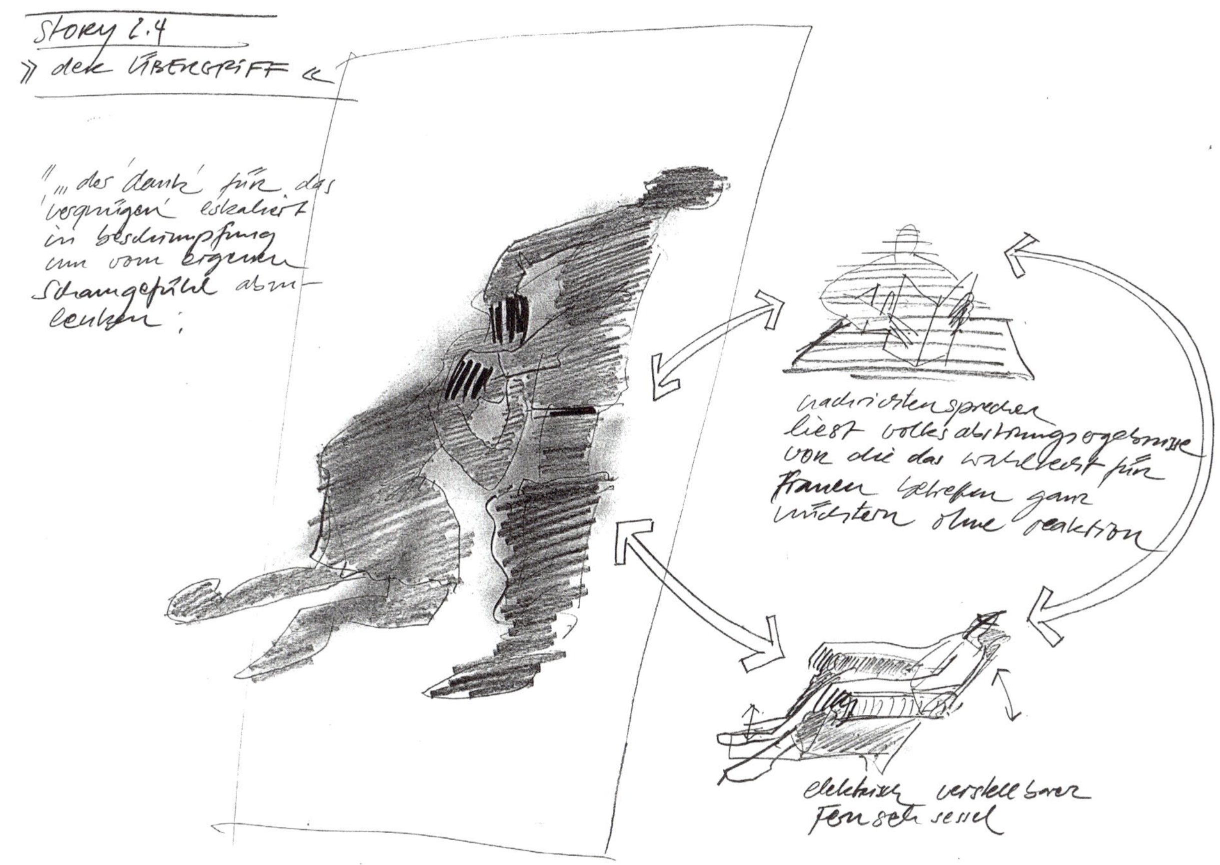

"Experiencing Frontiers"–Central panoramic projection–"Der Übergriff" ("The Rape"), 2002.

addressee

Good scenography always keeps an eye on the recipient and takes visitors seriously as addressees, as guests, as consumers, and as participants. The question is always how sustainable and memorable a staging is–how scenography creates a synaesthetic experience space charged with meaning in which visitors can immerse themselves, get carried away, and find their way back again.

Letztlich behält gute Szenografie stets den Rezipienten im Blick und nimmt die Besucher und Besucherinnen als Adressaten, Gäste und als Konsumierende, Partizipierende oder Akteure ernst. Es geht immer um die Frage, wie nachhaltig und erinnerungswürdig eine Inszenierung ist, wie Szenografie einen mit Bedeutungen aufgeladenen, synästhetischen Erfahrungsraum schafft, in den der Besucher eintauchen, in dem er sich verlieren und wiederfinden kann.

“In the democratic museum, visitors decide for themselves when, where, and how much information they want to receive.” Uwe R. Brückner

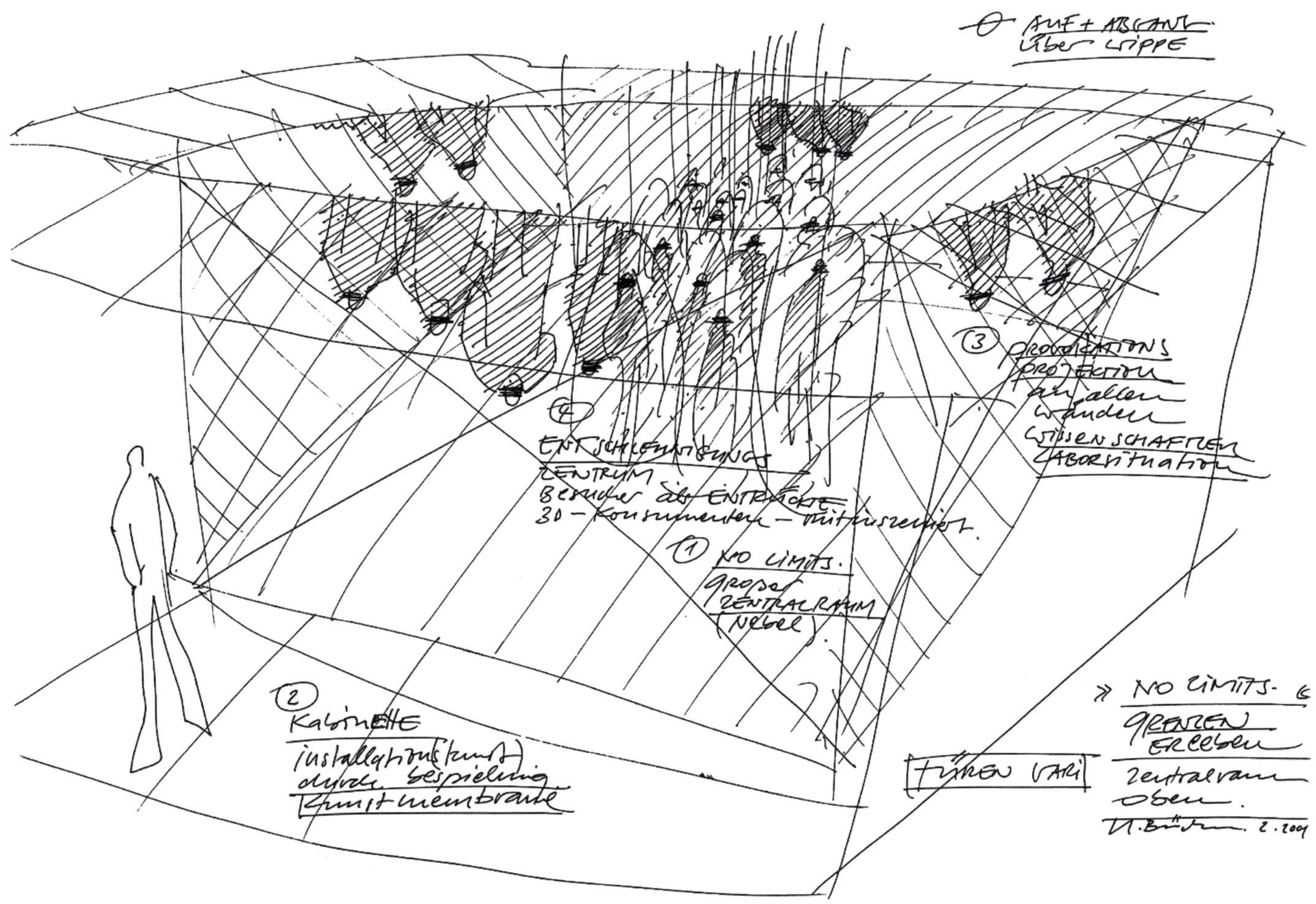

"Experiencing Frontiers"–"Central panorama (projection)," 2002.

FORMAT BRAND

Jochen Rädeker, Strichpunkt

BRANDS ARE RECOMMENDATIONS MANIFESTED IN SYMBOLS One hundred years ago, "Markenbutter" replaced the good advice of the sales assistant behind the shop counter. The trademark ensured that quality was given a name and kept plagiarists at bay. Those who could afford it used brand products, and this served them well. Over time, we came to understand: whether we like it or not, brands give us orientation, establish relationships, are a symbol of quality, love/hate objects, often for generations. Children whose parents had trusted in brand quality did the same–and guaranteed consistent added value at the producers, at the same time making their products a symbol and driver of affluence. For decades, static contact was sufficient to uphold this–a poster, an advertisement, a neon sign, and the urge to buy was triggered in our subconscious.

In today's world, the brand image has changed fundamentally. Brands have become omnipresent: an average inhabitant of a large city comes into contact with a brand around 3,000 times a day–that starts when they get up, when the alarm function of the smartphone is switched off. It continues with the clothing labels, the muesli package on the breakfast table, the jingle on the radio, advertising at the bus stop, getting into their own car. But above all these days, we experience brands in the digital space: intangible and abstract. And absolutely everywhere. In Europe alone there are more than ten million registered brands. Because every product is branded, competence as a recommendation no longer applies. And since our lives are taking place in disruptive contexts, we are losing faith in them.

Brands are no longer handed down–the family car is not necessarily the preferred brand of the children, if they want to own a car at all. Nowadays, brands have to present themselves in new guises, win over their customers again and again. The contact points this requires are far more comprehensive, deeper, more engaging, and multidimensional. It is about creating experiences: moments that stick in the mind. It is no longer about a logo. It is about form and content. Customers need to be astonished, touched, and thrilled. It is about scenography. And if the effect is to be long-lasting and work successfully across cultures, it has to be outstanding scenography. And therefore sooner or later it is about ATELIER BRÜCKNER.

MARKEN SIND IN SYMBOLEN MANIFESTIERTE EMPFEHLUNGEN Vor 100 Jahren ersetzte die „Markenbutter“ den guten Rat der Verkäuferin hinter der Ladentheke. Die „Schutzmarke“ sorgte dafür, dass Qualität einen Namen bekam, und hielt Plagiatoren auf Abstand. Wer es sich leisten konnte, nutzte Markenprodukte und war damit gut bedient. So lernten wir mit der Zeit: Marken geben uns – ob wir es wollen oder nicht – Orientierung, begründen Beziehungen, sind Qualitätssymbol, Liebes- oder Hassobjekt, oft über Generationen hinweg. An die Markenqualität, der die Eltern vertrauten, glaubten auch die Kinder – und sorgten so für beständigen Mehrwert bei den Produzenten, machten ihre Produkte gleichzeitig zum Symbol und Motor des Wohlstands. Dazu reichte über Jahrzehnte hinweg der statische Kontakt – ein Plakat, eine Anzeige, eine Leuchtreklame, und schon meldete uns unser Unterbewusstsein einen Kaufimpuls.

In der Welt von heute hat sich das Markenbild fundamental gewandelt. Marken sind allgegenwärtig geworden: Ein durchschnittlicher Großstadtbewohner kommt heute jeden Tag rund 3.000 Mal mit einer Marke in Berührung – das beginnt beim Aufstehen, wenn der Wecker des Smartphones ausgeschaltet wird. Es geht weiter mit den Labels der Kleidung, der Müsli-Packung auf dem Frühstückstisch, dem Jingle im Radio, der Werbung an der Bushaltestelle, dem Einstieg ins eigene Auto. Vor allem aber erleben wir Marken im digitalen Raum: unfassbar, nicht greifbar, abstrakt. Und: in Massen vorhanden. Allein in Europa gibt es über zehn Millionen registrierte Marken. Weil jedes Produkt gebrandet wird, entfällt die Empfehlungskompetenz. Und seit unser Leben in disruptiven Kontexten abläuft, schwindet das Vertrauen.

Marken sind keine Erbhöfe mehr – das Familienauto ist nicht zwangsläufig die präferierte Marke der Kinder, wenn sie überhaupt noch ein Auto besitzen möchten. Marken müssen sich deshalb heute immer wieder neu präsentieren, ihre Kunden neu erobern. Dazu bedarf es weit umfassenderer, tiefer gehender, involvierender, multidimensionaler Kontaktpunkte. Es geht darum, Erlebnisse zu schaffen: Momente, die in Erinnerung bleiben. Es geht nicht mehr um ein Logo. Es geht um Form und Content. Es geht um Staunen, um Berührung, um Begeisterung. Es geht um Szenografie. Um – wenn die Wirkung nachhaltig und kulturübergreifend erfolgreich sein soll – herausragende Szenografie. Und damit früher oder später um das ATELIER BRÜCKNER.

FORMAT BRAND

Jochen Rädeker, Strichpunkt

What possesses a Korean car maker to have its visitors' centre designed in Stuttgart? How come Brussels bureaucrats turns to Swabia in order to make the unpopular European Parliament more approachable? Why does a Scottish distillery with deeply regional roots entrust its brand space to a German agency?

The answer is simple: Because the team from ATELIER BRÜCKNER supplies convincing, disruptive, emotionalising, spectacular answers to the questions of their customers. Because they are able to conjure up archaic feelings with state-of-the-art technology. Because they do not present visitors to the Hyundai Motorstudio with neatly packed stories, but turn them into model builders, masters of the wind tunnel, rally drivers. Because they give visitors unforgettable moments. And because they constantly scrutinize their own benchmark–the BMW Museum sets standards in the industry to this day–and refine it. Because they do not shy away from difficult subjects. Because they constantly reinvent themselves and the brands they serve. Because ATELIER BRÜCKNER consists of inspired creative heads, uncompromising quality fanatics, and meticulous craftsmen who are passionate about their projects. And because long before–and to this day more systematically than–most others, they have made the brand appropriate for our times, creating a true "brand experience."

Was veranlasst einen koreanischen Autobauer, sein Besucherzentrum in Stuttgart planen zu lassen? Wieso kommen die Brüsseler Bürokraten nach Schwaben, um das ungeliebte Europäische Parlament nahbar zu machen? Wieso vertraut eine schottische Destillerie ihren zutiefst regional geprägten Markenraum einem deutschen Atelier an?

Die Antwort ist einfach: Weil das Team von ATELIER BRÜCKNER weltweit überzeugende, disruptive, emotionalisierende, überwältigende Antworten auf die Fragen der Kunden liefert. Weil es in der Lage ist, mit modernster Technik archaische Gefühle hervorzurufen. Weil es den Besuchern des Hyundai-Motorstudios nicht nett verpackte Geschichte präsentiert, sondern sie zum Modellbauer macht, zu Herrschern über den Windkanal, zu Rallyefahrern. Weil es ihnen unvergessliche Erlebnisse beschert. Und weil es seine eigenen Benchmarks – das BMW Museum setzt bis heute Maßstäbe in der Branche – beständig infrage stellt und weiterentwickelt. Weil es sich nicht vor schwierigen Themen scheut. Weil es sich und die von ihm betreuten Marken stetig neu erfindet. Weil das ATELIER BRÜCKNER aus inspirierten Kreativen, kompromisslosen Qualitätsfanatikern und akribischen Handwerkern besteht, die für ihre Projekte brennen. Und weil sie es sind, die weit vor den meisten anderen – und bis heute weit konsequenter als die meisten – die Marke so weiterentwickelt haben, wie es unserer Zeit gemäß ist: zur Erlebnismarke, zur wirklichen „Brand Experience“.

While the recipients to a museum are called visitors, in the brand area they are referred to as customers–who is being addressed and with what objective is thus clearly defined. The company wants to sell its products, and to do so wants to create an emotional relationship to the brand, thus triggering the desire to own it. This goal can be achieved by means of design, quality, or empathy, triggered by an individual or collective, sometimes associative staging of products or brand values. These values are not sold anonymously, but conveyed in a convincingly individual way with sustainable effect.

↗ p. 356

HYUNDAI MOTORSTUDIO GOYANG An ambitious automotive brand like Hyundai does not see the buyer only as customer, but as happy owner and thus ambassador of the brand. The desired loyalty is to be established by an impressive brand experience in an unusual visitors' centre. This requires expressive architecture and memorable scenography. The Hyundai Motorstudio Goyang in Korea (2017) offers both.

Während man im Museum die Rezipienten Besucher, und in der Architektur Nutzer nennt, spricht man im Brand-Bereich von Kunden – damit sind Ansprache und Zielsetzung klar definiert. Das Unternehmen will seine Produkte vermarkten, dafür eine emotionale Bindung zur Marke herstellen und den Wunsch auslösen, sie zu besitzen. Dieses Ziel kann über Design, Qualität oder Empathie erreicht werden, ausgelöst durch eine individuelle oder kollektive, manchmal assoziative Inszenierung von Produkten oder Markenwerten. Diese Werte werden nicht mehr anonym verkauft, sondern überzeugend individuell und nachhaltig vermittelt.

HYUNDAI MOTORSTUDIO GOYANG Eine ambitionierte Automobilmarke wie Hyundai sieht den Käufer nicht nur als Kunden, sondern als glücklichen Besitzer und damit Botschafter der Marke. Die gewünschte nachhaltige Bindung soll durch ein beeindruckendes Markenerlebnis in einem außergewöhnlichen Besucherzentrum erzeugt werden. Hier besteht der Bedarf an expressiver Architektur und erinnerungswürdiger Szenografie. Beides bietet das Hyundai Motorstudio Goyang in Korea (2017).

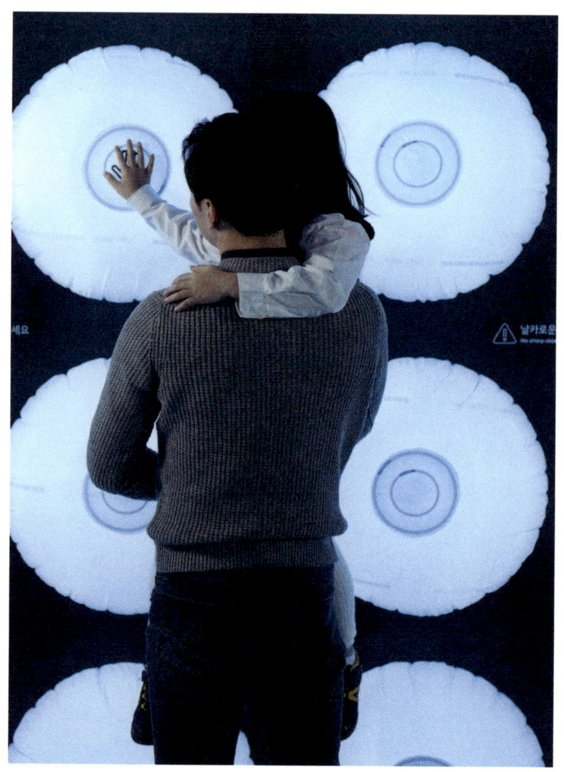

"Hyundai Motorstudio Goyang"–"Safety Room"–Reactive airbag installation, 2017.

In the "Safety Room," the walls are equipped with airbags, which respond to touch. They change their light intensity and thus trace the silhouette of the visitors–a self-explanatory staging. In a poetic way, the visitor is given a sense of personal safety through the reliable systems of Hyundai. An individually triggered interaction produces a narrative space quality that can be experienced collectively, placing the recipient in the centre, giving him a role and thus addressing him directly with a lasting effect.

The kinetic "Sculpture of Mobility" is an artistic translation of mobility and aesthetics. In reactive mode, this innovative construction as the result of high-tech and high-end engineering calls upon visitors to interact with the sculpture. It is not so much about function, technical details, or reliability, but about poetry, shared individually. The installation follows an aesthetic choreography of associative forms, at the same time as it reacts to visitors by assigning a personal wave to them based on their positions in the room, which follows them and whose form they can influence. Such an iconic and sensual installation shows the ambition of the company to place people at the heart of their technical development and aesthetic innovation.

Im „Safety Room" reagieren die mit Airbags bestückten Wände auf Berührung. Sie ändern ihre Lichtintensität und zeichnen so die Silhouette der Besucher nach – eine sich selbst erklärende Inszenierung. Dem Besucher wird auf poetische Weise ein Gefühl von persönlicher Sicherheit durch die verlässlichen Systeme von Hyundai vermittelt. Es entsteht eine individuell ausgelöste Interaktion, mit kollektiv erfahrbarer Raumbildqualität, welche die Rezipienten in den Mittelpunkt stellt, ihnen eine Rolle zuweist und sie damit gezielt und nachhaltig anspricht.

Die kinetische „Sculpture of Mobility" ist eine künstlerische Übersetzung von Mobilität und deren Ästhetik. Diese innovative Konstruktion als Ergebnis von Hightech- und Highend-Engineering fordert im reaktiven Modus die Besucher auf, mit der Skulptur in Interaktion zu treten. Hier geht es weniger um Funktion, technische Details oder Verlässlichkeit im Betrieb, sondern um Poesie, um individuelle Ansprache. Die Installation folgt einer ästhetischen Choreografie assoziativer Formen, gleichzeitig reagiert sie auf den Besucher, indem sie ihm über seine Position im Raum eine persönliche Welle zuordnet, die ihm folgt und die er beeinflussen kann. Eine derartig ikonografische und sinnliche Installation zeigt die Ambition des Unternehmens, den Menschen in den Mittelpunkt seiner technischen Entwicklung und ästhetischen Innovation zu stellen.

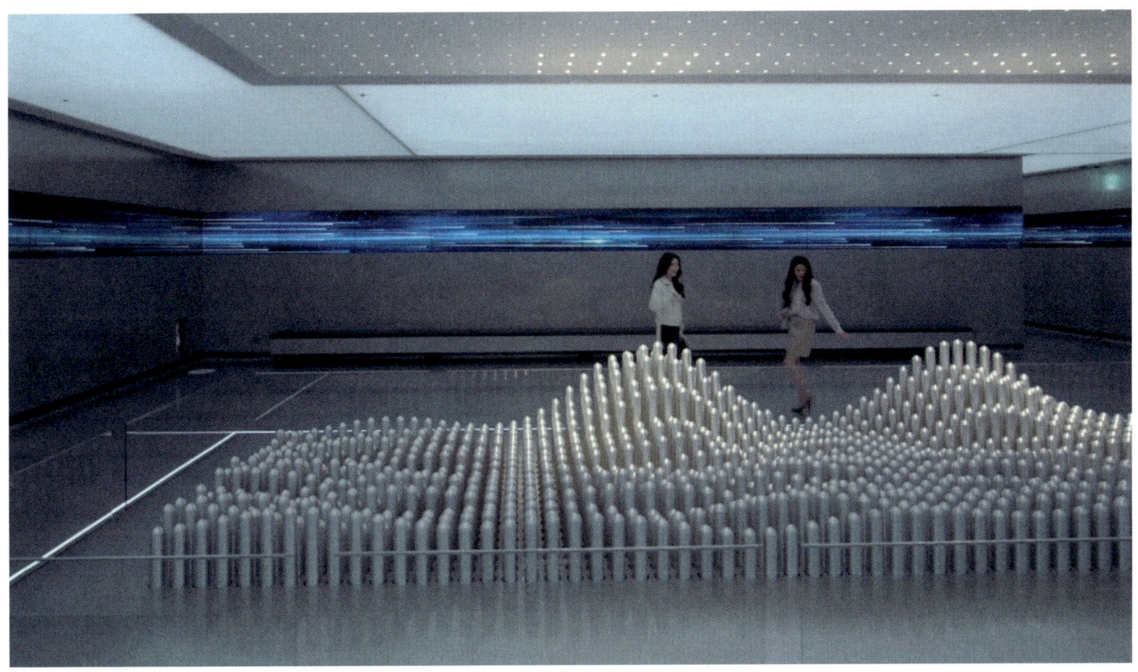

"Hyundai Motorstudio Goyang"–Reactive, kinetic installation–each visitor may trigger a wave, which follows the individual, 2017.

Autoactive, interactive, and reactive building–in the past twenty years, there has been a veritable explosion of media-based projections on architecture, however mostly focused on their skin. Using media to make buildings responsive was often initially limited to complex media installations with big budgets or artistic projects. As smart electronic systems have become widespread, the whole building is now able to become communicative and to react to the user, observer, or even intervener.

↗ p. 112

GS CALTEX PAVILION For the GS-Caltex pavilion at the Expo Yeosu 2012 in Korea this was precisely the intention. Instead of being a visually recognisable building, the pavilion disappeared in an abstract paddy field, the energy field of extra-long blades swaying in the wind. This was the scenographic translation of "I am your energy," the client's slogan. The actual architecture consisted of a star-shaped, completely mirrored building which multiplied the blades, thus visual-ly dissolving the building in the energy field. The 18-metre-high translucent blades could be illuminated by LED strips on the inside, which were equipped with various interfaces and could be played in

Autoaktive, interaktive und reaktive Gebäude – in den vergangenen 20 Jahren hat es eine wahre Explosion der medialen Bespielung von Architektur gegeben, die sich aber meist auf ihre Hülle konzentrierte. Oft war es zunächst aufwendigen Medieninstallationen mit üppigen Budgets oder künstlerischen Aktionen vorbehalten, Gebäude reaktiv zu bespielen. Mit der Ausbreitung intelligenter elektronischer Systeme ist nun das gesamte Gebäude in der Lage, kommunikativ zu werden und auf die Nutzer, die Betrachter oder gar Intervenierer zu reagieren.

GS CALTEX PAVILION Beim GS-Caltex-Pavillon auf der Expo Yeosu 2012 in Korea war genau dies die Absicht. Statt ein visuell erkennbares Gebäude zu sein, verschwand der Pavillon in einem abstrahierten Reisfeld, dem Energiefeld (Energy Field) aus sich im Wind wiegenden überlangen Halmen (Blades). Dies war die szenografische Übersetzung von „I am your energy", dem Slogan des Auftraggebers. Die eigentliche Architektur bestand aus einem sternförmigen, komplett verspiegelten Gebäude, das die Halme vervielfältigte und sich somit visuell völlig im Energiefeld auflöste. Die 18 innenliegender LED-Streifen leuchten. Sie waren

"GS Caltex Pavilion, Expo Yeosu 2012"–Energyfield light choreography depicts wave movements, 2012.

various modes. In the ideal mode, wave movements were transferred by sensors in the nearby sea to the energy field as light choreography. Five percent of the blades were equipped with sensors–touching them triggered different colours, and light patterns could be traced in the field. Moreover, with the help of a smartphone or tablet it was possible to activate the energy field with self-configured motifs.

Today, such an energy field can also emancipate itself algorithmically and enter into a creative dialogue with the recipients or players, that is, itself become a reactive medium.

The central 360-degree animated film, whose space-extending light lines continue the energy field virtually from the outside in, is also reactive. The film is only triggered when visitors have activated all the floor sensors. The visitor thus becomes an ally of the space, a trigger of the narration, and the recipient of the message.

mit verschiedenen Interfaces ausgestattet und in unterschiedlichen Modi bespielbar. Im sogenannten Ideal-Mode zeichneten sich, von Sensoren im nahen Meer übertragen, die Wellen als Lichtchoreografie im Energiefeld ab. Fünf Prozent der Blades waren mit Touch Points ausgestattet – Berührungen konnten unterschiedliche Farben auslösen und Lichtmuster in das Feld schreiben. Zudem war es möglich, von einem Smartphone oder Tablet aus das Energiefeld mit selbst konfigurierten Motiven zu bespielen.

Heutzutage kann sich ein derartiges Energiefeld auch algorithmisch emanzipieren und in einen kreativen Dialog mit den Rezipienten oder Spielern treten, also selbst zum reaktionsfähigen Medium werden.

Reaktiv ist auch der zentrale 360°-Animationsfilm, dessen raumerweiternde Lichtlinien das Energy Field von außen nach innen virtuell fortsetzen. Nur wenn die Besucher alle Bodensensoren aktiviert haben, startet der Film. Der Besucher wird so zum Verbündeten des Raums, zum Auslöser der Narration und zum Adressaten der Botschaft.

"GS Caltex Pavilion, Expo Yeosu 2012"–360-degree film igniting by the spectators, 2012.

Retrievable experiences for visitors are achieved via "information on demand." Since the more conventional additive attitude to design has been overcome and replaced by an integrative design approach–that is, objects can be staged both auratically and also contextualised–and access can be obtained to their hidden potential upon demand, we speak of responsible visitors who decidwe for themselves when, where, and how much information they want to receive.

↗ p. 60
↗ p. 240

RAUTENSTRAUCH-JOEST-MUSEUM In the Rautenstrauch-Joest-Museum in Cologne (2010) the "information on demand" strategy was developed in order to present an object from two different perspectives: on the one hand, as a work of art without context in a neutral showcase; on the other, as a ritual, religious object embedded in its cultural and historical context. The staging leaves it up to visitors to decide whether they want to enjoy the object in its mere aesthetic dimension or if they want to find out more about the origin and history of the object. By activating a sensor on the showcase, authentic photos become visible in the background showing the object in its original surroundings and in its former function.

Abrufbare Besuchererlebnisse erzielen wir durch „Information on Demand". Seit der eher konventionelle additive Gestaltungsansatz überwunden werden konnte und an seine Stelle eine integrative Gestaltungshaltung getreten ist – Objekte also sowohl auratisch als auch kontextualisiert inszeniert und der Zugang zu ihren verborgenen Potenzialen auf Wunsch abrufbar wird – sprechen wir vom mündigen Besucher: Er entscheidet selbst darüber wann, wo und wie viel Information er erhalten möchte.

RAUTENSTRAUCH-JOEST-MUSEUM Im Rautenstrauch-Joest-Museum in Köln (2010) wurde dafür die Vermittlungsstrategie „Information on Demand" entwickelt, um ein Objekt aus zwei unterschiedlichen Perspektiven zu präsentieren: einerseits als kontextloses Kunstobjekt in einer neutralen Vitrine, andererseits als rituelles religiöses Objekt, eingebettet in seinen kulturellen, historischen Kontext. Die Inszenierung überlässt dem Besucher die Entscheidung, ob er das Objekt in seiner rein ästhetischen Qualität wahrnehmen oder ob er mehr über dessen Geschichte und Hintergrund erfahren möchte. Durch die Betätigung eines Sensors an der Vitrine werden authentische Fotos im Hintergrund eingespielt, die das Objekt in seiner ursprüngli-chen Umgebung und in seiner ehemaligen Funktion zeigen.

"Rautenstrauch-Joest-Museum"– "Information on Demand"–Visitors may unveil background information, 2010.

↗ p. 290

SMAC–STATE MUSEUM OF ARCHAEOLOGY CHEMNITZ The staging at smac (2014) goes in a similar direction. The permanent exhibition over three floors of the listed Mendelsohn building shows objects from 300,000 years, from prehistory and early history through to the history of the state of Saxony. The highlight on the third floor is the 40-metre-long museum wall that was designed as a structured panorama showcase with around 1,000 everyday objects from the past 900 years. The exhibits are arranged both chronologically and grouped by usage.

Besides the strong visual presence, the idea was also to make the auratic potential of the individual exhibits accessible. Beyond the impressive narrative space with its aesthetically presented mass of exhibits, the individual quality of the items can be explored interactively and in detail at six media stations. With this media-based aid, visitors can dive into the deeper levels of meaning of the objects, thus obtaining an insight into the diversity of past everyday culture while at the same time experiencing them in their impressive materiality.

SMAC – STAATLICHES MUSEUM FÜR ARCHÄOLOGIE CHEMNITZ Die Inszenierung im „smac“ (2014) weist in eine ähnliche Richtung. Die im denkmalgeschützten Mendelsohn-Bau eingerichtete Dauerausstellung erstreckt sich über drei Etagen und zeigt Objekte aus 300.000 Jahren, von der Ur- und Frühgeschichte hin zur sächsischen Landesgeschichte. Highlight der dritten Etage ist die 40 Meter lange Museumswand, die als strukturierte Panorama-Vitrine mit rund 1.000 Alltagsgegenständen aus den vergangenen 900 Jahren gestaltet wurde. Die Exponate sind sowohl chronologisch als auch in Nutzungsgruppen geordnet.

Neben der starken visuellen Präsenz soll auch das auratische Potenzial der einzelnen Exponate zugänglich gemacht werden. Jenseits des imposanten Raumbilds mit seiner ästhetisierten Masse an Ausstellungsstücken sind die Exponate als Einzelstücke in ihrer individuellen Qualität über sechs Medienstationen interaktiv und im Detail explorierbar. Der Besucher kann durch diese mediale Hilfe individuell in die tieferliegenden Bedeutungsschichten der Objekte eintauchen. So erhält er einen Einblick in die Diversität vergangener Alltagskultur und erlebt zugleich die Inszenierung in ihrer beeindruckenden Materialität.

"smac–State Museum for Archaeology Chemnitz"–"Grand Showcase"–3rd floor, 1000 objects of 900 years perceivable as a whole or individual, 2014.

In theatre and opera productions, it is obligatory that the play describes the plot, the actors, and the message or moral and that the staging anticipates the reception. In exhibitions, the reaction and perception of the visitors are at best evaluated subsequently, but the visitor is rarely given a role to play. What if the visitor is to become an addressee, if a (distanced) spectator is to experience compassion, if one wants to provoke a reaction and empathy or cross emotional taboo boundaries? Is that possible in a format like an Expo pavilion designed to entertain?

↗ p. 32

EXPERIENCING FRONTIERS By placing the focus on personal borderline experiences such as those with the working poor, marital violence, transsexuality, clones, or euthanasia, "Experiencing Frontiers," the pavilion of the eight Swiss Border Cantons, had chosen one of the highest levels of difficulty for "entertainment" at an Expo (2002, Biel). Experiencing the personal borderline experiences of others, not experiences of one's own, had to be staged. Stories of seven protagonists in extreme mental and social border areas were to be narrated–the aim was thus to find a way of allowing visitors to experience the abstract, things that cannot be presented. This happens on two diffe-rent levels of experience, an individual one

In Theater- oder Operninszenierungen ist es obligatorisch, dass im Stück die Handlung, die Akteure und die Botschaft oder Moral beschrieben werden und bei der Inszenierung die Rezeption antizipiert wird. In Ausstellungen wird die Reaktion und Wahrnehmung der Besucher bestenfalls nachträglich evaluiert, aber selten wird dem Besucher eine Rolle zugeschrieben. Was also, wenn aus dem Besucher ein Adressat, wenn aus einem (distanzierten) Zuschauer ein Mitfühlender werden soll, wenn man eine Reaktion und Empathie provozieren oder Tabugrenzen emotional überschreiten will? Ist das in einem Format wie einem auf Entertainment ausgelegten Expo-Pavillon überhaupt möglich?

GRENZEN (ER)LEBEN Der Pavillon der acht Schweizer Grenzkantone auf der Expo.02 in Biel, hat sich mit dem Fokus auf persönlichen Grenzerfahrungen – etwa Working Poor, Gewalt in der Ehe, Transsexualität, Klonen oder Sterbehilfe – einen der höchsten Schwierigkeitsgrade der „Unterhaltung" auf einer Expo gestellt. Nicht das eigene Erlebnis, sondern das Erleben persönlicher Grenzerfahrungen anderer galt es zu inszenieren. Geschichten von sieben Protagonisten im extremen psychischen und gesellschaftlichen Grenzbereich waren zu erzählen – es sollte also das

"Experiencing Frontiers"–"Central Collective Experience," 2002.

and a collective one. The collective experience takes the form of a 360-degree panorama, that introduced the protagonists of the marginalised groups as anonymous silhouettes, before they interacted with one another to then take their position on the edge of society and to confront us spectators with a fragile mirror image of our own borderline experiences.

The projection surface was a translucent, permeable membrane, which combined the collective watching with individual reflection. As they passed through it, spectators not only changed their perspective, but also their role, changing from observer to accessory. The individual experience occurred in the twenty-eight cabinets (behind the membrane). In audio plays[88] (in five languages) visitors were sucked into the stories of the protagonists and reminded of their own experiences, while the projected silhouette entered into a connection between the images of the artistic translation and the images in the minds of the spectators. The visitors thus became an essential part of the staging, the recipient as intended addressee of his self-reflection.

88 "The eye takes a person into the world. The ear brings the world into a human being." Lorenz Oken.

Abstrakte, das nicht Darstellbare erlebbar werden. Das wurde auf zwei verschiedenen Erlebnisebenen erreicht, einer individuellen und einer kollektiven. Die kollektive Erfahrung erfolgte über ein 360°-Panorama, das die Protagonisten der Randgruppen in anonymisierter Silhouettenhaftigkeit vorstellte, bevor sie miteinander interagierten, um letztlich ihre Randstellung in der Gesellschaft einzunehmen und uns Zuschauern als fragiles Spiegelbild unserer eigenen Grenzerfahrungen entgegentreten.

Die Projektionsfläche war eine transluzente, permeable Membran, die das gemeinsame Schauen mit dem individuellen Reflektieren verband. Beim Durchschreiten wechselten die Zuschauer nicht nur die Perspektive, sondern auch die Rolle, wurden von Betrachtern zu Mitwissern. Die individuelle Erfahrung vollzog sich in den 28 Kabinetten (hinter der Membran). Dort wurden die Besucher in Hörspielen[88] (wahlweise in fünf Sprachen) in die Geschichten der Protagonisten hineingesogen und an eigene Erfahrungen erinnert, während die dazugehörige projizierte Silhouette eine Verbindung zwischen den Bildern der künstlerischen Übersetzung und den Bildern im Kopf der Zuhörer einging. Die Besucher wurden so zum unverzichtbaren Teil der Inszenierung, die Rezipienten zu intendierten Adressaten ihrer Selbstreflexion.

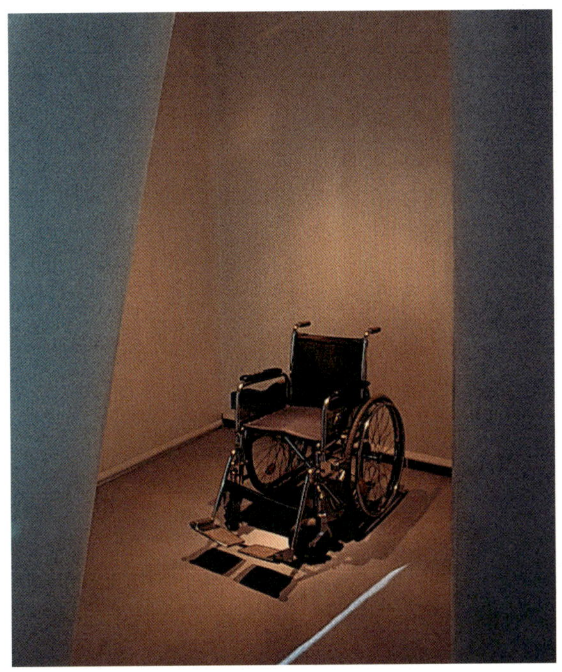

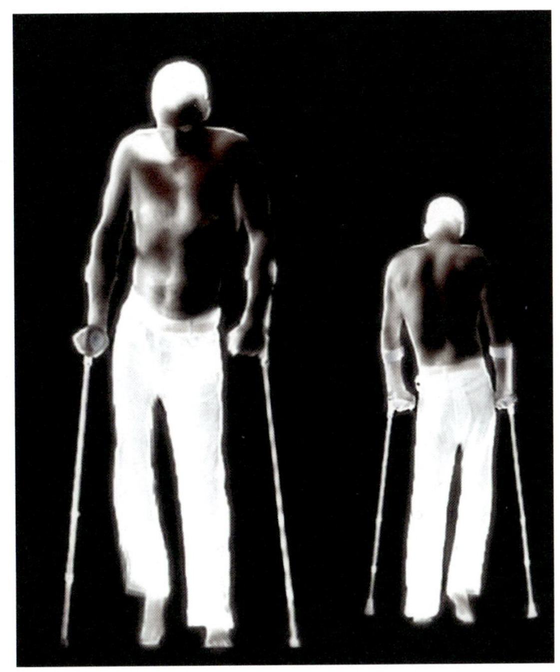

"Experiencing Frontiers"–Chamber "Valid–Invalid"–One of 28 cabinets that play audio dramas of the protagonist's stories, 2002.

DRAMATURGY

THE CHOREOGRAPHED PARCOURS

Uwe R. Brückner and Linda Greci

"Every space or architecture became a stage. Objects turned into artefacts and the scene was enriched by the actors or singers, who started to communicate with the audience. Finally all the action, the narrative, followed a dramatic structure fixed in a partitura." Uwe R. Brückner

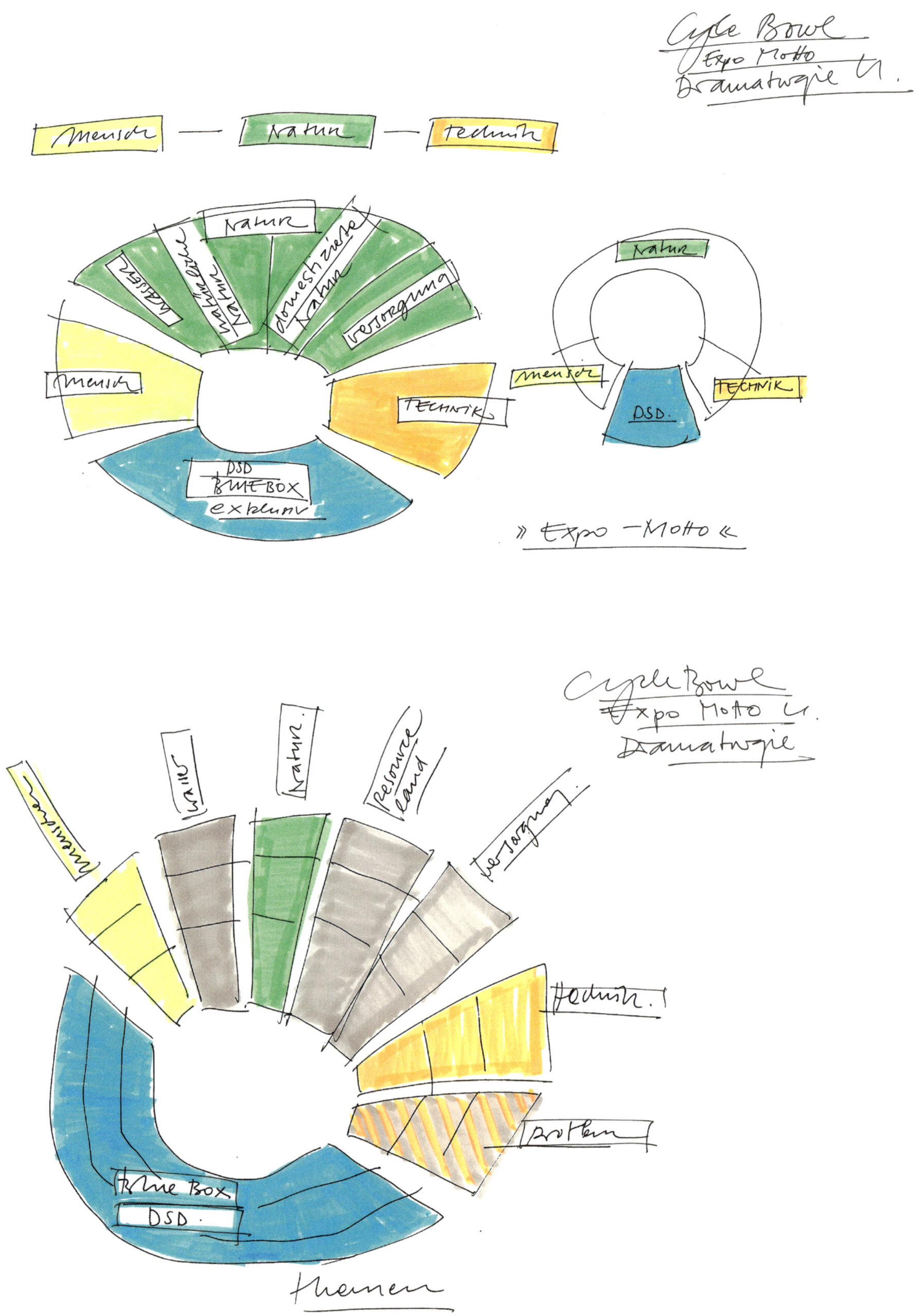

“Cyclebowl”–“Parcours,” 1998.

Scenographic design is a stage-setting act with its own dramaturgy. The term "dramaturgy" stems originally from theatre and is derived from the Greek "dramatourgia."[89] Dramaturgy is the theory of the external construction and the laws governing the inner structure of the drama. But it is also the art of telling good stories in staged spaces. The staging is defined by various elements such as space, stage set, actors, text, language, light, sound, costumes, and audience-elements each with their own, in some cases opposed, arc of suspense. As the staging of various social areas advanced, the term "dramaturgy" also found its way into these areas and has proved invaluable in arts such as film, dance, music, and audio drama.[90] Dramaturgy has also found its way into exhibition design; indeed, it has become one of the five central parameters of scenography that underpin our design philosophy. It determines the chronology of the content, the exhibits, and the reception; it defines the sequence of rooms and is manifested in the exhibition routing.

The dramaturgy of an exhibition is often structured much like a classical opera, a theatre play, a film, or a dance performance–with a prologue, a main part with various acts, and an epilogue. In the form of a narrative routing, it prescribes a reception chronology which is neither strictly one-dimensional nor will it be experienced by all visitors in the same way. Rather, it is to be understood as a kind of structure which connects complex, multidimensional narrative strands and visitor experiences and encourages an individual dynamic of walking and seeing. Dramaturgy forms the spatial and temporal flow of a story which visitors can walk through and experience autonomously–each with their own version of the story.[91] The exhibit also plays an important role as protagonist of the narrative; its staging by the scenographer can influence the attention of the visitors and thus control their movements in the space and their perception. Finally, the exhibition is based on a narrative structure, which unfolds as a story on the stage of the exhibition space and eliminates

89 Christel Weiler, "Dramaturgie", in Metzler Lexikon Theatertheorie, ed. Erika Fischer-Lichte, Doris Kolesch, and Matthias Warstat (Munich, 2005), pp. 80–83 and 146–153.

90 Ibid.

91 See Werner Hanak-Lettner, Die Ausstellung als Drama: Wie das Museum aus dem Theater entstand (Bielefeld, 2011), p. 22.

Szenografisches Gestalten ist ein inszenatorischer Akt mit eigener Dramaturgie. Der Begriff „Dramaturgie" kommt ursprünglich aus dem Theater und leitet sich vom griechischen „dramatourgia" ab.[89] Dramaturgie ist die Lehre von der äußeren Bauform und den Gesetzmäßigkeiten der inneren Struktur des Dramas. Sie ist aber auch die Kunst, gute Geschichten im inszenierten Raum zu erzählen. Die Inszenierung definiert sich über verschiedene Elemente, wie beispielsweise Raum, Bühnenbild, Schauspieler, Text, Sprache, Licht, Ton, Kostüm und Zuschauer – Elemente, die jeweils einen eigenen, teilweise auch gegenläufigen dramaturgischen Spannungsbogen haben. Mit der voranschreitenden Inszenierung verschiedener gesellschaftlicher Bereiche hat auch der Begriff Dramaturgie in diese Einzug gehalten und sich längst für Künste wie zum Beispiel Film, Tanz, Musik und Hörspiel bewährt.[90] Für das Ausstellungswesen hat sich die Dramaturgie nicht nur etabliert, sondern ist unserer Gestaltungsphilosophie zufolge als einer von fünf zentralen Parametern der Szenografie zu verstehen. Sie bestimmt die Chronologie der Inhalte, der Exponate und der Rezeption, sie definiert die Raumabfolge und manifestiert sich im Ausstellungsparcours.

Die Dramaturgie einer Ausstellung ist oft ähnlich strukturiert wie die einer klassischen Oper, eines Theaterstücks, eines Films oder einer Dance-Performance – mit einem Prolog, einem Hauptteil mit verschiedenen Akten und einem Epilog. In Form eines narrativen Parcours gibt sie eine Rezeptionschronologie vor, die weder streng eindimensional ist, noch von allen Besuchern gleichartig erlebt wird. Vielmehr ist sie als eine Art Struktur zu verstehen, die komplexe, mehrdimensionale Erzählstränge und Besuchererlebnisse verknüpft und eine individuelle Dynamik des Gehens und Sehens fördert. Dramaturgie formt den räumlichen und zeitlichen Ablauf einer Geschichte, die der Besucher selbstbestimmt abgehen und erleben kann – als seine eigene Version der Geschichte.[91] Dabei spielt auch das Exponat als Protagonist der Erzählung eine wichtige Rolle; seine Inszenierung durch den Szenografen kann die Aufmerksamkeit des Besuchers beeinflussen und somit seine Bewegung im Raum und die Wahrnehmung steuern. Der Ausstellung liegt schließlich eine Erzählstruktur zugrunde, die sich als Geschichte auf der Bühne des Ausstellungsraums individuell entfaltet und

dramaturgy

arc of suspense

reception chronology

narrative structure

the distance between visitor and exhibit.[92] Visitors can experience the exhibits, the content, and messages physically and emotionally, cognitively and associatively, authentically and auratically, actively and passively.[93] In 1993 Peter Greenaway, who uses two different formats of spatial narrative as filmmaker and exhibition designer, describes the exhibition from a comparative perspective as "a form of three-dimensional cinema with stimulus for all five senses where the viewer is not passively seated."[94] The comparison and the emphasis of the difference between exhibition and film reveal the scenographic potential of the exhibition space; at the same time, scenography borrows from other staging formats and consequently has much in common with them. Scenography uses dramaturgical structures and principles from literature, drama, theatre, film, dance, music, and opera, transferring them in an altered form to the exhibition format. What models does scenography draw on?

staging formats

dramaturgical structures

ELEMENTS OF DRAMATURGY BORROWED FROM THE THEATRE: ARISTOTLE AND BRECHT

teachings of Aristotle

plot

catharsis

epic theatre of Bertolt Brecht

Looking back at Ancient Greece, the focus is first trained on the teachings of Aristotle. In his poetics, he reflected on the nature of tragedy and named mimesis, the depictive representation of plots, as the defining characteristic. A good plot, according to Aristotle, has to be cohesive and has a beginning, a middle, and an end–that is, it has to have a dramaturgical structure: all the parts have to be logically connected to one another. According to Aristotle, a tragedy aims to purify the audience and their souls from states such as suffering, horror, pity–a process that he called "catharsis," as purification of the soul. In Aristotelian theatre it was thus about identification, empathy, and compassion. The epic theatre of Bertolt Brecht, by contrast, wanted the audience to consider what was happening on the stage from a distance and encourage criticism. He therefore created dialectic, stylised, and alienated performances, which aimed at socio-critical insights and distance rather than empathy and

92 Ibid., p. 9.
93 See Brückner and Greci 2016, p. 51.
94 David Pascoe, Peter Greenaway: Museums and Moving Images (London, 1997), p. 198.

die Distanz zwischen Besucher und Exponat aufhebt.[92] Die Besucher können die Exponate, die Inhalte und Botschaften physisch und emotional, kognitiv und assoziativ, authentisch und auratisch, aktiv und passiv erleben.[93] In diesem Sinne beschreibt 1993 Peter Greenaway, der als Filme- und Ausstellungsmacher zwei verschiedene Formate der räumlichen Erzählung nutzt, aus einer vergleichenden Perspektive die Ausstellung als „[…] a form of three-dimensional cinema with stimulus for all five senses where the viewer is not passively seated […]."[94] Dieser Vergleich und das Hervorheben der Unterschiede zwischen Ausstellung und Film verweisen auf das szenografische Potenzial des Ausstellungsraums; gleichzeitig gibt es zahlreiche Anleihen aus anderen Inszenierungsformaten und dementsprechend viele Gemeinsamkeiten. Die Szenografie bedient sich dramaturgischer Strukturen und Prinzipien aus Literatur, Drama, Theater, Film, Tanz, Musik und Oper und überträgt diese transformatorisch in das Format Ausstellung. Auf welche Vorbilder greift die Szenografie dabei zurück?

DRAMATURGISCHE ANLEIHEN AUS DEM THEATER: ARISTOTELES UND BRECHT

Mit Blick zurück auf das antike Griechenland steht zunächst die Lehre des Aristoteles im Fokus. Er hat in seiner Poetik über das Wesen der Tragödie räsoniert und die Mimesis, die nachahmende Darstellung von Handlungen, als maßgebliches Charakteristikum benannt. Eine gute Handlung, so Aristoteles, muss in sich geschlossen sein und einen Anfang, eine Mitte und ein Ende haben – also über einen dramaturgischen Aufbau verfügen, alle Teile sollen logisch miteinander verknüpft sein. Laut Aristoteles zielt die Tragödie auf eine Läuterung des Zuschauers und seiner Seele von Erregungszuständen wie Leid, Schrecken, Rührung ab – ein Prozess, den er als Katharsis, als seelische Reinigung, bezeichnet. Im aristotelischen Theater ging es also um Identifikation, Einfühlung und Mitleiden. Das epische Theater Bertolt Brechts dagegen wollte den Zuschauer zu einer distanzierten Betrachtung des Bühnengeschehens animieren und ihn zu Kritik anregen. Er schaffte daher dialektische, stilisierte und verfremdete Inszenierungen, die nicht auf Einfühlung und Nähe abzielen, sondern auf gesellschaftskritische Erkenntnisse und

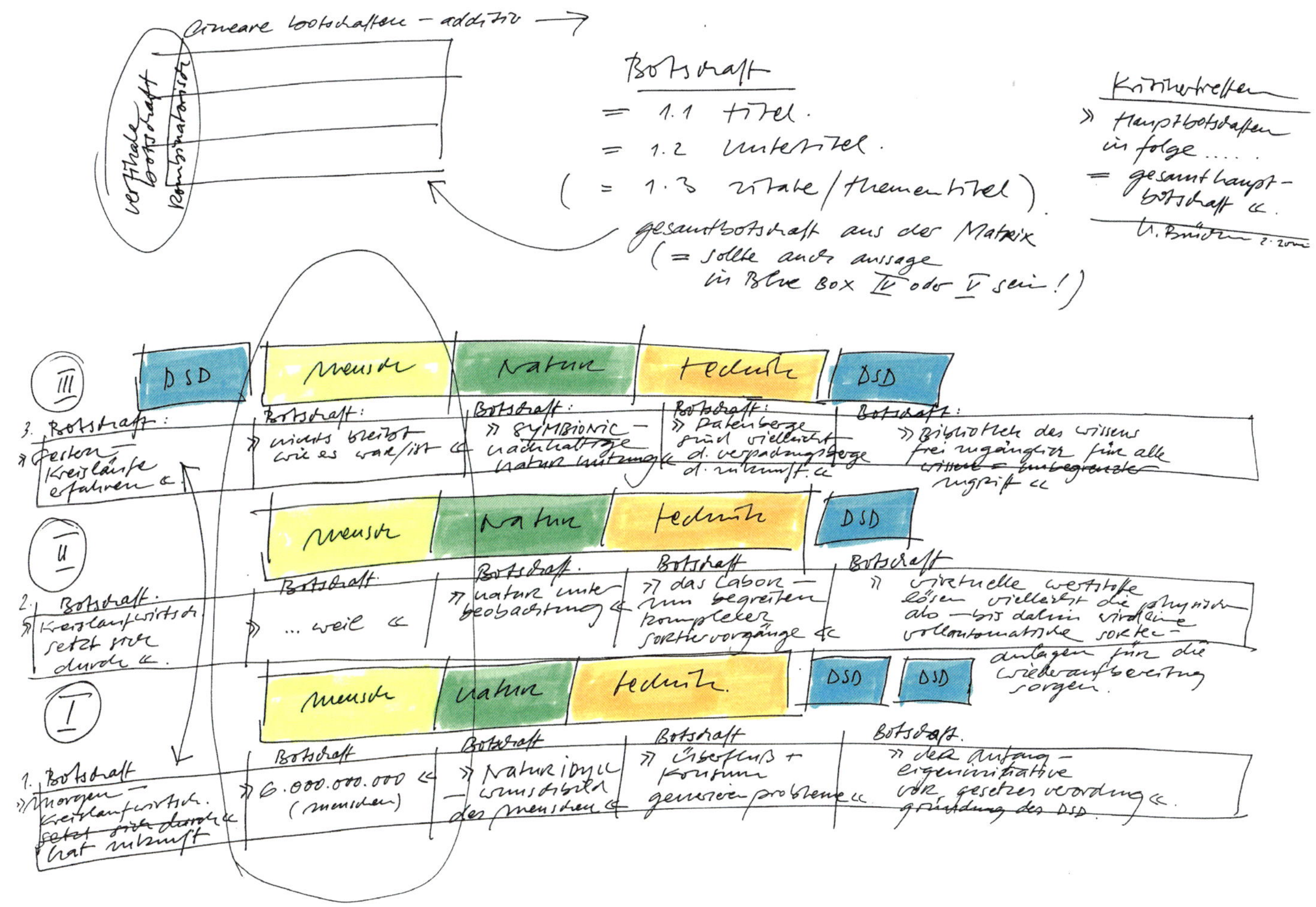

"Cyclebowl"–"Schematic Partitura," 1998.

illusion

closeness. While with Aristotle it is about emotional involvement, Brecht calls on the imagination of the audience and breaks away from the illusion. Werner Hanak-Lettner is therefore justified in asking whether the exhibition is moving towards the drama, inversely to the development of modern theatre, which is increasingly moving away from drama. His answer: "While the theatre of the twentieth century, in particular since Brecht, tried to establish an illusion-destroying distance between what was happening on the stage and the audience, exhibitions and other 'epic' media strive to overcome this distance, in order to involve their visitors and viewers, to encourage them to interact with a view to entering into a (albeit a controlled) dialogue."[95]

dialogue-based relationship

distortion

Following the Aristotelian principle, an exhibition involves a dialogue-based relationship between exhibit and visitor, and a reception space which creates a sense of closeness. At the same time, and without contradiction, the exhibition can also use the means of distortion in the sense of an unconventional, astounding staging from an unusual perspective which creates a critical distance, causes irritation, and encourages the visitor to

95 Hanak-Lettner 2011, p. 17 (translation of the German original quotation taken from this source).

Distanz. Während es bei Aristoteles um emotionales Miterleben geht, fordert Brecht die Imagination des Zuschauers ein und bricht mit der Illusion. Und so stellt Werner Hanak-Lettner berechtigterweise die Frage, ob sich die Ausstellung zum Drama hin bewegt, und zwar entgegen der Entwicklung des Gegenwartstheaters, das sich immer häufiger vom Drama verabschiedet. Und seine Antwort lautet: „Während also das Theater des 20. Jahrhunderts, insbesondere seit Brecht, versucht hat, eine illusionsbrechende Distanz zwischen dem Bühnengeschehen und dem Publikum aufzubauen, haben Ausstellungen und andere ‚epische' Medien danach gestrebt, diese Distanz zu überwinden, um ihre Besucher und Zuseher zu involvieren, zur Interaktion zu überreden, um letztlich mit ihnen in einen (wenn auch sehr einseitig kontrollierten) Dialog zu treten."[95]

Dem aristotelischen Prinzip folgend, geht es in der Ausstellung um eine dialogische Beziehung zwischen Exponat und Besucher und um einen Rezeptionsraum, der Nähe schafft. Gleichzeitig und nicht im Widerspruch dazu kann die Ausstellung aber auch das Mittel der Verfremdung nutzen – im Sinne einer unkonventionellen, verblüffenden Inszenierung aus einer ungewohnten Perspektive, die eine kritische Distanz erzielt, eine Irritation hervorruft und den Besucher zum Reflektieren, Hinterfragen und Weiterdenken anregt. Die gegensätzlichen Prinzipien des aristotelischen und des epischen Theaters vereint die zeitgemäße Ausstellung und transformiert diese auf der Bühne

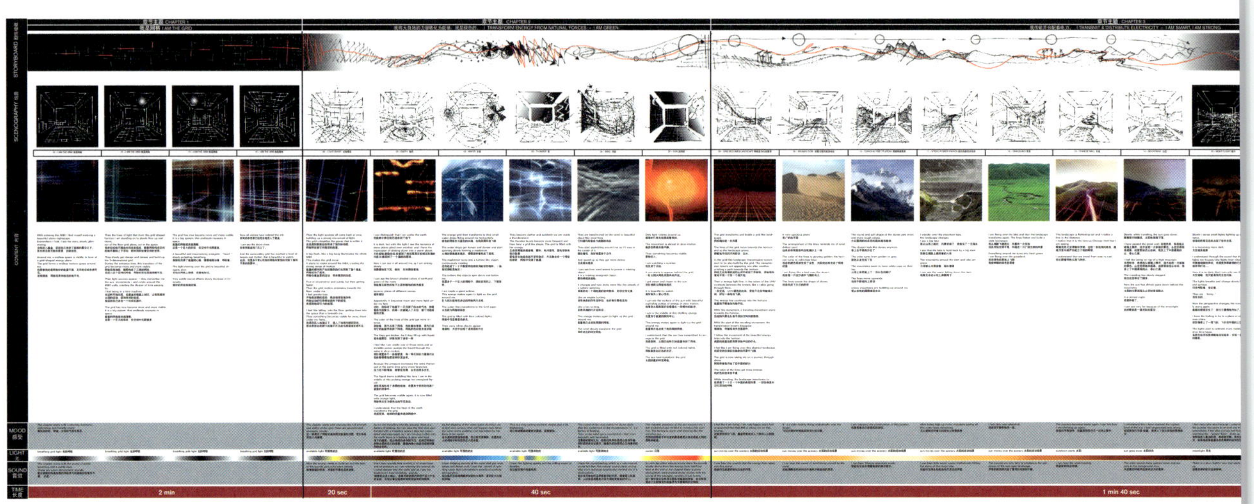

"State Grid Pavilion–Magic Box"–"Partitura" (extract), 2010.

reflect, question, and think further. The contradictory principles of the Aristotelian and epic theatre are combined in contemporary exhibitions, transformed on the platform of the staged space. In the exhibition, the story is not narrated behind the "fourth wall" but is penetrated as an invisible wall between actor and audience, between exhibit and visitor, similar to contemporary theatre, and thus creates a space for imagination and interaction, full of suspense.[96]

DRAMATURGICAL BORROWINGS FROM FILM: HITCHCOCK'S SUSPENSE

A similar form involving building suspense is to be found in the format of film, for example as seen in the suspense technique used by Alfred Hitchcock. Suspense is a term that stems from the theatre, film, and literature studies and in this context means the dramatization of the narrative material of a film or also the intense presentation of dramatic situations in a film.[97] In some ways, suspense scenes are privileged moments that have a longer effect and stick in the memories of the audience.[98] On the one hand, it is about getting the attention of the audience; on the other, it is about arousing

des inszenierten Raums. In der Ausstellung findet die Geschichte nicht wie im klassischen Drama hinter der „vierten Wand" statt, sondern jene wird als unsichtbare Wand zwischen Schauspieler und Zuschauer, zwischen Exponat und Besucher, ähnlich wie im Gegenwartstheater durchbrochen. Auf diese Weise entsteht ein spannungsgeladener Imaginations- und Interaktionsraum.[96]

fourth wall

DRAMATURGISCHE ANLEIHEN AUS DEM FILM: HITCHCOCKS SUSPENSE

Eine ähnliche Form des Involvierens und des Spannungsaufbaus findet sich im Format Film, beispielsweise bei der Suspense-Technik Alfred Hitchcocks. Suspense ist ein Begriff, der aus der Theater-, Film- und Literaturwissenschaft stammt und in diesem Kontext die Dramatisierung des Erzählmaterials eines Films oder auch die intensivste Darstellung dramatischer Situationen im Film bedeutet.[97] Suspense-Szenen sind in gewisser Weise privilegierte Augenblicke, die nachhaltig wirken und im Gedächtnis des Zuschauers haften bleiben.[98] Es geht einerseits darum, die Aufmerksamkeit des Zuschauers zu erhalten und andererseits seine Emotionen zu wecken und

Hitchcock

dramatization

96 The "fourth wall" is a term used in theatre. When the fourth wall, the imaginary wall of a proscenium stage, is broken, the actors enter into an interaction with the audience. See Herbert Willems, Theatralisierung der Gesellschaft, vol. 1, Soziologische Theorie und Zeitdiagnose (Wiesbaden, 2009), pp. 69–70.
97 See Francois Truffaut, Mr. Hitchcock, wie haben Sie das gemacht? (Munich, 1989), pp. 11–12.
98 Ibid.

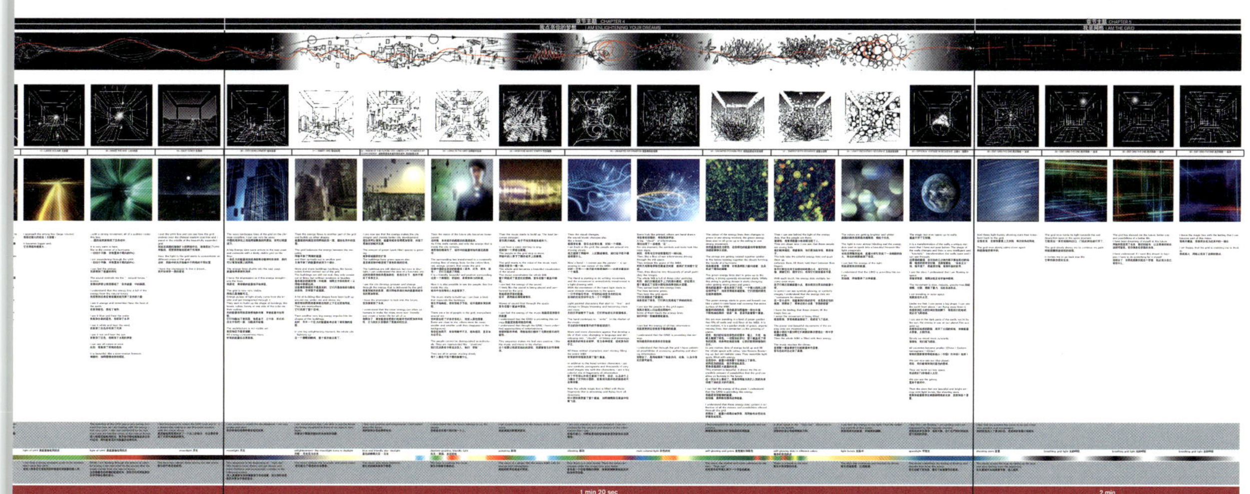

their emotions and building dramatic suspense. This is how Hitchcock does it:

"The bomb is under the table and the viewers know it. Let's assume because they saw how the anarchist put it there. [...] The same harmless conversation suddenly becomes interesting because the audience participates in the scene. They want to call out to the people on the stage: Don't speak about such everyday things, there is a bomb under the table and it is about to explode. In the first case, the audience has 15 seconds of surprise when the bomb explodes! In the second case, we offer them 15 minutes of suspense."[99]

The audience is better informed than the protagonist in the film itself; they share in the excitement and want to warn him. But unfortunately they can't intervene in the scene, as they are members of an uninvolved audience that is incapable of reacting. And this is where exhibitions differ decisively from film, because an exhibition allows interaction; visitors may act as protagonists and can influence what is happening on stage. These forms of dramatic climax and the building of suspense are central aspects of contemporary scenography which can be used to achieve precisely what Hitchcock aimed to do with his suspense scenes: attention, concentration, emotion, sustainability, memorability, and an individual, positive involvement which makes the recipient into an addressee. In the exhibition, this is achieved, for instance, by using narrative spaces which address the deeper layers of consciousness and the emotions of the visitor, thus conveying information directly and creating associations in the process. As soon as the narrative space arouses attention and has built up suspense, the visitor enters into a dialogue with the objects and is open for the content of the exhibition. The narrative space acts as the first dramatising moment which captures the imagination of the visitors, making them the addressee, the participant, or at least an accessory.

building of suspense

positive involvement

dramatische Spannung aufzubauen. Das schafft Hitchcock wie folgt:

„Die Bombe ist unter dem Tisch, und das Publikum weiß es. Nehmen wir an, weil es gesehen hat, wie der Anarchist sie dahingelegt hat. [...] Dieselbe unverfängliche Unterhaltung wird plötzlich interessant, weil das Publikum an der Szene teilnimmt. Es möchte den Leuten auf der Leinwand zurufen: Reden Sie nicht über so banale Dinge, unter dem Tisch ist eine Bombe, und gleich wird sie explodieren! Im ersten Fall hat das Publikum fünfzehn Sekunden Überraschung beim Explodieren der Bombe. Im zweiten Fall bieten wir ihm fünfzehn Minuten Suspense.“[99]

Der Zuschauer ist informierter als der Protagonist im Film selbst. Er fiebert mit und will ihn warnen. Nur leider kann er in die Szene nicht eingreifen, er ist unbeteiligter, reaktionsunfähiger Zuseher. Und hier unterscheidet sich die Ausstellung wesentlich vom Film, denn die Ausstellung ermöglicht Interaktion: Der Besucher ist selbst Protagonist und kann das Bühnengeschehen beeinflussen. Diese Formen der dramatischen Zuspitzung und des Spannungsaufbaus sind zentrale Aspekte einer zeitgemäßen Szenografie, mit der genau das erreicht werden kann, was Hitchcock mit seinen Suspense-Szenen anstrebt: Aufmerksamkeit, Konzentration, Emotion, Nachhaltigkeit, Erinnerungswürdigkeit und ein individuelles, positives Beteiligtsein, das den Rezipienten zum Adressaten macht. In der Ausstellung wird dies beispielsweise über Raumbilder erreicht, welche die tieferen Schichten des Bewusstseins und die Emotionen der Besucher ansprechen und dabei Informationen unmittelbar und assoziativ vermitteln. Sobald das Raumbild die Aufmerksamkeit geweckt und Spannung aufgebaut hat, tritt der Besucher in Dialog mit den Objekten und lässt sich auf die Inhalte der Ausstellung ein. Das Raumbild fungiert als erster dramatisierender Moment, der den Besucher in seinen Bann zieht und zum Gemeinten, zum Beteiligten, mindestens zum Mitwisser macht.

99 Ibid., p. 64.

DRAMATURGICAL BORROWINGS FROM MUSIC: BACH AND THE SCORE

In order to build the desired suspense and to arouse emotions, it will generally be necessary to compose a consistent, effective dramaturgy. An important resource to achieve this is “Die Kunst der Fuge” (The Art of the Fugue) from the late works of Johann Sebastian Bach. The musical composition principle of the fugue is one of the strictest forms of musical thought. As Bach, shortly before his death, almost blind, writes this cycle, he does this in the form of a score, contrary to customary practice, in order make clear the contrapuntal, dramaturgically choreographed logic of the work. The score (and its voices) does not specify the instrumentation of the work; it is rather a metastructure of a composition, a universally interpretable set of rules–a kind of open staging structure, an interpretable code with scope for perception, with fugues as interim spaces which hold the content, chapters, and narration together. An ideal-typical dramaturgical structure for ambitious scenography.

The score also serves as a methodical toolkit for the composition and presentation of exhibition dramaturgies. The score from the Italian “partitura,” meaning “division,” is used in music to describe the notation of instrumental and vocal parts in clear layers.[100] In a score, all the parts are recorded in a composition, stave by stave below one another so that their connection is clear both horizontally and vertically.[101] This makes it easier to read the course of the individual parts, their coordination and harmonies. The integrated libretto and any stage directions round off the complex structure and establish a synchronised relationship between all the elements–narration, cue, appearance, or theatrical procedures. The score is of central importance for the composition of music with several voices. In exhibition
design, we use it in order to orchestrate various design parameters and instruments into a holistic composition and to combine these interactively with one another. In this way, it is possible to map considered dramaturgies and very complex spatial installations or spatial choreographies.

100 See Ulrich Michels, dtv-Atlas Musik: Systematischer Teil: Musikgeschichte von den Anfängen bis zur Gegenwart (Kassel, 2001), p. 69.

101 See Wieland Ziegenrücker, ABC Musik: Allgemeine Musiklehre (Wiesbaden, 1997), p. 228.

DRAMATURGISCHE ANLEIHEN AUS DER MUSIK: BACH UND DIE PARTITUR

Eine konsistente, wirkmächtige Dramaturgie muss in der Regel komponiert werden, um die gewünschte Spannung aufzubauen und Emotionen zu wecken. Eine wichtige Ressource hierfür stellt „Die Kunst der Fuge“ aus dem Spätwerk Johann Sebastian Bachs dar. Das musikalische Kompositionsprinzip der Fuge gilt als eine der strengsten Formen musikalischen Denkens. Als Bach kurz vor seinem Tod schon fast erblindet diesen Zyklus notierte, tat er dies entgegen der gängigen Praxis in Partiturform, um die kontrapunktische, das heißt die wechselspielhafte, dramaturgisch choreografierte Logik des Werkes deutlich zu machen. Die Partitur (und ihre Stimmen) blieb(en) ohne Angaben zur Instrumentierung des Werks, als handele es sich um die Metastruktur einer Komposition – ein universal interpretierbares Regelwerk, eine Art offene Inszenierungsstruktur oder einen interpretierbaren Code mit Wahrnehmungsspielraum, mit Fugen als Zwischenräumen, die Inhalt, Kapitel und Narration zusammenhalten: eine idealtypische dramaturgische Struktur für eine ambitionierte Szenografie.

Als methodisches Instrumentarium dient die Partitur auch der Komposition und Darstellung von Ausstellungsdramaturgien. Die Partitur – italienisch „partitura“: Einteilung – bezeichnet in der Musik die Aufzeichnungsweise von Instrumental- und Vokalstimmen in übersichtlicher Schichtung.[100] In einer Partitur werden alle Stimmen einer Komposition erfasst und taktweise untereinander verzeichnet, sodass ihr Zusammenhang horizontal und vertikal deutlich wird.[101] Dadurch können der Verlauf der Einzelstimmen, ihre Koordination und die Zusammenklänge ablesbar werden. Das integrierte Libretto und eventuelle Regieanweisungen komplettieren die komplexe Struktur und setzen alle Elemente in eine synchronisierte Beziehung – Narration, Einsatz, Auftritt oder theatralische Vorgänge. Die Partitur hat zentrale Bedeutung für das Komponieren mehrstimmiger Musik. In der Ausstellungsgestaltung machen wir sie uns zunutze, um verschiedene Gestaltungsparameter und -instrumente zu einer Gesamtkomposition zu orchestrieren und diese in eine wechselspielhafte Beziehung zueinander zu setzen. Mit ihr können überlegte Dramaturgien und sehr komplexe Rauminstallationen oder Raumchoreografien dargestellt werden.

composition principle

staging structure

score

exhibition dramaturgies

holistic composition

"Spatial dramaturgy, that means a narrative parcours, a root of perception in a choreographed space or a choreographed order of spaces." Uwe R. Brückner

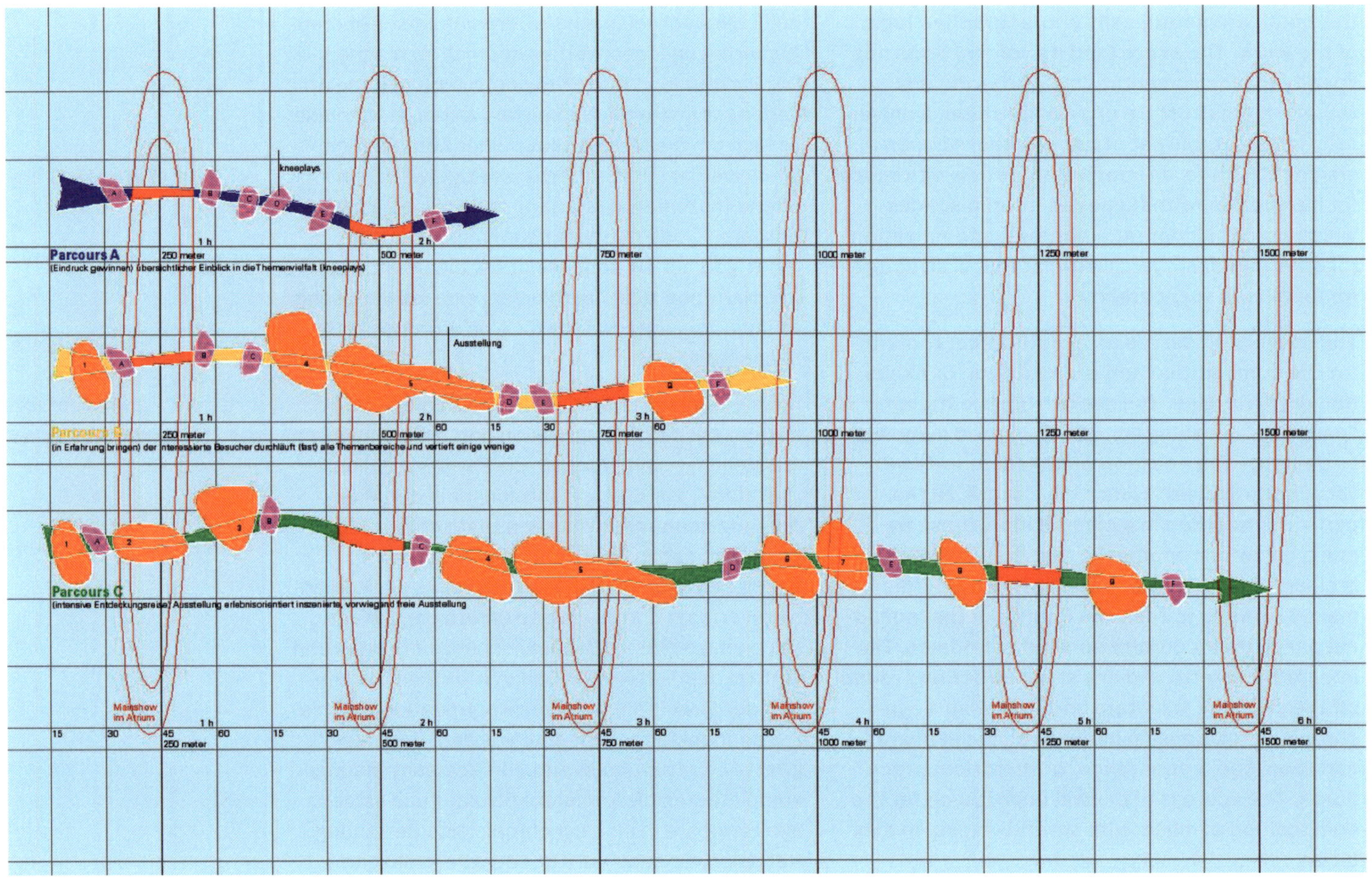

"O.VISION"–"The Transparent Human"–the parcours and routing based on three different durations, 2003.

DESIGN. Exhibition and Interior Design Solutions. Content Structure

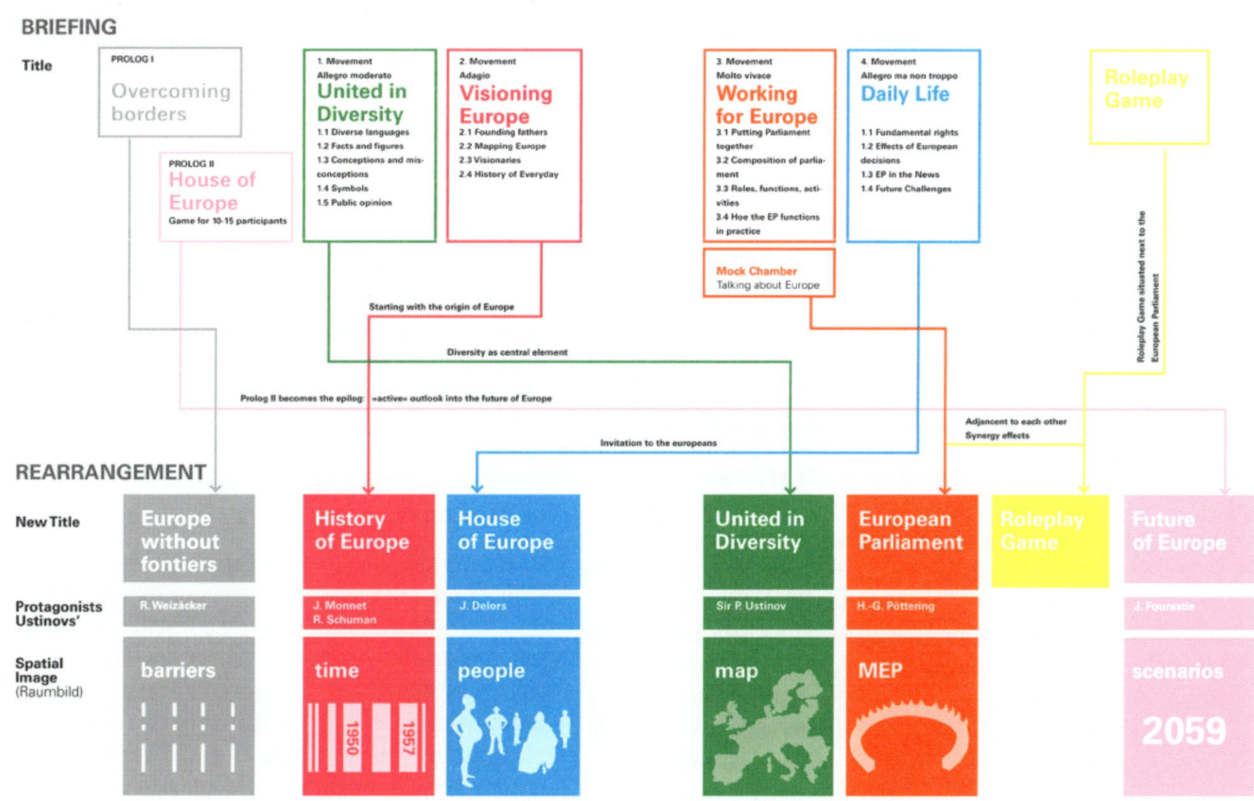

↗ p. 98

"Parlamentarium"–Dramaturgy based on order of content and perception, 2011.

DRAMATURGICAL BORROWINGS FROM DANCE: CHOREOGRAPHY

choreographed space

"The scenographic space is a choreographed space or a choreographed sequence of spaces."[102] Originally, the term "choreography" means the composition of a dance, that is, the movement of a body in space and time.[103] However, since the 1990s, the term "choreography" has not been limited to dance and to the movement of the human body and since then can also be applied to the arrangement of things in spaces or to the arrangement of spaces themselves and their readability in an intended order. Choreography and dramaturgy generate rhythm and dynamics; they play a decisive role in conditioning the visitor reception of space, exhibits, and content and create connections between them. In this field of tension, there arises a scenographical force field–space becomes a (physical) body space, a (dynamic) movement space, and an (interpretable) experience and meaning space. Scenographic design is accordingly dramatising, dynamic design.

dynamic design

DRAMATURGY MANIFESTED IN THE ROUTING

exhibition routing

Dramaturgy and choreography are manifested in the exhibition routing, which determines the space, time, and narration and includes all aspects such as duration, chronology, and pace, and, not least, structures the content, themes, and stories to be narrated. As a rule, the routing offers different routes through the walk-in exhibition space. There are three types of routing: with the "free flow" route, the decision as to how to walk through the exhibition is left up to the visitors, also the order in which they want to experience the space, content, and objects. A defined route prescribes a fixed pathway and follows a certain dramaturgy. Between these two is the optional route,

free flow route

defined route

optional route

102 Uwe R. Brückner
103 Per William Forsythe, "Choreography is about organising bodies in space, or organising bodies with other bodies, or a body with other bodies in an environment that is organised." See Steven Spier, "Choreographic thinking and amateur bodies," in William Forsythe and the Practice of Choreography: It Starts From Any Point, ed. Steven Spier (New York, 2011).

DRAMATURGISCHE ANLEIHEN AUS DEM TANZ: DIE CHOREOGRAFIE

„Der szenografische Raum ist ein choreografierter Raum bzw. eine choreografierte Abfolge von Räumen."[102]. Der Begriff „Choreografie" bedeutet ursprünglich die Komposition eines Tanzes, also die Bewegung eines Körpers in Raum und Zeit.[103] Doch seit den 1990er-Jahren ist der Begriff „Choreografie" in seiner Bedeutung nicht mehr nur an den Tanz und an die Bewegung eines menschlichen Körpers gebunden, sondern kann sich seither auch auf die Anordnung von Dingen in Räumen oder auf die Anordnung von Räumen selbst sowie deren Lesbarkeit in einer intendierten Reihenfolge beziehen. Choreografie und Dramaturgie erzeugen Rhythmus und Dynamik. Sie konditionieren entscheidend die Besucherrezeption von Raum, Exponat und Inhalt und stellen eine Verbindung zwischen ihnen her. In diesem Spannungsfeld entsteht ein inszenatorisches Kräftefeld – Raum wird zum (physischen) Körperraum, zum (dynamischen) Bewegungsraum und zum (interpretierbaren) Erfahrungs- und Deutungsraum. Szenografisches Gestalten ist entsprechend ein dramatisierendes, dynamisches Gestalten.

DIE MANIFESTIERUNG DER DRAMATURGIE IM PARCOURS

Dramaturgie und Choreografie manifestieren sich im Ausstellungsparcours, der Raum, Zeit und Narration bestimmt und sämtliche Aspekte mit einbezieht, wie Dauer, Chronologien und Geschwindigkeiten, und nicht zuletzt die zu erzählenden Inhalte, Themen und Geschichten strukturiert. Der Parcours bietet in der Regel unterschiedliche Routen durch den begehbaren Ausstellungsraum an. Im Sinne der Besucherführung wird zwischen drei Typen unterschieden: Als „free flow" wird dem Besucher die Entschei-

which offers an ideal line the visitor can follow but leaves freedom and space for excursions, and the reception chronology can be changed. A contemporary routing that works well is the circuit tour, which means that visitors do not have to return the same way they came. In addition to these three types of route, two main routing structures can be defined, the chronological routing and the thematic routing. Other options include topographical and hybrid routing.

Which routing structure is chosen depends on whether and how content is conveyed, how they build on one another, whether they should have an effect one after the other (chronological) or whether they are told in a self-explanatory manner, next to and independent of one another (thematic). The decision about which one or a combination of the two serves best depends on the focus of the exhibition in terms of content or concept and accordingly the narrative strand differs from the sequence of experiences.

A consistent routing choreographs the content of an exhibition, the (re-)presentation of the exhibits, the sequence of rooms, and the visitor experience. It conveys the overarching message and stages the plot. The routing gives the narrative structure a spatial dimension, lending the dramaturgy its material and walk-in form.

dung überlassen, wie er die Ausstellung durchlaufen und in welcher Reihenfolge er Raum, Inhalte und Objekte erleben möchte. Demgegenüber steht der definierte Parcours, der eine festgeschriebene Route vorgibt und einer bestimmten Dramaturgie folgt. Dazwischen ist der optionale Parcours angesiedelt, der eine Route als Ideallinie vorschlägt, dabei aber den Besucher selbst entscheiden lässt, an welchen Stellen er Exkursionen machen und die Rezeptionschronologie selbstbestimmt verändern möchte. Ein zeitgemäßer, gut funktionierender Parcours ist als Rundgang konzipiert, sodass der Besucher nicht die gleiche Route zurückgehen muss, die er bereits zurückgelegt hat. Darüber hinaus sind vornehmlich zwei Parcourstypen zu unterscheiden, nämlich der chronologische Parcours und der thematische Parcours. Weitere Optionen sind eine topografische oder auch eine hybride Tour.

chronological routing
thematic routing

Die Wahl hängt davon ab, ob und wie Inhalte vermittelt werden, wie sie aufeinander aufbauen oder nacheinander wirken sollen (chronologisch) oder ob sie selbsterklärend nebeneinander und unabhängig voneinander erzählt werden können (thematisch). Je nach inhaltlichem oder konzeptionellem Schwerpunkt kann der passende Parcourstypus gewählt – oder gar beide kombiniert – werden und entsprechend unterscheidet sich dann der Narrationsstrang von der Erlebnisabfolge.

narrative strand

Ein konsistenter Parcours choreografiert die Inhalte einer Ausstellung, die (Re-)Präsentation der Exponate, die Raumabfolge und das Besuchererlebnis. Er vermittelt die übergeordnete Botschaft und inszeniert den Plot. Der Parcours wird zur Verräumlichung der Erzählstruktur – zur begehbaren Materialisierung der Dramaturgie.

“It’s up to the visitor to either follow or ignore a dramatized route, to get involved in a narrative structure, a rhythm and suspense.” Uwe R. Brückner

We know that a stage can be a house; but can a house also be a stage, with a personality, a soul, a role to play, that can change dynamically, that follows the composition of a certain choreography? Can a building be transformed, take on various shapes, and follow an arc of suspense, like in a score, its own dramaturgy? Smart architecture whose innovation lies in its digital connectivity and whose mediality is not limited to a technical facade projection, but can follow composition, dynamically, interactively, or reactively?

↗ p. 20

CYCLEBOWL The Cyclebowl pavilion at the Expo Hanover 2000 was such a complex composition. In less than eight minutes, it could be transformed from a building illuminated by natural daylight with living plants into a black box of cinematic quality. The pneumatic facade could be shaded and blacked out by means of overlapping foils.

Inside, visitors wandered through an exhibition on a three-storey ramp, which followed the dramatic structure of a three-act opera and staged the expo theme "Man Nature Technology" along a highly interactive routing.

Wir wissen, dass eine Bühne ein Haus sein kann, aber kann ein Haus auch eine Bühne sein, die einen Charakter besitzt, eine Seele hat, eine Rolle spielen kann, die sich dynamisch verändert, die einer Komposition, einer bestimmten Choreografie folgt? Kann sich ein Gebäude verwandeln, verschiedene Gestalten annehmen und einem Spannungsbogen folgen wie in einer Partitur, einer eigenen Dramaturgie? Eine intelligente Architektur, deren Innovation auf digitale Vernetzung zielt und deren Medialität nicht auf eine technische Fassadenbespielung reduziert ist, sondern die sich dynamisch, interaktiv oder reaktiv verhalten, einer Komposition folgen kann?

CYCLEBOWL Die Cyclebowl auf der Expo Hannover 2000 war ein solcher durchkomponierter Pavillon. Er konnte sich in weniger als acht Minuten von einem Tageslichtgebäude mit lebenden Pflanzen in eine Blackbox mit Kinoqualität verwandeln. Die pneumatische Fassade ließ sich mittels überlagernder Folien stufenlos schließen, das Innere damit verschatten und verdunkeln.

Im Inneren wandelten die Besucher durch eine Ausstellung auf einer dreigeschossigen Rampe, die der Dramaturgie einer dreiaktigen Oper folgte und die Expo-Themen, „Mensch Natur Technik", in einem fast vollständig interaktiven Parcours inszenierte.

"Cyclebowl"–Central void with hourly appearing tornado, 2000.

Every hour on the hour, the whole light and sound choreography was synchronised with the circular film in the centre, the storytelling of which developed into the highlight of the show, a veritable physical tornado.

The whole routing followed a complex score which combined all the scenographic parameters–such as content, space, objects, visitors–and all the design instruments–like light, graphics, sounds, film–and the whole technical infrastructure–like a tornado, the twenty-four circular ventilators, the large ceiling ventilator, the rain machine, the whole facade and building control, and the sustainable air-conditioning system based on cooling by evaporation–to form a Gesamtkunstwerk.

In the end, the building itself became a walk-in opera, whose score formed the (built) interface for this innovative pavilion.

Jeweils zur vollen Stunde wurde die gesamte Licht- und Soundchoreografie mit einem zentralen kreisförmigen Film synchronisiert, aus dessen Storytelling heraus sich das Highlight, ein veritabler physischer Tornado, entwickelte.

Der ganze Parcours folgte einer komplexen Partitur, die alle szenografischen Parameter – Inhalt, Raum, Objekte, Besucher – und alle Gestaltungsinstrumente – Licht, Grafik, Sound, Film – und die gesamte technische Infrastruktur – den Tornado, die 24 Zirkularventilatoren, den großen Deckenventilator, die Beregnungsanlage, die ganze Fassaden- und Gebäudesteuerung und das nachhaltige, auf Verdunstungskälte beruhende Kühlsystem – zu einem Gesamtkunstwerk vereinte.

Letztlich war das Gebäude selbst eine begehbare Oper, deren Partitur das (gebaute) Interface des Pavillons darstellt.

"Cyclebowl"–"Black Box"– Pavilion opened by overlaying foils (left) | Pavilion closed by divided foils with 75 percent daylight (right), 2000.

Once a company decides to participate in an Expo, it aims to stage the brand and its appearance as spectacularly as possible in order to enhance the image of the brand. Theme parks tend to have a strong plot, with topics like "Man Nature Technology" (Expo Hanover 2000) or an overall artistic concept such as the "Arteplagen" of the Expo.02 in Switzerland. For scenographers, Expos are an experimental laboratory per se. Clients expect spectacular pavilions with fascinating routings full of surprises. The storylines and storyboards therefore need to be developed with a suspenseful dramaturgy, a high degree of fascination, and a sustainable result.

↗ p. 66

STATE GRID PAVILION—MAGIC BOX For the national Chinese electricity company State Grid, a 15 by 15 by 13-metre cube, the "Magic Box," (2010) was to be brought to life with LEDs. The only content: the transportation of electricity over 3,000 kilometres through using superconductivity from west to east, to the megacities on China's east coast. The big opportunity: the first cubic cinema in the world, a space-shaping screen, a walk-in 720-degree screen.

Sobald ein Unternehmen entschieden hat, sich auf einer Expo zu engagieren, gilt es, die Marke und ihren Auftritt möglichst spektakulär zu inszenieren, um einen entsprechenden Imagegewinn zu erzielen. Von Themenparks ist man einen starken Plot gewöhnt, mit Themen wie „Mensch Natur Technik" (Expo Hannover 2000) oder ein künstlerisches Gesamtkonzept wie den „Arteplagen" der Expo.02 in der Schweiz. Für die Szenografen sind Expos die Experimentierlabore schlechthin. Man erwartet aufsehenerregende Pavillons mit faszinierenden Parcours voller Überraschungen. Dementsprechend gilt es, Storylines und Storyboards mit einer spannungsreichen Dramaturgie zu entwickeln, die einen hohen Faszinationsgrad haben und ein nachhaltiges Erlebnis generieren.

STATE GRID PAVILION—MAGIC BOX Für den nationalen chinesischen Stromversorger State Grid sollte ein 15 auf 15 auf 13 Meter großer Würfel, die „Magic Box" (2010), mit LEDs bespielt werden. Einziger Inhalt: Der Stromtransport über 3.000 Kilometer via Supraleitung von West nach Ost, zu den Megacitys der chinesischen Ostküste. Die große Chance: das erste kubische Kino der Welt, ein raumbildender Screen, ein begehbarer 720-Grad-Bildschirm.

"Sate Grid—Magic Box"—Cubic Cinema featuring the main chapters of film narrative, 2010.

How do images look which not only surround us but in which we move around ourselves? What scene sequences, which video editing, what speed, what narration, and what spatial dramaturgy were needed in order to use the potential of the cubic cinema?

After the trial run in an improvised cube of five by five by five metres, it became clear that any narrative structure against the physical space would lead to irritation, but the development of the narrative out of the spatial grid even allowed a virtual extension of space, in which ultimately the imagined space replaced the physical space with spectacular narrative spaces. A 90-centimetre-thick and six-metre-longer score recorded the complex composition in detail.

The spatial dramaturgy thus came before the dramaturgy of the narrative, a kind of empirical tribute to the unusual holistic spatial film language.

Seventeen million LEDs with a 20 by 20 millimetre resolution, behind diffuse panels, and a 48-channel sound system allowed an impressive synchronicity of moving image, sound, and narration. In the end, the "Magic Box" was a huge success for the 3.2 million visitors, for a satisfied client, and for all the designers involved who were able to experience the potential of spatial dramaturgy at first hand.

Wie müssen Bilder aussehen, die einen nicht nur umgeben, sondern in denen man sich selbst bewegt? Welche Szenenfolgen, welche Bildschnitte, welche Geschwindigkeit, welche Narration und welche Raumdramaturgie sind nötig, um das Potenzial des kubischen Kinos zu nutzen?

Spätestens nach dem Probeaufbau in einem improvisierten Kubus von 5 Metern Kantenlänge war klar, dass jede Erzählstruktur gegen den physischen Raum nur zu Irritation führen würde, jedoch die Entwicklung der Erzählung aus dem Raumraster heraus sogar eine virtuelle Raumerweiterung erlaubt, bei der schließlich der imaginierte Raum den physischen Raum durch spektakuläre Raumbilder ersetzt. Eine 90 Zentimeter breite und 6 Meter lange Partitur hielt die komplexe Komposition im Detail fest.

Die Raumdramaturgie kam also vor der Dramaturgie der Erzählung, ein empirischer Tribut an die ungewohnte holistische Raum-Filmsprache.

17 Millionen LEDs mit einer 20 × 20-Millimeter-Auflösung hinter Diffusor-Panels und eine 48-Kanal-Soundanlage erlaubten eine beeindruckende Synchronität von Bewegtbild, Ton und Narration. Am Ende war die „Magic Box" ein riesiger Erfolg für 3,2 Millionen Besucher, für einen zufriedenen Auftraggeber und für alle beteiligten Gestalter, die in Erfahrung bringen durften, welches Potenzial Raumdramaturgie hat.

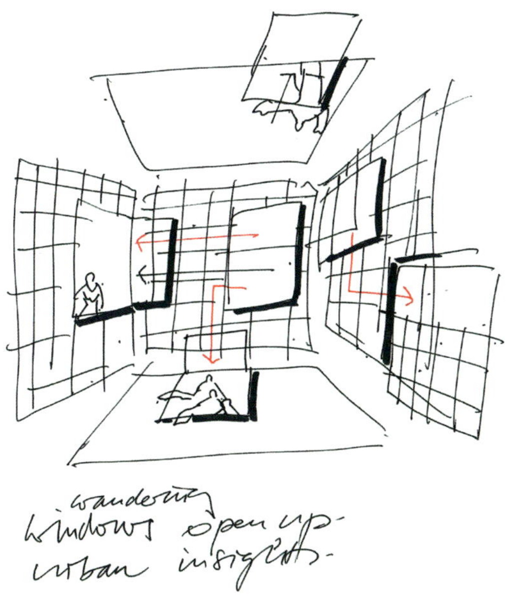

"Sate Grid–Magic Box"–Spatial dramaturgy derived from cubic grid, 2009.

Good scenography often borrows dramaturgical structures from literature, music, film, opera, or of course theatre. What happens, however, if the exhibition is about this very process, translating a performative format like an opera performance into a more static format like an exhibition?

One can use the composition principles and elements like the prelude, the libretto, the score, the stage set, the costumes, the singers and the performance as well as the finale for the composition of a scenography. All this, with the aim of getting even the Spotify generation excited about a genre like opera, which otherwise is reserved more for enthusiasts.

RICORDI–200 YEARS OF ITALIAN OPERA For "That's Opera" in Brussels (2008), the structure of a score became the structure of the exhibition itself. In addition to that, the routing reflects on the genesis of an opera in individual themed rooms.

The prelude begins with the visitor passing through several curtains, behind each of which one of five operas is playing. After a brief intermezzo, the introduction of Julio Ricordi and his family, followed by the room "Libretto," reminiscent of Rudolfo's attic room in "La Bohème." The subsequent acoustically dampened treasure chamber "Partitura" (score) shows, in respectful silence,

Gute Szenografie entlehnt oft dramaturgische Strukturen aus der Literatur, der Musik, dem Film, von der Oper und natürlich vom Theater. Was also, wenn es darum geht, genau diesen Prozess selbst auszustellen, also ein performatives Format wie eine Opernaufführung in ein eher statisches Format wie eine Ausstellung zu übersetzen?

Kompositionsprinzipien und -elemente wie das Präludium, das Libretto, die Partitur, das Bühnenbild, die Kostüme, die Sänger und die Aufführung oder Performance und das Finale lassen sich auch für die Komposition einer Szenografie verwenden. Das Ziel dabei ist, auch die Generation Spotify für ein Genre wie die Oper, das eher Liebhaberstatus genießt, zu begeistern.

RICORDI – 200 YEARS OF ITALIAN OPERA Für „That's Opera" in Brüssel (2008) wurde die Struktur einer Partitur zur Struktur der Ausstellung selbst. Zudem reflektiert der Parcours die Genesis einer Oper in einzelnen Themenräumen.

Das Präludium beginnt mit dem Durchschreiten mehrerer Vorhänge, hinter denen eine der fünf Opern angespielt wird. Nach einem kurzen Intermezzo, der Einführung zu Julio Ricordi und seiner Familie, folgt der Raum „Libretto", der an Rodolfos Dachkammer in „La Bohème" erinnert. Die darauffolgende akustisch gedämmte Schatzkammer

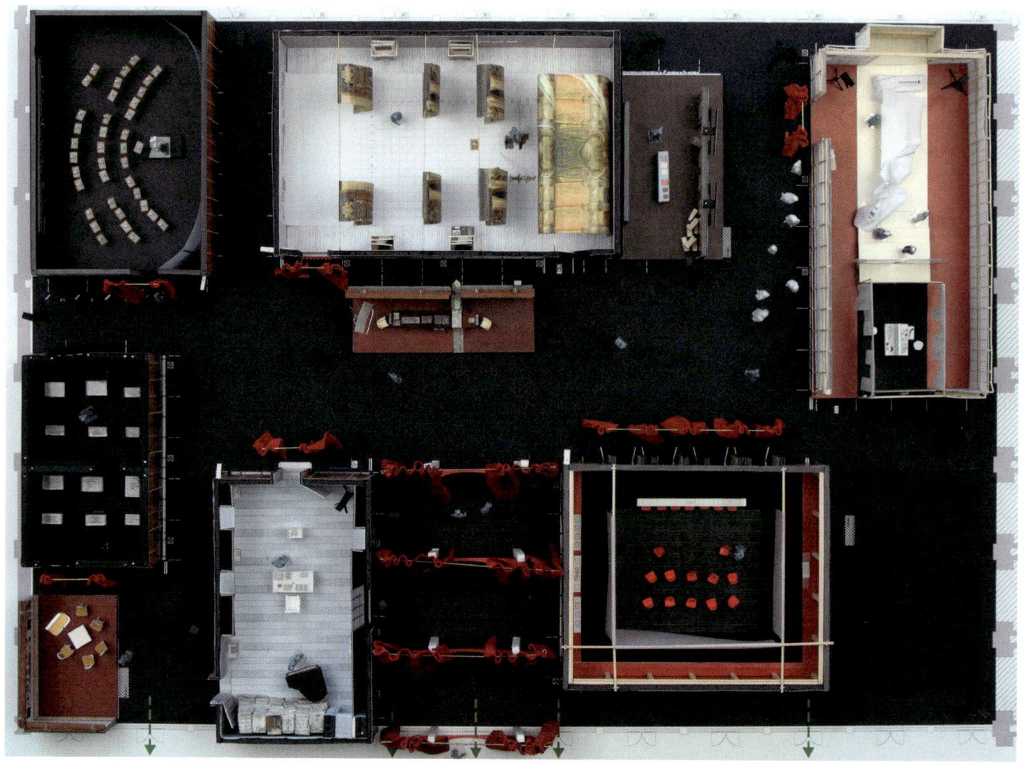

"That's Opera"–Model 1:50 shows the entire parcours with thematic stages on the larger exhibition stage, 2008.

various original scores from Donizetti to Luigi Nono—many of these on display for the first time. In the "walk-in orchestra pit," even the uninitiated can understand the performance of different operas from an "interactive score" and can easily follow the cues of the instruments and voices. The goal here is nothing less than to bring the notes on the paper to life and to make a complex score legible. Via the "Scenografia," a room with various stage set designs in mechanical stage boxes, and "Voci e Costumi," the tailor shop with costume designs, the visitors reach the performance ("Rappresentazione"). Probably the biggest challenge was to transform a two-and-a-half-hour opera of "Aida," that is, a performative format, into an approximately 13-minute installation in the exhibition. In preparation, we were allowed to film a performance at the Staatstheater Stuttgart with five cameras backstage and could arrange this material to form a 210-degree spatial projection so that visitors felt as if they could experience the performance from a surprisingly unusual perspective—on stage. In this case, the dramaturgy of experience follows the dramaturgy of staging.[104]

„Partitura" zeigt in respektvoller Stille verschiedene Original-Partituren von Donizetti bis Luigi Nono – viele davon erstmalig ausgestellt. Im „begehbaren Orchestergraben" können selbst Laien die Aufführung verschiedener Opern an einer „interaktiven Partitur" bestens nachvollziehen und die Einsätze der Instrumente und Stimmen mühelos verfolgen. Hier geht es um nichts weniger als darum, Papier zum Klingen zu bringen und eine komplexe Partitur lesbar zu machen. Über die „Scenografia", einen Raum mit verschiedenen Bühnenbildentwürfen in mechanischen Bühnenkästen, und „Voci e Costumi", der Schneiderei mit Kostümentwürfen, gelangen die Besucher zur Aufführung („Rappresentazione"). Die wohl größte Herausforderung lag in der Transformation einer zweieinhalbstündigen „Aida"-Aufführung, also eines performativen Formats, in eine circa 13-minütige Installation in der Ausstellung. Dafür durften wir eine Aufführung am Staatstheater Stuttgart mit fünf Kameras backstage filmen und konnten dieses Material zu einer neuen 210-Grad-Raumprojektion arrangieren, sodass die Besucher sich auf die Bühne gesetzt fühlten und die Aufführung aus überraschend ungewöhnlichen Blickwinkeln „on stage" erleben konnten. Hier folgt die Dramaturgie des Erlebens der Dramaturgie des Inszenierens.[104]

104 See Atelier Brückner 2016, pp. 258–263.

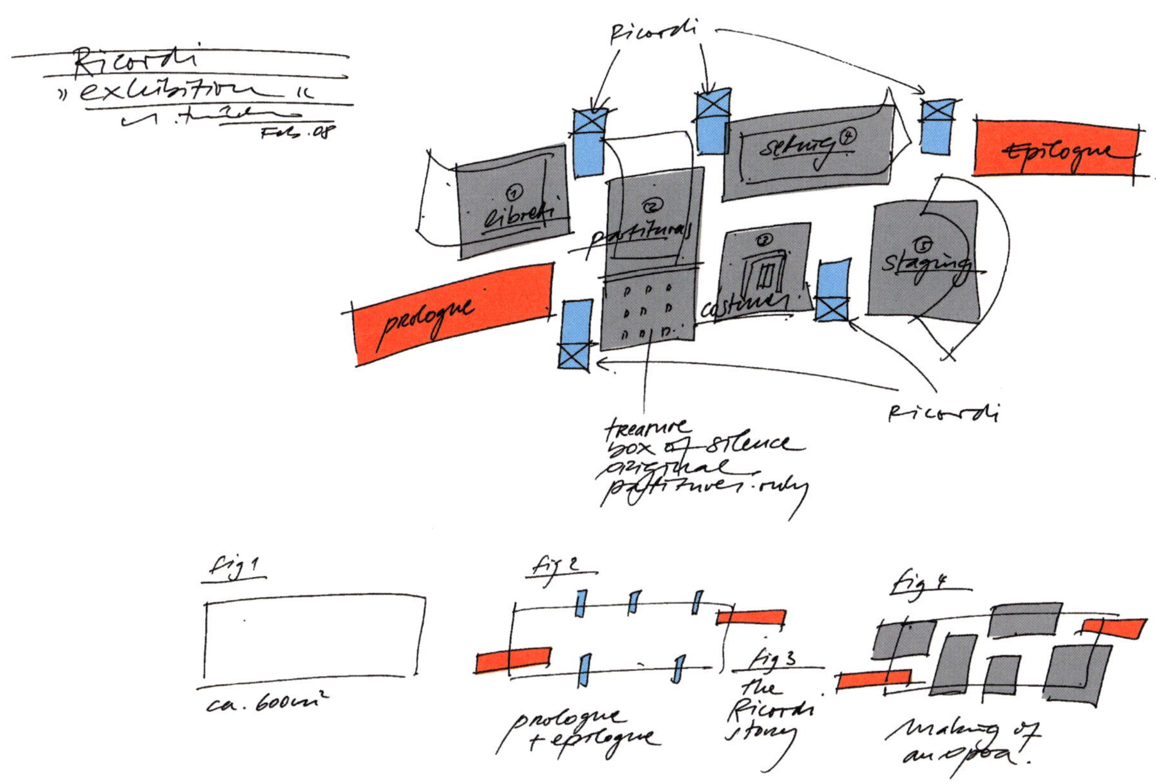

"That's Opera"–"Parcours" with thematic stages (grey) and interludes (red), 2008.

"It is not the virtual in the real but the real in the virtual that interests the addressees. We let them become involved in another, narrative space that attracts their attention and provokes diverse interpretation or associations. Due to the spatial narration, virtual extension of space is perceived as an enlargement of real space. Imagination takes the place of cognition. Scenography combines logic and magic."

Uwe R. Brückner

Scenography is not a static design philosophy, but a dynamic, narrative and, at best, holistic one. Clearly, contemporary scenography is no longer limited to the theatre and exhibition, but has gained influence in architecture and brand presentation and has conquered the public and social space.

Astonishingly, the questions about public or social scenography have remained unchanged over the years, as have the answers, in some places with more or less resounding success. A prime example that every city manager for construction likes to quote again and again, but that they rarely manage to realise in their own town, was actually realised in Copenhagen on Amager Island. The Maritime Youth House built there has created a public landscape with social function on a section of the coastline with contaminated soil (BIG).[105]

One of the most successful internal social scenographies is certainly the High Line in New York City's Meatpacking District.[106] To name but a few of the contributors, Diller, Scofidio + Renfro architects and Piet Oudulf landscape planners collaborated with the local initiative Friends of the High Line not only to rescue the district-shaping, steel fragment of the elevated track but they also cultivated the unique habitat that evolved there and presented it as an urban stage–a public, scene-creating space with social relevance and international reach.

For me, one of the most memorable urban scenographies is the Holocaust Memorial (Memorial to the Murdered Jews of Europe) in Berlin by Peter Eisenman.[107] An admonitory field of columns that demands respect, a sculpture of remembrance which appears to be self-explanatory and yet which loses none of its mysticism when visited–unfenced, freely accessible twenty-four hours a day–what a statement against political despotism, against state violence, for peace, freedom, and also reconciliation! The subterranean museum "Ort der Information" (information room) that follows the structure of the field of columns and the exhibition designed by Dagmar von Wilcken round off the holistic approach of an ingenious scenography, lest we forget.

This suggests that there is not one scenography, but many interpretations of a design approach which reinvents itself again and again and which allows countless new associations–but with the same signature. Good scenography also allows a Shakespeare drama to be translated and received in a different way for the hundredth time.

---

105 Bjarke Ingels Group, "Maritime Youth House" project: www.big.dk/#projects-mar, accessed August 21, 2018.
106 Diller, Scofidio + Renfro Architects, "The High Line" project: www.dsrny.com/project/high-line, accessed August 21, 2018.
107 Eisenman Architects, "Berlin Memorial of the Murdered Jews of Europe" project: www.eisenmanarchitects.com/Berlin-Memorial-the-the-Murdered-Jews-of-Europe-2005, accessed August 21, 2018.

Szenografie ist keine statische, sondern eine dynamische, narrative und im Anspruch holistische Gestaltungsphilosophie. Dass die vom Theater und der Ausstellung entfesselte zeitgemäße Szenografie nicht nur Einfluss auf die Architektur und die Markendarstellung gewonnen, sondern auch den öffentlichen und sozialen Raum erobert hat, ist evident.

Erstaunlicherweise sind die Fragestellungen zu „public“ oder „social scenography“ über die Jahre gleich geblieben, im selben Maße wie die Antworten, an manchen Orten mit mehr oder weniger durchschlagendem Erfolg. Ein Paradebeispiel, das jeder Baubürgermeister gern und häufig zitiert, aber selten in der eigenen Stadt durchsetzen kann, entstand in Kopenhagen auf der Insel Amager, wo mit dem „Maritime Youth House“ eine öffentliche Landschaft mit sozialer Funktion über einem Uferabschnitt mit kontaminierter Erde angelegt wurde (BIG).[105]

Als eine der international erfolgreichsten sozialen Szenografien kann die High Line von New York im Meat Packing District genannt werden.[106] Unter anderen haben dort Diller, Scofidio + Renfro Architekten und Piet Oudulf Landschaftsplaner in Kollaboration mit der lokalen Initiative „Friends of the High Line“ nicht nur das quartierbildende stählerne Fragment der Hochbahn gerettet, sondern das dort entstandene einzigartige Biotop kultiviert und als urbane Bühne inszeniert – ein öffentlicher Szenenraum mit sozialer Relevanz und internationaler Strahlkraft.

Eine der erinnerungswürdigsten urbanen Szenografien ist für mich das Holocaust-Mahnmal (Denkmal für die ermordeten Juden Europas) in Berlin von Peter Eisenman.[107] Ein mahnendes, Respekt forderndes Stelenfeld, eine Erinnerungsskulptur, die selbsterklärend scheint und bei ihrer Begehung mystisch bleibt – zaunlos, 24 Stunden frei begehbar – was für ein Statement gegen politische Willkür, gegen staatliche Gewalt, für Frieden, Freiheit und auch Versöhnung! Das in der Struktur des Stelenfelds konsistent und unterirdisch angelegte Museum „Ort der Information“ mit der von Dagmar von Wilcken gestalteten Ausstellung vervollständigt den holistischen Ansatz einer genialen Szenografie, die gegen das Vergessen gerichtet ist.

Es gibt demnach nicht die eine Szenografie, sondern viele Interpretationen einer Gestaltungshaltung, die sich immer wieder neu formiert und immer neue Assoziationen zulässt – bei gleichbleibender Handschrift. Gute Szenografie ermöglicht auch einem Shakespeare-Drama, zum hunderttausendsten Mal anders übersetzt und rezipiert zu werden.

Good scenography opens up new perspectives to interpret things and content from an unusual perspective–this “change of perspective” taps both new analytical as well as creative potential.[108] It allows journeys to inaccessible places, opens windows on hidden, maybe complex worlds. The staging of these worlds allows easier or more attractive access to complicated content or stories.

↗ p. 136

↗ p. 168

Its protagonist, the scenographer, is an author designer. He is able to employ various design disciplines at the same time and to stage content, object, space, and recipients using a suspenseful dramaturgy. The scenographer sees himself as the design lawyer for his own concepts and for those of his client.

Our interpretation of contemporary scenography aims neither to reinvent the wheel nor to repeat common patterns. It is more about finding a unique scenographic interpretation of content, information, and message in the space and with the space as design medium–in the virtual but above all in the physical space. It is about generating authentic experiences which address visitors as equals, which demand a lot of them but without overloading, which give them the possibility to participate or even give them a role, thus demanding their physical presence. It is about creating positive involvement in the recipients, that conveys that they are addressed and it concerns them.

Scenography is not a fad, not a “flash in the pan” with limited shelf life as Martin Roth postulated a few years after the Expo Hanover 2000. On the contrary, scenography is the contemporary answer to the changed reception behaviour of today’s generation and a future generation. In fact, its success story has only just begun …

108 See Uwe R. Brückner and Linda Greci, eds., EMEE Toolkit 4: Synaesthetic Translation of Perspectives. Scenography: A Sketchbook (Vienna, 2016), esp. pp. 17–31.

Gute Szenografie ermöglicht neue Sichtweisen, Dinge und Inhalte aus einer ungewöhnlichen Perspektive zu interpretieren – dieser „Change of Perspective" erschließt sowohl neue analytische als auch kreative Potenziale.[108] Sie ermöglicht Reisen zu unerreichbaren Orten, öffnet Fenster zu verborgenen, vielleicht komplexen Welten. Die Inszenierung dieser Welten ermöglicht einen leichteren oder attraktiveren Zugang zu komplizierten Inhalten oder Geschichten.

Ihr Protagonist, der Szenograf, ist ein Autorengestalter. Er ist in der Lage, verschiedene Gestaltungsdisziplinen simultan einzusetzen und Inhalt, Objekt, Raum und Rezipienten mittels einer spannungsreichen Dramaturgie in Szene zu setzen. Der Szenograf versteht sich als gestalterischer Anwalt seiner eigenen Konzepte oder der seiner Auftraggeber.

In unserer Interpretation kontemporärer Szenografie geht es weder darum, das Rad neu zu erfinden, noch, gewohnte Muster zu wiederholen. Es geht vielmehr um eine maßgeschneiderte szenografische Interpretation von Inhalten, Informationen und Botschaften im Raum, in den Raum und mit dem Raum als Gestaltungsmedium – im virtuellen, aber vor allem im physischen Raum.
Es geht darum, authentische Erlebnisse zu generieren, die den Besucher auf Augenhöhe ansprechen, die ihn fordern, aber nicht überfrachten, die ihm die Möglichkeit der Partizipation geben oder ihm gar eine Rolle zuschreiben und somit seine physische Präsenz einfordern. Es geht darum, eine positive Betroffenheit beim Rezipienten hervorzurufen, die ihm vermittelt, dass er gemeint ist, dass es ihn etwas angeht.

Szenografie ist keine Modeerscheinung, kein „Strohfeuer" mit limitierter Halbwertszeit, wie Martin Roth ein paar Jahre nach der Expo Hannover 2000 konstatierte. Im Gegenteil, die Szenografie ist die zeitgemäße Antwort auf das veränderte Rezeptionsverhalten der heute lebenden und einer zukünftigen Generation. Sie hat ihren Siegeszug erst begonnen ...

SMAC–STATE MUSEUM OF ARCHAEOLOGY CHEMNITZ

Permanent Exhibition, 3,600 sqm, Chemnitz, Germany, 2014

Where customers once bought suits, shoes, and dresses, visitors today find out how people in the area that now makes up the federal state of Saxony gradually transformed it into a cultural landscape. The former department store Schocken, which was designed in the 1920s by Erich Mendelsohn and has now been converted into a museum, presents 300,000 years of human history using the impressive collection of Saxon state archaeology. More than 5,200 excavated finds are on display.

The visitor journey starts in the foyer with two large staged settings: the 18-metre-tall stratigraphic diorama that accompanies the ascent to the three upper exhibition levels, and the time-dynamic model of Saxony. This spectacular interactive model connects the floors vertically and establishes a visual context to the respective topics of the three levels. On its journey, it passes through the millennia like in a time-lapse film.

The exhibition shows the development of Saxony from the Palaeolithic through to the nineteenth century. The journey of the visitor takes him through space and time. The floor graphics and showcases express the transformation: amorphous lines change into right-angled grids, thus visualising the growing structuring and urbanisation offered by progress and science. Panoramas that give the narrative space its character change from a natural landscape on the first floor via a settlement landscape on the second floor to a cultural landscape on the third floor. Here, the panorama consists of 40 metres of showcases with around 1,000 objects from the past 900 years.

Wo Kunden einst Anzüge, Schuhe und Kleider kauften, erfahren Besucher heute, wie Menschen auf dem Gebiet des Bundeslandes Sachsen die Natur- allmählich in eine Kulturlandschaft verwandelten. Das ehemalige Kaufhaus Schocken, das in den 1920er-Jahren von Erich Mendelsohn geplant und nun zum Museum konvertiert wurde, stellt 300.000 Jahre Menschheitsgeschichte anhand der beeindruckenden Sammlung der sächsischen Landesarchäologie vor. Über 5.200 Ausgrabungsfunde sind zu sehen.

Der Parcours wird im Foyer mit zwei großen Inszenierungen eröffnet: dem stratigrafischen, 18 Meter hohen Diorama, das den Aufgang zu den drei Ausstellungsebenen begleitet, und dem zeitdynamischen kinetischen Sachsenmodell. Dieses spektakuläre interaktiv-mediale Modell verbindet die Etagen vertikal und steht im visuellen Kontext zu den Themen der Ebenen. Auf seiner Fahrt durchläuft es die Jahrtausende wie im Zeitraffer.

Die Ausstellung zeigt die Entwicklung Sachsens von der Altsteinzeit bis ins 19. Jahrhundert. Der Weg der Besucher gestaltet sich als Gang durch Raum und Zeit. Die Bodengrafik und die Vitrinen drücken den Wandel aus: Amorphe Linien wandeln sich zum rechtwinkligen Raster und versinnbildlichen damit die wachsende Strukturierung und Urbanisierung durch Fortschritt und Wissenschaft. Raumbildprägende Panoramen ändern sich von einer Naturlandschaft im ersten über die Siedlungslandschaft im zweiten bis hin zur Kulturlandschaft im dritten Obergeschoss. Dort besteht das Panorama aus einer 40 Meter langen Vitrinenwand mit rund 1.000 Objekten aus den vergangenen 900 Jahren.

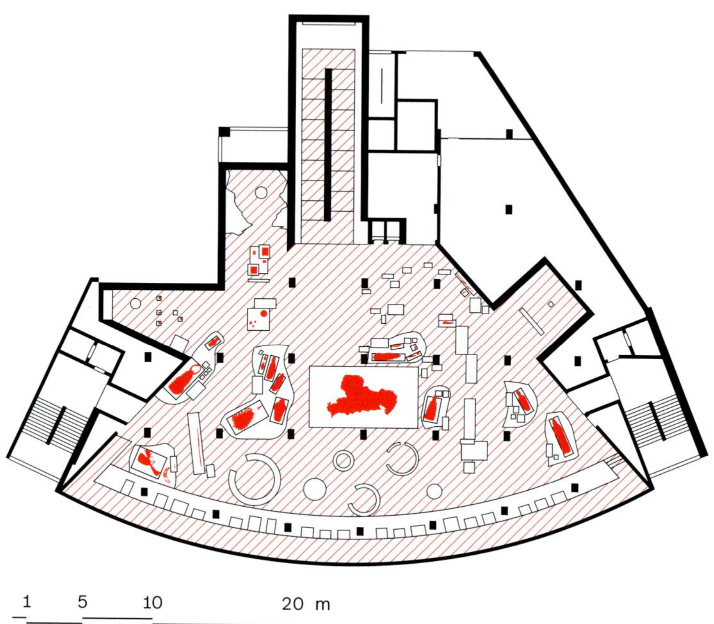

01 Floor plan–first floor.
02 Time-dynamic model of Saxony–moving up and down the three exhibition floors while objects and patterns are projected synchronously on the translucent silhouette representing the content shown in the exhibition.

03 Ramp-like stairs connect the exhibition floors accompanied by the "Stratigraphic Diorama"–an archaeological profile-cut representing the 300,000 years of human existence in Saxony.

Behind the panorama walls are three further exhibitions in the bay window area, which is suffused with light. These are dedicated to the architect Erich Mendelsohn, the department store tycoon Salman Schocken, and the once prospering Schocken department store group.

The panorama wall is an important conceptual device used to seperate the floors into two exhibition areas: archaeological content on the one side and building history on the other. Thus it maintains the glowing appearance of the facade windows, as they historically looked.

Hinter den Panoramawänden liegen drei weitere Ausstellungen im lichtdurchfluteten Erkerbereich. Sie sind dem Architekten Erich Mendelsohn, dem Kaufhausmagnaten Salman Schocken sowie dem blühenden Schocken-Warenhauskonzern gewidmet.

Mit dem konzeptionellen Kunstgriff der vielschichtig bespielten Panoramawand gelingt es, die Außenansicht der Architektur in historischer Anmutung zu rekonstruieren, die Geschichte des Hauses sowie seiner Protagonisten zu erzählen und im Inneren die Ausstellung zur Archäologie Sachsens autark zu inszenieren.

04 First-floor exhibition (300,000–7,000 BC)–hand axes and spears in front of an ice age panorama.

05 Authentic reconstruction of the historic facade of the department store building by Erich Meldelsohn, 2014.

06 The "Mendelsohn Schocken Gallery," featuring the history of both Erich Mendelsohn's influential architecture and Salman Schocken's department store concept.

07 The panoramic "Object Wall," a 40×3-metre showcase displaying more than 1,000 objects covering 900 years of everyday archaeology. Most of them are explorable in detail with a digital interface.

SHANGHAI AUTO MUSEUM – COLLECTION PAVILION

Permanent Exhibition, 2,300 sqm, Shanghai, China, 2014

The Collection Pavilion on the first floor of the Shanghai Auto Museum stages the milestones of the evolution of the automobile and supplements the permanent exhibition on the history of mobility that ATELIER BRÜCKNER had designed on the ground floor of the museum. Down below, there is an urban scene with roads and squares; up above is the exclusive parking level where the visitor saunters between "parked" cars.

The idea of the "Collection" is the guiding principle of the exhibition. Visitors first encounter it in the prologue with a collection of model cars. In the main room, the theme is reflected in the way the exhibits are arranged. The passion for collecting is tangible here.

The vintage cars from the years 1900 to 1975, including a Ford Mustang, a Porsche 356 C, and even a BMW Isetta 300, are chronologically ordered in six development lines on a row of flat, white plinths: from the "Age of Acceleration," which shows the beginnings of mobility, through to "Chinese Mobility," which presents the first Shanghai Sedan produced in China from 1970. The "Dream Machines"–cars which at any time were considered to be unaffordable–are given star treatment. Shiny aluminium plinths and light ceilings underline their prestige; interactive screens provide technical details. Like "Happy Family" cards, the data sheets can be compared with other vehicles.

The exhibition lets visitors dip into various eras and conveys the unbroken fascination that historical vehicles inspire to this day.

Der Collection Pavilion im ersten Obergeschoss des Shanghai Auto Museum setzt Meilensteine der Automobilentwicklung in Szene und ergänzt die Dauerausstellung zur Geschichte der Mobilität, die im Erdgeschoss des Museums gestaltet wurde: unten das Raumbild der urbanen Stadt mit Straßenzügen und Platzsituationen, oben das des exklusiven Parkdecks, auf dem Besucher zwischen „parkenden" Autos wandeln.

Die Idee der „Collection" ist das Leitmotiv der Ausstellung. Sie begegnet Besuchern bereits im Prolog mit einer Modellautosammlung und spiegelt sich in der Exponatanordnung im Hauptraum. Hier wird Sammelleidenschaft greifbar.

Die Oldtimer aus den Jahren 1900 bis 1975, unter anderen ein Ford Mustang, Porsche 356 C oder auch eine BMW Isetta 300, sind chronologisch in sechs Entwicklungslinien auf weiß akzentuierten, flachen Sockeln aufgereiht: von „Age of Acceleration", welches die Anfänge der Mobilität zeigt, bis hin zu „Chinese Mobility", das den ersten in China produzierten Shanghai Sedan von 1970 präsentiert.

Die „Dream Machines" – Traumautos, die zu jeder Zeit als unerschwinglich galten – erhalten einen Starauftritt. Glänzende Aluminiumpodeste und Lichtdecken heben sie als Hauptdarsteller hervor; interaktive Screens geben Auskunft zu den technischen Details. In Quartett-Karten-Manier können sie mit jenen anderer Fahrzeuge verglichen werden.

Die Ausstellung lässt die Besucher in verschiedene Epochen eintauchen und vermittelt die anhaltende Faszination, die mit historischen Automobilen verbunden ist.

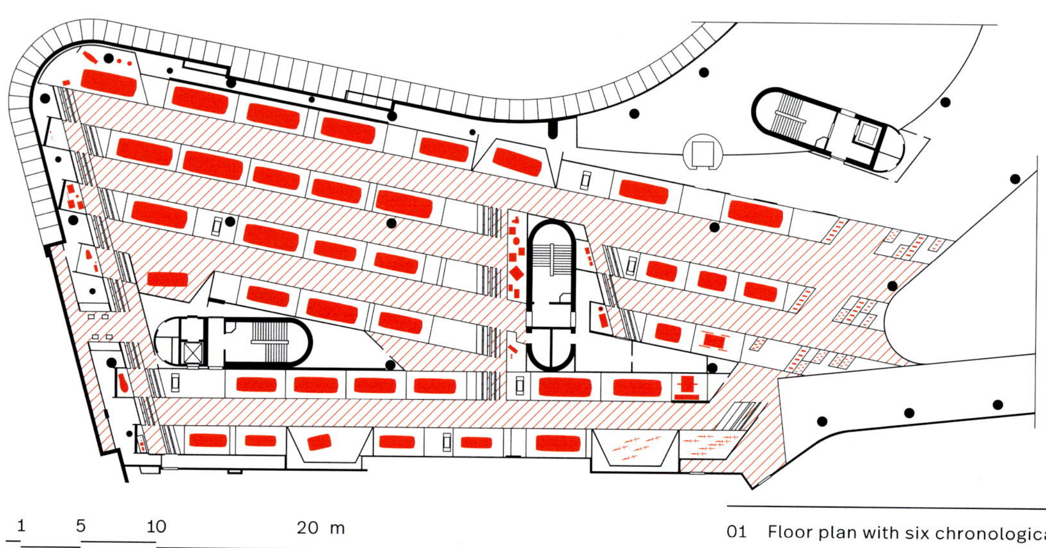

01 Floor plan with six chronological lanes.

02 The setting follows six chronological lines of vintage cars on abstract street lanes featuring a number of "Dream Machines"–cars of desires.

03 Historical objects act as contemporary backdrops to contextualize the past decades of car culture.

04 Film footage backdrops illustrate the rank of the cars in society.

SWISS CHOCOLATE ADVENTURE

Permanent Exhibition, 700 sqm, Lucerne, Switzerland, 2014

The Swiss Chocolate Adventure is the product of a partnership between the Lindt Chocolate Competence Foundation and the Swiss Museum of Transport. Both institutions represent typical Swiss values like tradition, pioneering spirit, and innovative drive and as such contribute to the strengthening of Switzerland as a brand. The exhibition connects a typical Swiss premium product–chocolate–with the subject of transport.

A themed journey whisks visitors into the world of famous Swiss chocolate and big-name chocolate-makers. The journey begins in the lift housed in a mobile freight container. A visual staging with panorama pictures is suggestive of a voyage on a freight ship over the seas from Hamburg to West Africa, where cocoa beans come from.

Having arrived at the exhibition level, travellers are transported in people movers–induction-controlled coffee beans–through a darkened room in which four protagonists speak about their work: the cocoa Administrator from Ghana, the buyer from Switzerland, the maître chocolatier, and the confiseur. Large-scale projections show the various stages involved in chocolate production.

Das Swiss Chocolate Adventure ist das Ergebnis einer Partnerschaft zwischen der Lindt Chocolate Competence Foundation und dem Verkehrshaus der Schweiz. Beide Institutionen vertreten typische Swissness-Werte wie Tradition, Pionier- und Innovationsgeist und tragen damit zur Stärkung der Marke Schweiz bei. So verknüpft die Ausstellung ein typisch schweizerisches Qualitätsprodukt - Schokolade - mit dem Thema Transport.

Eine Erlebnisreise entführt die Besucher in die Welt der berühmten Schweizer Schokolade und der großen Chocolatiers. Sie beginnt in einem mobilen Frachtcontainer, der als Aufzug fungiert. Dabei suggeriert eine visuelle Inszenierung mit Panoramabildern die Überfahrt auf einem Frachtschiff von Hamburg nach Westafrika, dem Anbaugebiet der Kakaobohnen.

Auf der Ausstellungsebene angekommen, bewegen sich die Reisenden in sogenannten People Movern - induktionsgesteuerten Kaffeebohnen - durch einen dunklen Raum, in dem vier Protagonisten von ihrer Arbeit erzählen: der Kakaoverwalter aus Ghana, der Einkäufer aus der Schweiz, die Schokoladenmeisterin und der Confiseur. Die Besucher erleben dabei in Großprojektionen die verschiedenen Produktionsschritte der Schokoladenherstellung.

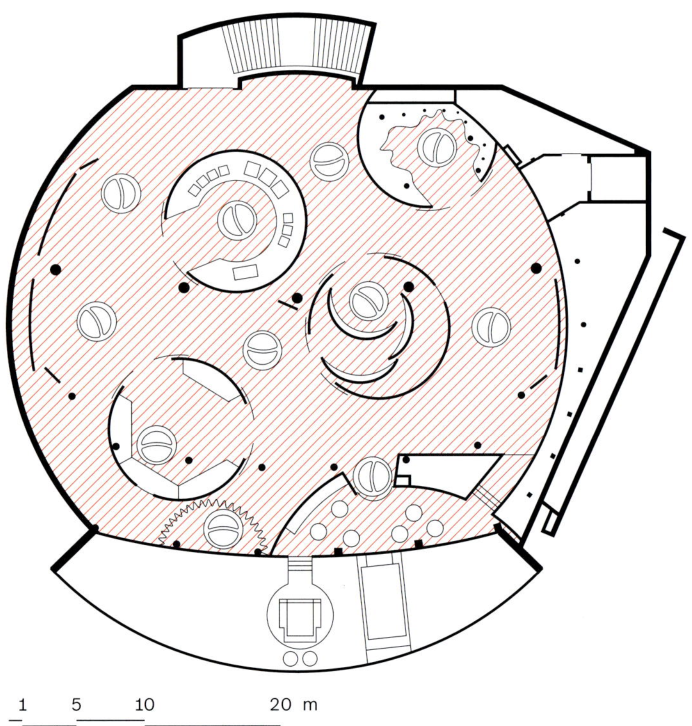

01 Floor plan with people movers and cylindric “Thematic Theatres.”
02 The “Praline-Theatre”–visitors are travelling in a self-driving “coffee bean” people mover.

03 The "Confiseur" introduces visitors to chocolate making and the art of creating pralines.

An immersive experience of a special kind is offered by four themed cylindrical islands whose rotating backdrops encircle the people movers to form panoramas as they enter: in the tropical rain forest the traveller finds out how cocoa beans are grown and harvested; in the Swissness diorama they learn which ingredients Swiss agriculture–milk and sugar–contribute to the chocolate; and in the world of the chocolate pioneers they encounter François-Louis Cailler, Philippe Suchard, and Daniel Peter, as well as Rodolphe Lindt and Rudolf Sprüngli. The destination of the journey is an oversized, drive-in chocolate box in which chocolates can be tasted.

The scenographically staged intermezzo of the journey is another special experience. In a joint choreography, the people movers glide together through the exhibition. Huge projections and sounds transport the travellers into a flowing chocolate world in which they have the opportunity to feel what it is like to be part of the cocoa paste in a chocolate drum.

They return in the mobile freight container, this time with projections showing how pralines are exported around the world.

Ein immersives Erlebnis besonderer Art bieten vier zylindrische Themeninseln in Form befahrbarer Bühnen, deren rotierende Kulissen die People Mover umschließen und sich zu Panoramen fügen: Im tropischen Regenwald erfahren die Reisenden, wie Kakaobohnen angebaut und geerntet werden, im Swissness-Diorama, welche Zutaten – Milch und Zucker – die schweizerische Landwirtschaft zur Schokolade liefert, und in der Welt der Schokoladenpioniere begegnen sie den Wegbereitern François-Louis Cailler, Philippe Suchard, Daniel Peter sowie Rudolphe Lindt und Rudolf Sprüngli. Ziel der Reise ist eine befahrbare, überdimensionale Pralinenschachtel, in der die Schokolade verkostet werden kann.

Ein besonderes Erlebnis ist zudem das szenografisch inszenierte Intermezzo der Reise. Dann gleiten alle People Mover in einer gemeinsamen Choreografie durch die Ausstellung. Raumgreifende Projektionen und Klänge entführen in eine fließende Schokoladenwelt, in der sich die Reisenden als Teil der Kakaomasse in einer Schokowalze fühlen dürfen.

Zurück geht es wieder im mobilen Frachtcontainer, der nun den Export der Pralinen in alle Welt zeigt.

04 The "Swissness Theatre" offers dynamic backdrops in motion collaging the typical charming Swiss clichés, including chocolate production.

05 "The Prologue" starts in a shipping container travelling to where the cacao beans were farmed.

06 Travel to "The Jungle Farm Theatre," where the cacao plants were cultivated.

ENERGETICON

Permanent Exhibition, 3,000 sqm, Alsdorf, Germany, 2014

Experiencing energy, understanding energy: on the grounds of "Anna," a former colliery and authentic mining site, the Energeticon is dedicated to fossil fuels and renewable sources of energy. The visitor route is guided by the idea "From the Sun to the Sun" and passes through three former mine buildings –forge, pithead, and coop–as well as two underground routes and the generously dimensioned outdoor area.

A huge, artistic sun installation forms the emotional prelude that identifies the sun as the source of all energy. This is the start and finish of the tour that expresses the power of the sun and carries with it the core message.

There follow two exhibition areas: "Energy of the Past" and "Energy of the Future," which differ both in terms of their spatial narrative and their didactic approach. First, the themes of the "Energy of the Past" are presented, subtly incorporated into the historical substance of the building: a staged lift uses sounds, media projections, and jolts and judders to simulate the journey down to the pit face. The atmosphere and working conditions of the arduous work belowground are experienced in films and audio recordings, incorporated in the underground parts of the routing. Reconstructed living rooms and expressive portrait photos offer visitors additional intuitive access to the miners. A highlight of the visitor's journey is the authentic changing room, referred to by the miners as the coop. Some 700 metal baskets hanging from the ceiling give a good idea of the size and importance of the former coal mine.

The themes of the renewable energy age are presented against the contrasting backdrop of the historical architecture. The look into the future is underlined by the use of expressive design elements. The interactive installations can be perceived as deliberate interventions, set apart from the historical rooms by use of colour. For example, on the upper level of the coop, an impressive, space-shaping sculpture conveys alternative possibilities of energy supply. Renewable energies are experienced in hands-on exhibits and media installations as a real alternative to fossil fuels.

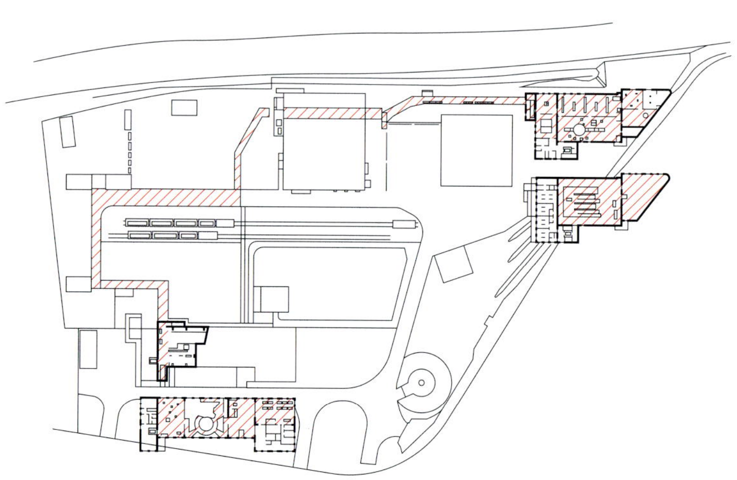

Energie erleben, Energie verstehen: Auf dem ehemaligen Zechengelände „Anna", einem authentischen Ort des Bergbaus, widmet sich das Energeticon den fossilen und den erneuerbaren Energieträgern. Der Parcours steht unter dem Leitgedanken „Von der Sonne zur Sonne" und führt durch drei ehemalige Zechengebäude - Schmiede, Fördermaschinenhaus und Kaue - sowie durch zwei Untertagestrecken und über ein großzügiges Außengelände.

Den emotionalen Auftakt bildet eine raumgreifende künstlerische Sonneninstallation, welche die Sonne als Quelle aller Energie ins Bewusstsein rückt. Hier ist der Start- und Zielpunkt des Rundgangs, der die Kraft der Sonne zum Ausdruck bringt und die Kernbotschaft in sich trägt.

Die daran anschließenden Ausstellungsbereiche „Energievergangenheit" und „Energiezukunft" unterscheiden sich hinsichtlich ihrer räumlichen und didaktischen Aufbereitung. Zunächst werden die Themen der „Energievergangenheit" vorgestellt, die sich subtil in den historischen Baubestand einfügen: Ein inszenierter Aufzug vermittelt über Geräusche, mediale Bespielung und Erschütterungen die Einfahrt in den Schacht. Atmosphäre und Arbeitsbedingungen der mühsamen Arbeit unter Tage werden über filmische Projektionen und Audiobeiträge, eingebunden in die Untertagestrecken, erlebbar. Rekonstruierte Wohnräume und ausdrucksstarke Porträtbilder bieten den Besuchern zusätzlich einen intuitiven Zugang zu den Bergmännern. Ein Höhepunkt des Rundgangs ist der authentisch belassene Umkleideraum, die sogenannte Schwarzkaue. Rund 700 Metallkörbe hängen hier unter der Decke und geben einen Eindruck von der Größe und Bedeutung des ehemaligen Bergwerks.

Kontrastierend zur historischen Architektur präsentieren sich die Themen des regenerativen Zeitalters. Der Blick in die Zukunft wird mittels ausdrucksstarker Gestaltungselemente unterstrichen. Die interaktiven Installationen sind als bewusst eingestellte Interventionen wahrnehmbar, die sich von den historischen Räumen farblich abheben. So vermittelt beispielsweise eine eindrucksvolle, raumprägende Skulptur im Obergeschoss der Kaue alternative Möglichkeiten der Energieversorgung. Erneuerbare Energien werden mittels Hands-on-Exponaten und Medieninstallationen als Alternative zu fossilen Energieträgern erlebbar.

5 25 50 100 m

01 Floor plan.
02 "From the Sun to the Sun"–where it all began and ends, both the source of all energy and the visitors' tour.

03 The upper level of the coop hosts various interactive stations which allow visitors to explore the possibilities of future energy sources.

The exhibition concept uses strong visual and diversely interactive formats in order to allow all different groups of visitors to experience this complex topic in a highly accessible way. Like a new layer of time, the themes of the "Energy of the Future" are superimposed on the historical location, giving it a new alignment and significance, a clear manifestation of the transition from fossil fuels to sustainable energy sources.

Das Ausstellungskonzept setzt auf starke visuelle und vielfältig interaktive Formate, um das komplexe Thema für unterschiedliche Besuchergruppen auf niederschwellige Weise erfahrbar zu machen. Wie eine neue Zeitschicht überlagern die Themen der Energiezukunft den historischen Schauplatz und geben ihm eine neue Ausrichtung und Bedeutung. Der Übergang von der Nutzung fossiler Energieträger zu einer nachhaltigen Energienutzung wird deutlich.

04 The black coop is left as an authentic space as it was during the operation of the coal mine. Stories of the former miners are made accessible with audioplays.

05 Tunnels with coal mining machinery featuring film footage of workers.

06 The photo gallery in the former coop. Motion detector-equipped light boxes show pictures featuring miners at work.

07 The authentic white coop hosts various interactive stations which allow visitors to explore the fundamentals of energy. The flight cycle provides the feeling of harnessing energy.

08 Game of energy density.

09 Hands on interactive table.

DIALOGUE WITH TIME

Touring Exhibition, 570 sqm, Frankfurt/Main, Germany, 2014.

How do I want to live when I am old? What challenges and what opportunities does ageing offer? These are questions which visitors to the exhibition "Dialogue with Time" can explore in an unusual way: in conversation with senior guides. They are ambassadors of this interactive exhibition format and convey a uniquely personal, authentic approach to being and getting old. Themed rooms in intensive colours (cyan, magenta, and yellow) structure the display and require openness. A dialogue between the generations emerges.

To kick things off, a video installation transforms the face of a young child successively into that of an old woman. In the "Blue Salon," visitors then playfully enter into a discussion with the guides. With a series of questions, the latter encourages self-reflection. The yellow area is all about mental and physical illness. At interactive stations, visitors can find out what it is like to unlock a front door with shaking hands or to climb stairs with heavy legs. Finally, the visitors themselves are placed in retirement and find out what older people experience when they reach this turning point and no longer play a full role in life. Finally, the magenta area shows old age through rose-coloured glasses. At five stations, this last section is devoted to the positive sides and potential that are associated with growing old.

Discussion and relaying of experiences take centre stage in the exhibition. This leads to empathy as old age and ageing is recounted to the visitor by real people.

Wie möchte ich im Alter leben? Welche Herausforderungen und auch welche Chancen bringt das Älterwerden mit sich? Diesen Fragen können Besucher der Ausstellung „Dialog mit der Zeit" auf ungewöhnliche Weise nachgehen: im Gespräch mit Senior Guides. Sie sind die Botschafter dieses interaktiven Ausstellungsformats, begleiten die Besucher durch die Ausstellung und vermitteln einen sehr persönlichen, authentischen Zugang zum Altsein und Altwerden. Expressiv farbig (Cyan, Magenta, Gelb) gestaltete Themenräume strukturieren die Schau und fördern Aufgeschlossenheit. Ein Dialog zwischen den Generationen entsteht.

Als Auftakt verwandelt eine Videoinstallation das Gesicht eines Kleinkinds sukzessive in das einer Greisin. Im blauen Bereich kommen die Besucher dann mit den Guides spielerisch ins Gespräch. Mit kleinen Fragerunden regen jene zur Selbstreflexion an. Im gelben Bereich geht es um psychische und physische Erkrankungen. An interaktiven Stationen können Besucher nachvollziehen, wie es ist, mit zitternder Hand eine Haustür aufzuschließen oder mit schweren Beinen eine Treppe hochzusteigen. Schließlich werden die Besucher selbst in den Ruhestand versetzt und erleben die Zäsur, die ältere Menschen empfinden, wenn sie nicht mehr gleichwertig am Leben teilhaben können. Der magentafarbene Bereich zeigt zuletzt den rosaroten Blick auf das Alter. Er widmet sich in fünf Stationen den positiven Seiten und Potenzialen, die mit dem Altern verbunden sind.

Die Ausstellung stellt nicht Exponate, sondern das Gespräch und das eigene Erleben ins Zentrum der Vermittlung. Über Interaktion entsteht Empathie – ein persönlicher, erlebnis- und erfahrungsorientierter Zugang zum Alter(n).

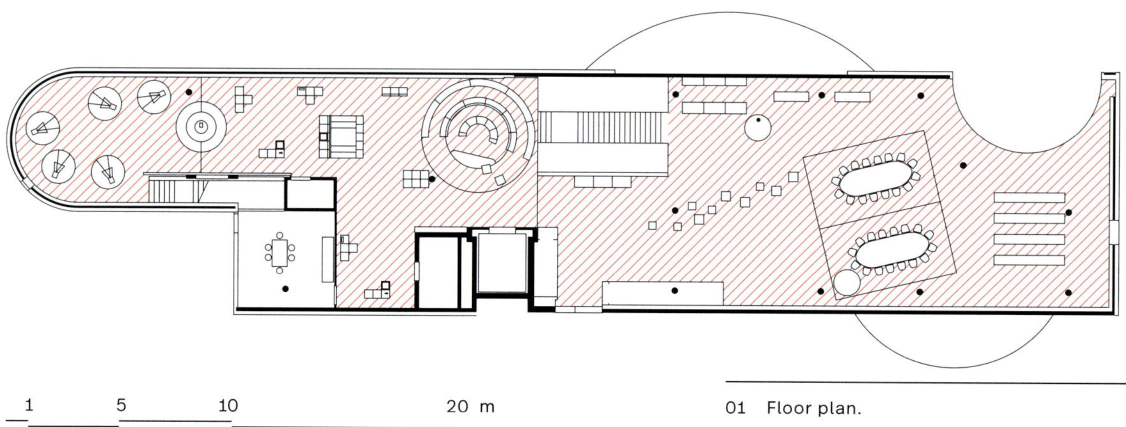

01 Floor plan.

02 Hourglasses, a metaphor for the passing of time, feature questions related to ageing. The colour coding indicates the thematic areas of the exhibtion.

03 Blue Salon–senior guides give visitors an authentic introduction to what ageing means. They involve them in discussion to challenge prejudices concerning the daily lives of the elderly.

04 Yellow Salon–first-hand experience of the physical challenges resulting from ageing. A wrist device worn by the visitor simulates tremors, and weighted stockings simulate heavy sensations while climbing stairs.

GERMAN HAT MUSEUM

Permanent Exhibition, 1,000 sqm, Lindenberg, Germany, 2014

Until into the 1970s, Lindenberg was one of the most important hat centres in Germany–known as far afield as the USA, not least due to the international export success: the matelot. The museum in the former Ottmar Reich hat factory enables visitors to experience the tradition of the place in a new way.

On the first exhibition level numerous exhibits, including unique hat models, tools, machines, and certificates, tell the story of 300 years of hat fashion and fabrication in Lindenberg. The focus of the stories is on the people who, in the early twentieth century, turned the small town in the Allgäu region into the petit Paris of hat fashion–hard-working home workers, feisty hat dealers, and powerful factory owners. At themed islands arranged prominently around a centrally positioned factory shelf, they all have their say. Numerous tools and artefacts from the production process are arranged on the shelf that is designed as a glazed walk-in cube and which conveys the technical steps involved in hat production. As soon as the panes of the cabinet change from transparent to translucent, thus offering a floor-to-ceiling projection surface for historical film material, the visitor is immersed in the working atmosphere of the former hat factory.

On the second exhibition level, which shows the cultural history of the hat, an impressive hat tornado acts as a counterpart to the factory shelf on the first level. The hats appear to be whirling upwards as if they were flying out of the production area. They arrive in their era and add dynamic movement to the surrounding space. The exhibits are contextualised by large-scale photographs that shape the narrative space and supplement the themed stagings in the surrounding showcases around the room.

Bis in die 1970er-Jahre war Lindenberg eines der wichtigsten Hutzentren Deutschlands – bekannt bis in die USA, nicht zuletzt aufgrund seines internationalen Exportschlagers, dem Matelot. Das Museum in der ehemaligen Hutfabrik Ottmar Reich macht die Tradition des Orts erneut erfahrbar.

Zahlreiche Exponate, darunter einzigartige Hutmodelle, Werkzeuge, Maschinen und Urkunden erzählen auf der ersten Ausstellungsebene von drei Jahrhunderten Hutmode und -fabrikation in Lindenberg. Im Fokus der Geschichten stehen Menschen, die Anfang des 20. Jahrhunderts aus der kleinen Stadt im Allgäu das „Klein-Paris" der Hutmode machten: tüchtige Heimarbeiterinnen, couragierte Huthändler und mächtige Fabrikanten. Sie kommen an den Themeninseln prominent zu Wort, die rund um ein zentral positioniertes Fabrikationsregal angeordnet sind. Es ist bestückt mit zahlreichen Werkzeugen und Artefakten aus dem Produktionsprozess und als gläserner, begehbarer Kubus gestaltet, der die technischen Abläufe der Hutherstellung vermittelt. Der Besucher taucht in die Arbeitsatmosphäre der ehemaligen Hutfabriken ein, sobald sich die Vitrinenscheiben von transparent zu transluzent wandeln und damit eine raumhohe Projektionsfläche für historisches Filmmaterial bieten.

Pendant zum Fabrikationsregal ist auf der zweiten Ausstellungsebene, die der Kulturgeschichte des Huts gewidmet ist, ein eindrucksvoller „Hut-Tornado". Gleichsam aus der Produktion heraus scheinen die Hüte nach oben zu wirbeln. Sie kommen in ihrer jeweiligen Epoche an und dynamisieren den umgebenden Raum. Kontextualisiert werden die Exponate durch großformatige Fotografien, die das Raumbild prägen und thematische Inszenierungen in den umgebenden Raumvitrinen ergänzen.

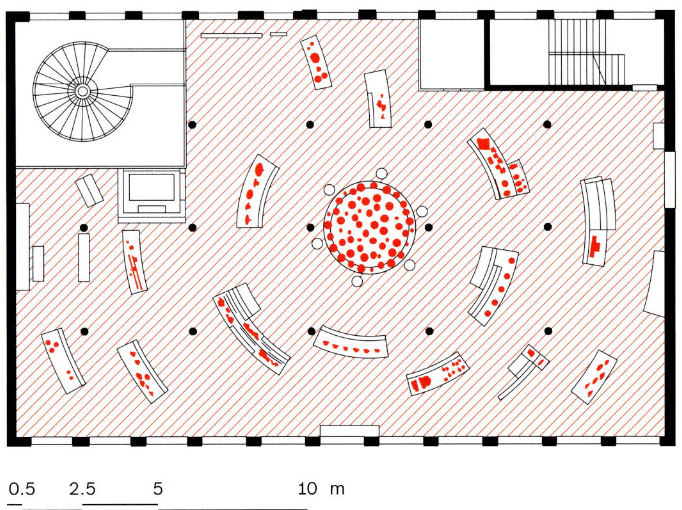

01 Floor plan–second exhibition level.
02 As an iconic installation, the "hat tornado" works like a symbol for the worldwide trading success of straw hats made in Lindenberg. In the circular periphery the historical context is conveyed by photographs which show how obligatory it was to wear hats until the late 1960s.

03 The thematically organised and impressive collection of hat fashion is arranged logically behind the Tornado scenery.

The hat museum allows visitors to immerse themselves in an authentic location in the craft of making hats and in 300 years of hat fashion. The hat tornado as an artistic installation stands for the movement and momentum that headgear–until this day–can trigger.

Numerous hands-on stations make the process of manufacturing a hat easy to understand–from straw to the finished pork pie hat, as the matelot was also jokingly called due to its shape. Join in and try it out: The museum conveys the regional and supraregional history of the hat.

Das Hutmuseum lässt Besucher an einem authentischen Ort in das Handwerk der Hutmacher und in 300 Jahre Hutmode eintauchen. Der „Hut-Tornado“ als künstlerische Installation steht für die Bewegung und Dynamik, die Kopfbedeckungen – letztlich bis heute – auslösen können.

Zahlreiche Mitmachstationen machen den Prozess der Hutherstellung nachvollziehbar – vom Strohhalm bis zur fertigen „Kreissäge“, wie der Matelot aufgrund seiner Form scherzhaft auch genannt wird. Mitmachen und ausprobieren: Das Museum vermittelt regionale wie überregionale Hutgeschichte.

04 A rectangular cube constructed like an industrial shelf displays tools and machinery for the production of hats. Inside, contemporary film footage shows the production of hats.

05 Immersive panoramic projection inside the cube.

06 Hands on station–tactile samples of the felt hat materials.

MEG—MUSÉE D'ETHNOGRAPHIE DE GENÈVE

Permanent Exhibition, 1,000 sqm, Geneva, Switzerland, 2014

The ethnological collection of the City of Geneva, with its more than 80,000 artefacts and around 15,000 film and audio documents, is one of the largest in Switzerland. More than 1,000 of these objects are now accessible to visitors. The spatial composition developed for this is based on the guiding principle of a display repository. The museum is an encyclopaedic archive of human diversity.

Visitors start off in the prologue room that prepares them for the variety of the collection and explains its origins. On a table reminiscent of an ark, the exhibits are presented in themed groups: curiosities, rarities, exotic objects, artwork with a market value, ambivalent objects collected by missionaries, diplomatic gifts, and finally artefacts from scientific field research. The treasures seem to be waiting to be unloaded from the vessel. They are components and sources of the ethnological collection and are combined to form a multilayered ensemble that is rounded off by the video installation "Mer" (Sea) by the artist Ange Leccia. With undulating waves on a black beach, it gives the room a contemplative, timeless atmosphere.

Behind the video wall lies the display repository that shows the collection items in large glass cabinets. They are colour-coded, allocated to various cultural regions: Africa, America, Europe, Asia, and Oceania. The department for music ethnology is also presented here in the form of instruments and acoustic examples.

The strict parallel arrangement of the display cabinets underlines the archival character. This is interrupted by one outstanding exhibit that is placed like a solitaire between the cabinets, an eye-catcher in every geographic department.

Die völkerkundliche Sammlung der Stadt Genf zählt mit über 80.000 Objekten und rund 15.000 Bild- und Tondokumenten zu den größten der Schweiz. Über 1.000 davon sind nun für Besucher zugänglich. Das dafür entwickelte Raumbild basiert auf der Leitidee des Schaudepots. Das Museum ist ein enzyklopädisches Archiv der menschlichen Diversität.

Die Besucher betreten zunächst einen Prolograum, der sie auf die Vielfalt der Sammlung einstimmt und deren Ursprünge veranschaulicht. Auf einem Tisch, der an eine Arche erinnert, werden Exponate in thematischen Gruppen präsentiert: Kuriositäten, Raritäten, Exotika, Kunstgegenstände mit Marktwert, von Missionaren gesammelte ambivalente Objekte, diplomatische Geschenke und schließlich Artefakte aus der wissenschaftlichen Feldforschung. Die Schätze scheinen darauf zu warten, von der Barke abgeladen zu werden. Sie sind Bestandteile und Quellen der völkerkundlichen Sammlung und fügen sich zu einem vielschichtigen Ensemble, das durch die Videoinstallation „Mer" (Meer) des Künstlers Ange Leccia vervollständigt wird. Mit ihren langsamen Wellenbewegungen auf einem schwarzen Strand verleiht sie dem Raum eine kontemplative, zeitenthobene Atmosphäre.

Hinter der Videowand liegt das Schaudepot, das die Sammlungsstücke in Großvitrinen zeigt. Sie sind, durch Farben codiert, den einzelnen Kulturräumen zugeordnet: Afrika, Amerika, Europa, Asien und Ozeanien. Zudem wird hier die Abteilung für Musikethnologie anhand von Instrumenten und akustischen Beispielen vorgestellt.

Die streng parallele Anordnung der Schaukästen unterstreicht den Archivcharakter. Diesen unterbricht jeweils ein herausragendes Exponat, das sich als Solitär zwischen die Vitrinen einordnet und in jeder geografischen Abteilung einen Blickfang bietet.

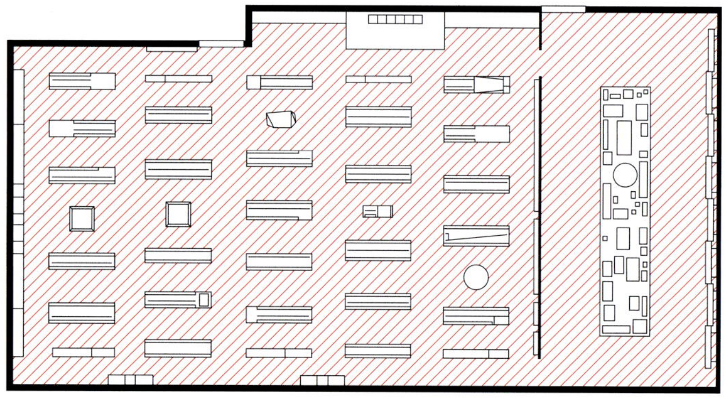

01 Floor plan.

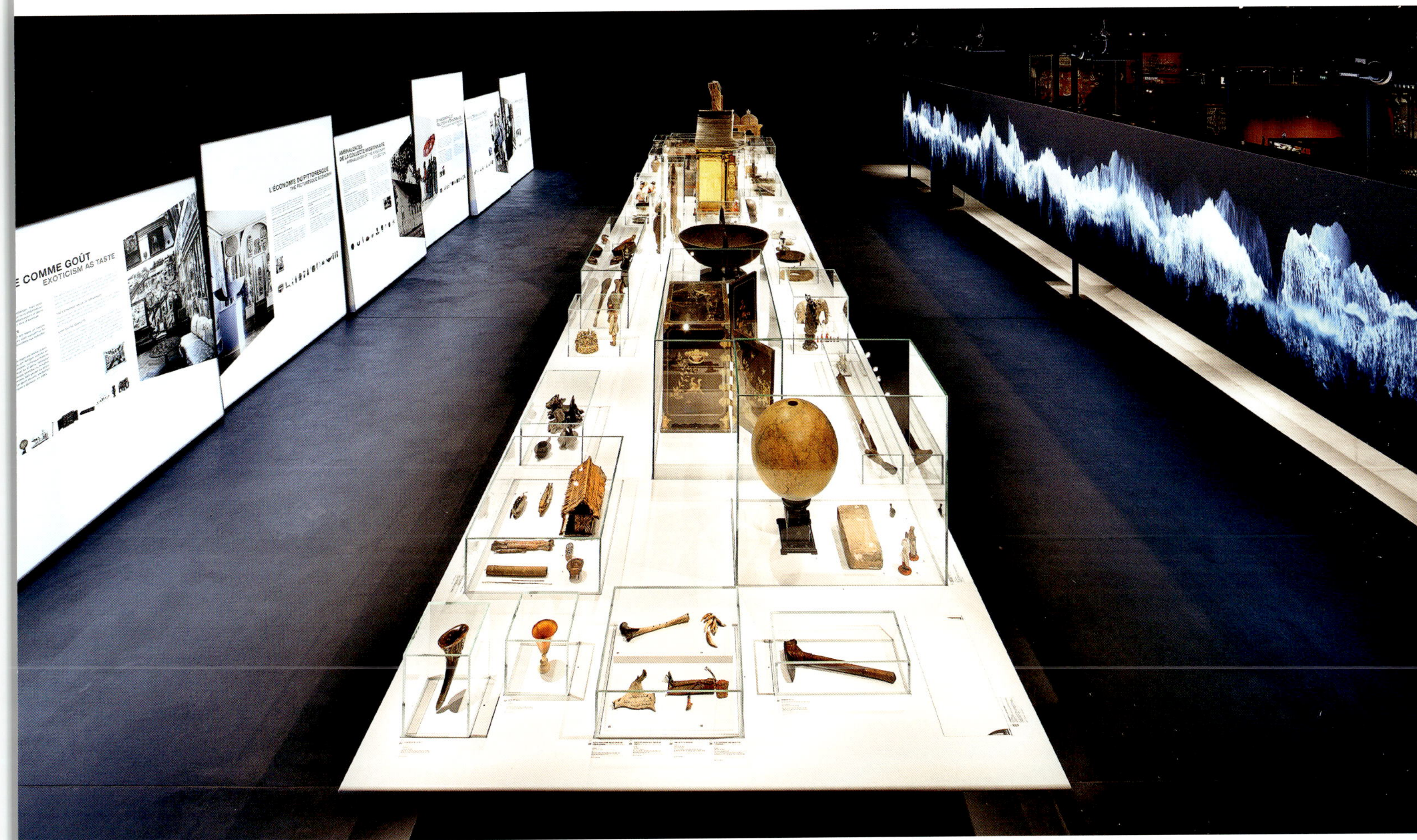

02 The prologue area is dominated by an ark-like table which displays the diversity of the collection arranged in thematic groups of the same origin.

03 The presentation of the objects allows a close relation to the visitors.

04 Ark-like table in front of the video installation “Mer” (Sea).

05 The accurate setting of the showcases emphasises the archival character of the exhibition. They are organised according to the cultural areas and provenance of the objects, balanced with highlight artefacts in solo vitrines.

The exhibits are ambassadors of the diversity of the peoples of the world and allow visitors to draw countless associations and cross-references between them. The display repository expresses their variety, scope, and quality and invites visitors to encounter the objects and the cultural history that goes with them.

Die Exponate erzählen als Botschafter von der Diversität der Völker der Welt, zwischen denen zahlreiche Bezüge und Querverweise möglich sind. Das Schaudepot bringt deren Vielfalt, Umfang und Qualität zum Ausdruck und lädt die Besucher zu einer Begegnung mit den Objekten und der zugehörigen Kulturgeschichte ein.

DEN BLÅ PLANET

Permanent Exhibition, 1,600 sqm, Copenhagen, Denmark, 2015

The largest aquarium in Northern Europe is one of Denmark's main attractions. To keep the existing building, designed in the form of a vortex, attractive and user-friendly for the unexpectedly high number of visitors–in excess of 600,000 per year–the routing was to be reorganised and the exhibition redesigned. The brief was to improve the orientation in the building and to find a playful way to encourage visitors to interact and participate.

The shaping element is a subtle visual language that was developed to incorporate all information levels. It allows visitors to immerse themselves in the fascinating underwater worlds of our blue planet by evoking the deep blue immensity of the ocean: dark interiors in which the light of the aquariums pulsates.

Graphic illustrations, up to 50 metres in length, swim in the black infinity. They show large-scale infographics and provide the backdrop for the colour coding, whose large, luminous figures and minimalistic typography give simple orientation. The thus classified themed areas are easy to find and self-explanatory. Interactive media installations are embedded in the graphic tableaus.

Das größte Aquarium Nordeuropas gilt als eine der Hauptattraktionen Dänemarks. Um das bestehende Gebäude, gestaltet in Form eines Wasserstrudels, für die unerwartet hohe Besucherzahl von über 600.000 Menschen pro Jahr attraktiv und benutzerfreundlich zu erhalten, sollte der Parcours reorganisiert und die Ausstellung neu gestaltet werden. Es galt, die Orientierung im Gebäude zu verbessern und über einen spielerischen Zugang die Besucher zu Interaktion und Partizipation anzuregen.

Als prägendes Element wurde eine feinsinnige Illustrationssprache entwickelt, die alle Informationsebenen erfasst. Sie lässt die Besucher in die faszinierende Unterwasserwelt unseres Blauen Planeten eintauchen, indem sie die blauschwarze Grenzenlosigkeit des Ozeans erzeugt: dunkle Interieurs, in denen das blaue Licht der Aquarien pulsiert.

Bildhafte Illustrationen, bis zu 50 Meter lang, schwimmen in der schwarzen Endlosigkeit. Sie zeigen großformatige Infografiken und stellen den Fond für die Farbcodierung, die mit großen leuchtenden Ziffern und minimalistischer Typografie für einfache Orientierung sorgt. So werden die Themengebiete auffindbar und selbsterklärend gegliedert. Eingebettet in die Grafiktableaus sind interaktive Medieninstallationen.

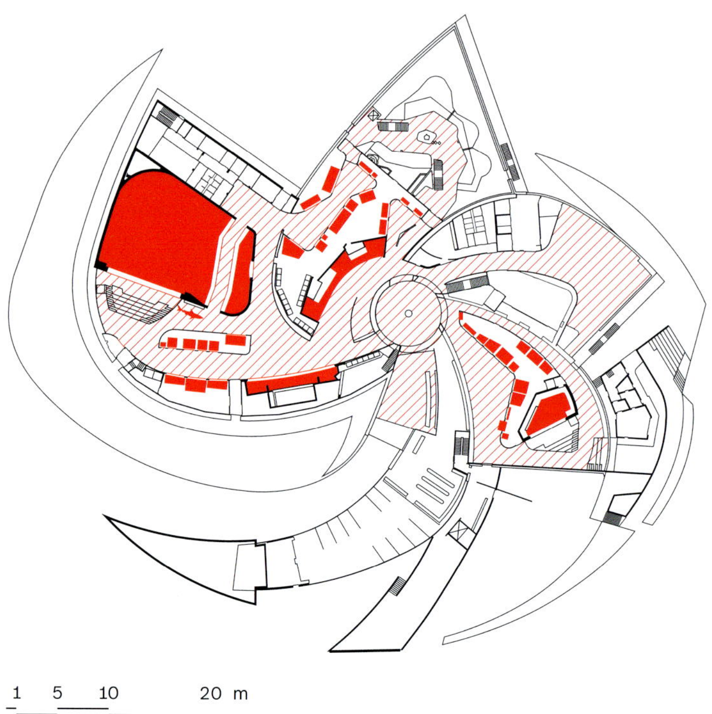

01 Floor plan.
02 The underwater tunnel offers an immersive view into the fish-tank ...

Gæller
Gälar
Gills
Hjerne
Hjärna
Brain
Mave
Mage
Stomach
Svømmeblære
Simblåsa
Swimbladder
Nyre
Njurar
Kidney
Urinblære
Urinblåsa
Urinary bladder
Ovary
Hjerte
Hjärta
Heart
Lever
Lever
Liver
Tarm
Tarm
Intestine
Fisken flyder med sin svømmeblære,
Fisken flyter med sin simblåsa, andas med gälarna
Skræl en fisk
Skala en fisk

03 ... and a preview of the next thematic area. The information system and wayfinding design are combined into one.

Visitors explore the aquarium with the "Blå Planet" app, which combines orientation and content sharing. Thanks to intelligent programming, the app recognises which aquarium the visitor is standing in front of and provides information about the species that live there.

Die Besucher erkunden das Aquarium mit der Blå-Planet-App, die Orientierung und Informationsvermittlung vereint. Dank einer intelligenten Programmierung erkennt die App, vor welchem Aquarium sich die Besucher befinden, und stellt Informationen zu den darin lebenden Spezies zur Verfügung.

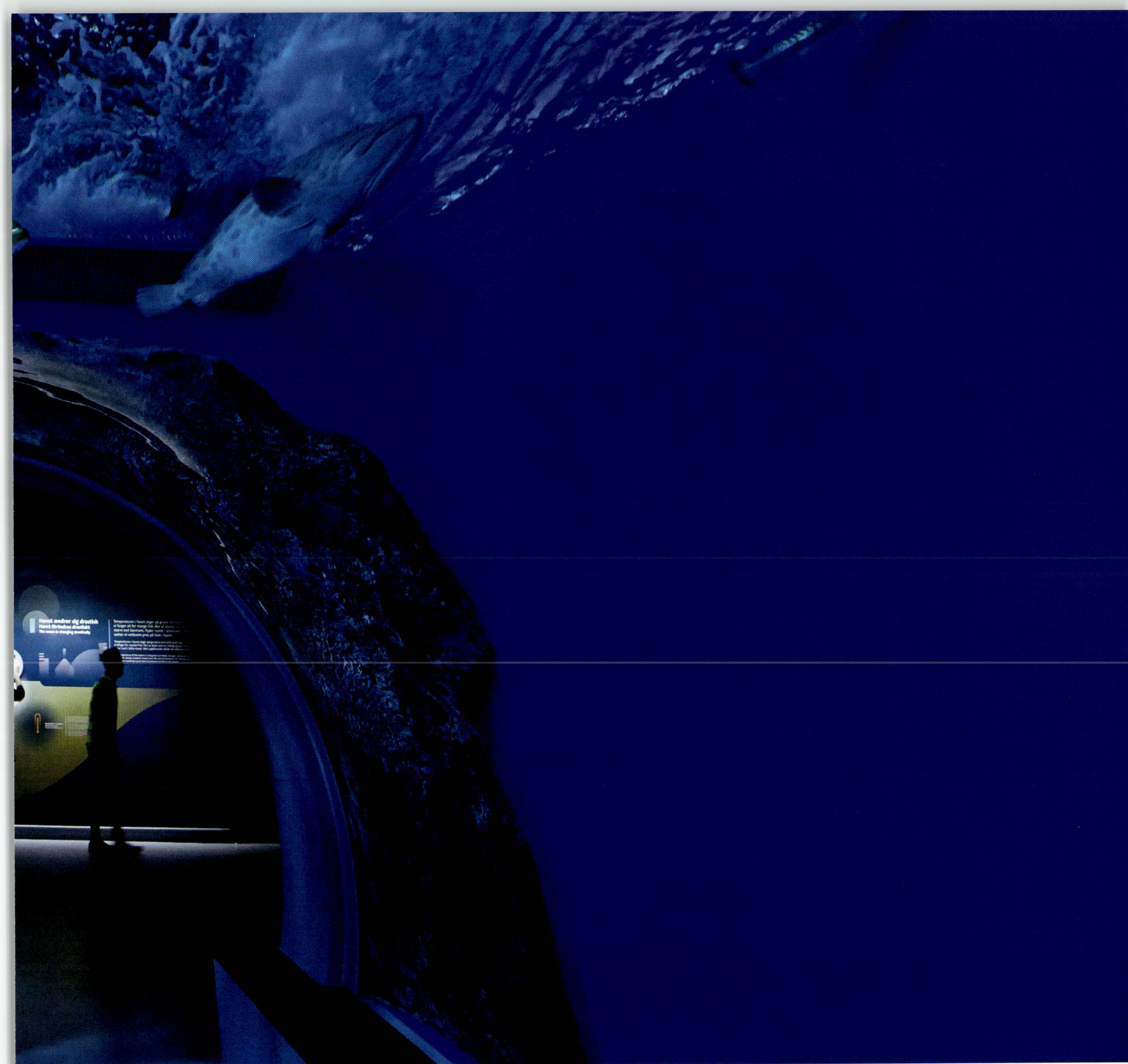

With “Create your own Fish,” it offers another fun feature. Visitors can playfully test their knowledge and win coloured fish parts that they can then piece together to form an individual imaginary fish. At the end of the tour, back in the circular foyer, it is then set free into a virtual aquarium. It swims out of the smartphone into its new, ceiling-high, projected habitat.

Every visitor can leave behind a new, self-created inhabitant, thus making a contribution to the flowing-pulsating experience of the aquarium.

Mit „Create your own Fish“ bietet sie noch ein weiteres Feature. Die Besucher können spielerisch ihr Wissen abfragen und einzelne, farbig gezeichnete Fischteile gewinnen, die sie dann zu einem individuellen Fantasiefisch zusammensetzen. Am Ende des Rundgangs, wieder zurück im kreisrunden Foyer, wird dieser in ein virtuelles Aquarium ausgesetzt. Er schwimmt aus dem Smartphone heraus in sein neues, raumhoch projiziertes Habitat.

Jeder Besucher kann einen selbst gestalteten neuen Bewohner hinterlassen und trägt so zum fließend-pulsierenden Erlebnis im Aquarium bei.

04 Colour coding, style and positioning of the graphics allow clear orientation in the complexity of the entire aquarium in an integrated way. It is designed as discreetly as possible and as self-explanatory as necessary–the reading direction is following the visitors' flow.

05 At the end of the journey, the visitors can assemble their individual fantasy fish and let them swim free in a virtual aquarium.

06 Kids may collect bits and pieces from the experiences made on their journey through the seas.

07 Information touch screen to explore ocean life.

MUSEUM OF TYROLEAN FARMS

Permanent Exhibition, Open Air Museum: 85,000 sqm, Kramsach, Austria, 2015

A new navigation system and a multilayered narrative structure provide access to the idyllic landscape with 14 historical farmhouses translocated from all over Tyrol. Four pavilion structures are designed as viewing and meeting points, each dedicated to a specific topic: landscape, economy, community, and rulership.

These four focal points are presented on the farms as living history/stories: Individual protagonists tell about their lives in films that are subtly incorporated into the scenery of the farms. A spinner, for instance, gives an insight into her everyday life or two brothers explain how inheritance law affected them.

At hands-on stations, children can discover the main topics in playful, interactive activities. For example, they learn on scales about the historical form of inheritance law "Realteilung," which divides the property among the heirs, and on a wheel of fortune they find out about another old form of inheritance law, "Anerbenrecht," under which just one person inherits everything.

In the entrance building, the history of the museum itself is told. A map shows the former locations of the farms.

The navigation system around the three-kilometre routing picks up the expressive design idiom of the pavilion. The angular forms and dashes of colour draw attention to the signposts, orientation plans, and information totems, but thanks to the use of wood, the construction material of the farmhouses, they nevertheless blend unobtrusively into the landscape. This leads to a dialogue between historical and contemporary design idiom. The scenography combines all the elements into a consistent, memorable experience. Both the expansive area with the consistently placed Tyrolean farmhouses and their social significance are revisited.

Ein neues Leitsystem und eine vielschichtige narrative Struktur erschließen die idyllische Landschaft mit ihren 14 translozierten historischen Bauernhöfen, die aus ganz Tirol stammen. Vier Pavillonbauten sind als Aussichts- und Anlaufpunkte konzipiert und jeweils einem Thema gewidmet: Landschaft, Wirtschaft, Gemeinschaft und Herrschaft.

Diese vier Schwerpunkte sind auf den Bauernhöfen als lebendige Geschichte(n) aufbereitet: Einzelne Protagonisten erzählen in Filmprojektionen aus ihrem Leben. Sie sind subtil in die Szenerie der Höfe eingebunden. So gibt etwa eine Spinnerin Einblicke in ihren Alltag oder zwei Brüder berichten, welche Auswirkungen das Erbrecht auf sie hat.

An Mitmachstationen können Kinder die Schwerpunktthemen spielerisch-interaktiv entdecken. Beispielsweise lernen sie an einer Waage die Realteilung kennen, bei der das Eigentum zwischen den Erben aufgeteilt wurde. Und ein Schicksalsrad vermittelt das Anerbenrecht, dem zufolge das gesamte Erbe einer einzigen Person zufiel.

Im Eingangsgebäude wird die Geschichte des Museums erzählt. Eine Bodenkarte veranschaulicht die ehemaligen Standorte der Höfe.

Das Leitsystem des über drei Kilometer langen Rundwegs greift die ausdrucksstarke Gestaltungssprache der Pavillons auf. Wegweiser, Übersichtspläne und Infostelen erregen einerseits durch kantige Formen und farbige Akzente die nötige Aufmerksamkeit, nehmen sich andererseits durch das Material Holz, das dem Baumaterial der Höfe entspricht, optisch zurück. Dies führt zu einem Dialog zwischen historischer und zeitgenössischer Formensprache. Die Szenografie verbindet alle Elemente zu einem nachhaltigen Erlebnis. Sowohl das weitläufige Areal mit den konsistent platzierten Tiroler Bauernhöfen als auch deren gesellschaftliche Bedeutung werden neu erlebbar.

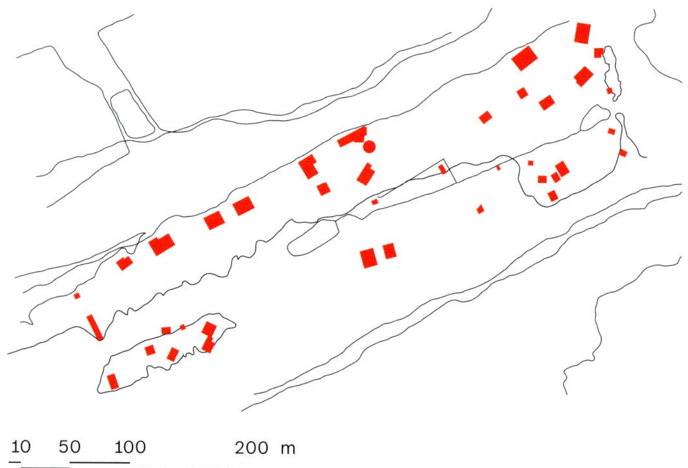

01 Site map.

02 The info-pavilions offer a great view over the site. While their materiality and construction take reference from the old farmhouses, their shape and proportion are clearly contemporary in order not to be mixed up with the historical buildings.

03 Information totem for each farmhouse provide photos of the former location and inhabitants, including basic information of the construction typology.

04 Empathetic stories of the tough and poor lifestyle of the past inhabitants are told on the authentic site.

ARCHAEOLOGY SWITZERLAND

Permanent Exhibition, 500 sqm, Zurich, Switzerland, 2016

The lightning-shaped new building of Christ & Gantenbein is home to some 1,400 archaeological artefacts from Switzerland, showcased in three expressive themed presentations—"Homo," "Natura," and "Terra."

The "Terra" room is devoted to the relationship between exhibit and site of the find. Visitors wander below an extruded landscape, a sculpture made of more than 3,000 shimmering aluminium parts suspended in mid-air which traces the silhouette of Switzerland. A dynamically moving light choreography poetically portrays the passing of time. Archaeological treasures which were discovered in places of geographical interest are illuminated by suspended lighting elements.

The centrepiece of the exhibition is the chronologically staged "Homo" section, which represents the 100,000 years of human history in Switzerland. Seven main works of the collection, including the gravestone with the oldest mention of Zurich, are arranged like solitaires in the centre of the room. When visitors touch the display cabinets, a window opens on the past: Animated films on the rear wall of the cabinets tell the story of the find and also the original purpose of the objects. They are thus put back into context. For example, visitors find out about a Celt who dedicated his gold treasures to the gods returning them to the earth before he started his journey over the Saint-Gotthard Massif.

Six ceiling-high pictures—each depicting an archaeological period—coupled with aesthetically arranged objects from the Palaeolithic to the Middle Ages shape the display cabinets on the longitudinal walls of the room. With movable scanners, visitors can explore the objects in more detail—for example, one of the oldest wagon wheels in Europe, which has been completed using media technology.

Im blitzförmigen Neubau der Architekten Christ & Gantenbein werden rund 1.400 archäologische Objekte der Schweiz in drei ausdrucksstarken Themeninszenierungen – Homo, Natura, Terra – gezeigt.

Dem Bezug zwischen Exponat und Fundort ist der Raum „Terra" gewidmet. Besucher flanieren unterhalb einer extrudierten Landschaft, einer im Raum schwebenden Skulptur, die mit mehr als 3.000 schimmernden Aluminium-Einzelteilen die Silhouette der Schweiz nachbildet. Über sie wandert eine dynamische Lichtchoreografie und inszeniert damit auf poetische Weise den Lauf der Zeit. Archäologische Schätze, die an geografisch markanten Fundorten entdeckt wurden, werden von abgependelten Lichtelementen beleuchtet.

Herzstück der Ausstellung ist der chronologisch inszenierte Themenbereich „Homo", der 100.000 Jahre Menschheitsgeschichte in der Schweiz repräsentiert. Sieben Hauptwerke der Sammlung, darunter ein Grabstein mit der ältesten Nennung Zürichs, sind als Solitäre im Raumzentrum angeordnet. Berühren Besucher die Vitrinen, öffnet sich ein Fenster in die Vergangenheit. Filmische Animationen auf der Vitrinenrückwand erzählen dann sowohl von der Fundgeschichte als auch von der ursprünglichen Nutzung der Objekte. Sie werden rekontextualisiert. Die Besucher erfahren zum Beispiel von einem Kelten, der seinen den Göttern gewidmeten Goldschatz der Erde übergibt, bevor er zu einer Reise über den Gotthard aufbricht.

Sechs raumhohe Epochenbilder mit ästhetisch arrangierten Objekten aus der Zeit vom Paläolithikum bis zum Mittelalter, die jeweils eine archäologische Zeitspanne abbilden, prägen die Wandvitrinen an den Längswänden dieses Raums. Mit beweglichen Scannern können Besucher die einzelnen Objekte vertiefend erkunden, beispielsweise eines der ältesten Wagenräder Europas, das sich medial vervollständigt.

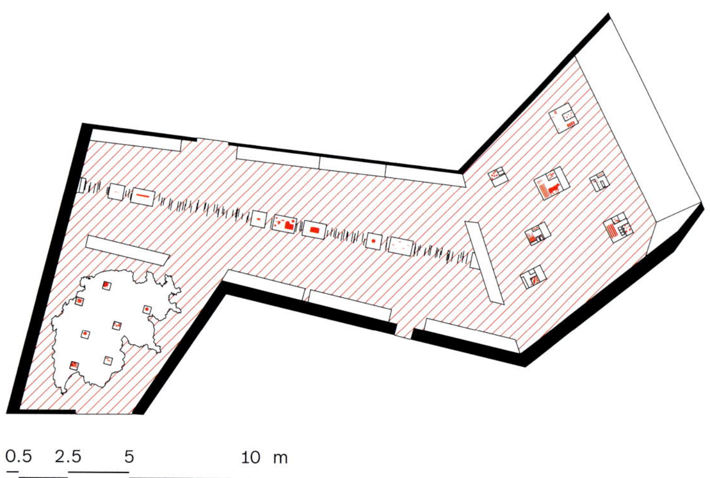

01 Floor plan.
02 One of six epochal wall showcases with a visual array of objects representing the Bronze Age. A movable scanner allows a detailed exploration of the objects.

Bronzezeit
Âge du Bronze
Età del Bronzo
Bronze Age
Neues Material
Nouveau matériau
Nuovi materiali
New materials

03 “Natura”–concentrating on natural resources and featuring archaeological finds like animal bones or seeds, which demonstrate the domestication of wildlife. This section offers seven interactive stations with artefacts. They come to life via a large format projection: an animated reconstruction of the environment and the daily struggle for survival.

The next themed room, "Natura," with its natural science exhibits, consists of seven themed stations presenting the domestication of wild animals and plants. An animated drawing, projected onto a monumental museum wall, transports the Swiss landscape directly into the museum. In interaction with the hands-on stations, visitors can bring the various scenes to life–for example, the horn of an aurochs is linked to a scene which shows the ox ploughing the first fields in the Neolithic.

Der anschließende Themenraum „Natura" mit naturkundlichen Exponaten präsentiert an sieben Themenstationen die Domestizierung von Wildtieren und -pflanzen. Eine animierte Zeichnung, großflächig projiziert auf eine monumentale Museumswand, bringt die Schweizer Landschaft direkt ins Museum. Besucher können darin durch Interaktion mit den Hands-on-Stationen verschiedene Szenen selbst zum Leben erwecken. So ist beispielsweise das Horn eines wilden Auerochsen mit einer Szene verknüpft, die Ochsen beim Pflügen der ersten Felder in der Jungsteinzeit zeigt.

04 “Terra”–the prologue area with seven highlight objects positioned under a stylised interpretation of Switzerland’s natural landscape expressed via topographic curves.

05 “Homo”–the central spine with showcases displaying highlight objects related to the evolution of the people living in the Swiss territory. They are related to the epochs shown in the flanked wall showcases.

The exhibition lives from its clear structure and its interaction with visitors. And it fits perfectly into the sculptural architecture.

Die Ausstellung lebt durch die klare Struktur und die Interaktion mit den Besuchern, und fügt sich in die skulpturale Architektur passgenau ein.

06 | 07 “Information on Demand” showcases reveal backdrop animations to re-contextualise the objects.

ERLEBNIS EUROPA– EUROPA EXPERIENCE

Permanent Exhibition, 450 sqm, Berlin, Germany, 2016

The exhibition “Erlebnis Europa–Europa Experience” offers surprising, direct, and fascinating access to the people, history, and politics of the European Union–and all that in 24 languages. Circular media tables and a 360-degree cinema set the stage for the exhibition dedicated to the EU slogan “United in Diversity.”

The slogan is the guiding principle of the very first media table. It reports on 90 EU success stories, pinpointed geographically on a three-dimensional map showing a Europe without borders. Visitors can explore various EU initiatives and programmes, for example the EU Daphne programme that promotes the internet skills of young people and supports the prevention of cyber mobbing.

The “Daily Life” panorama behind the media table shows the diversity of landscapes and the everyday life of Europeans. Two inhabitants from each EU country have their say, for instance the German Klaus Vogel, who on Europe Day 2015 founded the project “SOS MÉDITERRANÉE” to rescue boat refugees. The interviews are incorporated in the landscape picture and can be started via touch screens.

The highlight of the exhibition is, however, the 360-degree cinema that allows visitors to experience a plenary session at first hand. Seated in the middle of the plenum, they can immerse themselves in the world of politics and find out what it feels like to be a member of parliament.

Information about the history of the EU, the EU Parliament, and the EU Commission are clearly presented at further media stations. All the EU parliamentarians are present in text and images. Visitors can make contact with their European representatives and ask them a question by email.

In a playful, hands-on way, the interactive exhibition provides insights into the history and structure of the European Union and to the everyday life of the people of the EU member states: The idea of a united Europe is made transparent and comprehensible.

Die Ausstellung „Erlebnis Europa - Europa Experience“ bietet einen überraschenden, direkten und kurzweiligen Zugang zu Menschen, Geschichte und Politik der Europäischen Union - und dies in 24 Sprachen. Runde Medientische und ein 360-Grad-Kino bestimmen die Inszenierung, die unter dem EU-Motto „In Vielfalt geeint“ steht.

Diesem Leitsatz ist gleich zu Beginn ein Medientisch gewidmet, der von 90 EU-Erfolgsgeschichten erzählt, verortet auf einer dreidimensionalen Karte, die ein Europa ohne Grenzen zeigt. Hier können Besucher einzelne EU-Initiativen und Programme erkunden, beispielsweise das EU-DAPHNE-Programm, das die Internetkompetenz junger Menschen fördert und die Prävention von Cyber-Mobbing unterstützt.

Das Panorama „Daily Life“ hinter dem Medientisch zeigt die Vielfalt der Landschaften und des Alltagslebens der Europäer. Aus jedem Land der EU kommen zwei Einwohner zu Wort, so zum Beispiel der Deutsche Klaus Vogel, der das Projekt „SOS MÉDITERRANÉE“ zur Rettung von Bootsflüchtlingen am Europatag im Jahr 2015 gegründet hat. Die Interviews sind in das Landschaftsbild eingebunden und an Touch-Monitoren aufrufbar.

Höhepunkt der Ausstellung ist das 360-Grad-Kino, das Besucher eine Plenarsitzung immersiv erleben lässt. Mitten im Plenum sitzend, können sie in das politische Geschehen eintauchen und die Arbeit der Abgeordneten nachvollziehen.

Informationen zu Geschichte, EU-Parlament und EU-Kommission sowie zu den Etappen der Erweiterung Europas sind anschaulich an weiteren Medienstationen aufbereitet. Alle EU-Parlamentarier sind in Text und Bild präsent. Die Besucher können mit ihren europäischen Vertretern in Kontakt treten und ihnen per E-Mail Fragen stellen.

Die interaktive Ausstellung gibt spielerisch und erlebnisorientiert Einblick in die Geschichte und Struktur der Europäischen Union sowie in das Alltagsleben der Menschen in den EU-Mitgliedsstaaten. Die Idee eines geeinten Europas wird nachvollziehbar und verständlich.

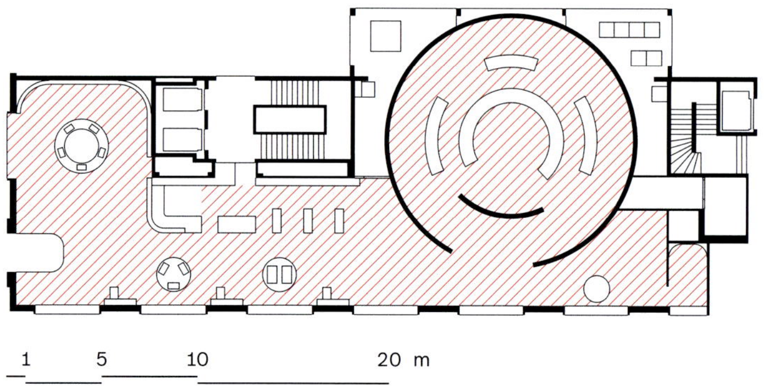

01 Floor plan.

02 The interactive media table “United in Diversity” invites visitors to travel over a 3-D European map conveying 90 locations of success stories. A panoramic backdrop talks of the environments and living conditions of European citizens.

03 A 360-degree cinema allows visitors to experience a plenary session at first hand.

04 Interactive media station presenting the enlargement of the European Union.

MILCHWERK

Redesign of the Entrance and Foyer, 1,200 sqm, Radolfzell, Germany, 2016

The Milchwerk in Radolfzell is today a venue for cultural events, conferences, and trade fairs. Since its conversion, it offers an attractive, appealing foyer and a welcoming, barrier-free entrance. The 48-metre red-walled ramp not only bridges steps in the interior and exterior area, it also optically accentuates the main entrance that until then had been hidden in the rear courtyard.

The new ambiance of the foyer now invites visitors to stay there a while before and after events. Shades of grey and black replace the previous colour scheme and allow certain areas to be accentuated. The white tiled floor was replaced by a matt, grey cast floor with an industrial flair. Amorphous shapes reminiscent of a large pool of spilt milk spread out over the floor. This flowing form is followed by a curtain system on rails. The white, translucent curtains that have been chosen can be used to zone and flexibly divide the foyer into individual areas.

A sophisticated changeable and dimmable light system sets off the space to great effect, underlining the pleasant atmosphere. The industrial character of the materials and colours reinforces the historical identity of the former milk-processing plant, paying homage to the original function of the building.

Das Milchwerk in Radolfzell ist heute ein Ort für kulturelle Veranstaltungen, Tagungen und Messen. Seit dem Umbau bietet es ein attraktives, ansprechendes Foyer und einen einladenden, barrierefreien Zugang. Die rote, 48 Meter lange Rampe überbrückt nicht nur einen Treppenabsatz im Innen- und Außenbereich, sie hebt auch den bisher versteckt im Hinterhof liegenden Haupteingang optisch hervor.

Das Foyer hat eine völlig neue Aufenthaltsqualität, die vor und nach Veranstaltungen zum Verweilen einlädt. Grau- und Schwarztöne ersetzen die bisherige Farbgebung und ermöglichen eine Akzentuierung einzelner Bereiche. Der weiße Fliesenboden wurde gegen einen grau gegossenen, matten Boden mit industrieller Anmutung ausgetauscht. Amorphe Formen, die an einen großen weißen Milchklecks erinnern, breiten sich darauf aus. Seine fließende Gestalt greift ein schienengeführtes Vorhangsystem auf. Mit den gewählten transluzenten weißen Vorhängen lässt sich das Foyer zonieren und flexibel in einzelne Bereiche unterteilen.

Ein ausgeklügeltes veränder- und dimmbares Lichtsystem setzt den Raum in Szene und unterstreicht dessen angenehmes Ambiente. Der industrielle Charakter der Materialien und Farben stärkt die historische Identität des ehemaligen Milchwerks – eine Reminiszenz an die ursprüngliche Funktion des Gebäudes.

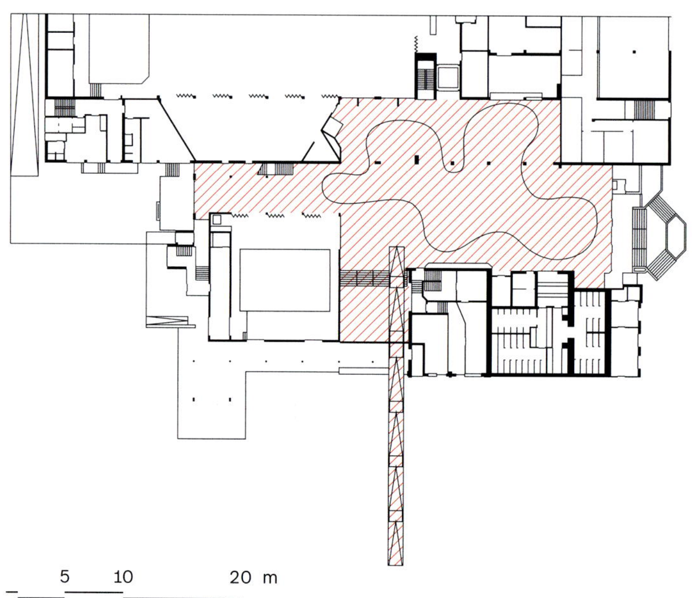

01 Floor plan.

02 A 48-metre-long red-walled ramp not only bridges steps in the interior and exterior area of the Milchwerk, it also becomes a stage for events and performances.

03 White, translucent curtains can be used to zone and flexibly divide the foyer into individual areas.

04 A pool of spilt milk on the floor is a memento to the former dairy.

KLS MARTIN WORLD

Permanent Exhibition, Showroom, 600 sqm, Tuttlingen, Germany, 2016

The main objective of the KLS Martin World comprising exhibition and training areas, including an operating theatre, is consultation and dialogue with specialist dealers and physicians.

The exhibition is devoted to the history of the company as well as its current medical-technical products. It is arranged in a horseshoe around the auditorium that is encircled at ceiling height by an impressive array of display cabinets–the knowledge archive. Here, product development since the foundation of the group in 1923 is showcased using important, chronologically arranged exhibits presented aesthetically with easy-to-read graphics like shiny bright gems against a dark satined rear wall. Milestones like the first electrical surgery device from 1923 or the first special laser for lung surgery from the year 2000 are graphically accentuated. This is counterbalanced by historical anatomical drawings on panel blinds.

Around the knowledge archive, visitors can get to know the latest product generations. More than 12,000 exhibits, classified into eight areas from hand surgery to gynaecology or electrical and laser surgery are to be found in drawers of high-quality table showcases. Screens incorporated in the tables provide important product information.

The demonstration operating theatre is used to present products in context. Large-scale backlit scientific images of human blood cells act as a backdrop.

Hauptanliegen der KLS Martin World, die Ausstellungs- und Schulungsflächen sowie einen Schau-OP umfasst, ist der Dialog mit Fachhändlern und Ärzten.

Die Ausstellung präsentiert die Geschichte der Firma sowie die aktuellen medizintechnischen Produkte. Sie ist hufeisenförmig um das zentrale Auditorium angeordnet, um das sich ein eindrucksvolles, raumhohes Vitrinenband – das Wissensarchiv – legt. Hier wird die Produktentwicklung seit Gründung der Firmengruppe 1923 anhand von chronologisch angeordneten Exponaten als helle Glanzstücke vor dunkler Rückwand ästhetisch und gut lesbar vorgestellt. Meilensteine wie das erste Elektrochirurgiegerät von 1923 oder der erste Speziallaser für Lungenchirurgie aus dem Jahr 2000 sind grafisch besonders hervorgehoben. Ein Pendant zu diesen Grafiken bilden historische anatomische Zeichnungen auf Schiebevorhängen an der Fensterfront.

Rund um das Wissensarchiv können Besucher die neueste Produktgeneration kennenlernen. Über 12.000 Exponate, gegliedert in acht Bereiche von Handchirurgie und Gynäkologie bis hin zu Elektro- und Laserchirurgie, sind in Schubladen hochwertiger Tischvitrinen untergebracht. Eingelassene Monitore liefern wichtige Produktinformationen.

Der Schau-OP ergänzt die Präsentation und zeigt die Produkte im Kontext. Hinterleuchtete wissenschaftliche Großaufnahmen menschlicher Blutkörperchen vermitteln eine angenehme Atmosphäre.

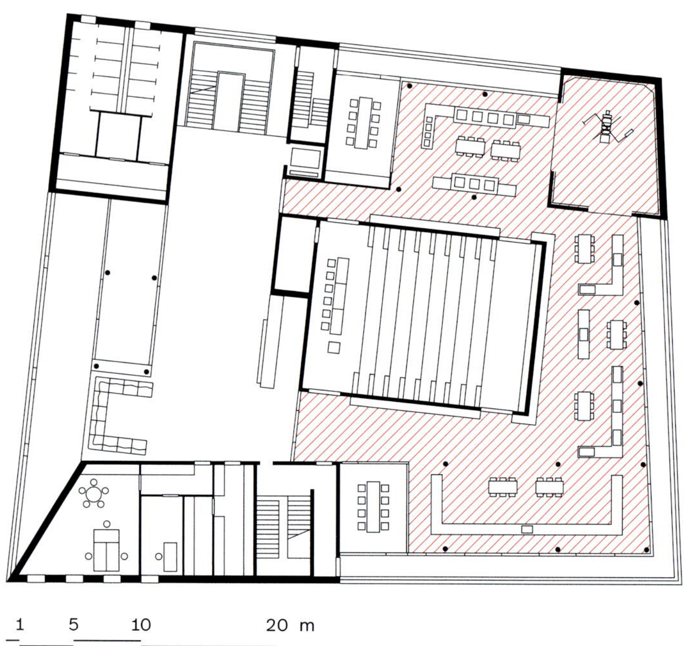

01 Floor plan.
02 The show operating theatre combines the latest technology with the demonstration of the medical tools, including light and backlit wall systems.

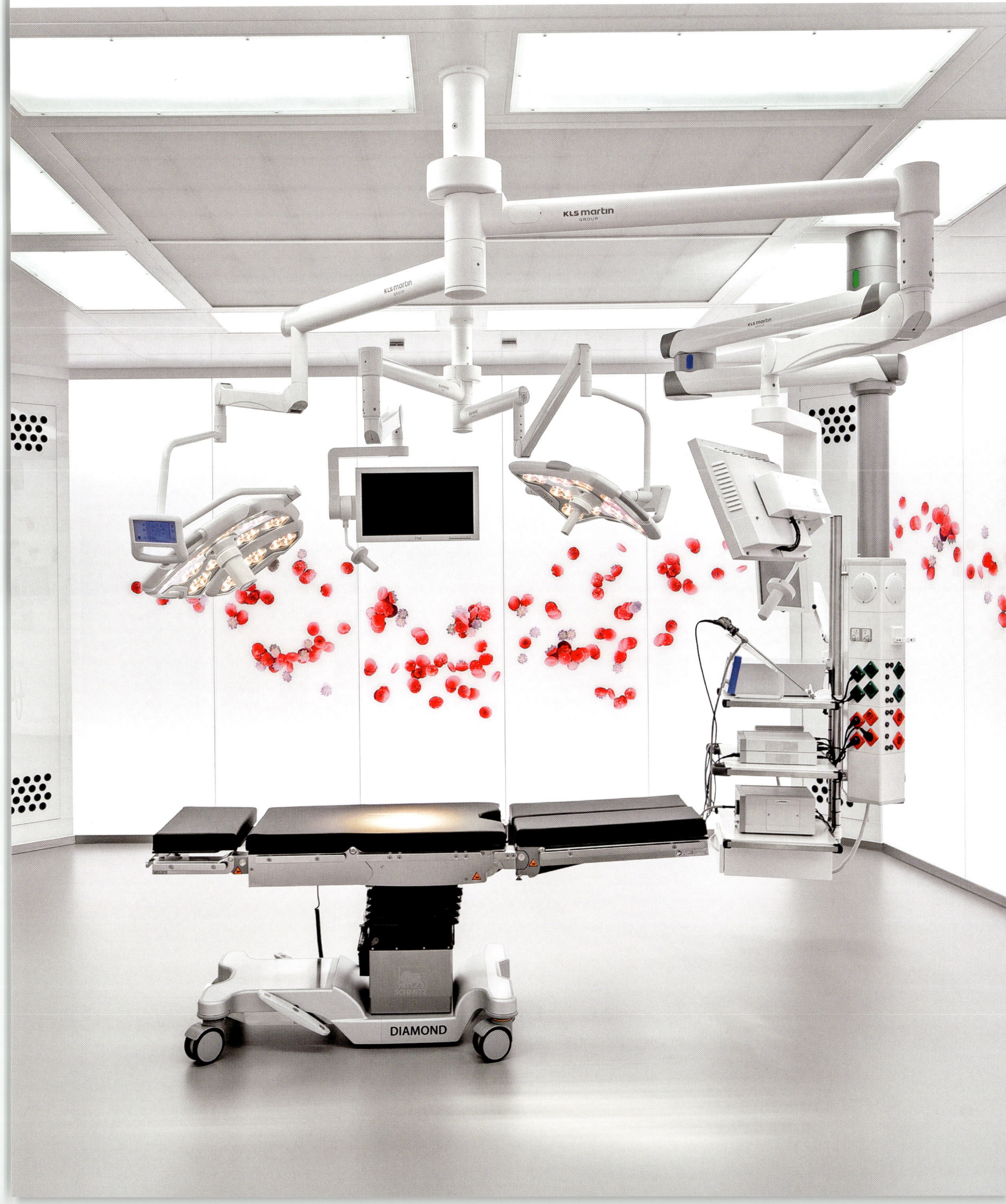
KLS martin
DIAMOND

03 An impressive shelf with numerous tools displayed in chronological order. This so-called "knowledge archive" embraces the entire exhibition.

The strict orthogonal arrangement of the table showcases, the precise, clear design idiom, and the clean-cut, bright impression of the room do justice to the precision of the high technology on display. In contrast to this, white-stained oak as well as translucent textiles and the lounge-like character provide a warm counterpoint to the coolness and soberness of the products and the operating theatre.

Die streng orthogonale Ausrichtung der Tischvitrinen, ihre präzise, klare Formensprache und die Sachlichkeit des hellen Raums werden der ausgestellten Hochtechnologie gerecht. Weiß gebeizte Eiche, transluzente Textilien und der Lounge-charakter bilden einen überzeugenden Kontrapunkt zur Kühle und Nüchternheit der medizintechnischen Produkte.

04 At the archive tables the potential client gets introduced to more than 12,000 objects via the instrument drawers and the retractable explanatory screens.

05 Consulting tables for customer meetings circle the central archive.

TRUCONNECT FORUM

Permanent Exhibition, Visitor Centre, 1,200 sqm, Trumpf, Ditzingen, Germany, 2016

The TruConnect Forum presents current topics and developments of connected production with a clear reference to Industry 4.0. It consists of an exhibition zone on the ground floor, a reception and lounge area on the upper level, and various stations in the demonstration hall where the machines can be experienced in action.

The stainless steel sculpture "Metamorphosis" in the atrium provides the emotional prelude to the exhibition and at the same time connects the floors. The individual elements that are punched, laser-cut, and bent using Trumpf machines and which develop step by step from a flat triangle into a three-dimensional icosahedron illustrate the various stages of the production process.

The sculpture is surrounded by various themed areas: the backlit prologue wall shows the changing demands placed on industrial production from the beginnings through to the twenty-first century. Impressively, two 7-square-metre multi-touch presentation walls show visions, products, and current best practice examples which customers can transfer to their own companies. In between, the central interactive media table demonstrates the individual process steps of intelligent connectivity.

Before the visitor gets to the machines, he sees production from the perspective of the factory manager–a transparent screen on the upper floor superimposes the process data in real time over the machines in the demonstration hall.

The TruConnect visitors' forum transfers technology from production into the exhibition. Industry 4.0. explains itself with the help of materials, production, and media content.

Das TruConnect Besucherforum präsentiert aktuelle Themen und Entwicklungen der vernetzten Fertigung – ganz im Zeichen von Industrie 4.0. Es besteht aus einem Ausstellungsbereich im Erdgeschoss, einem Empfangs- und Loungebereich im Obergeschoss sowie mehreren Stationen in der Vorführhalle, in der die Maschinen in Aktion erlebt werden können.

Die Edelstahl-Skulptur „Metamorphose" im Atrium bietet den emotionalen Auftakt der Ausstellung und verbindet gleichzeitig die Geschosse. Die einzelnen Elemente, die mit Trumpf-Maschinen gestanzt, gelasert und gebogen wurden und sich schrittweise vom flachen Dreieck bis zum dreidimensionalen Ikosaeder entwickeln, veranschaulichen unterschiedliche Stadien des Fertigungsprozesses.

Umgeben ist diese Skulptur von verschiedenen Themenbereichen: Die hinterleuchtete Prologwand verdeutlicht die sich ändernden Anforderungen an industrielle Fertigung von den Anfängen bis ins 21. Jahrhundert. Eindrucksvoll zeigen zwei über sieben Quadratmeter große Multitouch-Präsentationswände Visionen, Produkte und aktuelle Best-Practice-Beispiele, die der Kunde auf sein eigenes Unternehmen übertragen kann. Dazwischen demonstriert der zentrale, interaktive Medientisch die einzelnen Prozessschritte der intelligenten Vernetzung.

Bevor der Besucher zu den Maschinen gelangt, sieht er die Produktion aus der Perspektive des Fabrikleiters – ein transparenter Screen im Obergeschoss überlagert die Maschinen der Vorführhalle mit den Prozessdaten in Echtzeit.

Das TruConnect Besucherforum zeichnet sich durch den Technologietransfer aus der Produktion in die Ausstellung aus. Industrie 4.0 präsentiert sich hier selbsterklärend. Materialien, Herstellung und Medieninhalte tragen dazu bei.

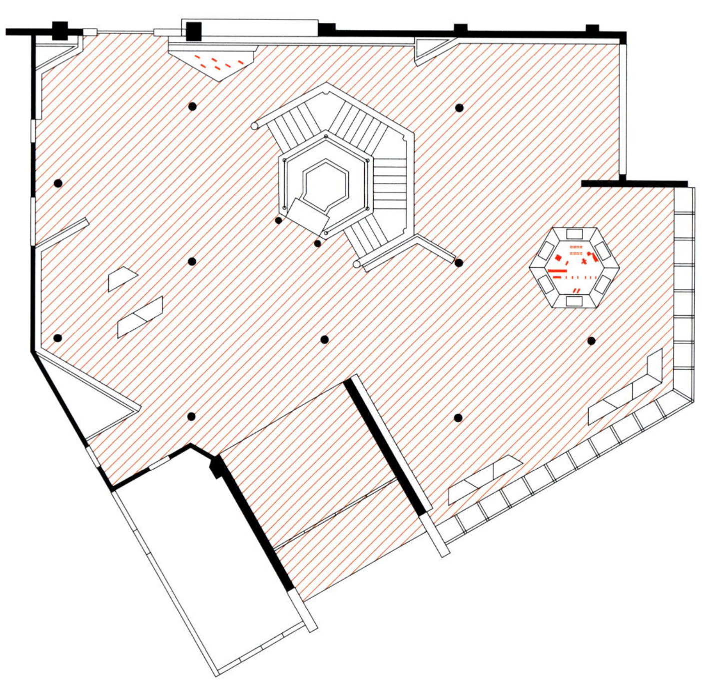

0.5 2.5 5 10 m

01 Floor plan–ground floor.

02 The central "Metamorphosis" sculpture shows a gradient from flat metal to 3-dimensional icosahedrons and connects the floors vertically.

03 The central interactive media desk provides insight in the various production processes and shows how smartly they can be digitally connected and improved.

04 The window to the production hall uses a transparent screen to augment the actual machines, give real-time information, and show animated processes.

AUGUST HORCH MUSEUM

Refurbishment and Extension of a listed Factory Building, 5,500 sqm, Zwickau, Germany, 2017

The expansion of the August Horch Museum consists of the restoration of the former Audi factory halls in line with heritage requirements and the addition of a new, sculptural building with museum café and kitchen. This connects the existing August Horch Museum that was opened in 2004 with the annex. The factory halls from the years 1912 and 1924, in which the first vehicles of the Audi marque were produced, are the shell and at the same time the biggest exhibit of the museum enlargement. Paying close attention to the requirements applicable to listed buildings, their clinker facades were renovated, the steel structure sandblasted and recoated, and the flat roof, consisting of a hollow brick ceiling with lines of skylights like those of a saddle roof, reconstructed. The delicate steel skeleton now offers the authentic framework for the new exhibition.

Drawn from the historical context, three aspects provide the source of inspiration for the new building: the industrial architecture, with shed roofs as the original form; the series production of vehicles, which stands for dynamic innovation and technical precision; and the emotional effect of the elegant and luxurious Horch automotive myths. But how can the character of a car be translated into architecture? The answer is a shaped metal shell to which a radiator grille has been attached. With a reference to car bodywork, the new building has been clad in sheet metal. The way it is shaped, the light reflections and its lightness are reminiscent of a vehicle that has drawn up and parked between the historical buildings. The generously glazed facade elements have broad, three-dimensional, steel plate frames, with a metallic lustre, like a radiator grille.

The new building respectfully docks onto the historical clinker facade via a narrow linking corridor, thus offering a largely unobstructed view of the original building. The shed roofs adopt the eaves' height of the museum and annex. With their sharp-edged, crystalline design idiom, the roofs at the same time provide a charming contrast.

Die Erweiterung des August Horch Museums umfasst die denkmalgerechte Sanierung der ehemaligen Audi-Werkhallen und einen skulpturalen Neubau mit Museumscafé und Küche. Er verbindet das bereits bestehende, 2004 eröffnete August Horch Museum mit der Erweiterungsfläche. Die Fabrikhallen aus den Jahren 1912 und 1924, in denen die ersten Fahrzeuge der Marke Audi produziert wurden, sind Hülle und zugleich das größte Exponat der Museumserweiterung. Ihre Fassaden aus Klinkermauerwerk wurden ertüchtigt, die Stahlkonstruktion sandgestrahlt und neu beschichtet sowie das Flachdach, bestehend aus einer Hourdis-Hohlziegeldecke mit satteldachförmigen Oberlichtbändern, denkmalgerecht wiederhergestellt. Der feingliedrige Stahlskelettbau bietet nun den authentischen Rahmen für die neue Ausstellung.

Für den Neubau waren drei aus dem historischen Kontext abgeleitete Aspekte die Inspirationsquelle: die Industriearchitektur mit Sheddächern als Urform, die Serienproduktion der Fahrzeuge, die für Dynamik, Innovation und technische Präzision steht, und die emotionale Wirkung der eleganten und luxuriösen Horch-Automobillegenden. Aber wie kann der Charakter eines Autos in Architektur übersetzt werden? Es besteht aus einer geformten Metallhülle und besitzt einen aufgesetzten Kühlergrill. So erhält der Neubau als Anleihe aus dem Karosseriebau ein Blechkleid. Durch seine Ausformung, Lichtreflexe und Leichtigkeit erinnert er an ein vorgefahrenes Fahrzeug, das zwischen den historischen Gebäuden parkt. Die großzügig verglasten Fassadenelemente haben breite, dreidimensional ausgebildete Stahlblechrahmungen, metallisch glänzend wie ein Kühlergrill.

Respektvoll dockt der Neubau mit reduzierter Gebäudetiefe an den historischen Klinkerfassaden an und bietet dadurch weitgehend freie Sicht auf die Bestandsgebäude. Die Sheddächer nehmen die Traufhöhen von Museum und Erweiterungsgebäude auf. Mit ihrer scharfkantigen, kristallinen Formensprache treten sie zugleich in einen reizvollen Kontrast dazu.

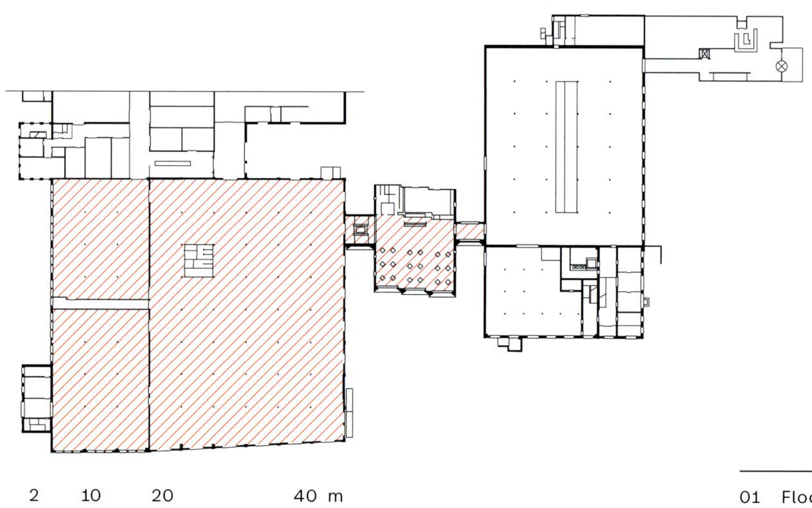

01 Floor plan.
02 Museum's Café–shed-roof-shaped corpus cladded with metal panels and positioned between two exhibition halls.

03 Museum's Café–the selected materials palette was inspired by automotive design: beech wood, chrome and leather.

04 The historical brick facades of the former factory building were carefully restored in close collaboration with the monument protection service.

The interior also draws its materials from the automotive industry. Oiled beechwood and grey leather framed in chrome dominate the room, reminiscent of the materials used inside luxurious limousines. The edgy architecture is in stark contrast to the warm wood. As the shed roofs point west and not, as is customary, north, they catch the light and offer special lighting moods whatever the time of day.

The new building adds a new time layer to the existing ensemble and puts a contemporary slant on the industrial design idiom.

Auch der Innenraum entlehnt seine Werkstoffe aus dem Automobilbereich. Er ist mit Materialien ausgestattet, die an das Interieur von Luxuslimousinen erinnern: Geöltes Buchenholz und in Chrom gefasstes graues Kunstleder prägen den Raum. Kontrastierend zum warmen Holz steht die kantige Architektur. Da die Sheddächer nicht wie gewöhnlich nach Norden, sondern nach Westen ausgerichtet sind, wirken sie als Lichtfänger und bieten zu jeder Tageszeit besondere Lichtstimmungen.

Mit dem Neubau wird eine neue Zeitschicht zum bestehenden Ensemble hinzugefügt und die industrielle Formensprache zeitgemäß interpretiert.

05 Historical flat roof with skylights provides an authentic ambience for the exhibition (exhibition design by ö_konzept).

06 Daylight exhibition in the former manufacturing plant.

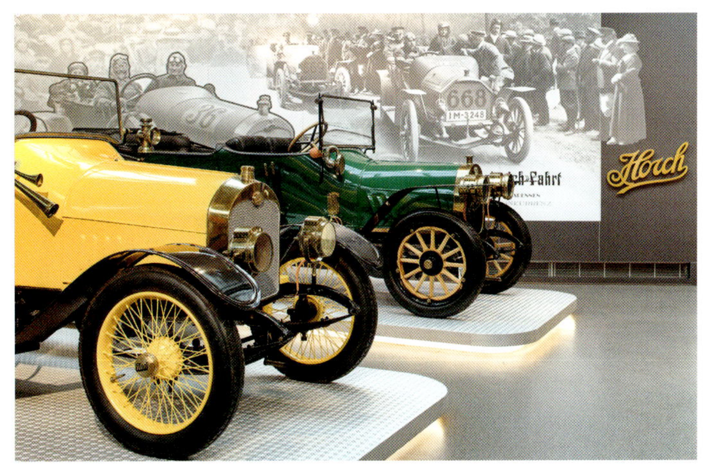

07 The radiator grilles of the historical Horch automobiles became the metaphor for the exterior facade of the new buidling–the Museum's Café.

WIELAND WAGNER

Temporary Exhibition, 500 sqm, Bayreuth, Germany, 2017

The Richard Wagner Museum dedicated an exhibition to Wieland Wagner to mark his one hundredth birthday. With his radically reduced production style, Richard Wagner's grandson revolutionised the work of his grandfather and is hailed as the renewer of Bayreuth and founder of New Bayreuth. The exhibition shows his personal and artistic development as a history of liberation and detachment of political and ideological convictions and constraints imposed by the family.

The staging of the exhibition allows the visitor to experience this difficult journey by translating the spatial concept, leading from the constrictions of history into the openness of the post-war period. Initially, the visitor moves between larger-than-life portrait photos, hung close together, which give a sense of the stifling presence of the family and the past burden of National Socialism.

Emerging from these constrictions, the exhibition room opens up and the visitor passes biographical landmarks–suspended textile panels which trace the career of the opera director. Early on, Adolf Hitler played a decisive role; later there was the influence of Adolphe Appia and the involvement of Wieland Wagner's wife, Gertrud Reissinger. Looking back, visitors see his parents' house that was destroyed in the Second World War and the opera "Parsifal" as a collage that expresses the turning point, the detachment of Wieland Wagner from the family.

The visitor routing opens up to show his productions. Here, visitors enter a circular stage and are immersed in Wieland Wagner's world of opera. Three large-scale gauzes create screens for a 360-degree film projection showing historical recordings of his opera productions, including "Parsifal," "Tannhäuser" and "Tristan und Isolde."

The exhibition is a critical tribute to an opera personality of the German post-war period who is as important as he is disputed.

Das Richard Wagner Museum widmet Wieland Wagner zu dessen 100. Geburtstag eine Ausstellung. Der Enkel Richard Wagners revolutionierte mit seinem radikal reduzierten Inszenierungsstil das Werk seines Großvaters. Er gilt als Erneuerer Bayreuths und Gründer von Neu-Bayreuth. Die Schau zeigt seine persönliche und künstlerische Entwicklung als eine Geschichte der Befreiung und Loslösung von politisch-ideologischem Gedankengut und familiärer Enge.

Diesen schwierigen Weg macht die Inszenierung eindrucksvoll erlebbar, indem sie ihn in das Raumkonzept übersetzt und aus der Beengtheit der Geschichte in die Weite der Nachkriegszeit führt. Zunächst bewegt sich der Besucher zwischen überlebensgroßen, dicht gehängten Porträtfotos, die ihn die erdrückende Präsenz der Familie und die belastende Vergangenheit im Nationalsozialismus spüren lassen.

Aus dieser Enge öffnet sich der Ausstellungsraum und der Besucher durchstreift biografische Wegmarken, hängende Stoffbahnen, die den Werdegang des Opernregisseurs nachzeichnen. Eine entscheidende Rolle spielte zunächst Adolf Hitler, später dann der Einfluss von Adolphe Appia und das Mitwirken von Wieland Wagners Ehefrau Gertrud Reissinger. Beim Blick zurück sieht der Besucher das im Zweiten Weltkrieg zerstörte Bayreuther Elternhaus und das collagierte Opernwerk „Parsifal", das die Zäsur, das Loslösen Wieland Wagners von der Familie zum Ausdruck bringt.

Der Parcours öffnet sich bis zum Inszenierungswerk. Hier betritt der Besucher eine kreisrunde Bühne und taucht immersiv in die Opernwelt Wieland Wagners ein. Drei großformatige Gazen bilden die Screens für eine filmische 360-Grad-Projektion, die historische Aufnahmen seiner Operninszenierungen zeigt, darunter „Parsifal", „Tannhäuser" sowie „Tristan und Isolde".

Die Ausstellung ist eine kritische Hommage an einen so wichtigen wie umstrittenen Opernmacher der deutschen Nachkriegszeit.

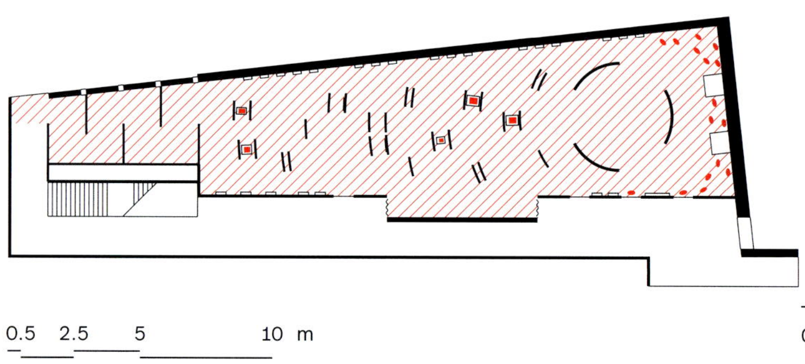

01 Floor plan.

02 Visitors can follow the steps of Wieland Wagner's (left) career by meandering through backdrops depicting his life's companions like Roller (right), Tietjen (centre), and others.

03 The central stage is formed by circular screens showing Wagner's revolutionary staging of "Parsifal," "Tannhäuser," and "Tristan und Isolde" (among others).

04 A selection of the very few historical costumes that survived the times, which were worn in Wieland Wagner's staged operas.

HYUNDAI MOTORSTUDIO GOYANG

Permanent Brand Exhibition, 4,000 sqm, Goyang, South Korea, 2017

The aim of the Hyundai Motorstudio Goyang is to support the desired transformation of the brand perception and to achieve long-term customer loyalty by addressing a younger target group. Hyundai wants to be perceived as a service-oriented brand with a personal touch.

Visitors to the largest centre of automotive culture in South Korea embark on an interactive journey of discovery through the production and development process of a vehicle. The journey begins with the finished car and leads them back via the individual production and development steps to the design concept.

The routing starts and finishes in the "Showcase" zone with the current vehicle range and a projection on a huge media facade that puts the vehicles in context. In the "Plant" section, visitors can actively get to grips with the production of a vehicle as they have the opportunity to control the industrial robots themselves: they experience the cutting and shaping of steel parts, direct welding robots, select the body paintwork, and install vehicle parts like windscreens and seats into a real car. Once an hour, the robots interrupt their work and perform a specially developed, synchronised choreography.

The second exhibition area, "Innovate," is devoted to vehicle development. In five themed rooms, visitors find out more about active and passive safety, aerodynamics, sound design, and energy efficiency. For example, 90 illuminated, reactive airbags give a feeling of safety. They define the narrative space. A spatial film combined with a real test car allows visitors to experience a crash test at first hand while wind tunnel tests in the "Wind" room convey the themes of air resistance and vehicle performance. In the next room, a spectacular "Sound Laboratory," visitors then explore the development of sound design and the huge effect it has on driving experience and product quality. A sophisticated 3-D sound system combines light animations with instrumentation and simulates the dynamic sound

Zielsetzung des Hyundai Motorstudio Goyang ist es, den angestrebten Wandel der Markenwahrnehmung zu unterstützen und eine langfristige Kundenbindung über die Ansprache jüngerer Zielgruppen zu erreichen. Hyundai möchte als serviceorientierte Marke wahrgenommen werden, die persönlich berührt.

Besucher des größten Zentrums automobiler Kultur in Korea begeben sich auf eine interaktive Entdeckungsreise durch den Herstellungs- und Entwicklungsprozess eines Fahrzeugs. Sie beginnt beim fertigen Automobil und führt über die einzelnen Produktions- und Entwicklungsschritte zurück zum Designkonzept.

Start- und Endpunkt ist der Bereich „Showcase" mit der aktuellen Fahrzeugpalette und einer kontextualisierenden Bespielung auf einer raumgreifenden Medienfassade. Im Bereich „Plant" können Besucher die Produktion eines Fahrzeugs aktiv nachvollziehen, indem sie selbst Industrieroboter steuern: Sie erleben das Stanzen und Formen von Stahlteilen, dirigieren Schweißroboter, wählen Karosserielackierungen und bauen Fahrzeugteile wie Frontscheiben und Sitze in ein reales Auto ein. Einmal pro Stunde unterbrechen die Roboter ihre Arbeit und führen gemeinsam eine eigens entwickelte, synchronisierte Choreografie auf.

Der zweite Ausstellungsbereich „Innovate" widmet sich der Fahrzeugentwicklung. In fünf Themenräumen erfahren Besucher mehr über aktive und passive Sicherheit, Aerodynamik, Sound-Design und Energieeffizienz. Beispielsweise vermitteln 90 leuchtende, reaktive Airbags ein Gefühl von Sicherheit. Sie prägen das Raumbild. Über einen Raumfilm, der mit einem realen Versuchsauto kombiniert ist, erleben Besucher hautnah einen Crashtest. Im Raum „Wind" vermitteln Windkanaltests die Themen Luftwiderstand und Fahrzeugperformance. In einem „Sound-Labor" erkunden die Besucher schließlich die Entwicklung und den großen Einfluss, den das Sound-Design auf das Fahrgefühl und die Produktqualität hat. Ein ausgefeiltes

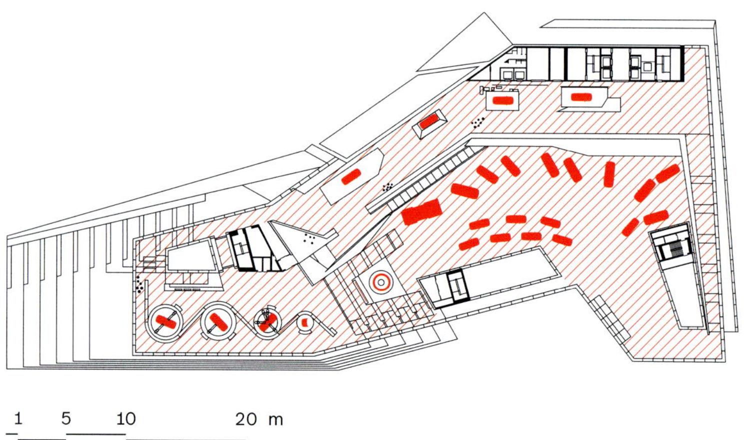

01 Floor plan–entrance level.
02 "Plant"–in this area visitors are able to choreograph four sets of robots which are programmed to run operations like forming, welding, painting, and assembling a real full-size car.

HYUNDAI
WIA-05
HYUNDAI MOTORSTUDIO

03 "Innovate/Safety Room"–90 illuminable, interactive airbags shape the room, which enable visitors to interact with the installation and leave their silhouettes for a moment.

of moving cars. The "Powertrain" room makes the function and processes in a running motor transparent: Five ceiling-high panels display a cross section of an oversized, walk-in engine in which animated light contours show what happens while the car is moving.

Visitors then enter a lift that presents a film to prepare them for the "Design" section. This is the highlight of the journey: an impressively staged, kinetic sculpture that expresses the Hyundai design philosophy, "Creating Design from Movement": 1,411 individually controlled tubes generate dynamically flowing movements and ultimately dovetail in the contour of a Hyundai automobile. In reactive mode, they pick up visitors' movements and translate them into individually visible forms.

With its innovative multimedia and interactive scenography, the visitors' centre is a new kind of hybrid of brand world, automobile exhibition, and service centre, in which tailor-made analogue and digital visitor experiences contribute to a comprehensive and holistic brand experience: corporate scenography for an aspiring brand.

3-D-Klangsystem kombiniert Lichtanimationen mit Instrumentenklängen und simuliert die dynamischen Geräusche fahrender Automobile. Der Raum „Powertrain" ermöglicht es, Funktion und Abläufe in einem laufenden Motor nachzuvollziehen: Fünf raumhohe Scheiben bilden Schnitte durch einen überdimensionalen begehbaren Motor. Animierte Lichtkonturen zeigen die Zusammenhänge und Vorgänge während der Fahrt.

Über einen Aufzug, der die Besucher mit filmischer Bespielung auf den Bereich „Design" einstimmt, erreichen die Besucher den Höhepunkt des Parcours: eine eindrucksvoll inszenierte kinetische Skulptur, welche die Hyundai-Designphilosophie „Creating Design from Movement" zum Ausdruck bringt. 1.411 einzeln gesteuerte Tubes erzeugen dynamisch fließende Bewegungen und führen schließlich zur Kontur eines Hyundai-Automobils. Im reaktiven Modus greifen sie die Bewegungen der Besucher auf und übersetzen diese in individuelle, nachvollziehbare Formen.

Das Besucherzentrum mit seiner innovativen, multimedialen und interaktiven Szenografie ist ein neuartiger Hybrid aus Markenwelt, Automobilausstellung und Service-Center, bei dem maßgeschneiderte analoge und digitale Besuchererlebnisse zu einer umfassenden und ganzheitlichen Markenerfahrung beitragen: Corporate Scenography für eine aufstrebende Marke.

04 “Innovate/Sound Laboratory”–the sounds of driving cars are enhanced by a synchronized light choreography, depicting travels through alleys, forest, or rain. This exhibit is an impressive demonstration of our senses’ being complexly connected–we can see with sound and listen to images.

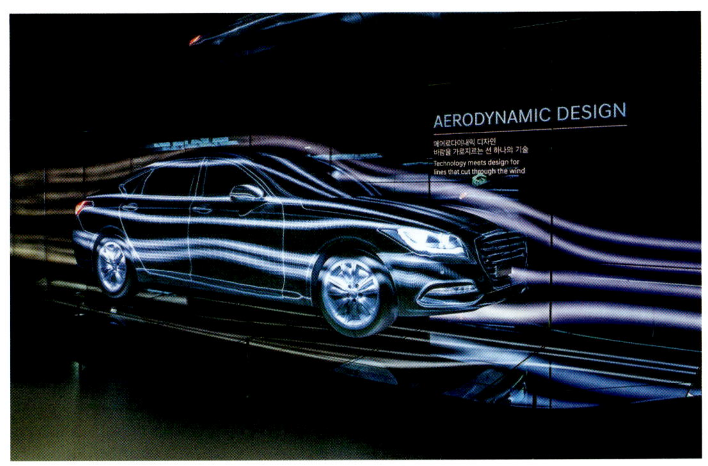

05 “Innovate/Aerodynamic”–animated aerodynamic installations show how the airflow helps to save fuel and how it influences the form-finding during the design process.

06 “Innovate/Powertrain”–this installation of laser-engraved glass panels invites visitors to walk trough a sliced motor while it is “running.”

07 “Creating Design from Movement”–a unique kinetic sculpture of 1,411 pins conveys the design philosophy of the company. ↗ 360

THE MACALLAN VISITOR EXPERIENCE

Permanent Brand Exhibition, 1,800 sqm, Craigellachie, UK, 2018

The Macallan whisky distillery was founded in 1824 as one of the first legal stills in the Scottish Highlands. As the "Rolls Royce among the malts," today The Macallan is one of the world's best-known single malt whiskies.

The visitors' centre greets its guests with an expressive brand wall. It prepares them for the brand and the product. The shelf filled with a vast number of original whisky bottles is set off by light and film projections. The associations with the authentic location and the long years of experience of distilling and perfect maturing of the single malt whiskies become apparent. The "Jewel Box," directly behind the brand wall, serves at the same time as confirmation of the claims: on display here is an incredible archive of Macallan whisky treasures, the oldest from 1841.

This is where tours round the distillery start. Groups of no more than 12 persons embark from here on a journey that impresses both with content and architecture through the spectacular production hall whose hilly grass roof merges seamlessly into the Scottish Highlands of the legendary Speyside. The tour is accompanied by interactive, kinetic pillars, information stations that offer visitors playful access to relevant content along the route. The tour kicks off with Easter Elchie's House, "Spiritual Home" of The Macallan, followed by "Curiously Small Stills," that shows the distilling process through to the "Finest Cut," that demonstrates the birth of the distillate with an impressive kinetic sculpture from the famous glass manufacturer Lalique.

Visitors reach "The Mastery," highlight of the Whisky Experience, after around 200 metres. All the production steps and components that lead to the legendary whisky are staged here as immersive experiences. The impressive spatial installations explain the significance of wood for the maturing in the oak barrel ("The Wood Story"); the magic of the "Blending," the composition of the whisky ("The Whisky Story") with its various colours from amber through to ruby red; and culminate in the longed-for end product, the whisky itself ("The Peerless Spirit"), staged as a dramatic moment: visitors can let a drop of whisky float in mid-air until it pours into the room.

Die Whisky-Destillerie The Macallan wurde 1824 als eine der ersten legalen Brennereien in den schottischen Highlands gegründet. Als „Rolls Royce unter den Malts" zählt The Macallan heute zu den bekanntesten Single Malt Whiskys der Welt.

Mit einer ausdrucksstarken Brand Wall begrüßt das Besucherzentrum seine Gäste. Sie stimmt auf die Marke und auf das Produkt ein. Das über und über mit originalen Whiskyflaschen gefüllte Regal wird mittels Licht und filmischen Projektionen in Szene gesetzt. Die Verbundenheit zum authentischen Ort, die lange Erfahrung in der Destillation und die perfekte Reifung der Single Malt Whiskys kommen hier zum Ausdruck. Die „Jewel Box", direkt hinter der Brand Wall gelegen, dient gleichsam als Bestätigung: Ein unglaublicher Archivschatz an Macallan-Whiskys, der bis in das Jahr 1841 zurückreicht, ist hier ausgestellt.

Touren durch die Destillerie beginnen an diesem Ort. Auf die Gruppen von maximal zwölf Personen wartet ein inhaltlich wie architektonisch eindrucksvoller Parcours durch die spektakuläre Produktionshalle, die sich mit ihrem hügeligen Grasdach wie selbstverständlich in die schottischen Highlands der legendären Speyside einfügt. Er wird begleitet von interaktiven kinetischen „Pillars" – Infostationen, die den Besuchern einen spielerischen Zugang zu den jeweils relevanten Inhalten des Rundgangs bieten. Den Auftakt macht das Easter Elchies House, „Spiritual Home" von Macallan, gefolgt von „Curiously Small Stills", das den Brennvorgang zeigt, bis zu „Finest Cut", das die Geburt des Destillats mit einer eindrucksvollen kinetischen Skulptur aus der legendären Glasmanufaktur Lalique veranschaulicht.

Die Besucher erreichen „The Mastery", den Höhepunkt der Whisky-Experience, nach rund 200 Metern. Hier sind alle Produktionsschritte und Komponenten, die zum legendären Whisky führen, als immersive Erlebnisse in Szene gesetzt. Die beeindruckenden Rauminstallationen erzählen von der Bedeutung des Holzes für die Reifung im Eichenfass („The Wood Story"), vom Zauber des „Blendings", der Komposition des Whiskys („The Whisky Story") mit seinen unterschiedlichen Farben von

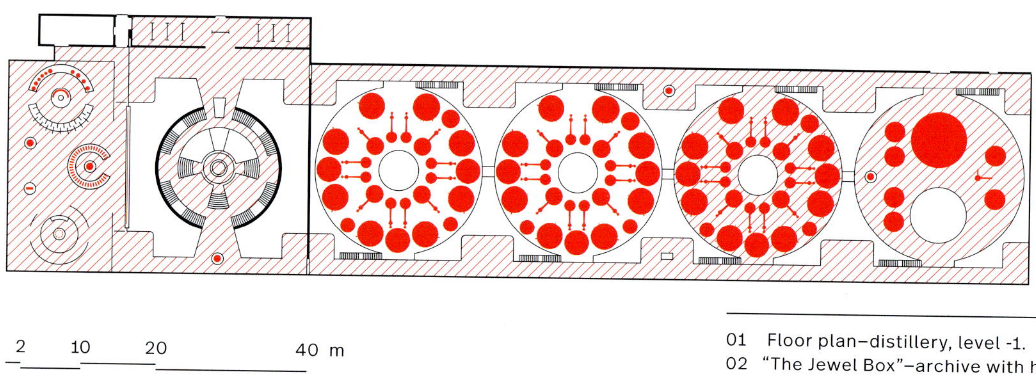

01 Floor plan–distillery, level -1.
02 "The Jewel Box"–archive with hundreds of bottles and other historical exhibits.

03 "The Whisky Story"–a pavilion built from authentic oak wood enclosed by a gallery displaying the full colour spectrum of the Macallan.

At the end of the tour, a light-symphonic event awaits visitors that underlines the authenticity and exclusivity of the place. Like a materialised score, the "Cave Privée" contains 150 original barrels in which the finest whisky slumbers, incorporated in an impressive composition of space, light, and sound. In a fleeting but memorable moment, visitors experience the "Macallan-Spirit."

Visitors can enjoy a tasting session at the bar that is situated directly above the "Cave Privée." The products can be tested here.

The scenography of the visitors' centre combines consistent storytelling with dramatic lighting and innovative media installations. The narrative space becomes the brand, and The Macallan brand becomes a multisensory and entertaining experience that will not be quickly forgotten.

Bernsteingelb bis Rubinrot, und gipfeln im ersehnten Endprodukt, dem Whisky selbst („The Peerless Spirit"), inszeniert als dramatischer Moment: Besucher können einen Tropfen Whisky schweben lassen bis dieser sich in den Raum ergießt.

Am Ende der Tour erwartet den Besucher schließlich ein lichtsymphonisches Ereignis, das die Authentizität und Exklusivität des Orts unterstreicht. Gleich einer materialisierten Partitur sind im „Cave Privée" 150 originale Fässer, in denen edelster Whisky schlummert, in eine eindrucksvolle Komposition aus Raum, Licht und Sound eingebunden. Die Besucher erleben einen nachhaltig flüchtigen Moment, in dem sich die Seele, der „Macallan-Spirit", manifestiert.

Abschließend geht es zum Tasting an die Bar, die direkt oberhalb des „Cave Privée" liegt. Hier können die Produkte verkostet werden.

Die Szenografie des Besucherzentrums verknüpft konsistentes Storytelling mit dramatischer Lichtführung und innovativen Medieninstallationen. So wird das Raumbild zur Marke und die Marke „The Macallan" zum multisensorischen, unterhaltsamen und nachhaltig-eindrücklichen Erlebnis.

04 “The Whisky Story”–following the film, the blending table with the taste-rose of scents completes and opens up to reveal a bottle of the selected blend.

05 “The Whisky Story”–an interactive media table synchronised with an impressive panoramic film showing the making of Macallan Whisky. This tells the entire story starting from the river Spey, the water, the barley, the mash, the distillation and finally the blending, how it all works and which criteria play a role to create an outstanding blend.

06 “Curiously Small Stills” (Pillar)—this scaled interactive model of the stills opens up by turning the handrail and shows the distilling process in progress.

JUNGHANS TERRASSENBAU MUSEUM

Permanent Exhibition, 830 sqm, Schramberg, Germany, 2018

Founded in 1861, Junghans is one of the world's most renowned watchmakers. At the headquarters of the company in Schramberg, in the Black Forest, the striking terrace construction by Philipp Jakob Manz climbs the incline in order to offer every single workplace in the long, narrow rooms ideal daylight conditions. This listed building in which watches and clocks were produced well into the second half of the twentieth century is now used as a museum.

A panorama lift brings visitors to the upper level. This is also the start of the thematic-chronological routing which meanders down through the individual levels.

The prologue in the head building of level nine uses a multisensory experience to get visitors in the spirit for the Black Forest, with the scent of a conifer forest heavy with resin in which arduous lumberjack work went on. This is in stark contrast with the finely designed watches and the delicate movements which farmers worked on in the evenings and in the winter, even before the watchmaking industry secured their livelihoods.

The exhibition shows a faithfully reconstructed workshop, a significant collection of Black Forest clocks, music boxes, and chronometers for sports events as well as the classic wrist watch, including the famous Max Bill collection for which Junghans is known.

The space-shaping design element consists of 40-metre panoramas that are found on all exhibition levels, giving the exhibits a content-generated backdrop. At first, these background pictures show the Black Forest: Visitors find themselves in the middle of the forest and then look at it from a greater distance. A collage of technical details like rollers and pipes replaces the Black Forest theme on level five that is about the technology of the movements, culminating in the treasure chamber on level three. Stainless steel, aluminium and brass stand for utmost precision, technology, and delicate design.

One hundred and fifty years of watchmaking and corporate history: the museum gives an insight and investigates the question why the Black Forest of all places became such an important centre of the German clock industry.

Im Jahr 1861 gegründet, zählt Junghans zu den weltweit bedeutendsten Uhrenherstellern. Am Firmensitz Schramberg im Schwarzwald steigt der markante Terrassenbau von Philipp Jakob Manz in neun Ebenen den Hang hinauf, um in seinen lang gestreckten, schmalen Räumen an jedem Arbeitsplatz optimale Tageslichtverhältnisse zu bieten. Das denkmalgeschützte Gebäude, in dem bis in die zweite Hälfte des 20. Jahrhunderts Uhren produziert wurden, wird nun als Museum genutzt.

Ein Panoramalift bringt die Besucher auf die oberste Ebene. Hier startet der themenchronologische Parcours, der mäandrierend durch die einzelnen Etagen nach unten führt.

Der Prolog im Kopfbau der Ebene 9 stimmt multisensorisch auf den Schwarzwald ein und vermittelt das Erlebnis von dichtem, nach Harz duftendem Nadelwald, in dem grobe Holzarbeit verrichtet wurde. Im Kontrast dazu stehen die feinsinnig gestalteten Uhren und kleinteiligen Uhrwerke, denen sich die Bauern am Abend und im Winter widmeten, noch ehe ihnen die Uhrenindustrie ein Auskommen sicherte.

Die Ausstellung zeigt eine originalgetreu rekonstruierte Werkstatt, eine bedeutende Sammlung an Schwarzwald- und Musikuhren sowie Chronometer für Sportveranstaltungen und die klassischen Armbanduhren, darunter auch die begehrte Kollektion von Max Bill, für die Junghans bekannt ist.

Prägendes Gestaltungselement sind 40 Meter lange Panoramen, welche die Ausstellungsetagen durchziehen und den Exponaten einen contentgenerierten Fond geben. Zunächst zeigen diese Hintergrundbilder den Schwarzwald: Die Besucher befinden sich mitten im Wald und betrachten ihn dann aus größerer Entfernung. Eine Collage aus technischen Details wie Walzen und Flöten ersetzt die Schwarzwaldthematik auf Ebene 5, auf der es um die Technik der Uhrwerke geht, und wandelt sich schließlich zur Schatzkammer auf Ebene 3. Edelstahl, Aluminium und Messing stehen für außerordentliche Präzision, Technik und filigrane Gestaltung.

150 Jahre Uhren- und Unternehmensgeschichte: Das Museum gibt einen Einblick und geht der Frage nach, warum gerade im Schwarzwald ein so bedeutendes Zentrum der deutschen Uhrenindustrie entstand.

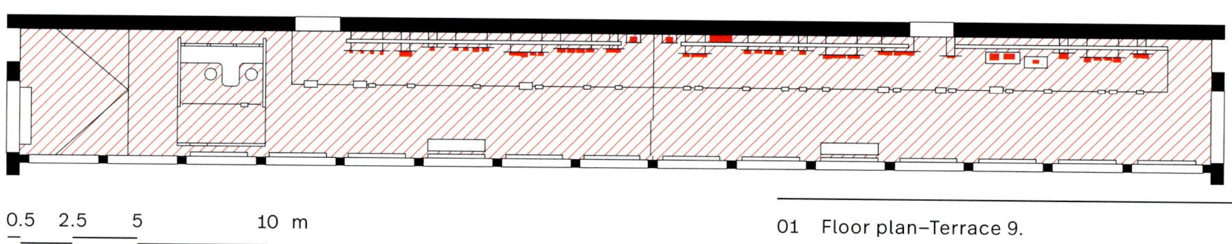

01 Floor plan–Terrace 9.

02 Terrace 5 displays the music clocks–most of them still functioning–which can be seen in action during guided tours.

03 On Terrace 8 the Black Forest cuckoo clocks–most of them in motion–form an immersive experience, enhanced by sounds from and a panorama of the forest.

04 The striking terrace construction by Philipp Jakob Manz climbs the incline in order to offer every single workplace in the long, narrow rooms ideal daylight conditions.

ITHRA–KING ABDULAZIZ CENTER FOR WORLD CULTURE

Architecture: Snøhetta, 100,000 sqm, Dhahran, Saudi Arabia, 2018

The national oil firm Saudi Aramco has set itself the task of making culture and knowledge accessible to the people of all social classes of the Kingdom of Saudi Arabia. The result, based on the plans of the Norwegian architects Snøhetta, is the country's first cultural centre, built in the middle of the desert.

The 70,000-square-metre centre houses numerous cultural offerings, including several museum galleries, a library, a creative laboratory, a cinema, an auditorium, and a theatre. All these areas are connected by a virtual knowledge stream that takes on a tangible form in informative themed stations, the "IT Exhibits."

Die nationale Ölfirma Saudi Aramco hat es sich zur Aufgabe gemacht, Kultur und Wissen im Königreich Saudi-Arabien für Menschen aller Bevölkerungsschichten zugänglich zu machen. Dafür ist inmitten der Wüste nach den Plänen des norwegischen Architekturbüros Snøhetta das erste Kulturzentrum des Landes entstanden.

Es beherbergt auf 70.000 Quadratmetern zahlreiche kulturelle Angebote, darunter mehrere Museumsgalerien, eine Bibliothek, ein Kreativlabor, ein Kino, ein Auditorium und ein Theater. Alle diese Bereiche sind mit einem virtuellen „Knowledge Stream" verbunden, der sich an informativen Erlebnisstationen konkretisiert – den sogenannten „IT Exhibits".

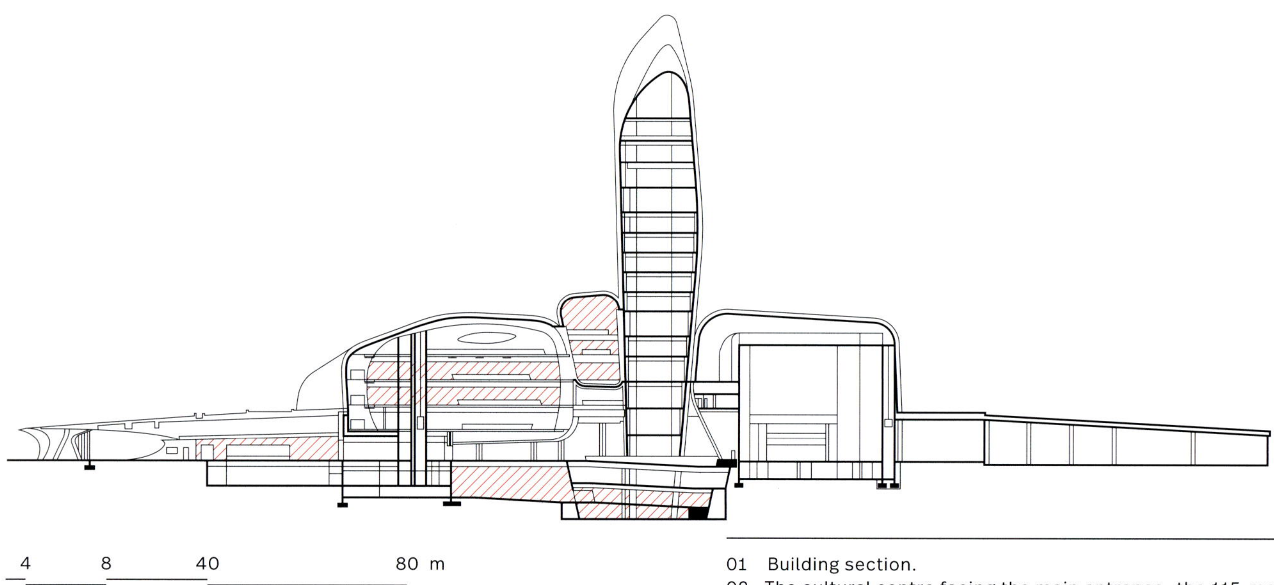

01 Building section.
02 The cultural centre facing the main entrance–the 115-metre-tall building functions like a landmark in the flat desert region.

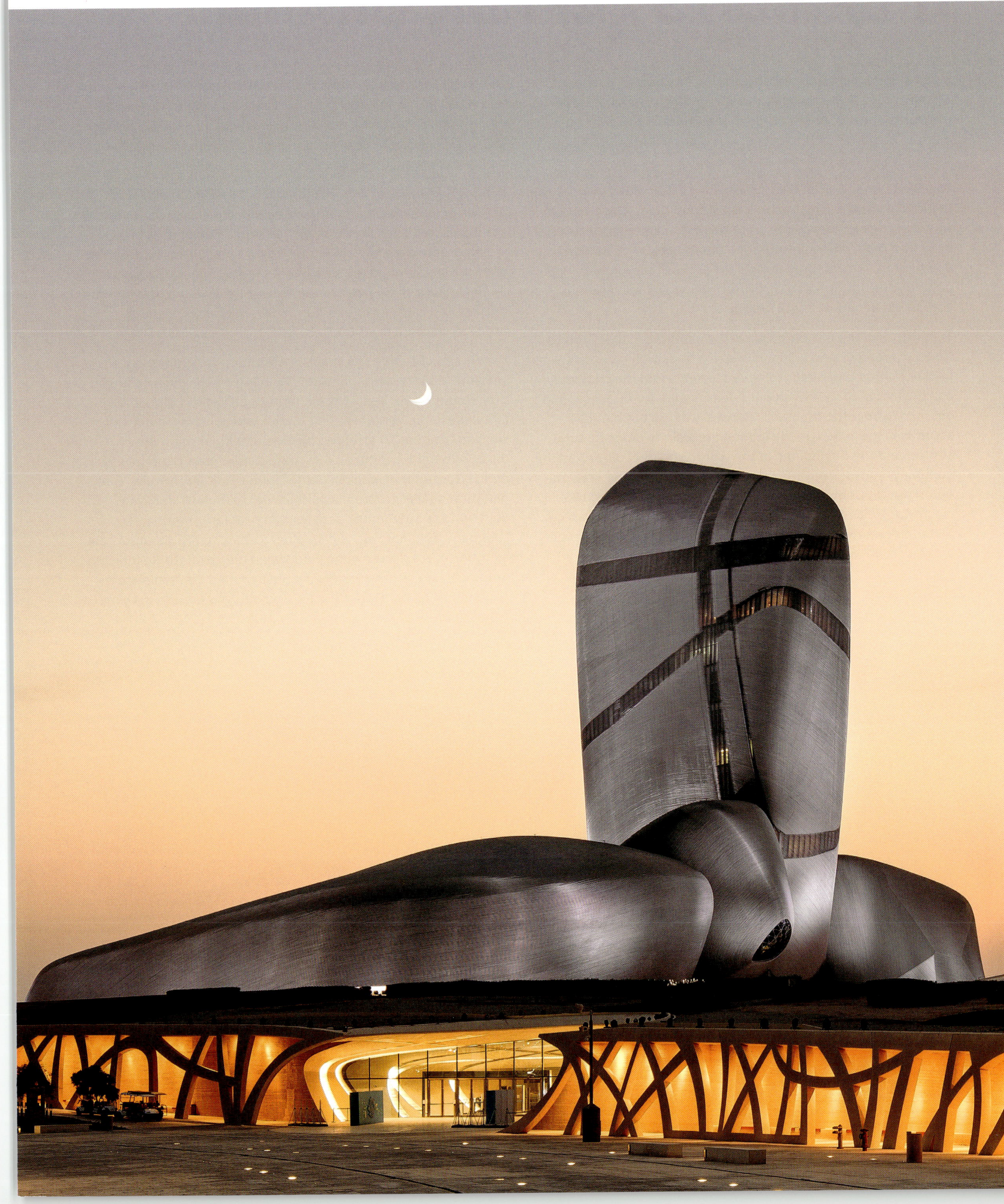

ITHRA–
IT EXHIBITS / ARAMCORAMA

Media Installations, 1,600 sqm / Permanent Exhibition, 540 sqm, Dhahran, Saudi-Arabia, 2018

Much like the blood circulating around our bodies, a stream of knowledge flows through the whole King Abdulaziz Center for World Culture, connecting all the areas of the cultural centre. The "IT Exhibits" reveal knowledge and at the same time collect information from visitors.

The "Welcome Wall" in the entrance area welcomes visitors as the virtual knowledge stream flows around them. The concrete wall, which conceals a huge, reactive video installation, is also used as a platform for information about current exhibitions and events. In real time, the visitor is thus immersed in the cultural world sponsored by the oil company Saudi Aramco, here in the desert of Saudi Arabia.

The history of the oil company can be explored in the "Archive Gallery: Aramcorama." Consisting of a huge wall equipped with backlit photos that offer preserved insights into the past and can be activated by movement. Visitors can, for instance, find out more about the dramatic discovery of the bubbling oil sources in the 1930s, in the immediate vicinity of the cultural centre, and the beginnings of the world's biggest oil-producing company, known from 1944 to 1988 under the name Arabian-American Oil Company. Like a timeline, the integrated, 100-metre-long video wall presents the whole history of Aramco. All the information that visitors can obtain at numerous touch screens is linked together in the knowledge stream.

Gleich einem zirkulierendem Blutkreislauf fließt ein Wissensstrom durch das gesamte King Abdulaziz Center for World Culture. Er verbindet alle Bereiche des Kulturzentrums. IT Exhibits bringen das Wissen zum Vorschein und nehmen zugleich Informationen der Besucher auf.

Zur Begrüßung lässt die „Welcome Wall" im Eingangsbereich den virtuellen Wissensstrom um die Besucher fließen. Hinter der Betonwand verbirgt sich ein riesiger, reaktiv bespielter Videoscreen, der auch als Plattform für tagesaktuelle Informationen wie Ausstellungen und Events genutzt wird. So taucht der Besucher in Realzeit in die kulturelle Welt ein, die hier in der Wüste Saudi-Arabiens durch den Ölkonzern Saudi Aramco ermöglicht wurde.

Die Geschichte des Ölkonzerns erkunden Besucher in der „Archive Gallery: Aramcorama". Sie besteht aus einer raumbildprägenden Wand, bestückt mit hinterleuchteten Fotos, die Einblicke in die Vergangenheit bieten und dynamisch aktiviert werden können. So erfahren die Besucher hier mehr über die abenteuerliche Entdeckung der sprudelnden Ölquellen in den 1930er-Jahren, ganz in der Nähe des Kulturzentrums, und die Anfänge der größten Erdölfördergesellschaft der Welt, die 1944 bis 1988 unter dem Namen Arabian-American Oil Company bekannt war. Gleich einer Zeitleiste repräsentiert die integrierte, 100 Meter lange Videowand die gesamte Geschichte Aramcos. Alle Informationen, die Besucher an den zahlreichen Touchscreens abrufen, sind im „Knowledge-Stream" miteinander verknüpft.

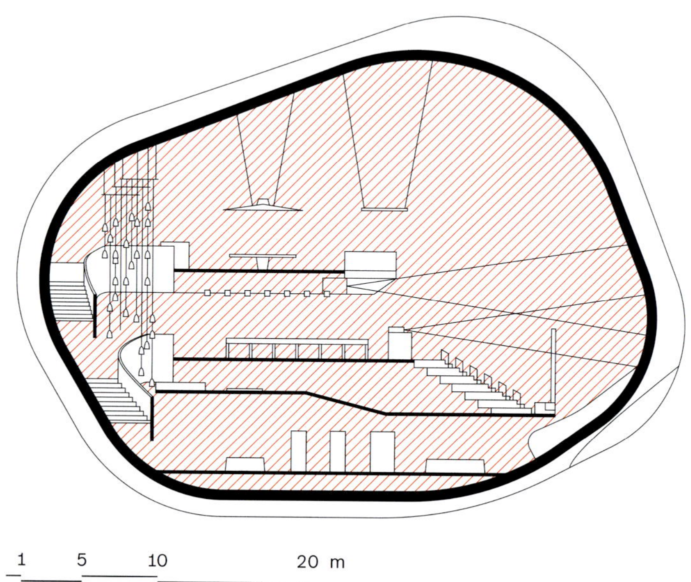

03 Section–"Keystone," the creative laboratory.
04 A reactive "Knowledge Stream" welcomes the visitors into the foyer and accompanies them through the entire centre, navigating them to various exhibitions, events or cultural activities.

أهلا بكم في إثراء
Welcome to Ithra

05 "Archive Gallery: Aramcorama"–"Knowledge Stream" fueling a 100-metre-long video wall showing the chronology of Aramco's heritage.

The exterior of the cultural centre is shaped architecturally by a central structure, flanked by the surrounding buildings. This "Keystone," shaped like a pebble, is the central thought room that invites visitors to enter into an interdisciplinary exchange of knowledge, supported by numerous high-tech features. Knowledge content can, for example, be saved in objects that pass on their information as soon as they are placed on the large meeting table. A multimedia knowledge network begins to develop.

The "Kids' Tables" in the library work in a similar way and thus introduce young visitors to the new, connected knowledge. Children place the book they have selected on a media table that then provides them with more information, such as a summary of the content, references to similar books and book topics or shows excerpts from the film version of the book. Children can also feed in their own content or leave drawings and comments that can in turn be retrieved at a later point in time.

The "IT Exhibits" offer unique possibilities to obtain information, to interact, and to learn. They correspond with the trend to convey knowledge and experiences digitally. Behind all this is the knowledge stream as a holistic IT structure and the synaptic digital network of an XL-sized building.

Nach außen ist das Kulturzentrum architektonisch geprägt durch einen zentralen Baukörper, gestützt von den umgebenden Bauteilen. Dieser wie ein Kieselstein geformte „Keystone", ist der zentrale Denkraum, der, ausgestattet mit allen technischen Raffinessen, zum interdisziplinären Wissensaustausch einlädt. Wissensinhalte lassen sich beispielsweise in Objekten speichern, die ihre Informationen weitergeben, sobald sie auf den großen Besprechungstisch gestellt werden. Ein multimediales Wissensnetzwerk entfaltet sich.

Auch die „Kids Tables" in der Bibliothek funktionieren ähnlich und führen so die jungen Besucher an das neue, vernetzte Wissen heran. Hier legen Kinder ihr ausgewähltes Buch auf einen Medientisch, der ihnen weiterführende Informationen liefert, wie zum Beispiel eine inhaltliche Zusammenfassung, einen Verweis auf vergleichbare Bücher und Buchthemen oder auch Ausschnitte aus Verfilmungen. Zudem können die Kinder ihre eigenen Inhalte einspeisen, Zeichnungen und Kommentare hinterlegen, die wiederum später abrufbar sind.

Die IT Exhibits bieten einzigartige Informations-, Interaktions- und Lernmöglichkeiten. Sie entsprechen der zunehmend digitalen Wissens- und Erlebnisvermittlung, hinter welcher der Wissensstrom als holistische IT-Struktur und zugleich synaptisch digitales Netzwerk eines XL-Size-Gebäudes steht.

06 "Archive Gallery: Aramcorama"–A large graphic wall shows historical maps of Arabia and Saudi Aramco's global organization while showcases in the foreground feature original instruments used in the geological expedition that led to the discovery of the first oil field.

07 "Keystone" Do Tank–library of smart and sustainable materials.

08 "Keystone" Think Tank–the discussion table enables new forms of collaboration and education.

ITHRA—ARABIAN JOURNEYS

Permanent Exhibition, 1,300 sqm, Dhahran, Saudi Arabia, 2018

In its permanent exhibition entitled "Arabian Journeys," the Rihlaat Gallery in the King Abdulaziz Center for World Culture conveys the natural history of Saudi Arabia and adaptation strategies of the flora, fauna, and people that live there. Visitors travel through the diverse landscapes of the Kingdom and also through the past, present, and future of the country.

A panoramic strip winds its way through the entire exhibition and, starting from a central "Connection Zone," creates five themed rooms: "Island Arabia," "Desert Trek," "Mountain Crossing," "Coastal Voyage," and "Into the Future." The amorphous spatial design is incorporated into the existing architecture. For each of the individual themes, impressively staged narrative spaces are generated from the respective landscapes, transporting visitors to the various regions of Saudi Arabia. Each area has its own colour scheme, a central media table, and hands-on stations.

Two virtual guides, a young and an old man, provide access to the themes and the objects on display. In each case, 30 to 50 exhibits have been integrated into the narrative space. Key objects lead visitors from the "Connection Zone" to the themed spaces.

The key object in "Island Arabia" is a mosasaur, an extinct reptile that invites visitors to take a journey back through 500 million years, conveying the geological development of Arabia in just a few minutes. In the themed area "Desert Trek," an Arabian horse whisks the visitor off to the Bedouin world: the tough habitat with its extreme climatic conditions requires special housing and means of transport. In the "Mountain Crossing" section, visitors follow a falcon and enjoy a bird's-eye perspective of the varied mountainous regions of Saudi Arabia. The edges and corners of polygonal display cabinets form the various altitudinal ranges of the mountains.

Die Rihlaat Gallery im King Abdulaziz Center for World Culture vermittelt mit der Dauerausstellung „Arabian Journeys" die Naturgeschichte Saudi-Arabiens und die Anpassungsstrategien der dort lebenden Flora, Fauna und Menschen. Die Besucher reisen durch die vielfältigen Landschaftsräume des Königreichs sowie durch Vergangenheit, Gegenwart und Zukunft des Landes.

Ein Panoramaband zieht sich durch die gesamte Ausstellung und bildet, ausgehend von einer zentralen „Connection Zone", fünf Themenräume aus: „Island Arabia", „Desert Trek", „Mountain Crossing", „Coastal Voyage" und „Into the Future". Die amorphe Raumgebung bettet sich in die bestehende Architektur ein. Entsprechend den einzelnen Themen sind eindrucksvoll inszenierte Raumbilder aus den jeweiligen Landschaftsformationen generiert, welche die Besucher in die verschiedenen Regionen Saudi-Arabiens entführen. Jeder Bereich hat seine eigene Farbgebung, einen zentralen Medientisch und Hands-on-Stationen.

Zwei virtuelle Guides, ein junger und ein alter Mann auf einem Screen, eröffnen einen Zugang zu den Themen und den ausgestellten Objekten. Je 30 bis 50 Exponate sind im Raumbild integriert. Key-Objects leiten die Besucher aus der „Connection Zone" in die Themenräume.

Für „Island Arabia" ist das Schlüsselobjekt ein Mosasaurier, ein ausgestorbenes Meeresreptil, das die Besucher auf ein Reiseerlebnis durch 500 Millionen Jahre einlädt und in nur wenigen Minuten die geologische Entwicklung Arabiens vermittelt. Im Themenbereich „Desert Trek" entführt ein arabisches Pferd in die Welt der Beduinen: Der entbehrungsreiche Lebensraum mit seinen extremen klimatischen Bedingungen fordert spezielle Behausungen und Fortbewegungsmittel. Im Bereich „Mountain Crossing" folgen die Besucher einem Falken und erkunden aus seiner Perspektive die abwechslungsreiche Bergregion Saudi-Arabiens. Polygonale Vitrinen bilden mit ihren Ecken und Kanten die unterschiedlichen Höhenzonen des Gebirges nach.

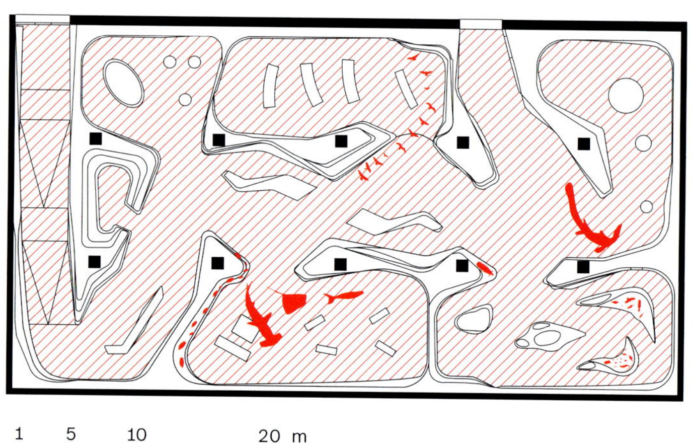

09 Floor plan.
10 The connection zone links five thematic areas—"Island Arabia," "Desert Trek," "Mountain Crossing," "Coastal Voyage" and "Into the Future."

People and navigation
Mountain Crossing

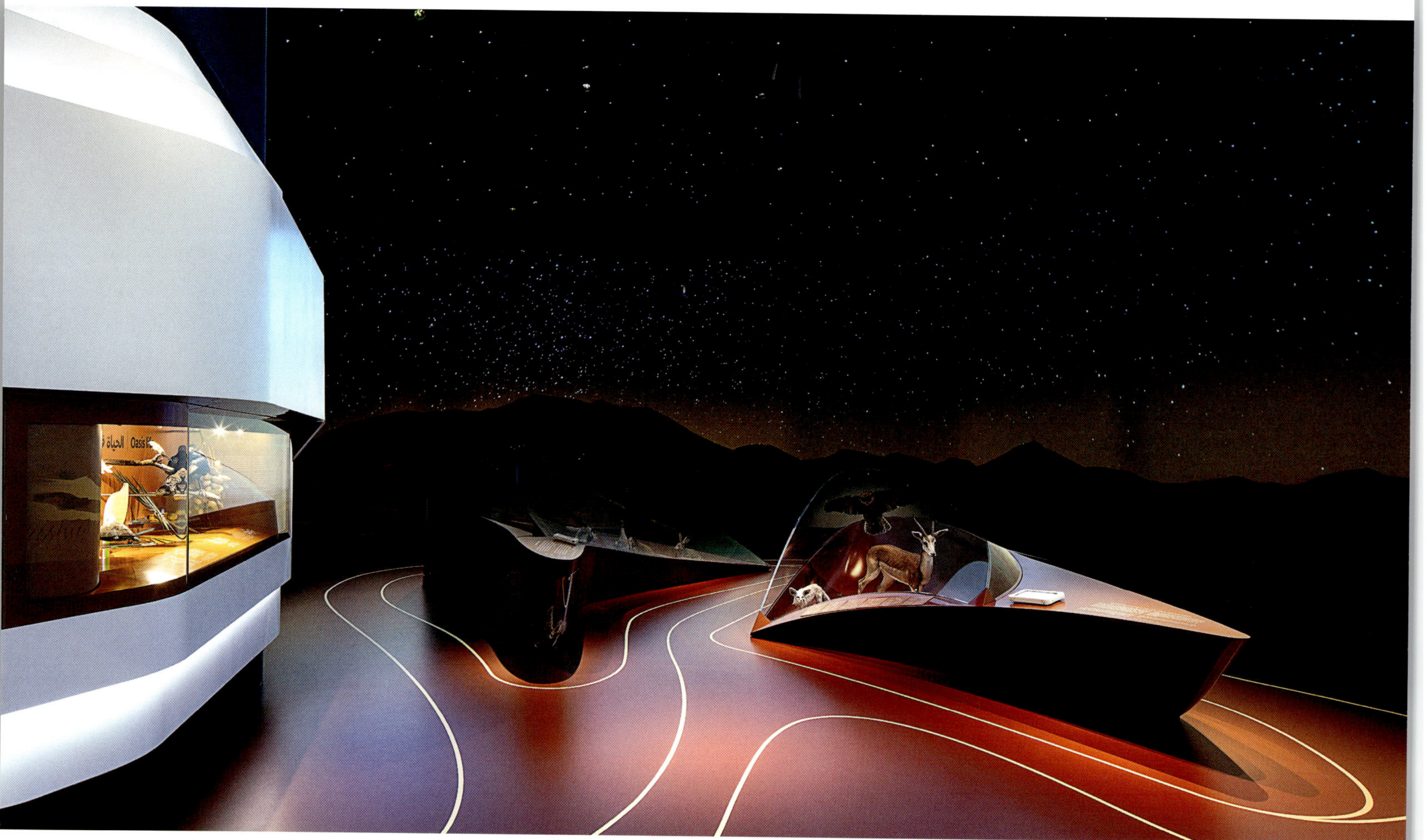

11 “Desert Trek.” Panoramic film projections on backdrop create an immersive feeling and atmosphere of a day and night cycle in the desert.

In the “Coastal Voyage” section, dhows, the typical sailing ships of the Arabian Sea, take visitors to the coastal region of Saudi Arabia that is dominated by fishing.

Finally, in the themed room “Into the Future,” visitors gather round the central media table. In a game with the guides, together they then venture a look into the future of the country. For example, they can fish rubbish out of the sea, applying themselves in the process to global challenges such as environmental protection and conserving resources.

While the impressive multimedia themed areas offer dynamic, multisensory impressions, the “Connection Zone” at the heart of the exhibition offers visitors a place to rest for a while, to reflect and to return to. The result is a varied spatial choreography and an unexpectedly immersive deep dive into the natural habitats of Saudi Arabia.

Bei „Coastal Voyage“ nehmen Dhaus, die typischen Segelschiffe des Arabischen Meeres, die Besucher mit zur Küstenregion Saudi-Arabiens, die von der Fischerei geprägt ist.

Im Themenraum „Into the Future“ versammeln sich die Besucher schließlich um den zentralen Medientisch, um in einem Spiel mit den Guides einen gemeinsamen Blick in die Zukunft des Landes zu werfen. Beispielsweise können sie Müll aus dem Meer fischen und sich so mit den globalen Herausforderungen wie etwa Umweltschutz und Ressourcenschonung auseinandersetzen.

Die eindrucksvoll multimedial inszenierten Themenbereiche bieten dynamische, multisensorische Eindrücke, während andererseits die „Connection Zone“ im Zentrum der Ausstellung ein Ort zum Verweilen, Reflektieren und Wiederkehren ist. Das sorgt für eine abwechslungsreiche Raumchoreografie und ein unerwartet immersives Eintauchen in die Naturräume Saudi-Arabiens.

12 "Mountain Crossing." A helicopter flight over the mountains filmed from a hawk's-eye perspective focuses on the rich natural life in the Dschabal Sauda region, an almost unknown region, up to 3,000 metres high.

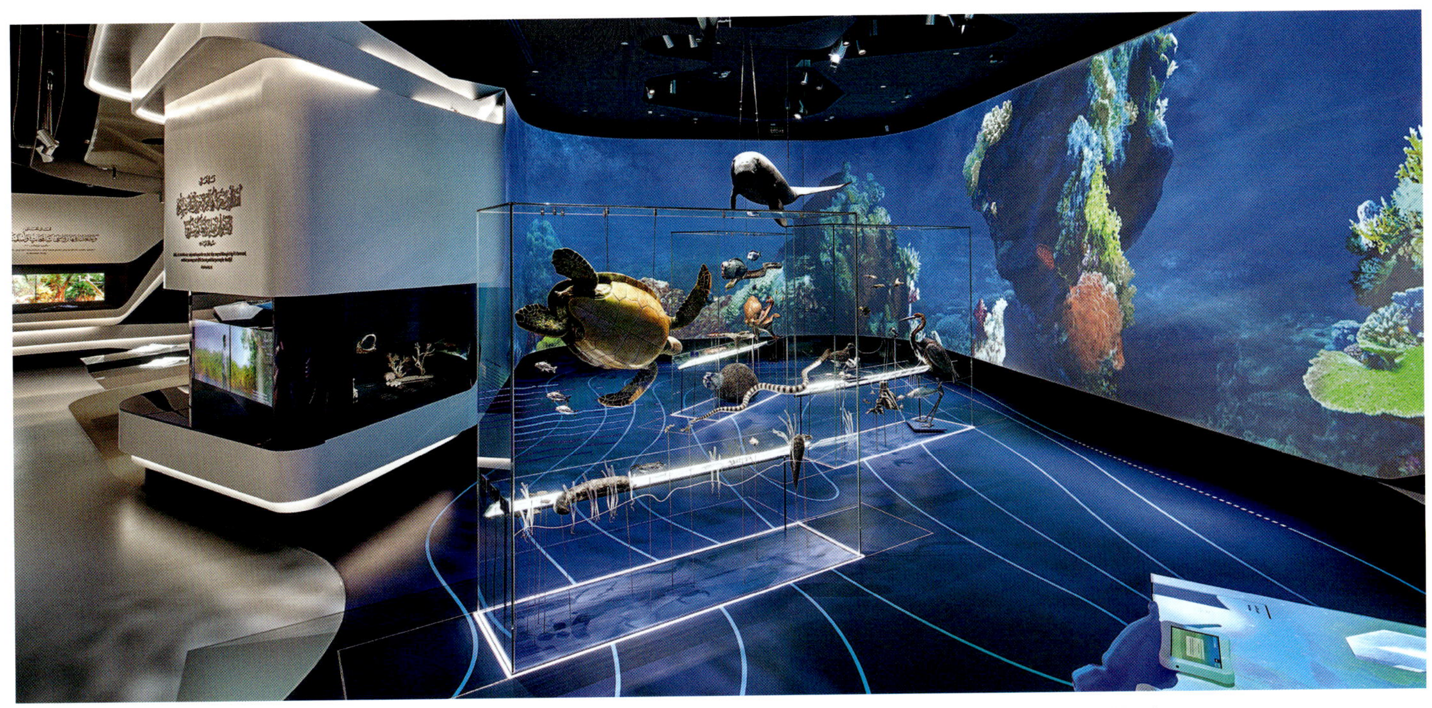

13 "Coastal Voyage" filmed from a submarine. Spectacular footage from the almost untouched underwater life of the Gulf Region acts as a dynamic backdrop for the exhibition space.

WAGENHALLEN

Refurbishment and a New Building with Studios, 14,000 sqm, Stuttgart, Germany, in progress

The former engine sheds, erected at the end of the nineteenth century and converted several times, were occupied by artists in 2003 and from then on developed into a lively hub for concerts and art events. After the renovation, the Wagenhallen will remain an attractive venue for Stuttgart's art and cultural community and the former users will move back in.

The historical building consists of four adjacent pitched roof halls. They were used as shelter and repair garages for locomotives and buses. Indeed, this original use provided the inspiration for the design idea and spatial conception. After an intensive analysis of the history of the building, the original design of the Wagenhallen was peeled out of the existing ensemble, the original substance carefully restored, and historical traces exposed. The living surfaces are retained; various time layers become visible and contrast with the additions to the building required by the new usages.

The building is now accessible via two main entrances at the side: on the western-facing side is the entrance for the event area that can accommodate up to 2,100 visitors. The main entrance for the Wagenhallen Art Association with its artists' studios is on the other side. A new, inviting urban square will also be established here. The square will be framed by the northern wing of the hall, home to a tango school, which has been raised to its original height. On the other sides are residential buildings from the nineteenth century and a new, two-storey building with studios. This new building picks up the new alignment of the Wagenhallen and respectfully moves away from the historical substance.

Die ehemalige Lokomotiv-Remise, Ende des 19. Jahrhunderts errichtet und mehrfach umgebaut, wurde im Jahr 2003 von Künstlern besetzt und entwickelte sich von da an zu einem lebendigen Hub für Konzerte und Kunstevents. Auch nach ihrer Sanierung sollen die Wagenhallen als attraktiver Ort der Stuttgarter Kunst- und Kulturszene erhalten bleiben und die bisherigen Nutzer wieder einziehen.

Das historische Gebäude besteht aus vier hintereinanderliegenden Satteldachhallen. Sie dienten Lokomotiven und Bussen als Unterstand und zu deren Wartung. Gestaltungsidee und Raumkonzeption sind aus der ursprünglichen Nutzung abgeleitet. Nach einer intensiven Analyse der Bauhistorie wurde die originäre Gestalt der Wagenhallen aus dem bestehenden Ensemble herausgeschält, die Originalsubstanz behutsam restauriert und historische Spuren freigelegt. Die lebendigen Oberflächen bleiben erhalten, verschiedene Zeitschichten werden ablesbar und kontrastieren mit notwendigen baulichen Ergänzungen, die sich aus neuen Nutzungen ergeben.

Das Gebäude erschließt sich nun über zwei seitliche Haupteingänge: An der westlichen Stirnseite liegt der Eingang zum Veranstaltungsbereich, der bis zu 2.100 Besucher fassen kann. Auf der gegenüberliegenden Seite befindet sich als Pendant der Haupteingang zum Kunstverein Wagenhalle mit seinen Künstlerateliers. Hier entsteht ein neuer, einladender urbaner Platz. Er wird umrahmt vom nördlichen Hallenflügel, der auf seine ursprüngliche Höhe aufgestockt wurde und eine Tangoschule beherbergt, von Wohngebäuden aus dem 19. Jahrhundert und einem zweigeschossigen Neubau mit Ateliers. Dieses neue Gebäude greift die Ausrichtung der Wagenhallen auf und rückt respektvoll vom historischen Bestand ab.

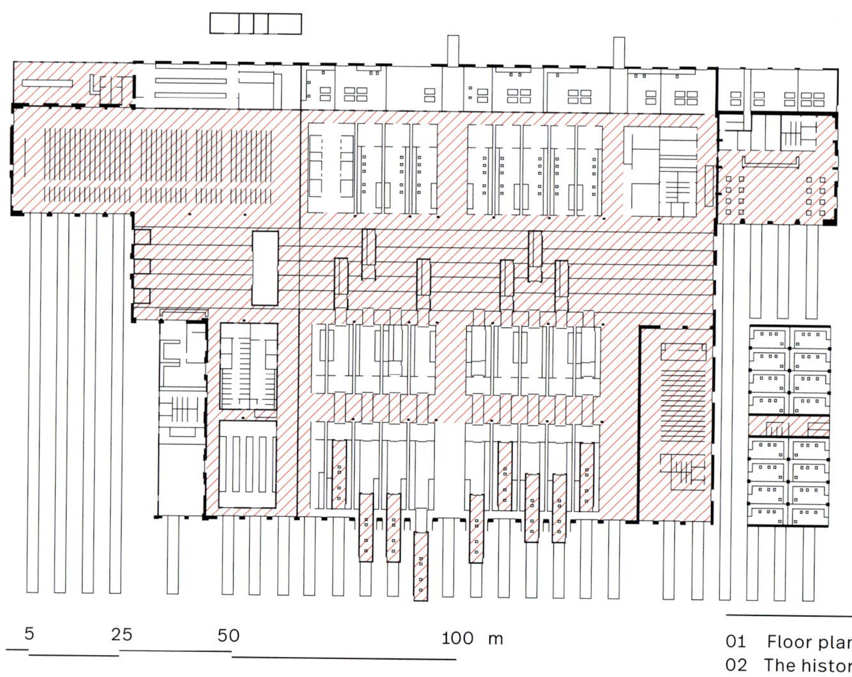

01 Floor plan.
02 The historical building seen from inside before renovation in 2017.

03 The walls of the Wagenhallen have been gently and cautiously refurbished. The grey walls indicate the reconstructed parts of the building.

Inside the Wagenhallen it is planned to install studios for artists in the form of cubes. This retains the original spatial impression of the generously dimensioned hall of up to ten metres in height, dominated by steel supports and rhythmically placed reconstructed skylights.

Reminiscent of the former engine sheds and the locomotives they housed, rail sections can be reactivated. Then studio cubes–for instance at events or for working outdoors–can be pushed outside. This makes both the former and the current usage visible in the outer space and allows those who visit to experience the design and function of the locomotive shed in its original form as a dynamic and lively building.

Im Inneren der Wagenhallen sind Atelierräume in Gestalt von eingestellten Kuben vorgesehen. Dadurch bleibt der authentische Raumeindruck der bis zu zehn Meter hohen, großzügigen Halle erhalten, der geprägt ist von Stahlstützen und rhythmisierenden rekonstruierten Oberlichtern.

Als Reminiszenz an den ehemaligen Lokschuppen und dessen Lokomotiven können Schienenstränge reaktiviert werden, um die Atelierkuben – etwa zu Veranstaltungen oder zum Arbeiten im Freien – nach außen zu schieben. Somit werden sowohl die ehemalige als auch die heutige Nutzung bereits im Außenraum sichtbar und die Lokomotiv-Remise gestalterisch und funktional in ihrer ursprünglichen Form als dynamisches und lebendiges Gebäude erneut erfahrbar.

04 The new highly flexible event area for 2,100 people will host various concerts and parties.

05 The cornice provides evidence of the ceiling of the garage formerly attached here.

06 The Wagenhallen event area with public plaza and future beer garden. ↗ 386

GEM–GRAND EGYPTIAN MUSEUM

Architecture: heneghan peng architects, 100,000 sqm, Giza, Egypt, 2018

The new, worldwide largest museum of Egyptian art and culture on a total area of 90,000 square metres is located near the pyramids of Giza. The building is the work of heneghan peng architects.

The designated exhibition space covers 40,000 square metres and houses more than 50,000 objects. It comprises the areas "Atrium" and "Grand Stairs," the "Tutankhamun Gallery," the children's museum, and the "Dynasty Galleries."

One of the central challenges was to design a visitor experience that does justice to the 15,000 visitors expected daily. Another was to present relatively small objects, tell complex stories in rooms with huge dimensions and extremely high ceilings, and last but not least to set the scene for one of the most valuable exhibits in the world–the Tutankhamun mask–in both a respectful and impressive way.

Das neue, weltweit größte Museum ägyptischer Kunst und Kultur mit einer Gesamtfläche von 90.000 Quadratmetern liegt unweit der Pyramiden von Gizeh. Geplant haben es heneghan peng architects.

Die designierte Ausstellungsfläche misst 40.000 Quadratmeter und beherbergt über 50.000 Objekte. Sie umfasst die Bereiche „Atrium" und „Grand Stairs", die „Tutankhamun Gallery", das Kindermuseum sowie die „Dynasty Galleries".

Zu den zentralen Herausforderungen zählt, die erwartete tägliche Besucherzahl von über 15.000 Menschen und die daraus abzuleitende Besucherführung zu konzipieren sowie in den Räumen mit riesigen Dimensionen und extremer Höhe vergleichsweise kleinformatige Objekte auszustellen. Zugleich gilt es, komplexe Geschichten zu erzählen, und nicht zuletzt ist eines der wertvollsten Exponate der Welt - die Tutanchamun-Maske - respektvoll und gleichzeitig beeindruckend in Szene zu setzen.

01 Bird's-eye view of the entire GEM construction site.
Photo: The Engineering Authority of the Armed Forces at the Grand Egyptian Museum.

02 The Statue of King Ramses II at its permanent display inside of the Atrium.

GEM—TUTANKHAMUN GALLERY

Permanent Exhibition, 7,500 sqm, Giza, Egypt, in progress

For the first time, the sensational grave treasure of Tutankhamun, whose untouched tomb was discovered by the Egyptologist Howard Carter in 1922, is on display in its entirety: a total of 5,600 objects which are divided into five themed areas: "Identity," "Funeral," "Rebirth," "Lifestyle," and "Discovery."

The routing begins with the theme "Identity," with Tutankhamun's life and the question who the young king was and why he died so young.

The "Funeral" theme shows how Tutankhamun was mummified and wrapped in 16 layers of material. Ritual objects and jewellery are arranged just as they were found on the corpse. The highlight is his golden mask that is displayed in a separate room. This emerges from the "Path of the Sun"–one of the two design elements that are found throughout the exhibition: a shiny gold ceiling of brass and bronze threads twinkling thanks to the dynamic light projections. On the floor is the counterpart, the "Flow of Life": a seven-metre-wide strip of blackened steel, the stage on which Tut's short life was played and on which exhibits have been placed accordingly. At turning points in the life of Tutankhamun, for example when he converted to monotheism it evolves into a wall.

From the "Funeral," the routing continues in one of the most poetic areas: "Rebirth," which is dedicated to the belief in the afterlife. The burial chamber is reconstructed with all the ritual objects in their original positions, like eleven paddles, four magical bricks or several wine amphoras.

In the fourth theme "Lifestyle," hunting scenes, weapons, and chariots are presented. In the palace, intimated by white-golden and shimmering gauze, the visitor finds tunics, wigs, 30 pairs of shoes, and 300 pairs of underpants. Musical instruments and board games have been provided to pass the time. The deceased should want for nothing in the hereafter.

The last area, entitled "Discovery," shows the search for and discovery of the tomb in the Valley of Kings. Staged as a scale-one contour model onto which media can be projected, the burial complex traces the discovery by Carter and Lord Carnarvon.

Erstmalig wird der sensationelle Grabschatz von Tutanchamun, dessen unberaubtes Grab vom Ägyptologen Howard Carter 1922 entdeckt wurde, vollständig gezeigt: insgesamt 5.600 Objekte, die in fünf Themenbereiche unterteilt sind: „Identity", „Funeral", „Rebirth", „Lifestyle" und „Discovery".

Der Parcours beginnt mit dem Thema „Identity", mit Tutanchamuns Leben und der Frage, wer der junge König war und woran er so früh verstarb.

Im Anschluss zeigt der Bereich „Funeral", wie Tutanchamun mumifiziert und in 16 Stofflagen eingewickelt wurde. Ritualobjekte und Schmuck sind so arrangiert, wie sie am Körper gefunden wurden. Den Höhepunkt bildet die goldene Maske, der ein eigener Raum gewidmet ist. Dieser formt sich aus dem „Path of the Sun" – einem der beiden gestalterischen Elemente, welche die ganze Ausstellung durchziehen: ein golden schimmernder Plafond aus Messing- und Bronzefäden. Er symbolisiert den Weg der Sonne und funkelt dank einer dynamischen Lichtbespielung. Auf dem Boden befindet sich als Pendant dazu, der „Flow of Life", ein sieben Meter breites Band aus geschwärztem Stahl. Es ist die Bühne, auf der sich das kurze Leben des Tut abspielte und auf dem entsprechend die Exponate platziert sind. Bei Einschnitten im Leben Tutanchamuns formt es sich zu einer Wand, etwa als er seinen Glauben zum Monotheismus wechselte.

Vom „Funeral" geht es weiter zu einem der poetischsten Bereiche, dem „Rebirth", der sich dem Jenseitsglauben widmet. Die Grabkammer ist mit allen rituellen Objekten an ihren Originalpositionen rekonstruiert, darunter elf Paddel, vier magische Ziegel oder auch mehrere Weinamphoren.

Beim vierten Thema, „Lifestyle", werden Jagdszenen, Waffen und Streitwagen präsentiert. Im Palast, angedeutet durch weißgoldene und durchscheinende Gaze, trifft der Besucher auf Tuniken, Perücken, 30 Paar Schuhe und 300 Unterhosen. Musikinstrumente und Brettspiele sind dem Zeitvertreib gewidmet. Dem Verstorbenen sollte es im Jenseits an nichts fehlen.

Der Bereich „Discovery" thematisiert schließlich die Suche und Entdeckung des Grabs im Tal der Könige. Die Grabanlage, inszeniert als medial bespieltes Konturenmodell in Originalgröße, zeichnet die Entdeckung durch Howard Carter und Lord Carnarvon als räumliches Erlebnis nach.

03 "The Mask Chamber" is the future home of the golden Tutankhamun Mask.

04 The “Path of the Sun” accompanies the golden coffins of King Tutankhamun.

05 The "Identity" area provides several installations talking about the young king and his family members.

The routing can be followed in two directions and tells the story of Tutankhamun from two different angles.

On one route, the visitor experiences the life and death of Tutankhamun, following him into the afterlife. He meets the young king, experiences his death, is witness to his mummification and burial, then his rebirth and his beliefs. He explores Tutankhamun's life after death and ends up at his grave.

The other way round the exhibition, the adventure of the discovering the tomb is narrated. After finding the grave, the visitor enters the antechamber, analyses the treasures like an archaeologist, unwinds the royal mummy, layer by layer, getting nearer and nearer to Tutankhamun, finally finding out who the young king was.

The complete and fantastic journey tracing the life and death of the legendary god king is tangible for the first time.

Der Parcours kann in zwei Richtungen begangen werden und erzählt die Geschichte Tutanchamuns dabei jeweils aus einer anderen Perspektive.

Einmal erlebt der Besucher den Weg vom Leben über den Tod Tutanchamuns bis zu seinem Leben im Jenseits. Er trifft zunächst auf den jungen König, wird Zeuge seines Begräbnisses, dann seiner Wiedergeburt. Er erkundet Tutanchamuns Leben nach dem Tod und stößt zuletzt auf sein Grab.

Umgekehrt wird das Abenteuer der Entdeckung des Grabs erzählt: Nach dem Aufspüren der Grabstätte tritt der Besucher in die Vorkammer, erforscht wie ein Archäologe den Grabschatz, wickelt die königliche Mumie Lage um Lage aus und kommt dabei Tutanchamun stetig näher, um schließlich herauszufinden, wer der junge Herrscher war.

Die komplette fantastische Reise auf den Spuren des sagenumwobenen Gottkönigs wird als stimmige Narration erlebbar.

06 The showcase installation “Burial Chamber” lights up all the walls of the shrine with hieroglyphs one by one.

“The Tutankhamun Collection is the Star of the Museum”

GEM Supervisor-General Director Dr Tarek Tawfik

GEM—GRAND STAIRS / ATRIUM

Permanent Exhibition, Grand Stairs 5,000 sqm, Atrium 8,000 sqm, Giza, Egypt, in progress

The Atrium welcomes visitors and connects all the areas of the museum complex. A more-than-11-metre-tall statue of Ramses II, standing in a pool of water, faces the entrance; his appearance is both eye-catching and imposing.

The exhibition areas are reached via a spectacular staircase. More then 180 metres in length, the Grand Stairs form the architectural backbone of the museum. The ascent via the stairs offers access to the children's museum, the "Dynasty Galleries," and the "Tutankhamun Gallery." Having arrived at the top, there awaits a breathtaking view of the pyramids of Giza.

The Grand Stairs present 90 immensely heavy, large-scale sculptures from the Nile region. Visitors wander from the Old Kingdom to the New Kingdom along a time axis of statues and objects which are divided into four themes, each arranged chronologically: "Royal Image," "Divine Houses," "Gods and Kings," and "Eternal Protection."

In the themed area "Royal Image," visitors encounter Egyptian rulers like the pharaohs of the three pyramids of Giza: Khufu (Cheops), Khafre (Chephren), and Menkaure (Mykerinos). Flawless and omnipotent, chosen by the gods, they are placed as the idealised representatives of the pharaohs: as Sphinx, as monumental statues, some standing, some sitting, as busts and sculptures on pedestals.

In the second theme, "Divine Houses," architectural fragments, pillars, and pedestals illustrate that one type of temple is dedicated to the gods, another to the cult of a deceased regent. Tables bearing sacrificial offerings and altars are testimony to religious rituals and cult-like actions.

In the next area, "Gods and Kings," visitors experience a scene of the divine family of Memphis—the goddess Sekmeth between two sculptures of the god Ptah. A triad of Ramses II, Sekmeth, and Ptah, by contrast, shows that the pharaohs put themselves on the same level as the gods and placed their images alongside those of the gods.

Das Atrium empfängt die Besucher und verbindet alle Bereiche des Museumskomplexes. Blickfang und imposante Erscheinung ist eine über elf Meter hohe Statue Ramses II. Sie steht in einem Wasserbecken, dem Eingang zugewandt.

Erschlossen werden die Ausstellungsbereiche über eine spektakuläre 180 Meter lange Treppe, die Grand Stairs, die das architektonische Rückgrat des Museums bildet. Dieser inszenierte Aufstieg bietet Zugang zum Kindermuseum, den „Dynasty Galleries" und der „Tutankhamun Gallery". Oben angekommen, öffnet sich ein atemberaubender Blick auf die Pyramiden von Gizeh.

Die Grand Stairs präsentieren 90 tonnenschwere Großskulpturen aus der gesamten Nilregion. Die Besucher wandeln vom Alten zum Neuen Königreich entlang einer Zeitachse von Statuen und Objekten, die in vier jeweils chronologisch arrangierte Themen unterteilt sind: „Royal Image", „Divine Houses", „Gods and Kings" und „Eternal Protection".

Im Themenbereich „Royal Image" begegnen sie ägyptischen Herrschern, wie den Königen der drei Pyramiden von Gizeh, Khufu (Cheops), Khafre (Chephren) und Menkaure (Mykerinos). Makellos und allmächtig, von Göttern erwählt, sind sie als die idealisierten Repräsentanten der königlichen Herrschaft platziert: als Sphinx, als monumentale sitzende und stehende Statuen, als Büsten oder Skulpturen auf Stelen.

Im zweiten Ausstellungsbereich, „Divine Houses", verdeutlichen Architekturfragmente, Säulen und Stelen, dass ein Tempeltyp den Göttern, ein anderer dem Kult eines verstorbenen Königs gewidmet ist. Opfertische und Altäre zeugen von religiösen Ritualen und kultischen Handlungen.

Im folgenden Bereich, „Gods and Kings", erleben Besucher eine Szene der göttlichen Familie von Memphis – die Göttin Sekmeth zwischen zwei Skulpturen des Gottes Ptah. Eine Triade von Ramses II., Sekmeth und Ptah dagegen verdeutlicht, dass sich Könige den Göttern gleichstellten und sich zusammen mit diesen abbilden ließen.

07 The Atrium's main attraction is the colossal statue of Ramses II.

08 The Digital Calender informs visitors about exhibitions and events taking place at the GEM.

The afterlife is the theme of "Eternal Protection." Sarcophagi and grave elements reveal to visitors that pharaohs became gods after death—that is why it is so important to prepare the corpse for a safe journey into the hereafter.

All the exhibits are on bases of green granite, and light has been used to underline their sculptural qualities. The way they are arranged, for example in family groups, triggers dialogues. The statues begin to communicate.

On the uppermost platform, the small pyramids of the pharaoh Hatshepsut are reference to the huge pyramids that lie behind the panorama window. And a fragment that broke off the original beard of the Sphinx of Giza is on display here. A 3-D model reveals the original connection and is an attractive addition, not only for people with impaired vision, who can approach the sculpture through the sense of touch.

The way the objects are arranged puts them in context and entices visitors to explore the galleries flanking the Grand Stairs.

Das Leben nach dem Tod ist in „Eternal Protection" thematisiert. Anhand von Sarkophagen und Grabelementen erfahren Besucher, dass Könige nach ihrem Tod zu Göttern wurden – das Wichtigste dabei war, den toten Körper für eine sichere Reise durch das Jenseits vorzubereiten.

Sämtliche Exponate haben Sockel aus grünem Granit und sind durch Licht in Szene gesetzt, das die bildhauerische Qualität der Skulpturen unterstreicht. Durch die Anordnung, beispielsweise in Form von Familienzusammenhängen, entstehen Dialoge. Die Statuen beginnen zu kommunizieren.

Auf der obersten Plattform verweist die kleine Pyramide der Königin Hatschepsut auf die riesigen Pyramiden, die hinter dem Panoramafenster liegen – hier befindet sich auch ein Fragment des originalen, schon vor langer Zeit abgebrochene Barts der Sphinx von Gizeh. Ein 3-D-Modell verdeutlicht den ursprünglichen Zusammenhang und ist eine attraktive Ergänzung, nicht nur für blinde Menschen, die sich auf diesem Weg der Skulptur haptisch annähern können. Braille-Texte treten unterstützend hinzu.

Das Arrangement der Objekte wirkt kontextualisierend und einladend, um von der Grand Stairs aus die flankierend angeordneten Galerien zu erkunden.

09 The Saqqara King List is a main attraction on the middle landing of the Grand Stairs.

"This is the world's largest museum devoted to a single civilisation." GEM Supervisor-General Director Dr Tarek Tawfik

10 Visitors can walk amongst 90 heavy artefacts from the Old Kingdom to the New Kingdom on the Grand Stairs.

الصورة الملكية
Royal Image
王のイメージ

ATELIER BRÜCKNER

ARCHITECTURE

EXHIBITIONS

SCENOGRAPHY

PARTNERS

Prof. Uwe R. Brückner

Prof. Uwe R. Brückner, founding partner, is held in esteem both in Germany and internationally as protagonist and opinion leader in the field of exhibition design. Studies of architecture at the TU Munich and stage design under Jürgen Rose at the Stuttgart State Academy of Art and Design precede his scenographic work: three decades of innovative projects and concepts. In 1997 he and Shirin Frangoul-Brückner founded ATELIER BRÜCKNER; in 2001 he co-founded the Institute for Interior Design and Scenography at the HGK Basel. Uwe R. Brückner is the creative director and visionary head of ATELIER BRÜCKNER.

Shirin Frangoul-Brückner

Shirin Frangoul-Brückner, managing director and founding partner of ATELIER BRÜCKNER, studied architecture at the universities of Kaiserslautern and Stuttgart. She has worked as an architect since 1994 and in 1997 co-founded ATELIER BRÜCKNER with Uwe R. Brückner. Guided by the principle "making the impossible possible" she systematically uses her competencies in project acquisition, conception, controlling, and realisation. As managing director she is responsible for positioning the Atelier, which has since developed into one of the world's leading offices for exhibition design.

Prof. Eberhard Schlag

Prof. Eberhard Schlag, project director, joined ATELIER BRÜCKNER in 1997 and has been partner since 2008. He studied architecture at the University of Stuttgart and at the IIT in Chicago. As project director, he is responsible for the complex museum, exhibition, and architecture projects at home and abroad, and also heads up the architecture department of ATELIER BRÜCKNER with a special focus on cultural buildings and refurbishment, of listed buildings. In 2018 he founded ATELIER BRÜCKNER KOREA, of which he is representative director. Eberhard Schlag is a professor for architecture and design at HTWG Konstanz, where he has built up an interdisciplinary course of studies in spatial design.

Britta Nagel

Britta Nagel, concept director, heads up concept development at ATELIER BRÜCKNER and in this capacity has been the creative lead responsible for the success of numerous projects. She is passionate about materializing content in space and inspiring visitors with a memorable experience. The architect studied at the University of Stuttgart and Bartlett School of Architecture in London. She sees her role as a creative designer as one that bridges exhibition, architecture, design, and art. Her strengths lie in her ability to guide her colleagues, collaborators, and clients towards an unexpected result. Britta Nagel has been a partner at ATELIER BRÜCKNER since 2011.

René Walkenhorst

René Walkenhorst, project director, is responsible for the development and management of complex construction and exhibition projects worldwide. He has many years of experience in planning and realising high-quality interior architecture and sees himself as a well-versed and highly structured project director, confidently managing even large teams. René Walkenhorst studied architecture at the universities of Hanover, Delft, and Helsinki and was co-founder of the office 5elf Architekten, before joining ATELIER BRÜCKNER in 2005. Since 2009 he has been an associate, and became partner in 2017.

ASSOCIATES

Bernd Möller

Bernd Möller completed his degree in interior architecture at the University of Applied Sciences Stuttgart in 1995. Since 2000 he has been a project manager and since 2009 an associate at ATELIER BRÜCKNER. The interior architect's approach to design and planning challenges is always solution-oriented in the context of sophisticated overall concepts. He strives to achieve the perfect implementation of materials and media. In presentations, workshops, and as jury member, Bernd Möller shares his knowledge and represents ATELIER BRÜCKNER.

Michel Casertano

Michel Casertano has been with ATELIER BRÜCKNER since 2005 and an associate since 2012. He studied architecture at the TU Munich and at the University of Bath. As main responsible in the architecture department, he is focusing on construction work in listed buildings and new builds in a cultural context. He is in charge of conception, planning, and realisation of architecture projects at ATELIER BRÜCKNER. From 2009 to 2013 he was a lecturer for media at the Stuttgart State Academy of Art and Design. He is regularly in demand as a speaker, guest reviewer, and jury member.

Dominik Hegemann

Dominik Hegemann finished his studies in architecture and design at the Stuttgart State Academy of Art and Design in 1999. Since then, he has managed complex exhibition projects for ATELIER BRÜCKNER at home and abroad, since 2013 as an associate. He is responsible for project management and planning across all project phases. His specialist expertise lies in the development and realisation of exhibitions with a strong media element. Experiential, target-oriented formats reflect the architect's passion for science and technology.

Marco Müller

Marco Müller studied architecture at the University of Stuttgart as well as industrial design at the Zurich University of the Arts. Since 2007 he has worked as a project architect at ATELIER BRÜCKNER and has been an associate since 2017. He is well versed in all project phases–from innovative design through to optimum implementation. His projects range from museum exhibitions and brand spaces to interior designs. He contributes his expertise in the field of interior and industrial design to projects the world over. Since 2016 he is a lecturer in design and media history at the HfG Schwäbisch Gmünd.

Kathrin Milic-Grunwald

Kathrin Milic-Grunwald is a communication designer with a master's degree in media and arts. She has been contributing her abilities in the field of design aesthetics and her strong conceptional and analytical skills to the work at ATELIER BRÜCKNER since 2010, since 2018 as an associate. She shapes and structures the content of complex exhibition and design projects, and in collaboration with museum curators and brand managers presents scientific and brand content in such a way that it is conveyed spatially in three dimensions. From 2014 to 2018 she was a visiting lecturer at the Royal College of Art in London.

TEAM

Adriana Castro
Alex Stütz
Alexander Baum
Alexander Frangoul
Alexander Schmid
Alexandra Vassilakou A
Amit Reshef D
Amy McDonnold A
Andrea Gehring O
Andrea Schmeckenbecher
Andreas Schirra A
Andreas Geissler
Andreas Goerke
Andreas Hoffmann-Daimler
Andreas Hummel
Andreas Martini
Andreas Pitteroff
Anette Moehle
Angela Kaaden
Angela Kettler-Bott
Anika Neugart O
Anita Wertiprach
Anita Widera A
Anja Haas
Anja Heinzel
Ann-Sophie Albrecht A
Anne von der Lippe A
Antonia Liebelt A
Aric Merz
Armin Schleicher
Benjamin Guschlbauer D
Benjamin Jagdmann
Bernd Möller A
Bernita Le Gerette
Bettina Johae
Bianca Döring
Birgit Kadatz
Birgit Kölz
Birgit Nädele-Gramling
Björn Müller-Weippert A
Britta Nagel A
Carina Ernst
Carmen Utz A
Caroline Wegener
Carsten Guth
Caterina De Manuele
Catharina Wegener
Cathérine François
Catrin Stahl
Cécile Offenhäuser
Céline Kruska
Charlotte Tamschick
Christian Fritz
Christian Geisser
Christian Kroh D
Christian Schmutz
Christian Stang
Christiane Forstnig
Christin Dotzel O
Christin Erdmann A
Christine Hebrank
Christine Kuss
Christine Knoll
Christoph von Bruchhausen
Christoph Emde
Christoph Längle
Christoph Wezel C
Claudia Frankenreiter
Claudia Kolbe A
Claudia Luxbacher P
Cord-Hinrich Grote D
Cuong Le
Dagmar Schmidt
Daniel Giordano D
Daniela Rebstock A
Daniela Tauscher
Daniela Valentini
David Kotz
Denada Dahriu D
Despina Simeonidou A
Deyana Stareva A
Diana Estabridis
Diana Kitzinski
Dieter Hellermann O
Dirk Bonfort
Dirk Olschewski
Dirk Schubert
Dominik Hegemann A
Dongho Nam A
Dorothea Hammer
Dorothee Silbermann
Eberhard Schlag A
Elaf Al-Kattan
Elisabeth Ramm C
Elli Panagakou
Emanuela Tierno
Emil Neumann
Emin Çimşir
Emma Kilday D
Eva Schrade
Eva-Maria Heinrich
Evelyn Heim D
Evelyn Prochota D
Ewelina Cis
Fabian Brenne
Fabian Schröder
Federica Chung Ferraro A
Felix Becker
Fernanda Reiss
Feyyaz Sözeri A
Florian Müller
Florian Widmann
Florian Wisotzki
Francesca Gotti D
Frank Forell
Franziska Götz C
Frauke Hildebrandt
Gabi Kümmerlin
Gala Marchal
Georg Penner
Gesa Dörfler-Gouverneur
Gesine Gennrich
Giulia Thieme
Giuseppe Mirko Cerami
Giusto Lo Bocchiaro
Gregor Hilpert
Harry Vetter
Haydar Dalci A
Heidemarie Zeh D
Helge Rösch
Hendrik Fischer
Holger Büttner
Ilham Bagdadi
Irene Kriechbaum
Isabel Reuter C
Jaap Vogel P
Jaione Cerrato D
Jan Hoos
Jan Maier
Jan Saggau
Jan Warnecke
Jana Fröhlich D
Jannis Renner A
Jassen Markov
Jelka Ottens A
Jiwon Yoon D
Jill Schwarzer
Johannes Vogt
Jörg Röhrich
Jörn Küsters A
Josipa Krizmanic
Judith Hummer
Julia Bialas
Julia Federhofer
Julia Leitmeyer D
Julia Walter A
Julian von Wolf
Juliane Kempe
Jutta Stüber
Karolina Bisewska
Katerina Krommyda
Katharina Bachtler
Katharina Hengel
Kathia Ecks
Kathrin Milic-Grunwald C

A Architecture and Interior Architecture
C Content and Interpretation
D Design and Scenography
O Office and Administration
P Public Relations and Business Development

Photos p. 405/406/407: Reiner Pfisterer

Kathrin Seitz A
Katja Kraiss D
Katrin Lessing
Katrin Stumpf
Kim Machielsen
Korkut Demirag
Kristina Feige A
Kristof Gavrielides
Laura Knüsel
Laura Lienert D
Laura Rottmann
Lea Spanke
Lech Grochola
Lejla Divanovic C
Lena Abdi
Lilian Fitch
Lilian Lautenschläger D
Linda Greci C
Liu Zhenyu
Ludmilla Knies
Luis Duarte
Manuela Gerold
Marc Dettinger D
Marco Brütsch
Marco Di Giacomo
Marco Gernt
Marco Müller A
Marco Vaccara A
Maren Vanessa Klotz O
Margareta Auer O
Maria Millan
Maria Murais
Marian Müller D
Mariane Ghafari D
Marianna Messina
Marie Rannou D
Marietta Fischer
Marina Klepka
Marion Kemmler-Fahrion O
Markus Selle
Martin Nielandt
Martin Grözinger
Martin Stoll
Martin Roth
Martina Grebenstein
Maryline Perrier
Matt Schwab
Maurice Kohl
Max Wuppermann
Meike Frankenhauser D
Meike Kerstin Kühn
Melanie Brugger
Melanie Kappes
Michael van Engelen
Michael Hoeschen
Michael Thomann
Michael Reiner D
Michael Volz
Michaela Ganter
Michaela Korb
Michaela Thrun
Michel Casertano A
Michelle Bühler Bauer
Mihai Vanca A
Milo Schwager D
Minne Schlag
Mirja Bekavac
Miruna Toma
Monika Goebel
Moritz von Sassen
Moritz Schneider
Moritz Reichartz
Muche Tamschick
Nadine Maier
Nadine Seidu
Nana Forell
Natalie Kleemann
Natalie Weinz A
Nelly Perrier
Nicole Liener O
Nicolo Piana D
Nils Scheffler A
Nuria Ferrer Paretas A
Oliver Kosic
Oliver Mack
Pamela Resuli A
Patricia Kaufmann
Patrizia Ambrisi
Patrizia Sahm
Peter Hufer
Petra Stojanik
Phil Püschel
Pia Weber
Priyank Soni A
Raed Caml
Rafal Klosinski
Raimund Docmac
Rana Rmeily D
Raya Hiyasat A
Reinhard Orlinski
Renate Stetter
René Walkenhorst A
Rischko Gutleber
Rudi Specht P
Ruiting Zhang A
Ruth Breidel
Sabine Binder
Sabine Hibler
Sabine Hug Schäfer
Sabine Loucka
Sabine Marinescu
Sami Karam D
Samir Saddi
Sandra Di Maria
Sandra Jirsch
Sandra Maier A
Sascha Bauer
Sayaka Koike D
Sayman Bostanci
Sebastian Schelling
Sebastian Schröter
Sebastian von Wolf
Seulbi Kim A
Shirin Frangoul-Brückner A
Sibylla Längle
Simon Bostanzi
Simone Baum
Sinan Apti
Stefan Schmotz
Sophie Horn A
Stefan Pinl
Stefan Schwab
Stefanie Brenner
Stefanie Klinge
Stefanie Naumann
Steffen Blunk
Stephan Obermaier
Steffen Vetterle
Stephanie Hoffmann A
Suee Chang
Sungha Kim A
Susanne Baiker
Susanne Heinrich
Susanne Pertschy A
Tanja Obergfäll
Tanja Hammerl
Tanja Zöllner D
Tatjana Triebelhorn
Thilo Albers
Till Nsoga-Zocher D
Tingting Zhang A
Tobias Geisler
Tobias Hegemann
Tobias Hoss
Tracy Krüger
Udo Kaiser
Ulrike Mumm
Ulrike Schlemm
Ulrike Schulmeister
Ute Bayer
Uwe R. Brückner D/A
Uwe Reinhardt
Valentin Kirsch
Valentina Reimer
Valeria Mogavero
Vera Zimmermann
Veronica Chini D
Vicky Berl A
Viktoria Schulze
Wassim Melki A
Wenke Merkel
Wenqian Luo A
Werner Gaiser
Whan Lee D
Wolf Kipper
Xiaoyi Gu P
Yijing Lu A
Yuchen Xie D
Yutong Chen A
Zaid Hammudeh A
Zeina Abdelkhalek D
Zeljana Holowitz
ZiYi Zhou
Zuhair Alam Baluch
Zoe Nann P

DISCIPLINES

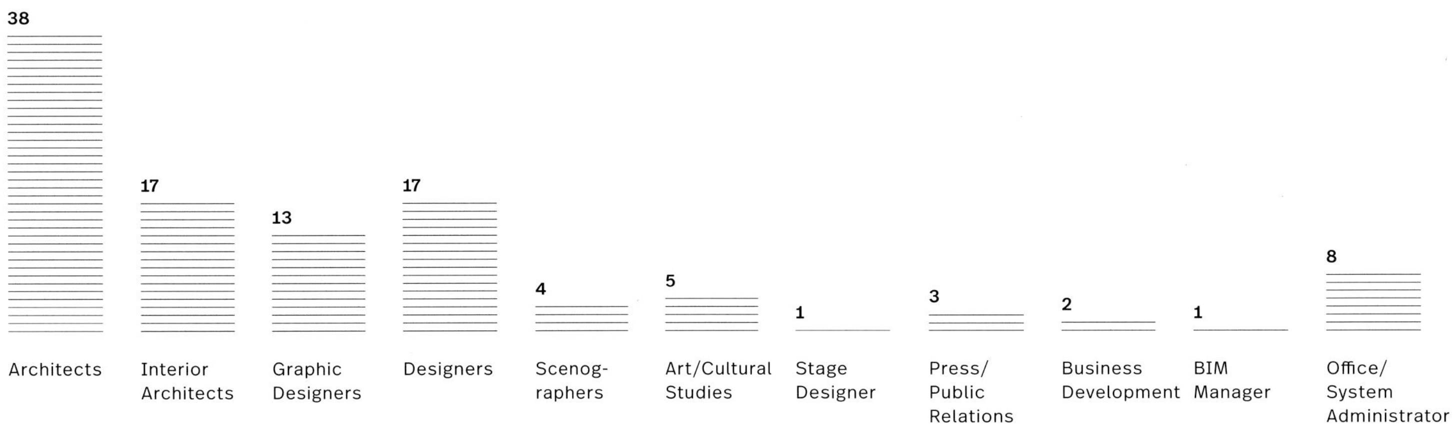

EVOLUTION

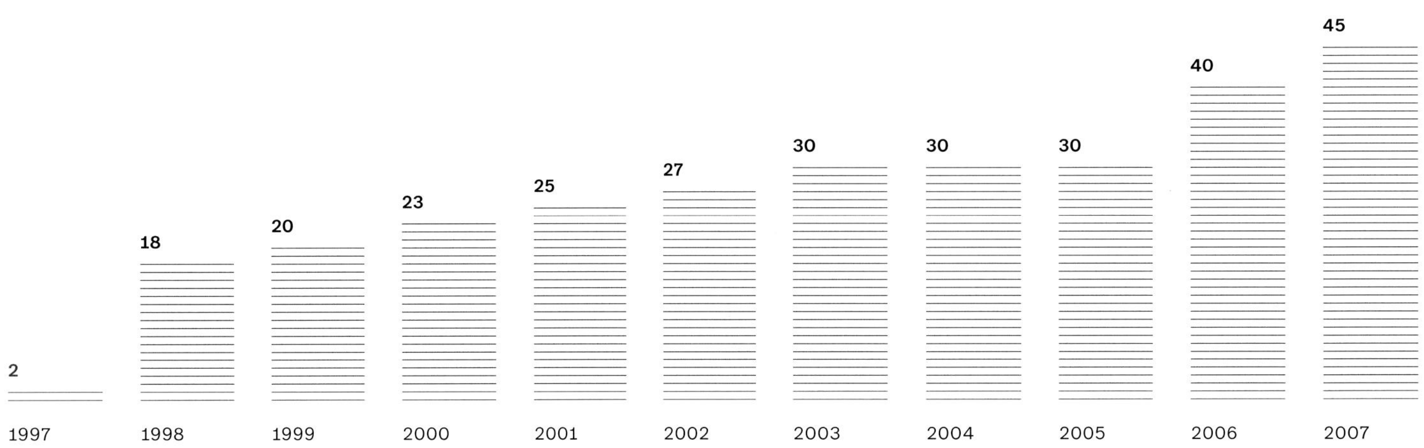

NATIONALITIES

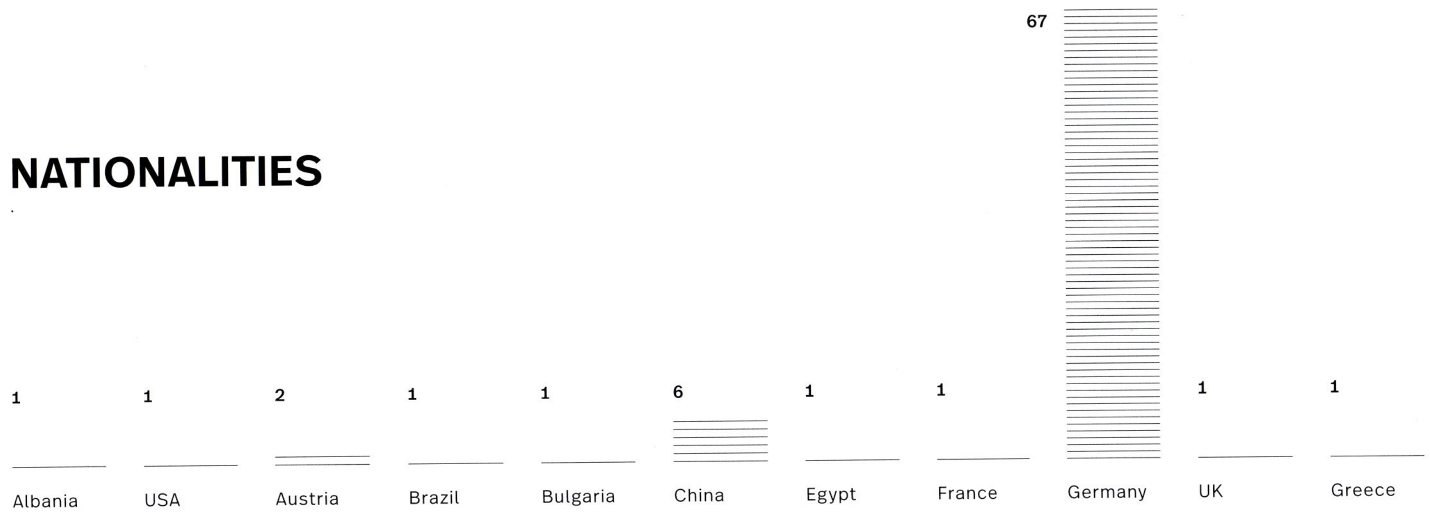

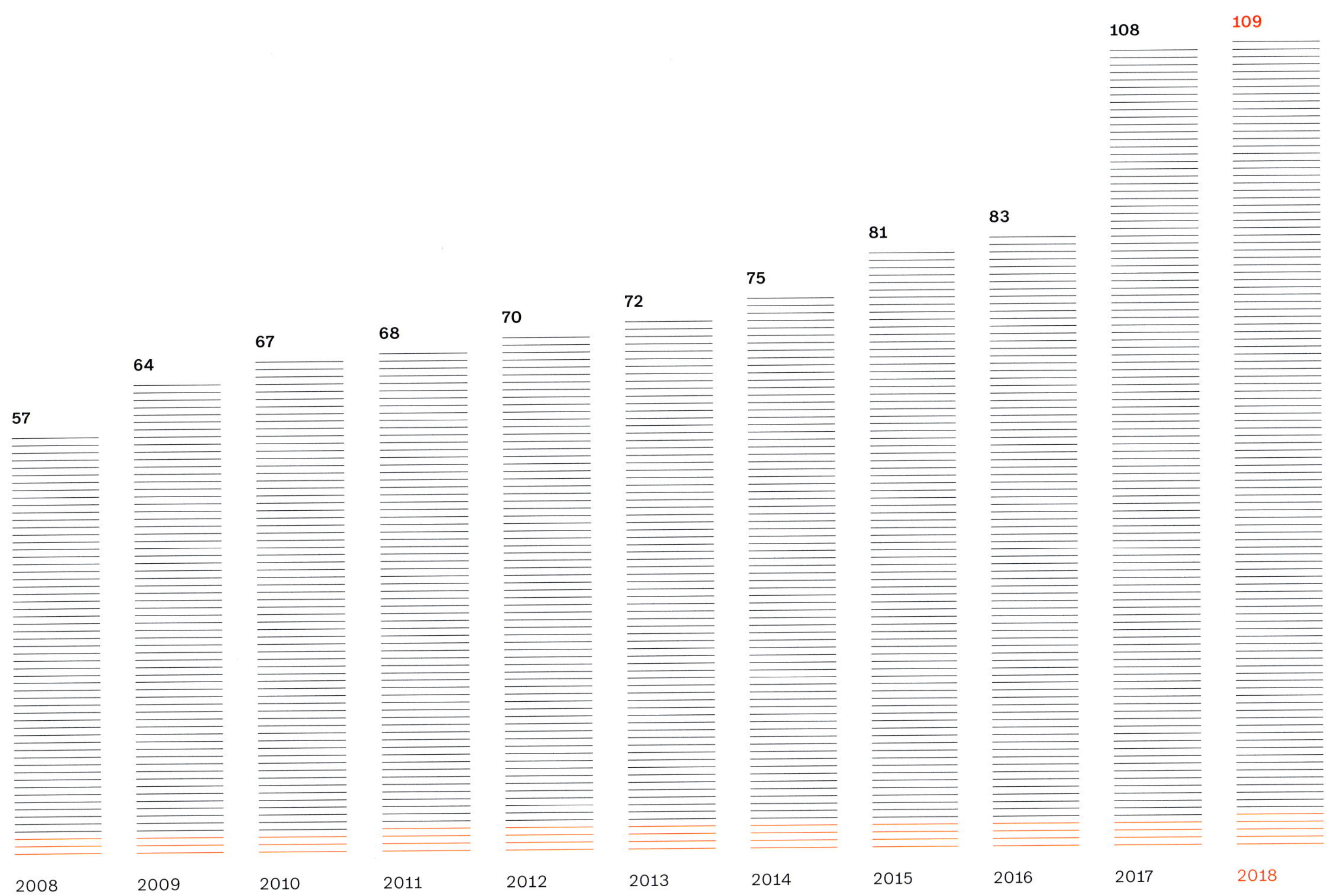

PROJECTS IN LOCATION

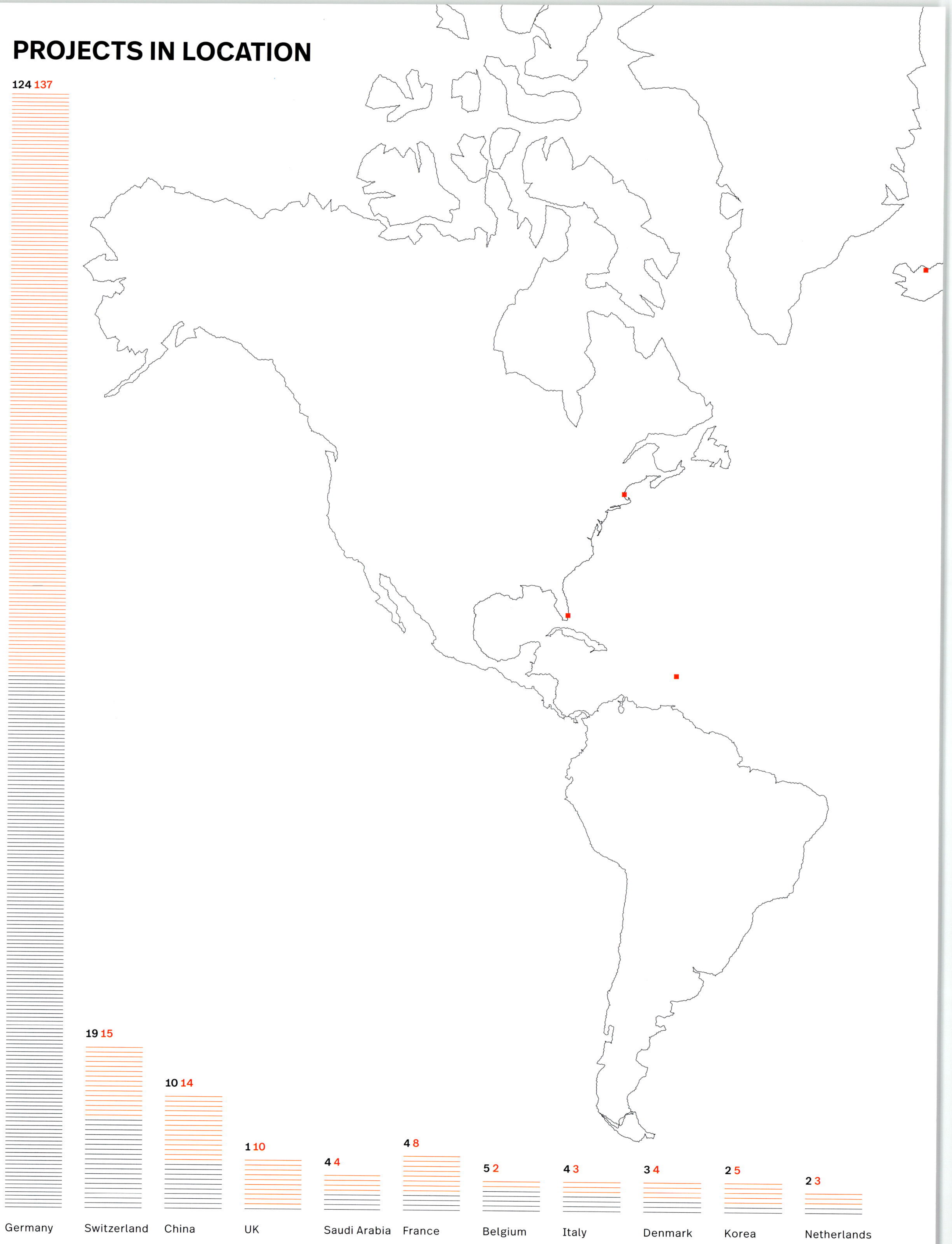

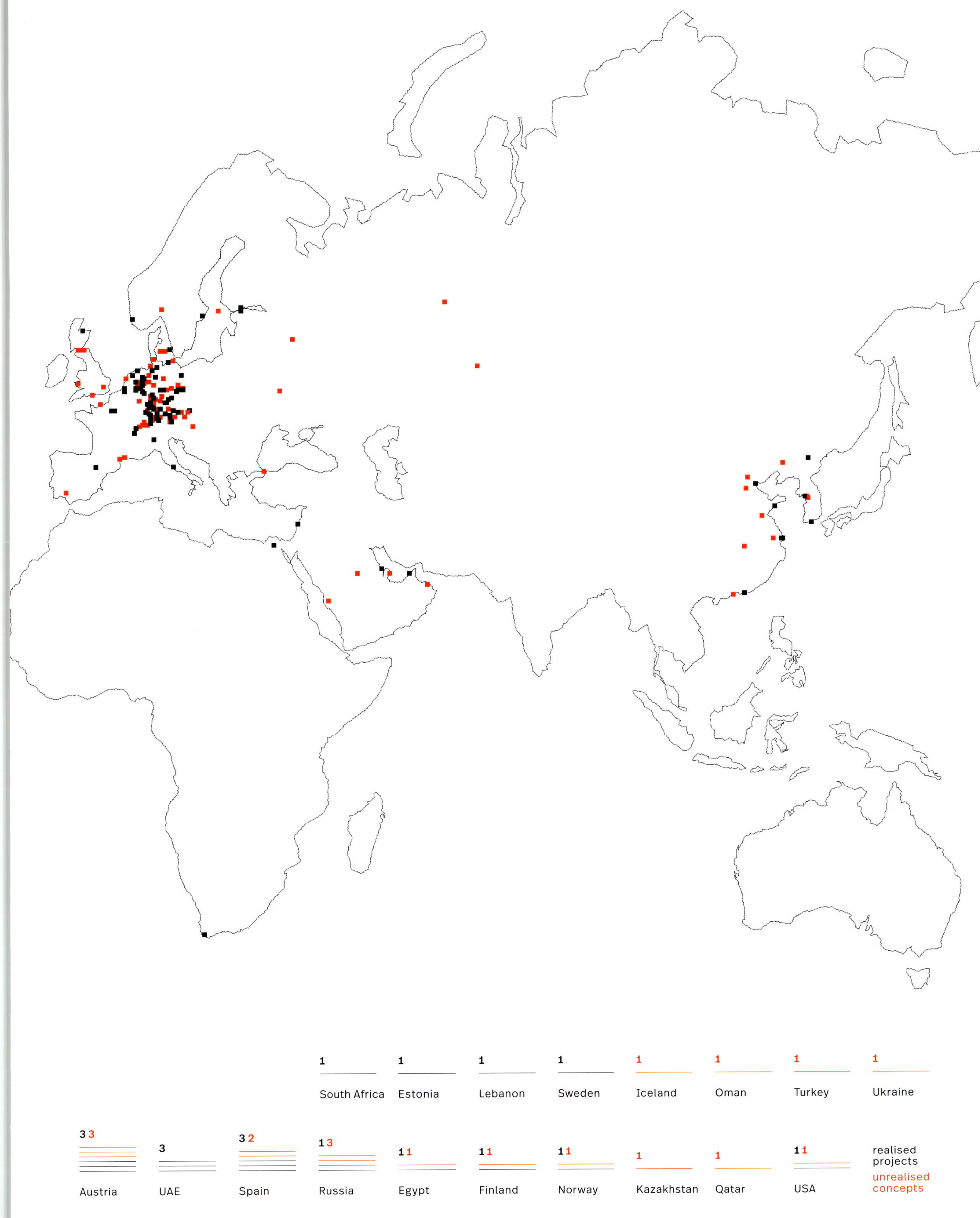
1 South Africa
1 Estonia
1 Lebanon
1 Sweden
1 Iceland
1 Oman
1 Turkey
1 Ukraine
3 3 Austria
3 UAE
3 2 Spain
1 3 Russia
1 1 Egypt
1 1 Finland
1 1 Norway
1 Kazakhstan
1 Qatar
1 1 USA
realised projects
unrealised concepts

PROJECT LIST

IN PROGRESS

ARCHÄOLOGIE
Permanent Exhibition, Badisches Landesmuseum, Karlsruhe, Germany T **Archaeology** C **Badisches Landesmuseum** A **500 sqm** R **Exhibition Design, Scenography** / Lighting Design: **LDE Belzner Holmes**; Media Planning: **medienprojekt p2**

AUDEMARS PIGUET – MAISON DES FONDATEURS
Permanent Brand Exhibition, Visitor Centre, Le Brassus, Switzerland T **Industry** R **Audemars Piguet** A **1,000 sqm** R **General Planning, Exhibition Design, Scenography, Experiential Graphic Design, Lighting Design, Media Planning** / Architecture: **BIG Bjarke Ingels Group**

BCM–BEIRUT CITY MUSEUM
Permanent Exhibition, Beirut, Lebanon T **Archaeology, History** C **Solidere, Kulturministerium DGA** A **5,000 sqm** R **Exhibition Design, Scenography** / Architecture: **Renzo Piano Building Workshop**

BUNKER STUTTGART
Conversion of an elevated bunker into a residential building, Stuttgart, Germany T **Architecture, Refurbishment** C **Private** A **900 sqm**

DEUTSCHES MUSEUM NUREMBERG – DAS ZUKUNFTSMUSEUM!
Permanent Exhibition, Nuremberg, Germany T **Science, Research, Technology** C **Deutsches Museum München** A **2,900 sqm** R **General Planning, Exhibition Design** / Collaboration: Lighting Design with **LDE Belzner Holmes**; Media Planning with **medienprojekt p2** / Architecture: **staab Architekten**

EUROPA EXPERIENCE
Permanent Exhibition, Copenhagen, Denmark T **History, Politics** C **European Parliament** A **130 sqm** R **General Planning, Exhibition Design, Scenography** / Collaboration: Lighting Design with **LDE Belzner Holmes**, Media Planning with **medienprojekt p2** / Media Production: **Markenfilm Crossing**

EUROPA EXPERIENCE
Permanent Exhibition, Helsinki, Finnland T **History, Politics** C **European Parliament** A **100 sqm** R **General Planning, Exhibition Design, Scenography** / Collaboration: Lighting Design with **LDE Belzner Holmes**; Media Planning with **medienprojekt p2** / Media Production: **Markenfilm Crossing** / Architecture: **ALA Architects**

EUROPA EXPERIENCE
Permanent Exhibition, Paris, France T **History, Politics** C **European Parliament** A **750 sqm** R **General Planning, Exhibition Design, Scenography** / Collaboration: Lighting Design with **LDE Belzner Holmes**; Media Planning with **medienprojekt p2** / Media Production: **Markenfilm Crossing** / Architecture: **Builders and Partners**

EUROPA EXPERIENCE
Permanent Exhibition, Tallinn, Estonia T **History, Politics** C **European Parliament** A **550 sqm** R **General Planning, Exhibition Design, Scenography** / Collaboration: Lighting Design with **LDE Belzner Holmes**; Media Planning with **medienprojekt p2** / Media Production: **Markenfilm Crossing** / Architecture: **HML Construction management**

FORUM WISSEN
Permanent Exhibition, Göttingen, Germany T **Knowledge** C **Georg-August-Universität Göttingen** A **1,400 sqm,** R **Exhibition Design, Scenography,** Collaboration: Lighting Design with **LDE Belzner Holmes;** Media Planning with **medienprojekt p2,** Architecture/Refurbishment: **gildehaus. partner architekten BDA**

FLIGHT, EXPULSION, RECONCILIATION
Permanent Exhibition, Documentation Center, Berlin, Germany T **Ethnology, Memory, History, Politics** C **Bundesstiftung Flucht, Vertreibung, Versöhnung** A **1,700 sqm** R **General Planning, Exhibition Design, Scenography, Lighting Design, Media Planning, Experiential Graphic Design** / Architecture: **Marte Marte**

↗ p. 388

GEM–GRAND EGYPTIAN MUSEUM
Permanent Exhibition, Giza, Egypt T **Archaeology, History** C **Ministry of Antiquities** A **90,000 sqm (Museum in total), 7,500 sqm (Tutankhamun Gallery), 5,000 sqm (Grand Stairs), 8,000 sqm (Atrium)** R **General Planning, Exhibition Design, Scenography** / Collaboration: Lighting Design with **Bartenbach**; Media Planning with **iart**; Corporate Design with **Tarek Atrissi Design** / Architecture: **heneghan peng architects**

HAIER – WORLD APPLIANCE MUSEUM
Permanent Exhibition, Company Museum, Qindao, China T **Home Appliance** C **Haier Electronics Group Co., Ltd** A **6,000 sqm** / Collaboration: Lighting Design with **LDE Belzner Holmes**; Media Planning with **medienprojekt p2**; Media and Film Production with **Gush Films**

KTM MOTOHALL
Permanent Brand Exhibition T **Industry, Technology, Brand, History** C **KTM AG** A **2,800 sqm** R **Exhibition Design, Scenography** / Collaboration: Lighting Design with **LDE Belzner Holmes**; Media Planning with **medienprojekt p2** / Architecture: **Hofbauer Architect, xarchitekten**

LIMES MUSEUM
Permanent Exhibition, Aalen, Germany T **Archaeology, History** C **Archäologisches Landesmuseum Baden-Württemberg** A **1,500 sqm** R **Exhibition Design, Scenography, Experiential Graphic Design, Media Software**

LINDT HOME OF CHOCOLATE
Permanent Brand Exhibition, Visitor Centre, Kilchberg, Switzerland T **History** C **Lindt Chocolate Competence Foundation** A **2,000 sqm** R **General Planning, Scenography** / Architecture: **Christ & Gantenbein**

MENSCHEN, RÄUME, SAMMLUNGEN
Permanent Exhibition, Swiss National Museum, Zurich, Switzerland T **Historical Rooms, Collections** C **Swiss Confederation, Federal Office for Property Construction and Logisitcs (BBL)** A **2,100 sqm** R **Exhibition Design, Scenography** / Collaboration: Lighting Design with **Atelier Derrer**; Media Planning with **medienprojekt p2** / Refurbishment: **Christ & Gantenbein**

MÜNCHNER STADTMUSEUM
Permanent Exhibition, Munich, Germany T **History** C **Münchner Stadtmuseum** A **4,200 sqm** R **General Planning, Exhibition Design, Scenography** / Collaboration: Lighting Design with **Bartenbach Lichtlabor**; Media Planning with **medienprojekt p2**

T Theme
C Client
A Area
R Responsibility
P Photography

MUSEUM MAISON JEAN MONNET
Permanent Exhibition, Bazoches-sur-Guyonne, France
T **Politics, Europe** C **European Parliament** A **400 sqm**
R **Exhibition Design, Scenography** / Collaboration: Lighting Design with **LDE Belzner Holmes**; Media Planning with **medienprojekt p2**

NOBEL CENTER
Permanent Exhibition, Stockholm, Sweden T **History, Science**
C **Nobel Foundation Stockholm** A **3,400 sqm** R **General Planning, Exhibition Design, Lighting Design, Media Planning** / Architecture: **David Chipperfield Architects**

NORWEGIAN PRINTING MUSEUM
Permanent Exhibition, Stavanger, Norway T **Industry, History**
C **Museum Stavanger** A Exhibition: **490 sqm**, Printing Works: **180 sqm** R **Exhibition Design, Scenography** / Collaboration: Lighting Design with **LDE Belzner Holmes**; Media Planning with **medienprojekt p2** / Architecture: **Eder Biesel Arkitekter AS**

PARLAMENTARIUM – MOBILE ROLE PLAY GAME
Travelling Exhibition T **History, Politics** C **European Parliament** A **100 sqm** R **Exhibition Design, Scenography** / Media Production: **Markenfilm Crossing**

SHENZHEN JEWELRY MUSEUM
Museum, Shenzhen, China T **Jewelry** C **Shenzhen Jewelry Museum Co. Ltd.** A **2,610 sqm** R **Scenography, Interior Design, Exhibition Design, Experiential Graphic Design, Lighting Design, Media Planning, Media Design** / Architecture: **Urbanus Architecture & Design**

STATE COLLECTION OF ARCHAEOLOGY
Permanent Exhibition, Munich, Germany T **Archaeology**
C **Bavarian State, represented by Archäologische Staatssammlung München** A **1,500 sqm** R **Exhibition Design, Scenography, Experiential Graphic Design** / Collaboration: Lighting Design with **LDE Belzner Holmes**; Media Planning with **medienprojekt p2** / Architecture: **Nieto Sobejano Architectos**

↗ p. 237
TROISDORF CITY GATE
Parish Centre St. Hippolytus, Architecture, Troisdorf, Germany
T **Community, Social, Eventspace, Office** C **Archdiocese of Cologne, Catholic Parish of Troisdorf** A **1,250 sqm** R **Architecture** / Collaboration: Structural Engineering: **Finck Billen Ing. GmbH & Co.KG**, Landscape Planning: **Jens Backhaus Landschaftsarchitekt BDLA**; Building Services: **Peter Zeiler + Partner Ing. GmbH**

TROISDORF KINDERGARTEN
Kindergarten St. Hippolytus, Architecture, Troisdorf, Germany T **Children, Architecture** C **Archdiocese of Cologne, Catholic Parish of Troisdorf** A **880 sqm**
R **Architecture** / Collabration: Structural Engineering: **Finck Billen Ing. GmbH & Co.KG**; Landscape Planning: **Jens Backhaus Landschaftsarchitekt BDLA**; Building Services: **Peter Zeiler + Partner Ing. GmbH**

↗ p. 223
↗ p. 382
WAGENHALLEN
Refurbishment and a New Building with Studios, Stuttgart, Germany T **Industry, Art, Mobility** C **City of Stuttgart**
A **14,000 sqm** R **General Planning, Architecture, Scenography** / Collaboration: Landscape Planning with **G2-Landschaftsarchitekten, Gauder+Gehring**; Structural Engineering: **Bornscheuer Drexler Eisele GmbH** P **Daniel Stauch** and **ATELIER BRÜCKNER**

2018

CONNECTING ELEMENTS – THE NOBEL PRIZE IN CHEMISTRY
Temporary Exhibition, Dubai City Walk, United Arab Emirates
T **Science** C **Nobel Museum Stockholm / Mohammed bin Rashid Al Maktoum Foundation** A **400 sqm** R **Exhibition Concept and Design, Scenography, Experiential Graphic Design** / Collaboration: Lighting Design with **Transpond** / Media Planning Hardware: **Transpond**; Software Design: **YOKE**; Content: **Nobel Museum Stockholm**

DIALOGUE WITH TIME
Permanent Exhibition, Dialoghaus Hamburg, Germany
T **Human** C **Dialogue Social Enterprise GmbH** A **390 sqm**
R **Exhibition Design, Scenography, Experiential Graphic Design, General Planning** / Collaboration: Lighting Design with **LDE Belzner Holmes**; Media Planning with **medienprojekt p2**

HAIER – COSMOPLAT
Trade Fair Stand, Hanover, Germany T **Industry, Technology**
C **Haier Electronics Group** A **360 sqm** R **Booth Design, Scenography, Experiential Graphic Design** / Collaboration: Media Design with **17K**; Lighting Design with **LDE Belzner Holmes**

IN SEARCH OF STYLE
Temporary Exhibition, National Museum, Zurich, Switzerland
T **History, Industry, Art, Mobility, Fashion, Technology** C **Swiss National Museum** A **1,100 sqm** R **General Planning, Exhibition Design, Scenography, Experiential Graphic Design** / Collaboration: Lighting Design with **Atelier Derrer** / Media Production: **17k**

↗ p. 378
ITHRA – ARABIAN JOURNEYS
Permanent Exhibition, King Abdulaziz Center for World Culture, Dhahran, Saudi Arabia T **Natural History** C **Saudi Aramco**
A **1,300 sqm** R **General Planning, Exhibition Concept and Design, Scenography** / Collaboration: Lighting Design with **LDE Belzner Holmes**; Media Planning with **medienprojekt p2**; Media Design with **iart**; Experiential Graphic Design with **Tarek Atrissi Design**; Film Production: **iart** with **Tamschick Media+Space**; Sound Design: **iart** with **idee und klang** / Architecture: **Snøhetta** P **Daniel Stauch**

↗ p. 374
ITHRA – ARAMCORAMA
Permanent Exhibition, King Abdulaziz Center for World Culture, Dhahran, Saudi Arabia T **History** C **Saudi Aramco** A **560 sqm**
R **General Contractor, Exhibition Design, Experiential Graphic Design** / Collaboration: Lighting Design with **LDE Belzner Holmes**; Media Planning with **Art+Com**; Structural Engineering with **Art Engineering GmbH**; Experiential Graphic Design with **Tarek Atrissi Design** / Architecture: **Snøhetta**
P **Daniel Stauch**

ITHRA – BEAUTY AND IDENTITY
Permanent Exhibition, King Abdulaziz Center for World Culture, Dhahran, Saudi Arabia T **Art** C **Saudi Aramco** A **545 sqm**
R **General Contractor** / Collaboration: Experiential Graphic Design with **Tarek Atrissi Design**; Lighting Design with **LDE Belzner Holmes** / Architecture: **Snøhetta**

↗ p. 374
ITHRA – IT EXHIBITS
Media Installations, King Abdulaziz Center for World Culture, Dhahran, Saudi Arabia T **Knowledge** A **1,600 sqm** R **General Planning, Experiential Graphic Design** / Collaboration: Lighting Design with **LDE Belzner Holmes**; Media Planning with **medienprojekt p2**; Experiential Graphic Design with **Tarek Atrissi Design** / Architecture: **Snøhetta** P **Daniel Stauch**

↗ p. 370

JUNGHANS TERRASSENBAU MUSEUM
Permanent Exhibition, Schramberg, Germany T **Technology** C **Immobilienverwaltung Geißhalde GbR** A **830 sqm** R **General Planning, Exhibition Design, Scenography** / Collaboration: Lighting Design with **LDE Belzner Holmes**; Media Planning with **medienprojekt p2** P **Daniel Stauch**

LUNENG CC PLAZA
Permanent Exhibition, Tianjin, China T **Children, Sport, Technology** C **Tianjin Luneng Property Ltd. Co.** A **1,300 sqm** R **General Planning, Exhibition Design, Scenography** / Collaboration: Lighting Design with **LDE Belzner Holmes**; Media Planning with **medienprojekt p2**

MONTBLANC HAUS
Concept for a Permanent Exhibition, Hamburg, Germany

↗ p. 238
↗ p. 364

THE MACALLAN VISITOR EXPERIENCE
Permanent Brand Exhibition, Visitor Centre, Craigellachie, UK T **History** C **The Edrington Group** A **1,800 sqm (Exhibition), 14,800 sqm (Distillery)** R **Exhibition Design, Scenography, Experiential Graphic Design, General Planning** / Collaboration: Lighting Design with **Speirs + Major**; Media Planning with **medienprojekt p2**; Media Design with **Tamschick Media+Space** P **Gyorgy Korossy**

2017

ATELIER BRÜCKNER | 20 YEARS
Temporary Exhibition, BDA Wechselraum, Stuttgart, Germany A **100 sqm** T **Architecture, Exhibition, Scenography** C **ATELIER BRÜCKNER GmbH** R **Concept, Exhibition Design, Scenography, Experiential Graphic Design**

↗ p. 348

AUGUST HORCH MUSEUM
Refubishment and Extension of a listed Factory Building, Zwickau, Germany T **Automotive** C **August Horch Museum Zwickau gGmbH** A **5,500 sqm** R **General Planning, Architecture and Refurbishment** / Collaboration: Structural Engineering with **RPB Rückert**; Landscape Planning with **t17 Landschaft** / Building Services: **INNIUS GTD**; Exhibition Design, Interior Design: **ö_konzept** P **Daniel Stauch**

CHANCELLOR ADENAUER HOUSE
Permanent Exhibition, Bad Honnef, Germany T **History, Politics** C **Stiftung Bundeskanzler-Adenauer-Haus** A **500 sqm** R **General Planning, Exhibition Design, Scenography, Experiential Graphic Design** / Collaboration: Lighting Design with **Licht Kunst Licht**; Media Planning with **medienprojekt p2**; Media Design with **tinetronics**

DAS GUTBROD
Lounge, Stuttgart, Germany T **Politics** C **Wirtschaftsförderung Region Stuttgart GmbH** A **240 sqm** R **General Planning, Interior Architecture** / Collaboration: Lighting Design with **LDE Belzner Holmes**; Media Planning with **medienprojekt p2**

ENIGMA KIDS
Concept for a Permanent Children's Exhibition, Enigma Museum of Post, Tele and Communication, Copenhagen, Denmark

FRANKFURT AIRPORT – WELCOME
Permanent Exhibition and Lounges, Frankfurt/Main, Germany T **Mobility** C **Fraport AG** A **2,000 sqm** R **Interior Architecture, Scenography, Graphics** / Collaboration: Lighting Design with **LDE Belzner Holmes**; Media Planning with **medienprojekt p2**

↗ p. 254
↗ p. 356

HYUNDAI MOTORSTUDIO GOYANG
Permanent Brand Exhibition, Goyang, Korea T **Mobility** C **Hyundai Motor Company** A **4,000 sqm** R **Exhibition Design, Scenography, General Planning** / Collaboration: Lighting Design with **LDE Belzner Holmes**; Media Planning with **medienprojekt p2**; Film Production and Choreography 'Design Room' with **Tamschick Media+Space**; Prototyping 'Kinetic Sculpture' with **MKT** / Media Production: **PYX Innovation Lab**; Audio Design: **Idee und Klang, Klangerfinder** / Architecture: **Delugan Meissl Associated Architects** P **Hyundai Motorstudio Goyang** / **Lim Juneyoung** and **Lee Junoh**

MIT MUSEUM
Masterplan for a Permanent Exhibition, MIT Museum, Cambridge, USA

PARLAMENTARIUM
Visitor Centre of the European Parliament, Strasbourg, France T **History, Politics** C **European Parliament** A **750 sqm** R **Exhibition Concept and Design, Scenography, Experiential Graphic Design** / Collaboration: Lighting Design with **LDE Belzner Holmes**; Media Planning with **Telmaco** / Media Production: **Markenfilm Crossing**; Role Play Game: **Mediafarm**

PETTING ZOO – ANIMAL & GOOD
Permanent Exterior Exhibition, Heidelberg, Germany T **Children, Natural History** C **Tiergarten Heidelberg** A **80 sqm** R **Exhibition Design, Experiential Graphic Design**

SENCKENBERG MASTERPLAN
Concept for a Permanent Exhibition, Senckenberg Museum, Frankfurt/Main, Germany

SMAC – STATE MUSEUM OF ARCHAEOLOGY CHEMNITZ INCLUSION
Extension of the Permanent Exhibition, Chemnitz, Germany T **Inclusion** C **Saxon Archaeological Heritage Office** A **3,600 sqm** R **General Planning, Developing and Design of a Tactile Guidance System including Touch Stations and Floor Markings** / Collaboration: Touch Stations with **tactile studio**

UNDERSTANDING MATTER – THE NOBEL PRIZE IN PHYSICS
Temporary Exhibition, Children's City, Dubai, United Arab Emirates T **Science** C **Nobel Museum Stockholm / Mohammed bin Rashid Al Maktoum Foundation** A **640 sqm** R **Exhibition Concept and Design, Scenography** / Collaboration: Lighting Design with **Transpond** / Media Hardware Planning: **Transpond**; Media Software Design: **YOKE**

VORWERK BRANDSPACE
Permanent Exhibition, Visitor Centre, Wuppertal, Germany T **Home Appliance** C **VORWERK & CO. KG** A **700 sqm** R **General Planning, Exhibition Design, Scenography** / Collaboration: Lighting Design with **LDE Belzner Holmes**; Media Planning with **medienprojekt p2**; Media Production with **2av**; Film Production with **EMENES**

↗ p. 354

WIELAND WAGNER
Temporary Exhibition, Richard Wagner Museum, Bayreuth, Germany T **Music, Theatre** C **Richard-Wagner-Stiftung Bayreuth** A **500 sqm** R **General Planning, Exhibition Design, Scenography** / Collaboration: Media Planning with **medienprojekt p2**; Lighting Design with **LDE Belzner Holmes**; Film Production with **fettFilm** P **Daniel Stauch**

2016

↗ p. 218
↗ p. 330

ARCHAEOLOGY SWITZERLAND
Permanent Exhibition, Swiss National Museum, Zurich, Switzerland T **Archaeology** C **Swiss Confederation, Federal Office for Property Construction and Logistics (BBL)** A **500 sqm** R **General Planning, Exhibition Design, Scenography, Experiential Graphic Design** / Collaboration: Lighting Design with **Atelier Derrer**; Media Planning with **medienprojekt p2**; Media Production with **2av** / Architecture: **Christ & Gantenbein** P **Daniel Stauch**

↗ p. 336

ERLEBNIS EUROPA – EUROPA EXPERIENCE
Permanent Exhibition, Berlin, Germany T **History, Politics** C **European Parliament / Bruns B.V. / STOFANEL Investment AG** A **450 sqm** R **Exhibition Concept and Design, Scenography, Experiential Graphic Design** / Collaboration: Lighting Design with **LDE Belzner Holmes**; Media Planning with **medienprojekt p2** / Media Production: **Markenfilm Crossing** P **Michael Jungblut**

EXPERTISIUM
Concept for a Permanent Exhibition, Showroom, Berlin, Germany

EXPLORING LIFE – THE NOBEL PRIZE IN PHYSIOLOGY OR MEDICINE
Temporary Exhibition, Children's City, Dubai, United Arab Emirates T **Healthcare, Medicine** C **Nobel Museum Stockholm / Mohammed bin Rashid Al Maktoum Foundation** A **640 sqm** R **Exhibition Concept and Design, Scenography** / Collaboration: Lighting Design with **LDE Belzner Holmes**; Media Planning with **medienprojekt p2**

FRAPORT BESUCHERZENTRUM
Concept for the Visitor Center of the International Airport, Frankfurt/Main

HOUSE OF PARLIAMENTARY HISTORY
Permanent Exhibition, Düsseldorf, Germany T **Politics** C **State Parliament of North Rhine-Westphalia** A **300 sqm** R **Exhibition Design, Scenography, Media Production** / Lighting Design: **Peter Andres**; Media Planning: **Erben Elektronische Medien**

↗ p. 340

KLS MARTIN WORLD
Permanent Exhibition, Showroom, Tuttlingen, Germany T **Healthcare, Technology, Science** C **Gebrüder Martin GmbH & Co. KG** A **600 sqm** R **Design of Foyer and Exhibition, Scenography, Experiential Graphic Design** / Collaboration: Lighting Design with **LDE Belzner Holmes**; Media Planning with **medienprojekt p2** / Architecture: **Architekturbüro Heinrich Binder** P **Daniel Stauch**

LANDTAG NRW – VISITOR CENTRE
Permanent Exhibition, Düsseldorf, Germany T **Politics** C **Landtag NRW** A **120 sqm** R **Exhibition Concept, Scenography** / Lighting Design: **Peter Andres**; Media Planning: **Erben Elektronische Medien**; Media Design: **Visuarte** / Architecture: **Eller + Eller Architekten**

LEICA THEME PARK
Competition for a Brand Experience, Wetzlar, Germany

↗ p. 338

MILCHWERK
Redesign of the Entrance and Foyer of a Convention Centre, Radolfzell, Germany T **Industry** C **Stadt Radolfzell** A **1,200 sqm** R **General Planning, Scenography** / Collaboration: Lighting Design with **LDE Belzner Holmes** P **Dirk Wilhelmy**

MOT – MUSEUM OF TRANSPORT
Architectural Competition for the National Museum of Transport, Doha, Qatar

MUSEUM AAN DE A
Concept for a Permanent Exhibition, Groningen, Netherlands

OCEAN EXPERIENCE
Concept for a Permanent Exhibition, Hjalteyri, Iceland

POMMERN
Concept for a Permanent Exhibition, Åland, Finland

THEODOR-HEUSS-HAUS
Concept for the Renewal of the Permanent Exhibition, Stuttgart, Germany

THE UNIVERSE
Permanent Exhibition, Science Center, Wuhan, China T **Science** C **Wuhan Science and Technology Museum** A **2,270 sqm** R **General Planning, Exhibition Design, Scenography**

↗ p. 344

TRUCONNECT FORUM
Permanent Exhibition, Visitor Centre, Ditzingen, Germany T **Industry, Technology** C **TRUMPF GmbH & Co. KG** A **1,200 sqm** R **Exhibition Architecture, Scenography, Experiential Graphic Design** / Collaboration: Media Planning with **medienprojekt p2**; Lighting Design with **LDE Belzner Holmes**; Media Design with **2av** P **Daniel Stauch**

VIA DEI FORI IMPERIALI
Competition for a Permanent Exhibition, Rome, Italy / Architecture: **David Chipperfield Architects**

VW GLÄSERNE MANUFAKTUR
Concept for a Brand Experience, Dresden, Germany

2015

ALIBABA
Concept for a Brand Experience, Beijing, China

AUDI ROADSHOW
Concept for a Roadshow, Germany

BAUHAUS
Concept for a Permanent Exhibition, Dessau, Germany

BLETCHLEY PARK
Concept for a Permanent Exhibition, Bletchley, United Kingdom

BMW UNTERNEHMENSGESCHICHTE
Concept for the Renewal of the Exhibition Space "House of the Company" in the BMW Museum, Munich, Germany

↗ p. 320

DEN BLÅ PLANET
Permanent Exhibition, Copenhagen, Denmark T **Children, Natural History** C **Danmarks Akvarium – National Aquarium Denmark** A **1,600 sqm** R **Exhibition Concept and Design, Orientation System, Scenography, Media Concept, Experiential Graphic Design** / Collaboration: Lighting Design with **Jesper Kongshaug**; Media Planning and Media Design including App with **Yoke Interaction Design** / Architecture: **3XN** P **Klaus Reinelt**

DIALOGUE WITH TIME
Touring Exhibition, Museum für Kommunikation, Berlin, Germany T **Human** C **Dialogue Social Enterprise GmbH** A **570 sqm** R **Exhibition Design, Experiential Graphic Design, General Planning** / Collaboration: Lighting Design with **LDE Belzner Holmes**; Media Planning with **medienprojekt p2**

ENERGY – DEUTSCHES MUSEUM
Concept for a Temporary Exhibition, Munich, Germany

EXPERTISIUM
Concept for a Permanent Exhibition, Showroom, Tuttlingen, Germany

FEATHERS TO THE STARS
Competition for a Permanent Exhibition in the Phillip and Patricia Frost Museum of Science, Miami, USA

FUTURIUM
Competition for the Permanent Exhibition in the Futurium, Berlin, Germany

GRÜNE ERDE ERLEBNISWELT
Competition for Architecture and a Permanent Exhibition, Corporate Headquater Scharnstein, Austria

HOUSE OF FUTURE
Concept for a Permanent Exhibition, Berlin, Germany

HOTEL SILBER
Concept for the Permanent Exhibition of a National Heritage Site, Stuttgart, Germany

HOUSE OF FAIRYTALES – HANS CHRISTIAN ANDERSEN MUSEUM
Competition for a Permanent Exhibition, Odense, Denmark

LERNWERK BOCHOLT
Architectural Competition for the Conversion of a former Spinning Mill into an Adult Education Centre, Bocholt, Germany

MUSEUM MENSCH UND NATUR
Concept for a Permanent Exhibition, Munich, Germany

↗ p. 326
MUSEUM OF TYROLEAN FARMS
Permanent Exhibition, Kramsach, Austria T **Ethnology, History** C **Museum of Tyrolean Farms** A **85,000 sqm (Open Air Museum)** R **Concept, Visitor Routing, Exhibition Design, Architecture** / Collaboration: Lighting Design with **LDE Belzner Holmes**; Media Planning with **medienprojekt p2** / Execution Planning Pavilions: **Wurzer Nagel ZT-GmbH** P **Gabriele Grießenböck**

NONGFU SPRING
Permanent Exhibition, Visitor Centre, Fusong, China T **Water** C **Nongfu Spring** A **2,500 sqm** R **Exhibition Design, Scenography** / Collaboration: Lighting Design with **LDE Belzner Holmes**; Media Planning with **medienprojekt p2** / Architecture: **Ware Malcomb Architect** / Landscape Architecture: **Jensen & Skodvin Architects**

NOVARTIS
Concept for a Permanent Exhibition, Basel, Switzerland

NY TRELLEBORG
Competition for a Permanent Exhibition, Slagelse, Denmark / Architecture: **3XN**

OMEGA – HER TIME
Temporary Exhibition, La Triennale di Milano, Milan, Italy T **Fashion** C **OMEGA SA** A **250 sqm** R **General Planning, Exhibition Design, Scenography, Experiential Graphic Design** / Collaboration: Lighting Design with **LDE Belzner Holmes**; Media Planning with **medienprojekt p2**

OSKAR SCHLEMMER INSTALLATION
Concept for a Temporary Installation with **Eric Gauthier**, Staatsgalerie Stuttgart, Germany

PARLAMENTARIUM 2.0
Concept for a Design Update of the Parlamentarium, Brussels, Belgium

RENQIU URBAN PLANNING EXHIBITION
Concept for a Permanent Urban Planning Exhibition, Renqiu, China

SAUDI ARAMCO – CHILDREN DISCOVERY ZONE
Concept for a Permanent Exhibition, Dhahran, Saudi Arabia

STIHL CONCEPT
Concept for a Brand Experience, Waiblingen, Germany

SUDETENDEUTSCHES MUSEUM
Competition for a Permanent Exhibition, Munich, Germany

SUVA
Concept, Lucerne, Switzerland

SWATCH
Competition for a Permanent Brand Exhibition, Biel, Switzerland

2014

AMERIKA – ÜBERSEE-MUSEUM BREMEN
Concept for a Permanent Exhibition, Bremen, Germany

ARBURG EVOLUTION
Permanent Exhibition, Visitor Centre, Lossburg, Germany T **Industry, Technology** C **ARBURG GmbH + Co. KG** A **850 sqm** R **General Planning, Exhibition Design and Scenography** / Collaboration: Lighting Design with **LDE Belzner Holmes**; Media Planning with **medienprojekt p2**

ARCHÄOLOGISCHES MUSEUM
Competition for the Permanent Exhibition in the Archäologische Museum, Bad Königshofen, Germany

↗ p. 308
DIALOGUE WITH TIME
Touring Exhibition, Museum für Kommunikation, Frankfurt/Main, Germany T **Human** C **Dialogue Social Enterprise GmbH** A **570 sqm** R **General Planning, Exhibition Design, Experiential Graphic Design** / Collaboration: Lighting Design with **LDE Belzner Holmes**; Media Planning with **medienprojekt p2** P **Uwe Dettmar**

↗ p. 302
ENERGETICON
Permanent Exhibition, Alsdorf, Germany T **Energy** C **ENERGETICON gGmbH** A **3,000 sqm** R **Exhibition Design, Scenography, Experiential Graphic Design** / Collaboration: Lighting Design with **LDE Belzner Holmes**; Media Planning with **medienprojekt p2** / Refurbishment: **Architekturbüro Heinrich Böll** P **Thomas Mayer**

ENERGY PAVILIONS
Competition for the Theme Park of the Expo Astana, Kazakhstan

ESA
Concept for a Permanent Exhibition, Darmstadt, Germany

EUROPEAN ELECTIONS SINCE 1979
Temporary Exhibition, Parlamentarium, Brussels, Belgium T **Politics, History** C **European Parliament / Bruns bv** A **150 sqm** R **Exhibition Concept and Design, Scenography**

↗ p. 310
GERMAN HAT MUSEUM
Permanent Exhibition, Lindenberg, Germany T **Industry, Fashion** C **City of Lindenberg** A **1,000 sqm** R **Exhibition Concept, Scenography** / Lighting Design: **LDE Belzner Holmes**; Media Planning: **intermediate engineering**; Media Design and Production: **2av**; Experiential Graphic Design: **emde gestaltung** / Architecture/Conversion: **JAUSS + GAUPP** P **Daniel Stauch**

HAMAM
Concept for a Permanent Exhibition and Interior Design, Reconstruction, Istanbul, Turkey

HOFFMANN GROUP AUSSTELLUNGS- UND SCHULUNGSZENTRUM
Concept for a Corporate Exhibition and Educational Centre, Munich, Germany

KAPELLBRÜCKE
Concept for a Scenograhic Intervention on a Historic Bridge, Lucerne, Switzerland

KOSMOS WEIMAR
Competition for a Permanent Exhibition in the Residenzschloss, Klassik Stiftung Weimar, Germany

LA CITÉ DU CORPS HUMAIN
Competition for a Permanent Exhibition, Montpellier, France / Architecture: **BIG Architects**

LE JAPONISME
Concept for the Temporary Exhibition Le Japonisme in the Musée D'Ethnographie, Geneva, Switzerland

↗ p. 314
MEG–MUSÉE D'ETHNOGRAPHIE DE GENÈVE
Permanent Exhibition, Geneva, Switzerland T **Ethnology** C **City of Geneva, Department of Culture** A **1,000 sqm** R **General Planning, Exhibition Design, Scenography, Experiential Graphic Design** / Collaboration: Lighting Design with **Atelier Derrer**; Media Planning with **Point Prod** / Video Art: **Ange Leccia** / Architecture: **Graber Pulver Architekten** P **Daniel Stauch**

MESHES FASHION MAKERS
Temporary Exhibition, TIM–State Textile and Industry Museum, Augsburg, Germany T **Industry, Fashion** C **TIM–State Textile and Industry Museum, Augsburg** A **1,000 sqm** R **General Planning, Exhibition Concept and Design, Scenography, Experiential Graphic Design**

MINISTRY OF FOREIGN AFFAIRS PAVILION
Competition for an Exhibition in the Ministry of Foreign Affairs Pavilion, Al-Jandria, Saudi Arabia

MUSEUM OF THE HUMAN BODY
Competition for the Permanent Exhibition in the new Museum of the Human Body, Montpellier, France

NATURALIS – THE ENCOUNTER
Concept for a Permanent Exhibition – The Encounter, Naturalis Biodiversity Center, Leiden, Netherlands

NATURE DETECTIVES
Competition for a Temporary Exhibition, Museum of National History, Stuttgart, Germany

OMEGA MUSEUM
Concept for a Permanent Exhibition, Biel, Switzerland

POP ART
Permanent Exhibition, Nijmegen, The Netherlands T **Art** C **Museum Het Valkhof** A **400 sqm** R **General Planning, Exhibition Concept and Design, Scenography, Experiential Graphic Design** / Collaboration: Lighting Design with **LDE Belzner Holmes**; Media Planing with **medienprojekt p2**

RATHAUS INGELHEIM
Concept for the Architecture of the Town Hall of Ingelheim, Germany

ROLLING STONES
Concept for a Temporary Exhibition, London, United Kingdom

↗ p. 296
SHANGHAI AUTO MUSEUM – COLLECTION PAVILION
Permanent Exhibition, Shanghai, China T **Mobility** C **Shanghai Auto Museum** A **2,300 sqm** R **Exhibition Concept and Design, Scenography, Experiential Graphic Design, General Planning** / Collaboration: Lighting Design with **LDE Belzner Holmes**; Media Planning with **medienprojekt p2**; Media Production with **Werksrakete** and **Gush Films** P **Shanghai Auto Museum**

↗ p. 259
↗ p. 290
SMAC–STATE MUSEUM OF ARCHAEOLOGY CHEMNITZ
Permanent Exhibition, Chemnitz, Germany T **Archaeology** C **Saxon Archaeological Heritage Office** A **3,600 sqm** R **General Planning, Exhibition Design, Scenography, Experiential Graphic Design** / Collaboration: Lighting Design with **LDE Belzner Holmes**; Media Planning with **medienprojekt p2** / "Time–Dynamic Model of Saxony": **MKT** with **Tamschick Media+Space** / Architecture: **Erich Mendelsohn** / Conversion: **AUER WEBER** and **KNERER UND LANG Architekten** P **Michael Jungblut**

SOCKS ORIENT BEFIT
Concept for a Showroom, Hangzhou, China

↗ p. 298
SWISS CHOCOLATE ADVENTURE
Permanent Exhibition, Lucerne, Switzerland T **Industry, Trade** C **Swiss Museum of Transport / iart** A **700 sqm** R **Exhibition Design, Scenography** P **Michael Jungblut**

THE ENCOUNTER GALLERY
Proposal for a Permanent Exhibition of a Biodiversity Center, Leiden, Netherlands

VIKING EXPLORER CRUISING SHIPS
Concept for Interior Design, London, United Kingdom

2013

↗ p. 136
CERN – VISIT POINTS
Permanent Exhibition, Geneva, Switzerland T **Science** C **CERN (Conseil Européen pour la Recherche Nucléaire)** A **800 sqm** R **General Planning, Exhibition Concept and Design, Scenography, Exhibition Graphics** / Collaboration: Light and Media Planning with **iart** / Media Production: **Media Lab CERN** P **Michael Jungblut, Phil Püschel**

↗ p. 130
EXPERTISIUM
Permanent Exhibition, Showroom, Aesculap Academy, Bochum, Germany T **Healthcare** C **Aesculap Akademie GmbH, Tuttlingen** A **650 sqm** R **General Planning, Concept and Exhibition Design, Scenography, Experiential Graphic Design** / Collaboration: Lighting Design with **LDE Belzner Holmes**; Media Planning with **medienprojekt p2** / Architecture: **Günter Hermann Architekten** P **Brigida González**

↗ p. 138
GERMAN PAVILION
Competition for the German National Pavilion, Expo Milano 2015, Milan, Italy

↗ p. 124
GERMAN STEAM LOCOMOTIVE MUSEUM
Permanent Exhibition, Neuenmarkt, Germany T **History, Mobility** C **German Steam Locomotive Museum Foundation** A **100,000 sqm (Open Air Museum), 3,000 sqm (Engine Shed)** R **General Planning, Concept and Exhibition Design, Scenography, Experiential Graphic Design** / Collaboration: Lighting Design with **LDE Belzner Holmes**; Media Planning with **medienprojekt p2**; Media Production with **Clarence Productions** / Architecture/Coversion: **Architekturbüro Schramm** P **Michael Jungblut**

↗ p. 132
HAUS DER BERGE
Permanent Exhibition, Visitor Centre of the National Park, Berchtesgaden, Germany T **Natural History** C **Bavarian State Ministry for Environment and Health** A **900 sqm** R **General Planning, Exhibition Design, Scenography, Experiential Graphic Design** / Collaboration: Lighting Design with **LDE Belzner Holmes**; Media Planning with **medienprojekt p2** / Media Design and Production: **Tamschick Media+Space**; Sound: **Klangerfinder** / Architecture: **Staatliches Bauamt Traunstein**; Execution Planning: **Leitenbacher Spiegelberger Architekten** P **Michael Jungblut**

HMEC–HYUNDAI MOTOR EXPERIENCE CENTER
Concept for a Brand Experience Centre, Ilsan, Korea

INSIDE THE STATION
Temporary Exhibition, Palais Tour & Taxis, Brussels, Belgium T **Natural History, Science** C **International Polar Foundation** A **700 sqm** R **General Planning, Exhibition Concept and Design, Scenography** / Collaboration: Lighting Design with **LDE Belzner Holmes**; Media Planning with **medienprojekt p2**

↗ p. 128
LIVING THE FUTURE – THE DEMOGRAPHIC OPPORTUNITY
Touring Exhibition, Museum für Naturkunde, Berlin, Germany T **Science** C **Federal Ministry of Education and Research / Leibniz Association** A **300 sqm** R **General Planning, Exhibition Concept and Design, Scenography** / Collaboration: Lighting Design with **Fischer+Partner**; Media Planning with **medienprojekt p2** P **Michael Jungblut**

NATURAL HISTORY MUSEUM
Concept for Permanent Exhibitions in the Natural History Museum, Oslo, Norway

PANASONIC – 4K
Trade Fair Stand, IFA, Berlin, Germany T **Consumer Electronics** C **Panasonic Marketing Europe GmbH** A **6,000 sqm** R **Booth Design and Scenography, Experiential Graphic Design** / Media Concept and Production: **Tamschick Media+Space**; Booth Construction: **Display International**

QATAR PAVILION
Concept for the National Pavilion, Expo Milano, Milan, Italy

↗ p. 140
VIKING
Temporary Media Installation, Copenhagen, Denmark T **Archaeology** C **National Museum of Denmark** A **1,000 sqm** R **Concept, Storyboard, Scenography** / Collaboration: Media Production with **Shilo** / Lighting Design: **National Museum of Denmark** P **Michael Jungblut**

2012

BAUERNHOF MUSEUM ILLBEUREN
Concept for a Permanent Exhibition, Kronburg, Germany

CARLSWORLD
Competition for a Permanent Brand Exhibition, Copenhagen, Denmark / Architecture: **BIG – Bjarke Ingels Group**

↗ p. 118
DARWINEUM
Permanent Exhibition, Rostock, Germany T **Natural History** C **Rostock Zoological Gardens** A **1,700 sqm** R **General Planning, Exhibition Concept and Design, Scenography, Experiential Graphic Design** / Collaboration: Lighting Design with **Licht Kunst Licht**; Media Planning with **medienprojekt p2**; Media Design with **2av** / Architecture: **Rasbach Architekten, Inros Lackner AG, Ingenieurbüro J. Döhler** P **Michael Jungblut**

EMEE: EUROVISION – MUSEUMS EXHIBITING EUROPE
International Research Project T **Science** C **EU Kultur Programm (EACEA)** R Project Partner: **ATELIER BRÜCKNER GmbH**, Stuttgart, Germany; **Nationalmuseum für Geschichte**, Sofia, Bulgaria; **University Paris-Est Créteil – IUFM**, Paris, France; **University Roma Tre**, Rome, Italy; **Archäologisches Nationalmuseum**, Lisbon, Portugal; **Museum für Zeitgenössische Geschichte**, Ljubljana, Slovenia; **monochrom Kunstverein**, Vienna, Austria

EULE
Concept for a Childrens Science Lab, Schwäbisch Gmund, Germany

EUROPEAN CENTRAL BANK
Concept for a Permanent Exhibition, European Central Bank, Frankfurt/Main, Germany

FIFA
Concept for the FIFA Museum, Zurich, Switzerland

FREISTADT LANDESAUSSTELLUNG
Concept for a Temporary Exhibition, Freistadt, Austria

GELDMUSEUM DEUTSCHE BUNDESBANK
Concept for a Permanent Exhibition, German Central Bank, Frankfurt/Main, Germany

GRIMM JUBILÄUMSAUSSTELLUNG
Concept for a Temporary Exhibition, Kassel, Germany

↗ p. 112
↗ p. 256
GS CALTEX PAVILION
Corporate Pavilion, Expo Yeosu, South Korea T **Energy** C **GS Caltex / Peopleworks Promotion Co. Ltd.** A **1,960 sqm** R **General Planning, Architecture and Scenography, Main Show** / Collaboration: Structural Engineering with **Knippers Helbig**; Media Planning with **medienprojekt p2**; Production Main Show with **Tamschick Media+Space** / Sound Main Show: **BLUWI** P **Nils Clauss** and **ATELIER BRÜCKNER**

HYUNDAI MOTOR STUDIO MOSCOW
Concept for a Brand Experience, Moscow, Russia

↗ p. 104
KUSCH+CO – PAST-PRESENT-FUTURE
Trade Fair Stand, Milan, Italy T **Furniture** C **Kusch+Co** A **180 sqm** R **Concept, Booth Design, Scenography** / Collaboration: **Film with M.A.R.K. 13** P **Michael Jungblut**

↗ p. 110
LASCAUX IV – INTERNATIONAL CENTRE FOR CAVE ART
Concept for a Visitor Centre with a Permanent Exhibition, Montignac-Lascaux, France / Architecture: **Auer Weber Architects**

LUMINALE – BLUE NIGHT
Event, Frankfurt/Main, Germany T **Finance** C **Deutsche Börse AG** A **1,500 sqm** R **Concept, Design, Scenography** / Collaboration: Lighting and Sound Design with **Ingo Bracke, Studio Kybra**

MUSEUM BURGHAUSEN
Concept for a Permanent Exhibition, Stuttgart, Germany

PORSCHE MOBILITÄTSZENTRUM
Concept for a Brand Experience, Stuttgart, Germany

STAGED SPACES
Temporary Exhibition, Architekturgalerie am Weißenhof, Stuttgart, Germany T **Architecture, Exhibition, Scenography** C **ATELIER BRÜCKNER GmbH** A **60 sqm** R **Exhibition Concept and Design** / Curator: **Carola Franke-Höltzermann**

STADTHALLE KARLSRUHE
Concept for the Interior Design and Orientation System, Karlsruhe, Germany

TETRA PAK
Concept for a Trade Fair Stand, Anuga FoodTec, Köln, Germany

2011

ABB LEARNING FACTORY
Competition for a Permanent Exhibition, Zurich, Switzerland

AMOREPACIFIC
Concept for a Brand Experience, Gyeonggi-do, Korea

ARCHAEOLOGISCHE ZONE KÖLN
Concept for a Heritage Site, Cologne, Germany

BIONIK
Concept for a Temporary Exhibition, Munich, Germany

CITÉ DE LA ROMANITÉ
Competition for a Permanent Exhibition, Narbonne, France

DEUTSCHER BUNDESTAG
Concept for a Permanent Exhibition, Berlin, Germany

ELTERNHAUS BRÜCKNER
Concept for a Family Home, Föhrenbach, Germany

↗ p. 82
GERMAN FILM MUSEUM
Permanent Exhibition, Frankfurt/Main, Germany T **History, Science** C **German Film Institute DIF/German Film Museum** A **800 sqm** R **Exhibition Concept and Design, Scenography** / Collaboration: Lighting Design with **Bartenbach Lichtlabor**; Media Planning with **medienprojekt p2**; Media Design with **jangled nerves** / Architecture/Conversion: **Blocher Blocher Partners** P **Uwe Dettmar**

GOETHE
Competition for a Permanent Exhibition of the Goethe National Museum, Klassik Stiftung Weimar, Germany

↗ p. 92
↗ p. 216
HET SCHEEPVAARTMUSEUM
Permanent Exhibition, Amsterdam, The Netherlands T **Navigation** C **Het Scheepvaartmuseum** A **1,230 sqm** R **Exhibition Concept and Design, Scenography** / Collaboration: Experiential Graphic Design with **attraktive grautöne** / Lighting Design: **Lichtontwerpers**; Media Production: **Kiss the Frog** / Architecture/Conversion: **Dok Architects** P **Michael Jungblut**

MERCEDES-BENZ CAMPUS
Concept, Stuttgart, Germany

MIGRATION – GERMAN HYGIENE MUSEUM
Concept for a Temporary Exhibition, Dresden, Germany

NAVAL GALLERY–MARITIME MUSEUM
Concept, London, United Kingdom

OHOHOPE WISH TREE
Concept for a Private Permanent Expo Park, Jiangmen, China

↗ p. 98
↗ p. 202
PARLAMENTARIUM
Visitor Centre of the European Parliament, Brussels, Belgium T **History, Politics** C **European Parliament** A **5,400 sqm** R **Exhibition Concept and Design, Scenography** / Lighting Design: **LDE Belzner Holmes**; Media Design: **jangled nerves**; Media Production: **Markenfilm Crossing**; Media Planning: **medienprojekt p2**; Experiential Graphic Design: **integral ruedi baur**; Role Play Game: **Mediafarm** P Rainer Rehfeld

RICHARD WAGNER MUSEUM
Concept for a Permanent Exhibition, Bayreuth, Germany

SAMSUNG BRAND SHOWCASE
Concept, Seoul, Korea

SAMSUNG HISTORY MUSEUM
Concept for a Permanent Exhibition, Yongin-si, Korea

SBERBANK MUSEUM
Permanent Exhibition, Sberbank, Moscow, Russia T **Finance** C **KnaufKassel GmbH / Sberbank** A **1,000 sqm** R **Exhibition Design, Experiential Graphic Design** / Collaboration: Lighting Design with **Licht Kunst Licht** / Media Planning: **Arora**; Content Development: **Stefan Paul-Jacobs**; Light Production: **Lichtfront Köln**

SEEUM
Concept for a Permanent Exhibition, Bodman-Ludwigshafen, Germany

SHANGHAI NATURAL HISTORY MUSEUM
Concept for the Permanent Exhibition, Shanghai, China

SPORTSCHECK FLAGSHIPSTORE
Concept for a Flagship Store, Munich, Germany

↗ p. 86
↗ p. 222
TEXTILWERK BOCHOLT
Architecture/Conversion, Bocholt, Germany T **Industry** C **LWL-Industry Museum** A **8,500 sqm** R **General Planning** / Collaboration: Lighting Design with **LDE Belzner Holmes**; Structural Engineering with **Ingenieurbüro Pross**; Electrical Planning with **Ingenieurbüro Kipp & Knuhr**; Building Services with **K&L Energietechnik** P **mac tanó, Holtappels/ LWL-Industriemuseum**

THE MONETARY UNIFICATION IN ITALY
Temporary Exhibition, Palazzo delle Esposizioni, Rome, Italy T **Finance** C **Banca d'Italia** A **560 sqm** R **Exhibition Design and Planning, Scenography** / Collaboration: Lighting Design with **LDE Belzner Holmes**; Media Design and Media Planning with **ToDo**; Sound Design with **Enrico Ascoli**

WUXI CONCEPT
Concept for a Permanent Exhibition, Wuxi, China

2010

AUFRUHR 1225! – RITTER, BURGEN UND INTRIGEN
Temporary Exhibition, LWL-Museum of Archaelogy, Herne, Germany T **History** C **Landschaftsverband Westfalen-Lippe (LWL)** A **1,500 sqm** R **Exhibition Design, Media Planning, Experiential Graphic Design** / Collaboration: Lighting Design with **LDE Belzner Holmes**

BLAUE NACHT: HANDELN
Event Design for Luminale, Main Trading Hall, Deutsche Börse, Frankfurt/Main, Germany T **Finance** C **Deutsche Börse AG** A **1,500 sqm** R **Concept, Design, Scenography** / Collaboration: Lighting and Sound Design with **Ingo Bracke**

BUTZWEILERHOF
Feasibility Study for a Permanent Exhibition incorporating the historic runway, the former hangar and tower of the airport Butzweilerhof, Cologne, Germany T **Aerospace** C **Landschaftsverband Rheinland (LVR)** A **890 sqm** R **Design Concept**

↗ p. 70
CERN – UNIVERSE OF PARTICLES
Permanent Exhibition, CERN Visitor Centre, Globe of Science and Innovation, Geneva, Switzerland T **Science** C **CERN (European Organisation for Nuclear Research)** A **450 sqm** R **Exhibition Design, Experiential Graphic Design** / Collaboration: Lighting Design with **Rolf Derrer**; Media Planning with **iart**; Film Production with **Tamschick Media+Space** P **Michael Jungblut**

PROJECT LIST

CHILDREN RAINBOW LAND
Permanent Exhibition, Shanghai, China T **Science** C **Shanghai Science and Technology Museum** A **2,500 sqm** R **General Contractor, Exhibition Design, Experiential Graphic Design** / Collaboration: Lighting Design with **LDE Belzner Holmes**; Media Design with **iart**

DEUTSCHE BÖRSE – THE CUBE
Corporte Interior Design for the Entrance and Lobby, Guidance System, Eschborn, Germany T **Finance** C **Deutsche Börse AG** A **1,500 sqm (Exhibition Area), 56,000 sqm (Total Area)** R **Concept, Construction Planning** / Collaboration: Lighting Design with **LDE Belzner Holmes**

DFB-FUSSBALLMUSEUM
Competition for a Permanent Exhibition, Dortmund, Germany

GASTEIG WEGE-, WERBE- UND LEITSYSTEM
Concept for a Signage System, Munich, Germany

GOLF – HALL OF FAME
Concept for a Visitor Centre, Deutscher Golf Verband, Röhrenfeld/Neuburg, Germany

HOUSE OF HISTORY EUROPE
Concept for a Permanent Exhibition, Brussels, Belgium

HUMBOLDT-FORUM
Competition for a Permanent Exhibition, Collection of the Ethnological Museum and the Asian Art Museum, Berlin, Germany

ICE CUBE
Temporary Exhibition, Belgian Pavilion, Expo 2010, Shanghai, China T **Natural History** C **International Polar Foundation** A **30 sqm** R **Exhibition Design, Experiential Graphic Design** / Collaboration: Lighting Design with **LDE Belzner Holmes**; Media Planning with **medienprojekt p2**

IN3 INTERNATIONAL SCENOGRAPHERS' FESTIVAL
International Conference for Scenography, Basel, Switzerland T **Science**

LG – FREEDOM THROUGH INFINITE POSSIBILITIES
Trade Fair Stand, IFA Berlin, Germany T **Consumer Electronics** C **LG Electronics / Display International, Communication Agency: LBest** A **2,600 sqm** R **Concept, Fair Stand Design, Event Architecture, Lighting Design, Experiential Graphic Design**

LIVING OCEAN AND COAST
Competition for a Theme Park, Expo 2012, Yeosu, Korea / In cooperation with **Nüssli AG**

LUDWIG II
Concept for a Temporary Exhibition, Landesausstellung Bayern, Chiemsee, Germany

MAN BUS FORUM
Brand Experience, Munich, Germany T **Mobility** C **MAN Nutzfahrzeuge Group** A **1,800 sqm** R **Exhibition Design** / Collaboration: Lighting Design with **LDE Belzner Holmes**; Media Planning with **medienprojekt p2**; Media design with **Medienlabor Schrem**; Film production with **Schokolade** / Architecture: **pmp Architekten**

MUSÉE-CITÉ DE L'ÉCONOMIE ET DE LA MONNAIE
Concept for a Permanent Exhibition, Paris, France

ODYSSEY 21
Competition for a Permanent Exhibition, Le Havre, France

PANASONIC CONVENTION 2010
Retailer Event, Event-Arena, Munich, Germany T **Consumer Electronics** C **Panasonic Deutschland GmbH** A **450 sqm (3D Experience Space), 300 sqm (Stage)** R **Concept, Design, Event Architecture** / Collaboration: Film Production and Animation with **Thauma Motion Design Studio**

POLARIS CLIMATE CHANGE OBSERVATORY
Concept for a Science Centre, Cape Town, South Africa and Brussels, Belgium

↗ p. 60
↗ p. 240
↗ p. 258

RAUTENSTRAUCH-JOEST-MUSEUM – CULTURES OF THE WORLD
Permanent Exhibition, Cologne, Germany T **Ethnology** C **City of Cologne, Department of Art and Culture** A **3,600 sqm** R **Exhibition Design, Scenography, Experiential Graphic Design** / Collaboration: Lighting Design with **LDE Belzner Holmes**; Media Design with **jangled nerves** / Architecture: **Schneider+Sendelbach Architekten** P **Michael Jungblut**

↗ p. 66
↗ p. 278

STATE GRID PAVILION – MAGIC BOX
Corporate Pavilion, Main Show and Exterior Facade, Expo 2010, Shanghai, China T **Energy** C **State Grid Corporation of China (SGCC), IBM China Company Limited, Shanghai** A **15 x 15 x 13 m (Interior Magic Box), 380 sqm (Facade Magic Box), 4,700 sqm (Facade Pavilion)** R **Concept, Design and Production of the Main Show and the Pavilion's Facade** / Collaboration: Spatial Media Design with **Tamschick Media+Space** in cooperation with **m box Bewegtbild GmbH**; Media Planning with **medienprojekt p2**; Sound design with **Idee und Klang** / Architecture: **CCDI** P **Roland Halbe**

STUTTGART TOURIST INFORMATION OFFICE
Concept, Stuttgart, Germany

↗ p. 74

TIM – STATE TEXTILE AND INDUSTRY MUSEUM
Permanent Exhibition, Augsburg, Germany T **History, Industry, Fashion** C **City of Augsburg** A **2,500 sqm** R **Exhibition Design, Experiential Graphic Design** / Collaboration: Lighting Design with **LDE Belzner Holmes**; Media Planning with **medienprojekt p2**; Software Media Stations: **2av** / Graces: General Concept: **ATELIER BRÜCKNER**; Software Production: **Tamschick Media+Space**; Figurines: **Anja Luithle** with **Hans-Martin Wagner** / Architecture/Conversion: **Klaus Kada** P **Volker Mai**

VIBRACIÓN – MODERNE KUNST AUS LATEINAMERIKA
Temporary Exhibition, Bonn, Germany T **Art** C **Kunst- und Ausstellungshalle der Bundesrepublik Deutschland** A **1,600 sqm** R **Exhibition Design, Experiential Graphic Design**

WATERCUBE
Design Concept for a Permanent Exhibition, Pumping Station Friedrichshain, Berlin, Germany

WELT DER KELTEN – LANDESAUSSTELLUNG
Concept for a Temporary Exhibition, Stuttgart, Germany

WELTSICHTEN
Concept for a Temporary Exhibition, Stuttgart, Germany

ZHONGTAI SHOWROOM BEIJING
Concept for a Brand Environment, Beijing, China

ZITADELLE SPANDAU
Competition for Architecture and Design of a National Heritage Site, Berlin, Germany

2009

ARCHE
Competition for a Signage System and a walkable Installation, Olgahospital, Klinikum Stuttgart, Germany

DIE WITTELSBACHER UND DAS REICH DER MITTE – 400 JAHRE CHINA UND BAYERN
Temporary Exhibition, Bayerisches Nationalmuseum, Munich, Germany T **History** C **Bayerisches Nationalmuseum** A **600 sqm** R **Exhibition Design** in collaboration with **Tanja Hammerl**

DORNIER MUSEUM FRIEDRICHSHAFEN
Permanent Exhibition, Friedrichshafen, Germany T **Aerospace** C **Dornier Stiftung für Luft- und Raumfahrt, Friedrichshafen** A **5,000 sqm** R **Exhibition Design, Experiential Graphic Design** / Collaboration: Lighting Design with **LDE Belzner Holmes**; Media Design with **jangled nerves** / Architecture: **Allmann Sattler Wappner Architekten**

ENBW
Concept for a Brand Experience, Karlsruhe, Germany

INFORMATIONS- UND DOKUMENTATIONSZENTRUM DER BSTU
Competition for a Temporary Exhibition, Berlin, Germany

INN-MUSEUM
Feasibility Study for the Re-Design of the Inn-Museum, Rosenheim, Germany T **History** C **Wasserwirtschaftsamt Rosenheim** A **845 sqm** R **Exhibition Design, Lighting Design, Media Design**

LIGHT OF WISDOM
Design Concept for a Permanent Exhibition, Shanghai, China

LOKI SCHMIDT HAUS – MUSEUM FÜR NUTZPFLANZEN
Permanent Exhibition, Hamburg, Germany T **Natural History** C **Loki Schmidt Haus** A **286 sqm** R **Exhibition Design, Lighting Design, Media Design, Experiential Graphic Design** / Architecture: **Bernhard Winking Architekten BDA**

MAN FORUM
Brand Environment, Munich, Germany T **Industry, Mobility, Technology** C **MAN Nutzfahrzeuge AG** A **450 sqm (Brand World), 2,000 sqm (Exhibition Hall)** R **Exhibition Design** / Collaboration: Lighting Design with **LDE Belzner Holmes**; Media Planning with **medienprojekt p2**; Media Design with **jangled nerves** / Architecture: **pmp Architekten**

MARITIME LEBENSWELTEN
Competition for Architecture and Exhibition Design, Cuxhaven, Germany

RESIDENZSCHLOSS DRESDEN
Competition for the Reconstruction of the North Wing of the Historic Castle, Permanent Exhibition

RÜSSELSHEIM CONCEPT
Concept for a Permanent Exhibition, Rüsselsheim, Germany

SEA CITY MUSEUM
Concept for a Permanent Exhibition, Southampton, England

STAATLICHES MUSEUM FÜR NATURKUNDE, STUTTGART
Entrance, Shop and Prologue of the Permanent Exhibition, Stuttgart, Germany T **Natural History** C **Staatliches Museum für Naturkunde, Stuttgart** A **300 sqm** R **Interior Design** / Collaboration: Lighting Design with **LDE Belzner Holmes**; Media Planning with **medienprojekt p2**; Experiential Graphic Design with **attraktive grautöne**

STADTMUSEUM IM WILHELMSPALAIS
Competition for Architecture and Exhibition Design, Stuttgart, Germany

STONEHENGE VISITOR CENTRE
Concept for a Visitor Centre for a National Heritage Site, Wales, United Kingdom

STUTTGART 21 – UNSERE GRÜNE STADT
Permanent Exhibition, City Hall, Stuttgart, Germany T **Urban Planning** C **City of Stuttgart** A **160 sqm** R **Exhibition Design, Media Design** / Collaboration: Lighting Design with **LDE Belzner Holmes**; Experiential Graphic Design with **attraktive grautöne**

VW PRÄSENTIERT SICH
Competition for the Architecture and Design Concept for Trade Fairs and Congresses, Leipzig, Paris, Shanghai

WASSERBURG HÜLSHOFF
Feasibility Study for a Literature Centre, Havixbeck, Germany T **Literature** C **Stiftung Westfalen-Initiative** A **2,800 sqm** R **Concept, Architecture, Exhibition Design**

WELT DER RELIGIONEN
Expertise for a Temporary Exhibition, Gasometer Oberhausen, Germany T **Religion** C **Wirtschaftsmetropole Ruhr** A **7,000 sqm** R **Exhibition Design, Experiential Graphic Design, Lighting Design** / Collaboration: Concept Development with **the International Consortium “Dynamics in the History of Religions”**; Media Planning with **medienprojekt p2**; Media Staging with **Tamschick Media+Space**; Kinetic Installation with **Arnold Walz**

WELTWISSEN – 300 JAHRE WISSENSCHAFTEN IN BERLIN
Competition for a Temporary Exhibition, Martin-Gropius-Bau, Berlin, Germany

2008

AFRICAN PAVILION
Competition for Exhibition Design and Facade Design, Expo 2010, Shanghai, China

↗ p. 50
BLAUE NACHT
Event Design for Luminale, Main Trading Hall, Deutsche Börse, Frankfurt/Main, Germany T **Finance** C **Deutsche Börse AG** A **1,500 sqm** R Concept, Design, Scenography / Collaboration: Lighting and Sound Design with **Ingo Bracke** P **Uwe Dettmar**

↗ p. 54
↗ p. 220
BMW MUSEUM
Architecture/Conversion and Permanent Exhibition, Munich, Germany T **Mobility** C **BMW AG** A **5,000 sqm** R **General Planning, Interior Architecture, Exhibition Design** / Collaboration: Structural Engineering with **Schlaich Bergermann und Partner**; Lighting Design with **Delux AG, Rolf Derrer** / Experiential Graphic Design, Visual Identity: **Integral Ruedi Baur**; Spatial Media Design, Interactive Installations: **Art+Com**; Visual Symphony: **Tamschick Media+Space** / Architecture: Karl Schwanzer P **Marcus Meyer**

BUCHENWALD
Concept for a National Memorial Site, Weimar, Germany

CHINESISCHER PAVILLON
Concept for the Chinese National Pavilion, Shanghai, China

CHIRON
Trade Fair Stand, AMB, Stuttgart, Germany T **Technology** C **Chiron-Werke GmbH & Co.KG** A **450 sqm** R **General Planning, Exhibition Design** / Collaboration: Fair Stand Construction with **Mühlich GmbH**; Media Production with **Thauma Motion Design Studio**

CULTURE CUTS
Design Concept for a Permanent Exhibition, Ethnological Museum, Kiev, Ukraine

DER FRÖHLICHE WEINBERG
Feasibility Study for a Permanent Exhibition, Vogau, Austria

↗ p. 50
DEUTSCHE BÖRSE – MAIN TRADING HALL
Corporate Scenography, Main Trading Hall, Frankfurt/Main, Germany T **Finance** C **Deutsche Börse AG** A **1,500 sqm** R **General Planning, Experiential Graphic Design** / Collaboration: Lighting Design with **Delux AG**; Media Planning with **medienprojekt p2** P **Uwe Dettmar**

DEUTSCHE BÖRSE – HEADQUARTERS
Driveway and Foyer, Eschborn, Germany T **Finance** C **Deutsche Börse AG** A **360 sqm** R **Concept, Construction Planning** / Collaboration: Lighting Design with **LDE Belzner Holmes**

DEUTSCHE POST – INNOVATION CENTER
Competition for a Brand Experience, Troisdorf, Germany

DEUTSCHES MUSEUM–CHEMISTRY
Competition for a Permanent Exhibition, Munich, Germany

DEUTSCHES UHRENMUSEUM GLASHÜTTE
Permanent Exhibition, Glashütte, Germany T **Industry** C **Glashütter Uhrenbetrieb GmbH** A **1,000 sqm** R **Exhibition Design, Experiential Graphic Design** / Collaboration: Lighting Design with **Anke Augsburg Licht**; Media Design with **jangled nerves** / Refurbishment of the Building: **Bauconzept Planungsgesellschaft mbH**

ENERGETICON – INFORMATION TOTEMS
Energeticon, Alsdorf, Germany T **Energy** C **LEG Stadtentwicklung GmbH & Co. KG** R **Concept, Lighting Design, Media Design, Experiential Graphic Design**

HAUS DES WALDES
Competition for a Permanent Exhibition, Stuttgart, Germany

HELLWEG-MUSEUM
Concept for a Permanent Exhibition, Unna, Germany

HOHENASPERG – EIN DEUTSCHES GEFÄNGNIS
Competition for a Permanent Exhibition, Hohenasperg, Germany

IN3 INTERNATIONAL SCENOGRAPHERS' FESTIVAL
International Conference for Scenography, Basel, Switzerland T **Science**

K32 – ATELIER BRÜCKNER
New Office, Stuttgart, Germany T **Office** C **ATELIER BRÜCKNER GmbH** A **1,600 sqm** R **Interior Design**

LWL-LANDESMUSEUM FÜR KUNST UND KULTURGESCHICHTE
Competition for a Permanent Exhibition and Signage System, Münster, Germany

MEILENSTEINE AUTOMOBIL-DESIGN, MERCEDES BENZ
Temporary Exhibition, Pinakothek der Moderne, Munich, Germany T **Automotive** C **Daimler AG** A **400 sqm** R **Design Concept**

MEMORIAL ACTE
Competition for the Design of a Slavery Museum, Guadeloupe / In cooperation with **Auer Weber Architects**

MOBILITÄTS-ENERGIE-ZENTRUM
Concept for a Communal Center for Sustainable Mobility and Energy, Stuttgart, Germany

MUSEUM DINGOLFING
Permanent Exhibition, Dingolfing, Germany T **Industry, Mobility** C **Stadt Dingolfing** A **1,000 sqm** R **Exhibition Design, Lighting Design, Media Design, Experiential Graphic Design**

↗ p. 204
PABELLÓN ESTEPAS, PRADERAS Y SABANAS – AFRICAN PAVILION
Temporary Exhibition and Facade Design, Expo 2008, Saragossa, Spain T **Natural History** C **Expo Zaragoza** A **2,500 sqm (Exhibition), 1,500 sqm (Facade)** R **General Contractor, Facade Engineering, Structural Engineering, Exhibition Design, Lighting Design, Experiential Graphic Design** / Collaboration: Media Facade with **Tamschick Media+Space**

PABELLÓN MONTAÑAS
Facade Design, Expo 2008, Saragossa, Spain T **Natural History** C **Expo Zaragoza, Nüssli AG** A Facade: **1,600 sqm** R **General Planning** / Collaboration: Experiential Graphic Design with **emde gestaltung**

PABELLÓN OASIS Y DESIERTOS
Facade Design, Expo 2008, Saragossa, Spain T **Natural History** C **Expo Zaragoza, Nüssli AG** A Facade: **820 sqm** R **General Planning** / Collaboration: Experiential Graphic Design with **designcoop** and **emde gestaltung**

RÖMER MUSEUM XANTEN
Permanent Exhibition, Xanten, Germany T **Archaeology** C **Landschaftsverband Rheinland (LVR)** A **2,400 sqm** R **Exhibition Design, Experiential Graphic Design** / Collaboration: Media Design with **jangled nerves** / Architecture: **Gatermann + Schossig Architekten**

STADTMUSEUM BERLIN – MARINEHAUS
Competition for an Architectural Concept, Berlin, Germany / In collaboration with **no w here Architekten**

STIFTUNG KLOSTER DALHEIM
Competition for the Permanent Exhibition, LWL-Landesmuseum für Klosterkultur, Lichtenau, Germany

SUPERFUND
Design Concept for the Flagship Store Investmentworld, Frankfurt/Main, Germany

T11
Design Concept for the Lobby and Public Spaces of a High-rise Building, Frankfurt/Main, Germany

↗ p. 280
THAT'S OPERA – 200 YEARS OF ITALIAN MUSIC
Touring Exhibition T **History, Music** C **Bertelsmann AG, Ricordi & C. SpA** A **1,600 sqm** R **General Planning, Exhibition Design, Experiential Graphic Design** / Collaboration: Lighting Design with **LDE Belzner Holmes**; Media Planning with **medienprojekt p2**; Media Design with **jangled nerves**; Communication with **Dorten**; Content and Research with **Institut für Kulturaustausch** P **A. T. Schaefer**

TROPENHAUS – BOTANISCHER GARTEN BERLIN
Competition for a Permanent Exhibition and Signage System, Berlin, Germany

2007

ADYTON
Research Project for an Interactive Sound Room

BACHHAUS EISENACH
Permanent Exhibition, Eisenach, Germany T **Music** C **Neue Bachgesellschaft e.V.** A **350 sqm (Historic Building), 290 sqm (Extension)** R **Exhibition Design, Lighting Design, Media Planning, Experiential Graphic Design** / Collaboration: Walk-in Composition with **Tamschick Media+Space** / Architecture: **Penkhues Architekten**

BRÜDER GRIMM-KULTURZENTRUM
Concept for a Permanent Exhibition, Hanau, Germany

CHINESE NATIONAL PAVILION
Competition for Architecture and Exhibition, Expo 2010, Shanghai, China

DAMOCLES
Touring Exhibition, Polar Year 2007/2008, Brussels, Belgium T **Natural History** C **International Polar Foundation** A **50 sqm** R **General Planning, Exhibition Design** / Collaboration: Lighting Design with **LDE Belzner Holmes**; Media Planning with **medienprojekt p2**; Experiential Graphic Design with **attraktive grautöne**

E.ON ENERGY TRADING – THE OFFICE OF THE FUTURE
Competition for Interior Design Concept, Medienhafen Düsseldorf, Germany

GERMAN PAVILION
Competition for Architecture and Exhibition Design, Expo 2010, Shanghai, China / In collaboration with **Auer Weber Architects**

GERMAN PAVILION
Competition for an Exhibition Design Concept, Expo 2008, Saragossa, Spain

HAGENBUCHER
Architectural Competition for a Science Centre, Heilbronn, Germany

HEINZ NIXDORF MUSEUMSFORUM
Concept for a Permanent Exhibition, Paderborn, Germany

KNAUF ACADEMY
Concept for a Training Centre and Showroom at Knauf Headquarters, Iphofen, Germany

LE CAURREAU DE TEMPLE
Competition for Refurbishment and Conversion into an Exhibition Centre, Paris, France / In cooperation with **Auer Weber Architects**

NATURKUNDEMUSEUM
Concept for a Permanent Exhibition, Tyumen, Russia

ORTE DER SEHNSUCHT – MIT KÜNSTLERN AUF REISEN
Competition for a Temporary Exhibition, LWL-Landesmuseum für Kunst und Kulturgeschichte, Münster, Germany

PANASONIC – BLUE BOX
Trade Fair Stand, IFA Berlin, Germany T **Consumer Electronics** C **Panasonic Marketing Europe** A **3,100 sqm** R **Fair Stand Design** / Collaboration: Experiential Graphic Design with **attraktive grautöne**; Film and Media Design with **Tamschick Media+Space**

RAUB & RESTITUTION
Competition for a Temporary Exhibition, Jüdisches Museum Berlin, Germany

ROBERT BURN BIRTHPLACE
Competition for a Permanent Exhibition, Murdoch's Lone, Alloway, Scotland, UK / In collaboration with **Nick Kapica, Ständige Vertretung Design und Kommunikation GmbH**

SANTA CRUZ – THE BIRTH OF WORLDTRADE
Competition for Design Concept for a Touring Exhibition; Martin-Gropius-Bau, Berlin, Germany

SAURIER – ERFOLGSMODELLE DER EVOLUTION
Temporary Exhibition, Staatliches Museum für Naturkunde Baden-Württemberg, Stuttgart, Germany T **Natural History** C **Staatliches Museum für Naturkunde Stuttgart** A **3,600 sqm** R **Exhibition Design, Graphic Gesign** / Collaboration: Lighting Design with **LDE Belzner Holmes**; Media Design with **jangled nerves**

SWISS PAVILION
Competition for Temporary Architecture and Exhibition Design, Expo 2010, Shanghai, China

SHENYANG CITY PLANNING EXHIBITION HALL
Concept for an Urban Planning Museum, Shenyang, China

TELEKOM
Concept for a Brand Experience, Berlin, Germany

THE POBL OF WALES
Competition for a Landmark, Wales, United Kingdom

VW NACHHALTIGKEIT
Competition for a Temporary Exhibition, Wolfsburg, Germany

2006

CLIMATE AND MAN
Temporary Exhibition, LWL-Museum of Archaeology, Herne, Germany T **Archaelogy** C **Landschaftsverband Westfalen-Lippe (LWL)** A **850 sqm** R **General Planning, Exhibition Design, Lighting Design, Media Design**

FC BAYERN MUSEUM
Concept for a Corporate Exhibition, Munich, Germany

GRUBE MESSEL
Competition for Architecture and Permanent Exhibition, Germany

HELLWEG-MUSEUM
Expertise for Re-Design of the Museum, Unna, Germany

IN3 INTERNATIONAL SCENOGRAPHERS' FESTIVAL
International Conference for Scenography, Basel, Switzerland T **Science**

KELTENWELT AM GLAUBERG
Competition for an Architectural Concept, Germany

KELVINGROVE INTERACTIVE LEARNING CENTRE
Competition for a Permanent Exhibition, Kelvingrove, United Kingdom

MUSÉE D'HISTOIRE NATURELLE
Competition for the Permanent Exhibition, Brussels, Belgium

REGENWALDHAUS
Competition for an Adventure Architecture at the Zoo Leipzig, Germany / In collaboration with **Auer Weber Architects**

REINEN WEIN EINSCHENKEN – WEINWELT IM WANDEL
Temporary Exhibition, Haus der Geschichte Baden-Württemberg, Stuttgart, Germany T **Agriculture** C **Haus der Geschichte Baden-Württemberg** A **500 sqm** R **Exhibition Design** / Collaboration: Experiential Graphic Design and Catalogue Design with **attraktive grautöne**

SHANGHAI AUTO MUSEUM
Permanent Exhibition, Anting, China T **Mobility** C **Shanghai International Auto City** A **2,500 sqm** R **General Planning, Exhibition Design, Experiential Graphic Design** / Collaboration: Lighting Design with **LDE Belzner Holmes**; Media Design with **jangled nerves** / Architecture: **IFB Dr Braschel AG**

ÜBERSEE-MUSEUM BREMEN – ASIEN, KONTINENT DER GEGENSÄTZE ↗ p. 46
Permanent Exhibition, Germany T **Ethnology** C **Übersee-Museum Bremen** A **1,800 sqm** R **Exhibition Design, Experiential Graphic Design** / Collaboration: Lighting Design with **LDE Belzner Holmes**

URWELT-MUSEUM HAUFF
Competition for the Museum's Extension and for a Permanent Exhibition, Holzmaden, Germany

WESTFÄLISCHES LANDESMUSEUM FÜR KUNST UND KULTURGESCHICHTE
Concept for the Permanent Exhibition, Münster, Germany

ZECHE ZOLLVEREIN
Competition for a Visitor Centre, Essen, Germany

2005

ABENTEUER RAUMFAHRT – AUFBRUCH INS WELTALL
Competition for a Permanent Exhibition, Landesmuseum für Technik und Arbeit Mannheim, Germany

ADIDAS PERFORMANCE STAGE
Brand Experience, Herzogenaurach, Germany T **Fashion, Sport** C **Adidas Salomon AG** A **900 sqm** R **Interior Design, Experiential Graphic Design**

ADIDAS – WALK OF FAME
Competition for a Portrayal of the Company's History, Herzogenaurach, Germany

CHIRON FORUM
Permanent Exhibition on the Company's History, Tuttlingen, Germany T **Technology** C **Chiron-Werke GmbH & Co.KG** A **400 sqm** R **Exhibition Design, Lighting Design, Experiential Graphic Design** / Collaboration: Media Design with **jangled nerves** and **Camflight**

DEUTSCHE BAHN – VIP-LOUNGE
Competition, New Central Railway Station, Berlin, Germany

GUTENBERG MUSEUM
Concept for a Permanent Exhibition, Mainz, Germany

HAITHABU
Concept for a Permanent Exhibition, Busdorf, Germany

KING ABDULLAH CENTER FOR LUNAR OBSERVATION AND STUDY
Design Concept for a Permanent Exhibition, Mecca, Saudi Arabia

K.L.I.M.A., LABOR ERDE
Design Concept for a Temporary Exhibition, Gasometer, Oberhausen, Germany

KONSTANTIN DER GROSSE
Competition for a Temporary Exhibition, Trier, Germany

MAHLE FIRMENMUSEUM
Competition for a Permanent Exhibition, Stuttgart, Germany

PANASONIC – BLUE WORLDS
Trade Fair Stand, IFA Berlin, Germany T **Consumer Electronics** C **Panasonic Europe GmbH** A **2,800 sqm** R **Fair Stand Design** / Cooperation: Media and Film Design with **Marc Tamschick** and **m box Bewegtbild GmbH**

SCIENCE LABORATORY
Permanent Exhibition, Herne, Germany T **Archaeology** C **Landschaftsverband Westfalen-Lippe (LWL)** A **140 sqm** R **General Planning, Exhibition Design, Experiential Graphic Design, Lighting Design** / Collaboration: Media Design with **jangled nerves** P **Andreas Plattner, Susanne Wegner**

SENTIR ANDALUCIA
Concept for a Temporary Architecture and Travelling Exhibition, Sevilla, Spain

SIXT AG KUNDENZENTREN
Competition for the Re-Design of the Customer Centres, Pullach, Germany

SUMMERLEE – MUSEUM OF SCOTTISH INDUSTRIAL LIFE
Competition for a Permanent Exhibition, Coatbridge, Scotland, UK

THIS IS THE BIZ
Temporary Exhibition, Basel, Switzerland T **Finance** C **Bank for International Settlements** A **600 sqm** R **General Planning** in cooperation with **Ständige Vertretung Design und Kommunikation GmbH**

WELTENRAUM
Concept for a Temporary Exhibition, Mannheim, Germany

2004

AM BALL DER ZEIT
Temporary Exhibition, Historisches Museum der Pfalz, Speyer, Germany T **Sport** C **Historisches Museum der Pfalz** A **1,800 sqm** R **Exhibition Design**

ARCHÄOLOGISCHES MUSEUM ZÜLPICH
Competition for a Permanent Exhibition, Museum der Badekultur, Zülpich, Germany

AUDI-PAVILION
Competition for the Re-Design of the Permanent Exhibition, Wolfsburg, Germany

ERINNERUNGSSTÄTTE MATTHIAS ERZBERGER
Permanent Exhibition, Münsingen-Buttenhausen, Germany T **History,** C **Haus der Geschichte Baden-Württemberg** A **200 sqm** R **Exhibition Design, Experiential Graphic Design** / Refurbishment: **Hartmaier und Partner**

HISTORISCHES MUSEUM SCHAFFHAUSEN
Competition for a Permanent Exhibition, Schaffhausen, Switzerland

KODAK – ANYTIME, ANYWHERE
Trade Fair Stand, Photokina, Cologne, Germany
T **Photography** C **Kodak GmbH** A **8,600 sqm** R **Fair Stand Design, Lighting Concept, Media Concept, Experiential Graphic Design**

MERCEDES-BENZ – FUEL CELL
Competition for a Pop-Up Exhibition / In cooperation with **Ruth Berktold, Yes Architecture**

MERCEDES-BENZ SHOWROOM
Concept for a Brand Showcase, Stuttgart, Germany

MUSEUM OF THE HARAMEIN PROJECT
Design Concept for a Permanent Exhibition on the Holy Places Mecca, Medina and Jerusalem, Mecca, Saudi Arabia

NATURKUNDEMUSEUM BERLIN
Competition for a Permanent Exhibition, Berlin, Germany

PORSCHE MUSEUM
Concept for a Permanent Exhibition, Stuttgart, Germany

PORSCHE-TECHNOLOGIEZENTRUM
Competition for an interactive LED Facade, Bietigheim-Bissingen, Germany

RÖMER AM OBERRHEIN
Concept for a Temporary Exhibition, Karlsruhe, Germany

STADTMUSEUM WIESBADEN
Competition for a Permanent Exhibition, Germany

THE WAHIBA SANDS PROJECT
Concept for a Desert Accommodation Camp, Oman

THE WORLD OF DURAVIT
Brand Experience, Hornberg, Germany T **Lifestyle** C **Duravit AG** A **1,200 sqm** R **Interior Design, Media Concept, Experiential Graphic Design** / Collaboration: Lighting Design with **Rolf Derrer** / Architecture: **Philippe Starck**

WIDAR SCHULE
Architectural Competition for a School Extension, Bochum-Wattenscheid, Germany

2003

BMW WELT
Competition for Interior Design, Brand Experience Centre, Munich, Germany

CSC–COLOGNE SCIENCE CENTRE
Concept for a Science Centre, Cologne, Germany

EUROPÄISCHES HAUS
Expertise and Exhibition Concept for the "Neue Mitte Passau", Passau, Germany

FASZINATION HANDELSWELTEN
Competition for a Temporary Pavilion and Exhibition for METRO Group, Düsseldorf, Germany

GRIMMS WELTEN
Feasibility Study for a Permanent Exhibition, Kassel, Germany

IMPERIUM ROMANUM
Competition for the Große Landesausstellung, Stuttgart, Germany

LIEBE.KOMM
Temporary Exhibition, Frankfurt/Main, Germany T **Love** C **Museum für Kommunikation Frankfurt** A **800 sqm** R **Exhibition Design, Lighting Design, Media Design, Experiential Graphic Design, Catalogue Design**

LOTHAR BÖHM
Consultancy for the Re-Branding of the Lothar Böhm Agency, Hamburg, Germany

↗ p. 42
LWL-MUSEUM OF ARCHAEOLOGY
Permanent Exhibition, Herne, Germany T **Archaeology** C **Landschaftsverband Westfalen-Lippe (LWL)** A **2,500 sqm** R **Exhibition Design, Experiential Graphic Design, Signage System** / Collaboration: Lighting Design with **Rolf Derrer**; Media Design with **jangled nerves** / Architecture: **von Busse, Klapp, Brüning Architekten** P **Stefan Brentführer**

ODYSSEUM
Competition for a Permanent Exhibition, Cologne, Germany / In cooperation with **FAW Ulm**

O.VISION – MARKET PLACE OF INNOVATIONS
Feasibility Study for a Theme Park, Oberhausen, Germany T Life, Science C **PBO Projektentwicklungs- und Beteiligungsgesellschaft Oberhausen** A **15,000 sqm (Exhibition Hall), approx. 9,000 sqm (Der Gläserne Mensch), approx. 12,000 sqm (Innovarium)** / Architecture: **Hegger Hegger Schleiff, Planer und Architekten**

PANASONIC – BLUE SCAPE
Trade Fair Stand, IFA Berlin, Germany T **Consumer Electronics** C **Panasonic Deutschland GmbH** A **3,800 sqm** R **Fair Stand Design, Experiential Graphic Design** / Collaboration: Media Planning with **AV Lang**; Film with **Mediamorph, Marc Tamschick**

PROJEKT TIROL – LA05, DIE ZUKUNFT DER NATUR (THE FUTURE OF NATURE)
Competition for a National Heritage Exhibition, Salzlager Hall, Austria

RÖMERMUSEUM OSTERBURKEN
Competition for Architecture and Exhibition Design, Osterburken, Germany

SCHLOSS DYCK
Permanent Exhibition, Jüchen, Germany T **Natural History** C **Stiftung Schloss Dyck** A **1,100 sqm** R **Exhibition Design, Lighting Design, Media Design, Experiential Graphic Design**

ÜBERSEE-MUSEUM BREMEN– OZEANIEN, LEBENSWELTEN DER SÜDSEE
Permanent Exhibition, Bremen, Germany T **Ethnology** C **Übersee-Museum Bremen** A **1,800 sqm** R **Exhibition Design, Experiential Graphic Design** / Collaboration: Lighting Concept with **LDE Belzner Holmes**; Media Design with **jangled nerves**

WEIHNACHTSBELEUCHTUNG ZURICH
Design Concept for the Illumination of the Bahnhofstraße, Zurich, Switzerland

WINGAS
Competition for a Modular Trade Fair Stand and a Show, Moscow, Russia

2002

AUDI
Concept for the Motorshow, Geneva, Switzerland

BORN IN EUROPE
Competition for an International Travelling Exhibition

BRIDGE
Concept for Expo.02, Arteplage Biel, Switzerland

BUNDESPAVILLON
Competition for a Temporary Architecture, IGA 2003, Rostock, Germany

CIMBRIA
Concept for a Travelling Exhibition, Germany

↗ p. 32
↗ p. 260
EXPERIENCING FRONTIERS
Cantonal Pavilion, Expo.02, Arteplage Biel / Bienne, Switzerland T **Human** C **Intercantonal Body representing eight Border Cantons** A **900 sqm** R **General Planning, Architecture, Building Automation, Exhibition Design, Experiential Graphic Design** / Collaboration: Structural Engineering with **3e**; Lighting Design with **Rolf Derrer**; Media Planning with **Light&Magic**; Film Production with **Mediamutant, Marc Tamschick** / General Contractor: **Nüssli Special Events** P **Peter Studer**

GEM – GREAT EGYPTIAN MUSEUM
Competition for an Architectural Concept, Giza, Egypt

HEIDELBERGER DRUCKMASCHINEN – COLOUR GARDEN
Competition for a Temporary Event Architecture, Heidelberg, Germany

↗ p. 36
↗ p. 200
HOUSE OF HISTORY BADEN-WÜRTTEMBERG
Permanent Exhibition, Stuttgart, Germany T **History** C **Haus der Geschichte Baden-Württemberg** A **2,400 sqm** R **Exhibition Design, Experiential Graphic Design, Catalogue Design** / Collaboration: Lighting Design with **Rolf Derrer**; Media Planning with **Light & Magic**; Interactive Media with **jangled nerves** / Architecture: **Wilford Schupp Architekten** P **Bernd Eidenmüller, Daniel Stauch**

IGA – BUGA PAVILLON
Concept for an Exhibition Pavilion, Munich, Germany

INFRASERV
Design Concept of a Modular Trade Fair Stand, Germany

KARMANN – THE LINE OF DESIGN
Design of a Modular Trade Fair Stand, Germany

KLIMAHAUS BREMERHAVEN
Competition for a Permanent Exhibition, Germany / Collaboration with **Auer Weber Architects**

KODAK – SHARE MOMENTS, SHARE LIFE
Trade Fair Stand, Photokina, Cologne, Germany T **Photography** C **Kodak GmbH** A **8,600 sqm** R **Fair Stand Design, Lighting Design, Media Design, Experiential Graphic Design**

KULTURZENTRUM SINSTEDEN
Competition for a Permanent Exhibition about large agricultural machines, Rommerskirchen, Germany

MENSCHEN ZEITEN RÄUME
Temporary Exhibition, Martin-Gropius-Bau, Berlin, Germany T **Archaeology** C **Verband der Landesarchäologen in der Bundesrepublik Deutschland; Stiftung Preußischer Kulturbesitz** A **2,500 sqm** R **Exhibition Design, Lighting Design, Media Design, Experiential Graphic Design**

MERCEDES-BENZ – DENKBAUKASTEN
Competition for International Car Shows

SITECO – LIGHT IS BUILDING
Trade Fair Stand, Light+Building, Frankfurt/Main, Germany T **Lighting** C **Siteco Beleuchtungstechnik GmbH** A **420 sqm** R **Fair Stand Design, Media Design, Experiential Graphic Design**

SWISSCOM.BOX
Concept for a Corporate Pavilion, Expo.02, Arteplage Biel, Switzerland

WOHNHAUS BRÜCKNER
Single-family Home, Stuttgart, Germany T Residential C **Private** A **257 sqm** R **Architecture, Concept and Scheme Design** / Collaboration: Planning with **Ruppe Architekten**

2001

AGI THINK TANK TASK FORCE AGENCY
Agency Premises, Stuttgart, Germany T **Office** C **AGI Think Tank Task Force Agency GmbH** A **2,000 sqm** R **Interior Design, Lighting Design, Experiential Graphic Design**

AIRPORT FORUM FRANKFURT
Lounge, Frankfurt Airport, Frankfurt/Main, Germany T **Mobility** C **Fraport AG** A **470 sqm** R **Exhibition Design** / Collaboration: Lighting Design with **Candela**

LITERATURMUSEUM DER MODERNE
Architectural Competition, Marbach, Germany / Construction of the New Museum in collaboration with **Behnisch Architekten**

MUSEUM DER RESSOURCEN
Concept for a Permanent Exhibition, Heilbronn, Germany

OZEANEUM
Competition for a Permanent Exhibition, Stralsund, Germany

↗ p. 30
PANASONIC – BLUE GARDENS
Trade Fair Stand, IFA, Berlin, Germany T **Consumer Electronics** C **Panasonic Deutschland GmbH** A **3,500 sqm** R **Fair Stand Design, Experiential Graphic Design** / Collaboration: Media Planning with **AV Lang**; Film with **Mediamutant, Marc Tamschick** P **Bitter Bredt**

PISA – HAFEN DER WUNDER
Temporary Exhibition, Unna, Germany T **Archaeology** C **Stadt Unna** A **600 sqm** R **Exhibition Design** in collaboration with **Bettina Ahring**

SITECO – LEUCHTENINFORMATIONSZENTRUM
Showroom and Conference Rooms, Traunreut, Germany T **Light** C **Siteco Beleuchtungstechnik GmbH** A **200 sqm** R **Concept, Interior Design, Lighting Design**

TURMFORUM
Competition for a Temporary Exhibition of Deutsche Bahn AG, Stuttgart, Germany

2000

↗ p. 20
↗ p. 276
CYCLEBOWL
Corporate Pavilion, Expo 2000, Hanover, Germany T **Waste Management** C **Duales System Deutschland AG** A **1,600 sqm** R **General Planning, Exhibition Design, Architecture, Facade Planning** / Collaboration: Structural Engineering with **Baustatik Relling**; Mechanical and Electrical Engineering with **Arup**; Lighting Design with **Luna Lichtarchitektur**; Media Planning with **Michael Neumann**; Interactive Media with **jangled nerves**; Experiential Graphic Design with **Projekt Partner**; Sound Design with **Filmreiff**; Tornado with **Ned Kahn**; Film Production with **Mediamutant** P **Uwe Ditz, Thomas Mayer**

DEUTSCHES GARTENBAUMUSEUM
Permanent Exhibition, Cyriaksburg, Erfurt, Germany
T **Culture** C **Stiftung Deutsches Gartenbaumuseum Erfurt e.V.** A **1,800 sqm** R **Exhibition Design, Experiential Graphic Design**

GARTEN EDEN – FASZINATION GESUNDHEIT
Competition for a Pavilion for Hoffmann-La-Roche AG, Expo.02, Arteplage Yverdon-les-Bains, Switzerland

GARTENKUNSTMUSEUM SCHLOSS BENRATH
Concept for a Permanent Exhibition, Benrath, Germany

HOHENHEIM
Concept for an Exhibition, Stuttgart, Germany / In collaboration with **Uwe Reinhardt**

↗ p. 26
INNOVARIUM
Feasibility Study for a Science Centre, O.Vision, Oberhausen, Germany T **Science** C **Duales System Deutschland AG** A **7,500 sqm** R **Design Concept** in collaboration with **Arup engineers**

KODAK – PICTUREWORLD
Trade Fair Stand, Photokina, Cologne, Germany
T **Photography** C **Kodak GmbH** A **6,200 sqm** R **Fair Stand Design, Lighting Concept, Media Concept, Experiential Graphic Design**

NET TRADE SPHERE
Competition for the Re-Design of the Trading Floor of Deutsche Börse AG, Frankfurt/Main, Germany

SEDUS STUDIO
Concept for a Show Room, Berlin, Germany

SITECO – LICHTRÄUME
Trade Fair Stand, Light+Building, Frankfurt/Main, Germany
T **Lighting** C **Siteco Beleuchtungstechnik GmbH** A **400 sqm** R **Fair Stand Design, Experiential Graphic Design**

SWISSCOM BOX
Concept for a Corporate Pavilion, Biel Expo.02, Switzerland

THEMENPARK UMWELT – ENVIRONMENT, LANDSCAPE, CLIMATE
Theme Park Pavilion, Expo 2000, Hanover, Germany
T **Sustainability** C **Expo 2000 GmbH; Baden-Württemberg Film Academy** A **6,200 sqm** R **Exhibition Design, Experiential Graphic Design, Sponsor Acquisition** / Collaboration: Lighting Design with **Rolf Derrer**

1999

DEUTSCHES SPORT- UND OLYMPIAMUSEUM – 200 JAHRE SPORTGESCHICHTE
Permanent Exhibition, Cologne, Germany T **Sport** C **Stiftung Deutsches Sport- und Olympiamuseum e.V.** A **2,800 sqm** R **Exhibition Design, Experiential Graphic Design**

EU-GIPFEL
Competition for the Temporary Press Centre for the EU Summit, Cologne, Germany / In collaboration with **Jochen Siegemund**

GRUNDIG – NEUE WELTEN
Trade Fair Stand, IFA Berlin, Germany T **Consumer Electronics** C **Grundig AG** A **3,600 sqm** R Fair Stand Design in collaboration with **TC Studios**

KU'DAMM KARREE PASSAGE
Re-Design of an Arcade, Lighting Design and Shop Design, Berlin, Germany

MAHNMAL TORGAU
Competition for the Design of a Memorial, Torgau, Germany

MUSEUM DER RESSOURCEN
Feasibility Study for a Museum and Exhibition, Heilbronn, Germany

MUSEUM KALKRIESE
Competition for a Permanent Exhibition, Bramsche-Kalkriese, Germany

1998

EXPEDITION TITANIC
Resumption of the Exhibition, Zurich, Switzerland
T **History** C **Voyager Titanic Exhibition GmbH** A **3,500 sqm** R **Exhibition Design** in collaboration with **Götz Schulz Haas Architects** and **Holger von der Ley**

GERMAN HYGIENE MUSEUM
Concept for the Permanent Exhibition, Hygiene Museum, Dresden, Germany

„MINDESTENS HALTBAR BIS …“
Competition of Duales System Deutschland AG, Design Concept for the World Environment Day, Kunst- und Ausstellungshalle der Bundesrepublik Deutschland, Bonn, Germany

1997

↗ p. 14
↗ p. 148
↗ p. 178
EXPEDITION TITANIC
Temporary Exhibition, Hamburg, Germany T **History** C **Voyager Titanic Exhibition GmbH** A **3,500 sqm** R **Exhibition Design** in collaboration with **Götz Schulz Haas Architects** and **Holger von der Ley** P **Uwe Ditz**

SISYPHUS – A FRENZY MACHINE – POWERSTATIONS
Sculpture for Mercedes-Benz, IAA, Frankfurt/Main, Germany
T **Art, Technology** C **Mercedes-Benz, Atelier Markgraph GmbH** A **225 sqm**, height: **18 m** R **Concept and Planning** / Structural Engineering: **Anspichler & Widerspan**; Kinetics: **Klaus Nißl**; Sound Design: **Heiner Reiff**; Lighting Design: **Rolf Derrer**; Choreography: **Samuel Jornot**

AUTHORS

Prof. Uwe R. Brückner
↗ p. 145–288

Prof. Uwe R. Brückner is considered an influential visionary in the world's design community and pioneer of scenography. Since the legendary Titanic Exhibition, his design philosophy "form follows content" and his design method "Creativ(e) Structur(e)" have played a key role in shaping exhibition design. As an interdisciplinary designer, Uwe R. Brückner sees exhibitions and architecture as a holistic experience both in terms of space and content, as staging with narrative and dramaturgical structure. Prof. Uwe R. Brückner is co-founder of ATELIER BRÜCKNER and of the Institute for Interior Design and Scenography at the HGK Basel. Unique concepts, lectures, seminars, and workshops as well as a large body of publications are manifestations of his demand internationally as a design expert.

Prof. Uwe R. Brückner gilt weltweit als einflussreicher Vordenker der Gestalterszene und Wegbereiter der Szenografie. Seit der legendären Titanic-Ausstellung haben seine Gestaltungsphilosophie „form follows content" und seine Gestaltungmethodik, die „Creativ(e) Structur(e)", das Ausstellungsgestaltung mitbestimmt. Als interdisziplinärer Gestalter denkt Uwe R. Brückner Ausstellung und Architektur als räumlich-inhaltliches Gesamterlebnis, als Inszenierung mit narrativer und dramaturgischer Struktur. Prof. Uwe R. Brückner ist Mitbegründer des ATELIER BRÜCKNER und des Instituts für Innenarchitektur und Szenografie an der HGK Basel. Einzigartige Konzepte, Vorträge, Seminare und Workshops sowie eine umfassende Publikationstätigkeit weisen ihn als international gefragten Gestalterexeperten aus.

Linda Greci
↗ p. 145–288

Linda Greci studied Historical and Cultural Anthropology (EKW) and Romance Philology with a special focus on museum science in Tübingen, finishing her degree with research work in the field of museum brand presentation on the topic exhibition conception and design. From 2012 to 2016, Linda Greci was Uwe R. Brückner's assistant, supporting him in all matters relating to the Atelier and his teaching at university. In parallel, she was project manager for ATELIER BRÜCKNER for the EU research project "EuroVision – Museums Exhibiting Europe," held presentations and was involved in various publications. From 2016 to 2018 she focused on scenography and its parameters and was co-author of "Scenography – the Art of Holistic Design." Since 2016 she has been working on exhibition projects in the area of content and conception.

Linda Greci studierte Empirische Kulturwissenschaft und Romanische Philologie mit Schwerpunkt Museumswissenschaft in Tübingen und schloss mit der Forschungsarbeit „Museale Markenpräsentation" zum Thema Ausstellungskonzeption und -gestaltung ab. Von 2012 bis 2016 war Linda Greci Assistentin von Uwe R. Brückner, unterstützte ihn in allen Atelierbelangen sowie in der Hochschultätigkeit. Parallel war sie für ATELIER BRÜCKNER Projektleiterin des EU-Forschungsprojekts „EuroVision – Museums Exhibiting Europe", hielt Vorträge und verfasste Publikationen. Von 2016 bis 2018 beschäftigte sie sich mit Szenografie und ihren Parametern und war Co-Autorin von „Scenography – the Art of Holistic Design". Seit 2016 arbeitet sie im Bereich Inhalt und Konzeption an Ausstellungsprojekten.

Prof. Dr Ruedi Baur
↗ p. 8

Prof. Dr Ruedi Baur was born in Paris in 1956. In 1979 he qualified as a graphic designer in Zürich. In 1983 he founded Atelier BBV in Lyon and in 1989 the Integral Concept network with the ateliers Integral Ruedi Baur in Paris and Zurich and the research institutes Design2context (2004) and Civic City (2011). He currently researches and teaches at the École nationale supérieure des Arts Décoratifs in Paris, at the Haute école d'art et de design in Geneva and at the University of Strasbourg. In 2018 he and Vera Baur launched the atelier for research and development "Dix-milliards-humains," which deals with necessary changes to the world. Important publications have been published by Lars Müller.

Prof. Dr. Ruedi Baur wurde 1956 in Paris geboren. 1979 erhielt er das Diplom als Grafikdesigner in Zürich, 1983 gründete er in Lyon das Atelier BBV, 1989 das Netzwerk Integral Concept mit den Ateliers Integral Ruedi Baur in Paris und Zürich sowie die Forschungsinstitute Design2context (2004) und Civic City (2011). Er forscht und lehrt derzeit an der École nationale supérieure des Arts Décoratifs in Paris, an der Haute école d'art et de design in Genf und an der Université de Strasbourg. 2018 rief er mit Vera Baur das Atelier für Forschung und Entwicklung „Dix-milliards-humains" ins Leben, das sich mit notwendigen Weltveränderungen auseinandersetzt. Grundlegende Publikationen wurden unter anderem bei Lars Müller verlegt.

Dr Karl Borromäus Murr

↗ p. 196

Dr Karl Borromäus Murr studied history, philosophy, and ethnology at the Munich School of Philosophy, the LMU, Oxford University, in Eichstätt-Ingolstadt, and at Harvard. From 2005 to 2008 he was a scientific assistant and since 2009 director of the State Textile and Industry Museum (tim). Since 2013 he has been chairman of the jury and since 2015 a board member of the European Museum Academy. He teaches at the LMU and the University of Augsburg and since 2015 has been a visiting lecturer at Libera università di lingue e comunicazione IULM in Milan; he is a member or chairman of various advisory boards. Murr has published widely on German history and museum studies.

Dr. Karl Borromäus Murr studierte Geschichte, Philosophie und Ethnologie an der Münchner Hochschule für Philosophie, der Ludwig-Maximilians-Universität (LMU), der Oxford University, in Eichstätt-Ingolstadt und Harvard. Von 2005 bis 2008 war er wissenschaftlicher Mitarbeiter, seit 2009 ist er Direktor des Staatlichen Textil- und Industriemuseums Augsburg (tim). Seit 2013 amtiert er als Chairman der Preisjury und seit 2015 als Board Member der European Museum Academy. Er ist Lehrbeauftragter der LMU und der Universität Augsburg und seit 2015 Gastdozent der Libera università di lingue e comunicazione IULM Mailand sowie Mitglied oder Vorsitzender verschiedener Beiräte. Murr verfasste zahlreiche Publikationen zur deutschen Geschichte sowie zur Museologie.

Prof. Fritz Auer

↗ p. 234

Prof. Fritz Auer, born 1933 in Tübingen, studied at the TH Stuttgart and at Cranbrook Academy of Arts in Bloomfield Hills, Michigan, USA. He graduated in Stuttgart in 1962. He worked for the Stuttgart-based architects Behnisch und Lambart until 1965, when he became partner of Behnisch & Partner. In 1980 Fritz Auer and Carlo Weber left this partnership and founded their own office, today Auer Weber, in Stuttgart. From 1985 to 1992 Auer was professor of building construction and design at the FH Munich, and from 1993 to 2001 he was a professor of design at the Stuttgart State Academy of Art and Design. He has been a member of the Academy of the Arts since 1993.

Prof. Fritz Auer wurde 1933 in Tübingen geboren und studierte an der Hochschule für Technik in Stuttgart sowie an der Cranbrook Academy of Arts in Bloomfield Hills, Michigan, USA. 1962 diplomierte er in Stuttgart. Bis 1965 arbeitete er beim Architekturbüro Behnisch und Lambart in Stuttgart und wurde 1965 Partner im Büro Behnisch & Partner. 1980 lösten sich Fritz Auer und Carlo Weber aus dieser Partnerschaft und gründeten ihr eigenes Büro – heute „Auer Weber" in Stuttgart. Von 1985 bis 1992 war Fritz Auer Professor für Baukonstruktion und Entwerfen an der FH München, von 1993 bis 2001 Professor für Entwerfen an der Staatlichen Akademie der Bildenden Künste in Stuttgart. Seit 1993 ist er Mitglied der Akademie der Künste.

Prof. Jochen Rädeker

↗ p. 250

Prof. Jochen Rädeker is co-founder and managing partner of Strichpunkt Design with offices in Stuttgart, Berlin, and Shanghai—one of the largest and most successful German offices for communication design. He is responsible for the global appearance of brands like Audi, DHL, Metro, Porsche, Vorwerk, and Germany's national football team. His work has won more than 800 international creative awards. After eight years on the board of the Art Directors Club für Deutschland (ADC), of which three were as president, Rädeker has been teaching at HTWG Konstanz as professor for corporate identity since 2012. He is in demand as a jury member and speaker at home and abroad and has written numerous books on design and corporate communication.

Prof. Jochen Rädeker ist Mitgründer und geschäftsführender Gesellschafter von Strichpunkt Design mit Sitz in Stuttgart, Berlin und Shanghai – eines der größten und erfolgreichsten deutschen Büros für Kommunikationsdesign. Er verantwortet den globalen Auftritt von Marken wie Audi, DHL, Metro, Porsche, Vorwerk oder der Deutschen Fußball-Nationalmannschaft. Seine Arbeit wurde mit über 800 internationalen Kreativ-Awards ausgezeichnet. Nach acht Jahren im Vorstand des Art Directors Club für Deutschland (ADC), davon drei Jahre als Präsident, lehrt Rädeker seit 2012 als Professor für Corporate Identity an der Hochschule Konstanz. Er ist gefragter Juror und Redner im In- und Ausland und hat zahlreiche Fachbücher zu den Themen Design und Unternehmenskommunikation verfasst.

ACKNOWLEDGEMENTS

Uwe R. Brückner and Eberhard Schlag

Following the success of volume 1, SCENOGRAPHY–MAKING SPACES TALK, which was devoted to projects of ATELIER BRÜCKNER until 2010 and its design philosophy, volume 2, SCENOGRAPHY 2–STAGING THE SPACE, is an appreciation of the complete works of the past twenty years. With the milestones, the most important projects from 2011 to 2018, the guiding principle "form follows content," and the design method "Creativ(e) Structur(e)," SCENOGRAPHY 2 gives an insight into the creative potential of the Atelier.

The book thus pays homage to the passionate, creative, and professional commitment of its 109 employees (of a total of more than 300 in 20 years) from 22 nationalities and 11 different disciplines who have made ATELIER BRÜCKNER what it is today. Its importance is expressed not least in more than 300 international awards. We would like to thank the external architects, designers, artists, engineers, curators, scientists, and freelancers who have supported us, often beyond the course of duty. But we also pay tribute to our courageous clients whose decision to work with us culminated in successful projects.

Special thanks to our co-author Linda Greci and our guest authors Ruedi Baur, Karl Borromäus Murr, Fritz Auer, and Jochen Rädeker, whose carefully worded forewords about the scenography formats have contributed an important external perspective.

And last but not least, we thank the SCENOGRAPHY 2 team members Jana Fröhlich, Claudia Luxbacher, Anika Neugart, Whan Lee, Oliver Furtak, and many more for their passionate commitment to this book. This also applies to our project authors, editors, translators, and proofreaders, not to forget all those who already contributed to the success of SCENOGRAPHY 1.

Nach dem erfolgreichen Band 1, SCENOGRAPHY – MAKING SPACES TALK, der sich den Projekten des ATELIER BRÜCKNER bis 2010 und seiner angewandten Gestaltungsphilosophie widmete, übernimmt Band 2, SCENOGRAPHY 2 – STAGING THE SPACE, die Würdigung des gesamten Werks der vergangenen 20 Jahre. SCENOGRAPHY 2 gibt mit den Milestones, den wichtigsten Projekten von 2011 bis 2018, dem Credo „form follows content“ sowie der Gestaltungsmethode „Creativ(e) Structur(e)“ einen Einblick in das kreative Potenzial des Ateliers.

Das Buch ist damit auch eine Hommage an das leidenschaftliche, kreative und professionelle Engagement seiner 109 Mitarbeiter (von insgesamt über 300 in 20 Jahren) aus 22 Nationalitäten und 11 verschiedenen Disziplinen, die das ATELIER BRÜCKNER dorthin gebracht haben, wo es heute ist. Sein Stellenwert drückt sich nicht zuletzt in mehr als 300 internationalen Auszeichnungen aus. Unser Dank gilt den externen Architekten, Designern, Künstlern, Ingenieuren, Kuratoren, Wissenschaftlern und Freischaffenden, die uns häufig – bis an die Grenzen ihrer Kapazität – unterstützt haben. Unser Respekt gebührt auch den couragierten Auftraggebern, die ihre Entscheidung, mit uns zu arbeiten, in erfolgreichen Projekten bestätigt fanden.

Besonderer Dank gilt unserer Co-Autorin Linda Greci und unseren Gastautoren Ruedi Baur, Karl Borromäus Murr, Fritz Auer und Jochen Rädeker, die mit ihren wohlformulierten Vorworten zu den Szenografie-Formaten den wichtigen Blick von außen beigesteuert haben.

Nicht zuletzt gilt unser Dank den SCENOGRAPHY-2-Teammitgliedern Jana Fröhlich, Claudia Luxbacher, Anika Neugart, Whan Lee, Oliver Furtak und vielen mehr für ihren passionierten Einsatz für dieses Buch. Das gilt auch für unsere Projektautoren, Lektoren, Übersetzer sowie Korrektoren und schließt auch alle diejenigen ein, die schon SCENOGRAPHY 1 zum Erfolg verholfen haben.

IMPRINT

Editor	ATELIER BRÜCKNER GmbH
Concept	Uwe R. Brückner, Eberhard Schlag
Editorial Team	Uwe R. Brückner, Eberhard Schlag, Jana Fröhlich, Linda Greci, Claudia Luxbacher, Anika Neugart
Project Management	Eberhard Schlag, Jana Fröhlich
Authors	
Philosophy	Uwe R. Brückner, Linda Greci
Projects	ATELIER BRÜCKNER GmbH
Prefaces	Shirin Frangoul-Brückner, Ruedi Baur, Karl Borromäus Murr, Fritz Auer, Jochen Rädeker
Design	Whan Lee, Oliver Furtak
Translation	
German – English	Beverley Locke / PLOT | Marinescu, Poesch GbR
Text Editing	
German Projects	Andrea Scholtz
Copy Editing	
English	Keonaona Peterson
German Projects	Claudia Luxbacher
German Philosophy	Felix Ruhl
Proofreading	
English	Keonaona Peterson
German	Gisela Faller / PLOT | Marinescu, Poesch GbR Susanne Mädger
Sketches	Uwe R. Brückner
Image Coordination	Whan Lee, Anika Neugart, Benjamin Guschlbauer
Text Coordination	Anika Neugart
Final Artwork and Prepress	Alfred Stiefel, Boris Wick
Paper	135 g/qm ProfiSilk 120 g/qm DesignOffset classic white
Typeface	FF Real
Production	Offizin Scheufele Druck und Medien GmbH+Co. KG

Library of Congress Control Number: 2018958404

Bibliographic information published by the German National Library.
The German National Library lists this publication in the Deutsche Nationalbibliografie; detailed bibliographic data are available on the internet at http://dnb.dnb.de.

ISBN 978-3-0356-1640-8

9 8 7 6 5 4 3 2 1

www.birkhauser.com